PSYCHOLOGY
and the problems of society

Editors:

Frances F. Korten, APA Research Psychologist
Stuart W. Cook, Convention Theme Committee Chairman
John I. Lacey, Convention Committee Chairman

Published by
American Psychological Association, Inc.
1200 Seventeenth Street, N.W.
Washington, D.C. 20036

PHILLIPS MEMORIAL
LIBRARY
PROVIDENCE COLLEGE

Copyright © 1970 by the
American Psychological Association, Inc.
1200 Seventeenth Street, N.W.
Washington, D.C. 20036

Library of Congress Catalog Card Number 72-115-967

Preface

With the growing realization that contemporary society's problems are human, not technological, a troubled society turns to psychology for help. In response, numerous psychologists are bringing their talents to bear on socially relevant problems. This emerging social relevance is reflected in the problem-oriented theme chosen for the 1969 American Psychological Association Convention from which this volume takes its title.

The volume brings together some of the many 1969 convention presentations bearing on society's problems. The contributions are diverse, ranging from descriptions and evaluations of concrete action programs, exemplifying what actually can be accomplished, to theoretical essays providing a more general framework for action. Apparent in each is the author's commitment to and involvement in the problem he discusses. Some express this in empassioned pleas, others in objective research reporting. But the sense of concern shines through each style, indicating that while many of these contributors are dispassionate, none are disinterested. Each offers some spark of hope that indeed there are solutions to the troublesome problems that beset our society, if only we dare to act.

The contributors represent the variety of fields that might be expected in the discussion of complex problems that crisscross the boundaries of academic disciplines. While most are psychologists, this volume also includes the perspectives of lawyers, sociologists, educators, economists, government officials, and others who bridge a number of fields.

The 1969 convention included much more socially relevant material than could possibly be presented in one volume. Thus, only two of the many types of relevant presentations are included. The convention-wide theme symposia comprise the first type. On each of the five convention days, attention was focused from 10 to 12 a.m. on a single symposium devoted to a specific social problem. This volume includes the material from all five of these symposia.

Second, the theme-related divisional addresses are included. Before the convention the chairman of each APA division was asked to choose the programs of his division which he felt were particularly relevant to the convention theme. These items were then indicated as theme-related in the convention program guide. Of the 97 items so indicated, only the 22 invited addresses are included here. Thus, numerous symopisa, research papers, workshops, and discussions presenting valuable and relevant material are unfortunately omitted.

Given these arbitrary criteria used in determining the contents of this volume, it is significant that the contributions focus on a comparatively small set of problems including those of our cities, compensatory education, black–white relations, violence, student disruptions and drug use, and the influence of society's structures on human relationships. These would appear to be areas where psychologists feel they can make their greatest contributions.

In his APA presidential address which opens this volume, George Miller stresses that psychologists must learn to give away their knowledge—to provide psychological insights directly to those who need them, whether they be ghetto mothers or college presidents. In the preparation of this nontechnical book directed especially to those interested and involved in social problems, we hope to have taken a small step toward "giving psychology away."

Numerous people have helped in bringing about this volume. I am indebted to John Lacey who suggested the production of this volume and who approved and implemented the proposal of the convention theme, and to Stuart Cook who turned the hazy notion of a convention theme into programs of interest and import and who provided the comprehensive account of the convention's background which appears in this volume's introduction. I also extend appreciation to the contributors for their responsiveness to my impatient efforts to produce this contemporary collection quickly. Helen Orr, APA Managing Editor, and Harold P. Van Cott, Director of the APA Office of Communication Management and Development deserve thanks for their continuing support throughout the production of this book. Most of all thanks are due to Estelle Mallinoff, Editor, Separate Publications, and to Patricia Walsh, Technical Editor, who have so untiringly applied their talents to the production and technical editing of this volume. Estelle's imagination in the book's design and both Estelle's and Pat's numerous constructive suggestions on all manuscripts and constant alertness to error have contributed substantially to the quality of this volume.

F. F. K.

Table of Contents

Psychology and the Social Change Process 1

Psychology as a Means of Promoting Human Welfare
    George A. Miller 5

Psychologists and Federal Legislation
    Introduction
        Launor F. Carter 22

    Congress and the Psychologist
        Donald M. Fraser 25

    The Social Relevance of the Psychologist
        John R. Kramer 32

    Evaluation of Social Legislation
        Marcia Guttentag 40

Organizational and Conceptual Barriers to Social Change
    Martin Deutsch 47

The Psychotherapist as an Activist in Social Change: A Proponent
    Fred E. Spaner 58

Where Angels Fear to Tread: Reply to Spaner
    Ernest S. Lawrence 63

Counseling's Social Response
    John F. McGowan 67

The Immorality of Irrelevance: The Social Role of Science
    Bernard H. Baumrin 73

The Scientist in a rapidly Evolving Society
    Introduction
        George A. Miller 84

    The Need for Social Engineering
        Jerome B. Wiesner 85

    Comments on Weisner's Paper
        Herbert C. Kelman 95
        Charles E. Osgood 99
        George A. Miller 101

Psychology and Urban Problems ... 103

Innovative Approaches to Urban Problems
    Introduction
        Stuart W. Cook ... 107
    The Urban Problem and Action Research
        Arthur Naftalin ... 108
    Alternatives to Urban Public Schools
        Kenneth B. Clark ... 115
    Psychologist to the Powerless
        Hannah Levin ... 121
    Alternatives to Traditional Law Enforcement
        Morton Bard ... 128
    The Metropolitan Educational Park
        Thomas F. Pettigrew ... 133
Separation of Work and Income
    Juanita M. Kreps ... 140
The Experience of Living in Cities: A Psychological Analysis
    Stanley Milgram ... 152

Psychology and the Challenge of Early Learning ... 175

Disadvantaged Families: Despair to Hope
    James O. Miller ... 179
Early Learning and Compensatory Education
    Introduction
        Lloyd N. Morrisett ... 198
    Early Learning and Compensatory Education: Contributions of Basic Research
        William Kessen ... 200
    Designing Programs for Classroom Use
        Carl Bereiter ... 204
    Designing a Program for Broadcast Television
        Gerald S. Lesser ... 208
    Evaluation of Educational Programs as Research on the Educational Process
        Samuel Messick ... 215
    Technological Innovations: Computer-Assisted Instruction and Compensatory Education
        Patrick Suppes and Mona Morningstar ... 221
Malnutrition, Learning, and Intellectual Development: Research and Remediation
        Henry N. Ricciuti ... 237

Psychology and Minority Groups ... 255

Psychologists, Psychology, and the Black Community
        Charles W. Thomas ... 259

Toward a New Social Order
   Charles E. Wilson 268
Minority Subcultures and the Law of Effect
   Robert J. Havighurst 275
Testing and Equality of Career Opportunity
   Robert E. Hampton 289
Sadean and Institutional Cruelty
   Philip P. Hallie 295

Psychology and the Reduction of Violence 305

Violence and Human Behavior
   Marvin E. Wolfgang 309
The Concept of Power
   Isidor Chein 327
Three Not-So-Obvious Contributions of Psychology to Peace
   Ralph K. White 344

Psychology and Campus Issues 357

Factors Underlying Student Unrest
   Introduction
      Kenneth E. Clark 361
   Establishing the Right to Be Heard: The Development of a
   Program Takeover
      Jack Sawyer 363
   Transcript of the Protestors' Session 366
   Campus Disruption, 1968–69: An Analysis of Causal Factors
      Alexander W. Astin 377
   The Student Protest Movement: Some Facts, Interpretations,
   and a Plea
      Richard E. Peterson 388
   Activist Students Challenge the Social Scientists
      Paul Heist 395
   Comments on the Symposium "Factors Underlying Student Unrest"
      M. Brewster Smith 406
Student Drug Use
   Helen H. Nowlis 408
Black–White Campus Issues and the Function of Counseling Centers
   Charles W. Thomas 420

Psychology and Society's Future 427

A Funny Thing Happened on the Way to the Future
   Warren G. Bennis 431
Man and Society: The Inauthentic Condition
   Amitai Etzioni 451

Introduction

In the history of the American Psychological Association's annual meetings the 1969 meeting was unique. Prior annual meetings had followed a well-established tradition of emphasis on scientific developments in the field. The 1969 meeting, by contrast, represented the first convention-wide dedication to an examination of psychology's usefulness to society. To be sure, the commitment to social usefulness is long standing. The purpose of the APA is "to advance psychology as a science, and as a means of promoting human welfare." The 1969 meeting took a hard look at our successes, failures, and opportunities in achieving the second of these two goals.

Like all events, the 1969 annual meeting had background conditions in terms of which the emergence of its program theme may be better understood. Since World War II, thinking people have lived with the specter of nuclear war and a sense of impotence in warding it off. To this there has been added in the last decade new problems, equally critical and equally beyond the ability of the individual psychologist to solve: deterioration of life in the big cities, race riots, a dead-end war in Vietnam, uncontrolled population growth, irreversible pollution of the environment—all potentially devastating and all out of hand. To make things worse, over and over, tragedy or defeat has put an end to developments that had given grounds for hope: in the presidency of John Kennedy, in Martin Luther King's appeal to the American conscience, in Robert Kennedy's bond with alienated American youth—and, for some, in Eugene McCarthy's brief but inspiring challenge to American policy in Vietnam.

Against this background and simultaneously with the 1968 APA Annual Convention in San Francisco, came the Democratic Convention and the demonstrations in Chicago. To many psychologists, television coverage of the convention and Chicago streets delivered one more blow. Party insiders could be readily observed controlling the convention with an iron hand. Outside, the Chicago police, with their mayor's encouragement, suppressed demonstrations with a degree of force that shocked many—and drew applause from others. As we gathered in San Francisco, it was becoming increasingly difficult to have faith in what in earlier years had been our prevailing position, namely, that we should first develop a science of psychology and then apply it where it promised to benefit society. For many it began to seem that time no longer permitted such an orderly development.

An early reflection of the climate of the San Francisco meeting was a proposal to remove the 1969 convention from its scheduled location in Chicago. Petitions supporting the change drew wide support. Despite the threat of lawsuits for breaking contracts with the convention hotels, the Council of Representatives decided to make the change. It reaffirmed the decision at its October meeting, choosing Washington, D. C., as the alternative site.

Credit for sensing the need for action and for suggesting the concept of a program theme in the 1969 meeting goes to a group of 27 psychologists calling itself the Ad Hoc Committee of Psychologists for Social Responsibility. In a letter dated August 13, 1968, that Committee proposed that action be taken in San Francisco on two resolutions. One had to do with the Vietnam war, militarism in general, racism, and poverty. The other dealt with the question of science and social responsibility. Among other things the latter proposed as a theme for the 1969 convention the topic, "Psychologists and Social Responsibility."

It was clear that the Ad Hoc Committee had itself been stimulated by the earlier actions of other psychologists. The Committee's letter, over the signature of its chairman, Ethel Tobach, called attention to the fact that the North Carolina State Psychological Association had recently taken the lead in urging all state associations to study possibilities for the greater fulfillment of psychology's social responsibility.

The Ad Hoc Committee's proposal found immediate support. In a letter dated August 31, Thomas Pettigrew, president of the Society for the Psychological Study of Social Issues, reported endorsement by the council of that division. His letter further suggested the method of implementation that was later adopted—namely, that the Convention Committee be directly responsible for the theme program. Other divisional councils soon added their support. Moreover, under the leadership of some of the members of the Ad Hoc Committee, a new organization was formed; it calls itself American Psychologists for Social Action. One of its first actions was to send to the APA Council of Representatives a resolution endorsing the theme proposal.

Meanwhile, on August 29, 1968, the Board of Directors of the Association discussed the theme proposal and referred it to the Convention Committee for action. Later during the 1968 meeting a petition of support carrying more than 1,000 signatures was presented to the Council of Representatives. Here it was sympathetically discussed, but the decision regarding it was left with the Convention Committee. At its own sessions in San Francisco the Convention Committee decided to proceed with the program theme for the 1969 meeting, subject only to a determination of the feasibility of locating appropriate material and securing informed speakers both from within and without APA.

Shortly after the San Francisco meeting, the Convention Committee, through John Lacey, its chairman, asked me to join Kenneth E. Clark and Henry W. Riecken in making the feasibility study. We accepted and began an intensive review of types of programs that it might be practical to arrange. While this review was in progress, we received many suggestions from concerned and interested persons. Among these were two detailed and helpful sets of recommendations, one from a group of psychologists in New York City (Harriet Linton Barr, Murray Glanzer, Julian Hochberg, Robert Holt, Nancy Israel, and John Sullivan) and the other from Howard Gruber, co-chairman of the new American Psychologists for Social Action. Notable in the first letter was a suggestion to prepare this book. This action was advocated, later, by John Lacey and, due largely to his backing, the idea for this book was adopted.

Our subcommittee concluded that it was feasible to mount a program on the social responsibility theme and so reported to the Convention Committee at its fall meeting on October 14. In our report we characterized the nature of the program as follows:

> We have assumed that the objectives of the social responsibility meetings should be to crystallize and make visible the concern of psychologists about current social problems, to inform A.P.A. members about such problems, and to suggest practical possibilities for future, more effective contributions by A.P.A. members to the solution of these problems. We have assumed further that the programs should focus on psychological contributions to social problems as contrasted with social action of the type in which any citizen, not a psychologist, might participate equally well.
>
> We have not assumed, however, that the meetings need be limited to those topics on which psychological contributions have already been made. Their purpose would include, as well, the presentation of problems on which psychological contributions might reasonably be expected and on methods through which psychologists might exert greater influence on policy and program than is now the case.

It was at this meeting of the Convention Committee that the final designation for the program theme, "Psychology and the Problems of Society," was chosen. We had come to see that the earlier label, "social responsibility," had for many people the more narrow connotation of the scientist's responsibility for the good or evil use to which society put his research findings.

It was also agreed at this time that the theme should be carried out in two ways. First, following a precedent set at an earlier annual meeting celebrating the William James centennial, five two-hour sessions were to be set aside for theme programs without competition from other scheduled meetings; the subcommittee, consisting of K. E. Clark, H. W. Riecken, and myself, was asked to arrange these sessions. Second, the divisional program committees were to be asked to cooperate by scheduling papers and symposia in harmony with the theme.

During the following months the final choice of topics for the program was influenced by several factors. One of these was the desire to have participants from across the spectrum of psychological specializations. A second was the availability of significant material and informed speakers. A third was negative: It seemed unwise to duplicate material from recent annual meetings no matter how significant this material had seemed in its earlier presentations.

These considerations led to the omission of a number of highly significant problems. For example, not enough new material was found on the work of psychologists in international negotiation to warrant repeating earlier meetings on this important topic.

A review of psychology and the problems of society may be approached from at least two directions. One has to do with the type of problem considered, the other with the means of bringing psychology to bear on change whatever the problem may be. Our final selection of topics for the theme symposia reflected both orientations. Topics such as urban problems, student unrest, and early learning and compensatory education exemplify the problem focus. The symposia "Psychologists and Federal Legislation" and "The Scientist in a rapidly Evolving Society" exemplify concern with the means by which the influence of psychology may be brought to bear on change. In each symposium there was, of course, a merging of these two orientations; in the symposium "Innovative Approaches to Urban Problems," for example, there was a secondary focus on the development by psychologists of innovative methods to deal with such problems.

The theme committee invested great effort in one aspect of the program plan which did not work out: small-group discussions after each session. From the start we had agreed that the desire for the theme program reflected several conditions. First, psychologists were unaware of the socially relevant contributions their colleagues were making. Second, many psychologists desired to make such contributions but were uncertain how to proceed. Third, if the prevailing sense of inadequacy and irrelevance were to be overcome, this would require not only additional information but also collaboration with colleagues. We felt sure that speakers and discussants addressing passive audiences would do little to remedy these conditions. Accordingly we formulated plans for discussion groups which were to follow each presentation. To conduct these discussions we recruited 170 psychologists with experience in group leadership. We were greatly assisted in this effort by Monroe Miller of the University of Colorado. However, with the notable exception of those attending the symposium "Innovative Approaches to Urban Problems," few persons took advantage of the discussion opportunity. Hindsight suggests that in the context of a crowded convention schedule our arrangements were not workable ones. Whatever the cause, we clearly failed in this one of our major objectives.

The publication of this book could compensate in part for this failure. It will provide source material for local discussions by psychologists. Such discussions might include possibilities for contributions by individual psychologists to the solution of major problems. In addition they should provide both the exchange of information and the opportunities for collaboration for which the convention discussions were intended.

S. W. C.

psychology and the social change process

Psychology and the Social Change Process

In the young discipline of psychology a whirlwind of controversy blows as psychologists apply their talents to solving social problems. For solving social problems means changing the status quo and the depth of society's problems may require changes deeper than those to which most psychologists are accustomed. As Cook points out in the section, "Psychology and Urban Problems," while psychology has always been involved in modifying established practices, it is now being called upon to initiate and develop new practices. In so doing the question arises as to just what are the appropriate ways for psychologists to bring about social change. Many dimensions of this basic issue are reflected in the contributions in this section.

One dimension concerns the question: How directly should psychologists involve themselves in effecting change in public policy? Should psychologists remain dispassionate scientists, only providing data for others to use? Or should they become actively involved as impassioned advocates of change, using whatever tactics may be most effective in bringing about the necessary changes? The members of Carter's symposium take the side of direct action, enumerating a number of avenues through which psychologists can directly influence public policy. Kramer, as a lawyer and political activist, exhorts psychologists to enter into the political arena by bringing to bear various pressure techniques from letter writing to boycotts. Fraser urges psychologists to testify in congressional hearings, although he stresses the need to separate the role of dispassionate scientist from that of political participant. Guttentag suggests that psychologists should play an important role in determining the questions to be asked in the evaluation of government programs, pointing out that the questions to be answered determine the shape of the resultant findings. As an example, she describes the overall evaluation of the Head Start Program as having been an efficient, well-executed search for the answer to a meaningless question.

Others see a different role for psychologists, a role more consistent with their traditional scientific stance, but ultimately relevant to public policy. Miller, in his presidential address opening this section, sees psychology's potential power lying in its ability to change man's conception of himself—a change with enormous policy implications. This theme is echoed in Deutsch's presentation. Deutsch stresses psychology's role in attacking faulty assumptions about man, assumptions on which policy is based. He cites the popular conceptions about the nature of intelligence as an example, indicating the policy implications of these conceptions.

This divergence of opinion concerning the role of psychologists in the social change process is seen not only in this section but also throughout the volume. In the section "Psychology and Campus Issues," we see the takeover of the student unrest symposium representing the extreme activist views of some, with Smith's remarks as discussant for that symposium representing the more dispassionate view. In the urban problems section, Levin describes her part in a community mental health program, and insists that in order to promote truly effective change, psychologists and other professionals must plunge directly into the political process. Other contributors are less explicit regarding their stands on this controversy. Yet some philosophy about the proper roles for psychologists in the social change process lies behind each contribution, from Milgram's theoretical speculations on the experience of living in cities to Bard's efforts to change the structure of the New York police department.

A second dimension of controversy is apparent particularly within the therapeutic branches of psychology. It involves the question of whether to focus effort on individuals or on social structures. The heat of this controversy is evident in the Spaner-Lawrence interchange. Spaner recommends that psychotherapists look beyond the client to the conditions perpetrating his problems while Lawrence contends that treating the client is enough of a burden for psychotherapists without taking on society. In his presidential address to the Division of Counseling Psychology, McGowan reflects this issue in pointing out that counselors are not only agents of their clients but also agents of society; hence, they must make their approaches more responsive to the needs of society as a whole, rather than only to the needs of a restricted segment.

Another dimension of controversy involves determining the criteria for judging research efforts. Should the criteria focus only on the quality of the work and the creativity of the researcher, or should some criterion of relevance be added? Baumrin brings the logical approach of a philosopher to this question, arguing that to pursue science for its own sake is immoral. He maintains the position that "foreseeable beneficial consequences" should be a crucial requirement of all research. No contributor in this volume speaks directly to the other side of this issue, although it is certain that many would find substantial areas of disagreement with Baumrin's adamant stance.

A final dimension of controversy evident in this section involves whether it is ethical to make large-scale use of social science knowledge. Wiesner spotlights the ambivalence felt by both the public and the professionals. The spectre of 1984 looms large when the broad application of psychology is discussed. We fear manipulation and may cringe at the term "social engineering." Yet, at the same time, we can foresee disastrous consequences of a laissez-faire attitude. Wiesner urges the development and application of appropriate social science knowledge which will allow us to manage our future and avoid the otherwise inevitable crises. The ambivalence about manipulation is one with which clinical psychologists have struggled for years. Now, as psychologists from other specialities apply their skills to social change, they too begin to experience this ambivalence.

Psychology as a Means of Promoting Human Welfare[1]

GEORGE A. MILLER

The author received his PhD in psychology from Harvard University in 1946. He is presently a professor at the Rockefeller University, where his major research interest is in the psychological bases for language and communication.

The most urgent problems of our world today are the problems we have made for ourselves. They have not been caused by some heedless or malicious inanimate Nature, nor have they been imposed on us as punishment by the will of God. They are human problems whose solutions will require us to change our behavior and our social institutions.

As a science directly concerned with behavioral and social processes, psychology might be expected to provide intellectual leadership in the search for new and better personal and social arrangements. In fact, however, we psychologists have contributed relatively little of real importance—even less than our rather modest understanding of behavior might justify. We should have contributed more; although our scientific base for valid contributions is far from comprehensive, certainly more is known than has been used intelligently.

This is the social challenge that psychologists face. In the years immediately ahead we must not only extend and deepen our understanding of mental and behavioral phenomena, but we must somehow incorporate our hard-won knowledge more effectively into the vast social changes that we all know are coming. It is both important and appropriate for us, on an occasion such as this, to consider how best to meet this social challenge.

In opening such a discussion, however, we should keep clearly in mind that society has not commissioned us to cure its ills; a challenge is not a mandate. Moreover, there is nothing in the definition of psychology that dedicates our science to the solution of social problems. Our inability to solve the pressing problems of the day cannot be interpreted as an indictment of the scientific validity of our psychological theories. As scientists we are obliged to communicate what we know, but we have no special obligation to solve social problems.

Our obligations as citizens, however, are considerably broader than our obligations as scientists. When psychological issues are raised in this broader context, we cannot evade them by complaining that they are unscientific. If we have

---

[1] Presidential Address presented at the Annual Meeting of the American Psychological Association, Washington, D. C., September 1, 1969. Originally published in the *American Psychologist*, 1969, **24**, 1063–1075.

something of practical value to contribute, we should make every effort to insure that it is implemented.

I believe that the majority of American psychologists have accepted this broader interpretation of our responsibilities and have been eager—perhaps, sometimes, overly eager—to apply our science to social problems. We have not been aloof or insensitive; the bulk of our profession works full time on exactly such problems. And I do not wish to discount the many and often successful efforts toward application that we have made already. Yet I cannot escape the impression that we have been less effective than we might have been. "Why" and "what more might be done" are questions that have troubled me increasingly in recent years.

First, however, I would like to raise a somewhat parochial question.

The Role of the American Psychological Association

If we accept this challenge to use psychology to solve social problems, what role should we expect the American Psychological Association to play? I raise this question because my experience as an officer of the APA has taught me that many of our members look to their national organization for leadership in insuring that our scientific and professional activities have greater social relevance.

Psychologists have been well represented among those who sign petitions of political protest (Ladd, 1969), and they have not failed to make their opinions heard in their own national headquarters. Scarcely a meeting of the Board of Directors in recent years has not featured one or more petitions from concerned members, committees, boards, divisions, or state associations requesting some action related to public affairs. These matters range all the way from the proper use of psychological tests, where the APA usually has something to say, to the endorsement of particular political candidates, where the APA usually does not.

These demands have imposed considerable strain on the Association, which was not created to be an instrument for social action and which responds hesitantly to any suggestion that it should become something more than a scientific and professional organization. But it does respond. I was surprised to discover how seriously the APA regards any legitimate request from its membership, and how sensitive it is to the social implications of its actions, policies, and communications. Some members wish the APA would do more, some less. On balance, I think the APA has reflected reasonably accurately the general consensus of its membership with respect to its role in public affairs.

It is not my intention to raise here any of the specific issues of public policy that have concerned the Board of Directors and the Council of Representatives, or even to offer a general formula for deciding what the public role of the APA should be. Procedurally, I am willing to stand on the thoughtful recommendations of the ad hoc Committee on Public Affairs (Tyler, 1969).

A point of general interest, however, and one that relates more directly to the theme I wish to discuss, is the frequently heard argument that the APA should take some action or other because the first article of our Bylaws states that the Association shall have as its object to promote human welfare, a goal that is echoed in our statement of the *Ethical Standards of Psychologists.*

This argument is usually made by those who recommend that the APA should publicly advocate some particular social reform. When these recommendations are appropriate, the action is adopted—the necessary letters are written, public statements are released to the press, etc. But not every recommendation is acceptable. It has been my impression that the less related the issue is to the scientific and professional interests of our membership, the greater is the likelihood that the promotion of human welfare will be invoked in the course of the discussion.

In most cases this argument has not persuaded me; I have traced my skepticism to two sources.

First, even the most cursory study of welfare economics will show that human welfare has never been operationally defined as a social concept. If there is such a thing as human welfare in the general sense, it must be some kind of weighted average. In difficult cases, where disagreement is most probable, something that advances the welfare of one group may disadvantage another group. The problem is to decide whose welfare we wish to promote. The APA is committed to advancing the welfare of psychologists, of course, but we dare not assume blindly that whatever is good for psychology must always be good for humanity.

Vague appeals to human welfare seldom answer specific questions, because we seldom have sufficient information to decide which actions will have the desired result. And even when we do have sufficient wisdom to know in advance which actions will promote human welfare most effectively, we still face the ethical question of whether such actions are morally permissible.

My first reason for distrusting appeals to human welfare, therefore, is that they do little to clarify the logical, informational, or ethical bases for making difficult decisions. Something more is required than a sincere declaration that our heart is in the right place.

My second reason has to do with the fact that the phrase is usually quoted out of context. At the risk of losing your attention, therefore, I would like to state Article I of our Bylaws in full:

The objects of the American Psychological Association shall be to advance psychology as a science and as a means of promoting human welfare by the encouragement of psychology in all its branches in the broadest and most liberal manner; by the promotion of research in psychology and the improvement of research methods and conditions; by the improvement of the qualifications and usefulness of psychologists through high standards of professional ethics, conduct, education, and achievement; by the increase and diffusion of psychological knowledge through meetings, professional contacts, reports, papers, discussions, and publications; thereby to advance scientific interests and inquiry, and the application of research findings to the promotion of the public welfare [APA, 1968, p. xii].

As I understand Article I, our corporate aim is to promote psychology. We justify that aim by our belief that psychology can be used for the public good. I do not understand Article I as a general license to endorse social actions or positions, however meritorious on other grounds, that do not advance psychology as a science and as a means of promoting human welfare. The APA is our own creature, of course; we can change our Bylaws any way we like. As presently conceived, however, the APA does not have a charter to intervene on behalf of every good cause that comes along.

There are many things of social value that the APA can do, and many that it has already done. If your officers have not always seemed hungry for innovation, eager to reshape the APA to meet every new social issue, they have certainly been open to constructive change within the scope of our charter. I believe they have reflected the wishes of the bulk of the membership, and I feel no need to apologize for what has been accomplished. The APA has been doing what its membership wanted it to do, and doing it rather well.

Of course, the membership has been far from unanimous in these matters. For example, there has been a running debate in recent years concerning the proper role for individual psychologists to play in the initiation of social reforms. We have been divided as to whether psychologists should remain expert advisers or should take a more active, participatory responsibility for determining public policy. An adviser is expected to summarize the arguments pro and con, but to leave the policy decisions to others; a participant wants to make the policy decisions himself.

Those who favor more active participation by individual psychologists tend to argue that the APA should also become directly involved in advocating particular social policies. This whole debate seems to presuppose, however, that social reforms can occur only as a result of policy decisions by government or industry. This presupposition should not go unchallenged. Perhaps our options for promoting human welfare are broader than this debate would suggest.

It was E. G. Boring who first impressed on me the importance of a clear distinction between Psychology with a capital P and psychology with a small p. Capital-P Psychology refers to our associations, departments, laboratories, and the like. Small-p psychology refers to the discipline itself. Capital-P Psychology can do little to promote human welfare, outside of its faithful promotion of small-p psychology. We should not, through impatience or bad judgment, try to use capital-P Psychology where only small-p psychology could succeed. Let us by all means do everything we can to promote human welfare, but let us not forget that our real strength in that cause will come from our scientific knowledge, not from our national Association.

In my opinion, our Association can never play more than a supporting role in the promotion of social change. I do not conclude from this that the APA has become irrelevant or useless, or, even worse, that it has tacitly endorsed a political bureaucracy that presides over the inequitable distribution of health, wealth, and wisdom in our society. The fact that the APA has not reformed society does not mean that it approves the status quo; it means simply that there is relatively little such an association can do. When one considers the magnitude and urgency of the problems mankind faces, the question of what positions APA takes is, after all, a minor matter.

The important question, to my mind, is not what APA is doing, but what psychologists are doing. What Psychology can do as an association depends directly on the base provided by psychology as a science. It is our science that provides our real means for promoting human welfare.

So let me turn now to broader aspects of my topic.

The Revolutionary Potential of Psychology

I will begin by stating publicly something that I think psychologists all feel, but seldom talk about. In my opinion, scientific psychology is potentially one of the most revolutionary intellectual enterprises ever conceived by the mind of man. If we were ever to achieve substantial progress toward our stated aim—toward the understanding, prediction, and control of mental and behavioral phenomena—the implications for every aspect of society would make brave men tremble.

Responsible spokesmen for psychology seldom emphasize this revolutionary possibility. One reason is that the general public is all too ready to believe it, and public resistance to psychology would be all too easy to mobilize. Faced with the possibility that revolutionary pronouncements might easily do more harm than good, a prudent spokesman finds other drums to march to.

Regardless of whether we agree that prudence is always the best policy, I believe there is another reason for our public modesty. Anyone who claims that psychology is a revolutionary enterprise will face a demand from his scientific colleagues to put up or shut up. Nothing that psychology has done so far, they will say, is very revolutionary. They will admit that psychometric tests, psychoanalysis, conditioned reflexes, sensory thresholds, implanted electrodes, and factor analysis are all quite admirable, but they can scarcely be compared to gunpowder, the steam engine, organic chemistry, radio-telephony, computers, atom bombs, or genetic surgery in their revolutionary consequences for society. Our enthusiastic spokesman would have to retire in confused embarrassment.

Since I know that rash statements about the revolutionary potential of psychology may lead to public rejection and scientific ridicule, why do I take such risks on this occasion? My reason is that I do not believe the psychological revolution is still pie in the sky. It has already begun.

One reason the psychological revolution is not more obvious may be that we have been looking for it in the wrong place. We have assumed that psychology should provide new technological options, and that a psychological revolution will not occur until someone in authority exercises those options to attain socially desirable goals. One reason for this assumption, perhaps, is that it follows the model we have inherited from previous applications of science to practical problems. An applied scientist is supposed to provide instrumentalities for modifying the environment—instrumentalities that can then, under public regulation, be used by wealthy and powerful interests to achieve certain goals. The psychological revolution, when it comes, may follow a very different course, at least in its initial stages.

Davis (1966) has explained the difference between applied social science and applied natural science in the following way:

Applied science, by definition, is instrumental. When the human goal is given, it seeks a solution by finding what effective means can be manipulated in the required way. Its function is to satisfy human desires and wants; otherwise nobody would bother. But when the science is concerned with human beings—not just as organisms but as goal-seeking individuals and members of groups—then it cannot be instrumental in this way, because the object of observation has a say in what is going on and, above all, is not willing to be treated as a pure instrumentality. Most so-called social problems are problems because people want certain things or because there is a conflict of desires or interests [p. 26].

Davis goes on to argue that once conflicts of interest have developed, applied social science is helpless; that it is only when people are agreed on their goals that our information can be usefully applied.

Although I agree with Davis that behavioral and social sciences cannot be applied to people and institutions in the same way physical and biological sciences are applied to objects and organisms, I do not agree with his view that we must remain impotent in the face of conflict. We know a great deal about the prevention and resolution of conflicts, and that information could certainly be put to better use than it has been. Indeed, sometimes what is needed is not to resolve conflict but to foster it, as when entrenched interests threaten segments of the public that have no organizational identity. And there, in turn, we know a great deal about the creation of appropriate constituencies to defend their common interests. Behavioral and social scientists are far from helpless in such situations.

More important, however, I believe that the real impact of psychology will be felt, not through the technological products it places in the hands of powerful men, but through its effects on the public at large, through a new and different public conception of what is humanly possible and what is humanly desirable.

I believe that any broad and successful application of psychological knowledge to human problems will necessarily entail a change in our conception of ourselves and of how we live and love and work together. Instead of inventing some new technique for modifying the environment, or some new product for society to adapt itself to however it can, we are proposing to tamper with the adaptive process itself. Such an innovation is quite different from a "technological fix." I see little reason to believe that the traditional model for scientific revolutions should be appropriate.

Consider, for example, the effect that Freudian psychology has already had on Western society. It is obvious that its effects, though limited to certain segments of society, have been profound, yet I do not believe that one can argue that those effects were achieved by providing new instrumentalities for achieving goals socially agreed upon. As a method of therapy, psychoanalysis has had limited success even for those who can afford it. It has been more successful as a method of investigation, perhaps, but even there it has been only one of several available methods. The impact of Freud's thought has been due far less to the instrumentalities he provided than to the changed conception of ourselves that he inspired. The wider range of psychological problems that Freud opened up for professional psychologists is only part of his contribution. More important in the scale of history has been his effect on the broader intellectual community and, through it, on the public at large. Today we are much more aware of the irrational components of human nature and much better able to accept the reality of our unconscious impulses. The importance of Freudian psychology derives far less from its scientific validity than from the effects it has had on our shared image of man himself.

I realize that one might argue that changes in man's conception of himself under the impact of advances in scientific knowledge are neither novel nor revolutionary. For example, Darwin's theory changed our conception of ourselves, but not until the past decade has it been possible to mount a truly scientific revolution based on biological science. One might argue that we are now only at the Darwinian stage in psychology, and that the real psychological revolution is still a century or more in the future. I do not find this analogy appropriate, however.

To discover that we are not at the center of the universe, or that our remote ancestors lived in a tree, does indeed change our conception of man and society, but such new conceptions can have little effect on the way we behave in our daily affairs and in our institutional contexts. A new conception of man based on psychology, however, would have immediate implications for the most intimate details of our social and personal lives. This fact is unprecedented in any earlier stage of the Industrial Revolution.

The heart of the psychological revolution will be a new and scientifically based conception of man as an individual and as a social creature. When I say that the psychological revolution is already upon us, what I mean is that we have already begun to change man's self-conception. If we want to further that revolution, not only must we strengthen its scientific base, but we must also try to communicate it to our students and to the public. It is not the industrialist or the politician who should exploit it, but Everyman, every day.

The enrichment of public psychology by scientific psychology constitutes the most direct and important application of our science to the promotion of human welfare. Instead of trying to foresee new psychological products that might disrupt our existing social arrangements, therefore, we should be self-consciously analyzing the general effect that our scientific psychology may have on popular psychology. As I try to perform this analysis for myself, I must confess that I am not altogether pleased with the results.

I would like now to consider briefly some of the effects we are having and where, in my view, our influence is leading at the present time. Let me begin with a thumbnail sketch of one major message that many scientific psychologists are trying to communicate to the public.

The Control of Behavior

One of the most admired truisms of modern psychology is that some stimuli can serve to reinforce the behavior that produces them. The practical significance of this familiar principle arises from the implication that if you can control the occurrence of these reinforcing stimuli, then you can control the occurrence of adaptive behavior intended to achieve or avoid them. This contingency between behavior and its consequences has been demonstrated in many studies of animal behavior, where environmental conditions can be controlled, or at least specified, and where the results can be measured with some precision.

Something similar holds for the human animal, of course, although it is complicated by man's symbolic proclivities and by the fact that the disparity between experimenter and subject changes when the subject is also a man. Between men, reinforcement is usually a mutual relation and each person controls the other to some extent. This relation of mutual reinforcement, which man's genius for symbols has generalized in terms of money or the promise of money, provides the psychological basis for our economic system of exchange. Psychologists did not create this economic system for controlling behavior, of course. What we have tried to do is to describe its psychological basis and its limits in terms sufficiently general to hold across different species, and to suggest how the technique might be extended to educational, rehabilitative, therapeutic, or even political situations in which economic rewards and punishments would not normally be appropriate. Once a problem of behavior control has been phrased in these terms, we may then try to discover the most effective schedule of reinforcements.

My present concern has nothing to do with the validity of these ideas. I am concerned with their effect on the public at large, for it is there, if I am right, that we are most likely to achieve a psychological revolution.

In the public view, I suspect, all this talk about controlling behavior comes across as unpleasant, if not actually threatening. Freud has already established in the public mind a general belief that all behavior is motivated. The current message says that psychologists now know how to use this motivation to control what people will do. When they hear this, of course, our scientific colleagues are likely to accuse us of pseudoscientific claims; less scientific segments of the public are likely to resent what they perceive as a threat to their personal freedom. Neither reaction is completely just, but neither is completely unjustifiable.

I believe these critics see an important truth, one that a myopic concentration on techniques of behavior control may cause us to overlook. At best, control is but one component in any program for personal improvement or social reform. Changing behavior is pointless in the absence of any coherent plan for how it should be changed. It is our plan for using control that the public wants to know about. Too often, I fear, psychologists have implied that acceptable uses for behavior control are either self-evident or can be safely left to the wisdom and benevolence of powerful men. Psychologists must not surrender the planning function so easily. Humane applications of behavior control must be based on intelligent diagnosis of the personal and social problems we are trying to solve. Psychology has at least as much, probably more, to contribute to the diagnosis of personal and social problems as it has to the control of behavior.

Regardless of whether we have actually achieved new scientific techniques of behavior control that are effective with human beings and regardless of whether control is of any value in the absence of diagnosis and planning for its use, the simple fact that so many psychologists keep talking about control is having an effect on public psychology. The average citizen is predisposed to believe it. Control has been the practical payoff from the other sciences. Control must be what psychologists are after, too. Moreover, since science is notoriously successful, behavior control must be inevitable. Thus the layman forms an impression that control is the name of the road we are traveling, and that the experts are simply quibbling about how far down that road we have managed to go.

Closely related to this emphasis on control is the frequently repeated claim that living organisms are nothing but machines. A scientist recognizes, of course, that this claim says far more about our rapidly evolving conception of machines than it says about living organisms, but this interpretation is usually lost when the message reaches public ears. The public idea of a machine is something like an automobile, a mechanical device controlled by its operator. If people are machines, they can be driven like automobiles. The analogy is absurd, of course, but it illustrates the kind of distortion that can occur.

If the assumption that behavior control is feasible in some precise scientific sense becomes firmly rooted in public psychology, it could have unfortunate consequences, particularly if it is coupled with an assumption that control should be exercised by an industrial or bureaucratic elite. Psychologists must always respect and advocate the principle of *habeas mentem*—the right of a man to his own mind

(Sanford, 1955). If we really did have a new scientific way to control human behavior, it would be highly immoral to let it fall into the hands of some small group of men, even if they were psychologists.

Perhaps a historical analogy would be appropriate. When the evolution of species was a new and exciting idea in biology, various social theorists took it up and interpreted it to mean that capitalistic competition, like the competition between species, was the source of all progress, so the great wealth of the new industrialists was a scientifically necessary consequence of the law of the survival of the fittest. This argument, called "social Darwinism," had unfortunate consequences, both for social science and for society generally (Hofstadter, 1944).

If the notion should now be accepted that is it a scientifically necessary consequence of the law of reinforcement that industrialists or bureaucrats must be allowed the same control over people that an experimenter has over his laboratory animals, I fear that a similar period of intolerable exploitation might ensue—if, indeed, it has not already begun.

The dangers that accompany a science of behavior control have been pointed out many times. Psychologists who study motivation scientifically are usually puzzled by this widespread apprehension that they might be successful. Control is not something invented by psychologists. Everyone is "controlled" all the time by something or other. All we want is to discover how the controls work. Once we understand that, society can use the knowledge in whatever manner seems socially advantageous. Our critics, on the other hand, want to know who will diagnose our problems, who will set our social goals, and who will administer the rewards and punishments.

All that I have tried to add to this familiar dialogue is the observation that the social dangers involved need not await the success of the scientific enterprise. Behavior control could easily become a self-fulfilling prophecy. If people generally should come to believe in the scientific control of behavior, proponents of coercive social programs would surely exploit that belief by dressing their proposals in scientific costumes. If our new public conception of human nature is that man's behavior can be scientifically controlled by those in positions of power, governments will quickly conform to that conception. Thus, when I try to discern what direction our psychological revolution has been taking, some aspects of it disturb me deeply and lead me to question whether in the long run these developments will really promote human welfare.

This is a serious charge. If there is any truth to it, we should ask whether any other approaches are open to us.

Personally, I believe there is a better way to advertise psychology and to relate it to social problems. Reinforcement is only one of many important ideas that we have to offer. Instead of repeating constantly that reinforcement leads to control, I would prefer to emphasize that reinforcement can lead to satisfaction and competence. And I would prefer to speak of understanding and prediction as our major scientific goals.

In the space remaining, therefore, I want to try to make the case that understanding and prediction are better goals for psychology than is control—better both for psychology and for the promotion of human welfare—because they lead us to think, not in terms of coercion by a powerful elite, but in terms of the diagnosis of problems and the development of programs that can enrich the lives of every citizen.

Public Psychology: Two Paradigms

It should be obvious by now that I have somewhere in the back of my mind two alternative images of what the popular conception of human nature might become under the impact of scientific advances in psychology. One of these images is unfortunate, even threatening; the other is vaguer, but full of promise. Let me try to make these ideas more concrete.

The first image is the one I have been describing. It has great appeal to an authoritarian mind, and fits well with our traditional competitive ideology based on coercion, punishment, and retribution. The fact that it represents a serious distortion of scientific psychology is exactly my point. In my opinion, we have made a mistake by trying to apply our ideas to social problems and to gain acceptance for our science within the framework of this ideology.

The second image rests on the same psychological foundation, but reflects it more accurately; it allows no compromise with our traditional social ideology. It is assumed, vaguely but optimistically, that this ideology can be modified so as to be more receptive to a truer conception of human nature. How this modification can be achieved is one of the problems we face; I believe it will not be achieved if we continue to advertise the control of behavior through reinforcement as our major contribution to the solution of social problems. I would not wish to give anyone the impression that I have formulated a well-defined social alternative, but I would at least like to open a discussion and make some suggestions.

My two images are not very different from what McGregor (1960) once called Theory X and Theory Y. Theory X is the traditional theory which holds that because people dislike work, they must be coerced, controlled, directed, and threatened with punishment before they will do it. People tolerate being directed, and many even prefer it, because they have little ambition and want to avoid responsibility. McGregor's alternative Theory Y, based on social science, holds that work is as natural as play or rest. External control and threats are not the only means for inspiring people to work. People will exercise self-direction and self-control in the service of objectives to which they are committed; their commitment is a function of the rewards associated with the achievement of their objectives. People can learn not only to accept but to seek responsibility. Imagination, ingenuity, and creativity are widely distributed in the population, although these intellectual potentialities are poorly utilized under the conditions of modern industrial life.

McGregor's Theory X and Theory Y evolved in the context of his studies of industrial management. They are rival theories held by industrial managers about how best to achieve their institutional goals. A somewhat broader view is needed if we are to talk about public psychology generally, and not merely the managerial manifestations of public psychology. So let me amplify McGregor's distinction by referring to the ideas of Varela, a very remarkable engineer in Montevideo, Uruguay, who uses scientific psychology in the solution of a wide range of personal and social problems.

Varela (1970, in press) contrasts two conceptions of the social nature of man. Following Kuhn's (1962) discussion of scientific revolutions, he refers to these two conceptions as "paradigms." The first paradigm is a set of assumptions on which our social institutions are presently based. The second is a contrasting paradigm based on psychological research. Let me outline them for you very briefly.

Our current social paradigm is characterized as follows: All men are created equal. Most behavior is motivated by economic competition, and conflict is inevitable. One truth underlies all controversy, and unreasonableness is best countered by facts and logic. When something goes wrong, someone is to blame, and every effort must be made to establish his guilt so that he can be punished. The guilty person is responsible for his own misbehavior and for his own rehabilitation. His teachers and supervisors are too busy to become experts in social science; their role to devise solutions and see to it that their students or subordinates do what they are told.

For comparison, Varela offers a paradigm based on psychological research: There are large individual differences among people, both in ability and personality. Human motivation is complex and no one ever acts as he does for any single reason, but, in general, positive incentives are more effective than threats or punishments. Conflict is no more inevitable than disease and can be resolved or, still better, prevented. Time and resources for resolving social problems are strictly limited. When something goes wrong, how a person perceives the situation is more important to him than the "true facts," and he cannot reason about the situation until his irrational feelings have been toned down. Social problems are solved by correcting causes, not symptoms, and this can be done more effectively in groups than individually. Teachers and supervisors must be experts in social science because they are responsible for the cooperation and individual improvement of their students or subordinates.

No doubt other psychologists would draw the picture somewhat differently. Without reviewing the psychological evidence on which such generalizations are based, of course, I cannot argue their validity. But I think most of you will recognize the lines of research on which McGregor's Theory Y and Varela's second paradigm are based. Moreover, these psychologically based paradigms are incompatible in several respects with the prevailing ideology of our society.

Here, then, is the real challenge: How can we foster a social climate in which some such new public conception of man based on psychology can take root and flourish? In my opinion, this is the proper translation of our more familiar question about how psychology might contribute to the promotion of human welfare.

I cannot pretend to have an answer to this question, even in its translated form, but I believe that part of the answer is that psychology must be practiced by non-psychologists. We are not physicians; the secrets of our trade need not be reserved for highly trained specialists. Psychological facts should be passed out freely to all who need and can use them. And from successful applications of psychological principles the public may gain a better appreciation for the power of the new conception of man that is emerging from our science.

If we take seriously the idea of a peaceful revolution based on a new conception of human nature, our scientific results will have to be instilled in the public consciousness in a practical and usable form so that what we know can be applied by ordinary people. There simply are not enough psychologists, even including nonprofessionals, to meet every need for psychological services. The people at large will have to be their own psychologists, and make their own applications of the principles that we establish.

Of course, everyone practices psychology, just as everyone who cooks is a chemist, everyone who reads a clock is an astronomer, everyone who drives a car is an engineer. I am not suggesting any radical departure when I say that nonpsychologists must practice psychology. I am simply proposing that we should teach them to practice it better, to make use self-consciously of what we believe to be scientifically valid principles.

Our responsibility is less to assume the role of experts and try to apply psychology ourselves than to give it away to the people who really need it—and that includes everyone. The practice of valid psychology by nonpsychologists will inevitably change people's conception of themselves and what they can do. When we have accomplished that, we will really have caused a psychological revolution.

How to Give Psychology Away

I am keenly aware that giving psychology away will be no simple task. In our society there are depths of resistance to psychological innovations that have to be experienced to be believed (Graziano, 1969).

Solving social problems is generally considered to be more difficult than solving scientific problems. A social problem usually involves many more independent variables, and it cannot be finally solved until society has been persuaded to adopt the solution. Many who have tried to introduce sound psychological practices into schools, clinics, hospitals, prisons, or industries have been forced to retreat in dismay. They complain, and with good reason, that they were unable to buck the "System," and often their reactions are more violent than sensible. The System, they say, refuses to change even when it does not work.

This experience has been so common that in my pessimistic moments I have been led to wonder whether anything less than complete reform is possible.

Deutsch (1969) has made an interesting case that competitive and cooperative social relationships tend to be mutually exclusive. He summarizes the result of considerable research in the following terms:

The strategy of power and the tactics of coercion, threat, and deception result from and also result in a competitive relationship. Similarly, the strategy of mutual problem solving and the tactics of persuasion, openness, and mutual enhancement elicit and also are elicited by a cooperative orientation [p. 4].

Each orientation has its own internal consistency; elements of one are not easily injected into the other.

Perhaps a similar pressure toward internal coherence lies at the root of public resistance to many of our innovative suggestions. It often seems that any one of our ideas taken alone is inadequate. Injected into the existing social paradigm it is either a foreign body, incompatible with the other presuppositions that shape our social institutions, or it is distorted and trivialized to fit the preexisting paradigm.

One of the most basic ideas in all the social sciences is the concept of culture. Social anthropologists have developed a conception of culture as an organic whole, in which each particular value, practice, or assumption must be understood in the context of the total system. They tell terrible tales about the consequences of introducing Western reforms into aboriginal cultures without understanding the social equilibria that would be upset.

Perhaps cultural integrity is not limited to primitive cultures, but applies also to our own society here and now. If so, then our attempts at piecemeal innovation may be doomed either to fail or to be rejected outright.

I label these thoughts pessimistic because they imply a need for drastic changes throughout the whole system, changes that could only be imposed by someone with dangerous power over the lives of others. And that, I have argued, is not the way our psychological revolution should proceed.

In my more optimistic moments, however, I recognized that you do not need complete authority over a social organization in order to reform it. The important thing is not to control the system, but to understand it. Someone who has a valid conception of the system as a whole can often introduce relatively minor changes that have extensive consequences throughout the entire organization. Lacking such a conception, worthwhile innovations may be total failures.

For example, if you institute a schedule of rewards and punishments in the psychiatric ward of a Veterans Hospital, you should not be indignant when the American Legion objects on the grounds that you cannot withhold food and clothing from veterans. If you had had a more adequate understanding of the hospital as a social system, you would have included the interests and influence of the American Legion in your diagnosis of the problem, and you would have formulated a plan to gain their endorsement as part of your task as a social engineer. You should not demand inordinate power just because you made an inadequate diagnosis of the problem. Understanding must come first.

In my optimistic moments I am able to convince myself that understanding is attainable and that social science is already at a stage where successful applications are possible. Careful diagnosis and astute planning based on what we already know can often resolve problems that at first glance seemed insurmountable. Many social, clinical, and industrial psychologists have already demonstrated the power of diagnosis and planning based on sound psychological principles.

Varela has illustrated such applications by his work in Uruguay. Diagnosis involves not only a detailed analysis of the social organization and of the perceptions and goals of all the people caught up in the problem, but also the description of their abilities and personalities. Planning involves the explicit formulation of a series of steps that will lead these people to consider the problem together and will help them to discover a solution that respects everyone's hopes and aspirations. If, in the course of this plan, it becomes necessary to persuade someone, this is not to be accomplished by coercion or by marshaling facts, but by a gradual, step-by-step process that enables him to reduce his reactance little by little as he convinces himself of the virtues of the alternative view and broadens his conception of the range of acceptable solutions (Zimbardo & Ebbeson, 1969, pp. 114–121). This is not the place and I am not the person to describe the ingenuity with which Varela has constructed such plans and carried them out, but such applications give me some reason for optimism.

Diagnosing practical problems and developing detailed plans to deal with them may or may not be more difficult than solving scientific problems, but it is certainly different. Many psychologists, trained in an empiricist, experimental tradition, have tried to serve two masters at once. That is to say, they have tried to solve practical problems and simultaneously to collect data of scientific value on the effects of their interventions. Other fields, however, maintain a more equitable division of labor between scientist and engineer. Scientists are responsible for the validity of the principles; engineers accept them and try to use them to solve practical problems.

Although I recognize the importance of evaluating an engineer's product, in this domain it is no easy thing to do. Assessing social innovations is a whole art in itself, one that we are only beginning to develop. Economic considerations are relevant, of course, but we must also learn to evaluate the subtler psychological and social implications of our new solutions (Bauer, 1966). Technological assessment in this sense will not be achieved by insisting that every reform should resemble a well-designed experiment. In particular, the need for assessment should not be allowed to discourage those who enjoy and have a talent for social engineering.

We are in serious need of many more psychological technologists who can apply our science to the personal and social problems of the general public, for it is through them that the public will eventually discover the new paradigm that psychologists are developing. That is to say, it is through the success of such practical applications that we have our best hope for revolutionizing public psychology.

Obviously, we must avoid the evils of superficiality; we must continue as scientists to refine, clarify, and integrate our new paradigm. Most importantly, we must self-consciously recognize that it *is* a new and revolutionary conception that we are working toward, so that isolated discoveries can be related to and evaluated in terms of that larger context. But all that would be futile, of course, if the general public did not accept it, or if public psychology were not altered by it.

There is no possibility of legislating the changes I have in mind. Passing laws that people must change their conceptions of themselves and others is precisely the opposite of what we need. Education would seem to be our only possibility. I do not mean only education in the schoolroom, although that is probably the best communication channel presently at our disposal. I have in mind a more ambitious program of educating the general public.

It is critically important to shape this education to fit the perceived needs of the people who receive it. Lecturers suitable for graduate seminars are seldom suitable for laymen, and for a layman facing a concrete problem they are usually worse than useless. In order to get a factory supervisor or a ghetto mother involved, we must give them something they can use. Abstract theories, however elegant, or sensitivity training, however insightful, are too remote from the specific troubles they face. In order to get started, we must begin with people where they are, not assume we know where they should be. If a supervisor is having trouble with his men, perhaps we should teach him how to write a job description and how to evaluate the abilities and personalities of those who fill the job; perhaps we should teach him the art of persuasion, or the time and place for positive reinforcement. If a ghetto mother is not giving her children sufficient intellectual challenge, perhaps we should teach her how to encourage their motor, perceptual, and linguistic skills. The techniques involved are not some esoteric branch of witchcraft that must be reserved for those with PhD degrees in psychology. When the ideas are made sufficiently concrete and explicit, the scientific foundations of psychology can be grasped by sixth-grade children.

There are many obvious and useful suggestions that we could make and that nonpsychologists could exploit. Not every psychological problem in human engineering has to be solved by a professional psychologist; engineers can rapidly assimilate psychological facts and theories that are relevant to their own work. Not every teaching program has to be written by a learning theorist; principles governing the design and evaluation of programmed materials can be learned by content specialists. Not every personnel decision has to be made by a psychometrician, not every interview has to be conducted by a clinical psychologist, not every problem has to be solved by a cognitive psychologist, not every reinforcement has to be supervised by a student of conditioning. Psychological principles and techniques can be usefully applied by everyone. If our suggestions actually work, people should be eager to learn more. If they do not work, we should improve them. But we should not try to give people something whose value they cannot recognize, then complain when they do not return for a second meeting.

Consider the teaching of reading, for example. Here is an obviously appropriate area for the application of psychological principles. So what do we do? We assemble experts who decide what words children know, and in what order they should learn to read them; then we write stories with those words and teachers make the children read them, or we use them in programmed instruction that exploits the principles of reinforcement. But all too often the children fail to recognize the value of learning these carefully constructed lessons.

Personally, I have been much impressed with the approach of Ashton-Warner (1963), who begins by asking a child what words he wants. Mummy, daddy, kiss, frightened, ghost, their own names—these are the words children ask for, words that are bound up with their own loves and fears. She writes each child's word on a large, tough card and gives it to him. If a child wants words like police, butcher, knife, kill, jail, and bomb, he gets them. And he learns to read them almost immediately. It is *his* word, and each morning he retrieves his own words from the pile collected each night by the teacher. These are not dead words of an expert's choosing, but words that live in a child's own experience. Given this start, children begin to write, using their own words, and from there the teaching of reading follows naturally. Under this regimen, a word is not an imposed task to be learned with reinforcements borrowed from some external source of motivation. Learning the word is itself reinforcing; it gives the child something he wants, a new way to cope with a desire or fear. Each child decides where he wants to start, and each child receives something whose value he can recognize.

Could we generalize this technique discovered by an inspired teacher in a small New Zealand school? In my own thinking I have linked it with something that White (1959) has called competence motivation. In order to tap this motivational system we must use psychology to give people skills that will satisfy their urge to feel more effective. Feeling effective is a very personal thing, for it must be a feeling of effectiveness in coping with personal problems in one's own life. From that beginning some might want to learn more about the science that helped them increase their competence, and then perhaps we could afford to be more abstract. But in the beginning we must try to diagnose and solve the problems people think they have, not the problems we experts think they ought to have, and we must learn to understand those problems in the social and institutional contexts that define them. With this approach we might do something practical for nurses, policemen, prison guards, salesmen—for people in many different walks of life. That, I believe, is what we should mean when we talk about applying psychology to the promotion of human welfare.

If you tell me that such a program is too ambitious or too foreign to our conception of ourselves as scientists and practitioners, I must agree that I do not know where to place our fulcrum to move the world. My goal is to persuade you that this is the problem we face, and that we dare not leave it for bureaucrats or businessmen to solve. We will have to cope with it however we can, and I hope that someone has better ideas than I about how to do it.

I can see some promise for innovations in particular subcultures. If we apply our new paradigm in particular institutions—in schools, hospitals, prisons, industries—we can perhaps test its validity and demonstrate its superiority. Many such social experiments are already in progress, of course. And much of the recent surge of interest in community psychology (Bennett, 1966) has been stimulated by the realization that we really do have something to contribute to community life. Perhaps all this work will eventually have a cumulative effect.

One trouble, of course, is that we are trying to reverse the natural direction of influence. Ordinarily, an institution or a community models its own subculture more or less automatically after the larger culture in which it is embedded, and new members require little indoctrination in order to understand the tacit assumptions on which the institution is based. Whether the new paradigm will be powerful enough to reverse this direction is, I suppose, a matter for pure speculation at the present time. It seems unlikely that we will succeed, however, if each application of the new paradigm is viewed as unrelated to every other, and no attempt is made to integrate these experiments into a paradigm for society as a whole.

It is possible, however, that our society may not be quite as resistant as we anticipate. The demand for social relevance that we have been voicing as psychologists is only one aspect of a general dissatisfaction with the current state of our society. On every hand we hear complaints about the old paradigm. People are growing increasingly alienated from a society in which a few wise men behind closed doors decide what is good for everyone. Our system of justice based on punishment and retribution is not working. Even those most blessed by economic rewards are asking for something more satisfying to fill their lives. We desperately need techniques for resolving conflicts, and for preventing them from becoming public confrontations from which reasonable retreat is impossible. Anyone who reads the newspapers must realize that vast social changes are in the making, that they must occur if civilized society is to survive.

Vested interests will oppose these changes, of course, but as someone once said, vested interests, however powerful, cannot withstand the gradual encroachment of new ideas. If we psychologists are ready for it, we may be able to contribute a coherent and workable philosophy, based on the science of psychology, that will make this general agitation less negative, that will make it a positive search for something new.

I recognize that many of you will note these ambitions as little more than empty rhetoric. Psychologists will never be up to it, you will say. We should stay in our laboratories and do our own thing. The public will work out its own paradigms without us. Perhaps such skepticism is justified.

On the other hand, difficulty is no excuse for surrender. There is a sense in which the unattainable is the best goal to pursue. So let us continue our struggle to advance psychology as a means of promoting human welfare, each in our own way. For myself, however, I can imagine nothing we could do that would be more relevant to human welfare, and nothing that could pose a greater challenge to the next generation of psychologists, than to discover how best to give psychology away.

References

American Psychological Association. Bylaws of the American Psychological Association. In, *1968 Directory*. Washington, D. C.:Author, 1968.

Ashton-Warner, S. *Teacher*. New York: Simon & Schuster, 1963.

Bauer, R. A. (Ed.) *Social indicators*. Cambridge: MIT Press, 1966.

Bennett, C. C. *Community psychology*. (Report of the Boston Conference on the Education of Psychologists for Community Mental Health) Boston: Boston University, 1966.

Davis, K. The perilous promise of behavioral science. In, *Research in the service of man: Biomedical knowledge, development, and use*. (A conference sponsored by the Subcommittee on Government Research and the Frontiers of Science Foundation of Oklahoma for the Committee on Government Operations of the United States Senate, October 1966) Washington, D.C.: United States Government Printing Office, 1967.

Deutsch, M. Reflections on some experimental studies of interpersonal conflict. Presidential address to the Eastern Psychological Association, New York, April 11, 1969.

Graziano, A. M. Clinical innovation and the mental health power structure: A social case history. *American Psychologist*, 1969, **24**, 10–18.

Hofstadter, R. *Social Darwinism in American thought*. Philadelphia: University of Pennsylvania Press, 1944.

Kuhn, T. *The structure of scientific revolutions*. Chicago: University of Chicago Press, 1962.

Ladd, E. C., Jr. Professors and political petitions. *Science*, 1969, **163**, 1425–1430.

McGregor, D. *The human side of enterprise*. New York: McGraw-Hill, 1960.

Sanford, F. H. Creative health and the principle of *habeas mentem*. *American Psychologist*, 1955, **10**, 829–835.

Tyler, L. An approach to public affairs: Report of the ad hoc Committee on Public Affairs. *American Psychologist*, 1969, **24**, 1–4.

Varela, J. A. *Introduction to social science technology*. New York: Academic Press, 1970, in press.

White, R. W. Motivation reconsidered: The concept of competence. *Psychological Review*, 1959, **66**, 297–333.

Zimbardo, P., & Ebbeson, E. *Influencing attitudes and changing behavior*. Reading, Mass.: Addison-Wesley, 1969.

Psychologists and Federal Legislation

We have an interesting and diversified group of discussants for our symposium "Psychologists and Federal Legislation." Congressman Donald Fraser of Minnesota will give the main address. Next, John Kramer, who is Executive Director of the National Council on Hunger and Malnutrition in the United States and who, by admission, is an activist and very concerned about this most serious problem, will discuss how he tries to influence legislation. He will be followed by Marcia Guttentag, a psychologist with the Graduate Center of the City University of New York who is very much concerned with problems of poverty and segregation and their influence on the psychology of perception, particularly in children.

I thought I would set the stage by posing the problems facing psychologists as we attempt to influence legislation at the national level. I have tried to systematize my thoughts under three major headings: (a) What legislation do we try to influence? (b) Having decided what legislation to try to influence, how do we go about exerting influence and making an impact? (c) Who among psychologists appropriately tries to exercise this influence?

Under the area of "What legislation do we try to influence?" there are three categories. First, psychologists try to influence legislation which directly affects them. There are problems of civil service pay rates which directly affect psychologists. There are public laws, such as Medicare, which affect how psychologists are paid. There are proposed laws regarding psychological testing. As a profession we have a very legitimate reason to be concerned with these aspects of legislation.

There is a second class of legislation with which we are concerned. It deals with general professional problems which are not unique to psychology. These are the broad classes of professional problems in which we join hands with other professions in expressing our point of view. For example, there certainly will be some kind of regulations of animal experimentation. This is of concern to psychologists, physicians, physiologists, etc. We need to be concerned, along with other professionals, about privileged communications. I think it is turning out that psychologists frequently are forced by courts to divulge information, privileged communications, whereas physicians would not be required to make such information available. We need to work toward common legislation in this respect.

There is a third category of legislation which is much broader; it is not of immediate and direct concern to our own profession or allied professions. This is in the broad area of the general public welfare. What do we think about President Nixon's new welfare programs? Do psychologists as an organized group concern themselves with them or are we only concerned as citizens? Consider the recent debate over the ABM. Should psychology have expressed a point of view? Some ad hoc professional groups did, for example, the ad hoc Committee of Computer Professionals against the ABM. There was no corresponding group of psychologists. Should there have been? Certainly the military-industrial complex is a matter of concern. Some of the actions at this convention have implied certain interests in that area. Many of you are concerned with the functioning of higher education. It has been estimated that within a few years the federal government will be providing 50% of all funds for higher education. How should psychologists stand on such issues?

Having decided the issues we want to influence, there are the questions: How do we influence? What do we do? There are many things we can do. We can draft bills, as we have done in some states, and ask friendly legislators to introduce these bills. How far should we go in this respect? There is the question of testifying at hearings. It is fairly easy to testify at a hearing; I have done it four or five times. You let the responsible congressman or his staff know you are interested in testifying, and they will usually invite you. Also, you can communicate with your own representative. That is the traditional way, but some of us wonder how efficacious it is.

There is a second layer or structure in Congress: the staffs of congressmen and other permanent committees, which have a great influence on what Congress does. We can get to know them and influence them. Perhaps most important, we can engage directly in political activities as individuals; we can go out and campaign. Perhaps we should run for Congress. I believe that 80% of all legislators are lawyers; shouldn't there be some psychologists?

Next, there is the question of "Who communicates for psychology?" We have identified various issues on which we wish to exert influence. We have the problem of how to exert this influence. Then there is the question of who does the influencing.

What role should the organized profession of psychology take in influencing legislation? Should the executive officer or his representative in the APA actively try to influence legislation and, if so, what kind of legislation? How should other psychologists exercise their responsibility in this role? Should our APA president and heads of committees feel an obligation to represent psychology in administrative halls? Then there is the specialist—the psychologist who has studied a particular problem intensively. Should he come forward? There are also our friends in the physical sciences and in other areas on whom we can exert influence and who often have greater power than we do. How should we relate to them? Finally, there is the out-and-out paid lobbyist. Should psychologists become associated with such lobbying? The California State Psychological Association has employed a paid representative from time to time. Should we do that on a national level?

These questions pose a number of the problems we need to be concerned with in furthering our interest in promoting the public welfare through our knowledge and skill in the practice of psychology.

Having made these introductory remarks, I would like to present Congressman Fraser. Congressman Fraser is one of the influential young members of the

United States House of Representatives. He has been in the House since 1962. His father was Dean of the Law School at the University of Minnesota. I gather he has spent much of his life around the University. He took his Bachelor and Law degrees at the University of Minnesota and entered the practice of law in the University district. He soon ran for the Senate of the State Legislature of Minnesota, where he served from 1954 to 1962. He then ran for election to the United States House of Representatives. He was elected and serves in a distinguished capacity in the House, being a member of a number of important committees. Most importantly, he is Chairman of the Democratic Study Group, a group of liberal congressmen who form a caucus which attempts to influence legislation coming to the House having to do with problems of broad public welfare.

LAUNOR F. CARTER
Symposium Chairman

The chairman received his PhD from Princeton University in 1941. He is currently a vice-president of the System Development Corporation and Manager of its Public Systems Division. This Division is concerned with the application of modern technology to education, health programs, and other public areas.

Congress and the Psychologist

DONALD M. FRASER

The author received his LLB from the University of Minnesota in 1948. He is presently a member of the United States House of Representatives, representing the City of Minneapolis, Minnesota's Fifth Congressional District. He serves on the Foreign Affairs Committee, the District of Columbia Committee, and is Chairman of the Democratic Study Group, the liberal caucus of House Democrats.

It has been suggested that I discuss the contributions a psychologist might make to the legislative process and, in this connection, that I mention what kinds of inputs to the legislative process are welcome, and what communications problems might be expected between the Congress and psychologists.

Thus, in preparation for this undertaking, I sent memos to some of my colleagues who chair subcommittees, asking them about their experiences, if any, with testimony by psychologists. The inquiry was more productive than I had imagined it would be. The role of the professional psychologist in congressional hearings is a valuable and expanding one. Let me give you some examples.

Examples of Psychologists as Witnesses

Representative Edith Green wrote me that her subcommittee of the House Committee on Education and Labor had heard numerous professional witnesses on such subjects as preschool problems, problems with dropouts and juvenile delinquency, vocational rehabilitation, and problems of the elderly. In particular, she cited an outstanding presentation by Dr. Bruno Bettelheim of the University of Chicago on the motivations that lie behind the unrest on our college campuses.

Other colleagues reported on their use of advice from psychologists on such subjects as (*a*) stresses in the work of Federal Aviation Agency controllers, (*b*) drug abuse, (*c*) human factors of manned space flight, (*d*) basic research in the behavioral sciences, (*e*) psychological and psychiatric problems connected with health, (*f*) education programs affecting American Indians and the peoples of Guam and Micronesia, and (*g*) psychological aspects of designing safety features of freeways.

Professor Carl Pfaffman of the Rockefeller University made an impressive contribution to a 1965 report to the House Committee on Science and Astronautics by the National Academy of Sciences. He wrote on the subject of research in the behavioral sciences as related to national goals.

A very serious problem explored by Representative Cornelius Gallagher, Chairman of a Special Subcommittee on Invasion of Privacy, brought forth testimony from Dr. Arthur H. Brayfield, a former executive officer of the American Psychological Association. The issue was whether the MMPI and other personality tests were valid measuring devices for administrative purposes, and whether they violated the right of the individual against invasion of his privacy. A subsidiary question was what qualifications a person needed in order to administer tests of this kind at various levels of sophistication.

A brief but interesting presentation by Professor David C. McClelland of Harvard was made to the Subcommittee on International Organizations and Movements of the House Foreign Affairs Committee in 1967 on the subject of the contribution of psychologists to policy planning in the foreign aid program. I might add that the speaker concluded his remarks by declaring that "It is time to get behavioral scientists in the government who know something about human motivation, who are there at the time policy decisions are being made."

Perhaps I should also mention the very eloquent statement by Dr. Karl Menninger before the Senate Foreign Relations Committee, June 1969, during hearings addressed to the "Psychological Aspects of Foreign Policy." He spoke about the inconsistent ways in which irrational political man was waging war in Vietnam, destroying natural beauty everywhere, educating our youth to the skills of crime in misnamed "houses of correction," and other social defects.

These examples of professional psychologists testifying before congressional committees illustrate the type of assistance your profession contributes to the making of the laws.

Congress

I next want to describe briefly the nature of Congress and especially the nature of committee hearings, the point at which the expert witness comes into contact with the congressional process.

Congress is made up mostly of lawyers—about two-thirds of its members are lawyers. This, by the way, I believe is a much higher percentage than one finds in a state legislature. But while a psychologist would find many common characteristics among lawmakers, a political scientist would find wide divergencies.

In fact, I was intrigued when I read the other day about a study of candidates for the Oregon legislature. The study revealed that candidates with low self-esteem tended to win in their races for the legislature. If that quality bears a linear relationship to the number of successful campaigns of an officeholder, that research may have a message for some of us who up to now were proud we had never lost an election. This may not be exactly the kind of expert testimony for which the Congress is looking.

It is almost always possible to find in Congress members with sympathetic views and understanding of a position a witness favors. It is also almost certain that there will be some whose views are decidedly unsympathetic. But on most issues, Members of Congress are looking for guidance. They are looking for evidence—factual information about the alternative possibilities, normative indications as to what the electorate (their constituents) want, and an indication as to what the leaders of Congress itself believe to be the proper course.

The appropriate and most accessible leader on any given issue is the chairman of the congressional committee that is holding hearings on relevant legislation, or, perhaps, the ranking minority member. Those witnesses who can present a carefully considered, soundly reasoned, and factually based case to such important leaders make an impact on the Congress.

One common characteristic of congressional hearings is that they do not follow a standard procedure. Some hearings are strictly for publicity purposes. Some are merely routine performances to document the history of noncontroversial legislation. Some serve to explore widely the ramifications of a legislative proposal that has been introduced merely to open up the subject for discussion. Some are to test out the market. Some are deliberately intended to demonstrate the strength of the opposition to the idea proposed. These are only a few of the many possibilities. The fact is that congressional hearings serve many purposes, and quite often several at once. It is also important to remember that only a small percentage of all the bills introduced reach the hearing stage, and many of them do not go on to become law.

Another peculiarity of hearings is that they are rarely attended by all members of the committee. Frequently, the chairman presides all alone—with the committee staff, but no other members. A cost/effectiveness analyst might well suggest that the public purposes of such a hearing might be served with more economy by recording a conversation in the chairman's office. While there is some truth in this, it is a matter of high policy to preserve the hearing procedure. To abandon open hearings before a committee would be like abandoning elections because many eligible voters choose not to exercise their franchise. Always remember that what is said remains on the record and reaches many eyes. Hearings are published, and the published results of some hearings become hot items on the Government Printing Office's list.

When the issue is important and opinions differ widely and strongly, the hearing is likely to be well attended by committee members and by the public, and also well covered by the press. All these tend to go together.

Expert Witnesses

Are there any general rules of behavior for expert witnesses? Not very many. The general rules are mostly a matter of common sense.

As an old trial lawyer, I always remember the sign on the back of one courtroom door. As you leave you see these words: "If you told the truth you don't have to remember what you said." I was impressed with one congressional witness who was confronted with a different opinion than the one he had just given, the different opinion allegedly being one he himself had given a year or so earlier. He laconically replied that he could not very well remember if the quoted words were his from an earlier time, but that it did not matter since he always testified to what he believed at the time of testifying, and that he may very well have changed his opinion since then.

A corollary, of course, is the advice a trial lawyer must always give a witness: "If you don't know the answer to a question, don't hesitate to say so."

Thus, the expert witness should qualify himself as an expert, establish the relevance of his expertise for the problem at hand, describe the alternative courses of action that are available, and present his data and their interpretation in terms of the probabilities of outcomes and their effects.

Perhaps I should say a word about jargon, the mystique of specialized languages, and their effects on the outside. As parents we encounter the frustrating experience of the verbal "generation gap." My son, John, who took driver training this summer, was describing one day his route from Minneapolis to our summer place. He kept using the expression "hang a left," which my wife, who bridges this gap more easily than I, told me means to make a left turn. In the same way, the jargon terms of a science can be frustrating to the legislator.

Members of Congress usually serve continuously on one committee and are often able to absorb the technical language associated with the business of that committee. The reason for this continuous service on one committee is to be found in the seniority concept that is commonly misunderstood to refer to length of service in Congress. Except for minor considerations, the real importance of seniority is on committees, and if you change a committee after 10 years, you start at the bottom. This is the reason why members rarely change committees after the first few years.

Even after such continuous service, however, members are not able to master all the special words and special meanings used by all the experts. Confusion over language can be a fundamental obstacle to communication. I refer to the basic working assumptions of the different disciplines and their potential for creating misunderstandings with the generalists in Congress. Congressmen assume that people will respond to such forces as pride, guilt, hope of gain, sense of responsibility, belief in equity, and the like. From the point of view of the psychologist this may be unscientific, but it appears to the congressmen that these forces relate to the way people actually behave. When psychologists come in contact with the legislative process, it is important for them to remember that their specialized attitudes toward these forces may differ from those held by the Members of Congress.

One way for psychologists to enhance their effectiveness as witnesses in congressional hearings might be for them to familiarize themselves with the psychological assumptions of the law, of jurisprudence, and of normative behavior. Behavioral psychology in particular will in time have a great impact on the content of the law. But it is necessary to understand what is to be changed before one tries to change it.

Specific Areas of Concern for Psychologists

Let me give you a concrete illustration of the way Congress needs to work with social scientists. In an address to the American Bar Association, August 11, 1969, Chief Justice Warren E. Burger proposed a review of all aspects of handling criminals, from conviction through their release from prison. The Chief Justice said there had to be a way "to make our correctional system better than the revolving door process . . . of crime, prison, and more crime." He called for experiments by society with incentive programs to encourage inmates in penitentiaries to prepare themselves for release into society, for special arrangements under which inmates might be permitted to leave confinement during working hours, and for investigation of the "abnormal psychology of the habitual offender."

Crime has become a deep concern of the electorate, and accordingly a priority matter for the national legislature. It is also—quite evidently—a subject with many facets of interest to psychologists. It is concerned with motivation, group behavior, the learning process, effects of punishment, attitudinal analysis, sex behavior, and many other matters. In the past, our treatment of criminals has been hung up on the horns of the dilemma between punishment and correction. Our language reflects this. Prisons are alternatively houses of correction and penal institutions. The inmates are paying their debts to society, but they may be placed on parole on evidence that some sort of a process of reform has occurred.

For years we have known we were doing something wrong—that our accumulated social wisdom embodied in the law was defective. On the one hand, we adhered to the doctrine that certain apprehension and severe punishment deterred crime. On the other hand, we adhered to the doctrine that criminal behavior was not inborn and could be corrected. The rising statistics of recidivism alarmed us; hopeful statistics of parolees who did not resume a life of crime reassured us.

Bit by bit, the public has grown in sophistication—has come to realize that the control of crime cannot be simple. It is complicated and costly. As our crime rate continues to rise, it is necessary that we find some new answers. Psychologists have a role to play in this matter.

Congress can only play its role of passing effective laws and financing an improved criminal justice system if a public consensus has developed. A public consensus based on our best knowledge depends greatly on effective communication from the social scientists who have studied these questions.

Crime is not the only area of concern, despite the immense public concern about crime today. Congress is dealing with many other areas of vital public interest.

The problems of education, especially for the disadvantaged child, are real to the Congress. Some of us believe that the difficulties facing the disadvantaged child must be viewed in a very broad context, arising out of major cultural, or subcultural, differences and not easily dealt with by eliminating some of our shortcomings in education. The entire antipoverty program with its varied and innovative programs needs far more understanding from the point of view of the social psychologist. I, for one, tend to be impressed with the self-redemptive qualities of militancy. But these are impressions gained from brief and sporadic reading plus experience and intuition, rather than from carefully documented research.

There are, of course, many other areas in which psychologists have important insights to contribute, and I shall not try for an exhaustive list. But before leaving this question of substantive areas in which the profession of the psychologist may have substantive contributions, I want to make two observations.

First, the executive branch tends, perhaps too often, to set the style for committee hearings. If the executive branch brings in a psychologist to back up its ideas or positions, it becomes both logical and legitimate for the committee to search out others who will contradict or challenge in some fashion the administration witnesses. The executive branch is often seen as having the best access to expertise; the pattern tends to be established by them. Thus at some point you may wish to inquire into the use by the executive branch of the expertise of psychologists.

The other observation that I wish to make has been impressed upon me with great force as we have moved into the great debate over defense spending. Perhaps

I can summarize the point by quoting an adage of uncertain vintage, namely, that to ask the right question is to be halfway to the answer. Often the problem of congressional committees is that they are not asking the right questions. The result is that they get answers that are either irrelevant or even misleading. This was one of my strongest impressions arising out of the infamous Camelot project in Latin America designed to identify, as I recall, factors leading to instability in these countries. Psychologists can help make us more aware of the reasons why wrong questions are asked.

Awareness of the Potential of Psychologists' Contributions

How are we as politicians in the Congress to profit by the accumulated wisdom of the professional psychologists? With all the problems that confront us in the Congress, we often lack information on how you as psychologists can help; we do not know which of you to believe; and we cannot wait for the tests of time to sort out the true doctrine from the false.

Every bureaucrat and every politician must make decisions of great social impact on the basis of incomplete information. I have no doubt that the psychological profession can greatly reduce the incompleteness of information about our problems.

That is why I make such a point of the need for your profession, and for other disciplines in the social sciences, to develop more statesmen who can be spokesmen for your sciences in dealing with the Congress.

For social scientists, including psychologists, to enlarge their rapport with the Congress, I suggest that three sets of actions would be helpful.

First, there must be a better understanding on the part of the scientist that Members of Congress are supreme generalists, whose days are crowded with an ever-increasing information overload and whose task involves a multifaceted bargaining process.

Second, in the presentation by the scientists of information to the Members of Congress, advocacy should not rise above objectivity. It is important for Congress to know the probable results of alternative courses, including those already adopted.

There may be some psychologists who have difficulty in choosing what role to play when they come before a committee of the Congress: whether they should be objective and dispassionate scientists, disciplined to receive and analyze and interpret factual evidence; or, on the other hand, whether they care so deeply about some particular program or outcome that they prefer to depart from the role of scientist to become emotionally committed participants, to engage in the political process, to involve themselves in an adversary relationship.

I do not mean to suggest that a scientist should not also be a citizen and a political participant. But I do suggest that it can sometimes be difficult for a scientist to be an advocate of a political position and a scientist at the same hearing. It is necessary for him to let the committee know which role he has chosen, and it is necessary for him to stick to that role. The scientist who presents technical data and analysis bearing on an issue before a congressional committee and then changes hats to become an advocate tends to cancel out all the value of his professional testimony. He compromises the value of his professional contribution.

Third, nothing is of more value to a legislator than sources of pertinent information on which he can depend. The converse is also true and more infuriating. If the professional societies—not just psychologists, but those in all the learned disciplines—would systematically determine what kinds of technical information are needed by the Congress, and would then systematically assemble this information in an objective and professional way, exposed to criticism and review from within each discipline, before making it available to the legislators, it is my view that the Congress would be better equipped to make the law, and the scientists and other professional people would be more comfortable with it.

The Social Relevance of the Psychologist

JOHN R. KRAMER

The author received his LLB from the Harvard Law School in 1962. He is Executive Director of the National Council on Hunger and Malnutrition in the United States. He is currently interested in reforming federal food programs and food marketing and distribution in the United States.

Every profession in this country is confronting the problem of justifying its own existence in terms of its contribution to the social and political here and now. No longer does an excellent track record obviate the necessity for constant self-examination to determine whether the profession's work product has any implications for, let alone impact upon, the dominant pressing concerns of the present. As the 1969 APA Convention has so dramatically demonstrated, even psychologists yearn to be "relevant" now that some form of revolution seems to be at hand. The real revolution, of course, is the surfacing of the insistent demand for "relevancy." This demand arises from the daily morass of jobbism, of salary, of office space, and of project grants and forces us to ask: Have I justified my existence during the past eight hours? Whose lives have I affected favorably? Does my output really make any difference to my fellow man?

This internal challenge is revolutionary because Socratic self-awareness directed at one's role and function has, until recently, scarcely troubled professionals. Only now are professionals recognizing that they must be responsible to a broader universe than their immediate paying clients, that their work has (or, at least, should have) a more significant public impact which they must seek to control for constructive purposes. Never forget that your research may seem like an end in itself to you, but, to rank outsiders with other agendas, it may be a means to other goals. The supervocal concern for "relevancy" represents an effort by professionals to drag themselves out of their private closets into the public arena. We have come all the way from Proust's cork-lined walls to the din of the demonstration.

Psychologists, of course, are not accustomed to being held accountable to society at large. Your findings and conclusions have normally been the subject of fierce intramural debate in the trade journals but not much beyond. In 1969, however, your data and analyses are not very meaningful apart from their social consequences. Making a telling point on the "Letters to the Editor" page no longer seems as satisfying as attempting gamely, if unsuccessfully, to speak out on and remedy the social condition. Objectivity suddenly has a different hue. Today it means pursuing ends. "Relevance" is synonymous with immersion in politics, and politics for psychologists involves the conscious manipulation of insight to achieve predetermined goals. After such research, what action?

Political Infection of Science

Certainly there should be little new or startling in the fact that politics infects science. Scientists have, in the past, sought to fight off that infection. What is novel is the concern that the infection be fostered, but be socially benevolent. The following is an example from the popular field of hunger and malnutrition in which my limited expertise lies.

The basic "scientific" instrument for determining what one ought to consume to maintain proper nutrition is a table known as the Recommended Daily Dietary Allowances (RDAs) formulated by the Food and Nutrition Board of the National Research Council of the National Academy of Sciences. Since 1940 these so-called RDAs have provided the standards upon which nutritionists have relied in judging adequate daily nutrient consumption. If you fail to meet your RDA in any particular vitamin or mineral for a prolonged period of time and if the deficiency is substantial from a percentage point of view, then you are probably malnourished, even though perhaps not seriously enough to evidence conditions requiring medical treatment. This Rock of Gibraltar of the RDAs is, however, encrusted with politics.

Ascorbic acid, or as we popularly refer to it vitamin C, is essential to human life. British sailors in the eighteenth century found that out when they had no access to citrus fruit for prolonged periods of time. After they discovered that, they became known as "Limeys." Research in the United States on the human body's need for and utilization of ascorbic acid was originally dominated by Dr. Charles King, who, during the crucial early years of the RDAs, was chairman of the subcommittee on ascorbic acid. We know something about ascorbic acid, but not too much. We know, for example, that if you failed to take approximately 10 milligrams of ascorbic acid per day over a considerable period of time, you would develop scurvy. We also know that if you drank enough orange juice to yield more than 70 milligrams, the excess would be eliminated by body functions. What we do not know is what the average adult male has to take in, although this is the essence of the RDAs. With Dr. King as chairman of the subcommittee, the original RDA standard for vitamin C was fixed at 70 milligrams, not because that much was known to be needed, but because Dr. King was known to be loved and admired. Dr. King no longer heads the committee. Accordingly, as of 1968, the RDA for ascorbic acid is 60 milligrams. Somehow the loss of a man meant that an adult male needed less milligrams of vitamin C daily. Dr. King holds no sway in the United Kingdom or in Canada. In Great Britain the RDA for vitamin C is 20 milligrams; in Canada, it is 30 milligrams.

In this instance (and I suppose if we were to scrutinize all of the RDAs with an equally jaundiced eye, some of the others would also evidence the strains of backslapping and determinations controlled by impure considerations) the great god Science has been had. Virtue is no longer triumphant. But the real vice would be if we could not make sure that from the rape of Science issued a praiseworthy child. The various citrus growers associations in this country owe Dr. King a debt of thanks. But so do those of us who try to prove to the country that millions of people are malnourished and in need of increased purchasing power to buy good food in quantities so that we can achieve a guaranteed income. We cannot afford to look unfavorably at any development, however "unscientific," that tends to increase the statistical incidence of malnutrition. Thus, the scientist, subject to personal political stresses, becomes "unwittingly" relevant to major social issues.

Potential Insights from Psychologists

Psychologists have a definite capacity to offer the rest of us fruitful insights into the social and political issues that appear on the front pages of our newspapers and are prominent on the six o'clock news broadcasts. There are many American dilemmas that cry out for psychological explanations, but that have been unfortunately ignored. For instance, who is there who has sought to explain to the American public the widespread "Moynihan syndrome," which is the tendency of the good guys and even the bad guys to waste all their energies attacking their best friends rather than their real enemies? The most immediate example is what has happened during this convention with the Psychologists for Democratic Action focusing exclusively on criticizing the sympathetic APA and ignoring the hostile world without. The classical example, of course, is what happened to Patrick Moynihan when he released his report on the status of the Negro family in late 1965. The black outrage that erupted led to the ultimate dissolution of the original civil rights movement, which went through its death throes at the White House Conference on Civil Rights in June 1966.

Why haven't psychologists sought to inform this country of why the black militants should hate the Uncle Toms and fellow traveling whites more than they hate the racists, or why one faction of the Students for a Democratic Society is more furious with the other than with the young Americans for Freedom or the John Birch Society? I do not know the answer, but I do know that psychologists have yet to explore in public forums the fruitfulness of employing the analogy of the family model, with its sibling hatreds and the patterns of father-son rivalry, in seeking to cast light on these characteristics.

Who has spoken out in a meaningful manner about what lies behind the sickening, familiar pattern of liberal guilt that results in automatic and unthinking kowtowing to demands for violence and reparations in place of reasoned consideration and that compels whites to allow themselves to be shut out of events and meetings and seem to enjoy it? Who has told us what this means about the psychology of liberals? Theologists, maybe; psychologists, no.

Who is there to reveal the blindness of the social myth makers, those rhetorical neo-Jeffersonians who loudly proclaim the charms of citizen participation and community control, but who fail to deal realistically with their Hamiltonian instincts when confronted with the logical consequences of their shibboleths for the few blacks living in white bigot neighborhoods in Queens, or intellectual freedom in anti-sex education areas in the Midwest, or minorities in any other place in this country in which the majority is constituted by people with whose values we strongly disagree?

Use of the Mass Media

The psychologist has a special role in explaining to the American public the whys and wherefores of these manifestations of prevalent American social diseases and in seeking to alleviate, if not cure, them. At the moment that role is almost entirely unfilled. You must come forward and fill it. You must educate the

American public and you must try to make your version of the truth stick. There is only one effective way to reach out with your knowledge to produce action, and that is to exploit the media before they exploit you. All the academic insight in the world represents only another addition to the card file in the local library unless it is disseminated ad nauseam over the airwaves and through nonelitist publications. You must always strive for a larger audience. If you talk to yourselves and only to yourselves, perhaps your minds will become sharper and your reasoning powers expanded, but the walls will surely close in on you and you will become what you fear most—100% irrelevant.

The importance of getting to the media as one component of a strategy to touch and affect the public beyond the academy should never be underestimated. You did not do so in your most recent major efforts at being relevant. You simply ignored the next step—employing your press and film coverage as leverage for escalating action rather than falling in love with publicity for its own sake. In 1968 the most dramatic action taken by APA to solve America's social crises was to decide to hold the next convention in Washington rather than in Chicago. In 1969 your highlight was the march to the White House to protest the war in Vietnam. Both of these actions, as you are well aware, had immense practical consequences. Mayor Daley has surrendered his throne in horror at the thought of losing the benefit of your hotel and meal bills. President Nixon has declared a moratorium in Vietnam.

The sarcasm is deserved. Each of the gestures was merely that—a good emotional release that had no impact on anything other than a column in a paper and a slot on the 11 o'clock news. Where is your long-range strategy for implementing the social changes you want? Did you talk to any other academic groups when you determined to sidestep Chicago? Did you ever attempt to generate a widespread boycott of the city? Did you ever try to plan other actions to effectively demonstrate your displeasure at what happened at the Democratic Convention? No, no, a thousand times no. You did your thing, your minds were relieved, and so that evening you dined at the Rive Gauche instead of the Pump Room, and Mayor Daley could care less. Did you talk to the leaders of the October Moratorium about or consider for yourselves escalating your Vietnam concern by, among other possibilities, concertedly refusing as a profession to accept any government contracts in the field of defense or foreign policy or at veterans' hospitals until the war was seriously en route to termination? Of course not, and President Nixon probably does not even know you are in town unless someone has digested the papers for him.

I do not know how many of you saw the movie, "The Graduate," but the magic word for you has to be "politics," not "plastics." What you must do to survive is to apply the same level of craftsmanship and planning that you apply to generating papers to the art of programming your social demands through a carefully conceived progression of tactics to achieve what you desire. You have to become technocrats of change, which means being fully apprised of every conceivable political pressure point and what peculiar abilities you have for capitalizing on them, perhaps in concert with other groups, as long as you are constantly wary of being used by them for their own purposes. Above all, try to remain the master in your house, even though politics and social action is the name of the game.

Psychologists do not always have to be consultants for some other entrepreneur. They can seek to control and direct their own activities in social problem solving.

A Model for Action

Enough exhortation. Now for a simple program—you embroider the frills. If psychologists wish to acquire that invisible Washington quality, "clout," you will have to abandon the peace and superscrupulousness of paper preparation and enter the noisy, "shoot from the hip" arena of domestic (or foreign) policy, but armed with a strong factual predicate for every claim and contention. You can stand the heat only if you come into the kitchen with your dishes partially prepared and their final execution thoroughly plotted. To be ad hoc is a delight, but it rarely budges bureaucratic opponents, who are truly frightened only when they realize that outside critics are either privy to inside information as to how programs are being strangled or else have a stockpile of expertise that is greater than theirs. But developing and documenting your case are second nature to you anyway.

What is more difficult to grasp and perform is the swift shuttle between securing continuous media coverage of your particular campaign and mounting a tri-tiered attack directed at all the levels of government—executive and legislative as well as judicial—to assure a multiplier pressure impact. Nothing prompts a legislature to move quicker than a highly publicized threat to sue to bring the judiciary in to oversee program failures, and nothing goads an administrator to remedy his behavior faster than the announcement of the possible filing of a law suit or a call for a congressional hearing into his domain, with TV cameras whirring at the hearing door. Your shotgun must have three barrels if it is going to jolt the target, and the three must shoot in timed escalation.

The model is not meant to be a blueprint, but try this example. Suppose you decided that you wanted to terminate the smothering of your profession for political ends that disguise themselves in the form of a clause in your contracts with the government. When you embark upon evaluation projects for the federal government, you bind yourself to forego release of your findings about the strengths and weaknesses of the programs you are investigating. The silence pledge, universally extracted by a contractor whose limitless bargaining power makes it awesome to oppose, could be attacked by psychologists from many directions.

Declaratory judgment litigation could be brought by a group of contracting psychologists seeking to overturn that clause on various first amendment grounds, including the public's right to know (especially when government money is paying for the knowledge), and on the professional man's right to disseminate his work product when the client is a public one. Congressmen concerned with the value of programs involved in the area blanketed in secrecy could be approached to push for release of final data and interpretations. Each agency involved could be confronted with a petitioned demand to eradicate the offending contractual provisions. The demand, if unsuccessful, could be further pressed by a dramatic mass withholding of services from difficult agencies that could prove efficacious, since some agencies rely heavily on psychologists. All of this would be orchestrated in tune with a miniature media blitz, which would make John Q. Taxpayer aware that he shells out thousands to feed young and old psychologists who monitor federal programs he also supports in the millions and is later denied any opportunity to learn the worthlessness of much that he has paid for.

The example illustrates the need to coordinate numerous avenues of approach to social action and the importance of confining that action to issues with which psychologists as a professional body do not merely have a concern (I am certain that each article in the morning paper arouses at least some of you, including the obituaries), but more significantly have something to say that ought to be heard because of its intellectual bite and distinction. That, of course, does not eliminate many issues, including the anality of water polluters and the states of mind of industries, such as coal mining, which seem to enjoy defiling the land. Yet, since your scope of legislative (not to mention judicial or executive) attack has been limited to almost nothing in the past, it is best to begin by thinking small and carving out special issues for your own. Professional housecleaning should be foremost on the list, which means search and destroy missions to root out the qualities of your profession that have kept you so solipsistic and apolitical for years. Your initial target should be your own attitudes toward your major client—the United States Congress, but on your terms as much as possible, and the range of possibility depends on a combination of your own imagination and drive. Twenty-nine thousand individuals may not necessarily be creative, but they have a lot of collective muscle.

Issues to Confront

Issues that directly affect psychology as a profession should be the start, not the end, and even they should be selected in light of their ultimate effect upon society at large. If secrecy inhibits you, down with it. If freedom to criticize is a price you must pay for the federal buck, then be a whore no more. If there is a structural racism in psychology as there is in every other profession that dwells inside the castle of accreditation, then blow down the walls or at least make them easy to scale. That task of self-analysis followed by internal change could probably last a lifetime. As an outsider, I cannot pretend to pinpoint all of the focal questions that you silently ignore every day in your careers. You mask them so well that only you can uncover the critical issues that inhibit your profession from becoming free, the complex chain of sell-outs that we label our work.

You cannot allow the rest of the world to rot while you scrub your floor clean, however. On to the hustings to tackle law and order (Have you nothing to tell us of the devastation wreaked by the snowballing psychology of fear?) with testimonial support for suits against the legal instruments of repression, efforts to treat and work with the police to extinguish the flames of bitterness toward youth and minorities, public education activities to convince rich whites that the only thing they have to fear is fear itself whereas poor blacks have legitimate qualms, and any other local political tactic you can devise to reverse the galloping trend of projecting onto those we view as enemies our desire to strike out and hurt them. Law and order should also encompass concerted efforts by psychologists to change this nation's drug laws with white papers released to the press, law suits bolstered by evidence developed by psychologists as to the ratio between the harm caused to the individual and society by subjecting users of certain drugs to the penal system and the harm flowing from use of the drugs, lobbying efforts to include middle-aged, upper class drug users as potential felons, and, again, anything else that makes sense and moves mountains. To date the fight has been carried entirely by hippies, students, and the "narcs." Psychologists merely get paid to conduct research.

The list of issues on which you could and should be effective is endless. Perhaps one of the most fundamental problems in this society is the problem of the meaningfulness of labor, which is an inevitable by-product of the current controversy over adequate income maintenance for all. Recently, I spoke to a college graduate returned from a year in Israel during which this bright young man, brimming over with excitement and concern about Vietnam, poverty, and anything else you could name, had to spend eight hours a day working at a dull, mindless job in a factory to support his continued education. He loved those eight hours. Why? Because his horizons were enlarged or his intellect challenged or his wallet replenished? No. Because he was caught up in the fervor of a society in which every bit of work, however trivial, seems to be imbued with the national will to survive and prosper. His work had meaning because he was convinced that it was part of this national effort.

In the United States we, and this probably means you, are going to have to develop our own work teleology unless we wish to confront a growing crisis of work disaffection at every economic level. The executive who plays golf because he is so bored is no different, except in terms of his compensation, from the laborer who demands a three-day week because he cannot stomach what he is compelled to do for more than 24 hours. Both require your help in restructuring work and the attitudes toward it, or else we will become a nation of destructive malcontents. The demand for jobs when satisfied with slots meant for animals, however well paying, quickly translates itself into Wallaceite anger toward those above and below. I enjoy working late on my job and maybe you do on yours (not to mention week-long parties and social gatherings known as conventions), but few others do. They deserve your serious attention.

Psychologists have been equally slow to speak out and act on their own on matters about which they could make waves: the legitimate frustrations of 19- and 20-year-olds on campus; the propriety of enforced day care for preschoolers; the importance of instilling self-respect, not discipline, as an integral part of the educational process; the manner of manipulating guilt as a mechanism to prod manufacturers who would rather save costs than consumers' lives and well-being; and all of the other areas previously mentioned.

Tactics

There are numerous tactical questions that I should refer to. There is the pivotal problem of who communicates for psychology or which psychologists are to be "relevant." The answer cannot simply be "those who want to wear red arm bands" or "those who give a damn." On occasion, psychologists may have to act en masse through the Association or risk being unheard, for example, on the issues that relate to your practice. I would recommend that you seriously consider hiring, if you have not already done so, APA staff to keep watch over all agency developments that could affect the nature, level, and conditions imposed upon your grants and contracts and who, in addition, could alert the APA membership on a divisional basis when there are useful opportunities to testify on issue-oriented legislation or on agency practices and regulations.

For the Association to lobby congressmen and committees would be to invite sudden death under the tax laws. You simply cannot do that with the Internal Revenue Service looking over your shoulder, although the Association itself might testify from time to time. The lobbying difficulty goes beyond tax-exemption to the ability of the Association to speak on behalf of all 29,000 of you with respect to controversial items. The Urban Coalition has proved that mixing a lot of divergent characteristics in one bowl leads to separation and no coalescence. Ten psychologists will undoubtedly have 10 different opinions. Accordingly, ad hoc collections of psychologists, hopefully encompassing a few big names in the trade, make more sense because there would be no tax or human limitations. The result might be less substantial pressure than if the APA made its weight felt as an entity, but it probably is the best you can expect.

Testifying at hearings is by no means the only outlet for influence. Campaign contributions are the best, but none of you ought to be rich. Personal contact is second best. Congressmen have time to listen to you in private and are normally willing to do so, particularly if you leave your picketing signs in the lobby and plan to leave after no more than half an hour. The most well-known senators tend to be inaccessible, but you may have a friend who has a friend who . . ., etc.

The art of letter writing is no art at all and is more likely to be a waste of time, but if you are so inclined here are some hints from Representative Morris Udall: Address the letter correctly; identify the bill you are writing about; write only your own congressman or senators; be reasonably brief; be personal (do not parrot a form letter); give reasons for your position; give constructive suggestions; do not threaten or call names or be pretentious. That seems obvious enough, but you will violate one or more of these rules before you get through.

The ultimate results of all this organizing and activity may be nonexistent, but you will have tried. By undertaking the effort, you will be relevant and sleep soundly. Or will you?

Evaluation of Social Legislation

MARCIA GUTTENTAG

The author is an adjunct associate professor at the Graduate Center, City University of New York. A social psychologist, she studied at the University of Michigan, Harvard, and Adelphi University, where she received her PhD in 1960. Her research interests are the evaluation of social programs, and the relationship between urban school structure and children's attitudes. She is the editor of the forthcoming *Handbook of Evaluation Research*.

Helping and being helped are two distasteful and difficult human activities. If President Nixon's four-billion-dollar proposals on welfare, manpower training, and day-care centers pass Congress, the government will be more deeply involved in the "helping" business than ever before. As citizens, we psychologists, of course, share the same concerns for social justice, equality, and the amelioration of poverty as other citizens. We do have a serious respect for data—for discovering the facts even about complex social issues. But in that we are not very different from the people in other disciplines.

As psychologists though, we do have some special knowledge. I will comment briefly on two quite different ways in which that knowledge can profitably be used in social legislation. My remarks are directed first to what psychologists can contribute, not so much to the substance of federal legislation, but to the ways in which federal programs, once enacted, are administered and become social realities. Current psychological research, especially in social psychology, contains a great deal that can be directly applied to the manner in which federal programs are administered. Psychologists could now urge that the principles that have emerged from research be considered a part of any new federal programs for social welfare. I will use just two principles as an example, out of the many more that could be mentioned. Then I will comment on psychologists as evaluation researchers. In this role, they are becoming increasingly involved in policy decisions. It is their data on how well a program works or does not work that are used by decision makers—often with immediate political consequences.

Inherent Dangers of "Helping" Programs

The first of the two principles bearing on social legislation has to do with the dangers inherent in "helping" programs. To be the one who gives help can be difficult, as the research of Kaufmann and Zener (1968), Berkowitz (1969), Pepitone (1969), and others on altruism has shown. The helper's perceptions of the aided person may become distorted through the act of giving help. He who is aided is often seen to be culpable for his own plight.

To be the one who receives help, especially if few or no choices are available, is sometimes even worse. From studies of fate control in children (Lefcourt, 1966) to studies of the rehabilitation of psychiatric patients (Redlich & Freedman, 1966), it is evident that experiences which lessen an individual's autonomy have harmful effects. Powerlessness corrupts and absolute powerlessness corrupts absolutely.

This is a paradox. The government is committed to ever more massive programs of social help. Yet, being either the helper or the helped has deleterious effects. The answer, of course, is to minimize both the number of people and situations in which direct giving of help occurs. The substance or aim of a piece of social legislation is often much less important than its method of implementation. A basic principle for the success of any new federal program is, therefore, that the program largely avoid situations in which the roles of "helper" and "helped one" are sharply distinguished.

The acceptance of a service, training, or other form of aid should not require a person to forego or to sacrifice significant choices in other areas of his life. Making the choice to accept a service or training should not mean that a wide range of other choices is taken away.

This is done when a person is uprooted, or taken out of his normal environment. He is then deprived of too much for the sake of a service. This is what the Job Corps did. It offered job training in the setting of a total institution hundreds or thousands of miles away from the youths' homes, and in rural rather than urban environments, although most boys came from urban ghettos. Every part of a young man's day, not just that given to academic and job training, but also that related to his social and sexual life, was made subject to the rules of the institution. I will not enter the controversy on how well the Job Corps succeeded in giving job training to its population. The figures do indicate (Levitan, 1969) that if a youth stayed in the Job Corps for at least six months, he could learn a skill and earn a higher income. More important is the fact that a great many youths could not stand the total institutional life and left long before the six-month period elapsed. They found that they had to give up too much in order to remain. On the other hand, part of the success of the community mental health centers is undoubtedly related to their offering help without demanding exorbitant sacrifices. People can receive treatment without giving up their autonomy.

It is not just a changed physical environment that limits choices. It is also the number of different areas of the person's life that are intruded upon. The present welfare system is infamous for its terrible violations of the privacy and personal lives of welfare clients. The Social Security System, in contrast, has been justly praised for its impersonal administration and its refusal to intrude in recipients' lives.

The first principle offers a guideline for new social legislation: The greater the number of choices a person must sacrifice in order to receive any service or training, the less likely it is that the service will meet the social aims for which it was designed. We must applaud President Nixon's attempt to provide an income floor as a replacement for the present welfare system. What remains to be seen is the *way* in which job training and work opportunity programs will be linked to the income proposals. One can now predict that if it is *necessary* to work, while receiving benefits or in order to receive benefits, there will be regrettable social consequences.

Governmental Accountability

A second principle that can be mentioned is that the more a government program is accountable to its *consumers,* the greater is the likelihood that it will succeed. Not only will it gain the acceptance of its clients, but it will also succeed in terms of congressional objectives.

President Nixon's message on the decentralization of the new manpower programs showed an awareness of the importance of local and regional decision making. This would keep manpower programs close to labor market conditions and would prevent the further growth of a distant and unresponsive federal bureaucracy. But decentralization is not enough. Money strengthens the power of whatever agency receives it. Local bureaucracies, like federal ones, can exercise arbitrary power and control over the choices of their clients. The people who are being served often know best what they need. They certainly know when they are being abused. Accountability is a vague term in current vogue. Accountability for federal programs must go in two directions—to the taxpayers and to the consumers of the programs.

Goldenberg's (1970, in press) work in New Haven provides an illustration of a recent, good appreciation of the principle of accountability toward consumers. About three years ago he became distressed by the lack of relationship between Job Corps training and local labor market conditions. Backed by the Department of Labor, he began an experimental job training center. It was staffed and run completely by the youths who were the consumers of the service. They decided what training was needed based on the local labor market and specified under what conditions they were to receive the training. Not only was the venture much less costly than institutionalized job training, but rates of the completion of training were much higher, there was considerable success in finding and holding jobs, and there was a drop in arrests and other contranormative behaviors.

In the past, minority groups that have vigorously survived poverty and maintained social cohesion and organization have usually had group control over their own social, economic, and educational institutions. Often they have had separate taxation powers. The Mennonites and the Jews of medieval Europe are just two of many examples. Before Reconstruction the black communities in northeastern cities were highly and successfully organized in self-help, economic, religious, and educational societies and were prime movers in the underground railway and in the abolitionist movement (Quarles, 1969).

In our centralized society, control of education, health, and social services has been monopolized by the government except for the groups that had sufficient funds and organization before the massive concentration of social, health, and educational power in government agencies occurred. Thus, the government itself must see to it that its own programs are at the least accountable to, if not controlled by, the people they serve, not because it is politically wise to do so, but because the social effects of not doing so on the group served are disastrous.

One last example. Medicaid is a program for which each state passes its own implementing legislation and administrative guidelines. In some states, the rights of the poor to privacy have been violated by provisions that link payments to reviews of individual case histories. A system of Medicaid that was accountable to its client population would not contain such provisions.

Federal programs that do not provide for accountability to consumers tend to limit the choices of their users. They will evoke as a consequence negative social and personal reactions. Before we leave this issue, just a word about "maximum feasible participation." In the language of the bygone war on poverty, "maximum feasible participation" referred to some form of accountability. The few research studies we have on the effects of "maximum feasible participation" show that it did *indeed* have the intended results (Zurcher, 1969, in press). Poor people who served on local poverty boards showed a decreased sense of alienation, an increased achievement orientation, and many other changes.

These two principles, that the success of many types of federal programs will be enhanced the less they limit the autonomy and choices of the people served, and the more they are accountable to the same people, are simply derived from what we know about how people behave. There are many other principles psychologists can provide to help the decision makers. Let us do this now. The alternative is to later shake our heads knowingly.

The Psychologist as Evaluation Researcher

Let us turn now to the way in which psychologists have become, wittingly or unwittingly, a direct part of the political process. As evaluation researchers, they provide data for hard choices between policy alternatives. New legislation is written with increased emphasis on the evaluation of the effectiveness of federal programs. The role of the psychologist as evaluation researcher will increase. Whether we like it or not, the results of our evaluations of programs will be used by federal agencies and Congress in making their decisions.

Evaluation research is now an underconceptualized field.[1] Psychologists, like technicians, have been inclined to accept the questions posed by policy makers. They have tried to provide answers without first questioning the questions themselves. There is no need to accept the questions that policy makers pose; some of their questions are unanswerable. Our first task must be to help them to frame questions that can be answered, and to discard the unanswerable ones. But to do so, we must be clear about the basics of evaluation research.

The national evaluation of Head Start programs (Cicarelli et al., 1969) offers an illustration of the problem. The Westinghouse study has been the target of considerable controversy. I have no argument at all with the methodology of the study; given the way in which the study was conceptualized, it was admirably well executed. The number of centers and children sampled was large, great care was taken in the selection of the control sample, and a large number of well-standardized tests were used. Both an analysis of covariance and a nonparametric method of analysis were used with essentially similar results. Given the short time within which the study was conducted, it was done with precision and care.

However, what is open to serious question, I think, is the conceptualization on which the study was based. The OEO research office decided that there are

---

[1] There are some notable exceptions, see Herzog (1959) and Suchman (1967).

three different and quite separable types of evaluation research. They called these: Type 1, or *summative* evaluation, in which a national program would be assessed as a whole with *variations* in implementation averaged; Type 2, or *formative* evaluation, in which the effects of different types of the program on outcomes would be evaluated; and Type 3, or *monitoring* evaluation, which would provide periodic review and feedback of results to local programs. Types 2 and 3 were left to the responsibility of separate programs. The OEO Office of Evaluation accepted Type 1 evaluation as its own task, and as the way to answer the question "Does Head Start work?"

There is good reason to doubt whether it is possible to distinguish between Type 1 and Type 2 research. In research we are interested in the relationship between independent and dependent variations. That Head Start funds went from Washington to places throughout the country is insufficient proof of a single independent variable, or treatment, called Head Start. The Westinghouse study, with the single exception of the comparison between summer and full-year Head Start programs, does not report any data on independent variables but simply reports dependent measurements. It cannot be assumed that there is a Head Start treatment if measurement of it is not provided. Generalizations about effects of Head Start cannot be made without relating independent to dependent variation.

I am reminded of what happened with a research institute in New York that received a contract to evaluate the effects of Title 1 programs in New York City. As a first step, the evaluators went to the schools that receive Title 1 funds. To their surprise, they found that in many of the schools teachers were unaware that Title 1 funds were being used and did not know of any Title 1 programs. Did it make any sense to treat Title 1 funds as an independent variable in this evaluation? One of the first rules of experienced evaluation researchers is that the financial and administrative realities of Washington are often unrecognizable in the field.

Because the Head Start study did not attempt to relate treatment differences to the dependent measures, it has, for such an expensive study, yielded pitifully little information that policy makers can actually use. Let us suppose that 25% of the centers sampled had programs that, because of a directed emphasis on cognitive skills, significantly improved children's learning, that another 25% of the centers, those which emphasized social adjustment skills, actually had harmful effects on later learning, and that 50%, which had typical prekindergarten programs, had no effect at all. This would be quite useful information for policy decisions on Head Start. But we do not have this kind of information. Measurement of the relationship between treatment variation and dependent measures (except for program duration) was not reported. Even if it had been measured and reported, according to the conceptualization of Type 1 research, such differences would be lumped together and averaged out. It was fortunate, in post hoc analyses, that differences were found on the single treatment variable that was measured—the duration of the programs—for this did yield one piece of information useful for policy. The Westinghouse study contains some intriguing data, for example, that black, urban children in southeastern states do show benefits, but there is no inkling as to *why* this is so.

Small budget, modest studies and analyses like those of Hawkridge (1968, 1968b) and McDill, McDill, and Sprehe (1969), which have looked at the relationship between different types of preschool programs and effects on children's learning, and have classified the characteristics of successful and unsuccessful programs, have given policy makers more relevant information for their decisions than the Westinghouse study has.

The Head Start study illustrates just one problem in the underconceptualized state of evaluation research. The Type 1, 2, or 3 distinction has, as far as I know, not been challenged, nor has its logic been carefully explored outside government. It continues to be the dominant way in which evaluation research is framed in OEO.

An evaluation plan for parent-child centers has been proposed that *does include* careful measurement of independent sources of variation in three distinct phases before any dependent measurements are made. The value of a plan that would relate treatments to outcomes and would relate settings to treatment effects has not been fully recognized. The proposed plan has had some rough sledding in government, although this is precisely the type of evaluation research that can provide the data decision makers require.

Decision makers should be told that the question "Does Head Start (and other national programs) work?" will not give them the information they want. They must ask instead, "Which Head Start programs work, which do not, and why?"

There are at least two conclusions that can be drawn. The implementation of federal programs is at least as important as legislative initiative. How government programs encounter the people they serve is an issue to which psychologists have much to contribute. These encounters can mean the life or death of the aims behind social legislation.

A more immediate task for psychologists is to help policy makers frame the right questions about the effectiveness of social welfare programs. Until they do, rational choices between policy alternatives will not be made. We shall all be the losers.

References

Berkowitz, L. Social responsibility, empathy, and altruism. Paper presented at the annual meeting of the American Psychological Association, Washington, D.C., September 1969.

Cicarelli, V., et al. *The impact of Head Start*. Athens, O.: Westinghouse Learning Corporation, Ohio University, 1969. 2 vols.

Goldenberg, I. *Gonna build a mountain: The clinician in the world of poverty, community action, and the creation of setting*. Cambridge: MIT Press, 1970, in press.

Hawkridge, D. G. *Foundations for success in educating disadvantaged children*. (Final report, Project No. 107143) Washington, D.C.: United States Office of Education, 1968. (a)

Hawkridge, D. G. *A study of selected exemplary programs for the education of disadvantaged children*. (Final Report, Project No. 89013) Washington, D.C.: United States Office of Education, 1968. (b)

Herzog, E. *Some guidelines for evaluative research*. Washington, D.C.: Children's Bureau, 1959.

Kaufmann, H., & Zener, L. Helper's resentment in help-giving situations. Unpublished paper, Hunter College, 1968.

Lefcourt, H. M. Internal versus external control of reinforcement: A review. *Psychological Bulletin*, 1966, **65**, 206–220.

Levitan, S. A. *Great Society's poor law: A new approach to poverty*. Baltimore, Md.: Johns Hopkins University Press, 1969.

McDill, E. L., McDill, M. S., & Sprehe, J. T. An analysis of evaluation of selected compensatory education programs. Paper presented at the Evaluation of Social Action Programs Conference, American Academy of Arts and Sciences, Boston, May 2–3, 1969.

Pepitone, A. Redistributing wealth unfairly gained. Paper presented at the annual meeting of the American Psychological Association, Washington, D.C., September 1969.

Quarles, B. *Black abolitionists.* New York: Oxford University Press, 1969.

Redlich, F., & Freedman, D. *The theory and practice of psychiatry.* New York: Basic Books, 1966.

Suchman, E. *Evaluation research.* New York: Russell Sage Foundation, 1967.

Zurcher, L. The poverty board: Some consequences of maximum feasible participation. *Journal of Social Issues,* 1970, **26,** in press.

Organizational and Conceptual Barriers to Social Change[1]

MARTIN DEUTSCH

The author received his PhD from Columbia University in 1951. He is presently a professor of early childhood education and Director of the Institute for Developmental Studies at New York University. Professor Deutsch's work centers around the relationship between environment and behavior with special reference to the effects of social conditions on development. He is the immediate Past President of the Society for the Psychological Study of Social Issues.

The orientation of this paper is consistent with, I believe, the statement of purpose of the Society for the Psychological Study of Social Issues. This statement reads in part: "In various ways, the Society seeks to bring theory and practice into focus on human problems of the group, the community, and the nation as well as the increasingly important ones that have no national boundaries."

This orientation is also reflected in Ferkiss' (1969) preface to his excellent discussion of the nature of man in a technological society, in which he says, "If one takes the task of the social scientist seriously, one must go where the problems are, and if one acts as a human being as well as a scientist, one must go where the relevant problems are [p. viii]."

In what follows, I have attempted to explore the perennially relevant problem of the role of the social scientist in helping to bring about rational social change with particular reference to the current concerns and changes in our society.

Two areas of central concern in psychology that have great social relevance are conceptions of the nature and evolution of intelligence and the impact of race and class membership on the life experiences of individuals. Major emphasis in the social sciences has been placed on categorizing types of relationships hypothesized to exist between various psychological characteristics and demographic classifications. Among these psychological characteristics is intelligence, a concept of prime importance. What is too infrequently recognized is that our construct of intelligence

---

[1] Presidential Address to the Society for the Psychological Study of Social Issues presented at the Annual Meeting of the American Psychological Association, Washington, D.C., September 1, 1969.

Reprinted and edited with permission from the *Journal of Social Issues,* 1969, Vol. 25(4). The title of this article has been changed in order to reflect its content. Copyrighted by the Society for the Psychological Study of Social Issues, 1969.

is heavily biased by preconceptions. These embrace temporal restrictions, biological assumptions, frequent overgeneralizations from genetic data, and a rigidity as to the parameters of intelligence. The latter comes from the reification of mental test scores and the mechanical equating of those scores with the entity they presumably represent. It is necessary to recognize that areas such as intelligence, race, demography, etc., have extremely high public visibility and that, as a result, published findings and theories related to them can have inordinate impact on social processes.

Controversy over Determinants of Intelligence

We have recently seen an example of this, and indeed are still in its backwash. With all due respect to that journal, an article in the *Harvard Educational Review* does not ordinarily attract the enormous publicity and discussion aroused by Jensen's (1969) paper. The article had both proximal and distal public and scientific impact; examination of the social repercussions of this impact provides considerable insight into the pressure of social forces within our current cultural matrix.

In the present discussion, I would like to explore the interactive characteristics of these phenomena and the changing role of the social scientist. It seems to me he is now in a position to make thunder, but not to change the annual rainfall: For that matter, he is just on the frontiers of adequately predicting it! I also want to consider some of the psychological and political ramifications of conceptions of intelligence as well as to question some more or less sacred cows. (My rather extensive discussion of the technical assumptions and deficiencies of Jensen's major thesis as well as the data he uses to support it appears in the summer, 1969, issue of the *Harvard Educational Review*.) Intrinsic to any such analysis is consideration of barriers to both social and conceptual evolution.

My own heavy involvement in scientific and professional work has related to the issues Jensen raises: the role of environment in behavior and intelligence; stimulation of intellectual development; and general compensatory intervention efforts. My work has consistently led to conclusions quite opposite of those drawn by Jensen about the processes involved in the acquisition of knowledge, the functional dynamics of intelligence, and the severe limitations of a psychometric approach to the description of intellectual performance in human populations.

"At the same time that I deplore the nature, conclusions, and effects of Jensen's article, I support the right of free inquiry into *all* issues, popular or unpopular. . . . One must deplore and reject the many *ad hominem* criticisms to which Jensen has been subjected. There are enough issues raised and arguments presented in his article to provide concrete bases for disagreement and the presentation of an alternative point of view. . . .

Jensen's article takes the basic position that intelligence test differences between groups—most particularly between black and white groups—are reflections of differences in genetic endowment. Since the average scores of blacks are rather consistently below the average [scores of whites his conclusion is that genetic differences presumed to exist between the two groups operate to make blacks inherently less competent.] Contrary to the impression given by the mass media, Jensen offers no new data to support this position, but only a reorganization of existing old data. (It is important to remember that the data are mostly psychometric and not experimental or genetic.) [The policy implications he derives from this conclusion involve implementation of different curricula for black children as well as different expectations of their eventual intellectual level.] Jensen includes numerous caveats with respect to not assuming a certain level on the part of any given *individual* on the basis of the known *group* differences, but he does not include any suggestions as to how one can identify a potential conceptual thinker in early childhood other than by his skin color.

In our present rather explosive social climate in the United States, it is not surprising that the publication of this argument and these views by a respected professor of education with extensive experimental productivity has been met by a storm of emotions and rhetoric.

In general, the published popular commentaries on the article have accepted most or all of Jensen's assertions regarding intelligence, many of his statements about the measurement of intelligence, most of his genetic discussions, and, with only a few [cautions], his verdict on compensatory education. The impression is created that the article is a fair and lucid discussion of the issues. In fact, however, the article falls into serious contradictions in a number of places, and completely lacks a sophisticated understanding of the magnificent complexity of environment—organism interactions. [Brackets indicate changes from the original text (Deutsch, 1969, pp. 4 and 5)].

Necessity of Considering Potential Impact of Research

"An important consequence of Jensen's article has been to focus attention on the role of social scientists in interpreting behavior. The article has also highlighted the implications of such interpretations for formulating social and educational policy. The responsibility thus assumed by social scientists is a grave one [Deutsch, 1969, p. 5]." [2]

There is a tradition of using public issues and controversies as the focus for investigating social process. Examples are readily available in studies of conflicts about fluoridation, activities of extremist or cultist groups, conflict resolution, etc. The recurring controversies about the nature of intelligence and the admixture of environmental and genetic components which influence it have special characteristics. They are not only social phenomena to be studied by social scientists, but they also derive from central issues and data in the social and behavioral sciences. Therefore, we in these fields have the task of concern with the basic data and their interpretation as well as with the study of the impact of the controversy. When school systems use a particular concept such as genetically determined levels of intelligence as the basis for educational policy, there exists more than a theoretical issue of the dissemination and use of scientific knowledge. We have perhaps lagged behind the physical sciences in considering the potential impact of our work on the attitudes, behavior, and opportunities of people, as well as on the operation of social systems. The mushroom cloud brought many physicists down from whatever ivory towers they may have been in. Psychologists as a group have so far resisted the journey which is just as urgently demanded by the dysfunctioning of so many aspects of our social organization. When atomic fission killed people,

---

[2] Reprinted with permission from the *Harvard Educational Review*, 1969, Vol. 39, No. 3. Copyrighted by the *Harvard Educational Review*, 1969.

physicists could no longer regard experimentation with it solely as a laboratory activity. While there is no direct correlate in psychology, we cannot ignore the fact that many widespread, but not validated, assumptions can and do have enormous impact on the experiences of individuals. In evaluating the question of the continued relevance of this issue, one should consider, for example, whether or not the mores of contemporary psychology are such that studies are more likely to focus on the pathologies of Kohl's 31 children rather than on the structure of the institutions that manhandled them.

In a sense, it is the job of the social scientist to question all sacred cows, roast most of them, and protect some. A problem in doing this is selecting and identifying the sacred concepts, as they are so influential in the delineation of issues that they tend to be invisible. Finding them can require crawling out of one's *Zeitgeist* and simultaneously reversing figure and ground, thus creating cognitive dissonance, which research indicates can be very anxiety provoking. It follows that maintaining the status quo is self-reinforcing and thereby retards any cognitive renegotiation. At times of social crises (historically, a more or less constant state), it can be even more difficult to risk dissonance with familiar concepts. At the same time, an atmosphere of uncertainty and change can make it easier to see contradictions in fundamental assumptions. Today's contradictions between man and machine, between a fortified institution like our educational system and the aspirations of minority groups, between the defense budget and urban decay, and between dignity and poverty facilitate the locating of incompatible or incongruent assumptions. In a sense, the social sciences and social scientists already reflect the dissonance, urgency, and alienation of the current social matrix. What better time is there, then, to identify some of the elusive implicit frames of reference and their ramifications in the total fabric of social theory and action?

Such activity certainly follows Ferkiss' dictum that the human scientist must go where the relevant problems are. But the human social scientist can, I think, play a unique role in lowering the barriers to social change by his activities when he arrives at the relevant problems. He can not only study them, but also, by the kind of questioning of tacit assumptions proposed, he can assault the obstacles to their solution. Indeed, many of the implicit assumptions of the social sciences buttress the barriers to change—or constitute major obstacles themselves.

In the last few years, discussions of barriers to social change have focused mainly on bureaucratic and institutional structures which operate in ways to perpetuate the status quo and to frustrate the initiation and later the continuation of innovations. Without denying the validity of those analyses—indeed, no one who has attempted to introduce innovations into an existing structure could fail to know the frustrating reality of such concrete obstacles—I should like to focus on the operation of implicit assumptions and sacred cows as barriers to change and innovation. Social scientists are best qualified to remove the obstacles created by their own assumptions, as well as the realities and pseudorealities of their cultural context. It would seem necessary that they do so if they are to participate actively in the evolution of a democratic society. It should be possible to gain perspective on sterile lines of investigation as well as to promote thinking and research in heretofore ignored or "irrelevant" areas in a variety of ways, which include: bringing frames of reference to the foreground, evaluating them logically in the light of current data, modifying some, and discarding many. In other words, we can get out of ruts we perhaps are not aware of being in. In the process we can influence, or at least bring into question, the many aspects of public policy which may rest on outmoded or invalid assumptions. The policies affected could range from the use of police power to the use of marihuana and from influencing environmental quality to influencing the quality of children's experiences.

Misinterpretations Caused by Implicit Assumptions about Intelligence

An influential area in which sacred cows abound is intelligence. How this human attribute is regarded has come to be more and more important as our society has become more technologically advanced and as specific training or educational experiences have become the requisites for a larger proportion of jobs and occupations. It is not the purpose of this paper to analyze or evaluate concepts of intelligence per se; I have selected a central assumption about it as an example of the barriers created by implicit frames of reference. It is an assumption which permeates much thinking and which, if allowed to remain unquestioned, can have increasingly critical effects on educational programs and policies.

This assumption is that intellectual capacity is inborn and simply released by experience (or by time). Despite small-print qualifications, this assumption has had a profound influence on educational policy as well as making possible the field of mental testing which has, in turn, determined the educational opportunities of individuals and their admission into or exclusion from particular schools and occupations. It is obvious that this assumption is only one of many interactive determinants: Economic, political, geographical, and historical factors also have major impact on life choices and opportunities. However, since assumptions about intelligence issue from psychology, they are our responsibility.

Let us dissect the anatomy of this particular golden calf, both as an example of a method of analysis and as frames of reference that are so frequently accepted. It is not an example chosen at random: This assumption carries with it many of the contradictions that so often make social science irrelevant to social reality. Further, its influence is felt in many areas of public policy and of psychological research: in terms of questions asked, data gathered, and the nature of interpretation.

The assumption rests on and leads to many subassumptions; their identification and analysis constitute a method for getting a concrete grasp on a diffuse and pervasive idea. Let me first list and then discuss the primary assumption and its subassumptions.

The primary assumption to be questioned is that intelligence is a kind of intrinsic attribute of the individual which either unfolds with the simple passage of time, or—a currently more popular idea—is stimulated to unfold by the individual's experiences.

The subordinate concepts to be questioned include:

1. Intelligence is a biological attribute, related to some degree to genetic endowment and to whatever other variables influence the biology and chemistry of the individual.

2. An individual's maximum intellectual capacity is thus fixed by his biological and chemical makeup. This capacity may or may not be achieved, de-

pending on a host of social, economic, familial, and experiential factors. (An analogy frequently used is height.)

3. Intelligence is normally distributed in the human population in the same way that other biological attributes—such as height—are distributed.

4. Intelligence is an entity that can be measured and related to and used to predict other variables and attributes.

These are only a few of the subconcepts that can be derived from the broader one, and it is evident that they are not wholly independent. But let us examine the implications and some of the practical effects of each.

The Biological Assumption

To consider the first and second subconcepts together, seeing intelligence as basically biological and intrinsic implies that variability in intelligence levels among individuals is "given" rather than developed. In turn, this places emphasis on static categorization of individuals' levels, rather than on finding ways to maximize intellectual development. While always acknowledging the role of experiential factors in influencing the achievement of the intrinsic (and preordained) capacity, the orientation toward environmental effects has been based on a threshold concept rather than on a concept of continuum; the environment has typically been seen as either facilitating or not facilitating the development of the intrinsic potential. Again using height analogously, deprivation of essential nutritional elements during childhood can insure that an individual will not reach the maximum stature which his genetic endowment would permit, but feeding a child a superenriched diet will not enable his surpassing that endowment. Similarly, the concept as applied to intelligence has attributed the major variability in intellectual level to the intrinsic and fixed factors with the experiential diet having only a narrow range of influence. Jensen (1969), in fact, states very explicitly that, "The environment with respect to intelligence is analogous to nutrition with respect to stature [p. 60]." This orientation places the ball game for any individual in the ninth inning at birth and somewhere in the seventh at conception.

Since it is the nervous system that is involved with intelligence, intrinsic variability must rest in essence on a concept of continua in neural functions or efficiency. To maintain stable life processes, however, the nervous system must function within quite a narrow range of variation. Given this fact, plus the very wide range of variability in environments and individual experiences, it would seem more parsimonious to attribute the major share of intellectual variance to environmental factors, reserving to the neural substratum the portion dependent on intactness and functional integrity. (Of course, if the results reported by Krech and Rosenzweig and their colleagues—e.g., Krech, Rosenzweig, & Bennett, 1966; Rosenzweig, 1966—are maintained and confirmed, there will be a basis for seeing experiential variables as actually influencing neural structure, and therefore for attributing even greater impact to the environment.)

Given the infinitely greater accessibility of environmental factors to measurement and experimentation, the persistence of the attribution of the major variance to intrinsic biology is remarkable. This is especially surprising, since for many years such a belief system substantially ruled out attempts to influence intellectual growth by manipulation of extrinsic factors. Time does not permit lengthy speculation on the possible reasons for such persistence, but it can be briefly noted that many relationships among people and groups of people are governed by fixed status considerations, and that status is to a large extent a function of educational attainment and occupation. A view of intellectual level as largely controllable by man would challenge social organization in a major way as well as pose a potentially intolerable threat to the educational establishment as currently constituted. The assumption that intellectual level has a low susceptibility to enhancement by environmental means has been modified very slowly and has been extremely unresponsive to contrary data. For example, when 30 years ago the Iowa studies reported successful raising of measured intelligence as a result of environmental stimulation (e.g., Skeels, Updegraff, Wellman, & Williams, 1938; Wellman, 1938, 1940), many commentators advanced explanations for the results which avoided recognition of the challenge to the idea of fixed intelligence—a central aspect of the Iowa investigators' interpretation of their own data.

It has been only in the last few years, with the increasing concern about the negative influence of disadvantageous environments, that some of the rigidity of the concept of fixed levels has begun to give way. And even now, Jensen, for example, dismisses compensatory education—the current form of the attempt to influence cognitive development by environmental means—as an "apparent failure" without critically examining the negative data he mentions or the nature or duration of the programs from which they were derived. If only one well-controlled program involving a substantial number of children over a period of time yielded significant and lasting change in measured intellectual level, the entire thesis would have to be reconsidered. Since current compensatory programs have not been in operation long enough to make such an evaluation, the issue can hardly be considered resolved. In fact, as I have pointed out elsewhere, considering the less than minimal resources our society has been willing to allocate, there is serious question if meaningful intervention in cognitive development really has as yet been tried. This is apart from the issue of whether its results have been appropriately evaluated.

It must be stressed at this point that questioning the assumption of the primacy of intrinsic factors in intelligence does not negate their role, but instead leaves as an open question the eventual ordering of primary and secondary influences. One does not eliminate barriers by simply switching biases. Instead, the function of questioning should be to open up previously ignored and potentially fruitful lines of thought and investigation. Part of this involves tracing the philosophical implications of different primary assumptions. Obviously, a theory of intrinsically determined intelligence leads to an educational orientation of imparting facts to essentially passive recipients, while an emphasis on potential environmental influence of intellectual level would promote an educational approach whose aim would be the fostering of intellectual growth and which would demand active participation in a learning process.

The Normal Distribution Assumption

Continuing with a consideration of the third subconcept, it can be seen that it contributes further barriers to change in basic orientation and social organization. The assumption that intelligence is normally distributed is in reality a tautology. Standardized intelligence tests yield a normal distribution of scores when applied to large populations. However, test development starts with the assumption that intelligence is a normally distributed attribute, and therefore one index of a test's adequacy typically is whether it reflects this phenomenon. When it is then applied to populations and the scores derived are found to fall into a bell-shaped distribution, all that has happened is the regurgitation of the original input. Again we have the status quo reassuring itself.

The Measurement Assumption

Stemming from the final subconcept is the phenomenon of the loud disclaiming that IQ and intelligence are identical, while at the same time they are being used interchangeably. This amounts to fine print serving as a substitute for a rigorous analysis of what is not being measured as well as for a clear delineation of what is measured.

Enough has been written about the problems and deficiencies of test construction, interpretation, and, more recently, test taking to make reiteration superfluous. At the same time, critical analysis has been absorbed without any noticeable influence on either the testing or the intelligence games. What is quite evident is that the real nature of the game is the assignment of individuals to cubbyholes with labels and predetermined status designations to be carried through life. This process is a major source of strength for the freezing of social boundaries, aspirations, and motivational systems. As a result, change becomes objectively increasingly difficult, as an undetermined proportion of the population find cozy corners in their cubbyholes. Operationally, this becomes an exclusionary system and a major avenue for the continuation of inequalities of access to the opportunity structure. Verbal recognition of the culturally bound nature of intelligence tests has not been sufficient to remove the obstacles they create for minority group members. Positions such as the one Jensen advances leave little room for consideration of the highly differential experiences which are a consequence of social class and racial group membership and for the extent to which this differential limits the validity of any group comparisons.

The removal of barriers to new modes of thought created by our own assumptions can be to some extent under the control of persuasive social scientists. However, as Clark pointed out in his Lewin Address (1965), the power for change in society obviously resides in other places. It would be self-defeating to delude ourselves into believing that our agonizing reappraisals themselves will have effects on public policy. If new or changing concepts are to bring alterations to society, the social scientist must find ways of exercising influence to bring them about. Campbell (1969) believes that recognition of the political realities of innovative programs will enable the social science research consultant to promote the kind of evaluation which can eventuate in retention of the truly effective programs. Sanford and Krech (1969) call for the development of "clinicians to society": a specific role designation which presumably would give the social scientist an avenue into the machinery which can bring about change. Here it should be understood that the social scientist is at best a secondary powerbroker in our society: Increased involvement could also have socially counterproductive consequences.

Using assumptions about intelligence as examples in the foregoing discussion also serves the purpose of emphasizing the impact of experience on individual development. However, exploring this area also highlights how little we know in any systematic manner about the differential encounters people have with their environments, and what makes some of these encounters more influential than others. Similarly, despite all the studies in which human behavior has been assessed, whether without reference to social context or with the acknowledgment of the influence of social factors, we still know nothing of the actualities of human potential.

Need for New Approaches and Development

The need both to learn about the specifics of individual experiences and their effects and to insure that these and other social science findings could have concrete effects on the direction of change in policies and organization clearly points to an emphasis on action programs and action research as fundamental tools of the social scientist. Instead of being defensive or apologetic about the deficiencies of these methods, he should see them as approaches of choice for the investigation of natural situations. A major avenue through which we might achieve the greatest insight into the dimensions of human potential might well be the formulation and operation of action programs designed to foster the cognitive development of the child from birth on. This would appear to be a potentially effective way of discovering the many mechanisms through which development can be stimulated in all youngsters. At the same time, it would be a method for gaining primary knowledge about the nature of development and the differential roles of intrinsic and extrinsic factors. Such emphasis and such methodology are consistent with the view that a proper role for the social scientist is the use of his skills to facilitate development, encourage growth, and build in greater degrees of freedom for the individual and for the organizations and structures with which he is surrounded. Specifically, perspectives might be modified so that administrative and routine procedures could be relegated in favor of substantive matters that would be more responsive to social growth. In modern social science, as in some contemporary architecture, it might be that form can follow function instead of administrative forms operating to constrict growth in both human and organizational potential.

The cognitive style of the social sciences—and of the mental health field—has too frequently been oriented towards posing questions in negative terms. Pathology tends to be given priority—but then, human society certainly provides more opportunities for interchange with the pathological. In a sense, though, we are going through a revolution on the behavioral level, in which students, minority group members, and females are demanding alternatives and are no longer formulating questions only in negative terms. The change is not coming from social scientists, but it is offering stimulation to us to make similar alterations in our orientations to the phenomena we study. The increasing asking of questions in multivariate terms and the acceptance of alternatives and probabilities as answers become themselves potent motivations for social change; constant discomfort and dissonance are thereby reflected as important attributes of the social structure. Primarily, individuals are more motivated to learn how to overcome the effects of systematic social discrimination or dysfunctional social institutions than they are to know the mode of operation of the antecedent experiences. What this might reflect is a change in cognitive style, where within the context of a technological society a shift in orientation is occurring from past to current to future. At the same time, the discriminatory barriers are becoming increasingly dysfunctional. The continual asking of questions and sharpening of reasoning processes create the constant discomfort referred to and make existing institutions such as the universities or the church increasingly irrelevant if they fail to respond to the present by ridding themselves of the encrustations of the past. Their irrelevance is in direct proportion to the rigidity and elaboration of past-oriented structure: It can be no accident that it is the monolithic Roman Catholic church that is experiencing the greatest upheaval.

The avenues of access to knowledge and information have gone far beyond the teacher-child one-way exchange. The essential unresponsiveness of the schools and the entire educational system to these changed conditions creates a situation of paralysis. By offering access to an increased variety of stimuli through new methods of information retrieval, modern technology can facilitate decreasing dependence of learning opportunities on the restrictions currently accompanying race and social class membership, as well as organizational rigidities. Currently an enormous number of youngsters is just bored by exposure to what is too frequently obsolete curriculum in outmoded structure. The minority groups are being even more proportionately shortchanged, and both groups are tending in the direction of "copping out of Dullsville." The tension and frustration created simply cannot be resolved within the existing structures. Thus, another force for change is mobilized. Whether this force operates toward disintegration or improvement is a different issue. Nevertheless, the opportunities for restructuring become enhanced. The question of whether in this restructuring we need to make current forms work better or to evolve new forms probably has different answers for different structures and areas. Both institutions and communities differ in their ability to absorb new methods of operation while maintaining their essential individual characteristics. If one acknowledges that the university should survive, the problem is whether it can if it maintains the rigid bureaucratic stratification which too frequently has come to characterize its operations, if it retains its present artificial curriculum requirements and admissions policies, and if it retains a general detachment from its environment.

Before the recognition that policy modifications would be requisite for survival, educational—or business—institutions could indulge in the ignoring of the realities of social stratification and discriminatory practices. Now, however, it is increasingly incompatible with their viability; they can no longer deny their own prior biases and the varying life styles of the younger generation or of individuals from differing cultural backgrounds. No longer can they impose a single behavioral standard or maintain more than a fixed and predetermined relationship to students or employees. In other words, there is a certain accelerating motion toward greater freedom from institutional boundaries and restrictions. A foundation has been created for a general opening of opportunity for individual determination of personal life styles; and evidence exists that this is true from the crib throughout the life span. At the same time, though, strong repressive forces exist that have a great investment in the world as it was. However, there have been such rapid changes in communications, technology, and almost all aspects of life that the forces with an investment in the past may have difficulty in the present in characterizing the past to which they wish to return.

All this is occurring in an atmosphere of urban decay and racial and class conflict; an idiotic war; deterioration of transportation and other services; increasing pollution of the air and water; and a simultaneous growth of bureaucratic substructures and of indices of social disorganization. In addition, in spite of the never-fought war on poverty, we have had a society committed to a multibillion dollar war on man supported by a fantastically inconsistent and biased tax system and a draft policy which is highly discriminatory in operation.

In this total matrix, it is difficult not to oscillate between optimism about the strength of the movement for positive changes and pessimism about the possibility of achieving it before some bureaucratic mistake gives rise to the final cataclysm. Please note that I remain optimistic enough to believe that the final cataclysm would be precipitated by an accident.

In a recent article I stated,

Our society is in a very critical state of dysfunctioning. Unlike Rome, it could fall to a Carthage, either internal or external. The minds and knowledge of social scientists can play an enormous role in restructuring our social system as mediated through all human organisms. Through the socialization and education of children especially, it would seem that a significant degree of saliency could be reestablished between personal experience on the one hand, and on the other, social evolution founded in the gathering of knowledge and its correct and parsimonious utilization [1969, p. 551].

The burden of discussion in the present paper is the necessity for looking more closely at our environment in order to understand better the aspects which most impinge on individuals and influence their development; in order to maximize those factors which exercise the most positive developmental influence; and in order to minimize the most negatively acting ones. This is a tremendous task, and one which could well involve a large number of social and behavioral scientists. For not only will it be necessary to develop the requisite knowledge and understanding, but it will also be necessary to feed the new knowledge past the organizational barriers and into the structures of society's institutions.

References

Campbell, D. Reforms as experiments. *American Psychologist,* 1969, **24,** 409–429.

Clark, K. B. Problems of power and social change: Toward a relevant social psychology. *Journal of Social Issues,* 1965, **21,** 4–20.

Deutsch, M. Happenings on the way back to the forum: Social science, IQ, and race differences revisited. *Harvard Educational Review,* 1969, **39,** 523–557.

Ferkiss, V. C. *Technological man: The myth and the reality.* New York: George Braziller, 1969.

Jensen, A. R. How much can we boost IQ and scholastic achievement? *Harvard Educational Review,* 1969, **39,** 1–123.

Krech, D., Rosenzweig, M. R., & Bennett, E. L. Environmental impoverishment, social isolation, and changes in brain chemistry and anatomy. *Physiology and Behavior,* 1966, **1,** 99–104.

Rosenzweig, M. R. Environmental complexity, cerebral change, and behavior. *American Psychologist,* 1966, **21,** 321–332.

Sanford, N., & Krech, D. The activists' corner. *Journal of Social Issues,* 1969, **25,** 247–255.

Skeels, H. M., Updegraff, R., Wellman, B. L., & Williams, H. M. A study of environmental stimulation: An orphanage preschool project. *University of Iowa Study of Child Welfare,* 1938, **15**(3).

Wellman, B. L. The intelligence of preschool children as measured by the Merrill-Palmer scale of performance tests. *University of Iowa Study of Child Welfare,* 1938, **15**(3).

Wellman, B. L. Iowa studies on the effects of schooling. *Yearbook National Society for Studies in Education,* 1940, **39,** 377–399.

The Psychotherapist as an Activist in Social Change: A Proponent[1]

FRED E. SPANER

The author received his PhD in clinical psychology from Purdue University in 1950. He is presently Chief of the Community Mental Health Center Consultation Section for the National Institute of Mental Health, where his major activity involves the encouragement, development, and evaluation of mental health services to communities.

To be a proponent of activism in social change is currently a popular position among most behavorial scientists and is probably particularly attractive for psychotherapists. Psychotherapists usually have a humanistic orientation and have probably been preselected by their choice to enter this field and further selected on this dimension by supervisors and teachers. Those students of psychotherapy who show concern for people and desire to help the troubled are more likely to be encouraged than those who do not. Since the psychotherapist's clientele consists of people who are experiencing difficulties in coping with problems related to day-to-day living, helping such people to change enables the psychotherapist to think of himself as an activist in their behalf. Hence, a "do-gooder" motivational pattern predominates among psychotherapists and predisposes many to become conscious of social issues and to desire to improve the general condition of humanity. This, however, is usually perceived as something to be done as a concerned citizen, rather than something fundamental to psychotherapy as an occupation. If a psychotherapist is an activist for social change, he and others can accept this role only on the basis that an informed, liberal-minded individual is expected to hold such views and as a private citizen he has the obligation to translate them into action. But neither he nor others usually believe that his mission as a psychotherapist demands that he be active in promoting beneficial social change. The citizen-activist and the psychotherapist-activist should be a difficult distinction to discriminate, yet many of us have no trouble making this dichotomy. I submit, however, that psychotherapy as a vehicle for individual change is not distinct from psychotherapy as a vehicle for social change. I see the psychotherapist as having an obligation to influence and promote the change process in society.

---

[1] Invited Address presented to the Division of Psychotherapy at the Annual Meeting of the American Psychological Association, Washington, D. C., September 2, 1969. The opinions expressed are those of the author and do not necessarily reflect policy or opinions of the National Institute of Mental Health.

Cultural Backdrop of Psychotherapy

Let me explain the context in which I see this occurring. I have at other times discussed my thoughts on the relationship of psychotherapy to the social setting in which it occurs (Spaner, 1968). I consider psychotherapeutic theories and procedures as reflecting society's current concepts of Man. In the past, when Man has been considered worthless and sinful, the psychotherapeutic philosophies and the procedures employed to implement them were consistent with that orientation. When Man has been considered worthwhile and an object to be respected, philosophies and procedures current at the time reflected that position. Our collective view of Man, as shaped by those who influence public thought, keeps changing. With these changes occur changes in our ethics and values, which are intimately related to the social, economic, cultural, and technological conditions of the time. Psychotherapeutic orientations are, therefore, influenced by these social forces and in turn help to maintain and shape them. This makes psychotherapy, as it is conceptualized and practiced, responsive to the needs of the Establishment and an instrument that tends to serve those needs.

We, as psychotherapists, may not recognize this phenomenon, because we focus on our relationship to our client and tend to believe that only the resolution of his conflicts and problems is what matters. We rarely pay attention to the fact that the psychotherapeutic encounter takes place against a background of social and cultural conditions. Since these conditions are very similar for the psychotherapist and client, they remain in the background and are not noticed. Hence, we fail to appreciate the implications that follow from them. For example, we may fail to recognize the significance of providing psychotherapeutic services as an occupation. We earn our living in this occupation, and our livelihood is subject to social sanctions and sensitive to existing social and economic forces that may effect our earnings. Hence, these forces, both subtly and sometimes not so subtly, may tend to influence the nature of our psychotherapy. Someone has said that "the treatment follows the buck"—what we do in each psychotherapeutic session cannot help but be influenced by the social and economic factors that will either enable us or prevent us from continuing to function as psychotherapists.

The forces that make up this intricate web of social and economic influences impose invisible limits on us. These forces have been simplistically termed "the Establishment." Whatever keeps social and economic relationships in their existing balance tends to perpetuate psychotherapeutic practices that are consonant with them. Therefore, innovations and changes that occur are those that will not seriously jeopardize this equilibrium. This means that the psychotherapist is a part of the Establishment and his psychotherapy, generally, does not upset social relationships. This is further assured by the conditions imposed on what role the psychotherapist shall play in regard to his clients and who shall be a psychotherapist.

Psychotherapists are expected to assume responsibility and be in charge of the situation and are held accountable for their clients' behavior. They are given this authority as a consequence of a professional status that they seek and that is conferred upon them. The credentials of professionalism become the Establishment's way of providing special recognition as well as special control. Such credentials and who may have them are arranged through a self-perpetuating system in which those members of the profession who are accredited determine who else should receive such status. Should anyone try to bypass this procedure or aspire to become a psychotherapist without being properly annointed, he is branded as unqualified and subject to punitive action.

Through a process of denigration, individuals without credentials, called "trainees," "interns," or "nonprofessionals," are controlled and supervised by members of the profession and are permitted by them to engage in psychotherapy. All of this makes it possible for those who are the designated professional psychotherapists to assure society that their occupation will not be destructive of existing social relationships. By society, I mean those value-setting interests in our culture that control the socioeconomic system. It is that group which needs assurance that social relationships will remain stable and predictable, and that change, when it occurs, can be incorporated so as not to disrupt this equilibrium or threaten their control.

Psychotherapists, who are properly designated as professionals, are generally safe and not likely to pose a threat. That may account for why psychotherapists can continue to engage in an occupation that encourages changes in the individual and yet has had relatively little impact on correcting the social deficiencies that are largely responsible for bringing the individual to their attention. Can it be that our efforts are geared to helping our clients find solutions that will enable them to live within the social system that produced the problems rather than to helping them change the system?

It seems that we are not about to threaten the Establishment, whether it be through change in the system of credentials for professionals, or change in the control of the mental health industry, or major changes in any other aspects of the status quo. Not posing a threat has permitted us to continue to practice, and in our practice we have incorporated the principles of the Establishment. These principles are so well ingrained in our psychotherapeutic concepts that even when we ask questions and study the process of psychotherapy, we stay within safe limits. A recent comprehensive report of research directions in psychotherapy (Strupp & Bergin, 1969) indicates that one of the principal trends in psychotherapy studies is to explore specific psychotherapeutic procedures and techniques applicable to specific patients. Not to discount the importance of this question, it seems to me that there is a basic assumption in it that accepts the relevance of psychotherapy as it is.

Issues Needing Study

There are many questions and issues in psychotherapy that need to be studied and that should question our generally accepted concepts. We might consider, for example, the significance of present psychotherapist-client relationships in terms of the status of the participants, or the influences of where psychotherapy takes place, or the nature of the preparatory arrangements for this encounter, or to whom psychotherapists are accountable. Other questions that could be explored are: How do psychotherapeutic procedures relate to social needs? How does the public make its needs known so that psychotherapy may attempt to meet them? Who comprises the public to which psychotherapists attend? To what extent are psychotherapeutic procedures responsive to the psychotherapeutic needs of the poor in general and the Chicanos, the Puerto Ricans, the blacks, and the American Indians in particular? How many members of these groups are practicing psychotherapists? How many are in training programs for psychotherapists? How proportionate are their numbers in these activities to their numbers in the general population? How proportionate are their numbers in the psychotherapy professions to the need for mental health services to their people? We may also ask to what extent have private psychotherapists participated in community mental health programs? These issues and questions should be as important to us as psychotherapists as what procedures should be employed for what specific symptom pattern.

Despite the failure to attend to these questions, psychotherapists continue to consider themselves scientists and change agents. As scientists, we consider many variables that affect our ability to produce psychotherapeutic change. Some of these are the interpersonal relationship between psychotherapist and client, the personality of the psychotherapist, and the personality of the client. These have been and are being studied and cover a respectable body of research. We need, however, to study also the broad social setting in which psychotherapy takes place. What is not being studied is the interaction of psychotherapy and the social system. We should be studying the psychotherapist's potential for effecting social change and should be concerned with producing the type of social change that could reduce the need for psychotherapy.

We need to examine and understand how we can provide our client with something that is meaningful for his full 168 hours a week rather than just the 1, 2, or 3 hours with us. We must also learn more about populations who do not avail themselves of psychotherapy and their reasons for not doing so. This latter is a most pressing issue to activists for social change. It is in the area of broadening our clientele to encompass members of social, ethnic, and cultural groups foreign to our practice that psychotherapists have been most uncomfortable and inept. There is legitimate reason for this. We are aware that the better the match between psychotherapist and client the more likely they are to find it a mutually rewarding relationship. Hence, it would follow that the greater the discrepancy in social and cultural backgrounds the more difficult it would be to establish a mutually effective psychotherapeutic relationship.

There is obviously a need to examine our role, our methods, and our procedures to determine their relevance in these new encounters. Some psychotherapists feel that the techniques of psychotherapy are not as important as the basic human relationships involved (Truax & Corkhuff, 1967) and that these should hold regardless of social class or other grouping. This would be so, except that the objectives of psychotherapy are different for these groups. A fundamental difference that the psychotherapist, as an activist for social change, recognizes, and many of his colleagues who do not consider themselves activists ignore, is that with disadvantaged groups our mission can no longer be just that of helping to resolve personal problems. What we are being asked to do when we attend to the broader population is to help individuals break the bonds of psychological slavery. To do this we must help them to change the system that imposes these bonds. Our psychotherapeutic orientation must, therefore, require outcome responses that emphasize active participation on the part of individuals in effecting social change, as well as personal change. Responses such as accommodation, submission, compromise, resolution of conflicts, recognition of the rights of others, and fairness as defined by the majority may not be the responses that will be most meaningful to a person whose problems and ineffectiveness stem from these virtues, so dearly held by those in power. It has been that power which has not permitted the clients from disadvantaged groups to acquire the basic early experiences upon which such a repertoire of responses depends. Can we as psychotherapists ignore this need to help a deprived individual make relevant responses to the cause of his deprivation?

We may feel unable to fulfill this need, because our experiential backgrounds are so different and, therefore, we may not be able to really understand. We may also feel fearful, because we as psychotherapists are identified with the power structure of society and are unintentional proponents of the system that has produced the problems. It is this bind that frustrates most psychotherapists when they sincerely wish to assume their rightful role as activists for social change, thus causing them to assume a less hazardous position of considering psychotherapy as applying only to intrapsychic phenomena. In that way a psychotherapist can concentrate on the psychotherapeutic hour to the exclusion of both the client's and his own real life.

If we are to truly fulfill our mission as psychotherapists, we must be activist oriented. This means recognizing and relating with our clients to the full scope of the situation in which we find ourselves now. It also means being able to accept our position as part of the Establishment and attempting to change the Establishment not by chance but by design. This will take much thought, an alteration of our present concepts, and a reexamination of all our procedures. We might start by asking ourselves the question: Where do we conduct our psychotherapy? On what basis does a person have access to us and is able to avail himself or our skills? Who, besides professional psychotherapists, can produce understanding and psychotherapeutic changes in an individual? How may we as psychotherapists become more responsive to the mental health needs of the community? Can our psychotherapeutic skills be employed in helping people effect needed social changes rather than merely attempting to help those who have been crippled as a result of the lack of that change?

Psychotherapists cannot separate themselves from the deep social and moral issues that pervade our current scene. We cannot delude ourselves into thinking that there is a neutral or "professional" position. We are activists whether we admit it or not. If we are not participating as activists to promote beneficial social change, we are participating as activists to maintain the social system as it is.

References

Spaner, F. E. Beyond the intra psychic. Presidential address to the Division of Psychotherapy at the 76th annual meeting of the American Psychological Association, San Francisco, August 30, 1968.

Strupp, H. H., & Bergin, A. E. Some empirical and conceptual bases for coordinated research in psychotherapy. *International Journal of Psychiatry,* 1969, **7**(2).

Truax, C. B., & Corkhuff, R. R. *Toward effective counseling and psychotherapy: Training and practice.* Chicago: Aldine Press, 1967.

Where Angels Fear to Tread: Reply to Spaner[1]

ERNEST S. LAWRENCE

The author received his PhD in clinical psychology from the University of Southern California in 1953. At present he is a consultant in clinical training at Cedars-Sinai Medical Center and the Los Angeles Psychiatric Service, is on the faculty of the Los Angeles Center for Group Psychotherapy, and is also in private practice. His major interest is in the relationship of psychotherapeutic processes to implicit philosophical positions.

The kernel of Spaner's presentation, it appears to me, is contained in the following statement:

Our mission *can no longer be just that of helping to resolve personal problems. What we are being asked to do . . . is to help individuals break the bonds of psychological slavery. To do this we must help them to* change the system that imposes these bonds. *Our psychotherapeutic orientation must, therefore,* require outcome responses that emphasize active participation on the part of individuals in effecting social change, as *well as personal change [1970, p. 61, nonitalics added].*

The call for a crusade by Spaner is a far cry from the depth therapists' attempts to analyze unconscious motivational conflicts in order to create a personal climate in which the client can be released from crippling ambivalence and enabled to exercise free choices. The more free-wheeling encounter/confronting psychotherapists are usually content if they can put a person in contact with his feelings and some essential aspects of interpersonal relationships in an authentic and open manner. Behavioral therapists work hard to accomplish a program of relief from symptoms and recurrent self-destructive behavior.

Is Spaner so far away from clinical work that he thinks that it is nothing to "just" resolve a disabling emotional problem? Is he suggesting that our technical skills are to the point where we can ignore the development of procedures and techniques for specific problems? Has his impatience with social progress blinded him to the problems of the psychotherapist in his effort to rehabilitate incapacitated individuals? Must we all abandon our clinical inquiries into the nature of mind?

---

[1] An extension of remarks made as the discussant of the paper by Fred Spaner, "The Psychotherapist as an Activist in Social Change: A Proponent," presented to the Division of Psychotherapy at the Annual Meeting of the American Psychological Association, Washington, D. C., September 2, 1969.

Influencers and Promoters

Spaner is after big game. He suggests nothing less than that psychotherapists in their infinite wisdom and using their unique and opportune position be *obligated* "to influence and promote the change process in society." Since he is speaking of psychotherapists qua psychotherapists, not of psychologists in social programs, what he must mean is that psychotherapists working with a troubled and confused population explicitly become "influencers" and "promoters"—wedded to a position of "beneficial social change."

One hardly need raise the perplexing and ubiquitous question of what beneficial social change position the psychotherapist should influence and promote his clients to adopt. The danger is clear and obvious. Spaner's *required* therapeutic outcome for his clients is to "change the system that imposes these bonds," and "to make relevant responses to the source of his deprivation." Disregarding for the moment the eloquent vagueness combined with "psychologeze," he sure wants his clients to come out of therapy doing something! By some curious strangulation of logic it becomes apparent that the therapist-activist position that Spaner so persuasively exhorts becomes one of getting clients to go out and do the work that Spaner feels so strongly has to be done.

If you want to make a revolution, go make it yourself; your clients have enough troubles without acting out your social perceptions and ideological biases while you sit around with the word "activist" emblazoned on your sweatshirt (proof that you are an activist—right?).

Perhaps Spaner is putting us on. As he somewhat circuitously gets to the end of his paper (touching all bases: selection and training procedures; humanity and humanism; the Great Big Thought—how psychotherapy reflects society's current conception of Man and serves the Establishment; a few swipes at the bad guys who do not seem to realize that their clients live *real* lives not just in their heads but in a "real world," and how psychotherapists also live in the "real world," etc.) something seems to happen to all his ginger and snap. The conclusions are downright pedestrian. Spaner admonishes us to accept our position as part of the Establishment and change it from within (while our clients ostensibly are proving their therapeutic improvement by changing the Establishment from without). He recites the litany of asking how the poor can avail themselves of our services, how we may become more responsive to their needs, and where we should conduct psychotherapy. So what else is new? Oh yes, further studies and research.

The specifics prove to be all old hat—even the rhetoric has an old, tired sound like something warmed over from the thirties. Today's radical/activist would neither buy Spaner's liberal grandiloquence nor subscribe to his restrained conclusions. I am afraid that Spaner, for all his honest passion about the social injustices of our time, and perhaps because of it, misses the point of psychotherapy and the larger question of the relation of the social sciences (or behavioral sciences as many prefer) to social, political, and moral issues. The latter question would require too much space for an adequate presentation, so I will confine myself to a few brief remarks regarding psychotherapy.

The Psychotherapist's Responsibility

What is immediately relevant for any psychotherapist of whatever persuasion is how to ease the pain and help his clients resolve the debilitating conflicts that have crippled their functioning (no mean trick in itself), and secondarily, and hopefully, to help them think through a meaningful course to their lives. Implicit in this is the therapist's resolve not to impose his life style, his biases upon his client. Freud warned us to be constantly alert not to use our clients for our own gratification (he did not mean the ordinary and very meaningful satisfactions of doing a good job), and the working through of transference phenomena was to this end. The client should not be obligated to act out of the therapist's needs, fears, or conflicts—neither about sex nor social action. Spaner's essential thesis is that psychotherapists "are held accountable for their clients' behavior." Are we really missionaries? The responsibilities are grave indeed and I would suggest a reading of Kaiser (1955) on the problem of responsibility in psychotherapy. The tradition of respect for the dignity and individuality of the client of whatever background and appreciation of his right of free choice is in the finest liberal humanistic spirit.

Spaner touches another problem at one point: "Can our psychotherapeutic skills be employed in helping people effect needed social changes rather than merely attempting to help those who have been crippled as a result of the lack of that change?" If we delete the last loaded phrase which creates an umbrella that may or may not be congruent with reality unless every psychopathological phenomenon is viewed as a result of an aberrant society, then Spaner is posing a choice for psychotherapists as to how they want to work. It would appear to me that psychotherapy now is not what Spaner is talking about. The use of group dynamics in a social action context is another ballpark, and if that is your thing, fine—do it. It certainly is a very civilized way of working and not in the strident and urgent style of the quote from Spaner offered at the beginning of this discussion. However, one should not be able to shift one's ground at will. If the ballpark is psychotherapy and he links therapy outcome with getting clients to be active in social change as well as to resolve internal conflicts, that is strikingly different from his recommendation that therapists act as group leaders for interested citizens who want to think through a position or action on a social level. Hopefully, at this latter level, Spaner would accept the goals of the group and not impose his own.

I must confess to some irritation with many of the offhand comments: "A 'do-gooder' motivational pattern predominates among psychotherapists." "The citizen-activist and the psychotherapist-activist should be a difficult distinction to discriminate, yet many of us have no trouble making this dichotomy." "This makes psychotherapy, as it is conceptualized and practiced, responsive to the needs of the Establishment and an instrument that tends to serve those needs." Whose psychotherapy? Whose conceptualization? Which establishment? The Skinnerian? The Freudian? The police? I suspect that most psychotherapists and people in the social sciences have more than a tint of antiestablishmentarianism in them. Governor Reagan of California this past summer accused those in the social sciences of being unbalanced to the left. Further on, Spaner states "we may fail to recognize the significance of providing psychotherapeutic services as an occupation." Yes, and vastly different from a mission.

I am distrustful of global indictments, sweeping statements, and evangelical fervor. The problems our society faces are serious ones: social, political, economic, and moral. They will not yield to slogans, the currently popular phrase, dangling thoughts, and well-meaning but empty and often reckless suggestions. Knocking down straw men may be fun, but is unworthy of a man in Spaner's position.

Social change is a meaningless concept unless tied to substantive material and articulated processes. We are all for God, motherhood, and beneficial social change. But if psychotherapy is to enter into the substance and process of social change, then it demands explicit and specific political positions. The morality and ethics of psychotherapy would then be reducible to politics in the last analysis—all in the name of beneficial social change, of course. It is at this point that psychotherapy would cease being an independent professional occupation in the service of individuals to use (or abuse) according to individual idiosyncracy.

Psychotherapy today is one of the few institutions in our culture that preserves the individual's sense of individuality, that gives value to his uniqueness, and that helps to resist the tide of the mass culture. Spaner's thesis would destroy this respect and tolerance for the intrinsic worthwhileness of each of us by sweeping us up in social outcome requirements. When psychotherapy becomes social and political, we will indeed be immersed in an Orwellian tragedy.

Our socially relevant problem is how to broaden the base of our services to the poor, the underprivileged, the black, to all individuals in need; to find techniques of communication that respect the differentness of people. Concern about the social inequities of our society does not mean abandoning the independent professional moral and ethical base of responsibility to our clients. No teacher requires of his students that they use their knowledge for social action. No physician requires that patients change the social conditions that produced the disease process. No lawyer defending a thief requires that the thief correct the social conditions contributing to his delinquency.

If a profession is responsible, it actively and conscientiously seeks to provide its services to all those in need. The profession alerts the community to the need; it enters into the social and political processes to help society recognize and supply the service. When necessary, the profession must even contribute its services. But under no circumstances must the professional qua professional obligate the needy as a condition of his services.

References

Kaiser, H. The problem of responsibility in psychotherapy. *Psychiatry,* 1955, **18,** 205–211.
Spaner, F. E. The psychotherapist as an activist in social change: A proponent. In F. F. Korten, S. W. Cook, & J. I. Lacey (Eds.), *Psychology and the problems of society.* Washington, D. C.: American Psychological Association, 1970.

Counseling's Social Response[1]

JOHN F. McGOWAN

The author received his PhD in guidance and counseling from the University of Missouri at Columbia in 1954. He is presently a professor of education at the University of Missouri at Columbia and Dean of the University Extension Division.

As outgoing President of Division 17, I have allowed myself the somewhat questionable privilege of sharing with you some of my personal concerns about the way in which many, or even most, members of the Division seem to be passing up an opportunity to respond to the needs of two expanded clientele groups—*the culturally disadvantaged and the culturally alienated*. I will warn you before I start that I have a message and that many or even the majority of you will not necessarily agree with either my perception of our discipline's lack of response or my conclusions.

The theme of this year's American Psychological Association Convention is "Psychology and the Problems of Society." I would like to comment on counseling's societal response to the expectations and needs of society. First, a few words about my personal background and work experience so that you can better understand my frame of reference as I discuss the problem. I entered the field of counseling working as a counselor for a Veterans Administration counseling center connected with the University of Missouri at Kansas City. After completing a doctorate at the University of Missouri at Columbia, I took a one year's internship in a VA hospital located at Wadsworth, Kansas. I then returned to the University of Missouri at Columbia and worked for the next 10 years as a counselor trainer, teaching courses in tests and measurements, counseling methods, and spending most of my time in the supervision of counseling practicum. I had administrative control of what we refer to as our out-of-school training program. We graduated, and are still graduating, students with special training in the areas of Veterans Administration hospital work, rehabilitation, and employment service counseling, in addition to our regular high school and college counselor personnel programs. I was also engaged in some private consulting work and served on numerous committees with the Department of Labor and the Department of Health, Education, and Welfare. Three years ago, I moved into a university administrative position on a full-time basis and am now teaching only one course, Advanced Counseling Theories. The point that I am trying to establish is that my training, experience, personal

---

[1] Presidential Address to the Division of Counseling Psychology presented at the Annual Meeting of the American Psychological Association, Washington, D. C., September 1, 1969.

interests, and preferences have emphasized a *service* orientation. I remain more product than process oriented and am interested in measurable outcomes. I also hold the hard to defend position that counseling and psychotherapy are *not* the same and that there are essential differences between the two. I am willing to concede that there is great overlap and that you can argue this point for a day, a week, or a month and never reach any firm conclusions.

Current Problems

It seems to me that the basic overall problem we face is how to offer either *new* or *better* services to an expanded clientele group. It is this demand to provide new or better services to a new audience that may well require some significant *changes* in counseling as we have traditionally thought of it. When I speak about new clientele, I am referring to any group other than our traditional middle class white clients who are capable of responding to the type of services that counselors have traditionally offered. More specifically, I am talking about the problems we counselors encounter in offering services to either the culturally disadvantaged or the culturally disillusioned. My own critical view is that we must examine what we have been doing and find ways of responding, as a discipline, to a wider group than the one we are now reaching. In essence, we continue to offer services to those who, although most able to profit from them, may need them the least, and are offering the least services to those who need them the most, but may not be able to profit from the traditional type of verbal help that you and I have been trained to provide.

What I am suggesting is that we may well have boxed ourselves in so tightly as a result of *not* modifying our traditional methods and techniques that we stand the risk of offering services that are no longer relevant to the needs of society, or at least to those members of society who are *most* in need of our help. I see our problems as falling within two areas: (*a*) problems related to training; (*b*) problems related to new clientele groups.

Problems Related to Training

There are several separate issues involved with training. The first is the issue of the counselor's role perception. Is he to serve *primarily* as an agent of the client, or as an agent of society, or, to word it another way, as an agent of social change? Our training programs over the years have produced counselors who see themselves as agents or representatives of the client. Nevertheless, society, as represented by schools and social agencies, pays us and thinks that it is hiring us as agents of society or social change. This results in conflict between schools and agencies, between graduates and agencies, and between training institutions and funding agencies. It appears to me that most training programs are graduating counselors who tend toward being therapists. While in school and upon graduation our graduates are rewarded by a pecking order within the field of psychology, which encourages and reinforces such a perception. Nevertheless, the vast majority of our graduates are going into schools or agencies whose general objectives are set by law, or at least where they are certainly very clearly established social objectives. These agencies are *funded* by state legislatures, by local school boards, or by federal monies on the basis of how well specific objectives are met. In the case of the employment service, rehabilitation, and public schools, I do not see how anyone could be naive enough to think that these services did not have direct political and social implications, that is, stopping crime, getting people off poverty rolls, and keeping youth in school.

From a *training* point of view the universities must reach some decision about what *changes* they are willing to make in the field of counseling, as they have traditionally perceived and taught it, and decide if they wish to adapt their training programs to meet agency needs. Even though this could be easily done by modifying the *practicum* setting, my own feeling is that the majority of universities are not doing so at the present time, and I would suspect that many of you in the audience will agree with me on this point.

Our other training issue relates to the application of emergence or reeducation theories of counseling. I am sure all of you recognize this as an old issue that I have merely dressed up with new labels. Unfortunately, it still exists as a major deterrent to the development of counseling as we consider a new emphasis, new groups, and a need for new techniques. As I perceive it, the old issue of directive versus so-called nondirective or Rogerian counseling has never been completely resolved. As a result, we are graduating two different types of counselors: one trained on the basis of a counseling theory which encourages and reinforces the emergence of feelings and attitudes within the individual versus one schooled in a theory based upon the idea of reeducation. One theoretical position and its resulting techniques assumes that good things will *always* emerge while advocates of the other theory are not quite so sure. My own personal experience has led me to believe that the vast majority of both counselor trainers and graduates of our training programs are *enamored* with the emergence concept. They have been trained to perceive all clients as positive, trustworthy, constructive, realistic, forward moving, etc. From my own critical and possibly even cynical point of view, this has resulted in the development of a discipline that we call "Counseling Psychology" based upon what I have come to refer to as the Boy Scout Oath Theory of Personality; that is, our clients, all of them under all conditions, are trustworthy, loyal, helpful, friendly, courteous, kind, obedient, cheerful, thrifty, brave, clean, and reverent. I think you will agree with me that this may well be true if we carefully restrict the clientele groups that we serve to middle class white college-bound students It may have little or no meaning as an attempt to answer the demands of society for expanded counseling services in the broad areas of the culturally disadvantaged, or in college of the culturally disillusioned. I suspect that a number of you in the audience whose jobs lead you into interaction with the slum dwellers of Newark, Chicago, Los Angeles, Denver, or Washington might better describe your clients, at least initially, as untrustworthy, discourteous, hostile, angry, disloyal, and conceivably even a little dangerous to you physically. I would call your careful attention to the fact that I have *not* denied this group's capacity of becoming, or better yet, learning to become, like the first group. Nevertheless, for reasons that I must confess I am unable to understand, many counselors seem fixated on two ideas. First, a terrific fear of ever being accused of controlling or manipulating client behavior within the interview. Yet, we obviously control the client's verbal production every time we select out of what he has said the material we choose to reinforce. And second, a feeling on the part of many counselors that they are counselors as a result of some mystical summons to "help people." Instead they need to hold a perception of themselves as trained behavioral scientists, who are trained to put in an eight-hour working day, in an established profession supported by a body of research knowledge offering professional services to a clientele group.

By way of further modifying what I have just said, I would point out to you that I am not denying that all good counselors should feel that their clients are capable of growth and development. Yet, I think data clearly support the fact that these potentials can be released in many different ways in addition to the traditional reflection or relationship method.

The publications of Truax and Carkhuff and their established conditions for counseling have brought still another issue to the surface as far as training is concerned. I would merely like to point out that it may be relatively easy to train a person to "look" like a counselor although he may not end up "acting" like one very long when he is bombarded with the force of the psychological data produced by clients.

Problems of Expanding Professional Counseling Services

We need to clearly identify what unique problems, if any, these groups present. I personally reject the concept of a ghetto problem, a hippie problem, or a Negro problem. I see it as people with problems who merely happen to belong to larger and more easily identified groups. I would point out to you that those of us working as college administrators these days are taking our share of abuse from both students and faculty. As a result and for our own general purposes and use, we have split our college groups into three classifications within the broad heading of the culturally disillusioned. First, an aggressive yet rational minority who accepts the goals of society and who merely wants its share. This includes most, or at least many, of your militant Negro groups, and we have had decent luck in working with them. Second, the culturally alienated or somewhat mixed-up students that we have always had with us; however, for the first time, their behavior and their dress are deemed socially acceptable. And third, a group of militant radicals or revolutionaries who are truly nihilistic and who want nothing from us except the destruction of our own system. In dealing with clients of this type, we have found that a very fine line exists between participating democracy, on the one hand, and *personal anarchy,* on the other. They represent a segment of society that has evaluated and then rejected the package that society has to sell. I need not point out to any of you that they have had considerable success in making use of the courts to militantly claim any rights that are due them under the law. In our own particular case at the University of Missouri, the surface issue that we are having difficulty with has been free speech versus obscene speech—while the real issue has been student power. In essence, we are finding out that as far as the courts are concerned, if material would not be considered pornographic in Kansas City, St. Louis, or Springfield, Missouri, it may well not be pornographic just because it is distributed by students on the campus. The basic question that I would raise with you as counselors is whether or not the basic criteria for counseling are being met when we attempt to offer any kind of services to a truly revolutionary or nihilistic clientele group. I would hold that in the majority of cases the criteria are not being met, and as a result you may have little or nothing to offer, at least if you stick to traditional methods and techniques. Nevertheless, college presidents, deans, boards of curators, governing boards, and boards of regents all look to college personnel services and college counseling bureaus for help with these groups. I do not think that we are being asked to control student unrest or guarantee student behavior; but we are being asked to serve as translators or intermediaries and to be willing and able to consult with college administrators. I think the college counseling service that is not in the position to play such a role may soon find itself short on operating budget.

What about the type of services we offer to minority or disadvantaged clientele groups? Data clearly support the fact that their culture is different, that their use of words has different meaning, and that their values are different. And, as far as I am concerned, their capacity to respond to reflective techniques or relationship counseling is either extremely limited or nonexistent. As an example, consider the problem of passive dependent clients or those whose past background and home life have resulted in a need for immediate gratification. Established personality disorders such as passive dependency are very subtle and hard to measure or identify yet have a powerful effect on outcomes. From the psychological point of view passive dependency represents an expression of hostility or inadequacy by not doing rather than by attacking. It is an extremely hard thing for an untrained counselor to recognize and respond to in an adequate and productive professional manner. I am sure that many of you know from personal experience a passive dependent personality person, who makes his living studying the responses that you and I want to hear and can do really fantastic things in his manipulation of a naive but well-intentioned counselor, particularly one who is waiting around for "good" to emerge.

Another group that we have to work into our counseling scheme is comprised of those people who are primarily concerned with immediate gratification or a "nowness" orientation. Many of these people have been raised in an environment which emphasizes and rewards immediate gratification. Yet, counseling as practiced today in most cases offers nothing but long-term delayed goals offered by ex-graduate students who themselves represent the extreme end of the continuum in a capacity to delay goals. We simply are going to have to get our counseling as well as our training programs set up to where there is a more immediate reward system involved if we hope to hold any of these people and do anything about the terrific dropout rate that we are encountering in many if not all of our social change programs.

Summary and Conclusions

Now a few concluding remarks. I hope by now that it is obvious to all of you that I do not think we are responding to the challenge to make counseling more relevant to the needs of a larger segment of society that needs our help. What do I feel that we can and should do?

1. See if we cannot work out a more acceptable middle role between serving as an agent of society versus an agent of the client. I think the roles can be made mutually compatible.

2. Do needed outcome studies on the results, or outcomes, of counseling—particularly studies designed to evaluate the effect of techniques on the process of counseling. In many cases, we are working on the basis of assumptions that we have very little data to support.

3. Reevaluate the relationship between current theories of personality and techniques of counseling.

4. Allow room for a good counselor who is not a therapist in our peer group pecking order.

5. Make readiness, or precounselor training, an acceptable part of the total process of helping, of which the formal counseling relationship is merely a part.

6. Develop a process of counseling which will allow us to respond adequately to the nowness, or immediate gratification needs, of many of our clients. We will fail with these groups if we do not. We simply have to give them a taste of success sooner than the end of the process since they lack the psychological capacity to delay goals for any long period of time.

7. Accept and be professionally proud of the fact that as behavioral scientists we do manipulate behavior towards socially acceptable goals. Learn to do it well. Do not allow yourselves or your counselors to be bound to ineffectiveness by a blind adherence to an old theoretical position that research has never really supported and that may be grossly inappropriate in today's society. As a counselor, you are establishing a professional contract between yourself and a client. Attempt to fulfill it by making use of the most appropriate sets of techniques and services, based upon the needs and resources of the individual client. In essence, loosen up and be willing to try new things.

The Immorality of Irrelevance: The Social Role of Science[1]

BERNARD H. BAUMRIN

The author received his PhD in philosophy from Johns Hopkins University in 1960 and has studied law at Washington University's and Columbia University's Schools of Law. He is presently an associate professor of philosophy at Lehman College (CUNY) and is on the Doctoral Faculty of the City University of New York. His major research has been in the philosophy of science and ethical theory, and he is currently studying the moral properties of social institutions.

The main thesis I wish to urge is that doing disinterested science or science for the sake of science is *likely to be* immoral, and that justifying that activity in terms of its benefit to mankind, or some portion of it, *is* immoral. This main thesis, stated above negatively and later to be restated positively and expanded, uses two well-known distinctions worth noting. The first is the distinction between *doing* an act and *justifying* it; the second is the distinction between what is *probably* the case and what is *absolutely* or certainly the case. This is not the place to propose a fully constructed ethical theory and so I use as the meaning of "immoral" a relatively noncontroversial one: "Something is immoral if it is a breach of duty; and something is immoral if, though not a breach of duty it has avoidable deleterious consequences." Clearly bad consequences by themselves do not make something immoral, since something done with the best intentions on the best evidence available may turn out to have thoroughly bad consequences, and something done thoughtlessly or with evil intentions may turn out to have thoroughly good consequences. Thus "avoidable" is the significant term in the definition; that is, if the agent could have foreseen the bad consequence and could have avoided its occurrence and nevertheless did not, then to that extent his act is immoral. If something is neither a breach of duty nor gives rise to avoidable deleterious consequences, then it is not immoral, though I do not go so far as to maintain here that it is moral per se. The tough case, which we will discuss later, is an act which is a fulfillment of a duty which nevertheless gives rise to avoidable deleterious consequences.

The main thrust of my argument will be to show first that the doing of disinterested science is quite likely to be immoral, that is, either a breach of duty or the

---

[1] Invited Address presented to the Division of Clinical Psychology at the Annual Meeting of the American Psychological Association, Washington, D. C., September 2, 1969.

cause of avoidable deleterious consequences; and though there are reasons why one might not thereby wish to discourage its pursuit, there is no reason for anyone to encourage its pursuit; and second that justifications for engaging in the pursuit of science for its own sake by reference to future hypothetical beneficial results is immoral because, first, it is generally a breach of duty, the duty to be honest, and second, it generally (perhaps always) does give rise to avoidable deleterious consequences. I do not think the proof of those rather radical views is very difficult or very long, but to avoid undue abstraction we shall first consider the standard theory of doing science as well as discuss some examples.

Science: The Gentleman's Pastime

The fundamental premise of the standard received view, at this juncture one might wish to say "the established view," is that the pursuit of scientific knowledge is a good activity in its own right, and even better since scientific knowledge is an absolute good apart from its consequences. This premise probably has as old a history as any piece of the collective wisdom one can state. I have never found a scientist that did not subscribe to it as a truism, or very close to one. It is fairly clear that somewhere around the time of Socrates, Plato, and Arisotle, it became an accepted part of the folklore of philosophy. But there is a difference between the pursuit of knowledge for its own sake and doing science for its own sake, and that difference can be illustrated by reference to Socrates' own activity. Socrates' major intellectual contribution was largely negative. He showed that most learned people who claimed to know things, people like Gorgias, Euthyphro, Thrasymachus, and Protagoras, were windbags. But the upshot of this could be very little more than knowledge for its own sake, for to know that Euthyphro did not know the truth about what the gods love does not tell us what they do love. Our object is knowledge about the gods, not about Euthyphro. Nevertheless, from a philosophic point of view to know that some theory is false and why it is false is to know quite a bit, and when science and philosophy were virtually indistinguishable, it was easy to import the highest philosophic value into anything barely in contact with it; and the highest philosophic value is to seek to know above all else the deepest mysteries even if they avail one nought in this world. In Plato's chief scientific work, *Timaeus,* he holds that searching for knowledge of nature (physics, psychology, astronomy) is "a recreation and a permissable pastime [Ryle, 1966, p. 13]." Aristotle recognized quite clearly that though philosophy (like science) begins in wonder, it requires leisure. And though science might begin in wonder, it could also begin with necessity, and though it can be pursued in leisure, it can also create leisure by replacing work with knowledge. Thus, though one can pursue science, like philosophy, for its own sake, science can also be pursued for the sake of what it can do. There is nothing new about this; many before have eloquently argued the point, Galileo, da Vinci, and Francis Bacon to name only an illustrious few. What calls for mention is that whether science was pursued for its own sake or for its fruits, in the beginning its gifts were great for, like many gems and minerals, much lay on or close to the topsoil for earlier generations. When men as foragers strode the earth, it lay festooned with discoveries that required little labor. It is very hard in retrospect to know whether early gems or discoveries were plucked for their beauty or their utility. But then again it hardly matters whether aristocratic (one may substitute "wealthy") Athenians, Romans, or Florentines wished to expend their time and wherewithal on the pursuit of knowledge.

Whatever the cost of such embellishments to prior societies we need not take seriously the ancient social imbalances they created. Our question is one of present and future imbalances. It does not matter now (perhaps it never did) that someone spent his fortune on astrologers, on measuring the ether, or on influencing genetic change by gross environmental differences. Goethe's Faust is dead; the question is this: Does Professor Faust still live within us all? I do not mean to be obscure; I mean to begin to focus our view not, for example, on the vast expenditure we have made to harness the energy of plasma at Oak Ridge, but on the vast expenditure of our time, energy, wherewithal, and talent on the pursuit and collection of scientific knowledge for its own sake, on massive technology for the sake of quixotic missions, on vast expenditures to pump people into some fields in preference to others. To object to personal scientific adventures at personal expense would be foolish and futile; to object to the use of public and institutional funds for similar adventures is not foolish but required by the recognition that not only is not all scientific knowledge valuable, but some is useless and some too dangerous to have. These facts, though well known, need to be kept constantly in view. Every researcher must be balanced enough in his perspective to be able to choose between getting information which is not useless and that which is. It is not good science to add marginalia to the well known, and it is of course suicidal to play with certain products that we can make but not control. One can go further and argue that some knowledge is harmful in itself, and, more importantly, that the search itself for more scientific knowledge is so costly to the species that even if the knowledge sought were to be obtained, it could never pay back its cost.

I have gone way ahead of myself for the subject has its own tempo of exposition. We have been looking at the fundamental premise of the received view; that is, that "the pursuit of scientific knowledge is a good activity in its own right, and even better since scientific knowledge is an absolute good apart from its consequences." Now if scientific knowledge is not always an absolute good apart from its consequences, then one must ask what justifies the belief that scientific investigation is a good in itself. It would follow from the fact that if its product were always good, it was good; but it is clear that the converse is not valid; that is, good activities can give rise to thoroughly undesirable products. Thus, there are two questions to be posed: First, is scientific knowledge absolutely good apart from its consequences? Second, if not, how would one defend the proposition that scientific activity is good in itself?

The Moral Neutrality of Science

The fact that the question is so rarely asked is related to the second basic premise of the received view. This premise is much more difficult to give a rigorous formulation to but an approximation to it might be: Since truth properly used can never lead to error, then the producers of truth are not and ought not to be accountable for its misuse, or for the consequences of its improper application. Scientific knowledge is a species of truth. Therefore, the discoverers of scientific knowledge are accountable for neither its use nor abuse, nor its consequences.

It is readily apparent that though most members of the scientific community subscribe to this article, nevertheless it is confronted with two obvious difficulties. First, some scientists acting on this principle produced knowledge that they later condemned themselves for having disseminated because those who used it were not capable of doing so properly. The principal, though by no means the only, case in point is that of the scientific producers of atomic energy. On the other hand, some atomic physicists [2] refused to cooperate with civilian and military authorities in providing the necessary scientific underpinnings for this venture and at least in some cases appeared therefore to contravene the second basic premise of the received view; that is, they held themselves accountable for its ultimate application and chose not to be responsible for its use. The second difficulty is that many scientists, indeed many kinds of scientists, are enthusiastic about taking credit for the "spin-off" from their discoveries. Medicine and chemistry afford only the more obvious cases: a surgical procedure, a new compound, a new drug. Indeed, the very purpose of some scientific disciplines is to effect cures, and it would hardly make sense to say of a psychologist or a physician who effected a cure that he was not responsible for it or was not the cause of it.

The usual intellectual gymnastic used to overcome this defect in the second premise is to hold that those whose aim is to "use" science to "do" things are merely technologists; and though science and technology are related, it is a confusion to think of technology as a part of science at all. This gymnastic has the well-known peculiar outcome that technologists are held accountable by scientists for the use of scientific knowledge, and technologists abjure that accountability wherever it is unprofitable by calling themselves "scientists" and their endeavors "science," and thus are able to cloak themselves in the rhetoric and the moral protection of the received view.

Riches beyond Their Wildest Dreams

The first premise stated as a sketch is that science is good, and the second is that science is morally neutral. The last premise that I intend to discuss might be thought of as science's faith in its own fecundity. On the established view every bit of data may, you can never tell, lead somewhere. Thus, though some knowledge is more immediately valuable, some more immediately useful, nevertheless in the long run every bit *may* be valuable, perhaps even more valuable than anyone can foresee. This belief, of course, is thought of as a basic prop to that part of the first premise, that scientific knowledge is absolutely good apart from its consequences, since if it is knowledge, it may in the future have very useful effects.

Unlike the first two premises for which no extratheoretical evidence can be given, the fecundity premise is usually supported with examples. The examples turn on the fact that once in a while some formerly irrelevant piece of data later comes in handy in the construction of a new theory, or in support of a new hypothesis. For example, prior sightings of bright stellar objects recorded in ancient Eastern sources lends support to the view that the Crab Nebulla is the remains of a supernova. Examples can be found in drug research, archeology, and botany. They

---

[2] Chiefly those outside the United States and the United Kingdom (cf., e.g., Junck, 1958).

are frequent in sciences related to the passage of long periods of time, and are rare in those that are relatively free of history. However, someone's long-forgotten nineteenth-century physics experiment on ether may come in handy, who knows? Let me emphasize here that point about the function of historicity in the usefulness of the forgotten. Every old science has accumulations of data whose relevance to the present depends on archival intellects or accidents of rediscovery, but the relevance of that data to present interests has never been decided upon since its ancient vintage obscures it from the view of all but a few. New sciences have short histories; most workers in those areas are still living and the data form part of their own personal histories. They are the monitors of their own disciplines. Thus, rarely do data get totally forgotten unless they are presently useless or in error. Price (1961, 1963) has shown that most scientific papers appear never to be noticed within as well as outside of their own discipline; and of those few that are noticed a very great proportion are no longer noted after a period of months, and further, the cost of researching the literature for relevant data is generally greater than the cost of recreating it. Taken together this information leads to the conclusion that the thesis of the cumulativity of science must be greatly modified for new disciplines and that data production is not a very important part of these scientific areas. Nevertheless, each piece of data *may* bear future fruit, who can tell?

Let us look at the established view as a piece. Science is good. Scientific knowledge is absolutely good, apart from its consequences. All scientific knowledge may ultimately be useful. Scientific knowledge since it is composed of the truth is morally neutral, only its misuse leads to deleterious consequences. Scientists are neither technologists nor politicians, therefore, they are not responsible for the misuse of what they have discovered (nor should they be rewarded for its utility except by academic and professional preferment commensurate with their demonstrated talent).[3]

It might be helpful here to juxtapose the thesis of this paper: Doing disinterested science is likely to be immoral and justifying that activity in terms of its future hypothetical benefit to mankind or some portion of it is immoral. Clearly the established view and the view proposed here are inconsistent and we shall forthwith dispatch one of them.

Science: Bread and Circuses

The established view has come in for comparatively little scholarly criticism since its Greek articulation. What scholarly criticism there has been has been either epigrammatic, as Marx's claim that it is time for philosophers to remake the world, or utopian as with Saint-Simon, August Comte, and other nineteenth-century utopian theorists intoxicated with technology. Aside from Luddite types few have challenged the established view. The challenge when made has not been very complicated and neither has the attempt at its rebuttal. In order to capture the flavor of such discussions what follows does not purport to be rigorous or exhaustive but reportorial.

The principal argument against the established view that there should be unstinting public support of disinterested science has been that limited resources

---

[3] For a recent critique of this intoxication in its present form see McDermott, 1969.

ought to be allocated to the solution of pressing social problems since scientific research for its own sake is a social frill and creation of public works, jobs, safety, and health are the chief responsibilities of those who have care of the common good.[4] The principal points made by those interested in public support for the pursuit of science for its own sake are (*a*) if the resources were not allocated to science, they would still not be allocated to pressing social needs; and (*b*) support of disinterested science is a good practical investment because it creates new knowledge which creates new products which creates new jobs and a better world. For Example, I quote from a General Electric advertisement in *The New York Times* (1969, p. 21) the day after Apollo 11's return:

Have you maybe heard a neighbor ask "So What?" about walking on the moon?
Some people think like that.
If it costs a lot of money and they don't see an immediate payoff, it's a So-What.
So when you see your neighbor tonight, tell him that for example here's what:
Scientists think the moon may offer clues to the secret of life.
The moon has no atmosphere. So the sun's hot rays come through loud and clear. Which means man can probably use the moon as a laboratory to perfect solar power and save mankind several billion dollars a year in the cost of energy. (Like cutting your neighbor's fuel bill drastically.)
The moon has a near-perfect vacuum that can't be duplicated here on earth. Which means that man can probably mass-produce important medicines on the moon at a fraction of the cost.
But that's only part of the Here's-What. There are plenty of immediate payoffs too. And they're already affecting life on earth more than your neighbor realizes.
Our own case is pretty typical.
The soles of the boots you saw walk on the moon are made of GE silicone rubber. And the Saturn booster, the Apollo spacecraft, the lunar module and the Astronauts' space suits also used silicone rubber, plus some of our space age silicone coatings, lubricants, sealants and electrical insulation.
The same silicone developments are also showing up in such down-to-earth uses as these:
Silicone membranes for artificial lungs. New building materials for new types of low cost housing. Coatings to increase rain water collection in arid regions. Improved components for safer, more reliable automobiles. Chemical additives to help control water pollution. New materials needed to find new food sources under the sea.
Sounds to us like the moon shot was a very smart investment.
We are proud to have had a small part in it. And we think every American should be.
Silicone Products Department
Waterford, New York
Lunar boots made with General Electric silicone rubber by ILC Industries, Inc., for NASA[5]

Here is the blatantly technological twist to the "disinterested science is a good investment" argument. Of course it is not an isolated appeal.

---

[4] This argument, of course, is much more impressive during periods of scarcity than those of plenty; so, for example, it was easy to publicly counter during the 1950s while it has lately begun to fall on some deaf ears.

[5] Reprinted with permission from *The New York Times,* July 25, 1969, p. 21. Copyrighted 1969 by The New York Times Company and the General Electric Company.

In this place was to be Ling-Tempco-Vought, Inc.'s advertisement on p. 18 of *The New York Times,* July 25, 1969. However, LTV has refused permission to reprint that material in this place. *For whenever and wherever man has gone looking before, to see what was there, he has been right to do so. And he has never gone unrewarded* [*Two sentences from LTV advertisement*].

To help us imagine the size of the investment and preoccupation involved the statistics of another advertisement in *The New York Times* (1969, p. 15) are instructive. Quoted in full, IBM, a company not reputed to be short of scientific respectability, had this to say:

The Questers

History's pages are illuminated with the names of men who journeyed into alien lands to make the unknown known. Marco Polo, to open the Far East. Columbus, to seek a New World. Magellan, to set sail around the globe. Lewis and Clark, to blaze a trail across our continent. Peary, to find the North Pole. A rare breed, these men who take the first step to bring more light into the world. Today IBM salutes all the astronauts who took historic first steps in our space program. And the people of NASA who guided them. And the some 20,000 companies in the Apollo program who helped. We are proud to be one of them.

IBM[6]

It is true that despite the expenditure of about 50 billion dollars, the Apollo program could have failed, as of course many voyages before have (though few were covered by television). But what must occur to the reasonable man is that an expenditure on the scale of the Marshall Plan could have gone a great distance in the creation of a livable world. We are 50 billion dollars further behind, and 10 more years, and thousands of men mistrained, and professionally narrow. To be an expert in a subject for which there is no basic need is to be a human frill in the class with circus freaks, eunuchs, and prostitutes past their prime.

Looked at in the clear light of day hardly anyone would espouse the view that "no matter what the cost, if it hasn't been done, it's worth doing." Indeed I do not think many would subscribe to the far weaker thesis that "if it hasn't been done, its worth doing."

One moral of this side trip to Apollo is that even if societal support of disinterested science does create new industries, jobs, and products, that support placed there effectively prevents its being placed elsewhere; for men, if nothing else, are funneled in the supported directions and away from the unsupported or lightly supported, and to the extent that this funneling takes place fewer people of energy and talent will tangle with increasingly massive and depressing problems like hunger, poverty, ugliness, pollution, ignorance, overpopulation, racial antagonism, etc. Of course, when these problems begin to threaten the foundation of any society, when ministers of state must avoid contact with the disenchanted multitude, then something must be done, and leaders all over wonder where the problems came from and quietly hope that they will fade away.

There is, however, a more fundamental moral that rests on a Luddite question. Are new industries and new products needed? Are they desirable? Do we require new kinds of public benefits rather than the expansion of the ones we have?

---

[6] Reprinted with permission from *The New York Times,* July 25, 1969, p. 15. Copyrighted 1969 by The New York Times Company and the IBM Corporation.

Must we not come finally to ask whether today's new product (like DDT) is tomorrow's disaster, whether today's profit is tomorrow's impossible cost? Beside insecticides having their now well-known pollutant effects,[7] have they done more than bring down the price of farm commodities, thereby increasing the cost of marginal farming, and thus emptying vast numbers of rural poor into urban ghettos and creating the necessity for the retirement of productive land to avoid vast agricultural surpluses? Has not DDT turned out to be a virtually unmitigated disaster?

New products create new waste. New industries strangle old ones. If private persons wish to gamble, so be it, but why should public resources be used in other than the public interest?

Of course, adherence to a principle of public support only for public interests will not serve to deter scientists as well as technologists from touting their special interests as having *incalculable* future benefits. It is just their incalculability that should always have made such appeals suspect. I remember reading wth great interest the interminable congressional hearings reports of the early 1960s on the support of high-energy accelerator construction, and there were only two arguments ever offered for the vast expenditures contemplated (running to well over one billion dollars): first, that one would (very rarely "might") find out something important about nuclear and subnuclear "weak" interactions; and, second, that one could never tell what untold riches might be developed from the knowledge gained from this investigation. The first point I am incompetent to comment on, but I did not find the argument persuasive, since it seemed then, at any rate, that high-energy physics theory was in chaos and scientists were likely in the dark about what they were talking about. Schwinger's (1969) recent paper in *Science* seems a first reasonable attempt to bring order out of chaos. As to the second, I am perfectly well able to comment on it, for it is a simple plea which is either made in ignorance or dishonestly. No one can ever tell what the remote consequences of anything will be, and very often one cannot tell what the propinquent ones will be either. Of course, we cannot tell what vast riches we might reap, but "So What?" to quote General Electric's primordial boob. What we want to know is whether or not the investment is worth making, and one thing we can calculate is that man hours spent in one place cannot be spent in another, no matter how much printing press money is created; and what ought to concern us above all else is how men spend their time. Thus to be told that great benefits might flow from X is to be told nothing; moral men must not play on the ignorance or gullibility of those who hold a public trust. If one can foresee no substantial benefits, one should say so or remain silent. If one can foresee them, then they should be unfurled for examination and evaluated against competing claims for support. To play upon ignorance of the history of science is dishonest, and to take advantage of those who are supposed to care for the public good is indirectly to take advantage of the public itself. It is, of course, also terribly odd that scientists, one of whose chief aims is to be able to predict what will occur, are incapable of articulating what social benefits will accrue from investing in the production of new knowledge.

---

[7] For an extensive discussion of mercury pollution from insecticides, see *Environment,* 1969.

The demonstration that it is immoral to *justify* doing science in terms of hypothetical future unknown benefits is therefore quite straightforward, as is the demonstration that it is sometimes immoral to do disinterested science. The latter is as clear as the former when one focuses on the choice being made to do what has no foreseeable benefit as opposed to doing what has. Of course, should one now argue, not the triviality that one cannot foresee, but that a particular investigation is interesting, beautiful, valuable in itself, etc., evaluators can appropriately contrast such claims with competing demands for support. The issue is, to put it another way, what ought to be the standards for selecting between competing demands for limited social resources. In general the answer is support those honest claims that promise to be more beneficial to society-at-large than others, for it is both immoral to take from society what it needs for oneself, and immoral to give society's wherewithal to those who are less deserving. Public resources belong to public projects.

Science and Relevancy

We come now to the question of relevancy. Demands on every side from blacks, hippies, college students, etc., for relevancy have been generally greeted by two kinds of responses: First, there is a kind of incredulity. What could be meant by calling English, chemistry, biology, or logic irrelevant? This response eventually leads to the giving of mere lip service to meeting such demands and the administrative burial of them. Second, there is the all too frequent crash program to meet the demand for relevancy by converting everything in sight to a social action or cultural information program. Here "relevancy" is interpreted as the "immediately useful." Such responses, of course, suffer directly from changed circumstances, for today's immediately useful is tomorrow's boringly passé. But the demands for relevancy are neither born of ignorance nor of misguided passion for application; they are, it seems to me, formed fundamentally from the insight that priorities have gone astray and some concerted effort must be made to get the engines of science and scholarship back on the right tracks. Enamored with atomic energy, insecticides, rapid travel, wonder drugs, computers, rockets, all of Western society has come to take for granted that every generation is intoxicated with progress, organization, and products, but the insight above is joined with the insight that hunger, poverty, and injustice, while perhaps tolerable in poor nations, or in times of drought and pestilence and general war, are intolerable in times of peace and plenty. Only misallocation of resources, or of energy, can account for such horrors, unless the world is run by evil men. So long as demands are for relevancy, those who demand still have hope for a better world within reach. Too long unfulfilled, the next cry will be "off with their heads."

Thus the point about relevancy is that however remote from one's scientific work, that work is relevant so long as the foreseeable consequences of its successful prosecution make headway in solving substantial extant problems facing men. If, on the other hand, its successful prosecution does not in any foreseeable way make a difference with respect to those problems, such work is irrelevant. The "degree of relevancy of an act" then it to be roughly defined as the "degree of articulable foreseeable consequences of that act with respect to substantial human problems." Scientific relevancy is then comprised of those relevant acts prosecuted within the house of and with the tools of science.

The immorality of irrelevance, then, has two sources. Its first source is in the subtraction of manpower, energy, and resources from the tasks that pressingly need to be attended to. Every frivolity has a cost, and great frivolities have great costs to nations and to the species. The second source is less global and more personal; each man of necessity makes his own professional choices, in choice of field, in choice of theory, in choice of experiment. To choose to do science for its own sake, or to choose to do science as if one were taking a hand in constructing a beautiful edifice, or to do it for one's own simple pleasure is to turn one's back on the world, to leave application to those who may be able to make something out of one's work never oneself knowing whether there is anything there to be useful. In short, to do irrelevant science is to make a moral choice; and if one can claim that ignoring the problems of one's fellow man is immoral, then doing science for its own sake is immoral. To take away from others one's own contribution to their well-being is immoral, particularly when it is done by deliberate choice.

Science, far from being morally neutral, is morally involved on two levels. First, it is our chief weapon in solving difficult problems. Second, the choice to join in that task or to abjure it is a moral one.

Let me try to make this point clear for it is crucial to an understanding of the seriousness of these issues. There are only a very few basic ways in which one can justify an action or a pursuit. One can claim as an egoistic justification that one engages in a certain activity because it is in one's own interest, whether psychologically or hedonistically. One can employ on the other hand an altruistic justification and claim that one engages in an activity for the betterment of some group or other or, stretched to its ultimate, as utilitarians would argue one must, for the betterment of the whole species. Both of these types of justification are consequential in character. They rest on the view that what is moral is to maximize a certain benefit for oneself, some group, or all mankind.[8]

Morality can be viewed, however, in a nonconsequential way. Foremost among nonconsequential views are those that hold (*a*) that one should engage in an activity because it is self-fulfilling, (*b*) that it is a fulfillment of a rightful command, for example, by God, and, finally, (*c*) that it is a self-imposed duty that derives its validity from its self-imposition and its universalizability (i.e., that everyone similarly situated could do likewise).[9]

Now a moral question before anyone, not excepting scientists, is whether or not any choice of pursuit, in general and in particular, is moral. The problem is unavoidable particularly if what one does has consequences to others. One complication to be kept in view is that the choice of justification having been made, one cannot without inconsistency shift to another, for then everything could be justified and nothing be immoral. What I have in mind here, for example, is that if one has chosen a pursuit because it gives one pleasure, then to ask for approbation for one's acts because of the potential or actual benefit to others is inconsistent.

---

[8] I think the foregoing classifications of egoisms, altruisms, and utilitarianism exhaust the range of teleological justification.

[9] These I think exhaust the nonconsequential views, though it is clear to me that the self-fulfillment view is deontological in the traditional sense.

Thus the egoist cannot justify his acts on utilitarian grounds nor can the utilitarian on egoistic grounds.

Now one can nail the flag to the mast: If scientists choose to justify their choice of engaging in disinterested science on the basis of its being pleasant for them, or its beauty or its self-fulfillment, then to ask for social support for their activity is facetious. For once we clearly recognize that they are in it for no public purpose, the denial of public support is no shocking deprivation. On the other hand, if they claim to be engaging in their pursuit of scientific knowledge because of the social value of its product, one has a right to expect an honest articulation of the beneficial consequences that are likely to flow from that pursuit. That of course is to demand of those who do *interested science,* science for the sake of its product, that they tell us what they aim at so that we can compare it with other competing claims on our human resources. Of course, one could argue that one might unconsciously choose to do science for its own sake, and indeed that is possible, or one might choose to do science for its own sake believing it to be one's duty, either imposed by a rightful command or self-imposed. In the former case, I suppose one could not condemn such a person, and perhaps it is not immoral for one to make unconscious choices, but I wonder whether any scientist or technologist would justify his activity this way.

In the latter and final case, the case in which one does science as a fulfillment of a duty, we have yet to hear an articulation of this interesting and engaging possibility.

References

Junck, C. *Brighter than a thousand suns.* New York: Harcourt, Brace & World, 1958.

McDermott, J. Intellectuals and technology. *The New York Times' Review of Books,* July 31, 1969, 25.

Novick, S. A new pollution problem. *Environment,* 1969, **2**(4).

Price, D. Science since Babylon. New Haven: Yale University Press, 1961.

Price, D. *Little science, big science.* New York: Columbia University Press, 1963.

Ryle, G. (Ed.) *Plato's progress.* London: Cambridge University Press, 1966.

Schwinger, J. A magnetic model of matter. *Science,* 1969, **165**, 757.

The Scientist in a rapidly Evolving Society

The principal speaker in this symposium is Dr. Jerome Wiesner, Provost of the Massachusetts Institute of Technology. Wiesner is a communications engineer who has demonstrated a very remarkable ability to organize and lead scientists and engineers. He has done this in the fields of research, development, education, and political public affairs. He was very influential, as you must know, in support of the atomic testing ban. Most recently, he put his scientific reputation on the line against the ABM system. But to the general public he is best known as an adviser to Presidents Kennedy and Johnson, an experience that provided the background for his book *Where Science and Politics Meet*; it was published in 1964, but the matters discussed in it seem to become more relevant each year.

I think as psychologists we owe Wiesner a special debt of gratitude. In 1961, acting as the President's Science Adviser, he organized a panel, through the Office of Science and Technology, under the chairmanship of Dr. Neal Miller, that prepared what I think has been a very helpful report (1962) "Strengthening the Behavioral Sciences." In this and many other ways, Wiesner has demonstrated himself to be a man who is not only one of our leading scientific statesmen, but a good friend of psychologists. His willingness to participate in this symposium is comforting evidence that this friendship has endured.

References

Miller, N. (Chm.) Strengthening the behavioral sciences. *Science,* 1962, **136,** 233–241.
Wiesner, J. *Where science and politics meet.* New York: McGraw-Hill, 1964.

GEORGE A. MILLER
Symposium Chairman

The chairman received his PhD in psychology from Harvard University in 1946. He is presently a professor at the Rockefeller University, where his major research interest is in the psychological bases for language and communication.

The Need for Social Engineering

JEROME B. WIESNER

The author received his PhD in electrical engineering from the University of Michigan in 1950. He is presently Provost of the Massachusetts Institute of Technology, where his major current interest is in seeking ways to use science and technology to create a decent world.

The operational mood for a panel such as this could well be that of Thurber's "Fables for Our Times" in which one of the more satisfying morals is that it is better to ask some of the questions than to know all of the answers. That is actually the way I feel about the issues raised in this symposium, but I am going to pretend that I know some of the answers as well in order to provide my colleagues on the program with some specific targets. In my view, we can hardly do better than to take George Miller's (see pp. 5–21) timely presidential address as the sermon for today; I think that his proposal is very nearly right—but too modest. He threw out the same challenge that I want to when he said, "The most urgent problems of our world today are the problems we have made for ourselves. . . . They are human problems whose solutions will require us to change our behavior and our social institutions." To do this he feels that we must foster some new public conception of man based on a deep understanding of psychology.

I believe that this is only part of the problem, though a vital part. We must, I am certain, foster a new public conception of man and his social system. In addition, we must develop a profession of social engineering that helps to plan, forecast, and provide feedback about social development. It would be a profession with all of the human sciences including psychology, but with a primary commitment to problem solving. I call this task social engineering because I want an engineering attitude. Technologists apply science when they can and in fact achieve their most elegant solutions when an adequate theoretical basis exists for their work, but normally they are not halted by the lack of a theoretical base. They fill in the gaps by drawing on experience, intuition, judgment, and experimentally obtained information. People working on social problems obviously follow this procedure, too, but it is safe to say that there is no generally recognized and well-organized discipline of social engineering. Experience, intuition, and prejudices are the principal resources of most people trying to solve social problems. Miller really laid the groundwork for an exploration of this question and I will push the issue further in my presentation.

My hope is that with a fuller understanding of the dynamics of our social processes, our human capabilities, and our needs much of the basis for reactionary stances in defense of the status quo will disappear and the basis for a much more satisfying society will exist. Most reaction is based on fear and lack of understanding of what is going on in our changing and evolving society.

The Relationship between Science and Society

There are two quite distinct though related facets to the relationship between science and technology and society: (*a*) the impact of science and its applications on the various aspects of society, and (*b*) the specific problems of the growth, direction, well-being, and support of research and development. We as scientists tend to think much more about this latter facet.

We tend mostly to think about the impact of science in terms of its potential for change, of the technological (that is, hardware), medical, and agricultural developments which research has made possible and we tend to underestimate the intellectual and psychological importance of the new understandings of man and his universe. We are conscious of the changing natural and man-made physical environments; but we rarely appreciate, I suspect, the rate of change of the psychological environment in which humans live or the fact that polluting man's psychological environment with television violence or cold war rhetoric can be as destructive as DDT in an estuary. One can push the similie further, too: Both forms of pollution have the most serious impact on the young of the species. Nor when we think of beautifying the environment, do we think of making a better home for our psyche.

Social Engineering

I was pleased to hear Miller's challenge to psychologists "to foster a social climate in which a new public conception of man based on psychology could take root and flourish." I believe that this is an essential precursor to the development and acceptance of the understanding and skills that I claim are necessary for the adequate management of change in our society. Certainly the social engineer would have to appreciate the overriding importance of the psychological environment as he explored the choices he was going to propose to the society. Since we seem to agree on this, the only issue left for us today seems to be how to do it. Perhaps as our first discussion point we might examine whether or not there is general agreement on this point and then explore how we might get ahead with the task. Actually, I intend to say a bit more about this point as I proceed. Incidentally, it would also be very constructive if men appreciated more the social, political, and technical interactions as well as their own nature.

Earlier I mentioned the two issues which naturally come to mind regarding science in relation to society: the social consequences of applied science and the problem of support and direction of science as separate matters. Clearly they interrelate. Modern society supports science on a grand scale largely because it has learned that scientific knowledge is a good investment. Though many scientists and many philanthropists who support science are motivated by the quest for understanding, the primary reason that a government or a private company spends money for research is the belief that in some sense it will pay off some day in new technology. Unfortunately our sights are too often on short-range goals and, all too frequently, the wrong ones, usually with initials. We get exactly the technology that we pay for—those things that have quick profits or for which it is easy to generate support such as space or military technology. Twenty-five billion dollars not only gets us to the moon, it creates an enormous and highly specialized technical capability—one might even say distortion—in engineering and the physical sciences in industry, government, and universities. The 10 million dollars in HUD for research on housing and urban development or the even smaller amounts in HEW for pollution control create proportionate capabilities for dealing with these problems and speak more loudly than presidential messages or congressional committee reports about national priorities.

Support for the Behavioral and Social Sciences

Even if you knew where to look, I doubt if you would be able to find many funds in the federal budget devoted to understanding the problems we are exploring today. In part this is because we have not been able to define or articulate them. Also, when we do articulate them, we arouse a general fear that understanding in the behavioral and social sciences would make possible manipulation and control of people, and this fear makes support hard to obtain. This is a more general expression of the specific problem of control relating to psychology that Miller talked about in his presidential speech. I certainly encountered much concern, particularly among Members of Congress, about the dangers implicit in developing behavioral science and social science knowledge when as President Kennedy's Science Adviser, I tried to increase the funds for the support of research in these areas. I am sure that the potential for abuse, both intentional and inadvertent, is great here just as in the physical sciences, but since we have cast our lots for survival with the creations of man's mind, it does seem rather dangerous to leave the social development to chance, while investing tens of billions of dollars each year to achieve greater and greater mastery of the physical world. Incidentally, last spring a group of our radical faculty and students visited me to protest a social science research project that involved the use of computers, and their true concern, they said, was that social science knowledge would lead to control and that such control would be exercised to preserve the status quo. The congressmen I referred to previously feared that knowledge inevitably led to socialistic management of our society. I suspect that both views have some validity. Miller ducked the matter of control by suggesting that new psychological knowledge be directed at people so that they know themselves better, but I doubt that this in an adequate answer. There will always be a need for administrative structures and governments and a need to make choices between disparate directions, and probably there will even be a need for gain-motivated individuals and larger social units. We cannot ever be certain that someone will not exploit knowledge improperly, but my worst fear is actually a different one, namely, that what we manage to do in creating social engineering efforts will be totally inadequate and will possibly make matters worse rather than better just from incompetence alone.

Mostly that is why we are in trouble now, because of our inadequacies rather than because of evil intent, though the results may be indistinguishable. Neither Vietnam nor Czechoslovakia was undertaken for destructive purposes, but each in its own way has done great, perhaps irredeemable damage to the psychological environment of the superpower involved.

The Need to Respond more rapidly to Social Problems

Most of us have the impression that the swarm of problems which technology has generated have arisen suddenly and with essentially no advanced warning so that there has been little or no time to prepare technically, politically, or organizationally to cope with them. Actually the shadows cast by many, though not all, of our most pressing problems have been visible for many years. Can you remember when you first heard about the population explosion or when you first heard Lewis Mumford deplore the accelerating decay of the environment? Can you recall when you first realized that the Bill of Rights was color blind and discriminated between rich and poor?

Gunar Myrdal spelled out the shame of our race problem 30 years ago, and Sigmund Freud even before that, in "Mankind and His Discontents," forecast the problem we are now examining, our failure to adjust psychologically and politically to the new world of technology.

We have not been totally blind or indifferent to these issues but in general our responses have come too late, have been inadequate and frequently just wrong. Though we are thoroughly conscious of the fact that we live in an age of very great change, we have done precious little to try to understand or direct that change to our liking or even to our true needs. This is, I have come to believe, the reason for the mass psychosis of our times. We are convinced that we have vast forces at our command to solve mankind's problems, and as we try to use them, the problems multiply in number and grow in size and complexity. Though the means exist for the first time in man's history to make a decent life for all on the planet, from these means flow greater horrors with which to contend.

In reflective moments, we must recognize that it is to this state of affairs that the young people of the world are protesting. Each in his own way and in his own culture has formed an image of modern society which revolts or, in modern jargon, radicalizes them. By some unconscious intellectual process worthy of investigation by psychologists—by some amazing integration of all they have seen, experienced, read, and heard—they have recognized that the parts of our society do not fit together and they are shocked to learn that we, their elders, do not even recognize these basic inconsistencies, or, even worse, that we do recognize them but in our comfortable adjustments cannot command the energy and courage to try to correct or reconcile them.

In an inspiring document made public by *The New York Times* about a year and a half ago, Academician Andreí Sakharov calls for cooperation between the United States and the Soviet Union so that the technical capabilities of the two superpowers can be directed to the solution of the multicrises of our times. He characterized the present period as a "hinge of history," by which he meant, I believe, a critical and decisive moment when decisions we make or do not make (for crimes of omission can be as deadly as crimes of commission, though you usually get promoted for committing crimes of omission) will point mankind on the path to greater fulfillment or doom it.

This may sound extravagant but I do not regard Sakharov's paper as overly dramatic and this moment in time should challenge us all to our best efforts. After I read the Sakharov paper, I dreamed that we were making our journey through time on a comet and that we are as close now as we will ever get to paradise. Awake, I do not believe this, but the reality truly depends on what we do about the problems we are discussing today. Why do I agree that this is such a critical moment, a hinge or possibly even a saddle point in history? You know the reason as well as I. Most phenomena associated with societies and people grow exponentially if not restrained. That is why crises appear to come on so suddenly, why problems seem unimportant one season and out of hand the next. It is probable that we can still control most of the serious problems we face, the population explosion and all of its by products, such as misery, crowding, famine, lack of education, poverty, or the spread of nuclear arsenals, or the pollution of the air and the seas. But this will not be true in another decade. Even on problems where we face no such final moments there are reasons for acting promptly. First of all, environmental and social diseases are much easier to prevent or arrest than reverse. Prevention requires legislation and restraint, while undoing environmental damage which requires vast physical projects and undoing the human damage of a social error, such as allowing children to grow up in poverty or without adequate proteins in their diets, may prove to be impossible. This may also be the case with taking DDT out of the seas, or strontium 90 from the atmosphere.

Furthermore, it takes time to develop new technologies and to put them to work, so that prompt recognition of work on the control of evolution is a necessity if we are to keep the society operating relatively evenly.

A Mechanism for Forecasting and Controlling Social Change

It should be clear by now that I am suggesting that we must develop a mechanism for fostering reasoned and continued examination of these social problems and controlled experimentation, so as to prevent the present almost totally blind and almost completely random decision-making process from ultimately leading to our destruction. I would like to suggest some possibilities for doing this and also to explore what has to be done to provide adequate financial support for the basic research and the experimentation needed to back up such efforts.

Before going on, though, I would like to make explicit the metaphor which guides my approach to these problems. It is a point of view derived from my long association with Norbert Wiener and my professional involvement with communication theory and computer design. By the uses of technology, man has set up a new evolutionary process in which adaptation is controlled in large measure by his perceptions of needs and his development of his technological capabilities to meet them. By a complex system of rewards and profits, we have a complex learning machine in which large numbers of individuals are trying to better satisfy the needs—or perceived needs—of the society or some component of it and by doing so serve their own ends as well. As in any learning system there must be feedback comparing the results with the goal. Here, of course, lies the problem. What are the goals? Who sets them and who measures success? How are conflicting goals of different individuals reconciled? In the private sector of a capitalist society, we have met this problem by using the feedback of the market system to measure the extent to which a given initiative meets social need hemmed about with control. In the public sector, there are many—the vote, the courts, etc. This arrangement has worked surprisingly well in the private sector. In fact, it is very clear that the socialist countries have not yet developed an adequate substitute for this particular elementary feedback. Unfortunately the system so far has tended to overemphasize those aspects that can easily be measured in monetary terms and allows activities which have many negative aspects. The monetary feedback is sensitive, the system is responsive. By way of contrast, in many areas involving the general public good, areas in which individual initiatives cannot be taken and a problem can be attacked only through community action, the system is much less adequate. It is hard to vote on the Vietnam war, social justice, pollution control, education, and conservation with one digit. It is clear also that one of the major sources of difficulty in our society arises because the only effective feedback on new private undertakings is economic.

In a very real sense a society is a coupled system so vast and intricate that no one can now or ever will be able to predict with confidence its response to a change. We will undoubtedly always be dependent upon experimental trial and error learning for dealing with our societal problems. But this does not mean that the situation is hopeless and we should despair. After all, this is just the normal learning process that sometimes works for us. Also, we have many tools to help us. We have learned how to analyze complex physical systems in order to understand their behavior. This is important in most physical design activities such as building large structures but it is essential in the design of dynamic systems that depend upon feedback control for stability, systems such as autopilots for aircraft, temperature and speed controls for turbines, etc. Without proper design such systems would be unstable and either hunt violently, that is, oscillate about the proper position, or just go as far in one direction or another as the situation permitted and stay there in an inoperative state. It now has become standard practice, as I am sure most of you know, to model or simulate complex physical systems on a computer as part of the design procedure before building them; in this way much developmental difficulty is avoided. I said much difficulty—not all—for frequently we discover modes of behavior in the real physical object after it is built that did not show up in the model because the model was imperfect.

Instabilities in coupled systems occur because of time delays in the transmission of feedback information so that corrective signals are in a sense misleading to the machine, corrective forces are applied after they are no longer needed and with a timing that exaggerates the error. We can see most of the pathological conditions of a poorly designed feedback system in human societies: insensitive feedback mechanisms, large time delays so the corrective actions are often the wrong one, etc. One particularly important fact that we have learned about physical networks is that there are certain modes in which they cannot be driven, certain forms of operation they cannot be made to assume. Similar effects can be found in social systems and frequently leaders are guilty of trying to induce or force modes of behavior which the system cannot accept. When we couple two complex systems, the modes of behavior become even more complex. For many, many years, 20 or so, the United States and the Soviet Union have been engaged in disarmament negotiations and one of the issues that arose at each new session was whether to negotiate about partial measures as we are doing now or whether to try for a staged, comprehensive disarmament plan. For years the two countries oscillated between these two approaches and stayed out of phase. It looked almost deliberate. The time constant for examining the issues and reaching a decision, in changing the posture of either country seemed to be between 12 and 18 months so that for many years we had the absurd spectacle of these great powers changing sides each time they got together. It was only when I began working as a presidential assistant trying to formulate negotiation positions that I appreciated that the long time delays were an inherent consequence of the internal decision-making process and that the instability I have described could only be overcome if one or preferably both of the countries engaged in efforts to predict the range of probable responses of the other and to approach negotiations with a broad range of possibilities. One of the strongest motives for the creation of the arms control and disarmament agency was to provide the basic understanding necessary for such flexibility. You can see a similar belated response in the current law and order emphasis as a response to black riots in the cities, which were being clearly abandoned as a principal mode of protest before the emphasis on police control really emerged.

Accepting my model of a society as a learning machine that, in spite of our best intellectual and planning efforts, is likely to continue to depend upon trial and error processes, we can proceed to specify some of the things we must do if we want to cope with the effects of change more satisfactorily.

1. We must develop better predictive capabilities. Long-range forecasting and resource allocation must become part of the ongoing business of the society.

2. We must create more sensitive feedback mechanisms for monitoring the evolving physical, social, economic, and psychological environments and they should function with appropriately short delays.

3. We should learn how to keep the early phases of social experiments small so as to avoid the human and fiscal costs, dislocations, etc., of major errors.

4. We should attempt many *different* experiments in parallel and learn how to intercompare them in order to maximize the real learning rate.

5. We must provide a more complete intellectual basis in the social, behavioral, analytical, and human sciences. Associated with this effort should be more individuals broadly trained in these fields to play a role in this social engineering effort.

6. We must develop some means of presenting the options to the general public in a comprehensible manner.

It is obvious that there are many more questions here than answers, and that there always will be, but I am certain that we are in a position to do much better than we are doing at present if we just use our existing knowledge to good advantage. Interdisciplinary groups within universities, in independent study centers, and within the government should be stimulated to do work on these planning and assessment problems with the same intensity devoted to the more traditional group development efforts. I believe that it is essential to have several independent groups involved in the prediction and feedback effort, too, if we are to avoid making gross errors and to provide a measure of protection against the misuse of behavioral science knowledge that concerns us all.

Research to Develop Adequate Tools for Social Engineering

The efforts I am proposing will have to be of a research nature, starting with the existing intellectual concepts and tools which the behavioral science knowledge already provides and adding to them. Fortunately we have a profound understanding of the economic aspects of society, a limited but increasing understanding of ecology (I will not presume to say here what we know about the individual human being), data banks providing factual information about many elements of the society, and an understanding of complex dynamic systems and how to model them which should prove of great value in studying aspects of social engineering problems. The first challenge is to use these resources effectively. At the beginning the learning aspects of the efforts and the insights they stimulate will be more valuable than the actual controls effected, but even raising questions will be a long step forward.

The Problems of Funding Research and Development

Returning now to the problem of obtaining adequate support for research and development activities, we can see that they are ideal subjects for the kind of rational study and decision making I have been talking about. The research establishment, of which we are a part, is in serious difficulty. In part, the problems stem from a general antiintellectualism in the nation but more importantly they arise from a failure on our part to understand, plan, and articulate goals for an ever expanding scientific enterprise.

We have many problems in our society—poverty, hunger, deterioration of the cities, pollution of the air and water, threats of war—and for each of these we see possibilities of technological assistance. However, if we pause and ask how well we are doing, how fast we are progressing toward solution of these most difficult problems, or even if we ask how effectively we are using our scientific and technological resources in the search for a solution to these problems, we are not very pleased with the answers.

Some important areas have never been properly managed or supported, particularly in those applied programs directed at finding solutions to our great social problems and in the basic research activities designed to support them. In this category I would include research in the behavioral and social sciences, already mentioned, as well as research related to the environment, and activities related to the urban setting.

The scientific establishment of the country is facing these severe, unsettling effects as a result of changing national interests, as well as the mounting government expenditures arising from the Vietnam war and the crisis in our cities. The difficulty has been made even more acute by a growing unwillingness on the part of some members of Congress to support university-based research through the Department of Defense. This exists because some legislators, resenting the antiwar attitudes prevalent on many campuses, have used cuts in research budgets as a way of expressing their dissatisfaction with campus activities; and, ironically, others have tried to reduce Defense Department academic research because they fear that DOD money is corrupting the universities.

Unfortunately, the impact of the antiscience sentiment in Congress is not restricted to programs sponsored by the Department of Defense. The National

Science Foundation, the National Institutes of Health, the Atomic Energy Commission, and the space agency, as well as many other agencies that sponsor R & D activities, have had their research support cut more severely than other parts of their budgets. The nation is planning to spend an additional 20 billion dollars on highway programs while 300 million dollars is being squeezed out for research support.

Much of this difficulty arises, I believe, because we do not have a sound strategy for science. Most of the R & D support of the past 20 years has been based on cold war incentives, that is, military requirements and the space race. Less than 2 billion dollars of the approximately 15 billion spent on research and development by the federal government in 1968 was undertaken to support other goals, and more than half of this remainder was for health-related activities.

This pattern of support has resulted, however, in a seriously lopsided research program. For example, the fields of chemistry and the social sciences have been regularly underfunded. The National Science Foundation, the agency that should have corrected these imbalances, has never been supported adequately. Those few federal programs that have been created to help, understand, and cope with the great social and technological problems of our times are not very well conceived or very well managed. The pollution control program, for example, is too gadget oriented, too short range, and lacks an adequate exploratory research base on which to build a sounder effort. The programs oriented to the many tough problems of the cities are similarly deficient. This difficulty arises, I suspect, because the agencies responsible for the related action programs are under great pressure to get quick results. What is more, they too are underfunded and, additionally, have no tradition of research support to guide their efforts.

Attempts to get agencies like HUD and HEW and the other missionary agencies to support the program have failed and they have failed more because of a lack of understanding of what research really is than from congressional antagonisms. I believe that until there is an agency such as the National Institutes of Health or the National Science Foundation whose primary mission is to focus on these social problems we will not develop an adequate quality of work in these fields.

Regardless of the current mood and attitudes, progress toward a decent society in the future will continue to depend upon a strong scientific program and its related educational activities, and so we must seek ways to remedy the present situation.

New Federal Science Arrangements

Given the present antagonisms and the considerable skepticism about the value of continued high-level research and development activities, I have concluded that the only solution is to strengthen the federal mechanisms for planning and supporting research and development.

I do not know what form the strengthened agency should take. There are several proposals for a department of science. I have felt that the proper route was to increase the role of the National Science Foundation so as to include a broad range of applied science and engineering efforts related to the important social problems. There is a proposal I find particularly intriguing to create a series of applied science and basic research institutes linked together much as the institutes in NIH are coupled, each with a great deal of independence but subject to overall planning and management. These would in effect constitute the National Institutes of Science.

With this arrangement, it might be possible to avoid the main danger of a single department of science, the forcing of most or nearly all of the nation's research and development effort into one mold. Probably this recent proposal is the most sensible to follow when all the issues are weighed. Thus, perhaps the first social engineering job we should undertake should be a serious look into the current problems of the research and development establishment.

Comments on Wiesner's Paper

HERBERT C. KELMAN

The author received his PhD in psychology from Yale University in 1951. He is presently Richard Clarke Cabot Professor of Social Ethics at Harvard University, where his major research interest involves experimental work on social influence and comparative studies on political legitimacy and national identity.

Let me begin by saying that I fully agree with several of the basic assumptions that I believe Dr. Wiesner made in his remarks: (*a*) that there is a great need for systematic social planning in our society; (*b*) that there is a need for adequate knowledge as the groundwork for such planning, including not only what we might call "basic" knowledge about man and society but also knowledge about social engineering; and (*c*) that this knowledge creates problems relating to the control of behavior, including the danger that the knowledge may be misused. In this connection, I am particularly concerned about the problems that arise from the fact that this knowledge may give undue advantage to some segments of society over others, by virtue of their greater access to the means of producing and utilizing the knowledge.

Within this context of general agreement, I would like to pick out three specific statements that Wiesner made with which I think I disagree, if I understand them correctly. Whether or not we really disagree, there is at least a difference in emphasis between what he said and what I would be inclined to say on these points. I am not all that concerned with the specific points per se, but I think they may serve as a springboard for approaching the problem of the role of social science in a changing society and the problem of control and manipulation that is linked to it.

1. In explaining the greater support that our society gives to the physical sciences as compared to the social sciences, Wiesner cited as one reason the fact that the physical sciences deal with things that are easy to make understandable, such as space and military technology. I am not sure exactly what he meant here: These things are easy to make understandable to whom and in what respects? At least in some respects, I would have made just the opposite statement. I would propose that it is easier to gain support for space and military technology precisely because they are *not* understandable to wide segments of the population. The ABM controversy is a good case in point here. It would have been much easier for the proponents of the ABM to gain support for the system if they had continued to maintain their virtual monopoly on the facts. It was only because

understanding of military technology was more diffused that it was possible to mount an effective challenge to the ABM, as Wiesner knows better than anyone else. In other words, by broadening the base of understanding, it was possible to undercut the support given to this project. In a sense, then, it can be argued that increased understanding—at least in the case of military expenditures and perhaps in the case of space expenditures as well—would be more likely to reduce rather than to increase support for these activities. I am not proposing here that we should therefore try to make social science less understandable, but I think it is important to keep in mind that, at least to some extent, social science is at a disadvantage precisely because Members of Congress and others *do* understand it—or think they do. The relatively unquestioning support that has been given to military technology and space exploration derives, of course, from the unique situation in which the sacredness of science is intimately linked with the sacredness of the nation-state and in which it is, therefore, not permissible to raise questions. It would not only be difficult for social science to gain greater support by tying itself to these sacred objects, but it would also be self-defeating, since the questioning of unquestioned assumptions about such sacred objects is one of the central purposes of social science. It is this role, in part, which makes it more difficult to gain support for the social sciences.

2. Wiesner mentioned that he encountered much concern, particularly among Members of Congress, that the development of social science would increase the dangers of manipulation and control. It is probably true that many congressmen do have genuine concerns about these dangers and that such concerns are one of the sources of opposition to the development of social science. In fact, there are some congressmen I like who have this concern, which obviously makes it legitimate. Among many congressmen, however, I would suspect that this concern about control is highly selective in nature. Many of those who are most vehement about the control implications of social science are quite ready to impose all kinds of controls on the political behavior, the freedom of expression, and even the private lives of the population. Clearly, their concern does not stem from their strong commitment to a libertarian kind of society. They are not so much concerned about preventing control as they are about the question of who is going to have that control. They are concerned about the fact that social science may constitute a threat to their particular control, because it may represent an independent source of analysis and influence which is not manipulable by them. This reaction is reminiscent of the attitude toward social planning that we often encounter in our society. Many of those who are most upset about social planning are themselves very much engaged in planning. The real issue concerns the kinds of planning they favor and oppose. They are often very willing to support planning for private profit or military development. It is only planning for public welfare that they are not willing to undertake.

3. Wiesner stated that we are in trouble now mainly because of our inadequacies rather than because of evil intent. I agree wholeheartedly with the second part of this statement. I think we are often terribly misled in our analyses of societal problems because we ascribe them to the evil motivations of individuals. It is precisely for this reason, for example, that many of the attacks on the military-industrial complex are very unproductive (which is too bad, because I

would like to see some *productive* attacks on the military-industrial complex). These attacks take off from the simpleminded assumption that this complex is the product of a conspiracy of evil-minded people. They fail to take into account that the problem is rooted largely in the operation of systemic forces, rather than in the motivations of individuals. The problem is actually more serious than the conspiracy theory implies. It cannot be resolved by deposing the evil men who are responsible for it, but requires a restructuring of those forces that automatically lead to a concentration of inordinate power in the hands of small segments of the society and to their mutual exchange and reinforcement. I agree with Wiesner, then, when he argues that the problem is not one of evil intent. As I understand his statement, however, his alternative analysis is not based on the operation of systemic forces; rather, it remains at the psychological level. When he says that we are in trouble because of our inadequacies rather than because of evil intent, he is still speaking, I believe, in psychological terms—merely substituting the concept of capability for that of intention. I would propose that our problem is not entirely one of inadequate knowledge—though God knows our knowledge *is* inadequate. Vietnam may very well be a product of our stupidity; but, if so, it is a product of systematic stupidity rather than of our low IQ. According to this view, what is required is an analysis of the *kind* of knowledge that is used in the policy process and the way in which it is used—or, in other words, of the communication processes that are involved in political and social decision making. This, in turn, requires an analysis of the distribution and operation of power within the social system. The special interests and built-in assumptions that guide the functioning of our institutions define the policy goals that are to be pursued, the options that are to be considered, and the means that are to be employed. At a later point in his paper Wiesner discusses these systemic considerations in his incisive and rich analysis of feedback processes and their failure. The only point I would want to add is that these feedback problems are not strictly technical problems of communication; to a large extent they are problems rooted in the special interests and built-in assumptions by which the system is run.

Now, let me draw out some of the general implications of the three points I have raised for the role of social science in a changing society and for the problem of control. I take as my basic point of departure Wiesner's statement that knowledge is power. Thus, to the extent that we can make social science knowledge more valid and more useful, we can transform it into power. This means that those who produce and use social science knowledge have a potential advantage over those who supply the data. Black people and poor people have become aware of this possibility and resentful of the fact that they are being used as subjects. More and more often one hears the complaint that, by focusing research attention on them, social scientists are placing them in a position where they can be more readily controlled and manipulated in the interests of the established powers.

Though I think it is wrong to identify social scientists as a group as tools of the Establishment and the status quo, I do feel that there is some merit to these concerns. Once again, I do not think the major problem is one of the use of social science for the deliberate manipulation of oppressed groups to suit the purposes of those in power. The problem is far more subtle and elusive. Those who do the research and those who sponsor it are in a position to define what is problematic—to decide what questions are to be asked and to provide the framework within which answers will be organized. They thus determine the range of the answers that are going to be obtained and set limits to the kinds of uses to which the research products can be put. Since the opportunities to define the questions to which social science research will address itself and to use social science knowledge are unevenly distributed within the society, we have a situation in which some groups may well be placed at a relative disadvantage; social research is more likely to be addressed to the problems as seen by other groups and may thus be irrelevant and at times even detrimental to their own needs.

Insofar as social research is sponsored, conducted, and used by the established segments of the society, it is more likely to support the status quo than it is to support social change—not primarily because of any deliberate attempt to uphold the status quo but because, as I have already said, status quo assumptions will tend to be built into the frame of reference within which the research is carried out and the questions to which it addresses itself. There are many forces pointing in the opposite direction. Not only have many social scientists traditionally been interested in social change, but the very methodology of social science is geared to questioning unquestioned (i.e., status quo) assumptions and to bringing independent, new perspectives to bear on matters of social policy. Yet I do think that the politics of social research often work against its methodology, by shaping the framework of research in terms of the requirements of the status quo.

These are some of the issues on which I think we should focus as we address ourselves to the problems of control. We should concern ourselves not merely with the manipulative implications of social science knowledge in general, but with the implications of such knowledge for differential control of some segments of the population over others.

I do not have precise solutions to these problems, but the direction in which I would want to look for solutions is one that might be called, for lack of a better phrase, the "democratization of social science." What I have in mind is a situation in which all segments of the population are in a position to produce and use social science knowledge and, at the same time, one in which all segments of the population (not only the disadvantaged) provide the data for social science. This is in contrast to the situation we have now in which the advantaged groups are able to use social science knowledge to maintain and extend (deliberately or otherwise) their advantaged position, while the disadvantaged groups have little opportunity to develop countervailing power through knowledge produced within their own frame of reference.

CHARLES E. OSGOOD

The author received his PhD in experimental psychology from Yale University in 1945. He is presently a professor of psychology and communications, and is in the Center for Advanced Study at the University of Illinois. His major research and scholarly interests are in psycholinguistics, crosscultural research, and problems in international relations.

I am not going to try anything in the way of a rebuttal of Dr. Wiesner's paper, since I generally agree with its content. But I do want to follow up some of the sparks he sent up in me—and I may not be entirely dispassionate.

Wiesner referred to the fact that as scientists we have done little. Despite knowing long in advance about the population explosion, pollution, etc., we have done very little to control them. I presume that by "we" he means our society in a broad sense. I think that use of this term "we" actually covers one of the most critical problems of all. This is what Kelman, I believe, was really focusing on. The fact is that "we" is a very complex pattern of interactions of many *different* people, with different kinds of knowledge, different kinds of motives, and very different amounts of political and economic power. And, unfortunately, as I see these things, depth of time perspective seems to be inversely related to amount of political and economic power.

There is also the fact that it is the people with the least power and economic well-being and the most grievous problems who characteristically are those who display adaptation to a very high degree. Adaptation to the military environment, to the pollution level of the air and water, and even to the ultimate dehumanization to which ABM systems lead us—adaptation to living like ants in a buried steel-tube culture.

The problem for psychologists is critical. We are right at the focus of many major issues. One of the roles psychologists adopt is simply tending to one's own knitting, on the general assumption that the more one contributes to a firm knowledge of man the better off society will eventually be. Up until about 1958 I played this null role, grumbling but doing nothing; but while at the Center in Palo Alto I decided there was not enough time for that type of approach. Another role—and one that is being adopted with very gratifying increasing frequency—is the role in which one's own knitting as a psychologist happens to be directly relevant to social issues. Peace research, in all of its many ramifications, is becoming a respectable specialization in psychology.

The newest role for psychologists is that of the activist, with direct participation at all levels—including the APA "Establishment"—designed to produce social change. Most of us, I guess, end up pretty schizophrenic, playing one role now and yet another then, as situations require.

I do think that the basic issue is education—the most rapid and effective education possible. In the long run, the more educated a public is, the more it is aware of the discrepancy between what is and what could be. And since ultimately in our society power, economic and political, resides in the governed, informed and aroused people can do much to change their own condition.

One thing I think social scientists can do is to try first to gain for themselves as broad a perspective of their own times as possible, which means correlating evidence over a wide spectrum and then transmitting it as widely as possible. This is something the layman seldom does but which the philosopher in all of us tries to do.

When *I* try to do this, I do not generate a very pleasant picture of our times. I am not very optimistic. We seem to be experiencing what, for lack of a better phrase, I would call a renaissance of the Neanderthal mentality. This kind of thinking characterizes both radical right and radical left. Extremism creates counterextremism, characterized by black-and-white thinking (I guess we will have to find a new term for this!), projection of one's own motives and values onto others, etc.

Look at the victories of so-called "law and order" in New York City and Minneapolis, the "holy wars" in Ireland and the Middle East, the increasing numbers of military dictatorships all over the world. Contrast our nuclear and space technology and the incredible precision with which we can put men on the moon and bring them back with the nearly complete lack of progress in human relationships for thousands of years. (It is a bit sobering to realize that this species has only had writing for 5,000 years.)

The decision to go ahead with the Safeguard ABM system, which was carried by the votes of a couple of old men, was accompanied by President Nixon's recent statement that the dreams people have for support of new and needed social programs for the cities once the Vietnam war is ended are "only dreams." This money is already committed through the decade of the seventies, mostly for the military. Compare the approximately 20 billion dollars that Safeguard will cost with the rot in our cities, the complete blocking of real movement on integration issues, the pollution of our air and waters, the widespread starvation in this most affluent of all societies, the population explosion, etc.—and then look at the infinitesimal support of all programs that are concerned with issues of this kind. The other day you may have read that one of our space gadgets misfired; it cost some 14 million dollars. What could social scientists do with money like this?

If we *do* go for another decade without pouring massive amounts of skill, effort, and money into these social problems, we shall have to ask ourselves just what on earth it is that we are "safeguarding." Are we "safeguarding" pollution? "Safeguarding" the rot in the cores of our cities?

GEORGE A. MILLER

Dr. Wiesner was kind enough to refer to my earlier remarks to the effect that we do need a new public conception based on the scientific conception of man, and, in a broader context, that I said that I wanted to give this conception to everyone, if possible, and to make psychology available to everyone who has a use for it. What Osgood said about the importance of education tends to confirm my view that we do face the important problem of getting the public to accept whatever new insights we arrive at in the social sciences and making them available everywhere that they can be used.

Wiesner, as I heard him, said that the notion that social science should be "given away," and that we should not let it fall into the hands of an exploiting minority, was not an adequate answer. Perhaps he is right, but it must be part of an adequate answer, I think. I would like to hear in more detail his thoughts about what a more adequate answer would be and what more psychologists could contribute to it.

Wiesner said that the need for a new public conception of man led him to think in terms of developing a new profession of social engineering. I have also felt for many years that we needed more social engineers. But almost every time I have mentioned this need, somebody has replied, "We already have social engineers. Lawyers are our social engineers." So I thought I should ask Wiesner what reply I should give to such critics. Is social engineering a course that should be introduced into the new curriculum?

The idea that lawyers are social engineers is a historical holdover from earlier days. Our government was created as a legislative government, and legislative government rests on two basic assumptions: first, that ordinary men of reasonable prudence and wisdom can understand any political problem that needs to be understood; and, second, that ordinary men are capable of passing laws that will deal with any problem. As Kelman said, one of the situations science puts us in is that the ordinary man (if he remains ordinary) simply does not understand the kind of issues that science is posing for us. I do not mean just technological problems having to do with weapons development; but the whole problem of ecological balance is very hard to appreciate unless you have some special training and can see it as a systems problem. It becomes perfectly clear, when you consider it as a systems problem, that every social problem we face is either directly caused by, or severely aggravated by, the frightening growth of world population. This is the source of most of our social problems. As a psychologist, I do not see what we can contribute to the solution. Is this where the lawyers might be better social engineers than the social scientists?

Wiesner invited such questions as these when he said that prevention is easier than cure in social problems, because prevention requires only legislation. It seems to me that the right legislation for prevention is obviously what we need, but how are we going to get that legislation without somehow getting the scientific ideas into the legislators' heads? Perhaps when they are in our classrooms, rather than later, when they have been elected to office.

psychology and urban problems

Psychology and Urban Problems

A sense of urgency permeates this section. The urban picture is dismal and getting worse. Schools deteriorate, crime rates rise, health services lag. Each of the authors in this section gives us a closer look at these problems, their depth and enormity. Yet the contributors' mood is one not of despair but of urgency. Each offers potential solutions and hence hope. But solutions can meet these massive problems only if backed by massive resources, and it is not yet clear that this society is ready to make such a commitment. Thus, the following authors not only present their ideas but also urge us to make use of them before it is too late.

Naftalin in his address opening Cook's symposium "Innovative Approaches to Urban Problems" speaks to us from the experience of having struggled for eight years with the problems of Minneapolis. He surveys the host of problems besetting urban communities, placing these in a broad, societal perspective. After noting the societal forces which perpetuate these problems, he sets forth five elements he considers critical to their solution. The five elements involve: (*a*) restructuring the government; (*b*) improving leadership and manpower resources in the public sector; (*c*) increasing knowledge and improving communication; (*d*) increasing funds available to the public sector; and (*e*) changing attitudes such that the other four needs can be met.

Naftalin proposes these critical elements in terms of broad changes applicable throughout the public sector. The other members of Cook's symposium describe plans and efforts to bring about such changes with regard to specific governmental services. While Naftalin sees restructuring local government as key to the success of other efforts, each symposium member sees restructuring a specific urban governmental service as key to improving that service. In the plans of each we see ramifications involving the other elements Naftalin views as so critical to the solution of our urban problems. The programs outlined are innovative, and along with the sense of urgency one finds a sense of excitement in the belief that solutions are possible if only we muster the will to use our knowledge.

Possibilities for restructuring the urban educational system are explored by both Clark and Pettigrew. Clark sees a structure of competing school systems as injecting needed vitality into the public educational system, improving education for both Negro and white children. For Pettigrew a beneficial restructuring involves pulling separate neighborhood schools together into metropolitan educational parks. The consequences of such restructuring he sees as extending into all of Naftalin's other four areas of critical need. He focuses particularly on the area of attitude change, noting that the desegregated nature of these parks would provide the context for changes in racial and ethnic attitudes.

Levin, calling herself a "radical professional," suggests a restructuring of the power relationship between the dispensers and consumers of community services. She describes a specific program in the health services where the community gained significant control of these services. Again the ramifications reached out into Naftalin's critical areas—including the development of leadership where none previously existed, the improvement of communication between professionals and nonprofessionals, the enlistment of the community in the search for resources, and a change in the attitudes of the consumers and dispensers of the services.

Turning to the urban police, Bard sees many of their problems as emanating from an antiquated structure based on a notion that police are primarily involved in law enforcement and crime suppression. He points out that in actuality most of the policeman's time is spent in interpersonal services for which he has no training. Bard suggests a restructuring of duty assignments which would allow greater specialization and hence more specific training appropriate to the policeman's particular duties. He describes such a training program which he has been involved in with the New York police department, discussing data supporting the effectiveness of this new approach.

Kreps, in her invited address to the Division of Maturity and Old Age, focuses our attention on the poor, and discusses possibilities for restructuring the framework within which the government provides them with income. She outlines various welfare proposals including the negative income tax, discussing the reasoning behind each along with its advantages and disadvantages. As an economist, she poses for the psychological community the question of what happens to people for whom work is separated from income.

In closing this section, Milgram brings a very different perspective to the urban context. He proposes no action programs and prescribes no solutions. Yet his observations on the effects of urbanization are relevant to both. He suggests that the concentrated nature of the city overloads the psyche of the city dweller, an overload with numerous behavioral consequences. He discusses a variety of studies indicating the effects of this overload on human interactions. Then shifting to a different psychological aspect of cities, he discusses the various images associated with different cities and the factors which affect those images. As planners become increasingly aware of psychological health as an important variable in designing environments, they may find in Milgram's theoretical speculations a framework for action.

Innovative Approaches to Urban Problems

"Innovative Approaches to Urban Problems" is a topic with two points of emphasis. One, obviously, is urban problems. The other, perhaps not so obviously, is the possibility of innovative contributions by psychologists to solving the problems of society.

In the past, psychologists have had some success in helping society *modify* practices. We are going to take a look at the possibility that, in addition, we may help by developing and initiating new practices.

To locate discussants for this two-faceted topic we looked in two directions—in one direction for a person who knew urban problems at firsthand; in the other, for psychologists making innovative approaches to these problems.

The first search led us to Arthur Naftalin who has recently retired, undefeated, from eight years of service as Mayor of the city of Minneapolis. Mayor Naftalin has served as vice-chairman of the organization of mayors of cities in the United States. Had he run for reelection, he would have been its next chairman. He is returning to the faculty of political science at the University of Minnesota from which he took leave to run for mayor eight years ago.

The search for innovative contributors led us to Hannah Levin of Albert Einstein Medical College; Kenneth B. Clark of the Metropolitan Applied Research Center who is represented in the symposium by Lawrence Plotkin of the City College of New York; Morton Bard, also of the City College of New York; and Thomas Pettigrew of Harvard University. I should note in passing that this latter search was encouraging. We found many more innovative activities than I had reason to expect.

STUART W. COOK
Symposium Chairman

The chairman received his PhD in psychology from the University of Minnesota in 1938. He is presently a professor of psychology at the University of Colorado, where his major research interest is in attitude change and attitude theory. He specializes in the study of race relations with a focus on the attitudinal outcomes of desegregation.

The Urban Problem and Action Research

ARTHUR NAFTALIN

The author received his PhD in political science in 1948 from the University of Minnesota, where he is presently a professor of public affairs. He previously served as Mayor of Minneapolis for eight years, retiring in 1969.

If I understand my assignment correctly, I am expected to open this symposium with a statement that will be essentially descriptive rather than prescriptive. I am invited to describe and analyze urban problems from the perspective of eight years as mayor of a major city and to identify points at which knowledge from psychologists and other social scientists might be helpful in dealing with them. The prescriptive part of the discussion, happily for me, will be provided by the other discussants as they review their efforts to develop innovative new approaches to these critical concerns.

Our assignment is a large one and it is not made easier by the fact that the urban crisis has been so widely reported by the media and so extensively analyzed and debated by researchers, politicians, and pundits. Every hour on the hour we hear the plight of our cities discussed. Each day there are fresh statistical series to terrify us anew. On all sides we are exhorted to take action that will quiet the revolutionary winds and rescue us from impending oblivion.

By now everyone is an expert on the urban crisis. The subject is so broad and wide and deep, affecting us in so many different ways, it has come to be all things to all men. It involves concerns that are at once governmental, economic, social, psychological, technological, moral, and philosophical, and it covers all aspects of community life and individual behavior: human relations, law enforcement, housing, sanitation, health services, education, income distribution—name it and you name a part of the urban crisis.

Therefore, I must make clear at the start that I view the urban crisis in a very broad context that reaches far beyond the problems of the ghetto. It involves the full sweep of our physical environment: growing congestion and pollution, the waste of our natural resources, especially our land, the critical lack of adequate housing, the failure to preserve open space, the growing problems of water supply, drainage, and waste disposal, and the baffling explosion of technology that has introduced speed and movement and change at a pace that confuses and bewilders almost everyone.

On the social side the crisis is not only a matter of poverty, although this is certainly its single most critical element. It involves a changing value structure that is fundamentally altering the nature of family life and the overall pattern of human relationships. It also involves an alarming increase in the use of alcohol and drugs, and mounting tensions that derive from growing insecurity and our inability to control or discharge hostility. It involves a general weakening of our major institutions of social control, especially the family and education.

Suddenly everything seems to have gone wrong. Police departments can no longer maintain law and order; our welfare system seemingly contributes to rather than checks social disorganization; the number of those suffering deprivation—even to the point of starvation—increases despite our unprecedented affluence; millions of our citizens remain victims of discrimination but we seem unable to reverse this historic pattern; we luxuriate in material goods to the point of surfeit and yet fail to support our educational system.

Why should we be in such difficulty? What happened to plunge this great nation into such deep trouble? Why do our efforts to cope with the urban crisis seem so faltering and ineffectual?

There are no simple answers. Our problems emerge out of deep-seated forces that assault all of our institutions and will not be contained until we have instituted reforms that are related to the new reality created by these forces.

Growing Impact of Modern Technology

The first of these forces is modern technology. It has relentlessly enlarged the scope and scale of economic organization and it has imposed an increasing need for human specialization and community interdependence. Yet, for all that has been written about the effect of technology on society, we are still not able, as a nation, to perceive how it has made our central institutions, especially government and education, increasingly irrelevant and unresponsive.

Our exploding technology produces increasingly a society in which man's worth turns on the special talents he brings to the marketplace. As specialization intensifies and as machines supplant human labor, man develops capabilities that can find an outlet only in the urban center. This is what is behind the movement from farms to cities all over the world and this is why training and education have become so indispensable for both individual and community survival.

This is only one dimension, however, of the change wrought by modern technology. It has also extended the span of life; suddenly we have millions of senior citizens living at or near the poverty level. The drugs that have added years of life have also created new problems by altering the range and quality of human experience and consciousness, introducing new and deeply unsettling patterns of behavior and threatening established moral codes.

In another direction our technology urges us on to an ever more feverish exploitation of our environment. New inventions, such as insecticides and nuclear energy, invade industry and agriculture with a momentum that seems irresistible, and before we can assess what is happening, we have major problems of air and water pollution and land contamination, to the point that some scientists fear we may be destroying the world's ecological balance.

Meantime, in our hunger to enjoy the new opportunities opened by technology and science, we recklessly squander our land and we permit our settlements to sprawl in all directions, creating still new problems for the urban centers.

The picture is, of course, familiar to you. I dwell on it because in my work as mayor I was continuously appalled by our inability to sustain an awareness of the devastation and imbalances that are coming to dominate our social and physical environment. The uses of technology and science cry out for some form of enlightened control that will preserve our natural and human resources, but the cry remains essentially unheeded.

Rigidity and Inadequacy of Government

This brings me to the second underlying force that, in my view, accounts for our inability to cope with our present ills—the rigidity, inadequacy, and unresponsiveness of our governmental structure. It is extremely important, I believe, that we come promptly to appreciate that, for all of the debate and dialogue and for all of the "viewing with alarm" by our mass media, as a nation we are retreating from our problems rather than mounting an attack upon them. The President and Congress acknowledge the need for new approaches and enlarged efforts but all that is proposed are programs that will do no more than nibble at the margins of the problems, and they are offered not to meet the urgent and immediate present but for the future when other needs—the Vietnam war, a larger defense establishment, a continuing space effort, and tax reduction for the affluent middle and upper classes—have been provided for. There is today an absence in our national leadership of a sense of urgency and an awareness of the need for redirecting the use of our enormous national resources and establishing national priorities that are aimed at preserving our strength as a nation.

If the national picture is discouraging, it is even more bleak at the state level. For many years now we have been bombarded by the call for a greater involvement of state governments in meeting our problems, the notion being that we can begin to reduce the size of the national bureaucracy by shifting responsibility to the states. This call is now being heeded under the name of the New Federalism, and it is, in my view, a snare. The plain and simple and unchallengeable fact is that our state governments are in default with regard to their responsibilities to the urban centers, and there is no evidence to suggest that this historic pattern of indifference will be reversed.

To round out the dismal picture, while the national government retreats and the state governments remain in default, the local governments are in a state of paralysis. Municipalities, counties, and school districts suffer in a tangled web of overlapping jurisdictions, competing fiercely for the tax dollar that comes for the most part from overburdened property in the form of the most regressive tax we know. Authority is fragmented among a maze of governmental units; leadership is in flight to the suburbs; the municipalities are unable to reach the resources of the area; the inner-city dweller and the suburbanite find their interests increasingly polarized; and, in the end, all of the critical problems appear no longer susceptible to local management or control.

I mean no partisan criticism in these observations concerning the unresponsive character of our government. Our failure is as much the responsibility of Democrats as of Republicans and it reflects a lack of popular support for measures that would shape a course of national action designed to take into realistic account the nature of modern technology, both its opportunities and its devastations.

Historical Basis of Governmental Unresponsiveness

It is this lack of popular support for institutional change that brings me to the third force that underlies our present predicament. This is the hold on our public consciousness of historic premises and biases that were tolerable—perhaps even to a degree valuable—in a nation with a primitive economic and social order in which men lived largely in isolation from each other. These biases derived largely from our emphasis on individualism, which conditioned us to accept competition as a way of life and to cherish the jungle's code of the survival of the fit as our creed. Thus, we rejected government as a positive and sanguine force; the very term "planning" has been anathema until quite recently. Throughout our history we have demanded that the community take no action that would impede the individual from exploiting his surroundings. We saw government action as destructive, regarding any action aimed at controlling individual excesses as containing the seeds of tyranny. As a result, from the start our institutions of government were never designed to regulate or to control or to govern. They were designed to blend and moderate clashing interests and not to exceed the minimal purpose of maintaining domestic tranquility and preventing external invasion.

Meantime, a related bias took hold. This was the nation's distrust of the urban center. From the beginning the American people have viewed the city as the source of all that is unwholesome in American life—sin, corruption, squalor, and lack of conformity. The countryside was perceived as pristine and wholesome, gentle and creative, where man lived at peace with a nature that carried Providence's special blessing. Thus, through the years we have been antigovernment and anticity. We gave over control of the government to rural forces and even today, in the aftermath of the Supreme Court's one-man, one-vote edict, control of Congress and of state legislatures eludes the city; we are governed by an alliance of rural and suburban legislators who cannot understand why our cherished institutions and our historic values should be under such fierce attack and who are united in their fear of the inner city and in their unwillingness to provide the massive resources needed to attend to urban problems.

Add to these biases our deep-seated yearnings to preserve our separate ethnic, religious, racial, and social groupings, our historic refusal to shape a society with a single standard of treatment and opportunity. Despite our lofty pretensions, we have been from the start a racist nation (Can slavery have any other explanation?) and our many diverse groups have been in a state of continuous warfare. Discrimination, deprivation, and division have been constant conditions in the American scene, constituting a major factor in the atmosphere of violence that has been characteristic of the nation.

These, then, are among the forces that have shaped the urban problem and that define the context within which the efforts of social scientists must, I believe, necessarily proceed if action-oriented research and experimentation are to have operational significance.

Critical Needs of Society

Within this context I identify a series of critical needs, each of which demands a vast enlargement of valid social theory and scientific knowledge.

The first of these is *the basic restructuring of government, especially at the local level*. Our formal public efforts to meet the urban crisis (antipoverty, urban renewal, public housing, aid to education, pollution control, planning assistance, civil rights legislation, and perhaps 150 or more federal grant programs) have been haphazard, underfinanced, duplicating, and fragmented. The city has remained essentially powerless in the face of mounting problems, lacking authority to develop cohesive and realistic programs and unable to reach the needed resources.

A restructuring of government is essential if new innovative efforts are to have a reasonable chance to survive and succeed. Urban problems are areawide problems, and a society that is so largely the product of social and economic organization based on an increasingly more sophisticated technology cannot deal with its problems except as it fashions a governmental organization that responds to the complexity of the larger society and can effectively innovate programs that are consonant with the prevailing scale of community activity.

The restructuring of government may appear to be the particular concern of specialists in government and administration and of only secondary interest to psychologists and other social scientists. This view, I believe, is too limited, because the lack of effective structure is pervasively impeding all innovative effort whether it be the fashioning of a decentralized storefront health center or little city hall, a training program for police officers, a remedial educational effort for delinquent or disadvantaged children, creation of an educational park, establishment of an areawide transportation system, or industrial development that creates job opportunities for the presently dispossessed. All require the resources of an area much larger than the inner city and none can succeed except as they are made part of a more cohesive and more comprehensive approach to a network of interrelated services and needs.

Government is the primary mechanism for the control of negative influences and the marshaling and unleashing of positive forces. If it is to fill its proper role in dealing with our urban problems, it must come to have a reasonable relationship to the nature of our industrial society. We must come to see that the economy of our nation is national, that it is only the national government that can direct the flow of income in a fashion that will alleviate the most troublesome of our inequities and disparities, and that it is only the national government that can reach the national wealth. It means, also, that we must come to see that our interrelated social and economic problems will be susceptible to control only through national programs based on national objectives enjoying national financing.

Once we have begun to develop viable local governments and once we have begun to establish realistic national programs based on meaningful commitments, we will be ready for further institutional rearrangements, such as devolving administrative responsibility on a regional basis, a more sensible involvement of state governments, and a vast enlargement of direct citizen participation.

The second critical need that should have the greatly enlarged attention of researchers is *a vast qualitative improvement in the leadership and manpower that serves the public sector*. One reason for the enormous success of the private sector of our economy has been the constant infusion of individuals of leadership capacity and imaginative force. The urban crisis today demands that we attract and retain a greatly enlarged number of such leaders for the public sector and that we devise the educational and training devices that will prepare them for innovative roles in government. This is an extraordinarily difficult objective because it involves not only adequate monetary reward and assurances of stable career opportunities but also the development of a general climate that regards public effort as meaningful and productive.

Effective structure and quality leadership are still not sufficient ingredients; they must be joined by a third critical factor, namely, *a vast increase in knowledge and a profound improvement in our systems of communicating information.*

Again and again we are told that a project has failed for lack of communication. Again and again we see that when information has been effectively organized even the most benighted among us respond constructively. The urban crisis is a crisis in knowledge and wisdom. One need not be of cynical temperament to entertain doubts concerning our capacity to survive, because the scope and complexity of our problems often make them seem beyond control and our efforts discouragingly ineffectual. Yet, man's successes in mastering his environment remain formidable and impressive. The moonshot is reassuring; it demonstrated what can be done when the commitment to achieve large and complex objectives is firmly made and the support unstintingly provided.

We need the same generous and spirited massing of information systems on our even more complicated and deeply threatening urban problems, and this massing requires new theoretical breakthroughs in our understanding of human behavior and in the interaction of technology and society—breakthroughs that can come only with the hard application of all of our intellectual resources.

Specifically, we must have new and more readily useful knowledge concerning the nature of social movements, concerning how to control and channel the discharge of hostility, how to influence belief structures so that prevailing attitudes are more consistent with the needs of the objective world and at the same time not do violence to the integrity and dignity of the individual, how to make education more vital and more relevant, how to release through planning those aesthetic elements that will improve the quality of life, and how to enhance the involvement and sense of personal worth for everyone in an increasingly impersonal society.

For all this we must have money, and this is the fourth critical need—*a massive increase in the resources available to the public sector.* If modern technology has taught us anything, it must be that we are irreversibly, irretrievably interdependent, that more and more we will do together what we once did as individuals, that the economic victims of the system are the community's responsibility, that the survival of our values demands an enormous program of catching up so that the dispossessed will be incorporated into the system before they destroy it, that education is the indispensable condition for establishing human worth, and that no cost is too great to prevent us from making certain that every individual has that opportunity.

This brings me to the fifth and the last need—*the unlearning of old destructive attitudes and the inculcation of new outlooks that are consonant with the urban condition,* because we shall meet none of the critical needs I have mentioned as long as there is no basic change in our prevailing national attitudes.

As a people we cling to old myths that blind us to reality. Even though, with only 8% of the world's population, we have 40% of the world's wealth, we stubbornly regard ourselves as impoverished. We spend only 27% of our gross national income for public services and public goods, while other nations spend vastly more; Sweden, for example, spends 43%. We are, in fact, a nation of unprecedented wealth; we can afford anything we are bold enough to want.

We cling to the notion that our urban ills can be cured by private action and that only those with a capacity to survive on their own initiative are entitled to public respect or community support for endeavors, such as education, that will help them to advance.

We remain bedeviled by emotions and fears of ethnic and racial differences; thus we drift ever more ominously towards the divided society reported by the Kerner Commission.

These are not optimistic judgments and my description of urban needs is distressingly hortatory. Yet, they are my honest views and they describe a framework for action that for me is a meaningful one, because I see little promise of success if we fail in this critical period to begin a fundamental transformation of our society.

I do not know whether science can save us from ourselves and I do not know what we can properly demand and expect from those who are engaged in the pursuit of new approaches to our problems. I can only say, as one who has viewed them from the firing line, where unreason and violence seem to be on the rise, that I see man's hope for conquering his future ever more dependent upon his capacity and willingness to face reality with all of his accumulated knowledge and to make adjustments that his reason shows him to be essential for survival.

Alternatives to Urban Public Schools[1]

KENNETH B. CLARK

The author received his PhD from Columbia University in 1940. He is presently a professor of psychology at the City College of the City University of New York, and President-Elect of the American Psychological Association.

Alternatives to the present public school system must be found because it is now clear that American public education is organized along social and economic class lines. The clearest manifestation of this fact is a biracial public school system in which approximately 90% of American children are required to attend segregated schools.

The less privileged schools consistently reflect a lowered level of educational efficiency. Schools attended by poor and Negro children have less adequate educational facilities than those attended by more privileged children. Teachers tend to resist assignments in these schools and generally function less adequately. Their morale is lower, they are not adequately supervised, and they tend to see their students as less capable of learning.

The pervasive educational inefficiency which characterizes these schools results in (a) marked and cumulative academic retardation; (b) a high proportion of high school dropouts who are unequipped academically and occupationally for a constructive role in society; and (c) a pattern of rejection, despair, and hopelessness resulting in massive human wastage.

American public schools have become significant instruments in the blocking of economic mobility and in the intensification of class distinctions rather than in fulfilling their historic function of facilitating mobility. Whether the United States government can afford, in the national interest, such waste of human resources is a serious question. Educational inefficiency contributes significantly to the cycle of pathology that weakens the fabric of the entire society.

Obstacles to the Attainment of Efficient Education

There are many obstacles to change. One is the dogma and the historical premises which exist about education. Here should be included the inviolability of the neighborhood school concept and the belief that schools should be economically and racially homogeneous.

---

[1] In Kenneth B. Clark's absence, his paper was presented by Lawrence Plotkin of the City College of New York.

There are also administrative barriers to change which favor the status quo. These can be seen in the problems incurred in the transportation of children from residential neighborhoods to other areas of the city.

Most important, however, in blocking educational efficiency are certain psychological assumptions and prejudices that probably underlie the apparent inability of society to resolve the historical and administrative problems. These residual psychological prejudices take many forms.

Initially, the academic retardation of Negro children was explained in terms of their inherent racial inferiority. More recently, the theory of biological inferiority has given way to more subtle explanations and support for continued inefficient education. Examples of this include theories of "cultural deprivation" and related beliefs that the culturally determined educational inferiority of Negro children will impair the ability of white children to learn if they are taught in the same classes. The theory of environmental deficits tends to support the pervasive rejection of Negro children and obscures the basic problem while intensifying it.

There are also more flagrant sources of opposition to any effective desegregation of American public schools. White citizens groups in the South, parent and taxpayer groups in the North, and the control of boards of education by whites who identify overtly or covertly with opposition to change are examples of effective resistance. School officials and professional educators have defaulted in their educational responsibilities to provide effective leadership. They have tended, for the most part, to go along with the level of community readiness and the "political realities." They have been accessories to the use of various subterfuges and devices to give the appearance of change without its substance and have failed to present the problem of necessary school reorganization in educational terms. This seems equally true of teachers and teachers' organizations.

Finally, we have seen in the past two years another formidable and insidious barrier in the way of movement towards effective, desegregated public schools—the black power movement and its demands for racial separatism. The black power demands are clearly a rejection of the goals of nonsegregated education and a return to the pursuit of the myth of an efficient "separate but equal" or the pathetic wish for a separate and superior racially organized system of education. There is no reason to believe, and certainly no evidence to support, the contention that all-Negro schools, controlled by Negroes, will be any more efficient in preparing American children to contribute constructively to the realities of the present and future world.

Attempts at Remedies

Despite the obstacles to desegregation and the attainment of effective non-racially constrained education for all American children, there have been persistent attempts to compensate for the deficits of racial isolation in the American public schools.

A tremendous amount of energy and money has been expended in the attempt to develop special programs to improve the academic achievement of Negro children. The report of the United States Commission on Civil Rights *Racial Isolation in the Public Schools* (1967) has presented facts which raise questions concerning the long-range effectiveness of these programs. Although there is some evidence that special programs do some good and help some children, they clearly underline the inadequacy of the regular education these children receive.

If one accepts the premise of the Brown decision, which is supported by much evidence, that racially segregated schools are inherently inferior, it should follow that all attempts to improve the quality of education in all-Negro schools would have necessarily limited effects.

Given the resistance to a racially heterogeneous school system, however, it may be necessary to increase the efficiency of education in all-Negro schools as a necessary battle in the larger struggle for racially desegregated schools. In spite of the basic premise of the Brown decision that racially segregated schools are inherently inferior, the extent to which it is possible to provide excellent education in a predominantly Negro school should be thoroughly reexamined.

The answers to two questions we must now dare to ask provide the basis for a new strategy in the assault against the inhumanity of the American system of racial segregation:

1. Is the present pattern of massive educational inferiority and inefficiency found in predominantly Negro schools inherent and inevitable?

2. Is there anything which can be done within the Negro schools to raise them to a tolerable level of educational efficiency or to a level of educational excellence?

If the answer to the first question is *yes* and to the second question, *no,* then the strategy of continued and intensified assault on the system of segregated schools is justified and should continue unabated since there is no hope of raising the quality of education for Negro children as long as they are condemned to segregated schools.

If, on the other hand, the answers are reversed, it would suggest that a shift in strategy and tactics would be indicated without surrendering the ultimate goal of eliminating racial segregation from American life. The suggested shift in emphasis from desegregation to quality of education is not a retreat into the blind alley of accepting racial separation as advocated by Negro nationalist groups nor is it acceptance of defeat in the battle for desegregation. It is rather a regrouping of forces, a shift in battle plans, and an attempt to determine the opposition's most vulnerable flank.

The shift demands a massive, system-wide educational enrichment program designed to obtain educational excellence in the schools attended by Negro children. This would mean that the bulk of the available organizational, human, and financial resources and specialized skills would be mobilized and directed toward obtaining the highest quality of education for Negro students without regard to the racial composition of the schools they attend.

The goals of high-quality education for Negro and lower class children and the goal of public school desegregation are inextricable—the attainment of one will lead to the attainment of the other. The Phase 1 struggle for excellent education for Negro children is not inconsistent with the Phase 2 struggle for nonsegregated education for all children. It is not likely that there would be effective desegregation without a marked increase in the academic achievement and the personal and social effectiveness of Negro and white children.

Problems of Educational Monopoly

It is possible that all attempts to improve the quality of education in contemporary racially segregated public schools will have minimal positive effects. The rigidity of present patterns of public school organization and the concomitant stagnation in quality of education and academic performance may not be amenable to any attempts at change working through and within the present system.

It is not enough that those responsible for our public schools assert passively that the schools merely reflect the pathologies and injustices of our society. Public schools and their administrators must assert boldly that education must dare to challenge and change society toward social justice as the basis for democratic stability.

There is also the disturbing question of whether the selective process involved in training and promoting educators and administrators emphasizes qualities of passivity, conformity, caution, smoothness, and superficial affability rather than boldness, creativity, substance, and the ability to demand and obtain those things essential for effective public education for all children. If this is true, all hopes for reform are reduced to a minimum if we are dependent upon the present educational establishment.

The hope for a realistic approach to saving public education in American cities seems to this observer to rest on finding the formula for demonstrating to the public at large that the present level of public school inefficiency has reached an intolerable stage of public calamity. It must be demonstrated that minority group children are not the only victims of the monopolistic inefficiency of our public schools.

It must be demonstrated that white children—whose privileged parents understandably seek to protect them by moving to suburbs and private and parochial schools—also suffer potentially and immediately.

It must be demonstrated that business and industry suffer double and triple taxation in seeking to maintain a stable economy in the face of public school inefficiency which produces human casualties rather than constructive human beings.

It must be demonstrated that the cost in correctional, welfare, and health services is intolerably high in seeking to cope with the consequences of educational inefficiency. It would be more economical to pay the price and meet the demands of efficient public education.

It must be demonstrated that a nation which presents itself to the world as the guardian of democracy and the protector of human values cannot itself make a mockery of these significant ethical principles by dooming one-tenth of its own population to a lifetime of inhumane futility because of remediable educational deficiencies in its public schools.

It does not seem likely that the necessary changes will come about because they should. To help one understand the ability of the educational establishment to resist change is the fact that the public school systems are protected public monopolies with only minimal competition from private and parochial schools. A monopoly need not genuinely concern itself with these problems. As long as local school systems can be assured of state aid and increasing federal aid without the accountability which inevitably comes with aggressive competition, it would be sentimental, wishful thinking to expect any significant increase in the efficiency of our public schools. If there are no alternatives to the present system, then the possibilities of improvement in public education are limited.

Alternative Forms of Public Education

Alternatives—realistic, aggressive, and viable competitors—to the present public school systems must be found. In thinking of alternatives all attempts must be made at the same time to strengthen our present urban schools. Such attempts should involve revision and strengthening of curricula, methods, personnel selection, and evaluation; the development of more vigorous procedures of supervision; reward of superior performance and the institution of a realistic and tough system of accountability; and the provision of meaningful ways of involving the parents and the community in the activities of the school.

The following are suggested as possible realistic and practical competitors to the present form of urban public school systems:

1. *Regional state schools.* These schools would be financed by the states and would cut across present urban-suburban boundaries.

2. *Federal regional schools.* These schools would be financed by the federal government out of present state-aid funds or with additional federal funds. These schools would be able to cut through state boundaries and could make provisions for residential students.

3. *College- and university-related open schools.* These schools would be financed by colleges and universities as part of their laboratories in education. They would be open to the public and not restricted to children of faculty and students. Obviously, public students would be selected in terms of constitutional criteria and their percentage determined by realistic considerations.

4. *Industrial demonstration schools.* These schools would be financed by industrial, business, and commercial firms for their employees and selected numbers of the public. These would not be vocational schools, but elementary and comprehensive high schools of quality. They would be sponsored by combinations of business and industrial firms in much the same way as churches sponsor and support parochial or sectarian schools.

5. *Labor union-sponsored schools.* These schools would be financed and sponsored by labor unions largely, but not exclusively, for the children of their members.

6. *Army schools.* The Defense Department has been quietly effective in educating some of the casualties of our present public schools. Schools for adolescent dropouts or educational rejects could be set up by the Defense Department adjacent to camps—but not necessarily an integral part of the military.

With a strong, efficient, and demonstrably excellent parallel system to public schools, organized and operated on a quasi-private level, with faculty control and professional accountability maintained by federal and state educational standards, it would be possible to bring back into public education the viability and dynamism that are now clearly missing.

American industrial and material wealth was made possible through industrial competition. American educational health may be made possible through educational competition.

If we succeed in developing better alternatives, we will not only save countless Negro children from lives of despair and hopelessness, and thousands and thousands of white children from cynicism, moral emptiness, and social ineptness: We will demonstrate the validity of our democratic promises; we will save our civilization through saving our cities.

Reference

United States Commission on Civil Rights. *Racial isolation in the public schools.* Washington, D. C.: United States Government Printing Office, 1967.

Psychologist to the Powerless

HANNAH LEVIN

The author received her PhD in social psychology from Rutgers University in 1964. She is presently an assistant professor of psychiatry at the Albert Einstein College of Medicine and Coordinator of Training for the Postdoctoral Program in Community Mental Health. Her major interests involve community development in urban ghetto areas.

Personality development is seen as the consequence of the decision-making process. One becomes actualized, becomes fully human, through making decisions and taking actions in important areas of one's life. Only by having control over planning, acting, and assuming responsibility for his actions does the child become the man.

Psychologists are concerned with human development. We know about the importance of physical health. We emphasize emotional integration and autonomy. Much has been written about cognitive stimulation and its function in developing conceptual skills. And recently, the effects of powerlessness have concerned us.

The psychological consequences of powerlessness for human development include alienation, anomie, deviance, hopelessness, less complex personality structure, and a lower level of cognitive functioning.

With the recognition of the damage that the sense of powerlessness induces in the individual it is surprising that psychologists have not paid more attention to the other side—to the concept of power. The concept of power, particularly political power, has a bad connotation for us. I maintain that without a certain amount of political and social power the phrase "having control over important decisions in one's life" is merely a loud shout in a vacuum. Nothing moves, not even hot air.

Therefore, our concern with human development dictates that we carefully examine the interface of individual autonomy and social and political power. The slogans "black power," "student power," and "power to the neighborhoods," that were popularized by Norman Mailer and Jimmy Breslin in the recent New York City mayoral primaries, spring from the public's frustration of its need for power. Their appeal is to all of us who feel alienated and isolated from society and who wish to try again to establish our stake in the future by becoming part of the political change process of the present.

Is "power to the people" a realistic slogan? Community corporations with elected indigenous leaders are one of the few existing institutional settings where the mechanisms of "power to the people" can be examined.

For the last two years, I have had the opportunity to work as an advocate and consultant to a community corporation in a low-income ghetto area in the Bronx. Our collective goal was to facilitate the growth of power in the community.

One outcome of the work of my staff and myself was the financing of the first community-controlled health delivery system in the country. Other direct outcomes were the National Institute of Mental Health's agreement to fund directly a community-controlled mental health unit (a first also) and the development of a community board with policy-making *power* for a five-million-dollar state children's mental hospital in the Bronx.

The indirect outcomes of our work are more difficult to pinpoint, but their significance may be greater. They include the development of a new community leadership, politicalization of residents, increased power for the Multi-Service Center and its community, and the spread to other community corporations of the demands which have already been realized at the Multi-Service Center where we work. This paper is based on these experiences.

The Radical Professional

Many professionals have worked in poverty areas before and if there is something innovative about our work it has to do not with where we work but rather our conceptualizations, our goals—our ideology.

Professionals traditionally have worked with individuals or groups to help them fit or adjust to society. As examples, we have manpower training programs, antidelinquency programs, and recreational activities to keep things cool.

Today, a new tradition for professionals is being molded. We call ourselves radical professionals; that is, we use our skills to help make social change. Thus as advocates for the powerless we assist these groups in gaining a redistribution of power rather than just a redistribution of services. We have given up our so-called professional neutrality for a partisan role. We believe that there is a conflict of interests between the groups we represent and other groups, and the recognition of this conflict is necessary in guiding our work. Our role has become that of aiding the poor in challenging society's standards rather than meeting them, and our relationship to the poor community and its organizations has been as employees rather than employers.

Since to us community development means a basic redistribution of power rather than a mere redistribution of services, our efforts are focused on initiating and supporting the move for community control of all public institutions and services. Power and conflict are the key concepts with which my staff and I work.

Community Power and New Processes

Now I would like to illustrate in a more concrete fashion the implications this ideology has for our work.

We were first called into the Hunts Point Multi-Service Center to write a proposal for a family care comprehensive health center. We might have accepted this assignment by merely producing a document that included better ways to distribute health care to the poor. Actually, NIMH in the Community Mental Health Act concerned itself with this very question of getting more and better mental health services to the poor. Taking as our primary goal the redistribution of power—in this case power in the health system—we worked in a different manner. This meant shedding the illusion that proposals and programs are panaceas. A great deal of emphasis was put on the process of working with community members rather than the outcome—the proposal. We began to work with a small committee. First they told us what they wanted; and interestingly enough although they came up with many ideas relating to better services, they made quite clear that the most important item was that they were to run the health center. They wanted the funds to come to the community corporation and they wanted the administration of the center to be manned by community residents.

Therefore, in working with this small group much time was spent in organizing meetings with city health officials who had no desire at all to give up their power. I said meetings—they were confrontations and they were consciously arranged to bring the various health agency power people face to face with the community so that the community's friends could be clearly distinguished from its enemies. Confrontations in which different elements of the system are brought together present an opportunity for perceptions to be grounded in reality. When everyone is together, it becomes difficult for agency people to pass the buck and say "it's not up to me." It becomes clear who is willing to take a stand for the community.

At these confrontations, when I became the professional advocate and stood up to argue loudly the community's case, I came face to face not with a neutral professional, but a partisan physician who passionately claimed that doctors must administer this program and the community could have an advisory board. This same scene has been replayed many times, and many of you are undoubtedly familiar with its dialogue: "Do you want a community person prescribing medicine, or taking out your appendix?" or "You can advise or even participate, but you can't control. Why isn't this enough?" They ask innocently, "What's the difference between participation and control?" Well, our answer has become "If you don't see any real difference between participation and control, then you can participate and the community will control."

Familiar as it may be, when a professional argues on the side of the powerless, it is a new scene for most community residents and many begin to gain confidence and speak up as well. We have now reached the point where the community organizes its own confrontations and has developed the confidence and knowledge so that it calls upon us less frequently. When I state that our recognition of conflicting interests guided our strategy, this does not mean that we saw any of the governmental agencies as monolithic entities. There were people in the Public Health Service, NIMH, and city government who favored community control. But only when the community began to demonstrate its very real concern with statements and bodies at meetings did these agency people openly support the community with actions.

The process of developing the proposal through a series of confrontations contrasts sharply with the more traditional approach of proposal writing that takes place when one's power base is the medical-academic rather than the community corporation.

With the community as the constituency there are no professional inhibitions against the use of politics. The power the community board has is based on the fact that it is elected annually by the community and is accountable to it. Therefore, politics is a daily and primary activity of the Multi-Service Center.

Pressure, whether it is on the city, or elected officials, or directors of multi-service programs, is exerted on the basis of the number of potential votes in the community, and these votes are collected through job patronage and improved services.

Community Power and New Priorities

The community-based power structure to which we were accountable influenced the substantive content of our work as well as our methods.

When you are a mental health professional whose base is in the profession, priorities of services are arranged differently than when your base is in the community. I was often asked by the directors of a medical school mental health center, "What are you going to do about the suicidal patients and the acutely disturbed?" They were concerned because they saw an emphasis in the Hunts Point program on consultation and educational services.

The main focus of the Hunts Point program was to be the youth. This is the community's priority. It is the community's feeling that the damage done their children is far more important than the few suicides, and they see it as irresponsible to ignore their children in school at the expense of psychotics. After all, they say, "It is the government who is forcing us to set priorities by limiting our funds."

The research enterprise is one that is acutely sensitive to the base from which one operates. In the past the Hunts Point community had been the focus of a highly competent medical school staff that had investigated the relationship of powerlessness and anomie to mental illness, and even the role of the spiritualist church as a mental health agent. These investigations represented the interests of the professional staff, and many community peoyple developed a very negative attitude towards this research. They had been questioned, often for an hour, about very personal areas in their lives and they had seen nothing flow from these studies which benefited them. Even when professionals have done research in a community which might be useful to the residents, there has been very little attention given to feeding back this information to those who could use it.

Research is a piece of social intervention in itself. One can study a community to find out things that will support one's own professional career and interests, or one can study a community to serve its interests and promote its development. I maintain that the latter can best be done when one is employed by the community in this role.

Professionals Need the Community

Over this two-year period, the community has had less need for our skills as it has developed its own. At the same time, mental health professionals began to become aware of how much they needed the community, as the following example illustrates.

New York State had just built a five-million-dollar children's hospital to serve all the emotionally disturbed children in the Bronx who needed partial or total hospitalization. A director and his two assistants were chosen from the faculty of the Albert Einstein College of Medicine. Two are child psychiatrists, and one is a psychologist. All are highly competent men anxious to make full use of a "community approach" in their program. Their hospital is a most magnificent structure with a swimming pool, gym, carpeting, and beautiful living quarters. The state somehow overlooked one important item: There was no budget to staff the hospital. The psychiatrist administrator came to visit me and asked whether I could help him get the community's support so that he could get some money to run this much needed facility. We brought his request to the members of the community; it was explained that he needed them badly and they were in a strong position to make their own demands.

Two meetings later, a community board of 21 was elected. Some of the power this board has relates to hiring personnel, planning programs, priorities of services, and geographic areas served. In return, the board is developing a strategy that will bring in money for staffing. At present the board has divided into three committees. One is developing a program proposal which will be used for additional funding, another is in charge of new personnel, and a third is working on bylaws for the group.

In the sphere of politics and power, attribution of causality is difficult, but let me mention one more episode at the children's hospital in which the community board seemed to make the vital difference.

For six months, the director had been trying to get supplementary training funds for the staff. The state's rejection of this request came before the community board was elected. Four weeks later the state suddenly reversed itself and granted the funds.

Usually, state hospitals are remote institutions whose goals and programs never become integrated with the lives of the families or communities from which they draw their patients. With this powerful community policy board and a responsive administration, each learning much from the other, there is an opportunity to overcome this isolation and facilitate the implementation of many mental health concepts that up to the present remain words in a proposal.

In the past in public institutions the lack of accountability of the professional to the client permitted in many instances the lowering of professional standards of practice. Psychiatrists in mental institutions and teachers in public schools are well aware of the dead wood that no accountability has allowed to accumulate. With a structure of accountability to the consumer built in, those professionals with a true commitment to the highest levels of service will receive renewed support from their community constituents.

Politicalization

One indirect accomplishment of our efforts was politicalization of community residents. I believe this took place first by bringing the different key political figures in the drama together so that the community became aware of not what they said or what they stood for, but what actions they were willing to take. Although the term "advocacy" comes from the legal profession, there is a great difference between legal and social advocacy. The practice of law takes place within a system of rules where there is a judge to adjudicate the dispute. Social advocacy takes place within a political context and the outcome is dependent on who can garner the most power. For the poor this power is mainly achieved through the development of aware constituencies. However, to leave the situation at a point where the community is only aware of how state and local figures stand on health or mental health is incomplete politicalization. As Mayors Naftalin of Minneapolis and Lindsay of New York have begun to point out, one reason more is not being done for our urban poor is that money has been drained off into the war and weaponry. Another effort of ours then is to point out the relationship between the immediate self-interests of the community, such as jobs, education, and health, and national policies. I maintain that if we do not direct the community's attention to these facts we merely become part of the Establishment machinery which redistributes the crumbs rather than the power. As examples of this kind of emphasis, members of the community went to Washington on a citizen's lobby for housing and against the ABM. The executive director of the Multi-Service Center wrote Senator Stennis asking for permission to testify before the Armed Services Committee at its ABM hearings, his letter stated in part:

> Dear Sen. Stennis:
> *I would appreciate an opportunity to testify when hearings are held on funds for the Sentinel anti-ballistic missile system. The threat that we poor people see is not from missiles. It is from big slum rats, small broken down schools, high food prices and low wages.*
> *The ABM won't fix this situation. The experts say it won't defend us either. But it will eat up money that could defend all of us from further decay and despair in the cities.*

Often we are asked "Isn't it difficult for white professionals to be accepted by the black and Puerto Rican communities? We believe that blacks and Puerto Ricans should administer and have the key roles in every program. When asked, we help the community to implement this policy by locating qualified personnel.

I believe the reason the community is willing to use us as consultants even though we are white is due to our relationship to them—that of employees. They hire us and if they are dissatisfied, they may discontinue our services. Although they were skeptical at first, trust has built up because of this relationship. Trust has developed because of the fact that we were able to produce results beneficial to them.

There is much more, but I shall be content if I have been able to communicate to you our ideology and new style of work, which included my submitting this paper to the leaders of the corporation for their thoughtful criticism.

But Is It Psychology?

All of what I have said may bring to your mind the question "But what has this to do with psychology?" There is much substantive knowledge we have which is useful to the community, for instance, presentation of results of different addiction treatment programs, information on factors that facilitate infant development, training of paraprofessionals, and effects of institutionalization. However, this information is always given within the frame of reference that the redistribution of power to our constituents is an absolute necessity. Although we are acutely aware that many mental health problems will not be solved by this increased acquisition of power, we consider it a prerequisite to the process of solving the other problems, and, therefore, it has top priority.

Those of us who believe that a measure of a man's development is the control he exercises over the important areas of his life can no longer close our eyes to power, for it sets the parameters of our work. Nor can we avoid the importance of conflict. Struggle is the key technique to gain power. It more clearly defines a man by defining his enemy.

Power is neither a positive nor a negative concept. Just as atomic energy can be used to advance man or to destroy him, so social and political power can be sources of either positive or destructive actions.

Those who now have power in our country have created need amidst plenty, destroyed our material resources, polluted our atmosphere, and turned our schools into a maze without a reward. With the most advanced technology in the world, capable of planning for every contingency in the flight of three men to the moon, we are incapable of planning for housing or mass transportation in our cities. The area in which we have most excelled is overkill.

The rationale for the redistribution of power is clear. Even our language reflects the basic conflict of interest that exists. *They* are the powerful. *We* are the alienated. No human relations techniques can change this. When power is abused by the few, a more equal distribution might act as a check on these abuses; and community control is one mechanism for the redistribution of power.

When I took the introductory course in psychology, I learned that the purpose of science was the understanding of the natural world. I was then taught that a good test of understanding was the ability to predict and control. Over 20 years ago I was being brainwashed to believe in the neutrality, the purity, of science. With my current value-laden approach, I now believe the mission of the scientist should be understanding the natural world so that he can improve the quality of life.

If some of the skills we have learned which give us the title "psychologist" are irrelevant to this mission, then we should forget about our professional title and learn what is necessary to fulfill our commitment as scientists. And let one measure of our understanding be a visible improvement in the distribution of power and resources in the areas in which we work.

Alternatives to Traditional Law Enforcement

MORTON BARD

The author received his PhD in clinical psychology from New York University in 1953. He is presently a professor of psychology at the City College of the City University of New York, where he also serves as Director of the Psychological Center. His major interests include the development of community psychology action programs and experimental social innovation.

Of the many facets of urban life, few are more likely to arouse a passionate response than the police. And understandably so, for in any changing society law enforcement, by its very nature a defender of the status quo, is forced to assume a critical role in the dynamics of change. Yet, in a strange way there is probably no clearer evidence of social growth than when a society relinquishes its usual attitude of indifference about its law enforcement institutions.

It goes without saying that the police are *the* instrument of power. Whether in Tokyo or Prague, Chicago or Peking, the police are and do what society defines for them. In more passive periods of social development, the exercise of police power is of little interest. For those who enjoy the privileges of power, indifference is a derivative of tranquility; for the powerless, indifference is born of a sense of fateful inevitability. But during periods of important social change, indifference about law enforcement disappears, as tranquility for the powerful and inevitability for the powerless are no longer predictable conditions of life.

In the place of indifference, one is either "for" or "against" the cop; each position is simplistically appealing and is equally destructive to destined social change. For those who are "against," the attitude is one of relentless criticism and faultfinding with an undercurrent of the promise that in utopia there will be no necessity for police. The "pros," on the other hand, express unquestioning support for all that is obsolescent and self-destructive within the police establishment in the absurd conviction that the methods of the past will reconstitute the past. For the object of this sudden attention, the individual police officer, neither friend nor foe offers any substantive relief in the face of a rising tide of social chaos.

The Social Scientist's Role in Law Enforcement

Unfortunately, psychologists and other social scientists have, in the main, succeeded in maintaining an attitude of indifference. Firmly rooted in a tradition of academic objectivity, the thought-oriented world of the intellectual-social disciplines is far removed from the action-oriented social discipline of the policeman. Recent events on many campuses, however, have forced the social scientist to consider the police as a social system, their presence on campus making them difficult, if not impossible, to ignore.

This situation, too, for all of its apparent turmoil, will prove to be a constructive development. Perhaps now there will be serious efforts to undertake objective assessment of the complexities of law enforcement, particularly as applied to urban areas. Perhaps it will now become academically respectable to examine the police establishment with a view to the development of constructive alternatives to traditional law enforcement. Perhaps the social sciences can thus avoid the trap of blanket condemnation of the police, with its accompanying fantasy that "somewhere beyond the rainbow" no police will be needed. Or perhaps students of social behavior can avoid the opposing but equally illusory belief that the kind of law enforcement typical of television westerns is a realistic possibility in today's world.

Little-acknowledged facts about law enforcement belie these polarized views. In our alienated, depersonalized, and often dehumanized urban centers, the police have taken on roles and responsibilities completely unforeseen even as recently as two decades ago. Most of these activities have become police functions through default. Many of the helping institutions in society have been unwilling or unable to adapt to changing conditions. While questions may be raised about the appropriateness of the police being involved in a wide range of service activities, the fact remains that, because of their instant availability night and day and because of the unavailability of other official agencies of government, the police function as a human resource agency without parallel. It is estimated that traditional law enforcing or property watching now occupies less than 20% of police man-hours. Maintaining order and providing interpersonal service—not law enforcement and crime suppression—are what modern police work is all about, particularly in the inner city. Yet the Marshal Dillon and Sherlock Holmes myths persist.

Even if one focuses on crime, traditional notions of law enforcement must be challenged. The notion of "crime in the streets" makes excellent media copy, but the fact remains that most criminal behavior occurs indoors, that is, off the street. The vast majority of homicides, assaults, and rapes take place indoors and between individuals who are related and who are known to each other. Most burglaries and robberies occur indoors and not on the street. But the traditional approach dictates that reduction of these crimes would best be accomplished by having more policemen and more hardware to do what the police have usually done in trying to achieve "safe streets." It is doubtful that increasing methods appropriate to the past can reduce those forms of behavior that contribute to constantly rising crime statistics today. But changing what the policeman does and how his system is organized may indeed serve to reduce apparently soaring crime. Even more important, perhaps, changes in method may serve a preventive function and lessen the increasing tension between police and community.

There is a strong suggestion that much of the existing tension between the police and the community results from the failure of the police to meet with skill and sensitivity the hopeful expectations of the citizenry. In the absence of other resources, the police are often expected to provide services that are, in the traditional sense, outside the realm of law enforcement. When the services are performed inappropriately because of inadequate preparation and because of a system that fails to acknowledge the reality of their existence, citizen resentment is understandably increased.

An Alternative Approach to Crime Prevention

At the City College in New York we have recently concluded an experiment to determine the parameters of a common police function—the family disturbance. The two-year program was supported by the United States Department of Justice and had the complete cooperation of the New York City Police Department. Its primary objectives were to demonstrate a viable community psychology program in preventive mental health and crime prevention. The project attempted to determine if, in a circumscribed urban area of about 85,000 population, a specially trained group of 18 patrolmen (about 10% of the regularly assigned complement of officers) could effect changes in homicides and assaults, as well as serve as a case-finding mechanism for families whose disorders required police intervention.

The 18 police officers were intensively trained for a full month and were then assigned to work in pairs to provide 24-hour coverage by one radio car for a 22-month period. On each tour of duty there were 2 members of the unit in the "family car," which was dispatched on all domestic disturbance calls regardless of the location in the precinct. A card index file in the car permitted each team to know of previous calls made to the same family and to follow up more effectively actions taken or recommendations made.

The heart of the program, however, entailed on-campus consultations for the men of the unit. On the theory that intensive training itself would not be sufficient to inculcate the highly sensitive skills necessary for family crisis intervention, the members of the unit engaged in weekly individual consultations with advanced doctoral students in clinical psychology and in weekly group discussions (in groups of six) with professional psychologists serving as group leaders.

One of the major challenges in the experiment was to see if policemen could be made psychologically sophisticated and be given highly technical skills without in any way confusing them about their professional identity. Throughout, every effort was made to preserve their identity as police officers and to avoid converting them into psychologists or social workers. In fact, they functioned throughout the program as general police officers and served as specialists *only* when dispatched on a specific family disturbance.

The final evaluation of the project, while completed, is too lengthy to report here, but will be available shortly from the National Institute of Law Enforcement and Criminal Justice, United States Department of Justice. However, there were some dramatic findings that can be noted briefly. The unit processed 1,375 interventions with 962 families. The community response to the unit was clearly a positive one by a variety of indirect measures. While homicides in New York City increased during the period of the project, there was not a single homicide in a family known to the unit. There was a reduction in assaults in the demonstration area and a drop in arrests for assaults, suggesting the positive effect of skillful police intervention and the use of mediation and referral rather than the usual inadequate use of the courts in such matters. Another striking finding was the total absence of injury to the policemen of the unit despite the high risk involved in being exposed more than would ordinarily be the case to emotionally volatile and potentially violent family crises. The danger to policemen in such situations is well known among policemen and is attested to by high police death and injury rates.

The experiment in police family crisis intervention suggests a constructive alternative to the traditionally military-modeled, crime-combat organization of virtually all police departments. It demonstrates the strong possibility that police departments might be structured along the lines of highly flexible service organizations without in any way compromising their basic law enforcement mission.

The approach taken in our project can best be described as conforming to the generalist-specialist model. Each officer was a general uniformed law enforcement agent performing patrol functions in keeping with the responsibility to keep the peace and enforce the law. However, each officer had, in addition, a highly trained skill in family intervention that could be called upon when required. The men in the unit were, in effect, on-call specialists who could render with competence a service that is ordinarily regarded by most policemen as an unwelcomed nuisance and not "real" police work.

Considering the highly complex demands made upon the police, it is ridiculous to expect each policeman to have the special skills required in the many situations that arise in a given area. However, as long as the system operates according to the assumption that each officer must be all things to all people, the men are forced to engage in appropriate behaviors that only serve to increase public disenchantment and widen the gap between the police and the community. Better community relations can be effected only by skillful performance of expected tasks, rather than the time-limited palliatives of special community relations programs.

The model presented by the family crisis program can be extended into other important areas. Disorderly adolescents, for example, are the bane of every police department. It would make better sense to dispatch a generalist-specialist skilled in dealing with youths than it would to send just any patrolman who happens to be in an area and who, because of personal limitations, might only worsen the situation. However, the same patrolman who has serious limitations with youngsters may have special talents in managing confused psychotics, and he could be effectively trained to be used as a generalist-specialist in that capacity.

Professionalization of the Police

In addition to the obvious organizational advantages in such an approach, there are distinct implications here for the issue of professionalization of the police. Despite frequent references to professionalization, if the present military system continues, the term must remain a fiction insofar as law enforcement is concerned. Authoritarian militarism is antagonistic to professionalism. The hallmark of the professional is his freedom to exercise his judgment and to use his discretion. The lawyer, the engineer, the psychologist, the physician, and the architect, once trained, are expected to exercise judgment in the discharge of their professional duties. A basic assumption of military organizations is that the practitioner does what someone hierarchically determines that he do. Supervision and control are omnipresent. However, the reality is that most of what a policeman does is done in isolation; he must perform in circumstances that preclude instruction and control. Yet the illusion persists that he always has a clear criterion in the law that he enforces without fear or favor. The usual authoritarian control, because it fails to provide the guidance officers really need, only serves to provoke passive-aggressive reactions to the system.

The criminal justice system, for which the policeman is an agent, winks at the issue of discretion. How well we all know how absurd is the classical belief that the policeman enforces the law without fear or favor. Even when a policeman decides *not* to write a traffic ticket because the female driver has broken down and cried, he has exercised professional judgment and has, in effect, dispensed discretionary justice. It is time for us to acknowledge that discretion and judgment are as much a part of a policeman's function as is their exercise by any other professional.

If we acknowledge this, then we must prepare the police officer to exercise this judgment and provide him with career incentives and rewards as we do in other disciplines. At the moment, all the brownie points in the police world relate to the ideal of strength through toughness; compassion and sensitivity in the present system only lend support for the adage "nice guys finish last." Freedom and independence are as much desired by policemen (psychological cliches about the authoritarian personality notwithstanding) as they are by other professionals.

A physician is an authority with the power of life and death in situations involving physical disorder. A policeman is a life and death authority in situations of social disorder. Yet physicians are trained, on the average, in 11,000 hours. The average policeman receives fewer than 200 hours of training. And, in the latter instance, most of the training is irrelevant to the functions to be performed.

It is time that psychologists attend to one of the most significant systems of social regulation—the police. Social psychologists, organizational psychologists, clinical psychologists, and educational psychologists can contribute much in the objective evaluation of police functions, in developing alternative organizational structures, and in designing training methods to enhance police performance. Continued faultfinding, on the one hand, or uncritical support, on the other, leaves the policeman in an increasingly untenable position—frightened, defensive, and alone while urban society continues to fragment.

We must begin to think of constructive alternatives in urban law enforcement. One possible alternative has been presented here. At the City College Psychological Center we are continuing to explore possibilities. Presently, for example, we are engaged in a program to train housing policemen for specialized functions in human conflict resolution. The possibilities are infinite.

Above all, however, we should remember that there is no better barometer of a society's condition than its police. If they fail, *we* have failed.

The Metropolitan Educational Park

THOMAS F. PETTIGREW

The author received his PhD in social psychology from Harvard University in 1956. He is presently a professor of social psychology at Harvard, where his major research interests involve race relations in education, politics, and public opinion.

The need for radically new designs for American public education was never more immediate and obvious. For a variety of reasons, only a few of which are racial in character, the present structure of our schools is inadequate to meet the heavy demands placed upon them by our society. But as a social psychologist who specializes in race relations, I shall dwell in this discussion principally on racial reasons for why I strongly support one possible new structural design for public education.

My reasoning begins with the following facts from relevant social science research:

1. Interracial schools featuring cross-racial acceptance have significant benefits, especially in the early grades, for both white and black children.

2. Schools with significant numbers of middle class children have significant benefits for less-advantaged children regardless of race.

3. Public schools in the United States are rapidly becoming *less,* not more, heterogeneous both in terms of race and social class.

4. In small cities and towns, the remedies for this growing separation are well known: district-wide redrawing of school lines within a district, the pairing of schools, careful placement of new schools, alteration of feeder systems, and conversion of more schools into district-wide specialized institutions.

5. The problem is most intense in the large central city and is brought about basically by: (*a*) the antimetropolitan manner in which our school districts are drawn and operated; (*b*) the growing racial and class ecological divisions between central cities and their suburbs; (*c*) the depletion of the central city's pool of middle class white children by large parochial and private school systems; and, finally, (*d*) the cynical and willful planning by major school systems to achieve maximum racial and class segregation. Here the techniques for heterogeneous schools in smaller localities are mere "band-aids" at best and counterproductive at worst.

A New Concept in Urban Education

Armed with these data-supported observations, one is soon led to considering new ways to structure our public schools in metropolitan areas which are not based on antimetropolitan, "neighborhood school" assumptions. Actually, the four basic reasons just cited for the growing intensity of big city race and class segregation of schools provide the form and direction for future efforts. Thus, large educational complexes drawing from wide attendance areas will be essential. These attendance areas will generally have to include both central city and suburban territory in order to ensure the optimal stable racial mix. The sites for these facilities must not only be convenient to the mass transit network but must also be on racially "neutral turf." Such locations would avoid immediate public labeling of the school as "white" or "Negro."

Racial specifications are by no means the only criteria for future remedies. Public schools in our largest cities have lost their former preeminence as the innovative educational leaders. Berkeley, California, Newton and Brookline, Massachusetts, and a host of other smaller communities are now the pacesetters. Thus, the plans for the future should accent and facilitate innovation. Indeed, future public schools should possess facilities which could rarely be duplicated by expensive private schools if they are to compete effectively for the children of advantaged parents. Such arrangements, of course, will cost considerable money; thus, a final criterion must be significant federal support of capital costs.

Several designs would meet these criteria; but let us consider one design as illustrative. Ringing our major cities with educational parks, each of which serves both inner-city and suburban students, offers one basic plan—*the metropolitan park plan*. Each park would be located on "neutral turf" in an inner-ring suburb or just inside the central city boundary; and it would be so placed that the same spoke of the mass transit system could bring both outer-ring suburban children into the park and inner-city children out to it. A few could also be located deep within the central city adjoining such key urban facilities as museums. The attendance area of each park would ideally cut out a metropolitan pie slice containing a minimum of 12,000-15,000 public school students, with the thin end of the slice in the more dense central city and the thick end in the more sparse suburbs.

An Incentive for Cooperation

What incentive could generate the metropolitan cooperation necessary for such a plan? A number of systems have considered educational parks, but they usually find the capital costs prohibitive. Moreover, many systems are currently hard pressed for expansion funds—especially as referenda for school construction bonds continue to be defeated throughout the nation. Federal funding, then, on a massive scale will obviously be needed, though it must be dispersed in a far more careful and strategic manner than the everybody-gets-his-cut, "river and harbors bill" principle of the 1965 Elementary and Secondary Education Act. As long as alternate federal funding for capital costs is available, many school systems—particularly those in bad faith—will not choose to join a metropolitan park plan. Therefore, future federal construction grants must: (*a*) involve more than one urban district and the consortium must always include the central city (note that any one park would not require the entire metropolitan area to join the proposal, though some coordination would be necessary, perhaps through review by each area's metropolitan planning commission); (*b*) require racial and social desegregation—and, hopefully, integration—in every school involved (metropolitan involvement makes this requirement feasible); and (*c*) exclude alternate routes for federal building funds (though if the first two criteria are met, the proposal need not adopt the metropolitan park plan as the model).

A 15,000-student, 40–50 million dollar park, 90% of it paid for by the federal government, would be a powerful inducement. But is such federal funding possible in the near future? The answer, as with many other domestic questions, rests with the termination of the Vietnam war. Nothing like the Vietnam war costs, of course, would become available for the domestic scene. Yet, at such a time, a two-billion-dollar-a-year school construction program, enough for building roughly 40 parks annually, is not unlikely. Here lie both a great opportunity and an equally great danger. If the money is distributed in the easy fashion of the 1965 Education Act to individual school districts, the antimetropolitan effects could be disastrous for both race relations and public education. Federal building money spent in such a manner would further insulate aloof suburbia and institutionalize de facto school segregation in the inner city for at least another half century. School construction money is likely to be made available by the federal government after Vietnam. The vital question is what will be its form and effects.

The educational park idea is not a panacea; there can be elegantly effective and incredibly ineffective parks. Yet ample federal funding combined with the nation's planning and architectural genius should be able to set a new standard and direction for public schools. This combination has successfully been applied to public facilities ranging from interstate highways to magnificent airports. Now the combination should be applied to the benefit of children.

Advantages of the Metropolitan Park Design

From high-rise structures to multiple-unit campuses, educational parks themselves can be planned in a variety of ways. The most widely discussed design would involve a reasonably large tract of land (80–100 acres as a minimum) and no fewer than 14 or 15 schools serving grades from kindergarten through high school. One educator has visualized a campus design for 18,000 students consisting of two senior high, four junior high, and eight elementary schools. If the park were to serve an especially densely populated section, it would be best if it did not include the entire grade spectrum so that it could still cover a reasonably expansive and heterogeneous attendance area. In general, however, an educational park resembles a public university. Both include a variety of educational programs for a large group of students of varying abilities. Like public universities in our major cities, some parks could consist of high-rise structures and some could develop a more spacious campus atmosphere with numerous buildings. Hopefully, the metropolitan park could usually follow the campus model since sufficient space would generally be obtainable at suburban-ring locations.

Apart from offering racial remedies, the metropolitan park concept has a number of distinct advantages. First, there are considerable savings that accrue from consolidation; centralized facilities, such as a single kitchen, need not be duplicated in each of the park's units. Savings on capital costs, too, would accrue from simultaneous building of many units at one location. These savings, however, do not necessarily mean that the total construction and operating costs would be less than those for the same student capacity spread out in traditional units. The advantage is that for essentially the same cost metropolitan parks could boast significantly better facilities than traditional schools. Consequently, each child would be receiving far more per educational dollar in the metropolitan park.

The improved centralized facilities of the park should maximize innovations and individualized instruction. It is difficult to institute new approaches to learning in old settings. A prime finding of social change research is that new norms are easier to introduce in new institutions. The metropolitan park offers a fresh and exciting setting that should encourage new educational techniques and attract the more innovative members of the teaching profession. In addition, the park presents a rare design opportunity for building innovation into the physical and social structures of the schools. This, of course, includes the latest equipment for aiding the teacher and the student. Centralization enhances this process, for example, by providing efficient concentration of all electronic information storage, retrieval, and console facilities. Yet such centralization of equipment should not be viewed as leading inevitably to a wide assortment of frightening Orwellian devices cluttering the school. Poor planning could lead to this result, but the accent should be on individualized instruction as the unifying and positive theme—a theme far more possible in the park design than in the present model of scattered "little red schoolhouses."

Many innovations made possible by the metropolitan park extend beyond the equipment realm. For instance, the teaching profession today suffers from being one of the most undifferentiated by rank of all professions, a characteristic which discourages a lifelong orientation to the field. While the medical profession has a graded rank order of roles from intern and resident to chief of a service, teachers must either enter administration and become principals or shift to more prestigious schools in order to move up the ladder. By concentrating a large number of teachers in a relatively small area, far more role differentiation becomes possible. Thus, a teacher might progress from an apprentice in a team-teaching situation to a master teacher in a team, to a supervisor of master teachers, etc. Faculty concentration also allows more intensive, across-school, inservice training and the formation of departments across schools with rankings within departments as in universities (e.g., a junior high history department consisting of all history teachers in the four or five junior highs on the campus).

Concentration of students also allows wider course offerings. Specialized classes, from playing the lute to seventeenth-century English literature, become economically possible when the students electing them are gathered from units throughout the park. Moreover, concentration makes possible some remarkable facilities that can be shared by all of the park's units (e.g., an Olympic-sized swimming pool, extensive auditorium, theatrical equipment, etc.). These special facilities could far surpass what is now available in all but the most affluent districts, become a source of student and community pride, and provide a competitive status advantage over private schools. They also would be used efficiently, rather than the minimal use expensive facilities receive in single-site schools.

The metropolitan park offers unusual opportunities for an effective liaison with a local university or college. Nova, the extensive educational park near Fort Lauderdale, Florida, even plans to include college and graduate work right on its campus. But direct contiguity is not necessary to develop a mutually beneficial coordination.

Recall that an important cause of public school segregation in many central cities is the enrollment of large percentages of white children in parochial schools. This fact suggests closer cooperation between public and parochial schools; and the metropolitan educational park could facilitate such cooperation under optimal conditions. Most parochial systems are currently in serious financial condition and tapping into the park's superior facilities should prove attractive. Roman Catholic educators point out that those items that cost the most—the physical science laboratories, gymnasium, and stadium—tend to be least related to the "moral training" that they believe to be the distinctive feature of their schools. Scattered-sites schools, public and parochial, make "shared time" and other cooperative arrangements awkward at best. And when parochial students come to take their public school class as a group, such segregation often reaps its usual harvest of intergroup tension and hostility.

A recent idea from Vermont introduces a more promising possibility. At the time of planning a large educational park, Roman Catholic educators are provided the opportunity of buying an adjoining plot of land and constructing a new facility of their own. As long as the land price is consistent with its true value, no constitutional infringements appear to be involved. The new parochial facility need only concentrate on housing courses directly needed for "moral training." Parochial pupils would be free as individuals, not as separated groups, to cross the park's grass, not urban streets, and attend physical education, science, and other public school courses when they fit their particular schedules. The Vermont Plan offers construction and operating savings to hard-pressed parochial systems, and it offers a greater race and class student balance to hard-pressed public systems.

Cost efficiency, educational innovations, more individualized instruction, wider course offerings, special facilities, and coordination with universities and parochial schools—all of these advantages of the well-designed metropolitan park are features that parents, white and Negro, would welcome in the schools of tomorrow. This is politically critical, for desegregation efforts of the past have seldom come as intrinsic parts of a larger package promising an across-the-board improvement in education for *all* children.

Major Objections to the Metropolitan Park Concept

In addition to the natural resistance to change, four major objections have been raised to the park concept: (*a*) excessive capital costs; (*b*) the phasing out of existing schools; (*c*) the problem of impersonalization in the large complexes; and (*d*) the loss of neighborhood interest and involvement in the school. Each is a serious objection and deserves comment.

The park *is* expensive, and major federal funding is necessary. Furthermore, mistakes in design and location could be disastrous. A park is an enormous commitment of resources, and, if poorly conceived, it could stand for years as a major mistake in planning. This is precisely what would happen if parks were operated totally within central city systems, for demographic projections prove the folly of building parks for a single central city system as a desegregation device. It is for this reason that the parks of the future must be *metropolitan* in character.

Present schools were expensive, too, and raise the problem of phasing out existing facilities. For many urban districts this is not a problem; they already have overutilized schools with double shifts and rising enrollments or old schools long past their usefulness. But some urban districts have many new schools and would be hesitant to join a park consortium. The program, however, is a long-term one. Hopefully, by the early 1970s most of the nation's leading metropolitan areas would boast one or more parks; these, in turn, could serve as models for completing the park rings in the decade. Moreover, elementary and secondary student enrollments will rise rapidly, from 48.4 million in 1964 to a projected 54.9 million in 1974 and 66 million in the fateful year of 1984. Metropolitan parks, then, could be phased in as older facilities are phased out and enrollments swiftly rise.

Such a process would be ideal nationally, but there will be special problems in localities with "planned de facto school segregation." These are cities, such as Chicago, that in recent years have purposely built new schools in the heart of their Negro ghettos in order to maximize racial separation. If racial progress is to be made in these cities, recent structures will have to be converted to new uses—perhaps, to much-needed community centers.

The third objection to parks centers on the impersonalization of organizational bigness—"the Kafka problem." Indeed, much of the park's description—15,000 students, a staff approaching 1,000, the latest electronic equipment—has a frightening Kafka ring; and one can easily imagine how an ill-designed park could justify these fears. But such a prospect is not inherent in the park plan; nor is bigness a park problem alone, for many of today's huge urban high schools accommodate many thousands of students in a single unit and arouse the same uneasiness. In fact, imaginatively designed parks could act to counter the urban trend toward ever larger public units. *Smaller* schools at each level can be economically built as units within the park, and careful planning can afford a reasonable degree of privacy for each unit while still providing access to the shared facilities of the park.

Some critics are particularly concerned about the park's loss of neighborhood interest and involvement. The criticism assumes that most urban public schools today are neighborhood based and that they generate considerable neighborhood involvement. Serious doubts can be raised about both assumptions; we may well be worrying about the loss of something already lost. In any event, there is no evidence to indicate that only a neighborhood-based school can generate parental concern, or that a metropolitan park could not duplicate this feat, or that there is a close and negative association between the size of the attendance area and the amount of involvement.

The criticism does raise an important planning issue: How can the park be initiated and planned to heighten parental and community interest? Certainly, the special facilities, the university liaison, and cooperation with parochial schools could help generate community pride and interest, as could smaller schools and a park school board of parents with wide authority short of taxing power. Furthermore, widespread use of the park for adult education, community affairs, etc., would also contribute to public involvement; indeed, the special facilities of the park lend themselves to such adult use more readily than the typical school today.

Finally, one might ask how such a metropolitan educational park plan fits with other such widely discussed possibilities as "decentralization" and "community schools." First, it should be noted that decentralization and community control are typically advanced either apart from integration considerations or as outright alternatives to integration. The Bundy Report (1967) for New York City, for instance, could well lead to racially homogeneous districts that would institutionalize racial segregation for generations to come. Yet there is an obvious need in such large and unwieldy systems as New York and Chicago to decentralize authority, as well as a general need to increase parental and community involvement in public education.

Similar to compensatory education, however, these possibilities acquire force and meaning when they *accompany* the drive for integration rather than substitute for it. Thus, effective decentralization need not take the form of isolated social class or racial islands, but should assume the metropolitan pie-slice shapes described earlier as ideal attendance areas for educational parks. New York City's schools *could* be organized along the lines suggested by the Bundy Report in such a way as to help rather than hinder integration.

In summary, then, those who say there is nothing we can do about the educational segregation of our major cities are wrong fortunately. This is not to say that desegregation progress will be easy, or even that we will do what is necessary to achieve such progress. But it is to say that potentially it *can* be done for a significant number of urban Americans, white and Negro.

Reference

Reconnection for learning: A community school system for New York City. New York: Mayor's Advisory Panel on Decentralization, 1967.

Separation of Work and Income[1]

JUANITA M. KREPS

The author received her PhD in economics from Duke University, where she is presently a professor of economics and Dean, The Women's College. Her major research has been in the fields of labor and manpower economics and in the economics of the aging.

"Pay, in one form or another, is certainly one of the mainsprings of motivation in our society. The drive for private money gains—the profit motive—provides the main ideological cleavage in the world today. Deep down, everyone assumes that we mostly work for money. The most evangelical Human Relationist insists that it is important, while protesting that other things are too (and are, perhaps, in his view, nobler). It would be unnecessary to belabor the point if it were not for a tendency for money drives to slip out of focus in a miasma of other values and other practices. As it is, it must be repeated: Pay is the most important single motivator used in our organized society [Haire, Ghiselli, & Porter, 1963, p. 3]."

Psychological research on pay is meager, despite the central role generally imputed to money incentives as a means of getting the world's work done. The authors cited above identify three major questions related to the operation of pay as an incentive. First, when does it provide a motivation for effort, before or after the reward? Does one work for a raise in pay, or having been given one, then try to live up to it? Second, how does the employee view his pay? How much of an annual increment does he expect? Third, how does he view his pay in comparison with that of others? One's pay is perceived as being equitable or not, depending largely on how it ranks him in the wage or salary hierarchy he considers appropriate.[2]

Incentive pay questions are of great interest to the economist as well as the psychologist, both for purposes of research and for the direction of social policy. For in economics, some of our most vexing current questions have to do with the provision of income in lieu of earnings: income transfers to persons who render no service, or at least render no service during the time period of the

---

[1] Invited Address presented to the Division of Maturity and Old Age at the Annual Meeting of the American Psychological Association, Washington, D. C., September 2, 1969.

[2] The authors suggest that this threefold division breaks the questions into three theoretical and methodological areas of psychology: motivation, perception, and social psychology (Haire et al., 1963, p. 4).

transfer. Such income maintenance for persons who are disabled, or who are too young or too old to work, does not raise the income-incentive question; no attempt is being made to entice the recipients into the labor force. But the man of working age is expected to work in our society. Support for the "able-bodied man" has not been condoned, except for periods of temporary unemployment. Moreover, unemployment and disability payments, financed by payroll taxes, are viewed as forms of insurance, and, hence, are available only to workers who have made tax payments, or have had employers who did so.[3]

Income without Work: The Rationale

How, then, have we come to the present stage of discussion of a guaranteed income for all? Is the emergence of new approaches to income maintenance due to a recognition of defects in the existing system? Or is the output of the economy now so large that the nation can "afford" to offer some minimum family income? To what extent does the widespread endorsement of such schemes as the negative income tax, which would be available without reference to employment, belie a belief that work is no longer necessary?

The workless society has been promised from time to time, usually on the basis that automation will soon eliminate the need for human labor. Robert Theobald, the widely quoted author of *Free Men and Free Markets,* maintains that "The guaranteed income is a philosophical principle which argues that every man is entitled to a minimum income at a time when machine can produce enough for all." Moreover,

Provision of income as a right will bring us to understand that money itself is an anachronism in a cybernated era. Money was needed to ration scarce goods and industrial services in the past, but it is a highly unsatisfactory means of determining priorities in a cybernated era. Society will find it more satisfactory, in terms of scarce resources, to distribute many types of goods and services without money payment [Theobald, 1968, pp. 64 and 71].

A constitutionally guaranteed income, he argues, is essential in an era when human labor is no longer necessary to the production of goods. But the fact that "man has a pathological desire to toil" means that he will not remain idle, but will turn his attention to those pursuits that interest him once his basic needs are assured. By eliminating money as a means of motivation, he concludes, people will do those things that make the best use of their talents.

---

[3] The rationale for retirement benefits is similar: Workers (and their employers) pay into the social security "fund" while working, and draw benefits when they retire. But since transfers can be made only out of current output, it must be recognized that the income shift is from workers to nonworkers, including retirees, of any given year. Boulding has summarized the nature of the intergenerational transfer as follows: "One of the things we know for certain about any age group is that it has no future. The young become middle-aged and the middle-aged become old, and the old die. Consequently, the support which the middle-aged give to the young can be regarded as the first part of a deferred exchange, which will be consummated when those who are now young become middle-aged and support those who are now middle-aged who will then be old. Similarly, the support which the middle-aged give to the old can be regarded as the consummation of a bargain entered into a generation ago [Boulding, 1961, p. 45]."

Although few economists agree with Theobald that work is on its way out, technology's role in the development and persistence of high levels of unemployment during the nineteen-fifties and early sixties has been the subject of some concern. Statistics showing that the number of jobs grows each year, despite the inroads of automation, are not completely reassuring; the question is not whether employment increases, but whether unemployment increases. During most of the two decades following the Second World War, the level of unemployment has been high, ranging from 7% to 5%. Only with the Vietnamese war did the rate fall below 4%.

Unemployment of such magnitudes in an era of prosperity and rising incomes and prices inevitably lends support to arguments for guaranteed family incomes. Whether the unemployment is an outgrowth of technological change or a result of lagging economic growth, the problem of providing income to the unemployed remains much the same. The National Commission on Technology concluded in 1966 that income maintenance arrangements needed to be reexamined, not because automation made human labor obsolete, but because we could afford to guarantee incomes to all persons.

We are convinced that rising productivity has brought this country to the point at last when all citizens may have a decent standard of living at a cost in resources the economy can easily bear . . . the road to satisfying life through work is not open to everyone: not to families without breadwinners, not to those whose productivity is reduced by physical or mental incapacity, not to people too old to work. . . . The Commission recommends that Congress go beyond a reform of the present structure and examine wholly new approaches to the problem of income maintenance. In particular, we suggest that Congress give serious study to a "minimum income allowance" or "negative income tax" program. Such a program, if found feasible, would be designed to approach by stages the goal of eliminating the need for means test public assistance programs by providing a floor of adequate minimum incomes [National Commission on Technology, Automation, and Economics, 1966, p. 38].

Thus, not out of fear of technology but because, as a gift of technology, the economy could afford to do so, the Commission proposed minimum guaranteed incomes; "to say don't worry about automation and computers as a cause of unemployment is not to say don't worry [Mangum, 1968, p. 98]." Moreover, the problem of low incomes extends to families whose heads are employed. Mollie Orshansky (1968) estimated that in 1966 one-fourth of all poor families were headed by a man who had worked throughout the year; among poor families headed by men under age 65, five out of six of the heads worked some time during the year. Supplements to the earnings of these workers are clearly a necessary part of any scheme designed to alleviate poverty.

Income without Work: The Schemes

In a recent discussion of income transfer programs, Henry J. Aaron identified three groups of poor: (*a*) the employed and employable (working age males and working age females without children); (*b*) those for whom employment is not feasible (the aged, the disabled, and the blind); and (*c*) mothers of working age, for whom jobs may or may not be available and appropriate. Income maintenance programs aim to replace income losses incurred primarily by the second group, who have suffered death of the breadwinner, retirement from work, disability, or some other termination or interruption of earnings. Income supplements, on the other hand, are provided because incomes are recognized as inadequate and are made without reference to any previous earnings records (Aaron, 1969).

Systems of transfers aimed at restoring income, in particular, the Old Age Survivor and Disability Insurance (OASDI) benefits, can of course be made to serve the poor aged to a greater degree than they now do. Aaron suggests (in addition to the removal of payroll taxes on the poor) that the scheme be reformed to increase the benefits of aged single persons whose incomes are lower than those of elderly couples, to raise minimum benefits, and to eliminate the practice of paying benefits to early retirees. As Eveline Burns has suggested, the payment of a demogrant to all aged persons, plus a wage-related benefit which restores some portion of previous earnings, would serve the poor without disturbing the present structure of social security payments.

Reforms in the present system of welfare payments are currently under discussion, in part because of obvious defects and in part because of the appearance of alternative proposals for guaranteeing minimum incomes. It is generally recognized that the public assistance programs as now run by the various states fail to meet the needs of the 35 million poor. Coverage is restricted, earnings are discouraged, and desertion of families is encouraged. Average benefits vary widely among the states: from a monthly $8.45 per person in Mississippi to $68.55 in New York.

Negative Income Tax Proposals

One of the earliest proponents of an alternative plan was Milton Friedman, who in *Capitalism and Freedom* proposed a simple negative income tax arrangement to replace the present proliferation of public assistance and government welfare programs.[4] Friedman's plan would apply a tax rate of, say, 50% to a family's unused exemptions and minimum standard deductions. If the minimum standard deductions for a family of five were $3,700, and its income, $2,000, unused exemptions and deductions would be $1,700. Fifty percent of this amount, or $850, would raise the family income to $2,850. The effective minimum income in this case would be $1,850, which would be the maximum payment going to a family with no other income.

Numerous variations on this theme have been composed. They involve a symmetrizing of the present income tax structure, with payments being made by the Internal Revenue Service upon the receipt of a statement of income similar to an ordinary tax form. They are noncategorical in coverage. Eligibility (in most proposals, based on the family as a unit) would be determined solely by income and family size; consequently, the problems of determining eligibility in exclusionary categories would be eliminated.

Although many variations have been suggested, they all require decisions on the base to which the rate is to be applied, the tax rate, the effective minimum, and a break-even point. Two possible *bases* have been under consideration: (*a*)

---

[4] This discussion of negative tax proposals and alternative schemes was published earlier (Kreps, 1967, pp. 103–109).

the unused exemptions and minimum standard deductions of a family with no taxable income and (*b*) the poverty-income gap, which is the difference between an officially established poverty line for a particular size family and that family's money income. Although the two bases differ substantially only for very small or very large families, the poverty-income gap is generally considered a better indicator of need.

As to tax rate, it should be noted that the present public assistance system operates under what amounts to a 100% tax—for every dollar earned, the public assistance allotment is reduced by $1.00. This provides a disincentive to work. The negative income tax attempts to provide some work incentive by allowing the poor to keep a percentage of their earnings in addition to the payment. This means a tax rate considerably lower than 100%. Not only does a 100% rate eliminate the monetary incentive to work, but it also could result in a much greater cost to the economy.

The effective *minimum income* can be either a stated floor or simply the amount paid on a particular scale to a family with zero income. The *break-even point* is that point at which a family's tax liability equals its guaranteed income, and thus the payment becomes zero.

While endorsing the principle of negative income taxation, Robert Lampman views the scheme as a supplement to other welfare programs. Public assistance payments should be greatly reduced by negative taxes under his proposals, but he would not eliminate Old Age Survivor and Disability Health Insurance (OASDHI) benefits, for example (Lampman, 1964, 1965). In one of his plans he suggests a $750 allowance for families with incomes up to $1,500, with a reduction of 50% in the allowance for any income over $1,500. In this manner, he would provide some work incentive for low-income workers. But since the benefits are clearly inadequate for families with the lowest incomes, the scheme relies on public assistance to supplement the allowance. Another of his plans calls for an effective minimum of $1,500, with the poverty-income level of $3,000 for a family of four, and negative tax rates that vary inversely with the income. If the family's income is $500, its poverty-income gap is $2,500, and payment at 45% of the gap would add $1,125, for a total income of $1,625. For a family with a $2,000 income, payment at 25% of the gap would add $250 to the income. This plan concentrates its benefits on the poorest of the poor, but like all negative income tax plans would reach many people who are working and not on relief yet whose incomes are considered inadequate by today's standard.

James Tobin would have an income guarantee high enough to raise those families with no other income out of poverty and a tax rate low enough to provide incentives for those who can work. For example, if the guarantee were to equal the $3,000 poverty line for a family of four, and the tax rate were set at 50%, a family with an income of $2,000 would receive $2,000 ($3,000 less 50% of its previous income), making its total income $4,000. He points out that if the income guarantee is to be sufficient to support a family, and still provide an incentive to work, it is impossible to avoid making payments to families who are above the poverty line. (In the preceding example, the break-even point would be an income of $6,000, Tobin, 1965.)

This can be avoided in any plan which provides a reasonable income floor and less than a 100% rate, but only at the cost of producing what has been called the "notch" effect. If a minimum of $3,000, for instance, is specified with a tax rate of 50%, and families with incomes over $3,000 are excluded, a family with a $2,000 income would receive $2,000 ($3,000 less 50% of $2,000), making its total income $4,000. This would be more than that of a family whose own earnings of $3,500 prohibited it from receiving any assistance. The logical thing for the second family to do would be to curtail its earnings until they dropped below the $3,000 level.

In his review of these and other negative income tax plans, Christopher Green points out that the schemes represent an attack on poverty with a minimum of income redistribution; further, that the plans allow the poor to benefit from tax cuts where the cuts include an increase in the negative rate. Tax reductions at present do not benefit the poor directly, whether the tax rate is being reduced or the level of personal exemptions and deductions is being raised (Green, 1967, p. 61). With Lampman, he emphasizes the fact that guaranteed incomes are not a substitute for long-range programs designed to increase labor productivity: "It is not inconsistent to provide money income for the poor and at the same time make government expenditures for raising the productivity of the poor [Green, 1967, pp. 8–9]."

Problems and Alternatives

The negative income tax shares with other guaranteed income plans an essential component: It involves a direct transfer of money to the poor. Consequently, the tax schemes face the same initial problem as other plans offering this guarantee, namely, that of avoiding payments to the nonpoor while at the same time making the guarantee adequate and avoiding the disincentive characteristic of public assistance programs. Moreover, any of the plans would be very costly even if restricted to those below the poverty line. (For cost estimates see Green, 1967, Appendix D, pp. 188–194.) Although calculations of cost must take into account the amount of reduction in public assistance expenditures, it is difficult to see how public assistance can be eliminated entirely without leaving some families worse off than they are at present.

There would also be difficulties in the administration of such a program. If payment were made at the end of a year on the basis of a statement of that year's income, the money would not be available when it was needed. Payment on the basis of estimated income would likely require adjustment at the end of the year, and it might be almost impossible for a poor family to return overpayments. This difficulty could be eased somewhat by quarterly or monthly statements.

Objections have been raised to having such a program administered entirely by the federal government, not only by opponents of "big government," but also by those who feel that local workers can do a better job. It is argued that the need is to individualize benefits not nationalize them, and that the Internal Revenue Service cannot be expected to be more sympathetic to the problems of the poor than present welfare officials.

Finally, criticisms of guaranteed income plans in general are relevant to the negative income tax. There is the question of whether a guaranteed income might lower the already low mobility of the poor, making it even less likely that they will move to sections of the country where jobs are more readily available. Congressman Thomas B. Curtis has suggested that any guaranteed income will lower the incentive to save, raise the propensity to consume, and thus threaten investment (Curtis, 1967).

Several alternatives to the negative income tax have been proposed; revision of the public assistance system is one suggestion. Benefits and coverage should be expanded, additional public services provided, and the means test simplified. The poor are not a homogeneous group, the argument runs, and a single program cannot be expected to meet the needs of all. Interestingly enough, the Advisory Council on Public Welfare has suggested a revision of the public assistance system which would turn it into a form of guaranteed income plan. The federal government would establish an income floor and provide the states with all the necessary funds. Eligibility would be determined entirely by need. This plan carries the same disadvantage as the present public assistance system or a negative income tax with a 100% rate: It eliminates the monetary incentive to work. Lowering the rate would lead to payments to families above the floor; excluding these families would result in the notch effect.

Some time ago Daniel Moynihan suggested a monthly family allotment of $10 per child, regardless of income; 60% of all poor families, he pointed out, have children. However, the objections were raised that this amount was not adequate for the poor, and also that it would help families who were not poor and who had 75% of the children.

Some economists, Leon Keyserling in particular, feel that while some forms of assistance are necessary and should be expanded for those who are unable or should not work, the emphasis on a guaranteed income is in itself defeatist. They would recommend instead guaranteed full employment with the government as the "employer of last resort." Keyserling points out that there are more than enough unmet needs in the public sector to avoid the inference of "make work" (Keyserling, 1967).

In rebuttal, proponents of the negative income tax argue that it would be an effective way of filling the poverty-income gap without discouraging the incentive to work. It would help the *working* poor—a group largely neglected by present assistance systems. It would eliminate the need for a huge welfare apparatus. It would provide a national assistance minimum, and the present wide state variations in welfare payments would be eliminated. Finally, it would be impersonally and impartially administered, with income and family size being the only criteria.

Income without Work: The Issues

Negative income taxation has been classified as a watered-down version of social dividend taxation, which in turn is defined as a

Tax-transfer system in which every family begins the year with an income guarantee . . . . The essence of social dividend taxation is that it combines negative and positive taxes in such a way as to build a floor under the income of every family. It requires the tax system to raise revenues to finance the guaranteed minimum income to everybody as well as to finance other public services [Green, 1967, p. 54].

The Question of Costs

The immediate objection raised to any scheme of guaranteed income is that of the cost involved. Cost estimates vary, depending largely on the size of the individual or family allowance. James Tobin's plan for a basic annual allowance of $400 per person, with an upper limit of $2,700 per family, was estimated to cost about 14 billion dollars based on 1962 income data (Tobin, 1965). In the early days of the antipoverty program, the Council of Economic Advisers' figure of 11 billion dollars was widely cited as the cost of raising families to a $3,000 and individuals to a $1,500 minimum. Translated into alternative uses, 11 billion dollars amounted to about one-fifth of the annual defense budget and less than 2% of the gross national product.

When the economy's output is growing and tax revenues are rising (even without increases in tax rates), aggregate costs of these magnitudes do not appear prohibitive. But an expenditure on any program can be judged as appropriate only when its advantages outweigh those accruing from a similar expenditure on some alternative program. A majority view would probably hold in favor of income supplements over military spending, space exploration, and, very likely, over foreign aid; but these budget items do not exhaust the list of possible priorities. What of an alternative expenditure to provide medical and dental care to low-income families? Would improved educational facilities make a more significant long-run contribution to the elimination of poverty? Rather than offer the income directly, would the provision for certain basic needs (housing, food, and health care) at public expense be a better use of the funds? Extending the range of social goals to other possible priorities, we find that

> We could rebuild all our cities or abolish poverty; or replace all the obsolete plant and equipment in private industry; or we could . . . develop the hardware to get us to Mars and back before the year 2000. We could make some progress on all the goals, perhaps substantial progress on many, but we cannot accomplish all our aspirations at the same time [Lecht, 1965, p. 5].

The question of costs is further complicated by the role of wage incentives. Will the guarantee of some minimum income reduce the amount of effort devoted to work, thereby reducing total output? To the extent that this reduction occurs, the cost of the income-supplement program is higher than the dollar cost of providing the allowance; it must include also the cost of the foregone output. Clearly, one's appraisal of the extent of our reliance on income as a motivating force in getting work done conditions his estimate of the true costs of income guarantees. Moreover, since income supplements must be paid for with tax revenues, one must reckon with a potential reduction in work effort on the part of the group whose incomes are being taxed to finance the allowances.

The Question of Incentives

The disincentive effect of income taxes has been exaggerated, according to George F. Break. From interviews with accountants and solicitors who were subject to high marginal and average tax rates (and who could control their work hours), he found the following attitude:

> When you get right down to it, I am working as hard as I ever worked. I complain bitterly about how little I am allowed to keep of every pound I earn, but I go on working just the same [Break, 1957, p. 548].

The author notes that several factors will tend to cause workers to offer the same amount of labor despite the imposition of income taxes: the tendency toward larger families, which increases commitments; higher divorce rates; increasing demand for consumer durables; the entrance of wives to the labor force, notwithstanding higher marginal tax rates; greater domestic and foreign travel which stimulates demand; greater urbanization, with the "bandwagon" effect on consumption patterns; decreasing flexibility of the individual's working habits, which reduces the individual's propensity to change his working hours in response to a tax increase.

The question of whether the members of low-income families would work less if they no longer had to rely on earnings to provide the basic necessities is difficult to subject to empirical test (David & Miller, 1968). The threat that certain jobs—the less pleasant and generally lowest paying ones—would not get done continues in many quarters to argue against income guarantees for the male of working age. Even though such jobs would presumably enable the family to achieve a level of living above the minimum standard, there persists some skepticism that the availability of additional income would provide adequate work incentive if a subsistence level of living is assured.

Conflicting views are currently being expressed as to the effect of public income subsidies on the supply of labor. Lowell Gallaway questions the contribution a negative income tax plan would make to the income of the poor, except for those poor whose labor force activity is quite limited; it is possible, he suggests, that the receipt of a transfer actually lowers a family's income by reducing work effort and lowering earnings (Gallaway, 1966). Brehm and Saving (1964), investigating the impact of general assistance payments, conclude that there are higher proportions of the population receiving payments in the states with higher average levels of general assistance payment transfers. By implication, work is more often withheld in order to receive the welfare check, when the check is larger. Kasper's (1968) study contradicts these findings, however. He argues that differences in labor market conditions, not differences in the level of welfare payments, are primarily responsible for interstate variation in the proportion of people drawing general assistance. Two other models again present diverse conclusions. Leuthold (1968) finds that, on the average, work effort increases somewhat for the population as a whole in response to the introduction of a formula transfer program. Perlman, in the same issue of the same journal, notes that in using a negative tax

The only possibility for maintaining labor supply would come about through a technique of making the marginal income received greater than the amount earned without a negative tax. This would require not only that the subsidy be graduated, but graduated in such a way that the extra amount received would increase with the number of hours worked near the full schedule for these workers receiving a subsidy [Perlman, 1968, pp. 298–299].

Except in some such plan as the one Perlman describes, it is generally thought that some work effort will be sacrificed in a program of subsidies to low-income families. Christopher Green, one spokesman for a negative income tax, summarizes the usual reasoning of the economist:

If both income and leisure are "normal" goods, and if preference patterns are not changed as a result of implementation of a negative income tax plan, utility maximizing individuals will choose to work less in the presence of negative tax payments than in their absence. How much less depends on the level of the income guarantee, the negative (marginal) tax rate, and the shape of the utility function [Green, 1967, p. 280].

Questions of Equity

Programs which might discourage work are seen as deterrents to a high rate of growth in output. Threats to the *size* of the nation's output are only one part of the objection, however; even stronger protests are heard because of the possible impact on the *distribution* of that output. In general, the distribution scheme espoused for our economy has been one which confers income in accordance with productivity. Such a reward system is found acceptable because it is thought to be fair—"a man gets what he is worth and he is worth what he gets." Leaving aside the difficulties of measurement, which might provide evidence as to whether productivity does in fact determine wages, equity under this distributive scheme is frequently challenged on the basis that inadequate educational opportunities limit the productivity and hence the earnings of certain groups. Expenditures made for the purpose of improving educational opportunities are thus generally acceptable, since they enable the citizenry to be self-supporting.

The idea of using public funds to provide income, rather than the means of learning to earn income, is in many circles vehemently opposed, as long as there is any work alternative. The work ethic lends strong endorsement to present wage-employment arrangements in which persons who receive income from public transfers are expected to be old or disabled. Any scheme which appears to be rewarding idleness by guaranteeing a minimum income is thus opposed by many who think of income as a reward for effort. In short, equity arguments against minimum income guarantees are similar to the protests against income redistribution in general: The receipt of earnings is *prima facie* evidence that the income is in fact earned, or deserved. By implication, those without earnings are undeserving, and our reward system cannot confer pay on the undeserving.

Some Points of Conflict

There is a conflict of objectives in the negative income tax proposals, a German economist noted recently. The antipoverty schemes, aiming for greater equality of income, call for subsidies with negative tax rates such as those proposed in the United States. The more assistance given to the very poor, the faster these rates drop with a rise in income. But a work-incentive scheme, designed to increase the total product available to all, calls for rising subsidies with rising income, in the manner of the German system. Clearly, these payments discriminate against the poor. "We are left with the conclusion," he writes, "that the incentive and distributional objectives of the negative income tax plans are inherently contradictory [Kisker, 1967, p. 104]."

We are caught in more than one contradiction, in fact. For one thing, we would like to guarantee a minimum income to all families regardless of current job status, and yet we are eager to preserve work incentives by making income depend on work. For another, we insist that the reward system pay for performance, which means it must penalize lack of performance if only by withholding payments, despite our recognition that human capabilities differ widely from one person to the next. Still a third set of problems arises from our ambivalence as to the meaning and role of work. In the best Puritan tradition, we claim that work is ennobling. But in all economic analysis, only income and leisure are desirable; the disutility of work is immediately recognized. Finally, we have given little thought to a possible substitute for pay, although there may be other equally strong motivating forces that would serve the interests of the individual and society.

In the midst of these conflicting notions, we are reminded by one economist of the constraints that have always been imposed on any move to separate income from work. Programs to provide income in lieu of work "have been established on the conviction that they will promote the efficiency of the economy or at least will not make it less efficient [Carlson, 1962]." Future measures, he predicts, will be subject to the same pragmatic test. If he is correct, it is difficult indeed to imagine any decisive move to sever income from work as long as we reason that "pay is the most important single motivator used in our organized society [Haire et al., 1963, p. 3]."

References

Aaron, H. J. Income transfer programs. *Monthly Labor Review,* 1969, **92,** 50–54.

Boulding, K. E. Reflections on poverty. In, *The social welfare forum.* New York: Columbia University Press, 1961.

Break, G. F. Income taxes and incentives to work: An empirical study. *American Economic Review,* 1957, **47,** 548.

Brehm, C. T., & Saving, T. R. The demand for general assistance payments. *American Economic Review,* 1964, **54,** 1002–1018.

Carlson, V. *Economic security in the United States.* New York: McGraw-Hill, 1962.

Curtis, T. B. Income guarantees: A spectrum of opinion. *Monthly Labor Review,* 1967, **90,** III–IV.

David, M., & Miller, R. F. The work leisure choice under a tax and transfer regime. University of Wisconsin, Social Systems Research Institute, Madison, 1968. (Mimeo)

Gallaway, L. Negative income tax and the elimination of poverty. *National Tax Journal,* 1966, **19,** 298–307.

Green, C. *Negative taxes and the poverty problem.* Washington, D. C.: Brookings Institution, 1967.

Haire, M., Ghiselli, E. E., & Porter, L. W. Psychological research on pay: An overview. *Industrial Relations,* 1963, **3,** 3–4.

Kasper, H. Welfare payments and work incentive: Some determinants of the rates of general assistance payments. *Journal of Human Resources,* 1968, **3,** 86–110.

Keyserling, L. H. Guaranteed annual incomes. *The New Republic,* 1967, **156**(March 18), 20–23.

Kisker, K. P. A note on the negative income tax. *National Tax Journal,* 1967, **20,** 104.

Kreps, J. M. Negative outlook for the negative income tax. In, *Increasing understanding of public problems and policies.* Chicago: The Farm Foundation, 1967.

Lampman, R. Programs for poverty. In, *Proceedings of the 57th Annual Conference of the National Tax Association.* Pittsburgh: National Tax Association, 1964.

Lampman, R. Approaches to the reduction of poverty. *American Economic Review, Papers and Proceedings,* 1965, **55,** 521–529.

Lecht, L. *The dollar cost of our national goals.* Washington, D. C.: National Planning Association, 1965.

Leuthold, J. H. An empirical study of formula income transfers and the work decision of the poor. *Journal of Human Resources,* 1968, **3,** 312–323.

Mangum, G. L. The computer in the American economy. In T. A. Naylor (Ed.), *The impact of the computer on society.* Atlanta: Southern Regional Education Board, 1968.

National Commission on Technology, Automation, and Economic Progress. *Technology and the American economy.* Washington, D. C.: United States Government Printing Office, 1966.

Orshansky, M. The shape of poverty in 1966. *Social Security Bulletin,* 1968, March, 14–15.

Perlman, R. A negative income tax plan for maintaining incentives. *Journal of Human Resources,* 1968, **3,** 298–299.

Theobald, R. The guaranteed income in perspective. In T. A. Naylor (Ed.), *The impact of the computer on society.* Atlanta: Southern Regional Education Board, 1968.

Tobin, J. Improving the economic status of the Negro. *Daedalus,* 1965, **94,** 889–895.

The Experience of Living in Cities: A Psychological Analysis[1]

STANLEY MILGRAM

The author is a professor of psychology at the Graduate Center of the City University of New York. In 1960 he received his PhD in social psychology from Harvard University, and in 1964 the American Association for the Advancement of Science awarded him its sociopsychological prize for his research on obedience to authority.

When I first came to New York it seemed like a nightmare. As soon as I got off the train at Grand Central I was caught up in pushing, shoving crowds on 42nd Street. Sometimes people bumped into me without apology; what really frightened me was to see two people literally engaged in combat for possession of a cab. Why were they so rushed? Even drunks on the street were bypassed without a glance. People didn't seem to care about each other at all.

This statement represents a common reaction to a great city, but it does not tell the whole story. Obviously, cities have great appeal because of their variety, eventfulness, possibility of choice, and the stimulation of an intense atmosphere that many individuals find a desirable background to their lives. Where face to face contacts are important, the city is unparalleled in its possibilities. It has been calculated by the Regional Plan Association (1969) that in Nassau county, a suburb of New York City, an official can meet 11,000 others with whom he may do business within 10 minutes of his office by foot or car. In Newark, a moderate-sized city, he could see more than 20,000 persons. But in midtown Manhattan an office worker can meet 220,000 persons within 10 minutes of his desk. There is an order of magnitude increment in the communication possibilities offered by a great city. That is one of the bases of its appeal and, indeed, of its functional necessity. The city provides options that no other social arrangement permits. But there is a negative side also, as we shall see.

Granted that cities are indispensable in a complex society, we may still ask what contribution psychology can make to understanding the experience of living in

---

[1] This paper is based on an Invited Address presented to the Division of General Psychology at the Annual Meeting of the American Psychological Association, Washington, D. C., September 2, 1969.

Barbara Bengen worked closely with the author in preparing the present version of this paper, and its expository values reflect her skill. The author wishes to express thanks to Gary Winkel, editor of *Environment and Behavior,* for useful suggestions and advice.

Reprinted with permission from *Science,* March 13, 1970. Copyrighted by the American Association for the Advancement of Science, 1970.

them. What theories are relevant? How can we extend our knowledge of the psychological aspects of life in cities through empirical inquiry? If empirical inquiry is possible, along what lines should it proceed? In short, where do we start in the construction of urban theory and in laying out lines of research?

Observation is the indispensable starting point. Any observer in the streets of midtown Manhattan will see: (*a*) large numbers of people, (*b*) high density, and (*c*) heterogeneity of population. These three factors need to be at the root of any sociopsychological theory of city life, for they condition all aspects of our experience in the metropolis. Wirth (1938), if not the first to point to these factors, is nonetheless the sociologist who relied most heavily on them in his analysis of the city. Yet, for a psychologist there is something unsatisfactory about Wirth's theoretical variables. *Numbers, density,* and *heterogeneity* are demographic facts, but they are not yet psychological facts. They are external to the individual. Psychology needs an idea that links the individual's *experience* to the demographic circumstances of urban life.

One link is provided by the concept of *overload*. This term, drawn from systems analysis, refers to the inability of a system to process inputs from the environment because there are too many inputs for the system to cope with, or because successive inputs come so fast that Input A cannot be processed when Input B is presented. When overload is present, adaptations occur. The system must set priorities and make choices. Input A may be processed first while B is kept in abeyance, or one input may be sacrificed altogether. City life, as we experience it, constitutes a continuous set of encounters with adaptations to overload. Overload characteristically deforms daily life on several levels, impinging on *role performance,* evolution of *social norms, cognitive functioning,* and the *use of facilities.*

The concept has been implicit in several theories of urban experience. Simmel (1950) pointed out that since urban dwellers come into contact with vast numbers of people each day, they conserve psychic energy by becoming acquainted with a far smaller proportion of people than their rural counterparts and by maintaining more superficial relationships even with these acquaintances. Wirth (1938) points specifically to "the superficiality, the anonymity, and the transitory character of urban social relations," and to the loss of community that produces "the state of *anomie,* or the social void." Simmel notes as well that the high density of cities encourages inhabitants to create distance in social contacts to counteract the overwhelming pressures of close physical contact. The greater the number and frequency of human contacts the less time, attention, and emotional investment one can give to each of them, thus, the purported blasé and indifferent attitude of city dwellers toward each other.

One adaptive response to overload, therefore, is that *less time is given to each input.* A second adaptive mechanism is that *low priority inputs are disregarded.* Principles of selectivity are formulated so that the investment of time and energy is reserved for carefully defined inputs (e.g., the urbanite disregards a drunk, sick on the street, as he purposefully navigates through the crowd). Third, *boundaries are redrawn in certain social transactions so that the overloaded system can shift the burden to the other party in the exchange*; for example, harried New York bus drivers once made change for customers, but now this responsibility has been shifted to the client who must have the exact fare ready. Fourth, *reception is blocked off prior to entering a system*; city dwellers increasingly use unlisted telephone numbers to prevent individuals from calling them, and a small but growing number resort to keeping the telephone off the hook to prevent incoming calls. More subtly, one blocks inputs by assuming an unfriendly countenance, which discourages others from initiating contact. Additionally, *social screening devices are interposed between the individual and environmental inputs* (in a town of 5,000 anyone can drop in to chat with the mayor, but in the metropolis organizational screening devices deflect inputs to other destinations). Fifth, the *intensity of inputs is diminished by filtering devices* so that only weak and relatively superficial forms of involvement with others are allowed. Sixth, *specialized institutions are created to absorb inputs that would otherwise swamp the individual* (e.g., welfare departments handle the financial needs of a million individuals in New York City, who would otherwise create an army of mendicants continuously importuning the pedestrian). The interposition of institutions between the individual and the social world, a characteristic of all modern society and most acutely present in the large metropolis, has its negative side. It deprives the individual of a sense of direct contact and spontaneous integration in the life around him. It simultaneously protects and estranges the individual from his social environment.

Many of these adaptive mechanisms apply not only to individuals, but to institutional systems as well, as Meier (1962) has so brilliantly shown in connection with the library and the stock exchange.

In summary, the observed behavior of the urbanite in a wide range of situations appears to be determined largely by a variety of adaptations to overload. We shall now deal with several specific consequences of responses to overload, which come to create a different tone to city and town.

Social Responsibility

The principal point of interest for a social psychology of the city is that moral and social involvement with individuals is necessarily restricted. This is a direct and necessary function of excess of input over capacity to process. Restriction of involvement runs a broad spectrum from refusal to become involved in the needs of another person, even when the person desperately needs assistance (as in the Kitty Genovese case), through refusal to do favors, to the simple withdrawal of courtesies (such as offering a lady a seat, or saying "sorry" when a pedestrian collision occurs). In any transaction more and more details need to be dropped as the total number of units to be processed increases and assaults an instrument of limited processing capacity. There are myriad specific situations dealing with social responsibility. Specific incidents can be ordered in terms of two dimensions. First, there is the dimension of the importance of the action in question. Clearly, intervening to save someone's life rates higher than tipping one's hat, though both imply a degree of social involvement with others. Second, one may place any specific incident in terms of its position on a social-anomic continuum. Thus, in regard to courtesy expressions, a person may extend courtesies (the social end of the continuum) or withhold them (the anomic end). Anomic conditions, up and down the spectrum, are said to characterize the metropolis in comparison with the small town.

The ultimate adaptation to an overloaded social environment is to totally disregard the needs, interests, and demands of those whom one does not define as relevant to personal need satisfaction, and to develop optimally efficient means of identifying whether an individual falls into the category of friend or stranger. The disparity in treatment of friends and strangers ought to be greater in cities than towns; the time allotment and willingness to become involved with those who can make no personal claim on one's time will be less in cities than in towns.

Bystander Intervention in Crises

The most striking deficiencies in urban social responsibility occur in crisis situations, such as the Genovese murder in Queens. As is well kown, in 1964, Catherine Genovese, coming home from a night job in the early hours of an April morning, was stabbed repeatedly over an extended period of time. Thirty-eight residents of a respectable New York City neighborhood admitted to having witnessed at least part of the attack but none went to her aid or called the police until after she was dead. Milgram and Hollander (1964) analyzed the event in these terms:

Urban friendships and associations are not primarily formed on the basis of physical proximity. A person with numerous close friends in different parts of the city may not know the occupant of an adjacent apartment. This does not mean that a city dweller has fewer friends than does a villager, or knows fewer persons who will come to his aid; however, it does mean that his allies are not constantly at hand. Miss Genovese required immediate aid from those physically present. There is no evidence that the city had deprived Miss Genovese of human associations, but the friends who might have rushed to her side were miles from the scene of her tragedy.

Further, it is known that her cries for help were not directed to a specific person; they were general. But only individuals can act, and as the cries were not specifically directed, no particular person felt a special responsibility. The crime and the failure of community response seem absurd to us. At the time, it may well have seemed equally absurd to the Kew Gardens residents that not one of the neighbors would have called the police. A collective paralysis may have developed from the belief of each of the witnesses that someone else must surely have taken that obvious step [p. 602].

Latané and Darley (1969) have reported laboratory approaches to the study of bystander intervention and have established experimentally the principle that the larger the number of bystanders the less likely it is that any one of them will intervene in an emergency. In any quantitative characterization of the social texture of city life a first order of business is the application of these experimental methods to field situations set in large cities and small towns. Theorists argue that the indifference shown in the Genovese case would not be present in a small town, but in the absence of solid experimental findings the question remains an open one.

More than just callousness prevents bystanders from participating in altercations between people. A rule of urban life is respect for other people's emotional and social privacy, perhaps because physical privacy is so hard to achieve. And in situations for which the standards are heterogeneous, it is much harder to know whether taking an active role is unwarranted meddling or an appropriate response to a critical situation. If a husband and wife are quarreling in public, at which point should a bystander step in? On the one hand, the heterogeneity of the city produces substantially greater tolerance of behavior, dress, and codes of ethics than does the small town, but this diversity also encourages people to withhold aid for fear of antagonizing the participants or crossing an inappropriate and difficult-to-define line.

Moreover, the frequency of demands present in the city gives rise to norms of noninvolvement. There are practical limitations to the Samaritan impulse in a major city. If a citizen attended to every needy person, if he were sensitive to and acted on every altruistic impulse that was evoked in the city, he could scarcely keep his own affairs in order.

Gaertner and Bickman (1968) have extended the bystander studies to an examination of help across ethnic lines. They arranged for blacks and whites, with clearly identifiable accents, to call strangers through an apparent error in telephone dialing. The caller indicates that he is attempting to contact a garage and that he is stranded on an outlying highway. He has just used his last dime attempting to reach a garage but received the present number instead by mistake. The caller then requests that the subject assist him in his predicament by calling the garage; he provides a telephone number and locational information to pass on to the service station.

The experimenters compared the number of persons who called the garage in response to white as opposed to Negro solicitation. White-accented callers had a significantly better chance of obtaining assistance than black callers. The findings of Gaertner and Bickman suggest that ethnic allegiance may well be another vehicle for coping with overload: The white, city inhabitant can reduce excessive demands and screen out urban heterogeneity by responding along ethnic lines; overload is made more manageable by limiting the "span of sympathy."

Favor Doing Based on Trust

We may now move away from crisis situations to less urgent examples of social responsibility; for it is not only in situations of dramatic need, but in the ordinary, everyday willingness to lend a hand, that the city dweller is said to be deficient relative to his small-town cousin. The comparative method must be employed in any empirical examination of this question. A commonplace social situation is staged both in an urban setting and a small town, a situation to which a subject can respond either by extending help or withholding it. The responses in town and city are then compared.

One factor in the purported unwillingness of urbanites to extend themselves to strangers may well be their heightened sense of physical and emotional vulnerability—a feeling that is supported by urban crime statistics. A key test for distinguishing between city and town behavior, therefore, is how city dwellers compare with town dwellers in offering aid that increases their personal vulnerability and requires some trust of strangers. Altman, Levine, Nadien, and Villena (1969) devised a study to compare city and town dwellers in this respect. The criterion used in their study was the willingness of householders to allow strangers to enter their homes to use the telephone. Individually the investigators rang doorbells, explained that they had misplaced the address of a friend nearby, and asked to use the phone. The investigators (two males and two females) completed a total of 100 requests for entry in the city and 60 in the small towns. The results gleaned from middle-income housing developments in Manhattan were compared with data gathered in several small towns in Rockland County, outside of New York City (Stony Point, Spring Valley, Ramapo, Nyack, New City, and West Clarkstown).

TABLE 1

Percentage of Entries by Investigators for City and Town Homes

Investigator	% entries	
	City (n = 100)	Small town (n = 60)
Male		
1	16	40
2	12	60
Female		
1	40	87
2	40	100

As Table 1 shows, in all cases there was a sharp increase in the proportion of entries gained by an investigator when he moved from the city to a small town. In the most extreme case the investigator was five times more likely to gain admission to a home in a small town than in Manhattan. Although the female investigators had noticeably higher levels of entry in both cities and towns than the male investigators, all four students did at least twice as well in gaining access to small-town homes than they did to city homes, suggesting that the city-town distinction overrides even the predictably greater fear of male strangers than of female ones.

The lower level of helpfulness by city dwellers seems due in part to recognition of the *dangers* of Manhattan living, rather than to mere indifference or coldness. It is significant that 75% of all city respondents received and answered messages either by shouting through closed doors or by peering through peepholes; in the towns, by contrast, about 75% of the respondents opened the doors, with no barriers between themselves and the investigator.

Supporting the investigators' quantitative results was their general observation that the town dwellers were noticeably more friendly and less suspicious than the city dwellers. Even city dwellers who allowed the investigators to use the phone appeared more ill at ease than their town counterparts; city dwellers often refused to answer the doorbell even when they were at home; and in a few cases city residents called the security police of the housing development. In seeking to explain the sense of psychological vulnerability city dwellers feel, above and beyond differences in actual crime statistics, Altman et al. (1969) point out that for a village resident, if a crime is committed in a neighboring village, he may not perceive it as personally relevant, though the geographic distance may be small. But a criminal act committed anywhere in the city, though miles from the city-dweller's home, is still verbally located within the city, "therefore . . . the inhabitant of the city possesses a larger vulnerable space."

Civilities

Even at the most superficial level of involvement, the exercise of everyday civilities, urbanites are reputedly deficient. Persons bump into each other and frequently do not apologize. They knock over another person's packages, and, as often as not, proceed on their way with a grump, rather than taking the time to help the victim. Such behavior, which many visitors to great cities find distasteful, is less common, we are told, in smaller communities where traditional courtesies are more likely to be maintained.

In some instances it is not simply that in the city traditional courtesies are violated; rather, the cities develop *new norms of noninvolvement*. They are so well defined and so deeply a part of city life that *they* constitute the norms people are reluctant to violate. Men are actually embarrassed to give up a seat on the subway for an old woman; they will mumble, "I was getting off anyway," instead of making the gesture in a straightforward and gracious way. These norms develop because everyone realizes that in situations of high-density people cannot implicate themselves in each other's affairs, for to do so would create conditions of continual distraction that would frustrate purposeful action.

The effects of overload do not imply that at every instant the city dweller is bombarded with an unmanageable number of inputs, and that his responses are determined by the input excess at any given instant. Rather, adaptation occurs in the form of the gradual evolution of norms of behavior. Norms are created in response to frequent discrete experiences of overload; they persist and become generalized modes of responding. They are part of the culture of the metropolis, and even newcomers may adapt to these manners in the course of time.

Overload on Cognitive Capacities: Anonymity

It is a truism that we respond differently toward those whom we know and those who are strangers to us. An eager patron aggressively cuts in front of someone in a long movie line to save time only to confront a friend; he then behaves sheepishly. A man gets into an automobile accident caused by another driver, emerges from his car shouting in rage, then moderates his behavior on discovering a friend driving the other car. The city dweller, when moving through the midtown streets, is in a state of continual anonymity vis à vis the other pedestrians. His ability to know everyone he passes is restricted by inherent limitations of human cognitive capacity. A continual succession of faces briefly appears before him then disappears. Minimal scanning for recognition occurs, but storage in long-term memory is avoided. (No one has yet calculated the number of faces scanned in a day by the typical midtown worker.)

The concept of "anonymity" is a shibboleth of social psychology, but few have defined it precisely or attempted to measure it quantitatively in order to compare cities and towns. Anonymity is part of a continuous spectrum ranging from total anonymity at one end to full acquaintance at the other, and it may well be that measurement of the precise degrees of anonymity in cities and towns would help to explain important distinctions between the quality of life in each. Conditions of full acquaintance, for example, offer security and familiarity, but they may also be stifling because the inhabitant is under continuous scrutiny by people who know him. Conditions of complete anonymity, by contrast, provide freedom from routine social ties, but they may also create feelings of alienation and detachment.

One could investigate empirically the proportion of activities in which the city dweller and town dweller are known by others at given times in their daily lives, and, if known, with what proportion of those the urbanite and town dweller interact. At his job, for instance, the city dweller may know fully as many people as his rural counterpart. While not fulfilling his occupational or family role, however—say, in traveling about the city—the urbanite is doubtlessly more anonymous than his rural counterpart. (One way to measure the difference in degrees of anonymity would be to display the picture of a New York inhabitant at a busy midtown intersection.

One could offer a significant reward to any passerby who could identify the person pictured. Calculation of the total number of passersby during a given period, coupled with the proportion who could identify the picture, provides one measure of urban anonymity. Results could then be compared with those gleaned by displaying the picture of a town dweller on the main street in his town. This test could also be used to define a person's "neighborhood boundary," that area within which a high proportion of people could identify the inhabitant's picture.)

Limited laboratory work on anonymity has begun. Zimbardo (1968) has conducted pilot studies testing whether groups asked to perform certain aggressive acts while wearing masks administer more shock than control groups without masks. The results were inconclusive, though Zimbardo's findings suggest that if we could create laboratory conditions of true anonymity, more aggressive behavior would result.

A related experiment by Zimbardo tested whether the social anonymity and impersonality of the big city encourage greater vandalism than found in small towns. Zimbardo arranged for one car to be left for 64 hours near the New York University campus in the Bronx and a counterpart to be left near Stanford University in Palo Alto. The license plates on both cars were removed and the hoods opened, to provide "releaser cues" for potential vandals. The results were as expected: The New York car was stripped of all moveable parts within the first 24 hours, and was left a hunk of metal rubble by the end of three days. Unexpectedly, however, most destruction occurred during daylight hours usually under scrutiny by observers, and was led by well-dressed, white adults. The Palo Alto car was left untouched (Zimbardo notes that when it started to rain, one bystander even lowered the car's hood to protect the motor).

Zimbardo attributes the difference in the treatment accorded the two cars to the "acquired feelings of social anonymity provided by life in a city like New York," and he supports his study with several other anecdotes illustrating casual, wanton vandalism in the city. Any study comparing the effects of anonymity in city and town, however, must satisfactorily control for other confounding factors: the large number of drug addicts in New York, the higher proportion of slum dwellers in the city, etc.

Another direction for empirical study is the investigation of the beneficial effects of anonymity. Impersonality of city life breeds its own tolerance for the private lives of inhabitants. Individuality and even eccentricity, we may assume, can flourish more readily in the metropolis than in the small town. Stigmatized persons may find it easier to lead comfortable lives without the constant scrutiny of neighbors. To what degree can this assumed difference between city and town be shown empirically? Waters (1969) hypothesized that avowed homosexuals would be more likely to be accepted as tenants in a large city than in small towns. She dispatched letters from homosexuals and normals to real estate agents in cities and towns across the country. The results of her study were inconclusive, but the general idea of examining the protective benefits of city life to the stigmatized ought to be pursued.

Role Behavior in Cities and Towns

Another product of urban "overload" is the adjustment in roles made by urbanites in daily interactions. As Wirth has said: "Urbanites meet one another in highly segmental roles. . . . They are less dependent upon particular persons, and their dependence upon others is confined to a highly fractionalized aspect of the other's round of activity." This tendency is particularly noticeable in transactions between customers and those offering professional or sales services: The owner of a country store has time to become well acquainted with his dozen-or-so daily customers; but the girl at the checkout counter of a busy A & P, handling hundreds of customers a day, barely has time to toss the green stamps into one customer's shopping bag before the next customer has confronted her with his pile of groceries.

In his stimulating analysis of the city *A Communications Theory of Urban Growth* Meier (1962) discusses several adaptations a system may make when confronted by inputs that exceed its capacity to process them. Specifically, Meier states that according to the principle of competition for scarce resources the scope and time of the transaction shrinks as customer volume and daily turnover rise (see Figure 1). This, in fact, is what is meant by the brusque quality of city life. New standards have developed in cities about what levels of services are appropriate in business transactions.

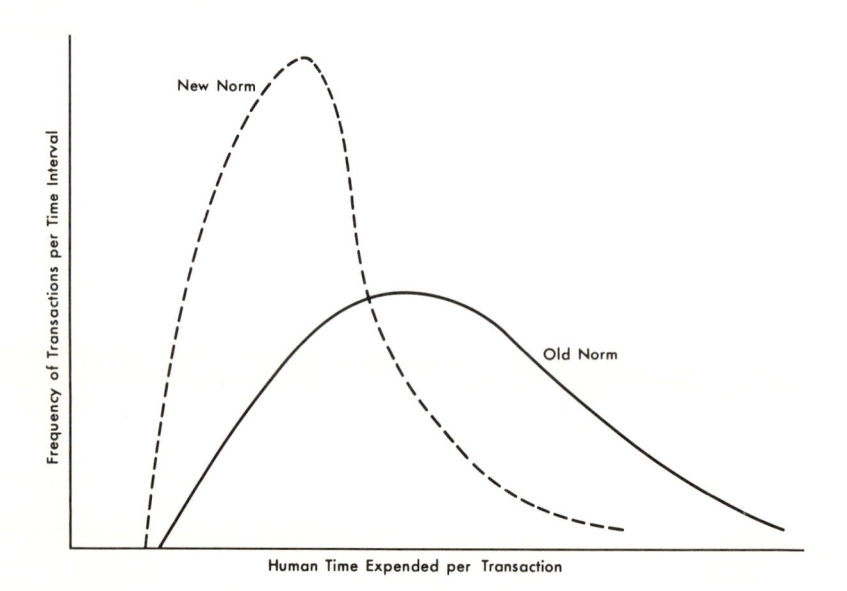

Fig. 1. Changes in the demand for time for a given task when overall transaction frequency increases in a social system. (Reprinted with permission from R. L. Meier, *A Communications Theory of Urban Growth*, 1962. Copyrighted by MIT Press, 1962.)

McKenna and Morgenthau (1969), in a seminar at the City University of New York, devised a study (*a*) to compare the willingness of city dwellers and small towners to do favors for strangers that entailed a small amount of time and inconvenience but no personal vulnerability, and (*b*) to determine whether the more compartmentalized, transitory relationships of the city would make urban salesgirls less likely than small-town salesgirls to carry out tasks for strangers not related to their customary roles.

To test for differences between city dwellers and small towners, a simple experiment was devised in which persons from both settings were asked to perform increasingly onerous favors for anonymous strangers. It was not possible for the investigators to travel around the country extensively, but by making use of a telephone they were able to reach persons in major cities (Chicago, New York, and Philadelphia) and 37 small towns in the same states in which the cities were located. The average population of the towns was 2,727 people, based on the 1960 census. Typical small towns used in the study were Coxsackie, Ravena, and Wappingers Falls (New York); Chenoa, St. Anne, and Fairbury (Illinois); and Doylestown, Sellersville, and McAdoo (Pennsylvania).

Within the cities, half the calls went to housewives, and the other half to salesgirls in women's apparel shops; the same division was made for the small towns. Each investigator represented herself as a long-distance caller who had mistakenly been connected with the respondent by the operator. The investigator began by asking for simple information about the weather for travel purposes. Next the investigator excused herself on a pretext stating "please hold on," put the phone down for almost a full minute, and then picked it up again and asked the respondent to provide the phone number of a hotel or motel in her vicinity at which the investigator might stay during a forthcoming visit. Scores were assigned to the subjects depending on how helpful they had been. Scores ranged from 1 (meaning that the respondent hung up without giving weather information and without an excuse) to 16 (meaning that the respondent remained on the phone during the delay and carried out all the requests).

McKenna summarizes her results in this manner: "People in the city, whether they are engaged in a specific job or not, are less helpful and informative than people in small towns. . . . People at home, regardless of where they live, are less helpful and informative than people working in shops [p. 8]." Representative quantitative results are shown in Table 2. It is important to note that the relatively high median for urban housewives and salesgirls alike does not jibe with the stereotype of the urbanite as aloof, self-centered, and unwilling to help strangers, and that the quantitative differences obtained by McKenna and Morgenthau are less great than one might have expected. This again points up the need for extensive empirical research on rural-urban differences, research that goes far beyond that

TABLE 2
People in Each Category with Scores above Overall Median

Category	City	Town
Home	13(11)	17(12.5)
Shop	16(11)	24(14)

Note.—Figures in parentheses indicate the median for that group. n = 34 for each cell.

provided in the few illustrative pilot studies presented in this paper. At this point we have very limited objective evidence on differences in the quality of social encounters in the city and small town.

The research on this subject needs to be guided by unifying theoretical concepts. As this section of the paper has tried to demonstrate, the concept of overload helps to explain a wide variety of contrasts between city and town behavior: (*a*) the differences in *role enactment* (the urban dwellers' tendency to deal with one another in highly segmented, functional terms; the constricted time and services offered customers by sales personnel); (*b*) the evolution of *urban norms* quite different from traditional town values (such as the acceptance of noninvolvement, impersonality, and aloofness in urban life); (*c*) consequences for the urban dweller's *cognitive processes* (his inability to identify most of the people seen daily; his screening of sensory stimuli; his development of blasé attitudes toward deviant or bizarre behavior; and his selectivity in responding to human demands); and (*d*) the far greater competition for scarce *facilities* in the city (the subway rush, the fight for taxis, traffic jams, standing in line to await services). I would suggest that contrasts between city and rural behavior probably reflect the responses of similar people to very different situations, rather than intrinsic differences between rural personalities and city personalities. The city is a situation to which individuals respond adaptively.

The Atmosphere of Great Cities

The contrast in behavior between city and town has formed a natural starting point for urban social scientists, but even among great cities there are marked differences in "atmosphere." The feel, tone, personality, pacing, and texture of social encounters are different in London than in New York, and many persons willingly make financial sacrifices for the privilege of living within a specific urban atmosphere which they find pleasing, stimulating, or in some way important to their lives. A second perspective for the study of cities, therefore, is to define exactly what is meant by the "atmosphere" of a city, and to pinpoint the factors that give rise to it. It may seem that urban atmosphere is too evanescent a quality to reduce to a set of measurable variables, but I do not believe the matter can be judged before substantial effort has been made in this direction. It is obvious that any approach in this vein needs to be comparative. It makes no sense at all to say that New York is "vibrant" and "frenetic" unless a specific comparison city is kept in mind.

In an undergraduate tutorial I conducted at Harvard University some years ago New York, London, and Paris served as the reference points for attempts at measurement of urban atmosphere.

We began with a simple question: Does any consensus exist about the qualities that typify given cities? To answer this question one could undertake a content analysis of travel books, literary descriptions, and journalistic accounts of cities. A second approach, which we adopted, is to ask people about cities they had lived in or visited. Advertisements placed in *The New York Times* and the *Harvard Crimson* asked persons to give us accounts of specific incidents in London, Paris, or New York that best illuminated the character of each city. Questionnaires were then developed and administered to approximately 60 persons who were familiar with at least two of the three cities. Some of the questions were:

1. Describe an actual event or incident from your experience that seems especially illustrative of the character of the city.
2. Explain what you think this experience reveals about the character of the city.
3. What did the city bring out in you? What did it inhibit?
4. What aspects of the city most lived up to your expectations? What surprised you?
5. Which of the following features—the city's police, taxis, passers-by, subways, retail personnel, bars, parks, traffic, etc.—had the greatest influence on your overall impressions of the city? What did they suggest to you about the city?
6. List about 10 adjectives or sensory descriptions that you consider good words to apply to this city. . . . Try to capture the city's essentials.
7. What marked differences or similarities did you find between this city and either of the other two?

Some distinctive patterns emerged for each city.[2] The distinguishing themes concerning New York, for example, dealt with its diversity, its great size, its pace and level of activity, its cultural and entertainment opportunities, and the heterogeneity and segmentation ("ghettoization") of its population. New York elicited more descriptions in terms of physical qualities, pace, and emotional impact than did Paris or London, suggesting that these are particularly important aspects of New York's ambiance. Most of the adjectives used in these categories illustrate agreement among respondents. The following are some of the adjectives that recurred often:

Sensory	Pace	Behavior
BIG	FAST	ALOOF
IMMENSE	BUSTLING	ANONYMOUS
VAST	HURRIED	IMPERSONAL
HUGE	RUSHING	COLD
MONUMENTAL	FRENETIC	RUDE
TALL	ACTIVE	
TOWERING	TEEMING	
CONGESTED	DYNAMIC	
CROWDED	SPIRALING	
SOUND-FILLED	INTENSE	
NOISY		

A contrasting profile emerges for London, for which respondents placed far greater emphasis on their interactions with the inhabitants than on physical surroundings. London elicited such themes as diversity and individuality, but these impressions seem to be drawn far more from the quality of Londoners themselves than from perceptions of the city's institutions or physical layout. On certain themes near unanimity emerged, those concerned with London's tolerance and courtesy. One respondent said: "People in London are more tolerant—whether about dress and hair styles or about the new homosexual set or reform of the penal code or allowing the Communist Party."

Another wrote: "Individuality, eccentricity, and non-conformity flourish. While on the one hand people mind their own business, they are generally more helpful than in New York, certainly more so than in Paris."

A third related: "When I was 12, my grandfather took me to the British Museum . . . one day by tube and recited the Aeneid in Latin for my benefit. . . . He is rather deaf, speaks very loudly and it embarrassed the hell out of me, until I realized that nobody was paying any attention. Londoners are extremely worldly and tolerant."

In contrast, respondents describing New York as aloof, cold, and rude referred to such incidents as: "I went to visit a friend of my father's who, to his knowledge, was staying at the Cloud Club, one of the more posh New York men's clubs. I was informed that the gentleman I sought was not in residence, had not been, and was

---

[2] The analysis of the adjectives used to describe New York, London, and Paris is based on a paper by Nancy Abuza (1967), a Radcliffe undergraduate in the tutorial. The profiles of each city also draw on observations and anecdotes from Donald Hooper (1967), a Harvard undergraduate in the tutorial.

not expected to be. I politely asked the secretary to check further, upon which request I was politely asked to leave the premises."

Another respondent recounts that he saw "a boy of 19 passing out anti-war leaflets to passers-by. When he stopped at a corner, a man dressed in a business suit walked by him at a brisk pace, hit the boy's arm, and scattered the leaflets all over the street. The man kept walking at the same pace down the block."

While New York evoked responses mainly to its institutions and pace, and London mainly to its people, Paris evoked responses divided about equally in number in regard to its inhabitants and its physical and sensory attributes. Cafes and parks were mentioned often as contributing to the city's sense of amenities, but there were many complaints about its taxis, traffic, and excessive tourists. Behavior was often characterized as inhospitable, nasty, and cold, while some found the city as a whole "refined," "charming," and "feminine." One female respondent combined both qualities in her account of an incident in Paris. She had been a regular customer at a dress store, where she saw a salesgirl surreptitiously put a higher price tag on an item as she entered the store. "I was outraged and walked out on principle. Halfway across the street, the girl came running out to re-negotiate. Parisians can be unbelievably avaricious, bitchy, and generally impossible—all superficially covered with a gentle charm."

Many more incidents of this sort need to be obtained, employing careful methods of sampling. By the application of factor-analytic techniques relevant dimensions for each city can be discerned.

We cannot be certain, of course, in what degree these statements reflect actual characteristics of the cities in question or simply tap the respondents' knowledge of widely held preconceptions. Indeed, one may point to three factors apart from the actual atmospheres of the cities that determine the subjects' responses:

1. *A person's impression of a given city depends on his implicit standard of comparison.* A New Yorker who visits Paris may well describe that city as "leisurely," while a compatriot from Richmond, Virginia, may consider Paris too "hectic."

In the questionnaire study, the responses to the questionnaire by the Londoners illustrate the impact of implicit base lines on perceptions of other cities. Londoners described New York as dirty, hectic, rude, intolerant, noisy, etc. Similarly, Londoners found Paris showy, intolerant, dishonest, and rude.

When we examine the impressions of London itself (by Londoners), we get a clear picture of the Londoner's orientation point in evaluating other cities. The following adjectives were specifically listed to describe London:

Behavior	**Tone and Orientation**
COURTEOUS	CLASSIC
RESERVED	SENSE OF TRADITION
RESTRAINED	URBAN
KIND	COSMOPOLITAN
TOLERANT	METROPOLITAN
HELPFUL	

Reciprocal judgments, therefore, seem a useful way to get at not only the city being judged, but the home city that serves as the visitor's base line.

2. *Perceptions of a city are also affected by whether the observer is a tourist, a newcomer, or a longer term resident.* A prerequisite of adapting to continuing life in a given city seems to be the filtering out of many observations about the city that the newcomer or tourist finds particularly salient. This selective process of observation seems to be part of the long-term resident's mechanism for coping with overload.

When my brother last came to New York, he noted the following events:
1. A man drawing circles in the dust on store windows on Fifth Avenue, where the window cleaners had been on strike for some time;
2. A man in Grand Central Station dangling a telephone receiver, still attached to the phone, down inside his pants;
3. A lady sitting at a table in the self-service automat mumbling that she had been waiting three years for her baked beans to be served.

After living in the city for two years, I am no longer attentive to details of this type, though initially they were highly salient. In the interest of psychic economy, the resident simply learns to tune out many aspects of daily life.

One method for studying the specific impact of adaptation on perception of the city is to ask several pairs of newcomers and old-timers to walk down the same city blocks and then report separately what each observed.

Additionally, many persons have noted that when travelers return to New York from an extended sojourn abroad, they are often confronted with "brutal ugliness" (Abelson, 1969) and a distinctive, frenetic atmosphere whose contributing details are, for a few hours or days, remarkably sharp and clear. This period of fresh perception ought to receive special attention in the study of city atmosphere; for in a few days, details which are initially salient become less easy to specify. They are assimilated into an increasingly familiar background atmosphere which, though important in setting the tone of things, is difficult to analyze into its constituent parts. There is no better point to begin the study of city atmosphere than at that moment when travelers have just returned from abroad.

3. *The popular myths and expectations each visitor brings to the city will also affect how it is perceived* (see Strauss, 1968). Sometimes a person's preconceptions about a city are relatively accurate distillations of a city's character, but preconceptions may also reinforce the city's "myths" by filtering the visitor's perceptions of the city to conform to his expectations. American visitors to Paris expect to be cheated by shopowners, taxi drivers, and the man in the street alike. As Feldman's (1968) studies have shown, some of these preconceptions are accurate, but others clearly are not.

The influence of a person's urban base line on his perceptions of a given city, the differences between the observations of the long-time inhabitant and those of the newcomer, and the filtering effect of personal expectations and stereotypes raise serious questions about the validity of travelers' reports. Moreover, no social psychologist wishes to rely exclusively on verbal accounts if he is attempting an accurate and objective description of the city's social texture, pacing, and general atmosphere. The researcher must devise a means of embedding objective measures in the daily flux of city life, measures that can accurately index qualities of a given urban atmosphere.

Experimental Comparisons of Behavior

Feldman (1967) incorporated these principles in a comparative study of behavior toward compatriots and foreigners in Paris, Athens, and Boston. Feldman wished to see (*a*) whether absolute levels and patterns of helpfulness varied significantly from city to city, and (*b*) whether inhabitants in each city tended to treat compatriots differently from foreigners. He examined five concrete behavioral episodes, each carried out by a team of native and a team of foreign investigators in the three cities. In Paris and Athens the foreign teams were American, while in Boston the foreigners were French. The episodes involved: (*a*) asking natives of the city for street directions; (*b*) asking natives to mail a letter for the investigator; (*c*) asking natives if they had just dropped a dollar bill (or the Greek and French equivalent) when the money actually came from the investigator himself; (*d*) deliberately overpaying for goods in a store to see if the cashier would correct the mistake and return the excess money; and (*f*) investigating whether taxicab drivers overcharged strangers and whether they took the most direct route available.

Feldman's results suggest some interesting contrasts in the profiles of the three cities. In Paris, for instance, certain stereotypes were borne out: Parisian taxidrivers overcharged foreigners significantly more often than compatriots. But other aspects of Parisian behavior contradict American preconceptions: In mailing a letter for a stranger (Experiment 2), Parisian treatment of foreigners was significantly better than Athenian or Bostonian behavior toward foreigners, and when asked to mail letters that were already stamped, Parisians actually offered better treatment to foreigners than to compatriots. Similarly, Parisians were significantly more honest than Athenians or Bostonians in resisting false claims to money (Experiment 3), and Parisians were the only citizens who treated foreigners better than compatriots in this experiment.

The distinctive feature of Athens in Feldman's experiments was that, in general, differences in Athenian behavior toward compatriots and foreigners tended to favor *foreigners* significantly, and in percentage terms, compatriots in Athens received worse treatment than their counterparts in Paris or Boston in most experiments.

Feldman's studies not only begin to quantify some of the variables that give each city its distinctive texture, but they provide a methodological model for other comparative research. His most important contribution is his successful application of objective, experimental measures to everyday situations, thus providing more pertinent conclusions about urban life than those achieved through laboratory experiments.

Tempo and Pacing

Another important component of a city's atmosphere is its tempo or pace, an attribute frequently remarked on but less often studied. Does a city have a frenetic, hectic quality, or is it easygoing and leisurely? In any empirical treatment of this question it is best to start in a very simpleminded way. Walking speeds of pedestrians ought to be measured from one city to the next, and from city to town. Students in my undergraduate tutorial filmed pedestrians in downtown Boston and in the town of Concord, and concluded that the mean walking speed of Bostonians was slightly greater than the residents of Concord. Berkowitz[3] has undertaken an extensive series of studies of walking speeds in Philadelphia, New York, and Boston, as well as in small and moderate-sized towns. Berkowitz states that "there does appear to be a significant linear relation between walking speed and size of municipality, but the absolute size of the difference varies by less than ten percent."

Perhaps the feeling of rapid tempo is due not so much to absolute pedestrian speeds as the constant need to dodge others in a large city to avoid pedestrian collisions. (One basis for computing the adjustments needed to avoid collisions is to hypothesize a set of mechanical manikins, sent walking along a city street, and to calculate the number of collisions when no adjustments are made. Clearly, the higher the density of manikins the greater the number of collisions per unit of time, or conversely, a greater frequency of adjustments is needed in higher densities to avoid collisions.)

Patterns of automobile traffic contribute to a city's tempo. Driving an automobile provides a direct means of translating feelings about tempo into measurable acceleration, and a city's pace should be particularly evident in vehicular velocities, patterns of acceleration, and response latencies to traffic signals. The inexorable tempo of New York is expressed, further, in the manner in which pedestrians stand at busy intersections, impatiently waiting for the traffic light to change, making tentative excursions into the intersection, and frequently surging into the street even before the green signal light is activated.

Finally, measurements should be made of the time it takes to conduct simple social transactions, such as buying a newspaper or shopping in a store. Admittedly, this is simpleminded empiricism. However, if the city is indeed "fast," the speed must reside somewhere, probably in the actions of people, and we had best begin searching for it in our attempt to find a quantitative basis for the myth of urban tempo. Perhaps we shall find that a city's pace expresses its values: Time is another scarce resource to be competed for actively among its inhabitants.

Cognitive Maps of Cities

When we speak of "behavioral comparisons" among cities, we must specify which parts of the city are most relevant for sampling purposes. In a sampling of "New Yorkers" should we include residents of Bay Ridge or Flatbush as well as inhabitants of Manhattan? And if so, how should we weight our sample? One approach to defining relevant boundaries in sampling is to determine which areas form the psychological or cognitive core of the city. Which locales are most often identified and accurately located by respondents? The pattern of these well-known geographic locales, coupled with their connecting pathways, creates a "psychological map" of the city, indicating its core and allowing us to weigh our samples most heavily toward the areas considered by most people to represent the "essence" of the city.

---

[3] W. Berkowitz, personal communication, 1969.

The psychologist is less interested in the geographic layout of a city or its political boundaries than the cognitive representation of it. Blumenfeld (1969) points out that the perceptual structure of a modern city can still be expressed by the "silhouette" of the group of skyscrapers at its center and of smaller such groups at its "subcenters" but that urban areas can no longer, because of their vast extent, be experienced as fully articulated sets of streets, squares, and spaces.

In *Image of the City* (1960) Lynch created a cognitive map of Boston by interviewing Bostonians. Perhaps his most significant finding was that while certain landmarks, such as Paul Revere's house and the Boston Commons, as well as the paths linking them, are known by almost all Bostonians, vast areas of the city were simply unknown to its inhabitants.

Using Lynch's technique, Hooper (1967) created a psychological map of New York from the answers to the questionnaire study on Paris, London, and New York. Hooper's results were similar to those of Lynch: New York appears to have a dense core of well-known landmarks in midtown Manhattan, surrounded by the vast unknown reaches of Queens, Brooklyn, and the Bronx. Times Square, Rockefeller Center, and the Fifth Avenue department stores alone comprise half the total places specifically cited by respondents as the haunts in which they spent most of their time. (Other midtown symbols were Central Park, Columbus Circle, Lincoln Center, Madison Square Garden, Pennsylvania Station, the Empire State Building, Grand Central Station, and the United Nations Plaza.) Outside the densely packed icons of the midtown area, however, only scattered landmarks achieved recognition: to the south, Greenwich Village, the Brooklyn Bridge, the Statue of Liberty, Wall Street, the Bowery, and the tenements of Brooklyn; to the north, the Guggenheim Museum, Columbia University, the tenements of Harlem, the George Washington Bridge, and Yankee Stadium in the Bronx. Another interesting pattern is that even the best known symbols of New York are relatively self-contained, and the pathways joining them appear to be insignificant on the map.

The psychological map can be used for more than just sampling techniques. Lynch argues, for instance, that a good city is highly "imageable"—with many known symbols joined by widely known pathways—while dull cities are gray and nondescript. We might test the relative "imageability" of several cities by determinining the proportion of residents who recognize sampled geographic points and accompanying pathways. If such a comparison were made, Paris, I would guess, would emerge as the most imageable major city, yielding a cognitive map that showed not only many famous symbols (as does New York) but a cohesive network of pathways linking them as well.

If we wish to be even more precise, we could construct a cognitive map that would not only show the symbols of the city but would measure the precise degree of cognitive significance of any given point in the city relative to any other. By applying a grid pattern of points to New York City, and by taking photographs from each point, we could then determine what proportion of a sample of the city's inhabitants can identify the locale specified by each point on the map. We might even take blindfolded subjects to each point on the map and ask them to identify their location from the view around them.

PSYCHOLOGY AND URBAN PROBLEMS 169

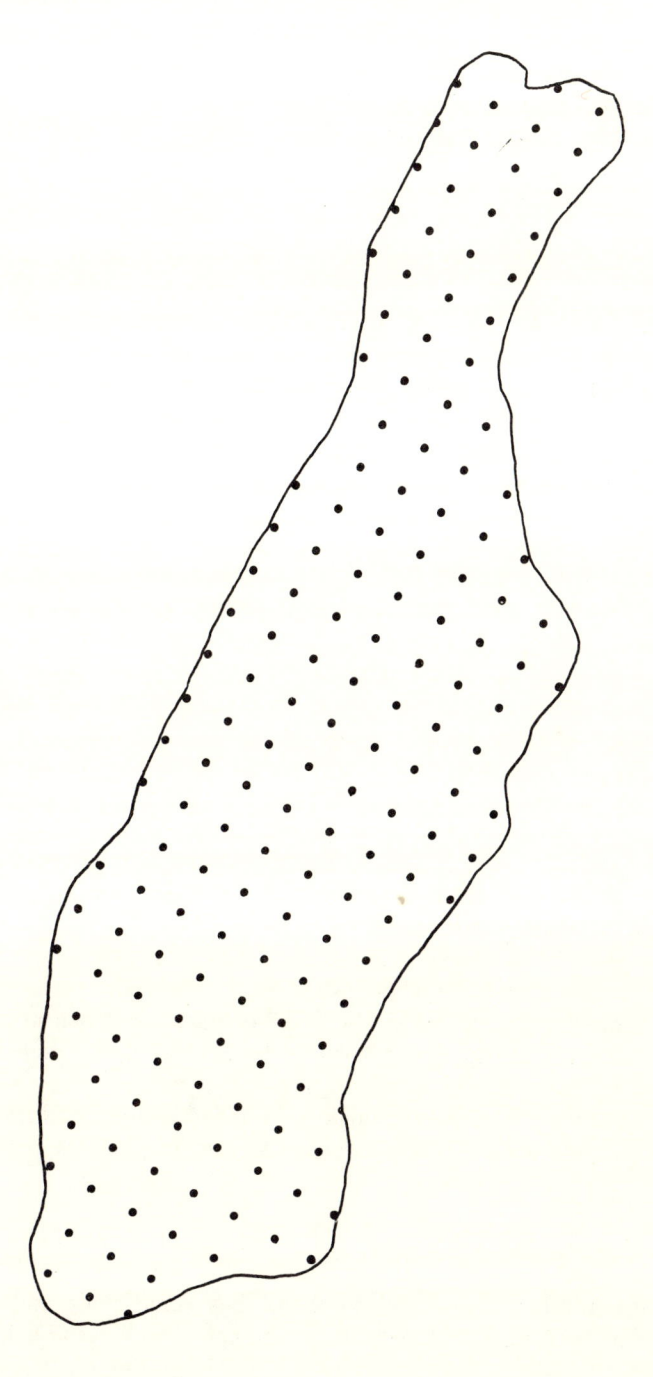

Fig. 2. Psychological map of Manhattan, points are sampled, and on the basis of photographs subjects attempt to identify where each point is located. To each point a numerical index is assigned indicating the proportion of persons able to identify its location.

One might also use psychological maps to gain insight into the differing perceptions of a given city held by members of its cultural subgroups: A map of New York created by a Harlem teenager would no doubt differ significantly from that of an elderly shopowner in Chinatown or a middle class Irish family in Queens. Cognitive maps might even be used to define the boundaries of a person's "neighborhood"—that area within which he is able to identify most of the streets and landmarks.

Application of cognitive maps of cities to current social issues are evident. One could determine whether there is a developmental divergence in the cognitive representations of the cities held by white and Negro adolescents. In the earlier stages of life each holds only a limited view of his city, centering on the immediate neighborhood in which he is raised. In adolescence, however, the white teenager probably undergoes a rapid enlargement of his field of knowledge, learning of opportunities in midtown and outlying sections, and comes to see himself as functioning in a larger urban field. But the process of ghettoization, to which blacks are subjected, may well hamper the expansion of a black adolescent's city. These are speculative notions but are readily subject to precise test.

Cities of the Blind

Finally, the visual aspects of the city are extremely important in contributing to its ambiance. Some would argue that this component is all important—that the "look" of Paris or New York can almost be equated with its atmosphere. To investigate this hypothesis, we might conduct studies using only blind or at least blindfolded respondents—we would no doubt discover that the texture of each city is distinctive even without its visual component.

As E. T. Hall has remarked (1966) the physical layout of the city also affects its atmosphere. A gridiron pattern of streets gives the visitor a feeling of rationality, orderliness, and predictability but is sometimes monotonous. Winding lanes or streets branching off at strange angles, with many forks (as in Paris or Greenwich Village), create feelings of surprise and aesthetic pleasure, while forcing greater decision making in plotting one's course.

Abstractly considered, street patterns are formally identical to a laboratory maze. For 50 years or more, psychologists have studied how a rat moves from one point in a maze to another. He ought to do as much for urban man struggling with complex street layouts in Paris, Tokyo, and Boston. One practical problem psychologists might consider in regard to physical layout is this: In cities with irregular street patterns, what system might be applied in naming streets to make remembering them and locating them as easy and unambiguous as possible?

Sources of Ambiance

Thus far we have tried to pinpoint and measure some of the factors that contribute to the distinct atmosphere of a great city. But we may also ask: Why do differences in urban atmosphere exist? How did they come about and are they in any way related to the factors of density, large numbers, and heterogeneity discussed previously.

First, there is the obvious factor that even among great cities populations and densities differ. The metropolitan areas of New York, London, and Paris, for example, contain 15 million, 12 million, and 8 million persons, respectively. London possesses average densities of 43 persons per acre, while Paris is more congested with average densities of 114 persons per acre (P. Hall, 1966). Whatever characteristics are specifically attributable to density are likely to be more pronounced in Paris than in London.

A second factor affecting the atmosphere of cities is the sources from which the populations are drawn (See Park, 1925). It is a characteristic of great cities that they do not reproduce their own populations, but that their numbers are constantly maintained and augmented by the influx of residents from other parts of the country. This can have a determining effect on its atmosphere. For example, Oslo is a city in which almost all of the residents are only one or two generations removed from purely rural existence, and this contributes to its almost agricultural norms. It is a slow-paced city that lacks sophistication and wit (compared to Paris, a far older city, in which a smaller proportion of inhabitants are of recent rural origin).

A third source of atmosphere is the general national culture the city participates in. Paris is a combination of the adaptations to the demography of cities *and* certain values specific to French culture. New York is an admixture of American values and the peculiar needs of an extraordinary high density and large population.

Finally, one could speculate that the atmosphere of one great city relative to another is traceable to the specific historical conditions under which adaptations to urban overload occurred. For example, a city which acquired its mass and density during a period of commercial expansion will respond to the new demographic facts by adaptations which are designed to serve purely commercial needs. Thus Chicago, which grew and became a great city under a purely commercial stimulus, adapted in a manner that emphasizes business needs. European capitals, on the other hand, incorporate many of the adaptations which were appropriate to the period of their increasing numbers and density. The prevalence of aristocratic values at the time of their growth turned coping mechanisms away from pure considerations of efficiency. Thus the manners, norms, and facilities of Paris and Vienna continue to reflect the idealization of leisure and aesthetic values.

Additional Problems and Opportunities

There are numerous other psychological questions centering on the city that cannot possibly be treated at length in this paper. The personality theorist may wish to ask what part the city plays as a component of individual identity. We know that for many persons who live in great cities it is important that they think of themselves as Parisians, New Yorkers, or Bostonians. Only a few cities so capture the imagination that they come to be integrated in this personal fashion, and we may ask what is distinctive about them.

Cities, by the very fact of their heterogeneous populations permit extension of psychological inquiry. Thus, in New York City we find thousands of Chinese, Ukrainian, American Indian, and Arab peoples. The study of white attitudes toward Negroes (which has dominated the psychological literature on prejudice) can readily be extended to expose the full matrix of attitudes of each ethnic group toward every other. Studies of Chinese attitudes toward Negroes, Negro attitudes toward American Indians, and Ukrainian attitudes toward Jews would provide a broader base from which to understand the principles of ethnic prejudice.

Attention to phenomena of city life will quite naturally give rise to new areas of basic research in psychology which are not limited to urban phenomena. One of the problems concerns the perception of aggregates. We do not know very much about the psychophysics of distinguishing between groups of stimuli. For example, given a series of tones that vary about a mean frequency, what are the main variables that determine whether that series will be perceived as different from or the same as another series that varies about another mean. Obviously, the range, length of the series, and differences between means will be important. But the psychophysics of perceiving aggregate differences has not yet been studied in psychology in any detail. And we need to know more about this basic problem before we can attain a very good understanding of how people perceive and form judgments on the aggregate stimuli of one city relative to another.

Conclusion

I have tried to indicate some organizing theory that starts with the basic facts of city life: large numbers, density, and heterogeneity. These are external to the individual. He experiences these factors as overloads at the level of roles, norms, cognitive functions, and facilities. These lead to adaptive mechanisms which create the distinctive tone and behaviors of city life. These notions, of course, are largely speculative, and need to be examined by objective comparative studies of cities and towns.

A second perspective concerns the differing atmospheres of great cities, such as Paris, London, and New York. Each has a distinctive flavor, offers a differentiable quality of experience. More precise knowledge about urban atmospheres seems attainable by applying tools of experimental inquiry.

References

Abelson, P. Microcosms in a world apart. *Science,* 1969, **165**, 853.

Abuza, N. The Paris-London-New York questionnaires. Unpublished paper, Social Relations 98, Harvard University, 1967.

Altman, D., Levine, M., Nadien, M., & Villena, J. Trust of the stranger in the city and the small town. Unpublished research, Graduate Center, City University of New York, 1969.

Blumenfeld, H. Criteria for judging the quality of the urban environment. In H. Schmandt & W. Bloomberg, Jr. (Eds.), *The quality of urban life.* Beverly Hills, Calif.: Sage, 1969.

Feldman, R. E. The response to compatriot and foreigner who seek assistance: Field experiments in Paris, Athens, and Boston. Unpublished doctoral dissertation, Harvard University, 1967.

Feldman, R. E. Response to compatriot and foreigner who seek assistance. *Journal of Personality and Social Psychology,* 1968, **10**, 202–214.

Gaertner, S., & Bickman, L. The ethnic bystander. Unpublished research, Graduate Center, City University of New York, 1968.

Hall, E. T. *The hidden dimension.* New York: Doubleday, 1966.

Hall, P. *The world cities.* New York: McGraw-Hill, 1966.

Hooper, D. A pedestrian's view of New York, London and Paris. Unpublished paper, Social Relations 98, Harvard University, 1967.

Latané, B., & Darley, J. Bystander apathy. *American Scientist,* 1969, **57**, 244–268.

Lynch, K. *The image of the city.* Cambridge: MIT Press & Harvard University Press, 1960.

McKenna, W., & Morgenthau, S. Urban-rural differences in social interaction: A study of helping behavior. Unpublished research, Graduate Center, City University of New York, 1969.

Meier, R. L. *A communications theory of urban growth.* Cambridge: MIT Press, 1962.

Milgram, S., & Hollander, P. Paralyzed witnesses: The murder they heard. *The Nation,* 1964, **25**, 602–604.

Park, R. E. The City: Suggestions for the investigation of human behavior in the urban environment. In R. E. Park, E. W. Burgess, & R. D. McKenzie (Eds.), *The city*. Chicago: University of Chicago Press, 1967. (Originally published 1925.)

Regional Plan Association (1969). The second regional plan. *The New York Times,* June 15, 1969, **119,** Section 12.

Simmel, G. The metropolis and mental life. In K. H. Wolff (Ed.), *The sociology of George Simmel*. New York: The Free Press, 1950. (Originally published: *Die Grossstadte und das Geistesleben die Grossstadt*. Dresden: v. Zahn & Jaensch, 1903.)

Strauss, A. L. (Ed.) *The American city: A sourcebook of urban imagery*. Chicago: Aldine, 1968.

Waters, J. The relative acceptance accorded a discreditable person in rural and metropolitan areas. Unpublished research, Graduate Center, City University of New York, 1969.

Wirth, L. Urbanism as a way of life. *American Journal of Sociology,* 1938, **44,** 1–24.

Zimbardo, P. G. The human choice: Individuation, reason and order as deindividuation, impulse and chaos. *Nebraska Symposium on Motivation,* 1969, **17,** in press.

psychology and the challenge of early learning

Psychology and the Challenge of Early Learning

"Every once in a while, a culture commits itself to an idea. We seem to have decided that the hope of the future is in the education of the very young." With these words, Kessen opens his remarks contained in this section. The magnitude of the governmental commitment to this idea is indicated in Morrisett's outline of major federal programs devoted to enhancing early learning. The popularity of mass media discussions on how parents can boost their children's IQs gives evidence of the general public's increasing commitment to this notion. Even toy manufacturers reflect an awareness of this trend in their increasing emphasis on the educational qualities of their products.

This commitment to early education presses "the experts" for answers about how best to accomplish it. The papers in this section indicate a variety of ways in which psychological knowledge has contributed to the programs designed for the very young. However, the contributors to this section also point out that there are numerous unresolved issues regarding early education. Exactly what kinds of early learning should we try to enhance? What approaches should be used? How should the outcomes of these approaches be evaluated? The authors that follow speak to these issues, raising further questions and offering constructive suggestions.

Miller opens the section with a discussion of research on the environmental inadequacies many poor children experience. He then describes a carefully designed educational program involving both preschool children and their mothers. The vivid descriptions of his action program and evaluation research provide a useful concrete example of an action program designed with research objectives in mind. It adds a richness of meaning to the more general discussions of Messick and Kessen regarding research on early education.

Both Messick and Kessen point to the need for systematic integration of the research and operational aspects of early educational programs. Properly designed, such integration can allow basic research questions to be conducted in the realistic setting of action programs, thus producing maximally meaningful results. Messick stresses that a simpleminded "Does it work?" question does not result in meaningful answers. (This point is echoed by Guttentag in another section of this book, pages 40–46. She cites the evaluation of Head Start as an example of too simpleminded an approach to evaluation.) Questions that Messick considers more meaningful include: How do the effects of an educational approach vary with the differing characteristics of those being educated? What underlying processes are contributing to the outcome effects observed? What side effects does the educational approach produce? Miller's research provides us with useful examples of such side effects, especially in his data on the effects of mother-child training programs upon other children in the family.

Lesser and Bereiter are both concerned with the content of early educational programs. Bereiter's own research as well as that of others has indicated the importance of education in concepts such as color, size, shape, location, and part-whole relations—especially for disadvantaged children. These are among the concepts approached in novel ways by the "Sesame Street" Educational TV series, discussed by Lesser. He describes how observing the children while they watched the film sequences helped in determining the ultimate content of the material.

Suppes and Morningstar provide a glimpse of the future in their discussion of the use of computers to individualize instruction for each learner. They stress the advantages of computer-assisted instruction particularly for children in educationally deprived areas, citing supporting data from their projects in California and Mississippi which revealed that computer-assisted instruction produced greater enhancement of learning in Mississippi than in California.

In his research overviews, Miller touches on the learning problems which malnutrition may cause. Ricciuti develops this theme more fully as a problem facing the disadvantaged throughout the world. He discusses the evidence of the effects of malnutrition, particularly of protein-calorie deficiencies, concluding that severe malnutrition—especially in the first years of life—is likely to have detrimental effects upon learning. He points out the difficulties inherent in field research on the effects of malnutrition and cautions us against a premature conclusion that mild malnutrition impairs intellectual development, lest we develop unrealistic expectations for the results of a school lunch program.

Disadvantaged Families: Despair to Hope[1]

JAMES O. MILLER

The author received his PhD in psychology from George Peabody College for Teachers in 1963. He is presently a professor of educational psychology at the University of Illinois and Director of the National Laboratory on Early Childhood Education. His major research interests involve variables affecting school achievement and cognitive and motivational development of culturally disadvantaged children.

Before describing the instructional programs and results of a second major longitudinal intervention program carried out at Peabody College, I would like to present the rationale and assumptions underlying this work. Growing logically out of an earlier study, the Early Training Project (Gray, Klaus, Miller, & Forrester, 1966; Klaus & Gray, 1968) conducted by Gray and Klaus, the second program addressed itself to different research questions and developed more extensive and systematic instructional programs.

Rationale

In our work with disadvantaged children and their families, we have taken the stand that environmental inadequacy is the primary factor leading to progressive intellectual retardation and the inability to cope effectively in an increasingly complex society. The cycle of defeat and failure is self-perpetuating, creating an ever more apparent gap between those caught in its grip and those reaping the benefits of an affluent society. The choice point for intervention in the cycle has been during early childhood, around three years of age.

In designing an intervention strategy based on the assumption of environmental inadequacy, two major dimensions of the environment have received attention. The first of these dimensions I shall call the objective environment, or the world of things which the child manipulates. The objective environment provides stimulus input which must be processed, contributing materially to intellectual and motivational development. The objective environment provides feedback to the child as to the relevance of his attending and exploratory behavior, which in turn affects his ability to process information efficiently and to use it effectively. It provides reinforcement for his manipulative behaviors, and this helps to develop a concept of personal control over his world and himself.

---

[1] Invited Address presented to the Division of General Psychology at the Annual Meeting of the American Psychological Association, Washington, D. C., September 1, 1969.

The second dimension, perhaps the more important, is the instrumental environment, or the world of people. The instrumental environment consists of those significant others who mediate between the child and the objective environment by imposing temporal and spatial order upon it. The effective instrumental agent interacts with the child, continuously providing behavior models and arranging appropriate reinforcement contingencies that encourage and sustain continued development and motivation. These considerations mediate for an active, or participating, involvement with a child rather than a passive, or observing, detachment if positive change is to occur.

The child, then, is seen as a part of an ecological system whose elements are in continuous interaction. This interchange can be stimulating and supportive, providing the conditions for continued growth and development of competency, or if either of these major environmental dimensions is inadequate, the interaction will inhibit, restrict, or pervert development. Only by attending to all the essential elements of the system can we expect positive development to occur and to be sustained.

During the child's early formative years, the instrumental environment is primarily the family and, more specifically, the effective instrumental agent is the mother. Our intervention strategy has been directed at the mother as well as the child while we self-consciously recognize that our intrusion adds another factor in the basic ecological system.[2]

A prime source for identifying the variables associated with the development of competency has been the research literature. Particularly, the body of comparative literature which has lent support to the hypothesis of environmental inadequacy has given direction to the development of the instructional programs for both the mother and the child. For purposes of organization, these variables have been divided into four major classes: (*a*) cognitive variables, those skills and abilities which are necessary to function at a level of abstraction required to be competent in a highly technical society, including such abilities as language and conceptual and perceptual skills; (*b*) motivational variables, sustaining states which support continued skill development and maintenance and orient the individual toward a high level of task performance, including such things as need achievement, persistence, delay of gratification, and interest in cognitively stimulating tasks; (*c*) personal style variables, those variables which define approach behaviors in problem-solving situations such as self-concept, success-failure orientation, impulsivity-reflectivity, and time orientation; (*d*) physical variables, such variables as nutritional conditions, large- and small-muscle coordination, and other physiological factors which are necessary to sustain continued performance output.

---

[2] I have come to believe that an essential condition for systematic development is the capacity to accommodate change rather than resist it if the system is to be effective in its mission. It might be taken one step further. Not only must it be able to *accommodate* change (essentially a respondent position), but it must be able to utilize the effects of change to manage and optimize the development of the total system. This concept might be generalized to more molar systems than that of the child. Our institutions, specifically our educational system, seem to be caught up in this very problem, an inability to accommodate and utilize change. The system seems to be much more geared to resisting change and retaining the status quo.

An exhaustive survey of the literature is not presented on these four functional categories related to competence, but some representative research findings are presented as the cornerstone for the development of intervention strategies with both the children and their mothers in our second major project.

Cognitive Variables

Lesser, Fifer, and Clark (1965) studied differential mental abilities, including verbal ability, reasoning, number facility, and space conceptualization as they relate to social class and ethnic group membership. A large group of first-grade children was divided into middle and lower class socioeconomic groups according to their ethnic background: Chinese, Jewish, Negro, or Puerto Rican. Social class placement was associated with significant differences in ability patterns. Ethnic group differences were related to both absolute level of each mental ability and the patterns among these abilities. Interestingly, social class and ethnicity interacted to affect absolute ability *levels* but not to affect ability *patterns*. Since the pattern of performance within ethnic subgroups was similar across social class levels, it appeared that a selective perceptual and learning set was exerted upon the membership. Ethnic groups also apparently place differential importance on skills, depending on the child's sex. The findings of these investigators suggest that ethnic group membership, the child's sex, and patterns as well as level of performance must be taken into consideration when planning intervention programs.

When compared with middle class subjects, disadvantaged children have been shown to be deficient in many aspects of language ability, both qualitatively and quantitatively (Bernstein, 1961, 1962; M. Deutsch, 1965; Irwin, 1948a, 1948b; Jensen, 1963; Siller, 1957). Lower class children spend less time in interaction with adults (Keller, 1963); and when in communication with adults, their verbalizations are significantly shorter (C. Deutsch, 1964). Hess and Shipman (1965) believe that the paucity and impoverishment in the mother-child communication system is the heart of the lack of language development among the disadvantaged. Their assessment of mother-teaching styles and information-processing strategies clearly indicated that the verbal output, the level of conceptualization, as well as the quality and focus of the mother-child interaction, are significantly poorer among lower class subjects. On tasks which require precision and abstract language and conceptualization, M. Deutsch (1965) found that middle class children were superior. Their superiority increased from the first to the fifth grade, leaving him to conclude that early intervention is necessary to offset the accumulative deficit these data reveal.

Recognition vocabulary, vocabulary of use, length of remark, and complexity of sentence forms are all significantly below norms for disadvantaged children (Jones, 1966). These findings are consistent with those of Bernstein (1965), who interpreted his findings as indicative of differential encoding processes between classes. It is his observation that lower classes use a restricted language pattern which functionally retains group integrity and status. Group solidarity is maintained through such a restricted encoding pattern by excluding nongroup members from sharing in the ingroup communication. It restricts the ability of the lower class person to communicate effectively with those outside the group. On the other hand, the middle class develops elaborated codes which are capable of transmitting information at high levels of intensity and meaning within a variety of social contexts.

Such elaborated codes require a high level of abstract usage. The ability to label and classify, to use hierarchial categorization, and to discriminate relevant stimulus cues and dimensions is related to effective informational processing and is substandard among the disadvantaged (Clark & Richards, 1966; Jensen, 1966; Ryckman, 1966; Spain, 1962). Ryckman concludes from his factor analytic study of cognitive abilities, "Since general language ability is the major differentiating characteristic between class groups and is a central element for information processing, it appears highly essential to give language training a central place in the [intervention] program framework [p. 2077]."

Motivational Variables

This category consists of those learned attitudes which maintain the task orientation of the individual and retain task-relevant involvement necessary for achievement. They seem to be highly related to reinforcement contingencies and types of rewards available in the environment. Disadvantaged children prefer concrete rewards over more abstract reinforcement in learning tasks (Terrel, Durkin, & Wiesley, 1959), while advantaged children perform at a higher level and prefer abstract reinforcement (Zigler & de Labry, 1962). Disadvantaged children prefer immediate reinforcement over delayed reinforcement even when greater rewards would be obtained under the delay condition. The ability to delay gratification is related to socioeconomic status, higher intellectual functioning, and such family variables as father's presence or absence and conditions of family disorganization (Kahl, 1965; Maitland, 1966; Mischel, 1961; Mischel & Metzner, 1962; Steen, 1966). Strauss (1962) has documented the relationship of deferred gratification and need achievement to social class.

The affluent society has been characterized as an achievement-oriented society. It is not surprising to find that members of the affluent mainstream would evidence a high degree of achievement motivation. McClelland (1955) and his associates have provided much of the stimulation for the study of n achievement. Of particular interest is the relationship of n achievement to family variables. Rosen and d'Andrade (1959) demonstrated that parents of high n-achievement boys were more competitive, took more pleasure in problem-solving experiments, and were more involved with their children than parents of low n-achievement boys. Fathers of high n-achievement boys stressed independence and tended to let their sons develop self-reliance by giving hints to the solution of problems, rather than doing the problems for them. This is an interesting contrast to the mother-teaching styles of Hess and Shipman's (1965) lower class subjects. Just as Hess and Shipman found greater language facility with their middle class subjects, who presumably showed greater n achievement, so Buehr (1965) found that high n-achievement boys manifested less dialect in their speech under achievement-oriented situations.

Personal Style Variables

It is much more difficult to draw a direct line between this group of variables and adequate achievement. Gordon and Wilkerson (1966) suggest that such a variable as self-concept may not be an important dimension of the problem since either positive *or* negative self-regard may be related to high achievement. With that word of caution in mind, we can say that disadvantaged children do evidence significantly lower self-esteem than more advantaged children (Coleman, 1966; Keller, 1963; Long & Henderson, 1967). These feelings of inadequacy seem to be related to failure experiences in the school environment. The concept of personal control implies a feeling of responsibility for that which happens to oneself and is related to social class (Battle & Rotter, 1963). Disadvantaged boys lack persistence in a school-related task and evidence a lower sense of control over the environment than more advantaged children. Poor achievers among the disadvantaged groups give higher evaluative ratings for school subjects in which they are achieving poorly than do better achievers (Greenberg, Gerver, Chall, & Davidson, 1965). These findings seem to be consistent with a greater discrepancy between actual performance and level of aspiration found among the disadvantaged (Hieronymus, 1951; Keller, 1963).

Academic achievement is related to a personal style dimension which Kagan has labeled "impulsivity-reflectivity." The more reflective response tendency is related to higher reading achievement, social class, and intellectual ability (Kagan, 1965; Miller & Mumbauer, 1967).

Disadvantaged children are more present oriented than future oriented (LeShan, 1952). In a study of the relationship of home environmental variables to high- and low-potential success in school among Mexican-American children, Henderson (1966) found that the low-potential families were more concerned with meeting daily needs than providing experiences that would have a future educational payoff.

Schoggen (1967), of our laboratory, in her ecological studies of disadvantaged homes, reports that disorganization can be characterized in terms of lack of temporal and spatial organization. The most disorganized homes do not even have a regular mealtime. Regular mealtime represents the most basic time ordering event by which one can begin to develop time concepts and a future orientation.

Physical Variables

A basic need for productive achievement is a reasonable state of physical health. However, among the disadvantaged, the wherewithal to provide adequate medical care is unavailable. The proportion of the population suffering from chronic ill health because of the lack of medical care rises sharply as income decreases. MacDonald (1966) found that the incidence of chronic health problems is almost four times as great among disadvantaged families (income under $2,000) when compared with more advantaged families ($7,000 annual income and up).

Nutritional deficiencies are probably the greatest single deterrent to adequate physical health. Inadequate and substandard diets, particularly when sustained by pregnant women, are the cause of the higher rate of infant mortality, prematurity, and birth defects among the disadvantaged than any other single cause. Liebow (1967) points out that pregnant disadvantaged women often eat as many as four boxes of Argo laundry starch a day.

Before describing the instructional programs, I would like to describe the research problems to which this intervention project was and is directed. From the experimental standpoint, we have been attempting a systematic assessment of the agents and conditions of change which enhance the diffusion of competency within a family. We are concerned with a spread of effect phenomenon, if you will, within a family as a consequence of active intervention with one or more other members of the family. We have labeled this "vertical diffusion" because the evidence thus far seems to indicate that it is an effect that moves downward. The vertical diffusion effect was first noticed in the Early Training Project (Klaus & Gray, 1968), in which two groups of preschool children had been provided two- or three-week summer school programs and regular between-session home contacts to maintain the progress gained during the summer. The summer program objective was to provide organized experiences designed to enhance the child's chances of coping effectively with formal schooling.

Following the experimental program it was found that the younger siblings of the experimental groups, when compared with the younger siblings of the control or comparison groups, showed a significant 13-point IQ differential in favor of the experimental children. This intriguing post hoc finding was attributed to the intersession contact the project home-visiting teacher had had with the mothers of the experimental children. The home-visiting program had been designed to maintain the effects of summer intervention itself by providing skill development for the mother so that she could be a more effective agent in structuring and implementing activities similar to those which the children were having during the summertime.

Accepting the significant performance difference as the result of a change in the child's ecological system along at least one of the critical environmental dimensions I have suggested earlier provides the raison d'etre for the experimental questions: (*a*) Is the effect of diffusion reliable? (*b*) Is the mother the crucial instrumental agent? (*c*) Will early intervention in the system provide the sustaining conditions for continued growth and development of the child? Assuming the relevant dimension is that of the instrumental environmental agent, the mother, our strategy has been to systematically include her in an instructional program designed to enhance her ability to cope more effectively in the child's ecological system.

The general design of the study included four groups, each receiving a different treatment or intervention program. I will describe each of these four groups but again call to your attention that it is the younger siblings in the family who, while not directly the targets of the intervention program, form the experimental groups with whom we are most concerned from an experimental standpoint. The first group was designated the Maximum-Impact group, in which both the mother and a target child of the family came to the Center for a training program. The mother came to the Center once a week; the child, five days a week. The mother's training program was a sequential process of skill development and movement from directed observations to actual classroom participation in a teaching role. In addition, a home-visiting teacher called at the home to stimulate use of the mother's newly learned skills in the training program. Continual reinforcement was provided in group session meetings, in which the mothers shared successes with their peers. The children's program was a comprehensive developmental curriculum to foster socialization for competence. It centered on the development of aptitudes of skills for environmental mastery and the development of sustaining attitudes necessary for continued growth.

In the second group, the target child of the family was the only member enrolled in a program. In this curriculum group, the child was provided a classroom program which was a replication of that received by the Maximum-Impact target child.

The third group was designated the Home-Visitor group. Here the family had no direct contact with the Early Training Center but was visited in the home once a week by a home-visiting teacher who worked directly with the mother and used the child to demonstrate the techniques and procedures consistent with the classroom programs.

The fourth group was a natural environmental group carefully chosen to match the demographic characteristics of the treatment families. But members of this group received no planned intervention other than periodic assessment and testing.

The children within the classroom groups were at an age which permitted them to begin the first grade in a regular elementary school in September 1968, after being enrolled for two and a half years in the Early Training Centers. Each of the children in the program who was to be a target of one of the intervention programs had to have at least one younger sibling. Preferably the mothers were young and relatively early in their child-bearing careers in order to insure follow-up potential with younger children. Subjects who met these criteria completely exhausted the available population in the 640-unit housing project. We were able to obtain 40 children for our two classroom groups and 20 for our visiting group, however, and on March 21, 1966, the intervention project began.

The specified formal areas of concern have been language maturity, intellectual functioning, concept formation, cognitive style, and variables, such as achievement press, in the home environment conducive to development. While these formal areas of concern have kept us scientifically legitimate, we have collected data on such informal and unobtrusive indices of improved adequacy as the mother's ability to plan, to organize, and to implement appropriate objectives in the home, the upgrading of her own level of aspiration as reflected in improved occupational status, and her use of classroom-learned methods and procedures in instructing her children at home. These may prove to be much more important markers of experimental effectiveness than the traditional psychometric measures.

Instructional Programs

Now to the instructional programs. Because of the differential effect upon the younger siblings in the family, I believe it is crucial to describe both the program for the mother and the program for the target child (not the younger sibling).

Support System Mothers' Program

Most of the mothers were employed as domestic or kitchen help at the beginning of the project. In order to insure that they would not be penalized for participation in the program, they were reimbursed $5.00 for their one-day-per-week participation. In addition, cooperative babysitting arrangements were made in the mothers' groups so that they could attend the training program at the Center. It might be observed that mothers from disadvantaged environments are sometimes criticized for lack of interest in their children when they fail to attend afternoon meetings of the local PTA. To attend the meetings, however, might mean the sacrifice of a day's wages from an already marginal income.

The major objective in the cognitive domain for the mother was to change her pattern of interaction with the child by providing skills and resources which she could call upon to stimulate her child intellectually. Such activities as learning how to read pictures to a youngster, to read storybooks, to play counting and singing games, and to take advantage of those opportunities for intellectual enrichment ever present in the environment were actively stressed in the mother's curriculum. In the motivational domain, the major objective was to develop a better support system for the child, a system supportive of his inquisitiveness, his accomplishments, and his aspirations. Through observation and active classroom participation, the mothers were encouraged to use the positive reinforcement techniques demonstrated for them by the teachers. They were encouraged in their observations to be aware of the child's progress and to support continued development actively. Indeed, the curriculum was so designed that many self-help skills for the mother were included. Planned to develop her own motivations, they were carefully woven into the curriculum. Many opportunities to develop skills in food purchasing, budget management, homemaking tasks, and personal care were included.

The major objective for the personal style variables was to improve the mother's self-concept through the development of skills and to provide a better approach to home management through planning. Thus, predictable mealtimes, more efficient use of her food dollar, and more attractive physical surroundings gave her a feeling of accomplishment and the approbation of her family members as a successful homemaker.

In the fourth domain, physical variables, the development of more nutritional meals is apparent from the foregoing. However, more active family outings and the development of a mother-father bowling league toward the end of the program attest to their growing interest and concern with physical development. They were introduced to agencies such as the medical and dental clinic, where some of them made arrangements for their own medical and dental care.

During the first phase of the mothers' program, the overriding goal was to develop planfulness as the key to development of self- and family organization.

The physical facilities at the Early Training Center include space for observation through a one-way glass around two sides of the classroom. Initially the mothers observed from this area under the guidance of the home-visiting teacher in charge of the mothers' program. She encouraged and reinforced any verbalization the mothers made concerning the ongoing activities in the classroom. As they began to be more comfortable in the setting, the home visitor began to point out the more relevant aspects of the children's classroom program. Of particular concern were the control and management techniques, where positive reinforcement was emphasized for work well done and for the specific accomplishments of the children as they went about their classroom tasks. As the mothers became more attuned to the organization of the classroom for instruction and the purposes the activities were designed to accomplish, they were led in their observations to diagnose specific situations, to anticipate the outcomes, and to predict how the teacher would manage the problems she would meet.

At the same time, the mothers engaged in role-play activities to develop a repertoire of appropriate behavior to work in the classroom. Modeling upon the teacher's techniques and methods, they moved from reading stories to planning an activity lesson and carrying it out with their peers as their students. The observation and role play served to complement each other and to provide a concrete situation in which they could practice their skills.

As the program moved along and as individual mothers were judged to be ready for classroom participation, their initial experience was planned. Their first entry into the classroom was always at the snack period. This provided them the opportunity to interact with the children as they were engaged in a self-reinforcing activity in which behavior control was not a problem. They were encouraged to talk with the children about what they were eating, where it came from, and how it grew.

As they became facile in their interactions with a group of children, they were then introduced to a large group activity in which they had no responsibilities for instruction but assisted in organizing and participated with the children in circle games. This kind of activity gave them more experience with anticipating behavioral difficulties and using positive behavior management procedures.

Next they graduated to an activity in which they had to provide the structure for the situation. Here they could be in charge of a housekeeping corner, a block-play group, or the communications corner with telephones and recording devices. At this step it was necessary for them to plan the activity to some extent and to be resourceful in creating an inviting and stimulating situation for the children.

Finally, a formal lesson was their responsibility. At this level they prepared written lesson plans and carried them out. Following the lesson they evaluated it as the regular classroom teachers did.

The overall objective of the second phase of the mothers' program was to provide a variety of contexts in which skills and abilities learned during the first phase could be generalized. The mothers continued their classroom participation on a regular basis, but small group meetings were held in individual homes on a rotating basis. These were supplemented by individual tutorials. Thus, the social responsibility of organizing and planning a meeting in one's home developed additional skills and provided the opportunity to implement and augment many of the instructional units on home management.

I have gone into the mothers' program at some length in order to develop some crucial points, which I believe are in keeping with the research literature of general psychology. (*a*) The activities were concrete and close to the day-to-day experience of the mother. They were designed to be intrinsically interesting and helpful. The average WAIS IQ of these mothers was approximately 85 at the beginning of the study, suggesting the level of operation that might be expected from them. (*b*) The program had specific objectives, which meant that the operations necessary to obtain those objectives could be clearly delineated. (*c*) The program was planned. Each step in the sequence was carefully designed to provide continuous movement and feedback to the subjects and allow accommodation of unanticipated contingencies. (*d*) The steps in the program were sequential and carefully monitored and guided. Careful program monitoring was important because one could be sensitive to individual differences within the group, providing the support necessary to build in intrinsic motivation for accomplishments. The steps in the program were of just manageable difficulty to insure success, often a new experience to women who have had a long history of failure. (*e*) The program was geared toward self-help, an important factor in providing the basis for developing competency and a feeling of self-worth. (*f*) There was rapid feedback concerning performance. Since the program was so geared that success was almost inevitable, feedback was most often positive, indicating to the mother that she was a competent person.

Socialization for Competence—The Children's Program

The ecological observations which Schoggen has been conducting in the homes of disadvantaged families confirms our assumptions concerning the inadequacy of the role the mother takes as an instrumental agent in the child's ecological system. Perhaps the observation of greatest impact has been the relative lack of structure or organization evident. Few attempts have been observed to impose order upon the physical and temporal environment of the kind with which we are familiar. Certainly this is not confined to the homes of lower socioeconomic groups, but it is an observation that is relatively general among them. It may well be a crucial defining variable in the operational definition of disadvantage.

Following Kelly's (1955) thesis that man is basically a scientist and predictor, I would suggest that structure, order, indeed, redundancy are necessary to developing predictive accuracy. When he can predict events, he can choose appropriate behavioral alternatives to cope with the events, thus exercising a minimal control over them. As predicting skills increase both in accuracy and over greater intervals of time, he is able to exercise even greater control, increasing his opportunity for innovative and creative solutions to the problems which confront him. This is the essence of competency.

Evidence from a variety of sources in the psychological literature suggests that man strives to impose order and structure on the environmental chaos in which he finds himself. More important, there is evidence to suggest that organizing and structuring skills are learned. As the child learns to impose order and structure on his environment, he is able to process information much more economically and efficiently. Efficient informational processing is essential to predicting environmental events. We have assumed that this learning takes place relatively early and is particularly susceptible to retarded development given an inadequate instrumental agent.

Using an informational processing model, the skill development program was carefully constructed to consider all of the conceptual dimensions used by the major sense modalities in the ordering process. For instance, color, shape, size, volume, time, numerical, positional, and whole-part-whole relationships representing relatively invariate conceptual areas were task analyzed according to the molar sensory processes needed to assimilate information. In this fashion the decoding skills for each of the major sense modalities were specified. Once these specifications were made, the abstracting skills necessary for appropriate responses could be generated. On an a priori basis, the developmental sequence of matching (simple discrimination), recognition (appropriate response to a verbal label or command), and identification (appropriate response to introduction of the stimulus) to response of choice (appropriate initiatory activity) became an instructional strategy. Evidence subsequently collected empirically demonstrated such ordering to be correct (Gilmer, 1969).

This elaborate and detailed work, when accomplished, provided a sequential road map around which appropriate activities could be designed to develop the complex of skills we feel are necessary for the child to be competent and able to cope effectively with later school activities.

Careful introduction and ordering of new material and steps of just manageable difficulty helped in moving motivations from an extrinsic to an intrinsic locus. Such a strategy also insured success, which helped to develop task orientation in school-related activities. Since the curriculum was directed toward developing skills and placing order upon one's environment, content—as such—took a secondary role. The basic conceptual skills were assumed to be relatively invariant while content changes over time. Much more important than changing content is the ability to recognize a set of three or five, to understand the positional concepts before, behind, or through, and to discriminate rough from smooth or hot from cold. Content then became a vehicle for the development of skills. A unit approach was adopted which moved from the child himself through the family, school, and local community to urban and farm life. The unit emphasis was on social studies, language, and science. Thus, within the context of ever broadening content areas, the skill development program increased in scope and the child developed ever more finely tuned capabilities.

Equally important to the development of coping skills was the development of attitudes necessary for sustaining developed skills and continuing the developmental momentum. Positive attitudes relating to school-type activities, ability to delay reward, persistence, achievement motivation, etc., were a few of the major sustaining attitudes which were systematically programmed into the curriculum. By carefully sequencing activities and tasks to develop these motivations, the child gained greater control over himself and his environment.

Central to aptitude and attitude development was the careful programming of reinforcement schedules to move the child from a concrete and extrinsic reward system to an abstract and intrinsic one. Careful contingency management was critical to the child's progress and his rapid development in the program.

Our goal has been to develop a curriculum based on substantive research and theory with clearly defined goals and objectives. In this way we believe we are able to delineate the step-by-step procedures for obtaining our objectives which can be communicated easily for application in other contexts and with other populations.

Partial Interim Results

As you might imagine, the mountains of data which have accumulated over the two and a half years that the project has been under way give rise to great fears that we may be buried alive in our own data. First, a few general observations. In our work with various groups of children from disadvantaged environments, we have found that it is not much of a trick to obtain an average Binet IQ score gain of 10–15 points over a year of intervention. This is consistent with the findings of other intervention programs and appears to be about the asymptote which is generally obtained. The real trick is to maintain those gains over a period of time so that the usual picture of progressive decline does not emerge, thus the strategy of a broad program of skill development with a fundamental stress on the sustaining motivations and the support systems with the family to insure continued development. The conclusion of whether or not the approach is sound, however, must wait for several years to follow the children in their careers.

First, let us address ourselves to the question of vertical diffusion within the family. As the younger siblings in various groups have reached an age at which they are capable of taking a test such as the Binet or a comprehensive skill development test based on our curriculum, at least those two instruments have been administered.[3] (See Table 1 and Figure 1.) In all comparisons of the younger

TABLE 1

Orthogonal Comparisons of Younger Siblings' Performance on Basic Concept Test Subtests

Source of variation	df	MS	F
Matching subtest			
$H_1: G_1 + G_2 = G_3 + G_4$	1	1.57	16.18*
$H_2: G_1 = G_2$	1	.006	1.00
$H_3: G_3 = G_4$	1	.002	1.00
Error (w)	76	.097	
Recognition subtest			
$H_1: G_1 + G_2 = G_3 + G_4$	1	12.94	71.88*
$H_2: G_1 = G_2$	1	.004	1.00
$H_3: G_3 = G_4$	1	.05	1.00
Error (w)	76	.18	
Identification subtest			
$H_1: G_1 + G_2 = G_3 + G_4$	1	18.29	65.32*
$H_2: G_1 = G_2$	1	.0001	1.00
$H_3: G_3 = G_4$	1	.28	1.00
Error (w)	76	.28	

Note.—Groups G_1 and G_2—parental involvement; Groups G_3 and G_4—no parental involvement. H represents hypothesis. Adapted from Gilmer, 1969.
* $p < .001$.

siblings in which the mothers have been enrolled in a training program, the younger sibling groups are superior to those in which no parental contact has been maintained. The differences are particularly striking in more specific measures of concept development. In tasks requiring the child to engage in a series of match-to-sample problems, the two mothers' training groups are significantly superior to the non-involved parental groups. These findings are relatively uniform across such tasks as recognition of choice problems involving the examiner's verbal command and identification tasks in which the child must produce the proper abstract label. This would seem to lend evidence to the hypothesized critical role the mother plays as instrumental agent in structuring and ordering the environment. On the basis of these data, it seems safe to conclude that the first of our two experimental questions (Is the effect of diffusion reliable? and Is the mother the crucial instrumental agent?) can be answered in the affirmative.

---

[3] Gilmer (1969) has just completed an extensive analysis of the performance of younger siblings as a doctoral dissertation.

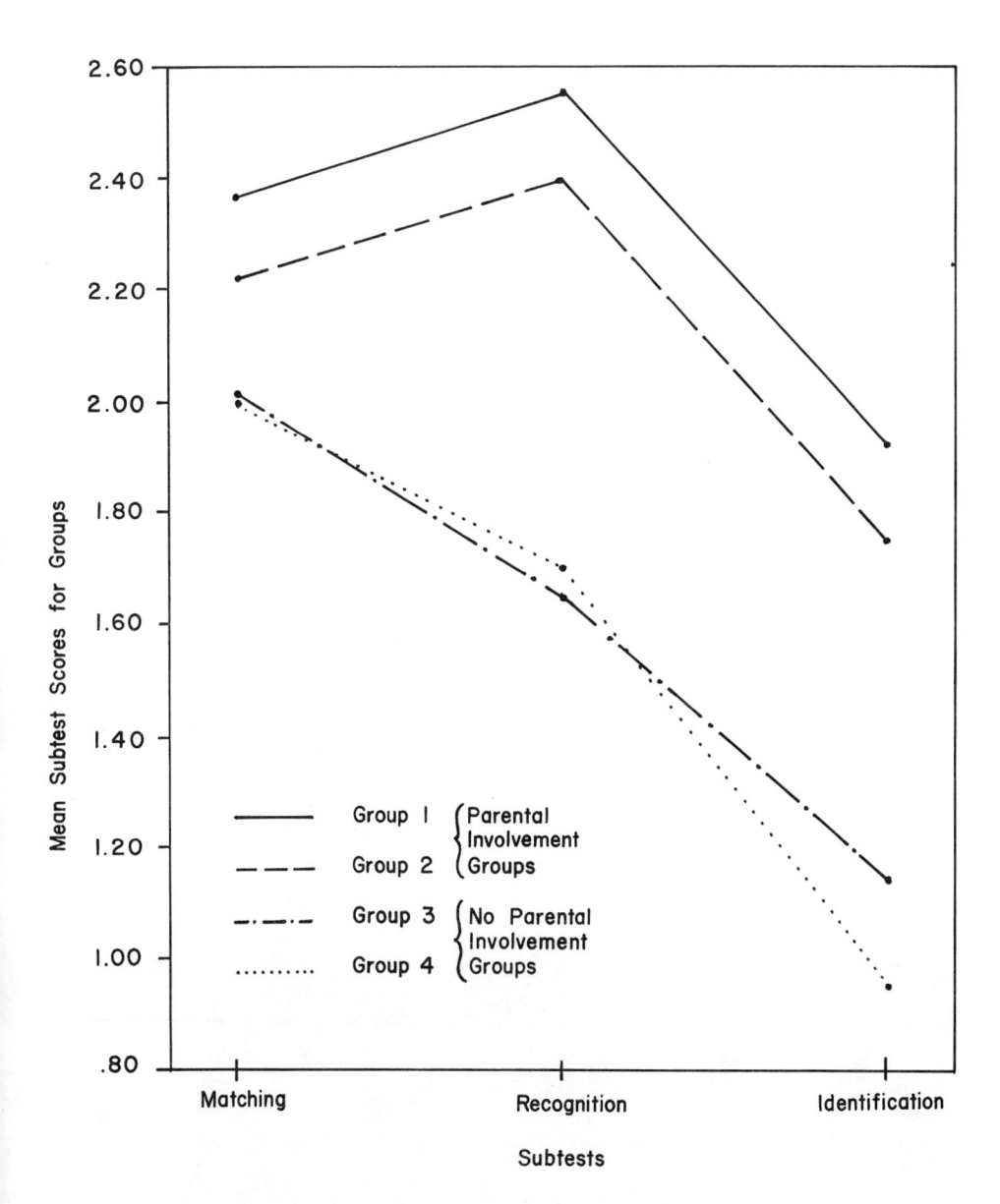

Fig. 1. Performance of younger siblings on Basic Concept Test. (Adapted from Gilmer, 1969.)

One additional bit of evidence which underscores the importance of parental involvement is an analysis of the attendance records of the classroom groups. The absence ratio to attendance days was significantly greater for the uninvolved parental group when compared with the groups whose mothers were enrolled in the training program. The absence ratio was almost twice as high for non-involved parental subjects. Equally interesting is the unaccounted for finding that the absence ratio was significantly greater for girls than boys in those groups. The girls had almost twice as high a ratio as the boys.

Second, an analysis of the psychometric data for the classroom-aged target children indicates performance of the two classroom groups to be significantly greater than that of the nonintervention groups, as well as that of the one which had only minimal intervention. However, in the spring testing, the classroom children with parental involvement continued to retain the original gains obtained while the group without parental involvement had begun to drop off. The interaction effect has not reached significance but the trend is apparent. (See Figure 2.)

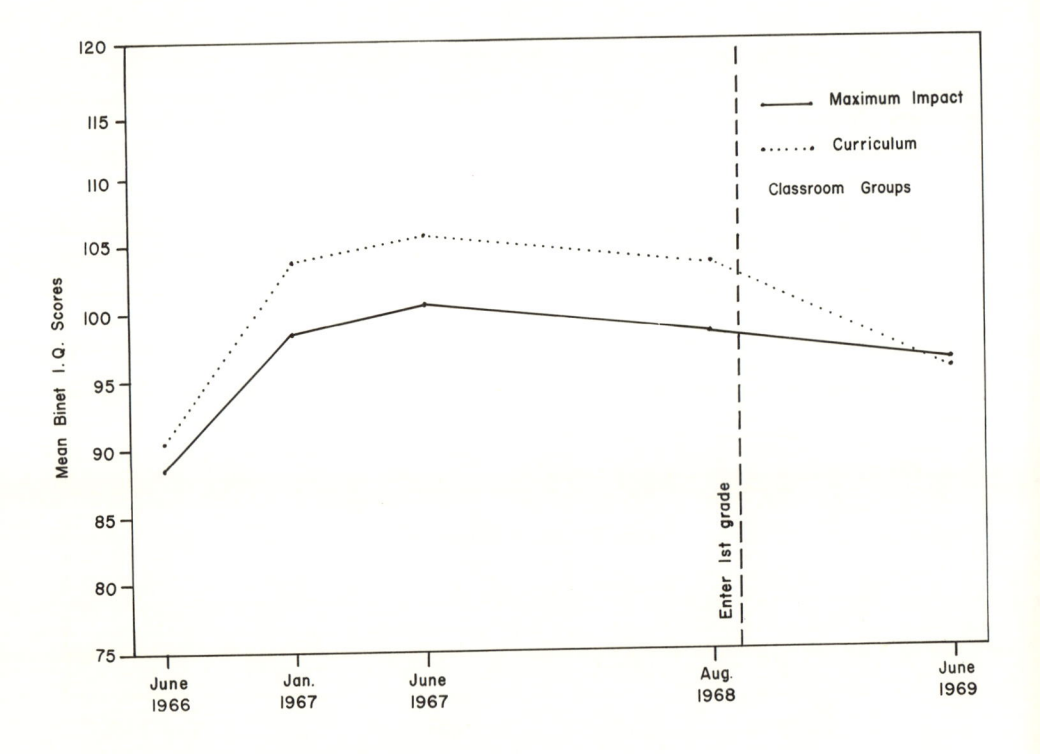

Fig. 2. Binet IQ means for classroom intervention groups over five administrations. (Adapted from Gilmer, 1969.)

Again these findings are not unexpected. The acid test will be whether or not the comparisons continue to hold up as the children progress through school and their gains are maintained over time. The answer to the third question then awaits the passage of time.

Far more interesting and perhaps far more important are the observations which have been made concerning the change in the life styles of these families.

Over 50% of the mothers have gone on to finish their high school education or have enrolled in training courses to upgrade their vocational skills. Several have finished courses in cosmotology, while almost a fourth of the mothers have enrolled in and completed nurse's aide or nursing technician courses and have become licensed practical nurses. At the present time none of the Maximum-Impact mothers are employed as domestics. Half of those who were employed as domestics at the beginning of the program have upgraded their employment status, while the other half have returned to their homemaking responsibilities on a full-time basis. During the summer of 1967, two of the Maximum-Impact mothers worked in Head Start centers as instructional aides, while another has taken on full-time work in a child day-care center. Two of the mothers who were originally functionally illiterate have gained reading skills to a third- or fourth-grade level through the help of other mothers in their group and the home-visiting teacher.

Their interest and concern in community affairs has also broadened. Several have served on their church boards for the first time after beginning work in the program. One has worked in Metropolitan Action Council elections, and two mothers have served as representatives on the Council's board for the Head Start program.

The social contacts between the parents and with other members of the community have increased markedly. On their own volition they developed a parent organization which has organized cooperative picnics and outings for the families on weekends, developed a rotating book library, and organized a mother-father bowling league in order to continue the relationships which have developed over the past two years.

One of our greatest problems has been to keep the members of our groups in the housing project until the completion of the intervention. They have developed a marked interest in buying their own homes. Indeed, two families have bought homes while continuing their children in the classroom program by providing their own transportation. At the end of the 1968 summer, many suggested the desire to move on to better housing of their own.

The increase in savings accounts and checking accounts has been marked. In each instance they cite this as an aid in helping them to budget their income. This outcome is interesting since few of the mothers were able to define the term budget when we began our program.

The family of most desperate means has shown such a remarkable change in furnishing its home and taking responsible care of the grounds around its apartment that neighbors have contacted the home visitor to remark about the family's progress since its involvement with the project.

In addition to these observations, which are but a few of the markers of change since the beginning of the program, our staff continually reports being asked into the homes of nonparticipating families to evaluate educational experiences being provided their children—a "horizontal diffusion effect," if you will.

While it is impossible to point with certainty to these events as being directly caused by our intervention program in the housing project, we would claim at least indirect influence. These results lead us to have greater confidence in our objective data. Certainly the manifest change in the life styles of these families—from the status of environmental victims to people who are beginning to develop environmental mastery—should have a supporting effect on their children's continued development.

The accumulated evidence of the impact of environment on the development of competency has led too many to close the case on circumstantial evidence alone. There is a quantum leap from establishing the case for environment to implementing programs to ameliorate environmental inadequacy. Two major problems evolve when we take such a leap:

1. We are vulnerable to the resurrection of old arguments, nature versus nurture, heredity versus environment. To date this battle has been the pet of those who would roll social responsibility back to the dark ages on the one hand and the ultimate utopians on the other. It provides the fertile ground for continued support of a racist mentality or a fuzzy-headed nirvana on earth. The question, it appears to me, that we must come to grips with is one of *rate* and *course* of development as influenced by environment. These are proper, answerable questions for psychology. Thus, the processes underlying development are of first concern. We must not get bogged down by misleading questions. The chief of these involves the heredity question of *sequence* and *limits* of development. The problems of *rate* and *course* are environmentally dependent variables which can be changed through environmental manipulation. It would appear that *sequence* and *limits* are not manipulated, and consequently are of lesser concern to the behavioral scientist.

2. Our leap to mass institution of programs of amelioration without intervention being based on the best knowledge we presently have available leads to a hodgepodge of doing nice things for needy little kids based on the assumption that anything is better than nothing at all (Miller, 1970). This leads directly to the disasters of a Westinghouse report (Cicarelli et al., 1969) and sets back progress in assuming our social responsibility for all the wrong reasons one could muster.

Let us come to grips with the fact that social need and the ameliorative necessity have outstripped our ability to supply *the* intervention program based upon sound, tested, and validated knowledge. We *must* take an *iterative* strategy, providing intervention models based on the best available knowledge while *simultaneously* investing heavily in discovery of the processes underlying the development of competency.

Such a strategy implies pluralism of intervention programs based on a comprehensive integrated system of research and development.

We must develop institutions which are anticipatory and future oriented rather than merely respondent if we are to meet the needs of a rapidly changing society.

The research I have discussed here offers hope for a few families. The challenge is to bring such knowledge to others. The social and behavioral scientist can ill afford to avoid the challenge and imperative of his social responsibility.

A question that often arises in discussions of intervention research is that of values. The question is usually raised by some well-meaning but misguided person that we are changing the value system of our families to that of the middle class. In working with families from disadvantaged backgrounds, we have taken the stand that there is nothing quaint about poverty, nothing socially uplifting about hunger, nothing self-rewarding about hopelessness, nothing inspiring about ignorance, and nothing culturally valuable about despair. We have assumed that to have the freedom of choice one must have the skills to make decisions. If one is going to have the right opportunity, one must be prepared adequately to take advantage of it. To be socially competent, one must be able to compete effectively for the rewards society has to offer. One must also be able to forge new roles which enhance oneself. This intervention research then is value oriented in the sense that it is based on the notion that social competency emanates from the development of adequate cognitive skills and the sustaining motivational states upon which self-development depends.

References

Battle, E. S., & Rotter, J. B. Children's feelings of personal control as related to social class and ethnic group. *Journal of Personality*, 1963, **31**, 482–490.

Bernstein, B. Social class and linguistic development: A theory of social learning. In A. H. Halsey, J. Floud, & C. A. Anderson (Eds.), *Education, economy, and society*. New York: Free Press of Glencoe, 1961.

Bernstein, B. Linguistic codes, hesitation phenomena and intelligence. *Language and Speech*, 1962, **5**, 31–46.

Bernstein, B. A socio-linguistic approach to social learning. In J. Gould (Ed.), *Penguin survey of the social sciences*. Baltimore, Md.: Penguin Books, 1965.

Buehr, R. F. Need achievement and dialect in lower-class adolescent Negroes. In, *Proceedings of the 73rd annual convention of the American Psychological Association*. Washington D. C.: APA, 1965. (Summary)

Cicarelli, V., et al. *The impact of Head Start*. Athens, O.: Westinghouse Learning Corporation, Ohio University, 1969. 2 vols.

Clark, A. D., & Richards, C. J. Auditory discrimination among economically disadvantaged and nondisadvantaged preschool children. *Exceptional Children*, 1966, **33**, 259–262.

Coleman, J. S. *Equality of educational opportunity*. Washington, D. C.: Office of Education, United States Government Printing Office, 1966.

Deutsch, C. P. Auditory discrimination and learning: Social factors. *Merrill-Palmer Quarterly*, 1964, **10**, 277–296.

Deutsch, M. The role of social class in language development and cognition. *American Journal of Orthopsychiatry*, 1965, **35**, 78–88.

Gilmer, B. R. Intra-family diffusion of selected cognitive skills as a function of educational stimulation. *DARCEE Papers and Reports*, 1969, **3**, No. 1.

Gordon, E. W., & Wilkerson, D. A. *Compensatory education for the disadvantaged: Programs and practices—preschool through college*. New York: College Entrance Examination Board, 1966.

Gray, S. W., Klaus, R. A., Miller, J. O., & Forrester, B. J. *Before first grade: The early training project for culturally disadvantaged children*. New York: Teachers College Press, 1966.

Greenberg, J. W., Gerver, J. M., Chall, J., & Davidson, H. H. Attitudes of children from a deprived environment toward achievement concepts. *Journal of Educational Research*, 1965, **58**(2), 57.

Henderson, R. W. *Environmental stimulation and intellectual development of Mexican-American children: An exploratory study.* (Doctoral dissertation, University of Arizona) Ann Arbor, Mich.: University Microfilms, 1966. No. 66–15, 258.

Hess, R. D., & Shipman, V. C. Early experience and the socialization of cognitive modes in children. *Child Development,* 1965, **36,** 869–886.

Hieronymus, A. N. Study of social class motivation: Relationships between anxiety for education and certain socio-economic and intellectual variables. *Journal of Educational Psychology,* 1951, **42,** 193–205.

Irwin, O. C. Infant speech: The effect of family occupational status and of age on use of sound types. *Journal of Speech and Hearing Disorders,* 1948, **13,** 224–226. (a)

Irwin, O. C. Infant speech: The effect of family occupational status and of age on sound frequency. *Journal of Speech and Hearing Disorders,* 1948, **13,** 320–323. (b)

Jensen, A. R. Learning in the preschool years. *Journal of Nursery Education,* 1963, **18,** 133–138.

Jensen, A. R. Social class and perceptual learning. *Mental hygiene,* 1966, **50,** 226–239.

Jones, K. L. *The language development of Headstart children.* (Doctoral dissertation, University of Arkansas) Ann Arbor, Mich.: University Microfilms, 1966. No. 66–11, 609.

Kagan, J. Reflection-impulsivity and reading ability in primary grade children. *Child Development,* 1965, **36,** 609–628.

Kahl, J. A. Some measurements of achievement orientation. *American Journal of Sociology,* 1965, **70,** 669–681.

Keller, S. The social world of the urban slum child: Some early findings. *American Journal of Orthopsychiatry,* 1963, **33,** 823–831.

Kelly, G. A. *The psychology of personal constructs.* Vol. 1, New York: Norton, 1955.

Klaus, R. A., & Gray, S. W. The early training project for disadvantaged children: A report after five years. *Monographs of the Society for Research in Child Development,* 1968, No. 120.

LeShan, L. L. Time orientation and social class. *Journal of Abnormal and Social Psychology,* 1952, **47,** 589–592.

Lesser, G. S., Fifer, G., & Clark, D. H. Mental abilities of children from different social-class and cultural groups. *Monographs of the Society for Research in Child Development,* 1965, **30**(4), No. 102.

Liebow, E. *Tally's corner: A study of Negro streetcorner men.* Boston: Little, Brown, 1967.

Long, B. H., & Henderson, E. H. Social schemata of school beginners: Some demographic correlates. *Proceedings of the 75th Annual Convention of the American Psychological Association,* 1967, **2,** 329–330. (Summary)

MacDonald, D. Our invisible poor. In L. A. Ferman, J. L. Kornbluh, & A. Haber (Eds.), *Poverty in America.* Ann Arbor, Mich.: University of Michigan Press, 1966.

Maitland, S. C. *The perspective, frustration-failure and delay of gratification in middle-class and lower-class children from organized and disorganized families.* (Doctoral dissertation, University of Minnesota) Ann Arbor, Mich.: University Microfilms, 1966. No. 67–866.

McClelland, D. C. *Studies in motivation.* New York: Appleton, 1955.

Miller, J. O. Cultural deprivation and its modification: Effects of intervention. In H. C. Haywood (Ed.), *Proceedings of the conference on social-cultural aspects of mental retardation.* Nashville, Tenn.: George Peabody College for Teachers, 1970, in press.

Miller, J. O., & Mumbauer, C. Intellectual functioning, learning performance and cognitive style in advantaged and disadvantaged preschool children. Unpublished manuscript, George Peabody College for Teachers, 1967.

Mischel, W. Preference for delayed reinforcement and social responsibility. *Journal of Abnormal and Social Psychology,* 1961, **62,** 1–7.

Mischel, W., & Metzner, R. Preference for delayed reward as a function of age, intelligence, and length of delay interval. *Journal of Abnormal and Social Psychology,* 1962, **64,** 425–431.

Rosen, B. D., & d'Andrade, R. The psycho-social origins of achievement motivation. *Sociometry,* 1959, **22,** 185–218.

Ryckman, D. B. *Psychological processes of disadvantaged children.* (Doctoral dissertation, University of Illinois) Ann Arbor, Mich.: University Microfilms, 1966. No. 66–12, 417.

Schoggen, M. Research, change, and social responsibility: Studies of imprint of the low-income home on young children. Part of papers on Research, change, and social rseponsibility: An illustrative model from early education. *DARCEE Papers and Report,* 1967, **2,** No. 3.

Siller, J. Socio-economic status and conceptual thinking. *Journal of Abnormal and Social Psychology,* 1957, **55,** 365–371.

Spain, C. J. Definition of familiar nouns by culturally deprived and nondeprived children of varying ages. Unpublished doctoral dissertation, George Peabody College for Teachers, 1962.

Steen, M. T. *The effects of immediate and delayed reinforcement on the achievement behavior of Mexican-American children of low socioeconomic status.* (Doctoral dissertation, Stanford University) Ann Arbor, Mich.: University Microfilms, 1966. No. 66–8594.

Strauss, M. A. Deferred gratification, social class, and the achievement syndrome. *American Sociological Review,* 1962, **27,** 326–335.

Terrel, G., Jr., Durkin, K., & Wiesley, M. Social class and the nature of the incentive in discrimination learning. *Journal of Abnormal and Social Psychology,* 1959, **59,** 270–272.

Zigler, E., & de Labry, J. Concept-switching in middle-class, lower-class, and retarded children. *Journal of Abnormal and Social Psychology,* 1962, **65,** 267–273.

Early Learning and Compensatory Education

The magnitude of the national effort in early learning and compensatory education has drawn psychologists, along with many other scientists, deeply into both theoretical and applied issues. Prior to 1965, there was no real national effort in early learning and compensatory education, but in that year the Elementary and Secondary Education Act and the Economic Opportunity Act were passed by Congress and signed by the President. In the ensuing years, many programs of research and application have been started, and now attempts to achieve goals of equal educational opportunity extend from birth through adulthood.

Many of the major federal programs in early learning and compensatory education are well known. They include:

1. The Regional Laboratories for Research and Development, seven of which are specifically concerned with preschool learning and compensatory education;

2. The National Laboratory on Early Childhood Education, involving at least six universities in research and development in preschool and primary grade programs;

3. Project Head Start which, in fiscal year 1969, helped over 600,000 children in academic year and summer programs at a cost of 275 million dollars;

4. Project Follow Through programs, of which there were 91 in fiscal year 1969 affecting over 15,000 children.

This brief summary of some of the federal programs does not begin to list many of the state and local efforts which, together with the federal programs, make up a massive national commitment to early learning and compensatory education.

Although much psychological knowledge is immediately useful in educational programs, much research remains to be done. William Kessen discusses contributions of basic research and points to long-term strategies that will need to be followed if we are to provide fundamental knowledge to guide ever-improving programs of early learning and compensatory education. Both Carl Bereiter and Gerald Lesser are involved in helping to design and conduct programs for early learning. Bereiter's work has been principally in the classroom; Lesser has been

---

[1] James Gallagher, Deputy Assistant Secretary for Research, Planning and Evaluation in the United States Office of Education, reacted to some of the points made by the symposium's five participants and talked about the present and future involvement of the federal government in these programs. Due to pressures of work he was unable to prepare his comments for inclusion in this publication.

helping to develop a national television program. Each shows how the psychologist can function effectively with educators and program designers to implement new programs. Patrick Suppes is applying computer technology to programs of early learning and compensatory education. He discusses the role of technological innovation in improving work in this area. Possibly the most frequent involvement of psychologists with early learning is the evaluation of programs. Finally, Samuel Messick analyzes productive and unproductive approaches to evaluation.

LLOYD N. MORRISETT
Symposium Chairman

The chairman received his PhD in experimental psychology from Yale University in 1956. He has recently become President of the John and Mary Markle Foundation, where his current major interest is in the educational uses of mass media and communications technology.

Early Learning and Compensatory Education: Contributions of Basic Research

WILLIAM KESSEN

The author received his PhD in experimental psychology in 1952 from Yale. He is presently a professor of psychology and a research associate in pediatrics at Yale, where his major research interest involves the psychology of human infancy.

Every once in a while a culture commits itself to an idea. We seem to have decided that the hope of the future is in the education of the very young. The Head Start program, which we continue and amplify in spite of mixed evidence of its success, the establishment of an Office of Child Development, the implications of the President's message on welfare for vastly enlarged day care, the increasing interest of professional people in early childhood, all testify to our decision—partly theoretical, partly political, and partly magical—to study and to educate infants. More—we have an analogy. Often during the convention one could hear, "If we can put a man on the moon, surely we can save the children." It is a revealing and instructive analogy. What did it take to put man on the moon? Scientifically, Newton's laws of motion (and a little help from James Clerk Maxwell), 24-billion-dollars worth of technology, and a firm goal—the moon. With proper respect for the advances of the social sciences over the last years, we have not had our *Principia* and, more vividly, we do not know where we are going. Consider for a moment the variety of ends that have been proposed for early childhood education: improvement of maternity, extension of group care, embedding of child care in a comprehensive system of social change, cognitive change, affective change, assimilation into the mainstream, protection of indigenous culture, early reading, early ecstacy, early political sense. The divergency and confusion of educational goals for the child make it no exaggeration to say that, if we are to follow the example of Apollo 11, we must head into space with neither Newton nor the moon.

Role of the Psychologist in Basic Research

The truth is not altogether bleak, however. The concern with infancy and the education of babies represents a too long delayed recognition that the problems of the nation posed by poverty and racial discord require attention from all of us and much hard thought. Something must be done. But the very importance of early childhood education should warn us to be wary, especially about the different jobs we do. Psychologists are n-headed men like other professionals and, in the field of early education, the psychologist may serve as a setter of goals, as a source of innovative educational ideas, as a repository of knowledge, and as an information gatherer. I believe that so elemental a reminder is necessary because of a remarkable tendency for the several tasks to become conflated. Information that we gather becomes—in ways that no one has systematically analyzed—support for our system of educational values. Examples of the tendency abound, but let me try to form a fictitious case. If we believe that early reading is a social value, the finding that children of two *can* read becomes somehow relevant to and supportive of the initial *belief* that early reading is valuable.

I do not mean to suggest that psychologists keep their opinions about values and directions to themselves, but I, with many others, most warmly urge that we do not pose as especially competent in matters of ultimate value. Psychologists do not have, more than other citizens, the right to decide about the directions of our lives together. In particular, I am concerned about the game that can only be called "black fixing"—the usually implicit, sometimes explicit assumption that all we need do is modify the environment of poor black people to make it more like the environment of middle class whites and the world will be made whole. I am afraid it is a dominant principle of remedial education nowadays and I am even more disturbed to see psychologists maintaining that they can document the virtues of such cultural intervention. But, beyond this specially crucial matter of value, it is important to raise the general issue of the competence of experts. To the degree that we confuse, for ourselves and others, the several tasks psychologists have in early education, to that degree we will often invite and will deserve false expectations, disappointment, and resentment.

Need we be as gloomy as I indicate? Well, let us go to the psychologist as a repository of information and ask just a few questions about early education.

1. What are the differences in handling and outcome between group day care of young children, full-time boarding care, and home rearing?

2. How do such differences vary with age, with prior environment, with training of caretakers, with physical setting, to name only a few?

3. What reliable and predictive measures of behavior before the second birthday can we use to study our educational procedures?

4. How does the evidence look on training the child to be cognitively competent in comparison with training him to be emotionally sensitive?

5. What are the implications of instituting educational changes without modifying the political and economic context?

Again, I rush to say that we are not totally in ignorance about these issues, but, at the very least, the evidence of basic research is insufficient to make clear-cut defensible decisions about any of the questions I posed. As a colleague has noted, our evidence about early education is of the sort that is adequate if you are deciding whether to package your new cereal in red boxes or blue boxes but hopelessly inadequate if your task is fixing tolerances on a new suspension bridge. In compensatory education, we are about to build bridges with cereal-box technology. For many complicated reasons, the world of educational reform will not wait for us and (in my opinion at least) it should not. What needs emphasis is that the basic research that is currently available is most valuable as it inspires and provokes sensitive and talented educational innovations, rather than as it prescribes solutions.

When we come at last to the place of the psychologist as information gatherer, the cloud lifts a bit. Surely, our special contribution to educational reform will be as designers of research that will, over a time scale fundamentally different from the time scale of reform, begin to provide the firm answers we require. Perhaps the most important function of research is to protect good ideas, and the diversity of ideas in compensatory education nowadays suggests that some of them, at least, need protection.

Proposed Innovations in Basic Research

I would like to propose an arrangement for research on early childhood that may also hold promise for a more efficient attack on the questions facing us. One way of expressing the research dilemma is that we need to bring the precision and objectivity of the laboratory into realistic settings, to supplement essential small-scale laboratory work and essential demonstration and innovation with large-scale rigorous research. Morrisett and I have explored this possibility for some time now and I believe that the primary need is for a few *experimental schools*, not demonstration schools where a new idea is installed full sweep, but schools where experiments, both in the long term and in the short term, are carried out. There can only be several such schools—there are preciously few educational researchers available—but there probably ought to be more than one in order to insure diversity. Early childhood education, because the institutional forms are not set yet and because the research problems are exquisitely important, would be an ideal setting for experimental schools. What is proposed here is not the same old limp appendage of research on an operational program; rather, true experimental schools would have two staffs, one for instructional operation and one for research. Research questions would be systematically addressed; for example, the schools would permit varying more values of a dimension of treatment than the something-versus-nothing designs now forced upon us by limited funds and limited control. Curriculum innovation, teaching techniques, power arrangements in class, administrative structures, all could be studied realistically and with sufficient control.

Let me cite an example. Particularly with very young children, a great deal of educational theory and a number of recent proposals rest on assumptions about the child's response to richly varying materials and about the educational effectiveness of such materials with and without adult tuition. In an experimental school (or school system if problems of pupil placement can be managed), a number of classrooms varying in the admixture of people and things, and with realistic budgets, could be established. The research would not aim to validate one procedure and invalidate another, but rather to permit the careful analysis of the *dimensions* of intervention and their effects.

In spite of much good work by many good people, dimensional analysis is far too rare for basic research to be closely relevant to the design of educational change. I recognize full well the difficulties such a proposal raises for issues of community participation, relations with teachers and educational administrators, and connections with university researchers. The problems, as a matter of fact, may be irretrievably difficult, but the attempt to establish research schools of this sort seems necessary if we are to avoid the frustrating disconnection between basic research and educational innovation.

Designing Programs for Classroom Use

CARL BEREITER

The author received his PhD in educational psychology from the University of Wisconsin in 1959. He is presently a professor of applied psychology at the Ontario Institute for Studies in Education, where he is mainly involved in developing programs for the teaching of conceptual skills.

A psychologist looking from the outside at what has been going on in early compensatory education during the past five years would probably be impressed by the variety of approaches and orientations that have been tried, and then would ask to see evidence as to whether they differ in their effects. Such a leap from procedures to results would be a little hasty, however, for it leaves unspecified what sorts of differences, if any, are at issue in such comparisons. To be sure, most of the evaluations carried out during this semidecade have been at no higher level of conceptualization than "What's your idea? How well does it work?" In the meantime, however, some interesting things have gone on.

Most striking, perhaps, has been the gradual convergence of a number of nominally different approaches upon a common set of instructional goals. This is a new development in early education and may well prove to be the only enduring change wrought by the large investment of developmental effort that accompanied the initiation of Project Head Start. In the elementary schools one also finds a variety of educational approaches, but most of them have in common a set of instructional goals and expectations that has acquired considerable force of tradition. Children in the primary grades are expected to learn to read and write, to add and subtract, to learn something about the geography of their nation, etc. No new approach can entirely avoid being judged by these time-honored expectations. Nursery schools and kindergartens, on the other hand, have not operated under a corresponding set of expectations for learning. Although nursery schools from Rome to Seattle are surprisingly similar, their communality resides not in what they are trying to get children to learn but rather in a set of activities, such as free play, certain games, story reading, painting, housekeeping and dress-up play, field trips, etc., that constitute the traditional school fare.

When Project Head Start began, this fund of common activities was about all there was to draw upon in forming a compensatory educational program for young children. Since then, in an effort to put wheels under one or another view of the cognitive needs of disadvantaged children, educators have begun to introduce new elements into the preschool curriculum that were not merely considered to be good things for children to do but that were intended to produce particular effects. Now, regardless of what long-range effects one wishes to produce, it is necessary to have the children doing something in the short run that entails learning, that is, a more than momentary change in behavior. No matter how general the long-range goal, in the short run the child must learn something in particular. Mere common sense and practicality require that this be something (*a*) that the child does not already know, (*b*) that he is capable of learning, and, other things being equal, (*c*) that is worth learning for purposes aside from those of the long-range goals.

Convergence of Approaches

These simple requirements account for the convergence of a number of dissimilar approaches on the same set of immediate learning objectives. Some psychologists have begun with the notion that what disadvantaged children lack is the development of certain central intellectual processes, such as auditory discrimination. In principle, training in any kind of sound discrimination would do, but this being the case it is only good sense to use auditory stimuli that have some practical significance—so why not use words? Other psychologists, taking a Piagetian approach, have been concerned with developing basic cognitive structures. Again, the specific content of day-to-day learning is incidental, and so out of the limitless range of possibilities these psychologists have settled upon familiar concepts of size, shape, use, classification, and order, which many children have not yet mastered but are able to learn. My co-workers and I have employed two different approaches to specifying curriculum content. One was to look at the kinds of things children are expected to know when they encounter first-grade curriculum materials (Bereiter, Engelmann, Osborn, & Reidford, 1966). Another was to work backward from the content of the Stanford-Binet Intelligence Test to define a universe of conceptual content that the Stanford-Binet could be said to sample (Washington, Engelmann, & Bereiter, 1969). Both routes led to much the same specifications and they are quite similar to the ones Sonquist, Kamii, and Derman (1970, in press) derived from Piaget's concepts. They involve the concepts of color, size, shape, location, number, order, class, action, use, material, and part-whole relation as applied to concrete objects and events. This, in brief, is the core content on which preschool programs seem to be converging.

There remain substantial differences in what people feel is important in this content and in how they think it should be taught. The differences are as great as those, say, between new math and old math, but the similarities are also as great, and this represents a substantial convergence, indeed, for an area of education that has been essentially devoid of content in the usual sense.

Problems with the Resulting Curriculum

Settling on a common body of curriculum content is not necessarily a good thing. The criticism has often been leveled against the existing school curriculum that it has grown up largely by accident and that it reflects the bourgeois biases of the group that has controlled education. The same could be said of the emerging preschool curriculum, with the added complaint that this is a poor way to meet the needs of minority group children for whom the existing school curriculum has already proved inadequate and irrelevant. Ideology aside, it can be predicted that the emerging preschool curriculum will resemble existing curricula at higher levels in that middle class children will start out more advanced in their mastery of it and better disposed to learn it than their lower class age-mates. Thus, what began as an effort at compensatory education may turn out to be a mechanism for producing an earlier and thus eventually greater separation in academic achievement between socioeconomic groups. On the other hand, it is not fair on these grounds to condemn an effort to discover worthwhile things for your children to learn and effective ways to teach them.

A fairer assessment might be that the effort to develop preschool programs for disadvantaged children has succeeded in giving more worthwhile substance to preschool education but it has not done anything much to alleviate the plight of poor and minority group children. Having accomplished this much, however, we are now in a better position to see the task that remains to be done. We know that the basic content of the preschool curriculum can be taught to children of all backgrounds. Finding better ways to do it is not essentially a psychological problem. It is an important task, but it can be left in other hands, and, fortunately, it is not only psychologists who have gotten involved in preschool education as a result of Head Start but a number of competent teachers and program writers as well.

The task remaining for psychologists is perhaps best seen in light of Jensen's (1969) recent paper entitled "How Much Can We Boost IQ and Scholastic Achievement?" Jensen has argued that we can make much better use than we do now of the learning abilities children possess in teaching them basic scholastic skills; and I see the emerging preschool curriculum as a step in this direction. It amounts to bringing deliberate teaching to bear on significant kinds of learning that have been left to happenstance. But Jensen has further charged that nothing educators are able to do at present makes much difference in the child's ability to reason and solve problems. This is apparently something that goes beyond the learning of concepts and ordinary scholastic skills, beyond the accumulation of experiences and interests.

Whether or not we can teach children to think along the lines that are required in academic disciplines and, if so, how are clearly problems for psychologists, and ones that remain virtually untouched. They require new paradigms. Small laboratory experiments concerned with improving performance on specific problems do not take us beyond the point where we are now, where we are able to teach specific skills but are unable to produce more far-reaching effects on competence. The problem for psychologists is not to find better ways of teaching what children will learn anyway, but to identify and find ways of teaching what some children do not learn at all. The task is not a popular one at this moment. One earns more applause by questioning the legitimacy of academic disciplines and the kind of thinking they entail than by worrying about how to enable more children to master them. But the problem of how to teach children to think remains a basic and significant one, which is bound to outlast the current social upheavals, and I hope more than a few psychologists will consider it worthy of their attention.

References

Bereiter, C., Engelmann, S., Osborn, J., & Reidford, P. An academically-oriented preschool for culturally deprived children. In F. M. Hechninger (Ed.), *Pre-school education today*. Garden City, N. Y.: Doubleday, 1966.

Jensen, A. R. How much can we boost IQ and scholastic achievement? *Harvard Educational Review*, 1969, **39**, 1–123.

Sonquist, H., Kamii, C., & Derman, L. A Piaget-derived preschool curriculum. In I. J. Athey & D. O. Rubadeau (Eds.), *Educational implications of Piaget's theory: A book of readings.* Waltham, Mass.: Blaisdell, 1970, in press.

Washington, E. D., Engelmann, S., & Bereiter, C. Achievement components of Stanford-Binet performance. In M. B. Karnes (Ed.), *Research and development program on preschool disadvantaged children.* Vol. 2. (Final Report, Project No. 5-1181) Washington, D.C.: Bureau of Research, United States Office of Education, 1969.

Designing a Program for Broadcast Television

GERALD S. LESSER

The author received his PhD in psychology from Yale University in 1952. He is presently Charles Bigelow Professor of Education and Developmental Psychology and Director, Laboratory of Human Development at Harvard University, where his major research interests include cultural influences upon learning and effects of visual media upon children.

On November 10, 1969, a series of 130, one-hour television programs for young children, an experimental series called "Sesame Street," began broadcasting over the 170 educational channels throughout the country.

With grants from both private and public agencies—Carnegie, Ford, the Office of Education, the Office of Economic Opportunity, and the National Institute of Child Health and Human Development—a group called the Children's Television Workshop currently is producing this five-day-a-week, 26-week television series for 3–5 year old children, primarily but not exclusively from urban families, and then will assess the impact that viewing these programs has on the development of these children. This paper focuses on the role that child watching, or formative evaluation, has been playing in guiding the design and construction of the television programs.

"Sesame Street" is not intended as a substitute for other forms of early childhood education, some of which you are hearing about in this symposium. Nor is it intended as a comprehensive program of early education. But there are some compelling facts about the television viewing of very young children which led us to consider national television programming as a complement and supplement, as one option to be added to other approaches to early education, an option that might achieve certain limited, selected goals quite well.

Television sets are in greater supply in American homes than bathtubs, telephones, toasters, vacuum cleaners, or newspaper subscriptions, Even for households with less than five-thousand-dollar incomes, over 90% own at least one television set. For example, in the "hollers" of Appalachia, where the median income is about three thousand dollars a year, and where homes are in such remote locations that preschool children cannot possibly reach an organized school, over 95% of the families have at least one television set, and these sets are on for an average of over 50 hours a week. By the time a child born today reaches age 18, he will have devoted more of his life to watching television than to any other single activity except sleep.

Over four-fifths of the three- and four-year-old children in this country do not attend any organized form of school, but the television medium is used by these young children for enormous numbers of viewing hours. What can we do with its message to capitalize on the inherent fascination that television seems to hold?

A compelling fact about television is its capacity to show children events that they have never seen before and are unlikely to ever have the opportunity to see in person. These events, in sequence, can add up to stories, and these stories can contain and convey ideas. With these stories and ideas, conceivably (with luck) we can touch the child and catch his imagination. We all know the power of the television medium to succeed in that most difficult accomplishment—catching the child's imagination—sometimes accidently and perhaps sometimes in ways that seem trivial or unworthy. But if we only can begin to understand what really moves a child and what really excites him to want to know more about what he sees and hears, that would be an achievement worth any investment.

The film sequences I will discuss illustrate the role of formative evaluation in program design. Of course, they will be out of the context of the total show, which combines warm human beings (who treat each other and their viewers in a gentle, dignified way) with puppets, live-action films, and short, animated segments.

Anyone who has children knows—mostly to his anguish—how readily young children learn commercials, in which pace, style, repetition, and the use of jingles are key elements. We are experimenting with short commercials to teach letters and numbers, and one of our early efforts is a commercial to teach the letter J.

The J commercial is a cartoon animation in which the letter J appears from the top of the screen to two boys resting on the ground and talking. The boys ask each other what it is, suggest that it looks like a fishhook, and the J replies that it is the letter J. Thereupon, the J recites a nonsense rhyme containing a number of words which start with the letter J. The narration is accompanied by illustrative animation. At the end of the story, the boys discuss the letter J, one saying, "So that's the letter J," while the other consolidates the little story with a nonsense rhyme of his own using words which start with J.[1] (Figure 1 shows the boys' first reaction upon encountering the letter J.)

We have had considerable criticism of the J commercial from adult audiences, who do not like the slang, the Judge hitting someone on the head, and the "negative attitude toward jails." More important, of course, were the reactions of young children, who take it simply as a nonsense rhyme—which is the way it was intended. They watch it and enjoy it, but some child watching told us that, despite its ability to hold the child's attention, it was not a really effective teaching device. One of our premises is that entertainment and instruction can complement each other, but we now find from watching children that we sometimes create a competition between the two—that because the animated characters in the J commercial, for example, are so successful and appealing to the child, and

---

[1] The material in reduced type was inserted in the text after the paper was delivered verbally in order to describe briefly the films that were shown to the audience.

210   PSYCHOLOGY AND THE PROBLEMS OF SOCIETY

Fig. 1. The opening scene from the J commercial.

draw his attention so strongly, he is distracted from the letter we are trying to present. So the next approximation tried to maintain the appeal of animation, but to make the letter more salient to the child. The animated sequence about Wanda the Witch is an effort to teach the sight and sound of the letter W.

Like the J sequence, Wanda the Witch is an animated cartoon sequence with rhyming narration. Here, however, the letter W is significantly more mobile and plays a larger role in the animation than the letter J did in its first usage. Ws were used in the animation whenever possible to represent the wig Wanda wore, and such things as snowflakes and the potion she brewed. Many of the key words which are in the rhyme are illustrated. (Figure 2 describes some scenes from Wanda the Witch, including the rhyme containing numerous W sounds.)

PSYCHOLOGY AND THE CHALLENGE OF EARLY LEARNING 211

The Story of... Wanda The Witch

This is how "Sesame Street," the new daily TV series for preschool children, teaches one of the letters of the alphabet. Cartoonist Tee Collins and Anne Bower, associate producer at the Children's Television Workshop, collaborated in the creation of this catchy, 60-second animated cartoon which not only introduces the shape of the letter but uses many words which employ the sound as well.

Wanda the Witch lived somewhere west of Washington.

Around her waist instead of a belt she wore a worm.

Wanda had a pet weasel. And on her head a wiry wig.

One Wednesday in the middle of winter, Wanda walked to the well to get water to wash her wig.

But the wheel on the well was worn and Wanda grew weary.

So she waved her wand and her washtub filled with warm water.

But just as Wanda dropped her wig into the warm water, a wild wind whipped the wig from her hands and blew it away.

Which taught Wanda this lesson: witches who wash their wigs on windy winter Wednesdays are wacky.

Fig. 2. Scenes from Wanda the Witch and the letter W. (Reprinted with permission, 1970. Copyrighted 1969 by the Children's Television Workshop.)

An even more direct focusing of the child's attention on the material to be learned is achieved in this next segment. Here, the letter itself is an actor and the child has an opportunity to get a good, long look at it. You also meet Kermit, an important member of our repertory company.

In this live, videotaped sequence Kermit the Frog, a Muppet puppet, delivers a lecture on the letter W, represented in the scene by the letter itself, made of foam rubber and therefore movable. As Kermit begins, unaware that the letter is capable of moving, he mentions words which start with W such as Wiggle and Wobble, and the letter reacts accordingly. Kermit is startled by the W's behavior, but passes it off as a figment of his imagination, then continues his lecture, mentioning words such as Walk and Wander. At this point the letter begins wandering toward Kermit, who is nonplussed. The letter moves in closer to Kermit and attacks him. Kermit explains to his audience that words like Wrestle and Wack start with W as well. The scene ends with the letter W victorious and Kermit saying, "Woe is me." (Figure 3 shows some segments from Kermit's lecture and the letter W's unexpected antics.)

212   PSYCHOLOGY AND THE PROBLEMS OF SOCIETY

3a. Kermit the Frog delivering his lecture on the letter W. As Kermit says that the letter W is used in the words Walk and Wander, the W approaches him.

3b. Kermit is surprised by the letter's behavior.

3c. The letter begins to pummel Kermit.

3d. Kermit, about to succumb to the W's attack, sighs, "W is for weakening. Woe is me!"

Fig. 3. Scenes from Kermit the Frog's lecture on the letter W.

The Role of Formative Evaluation

Let us return now to the function of formative evaluation in the design of children's television. The ultimate success of "Sesame Street" will depend upon the appeal of the programs and the impact they have on children. But there already has been one highly successful result of this experiment. Children's Television Workshop has a research staff responsible for child watching to get a detailed, moment-to-moment view of what goes on in the child's mind—what he actually sees and hears—when he is watching "Sesame Street," and to convey this information to the producers of the show to guide their efforts in building progressively better shows. The remarkable achievement is this: The researchers and producers actually have learned a great deal about how to be useful to each other. The researchers not only have learned to make useful observations about what works or does not work with children, but to convey this information in a usable form to the producers. Equally remarkable is the producers' ability to absorb and use this information and to ask reasonable questions of the research staff.[2]

The general function then of formative evaluation is to serve production. As the shows have been developing, research is assessing both their appeal for children and what children learn from them. To accomplish this, Edward Palmer and his group have developed several techniques of child watching, one simple but very effective one being the "distractor." Here, a child can watch either the television set or a television-sized projection screen on which slides are changing constantly. Fluctuations in the child's attention are recorded and graphed, and then reviewed in detail with the producers.

These and other techniques of child watching are yielding much specific information about program elements and some general understanding of children's viewing behavior: the roles of context, pace, and repetition, of familiarity and incongruity; the appeal of animation and pixilation (an old Buster Keaton, speeded-up action technique); the attentional drifts of the child; and the cues he uses in deciding very selectively whether he should watch or not. When television sets are turned on for an average of 50–60 hours a week in the homes of young children, they must become highly selective in monitoring what to watch, and they do. For example, very rarely will a young child watch for long if an adult is on the screen talking full-face to him. In contrast, contrary to the ancient folklore among television producers, children do enjoy watching other children in action and listening to their talk.

Another effort—in this instance, an effort to teach the concept of "round"—illustrates some of these general observations through its relative failure.

Using live-action film this short essay depicts objects with round shapes, such as manhole covers, Frisbies, clocks, soap bubbles, car wheels, holes, marbles, telephone dials, etc. This film is fast paced with lively music.

Although this segment does hold the children's attention and creates many images that they can recall and describe, child watching indicates that it fails to

---

[2] Those interested in how this successful collaboration between researchers and producers is coming about please contact Dr. Edward Palmer, Research Director, Children's Television Workshop, who is responsible for the formative evaluation phase of its operation.

teach the concept of round. Many round objects are depicted, but children apparently fail to abstract the concept of roundness from those objects.

Thus, in attempting to teach other concepts—around, through, and over—the action and language of children were added, with considerable repetition and redundancy.

In another live-action film, a group of children demonstrates by playing "follow the leader" the concepts of *around, through* and *over*. The children first go *around* some sheets hung on a clothesline but the smallest child does not understand and runs into them, getting tangled up in the clothes. The older children return, untangle him, and then go around the clothesline again so that the little child can learn correctly. He does, and they go on to the next two tests which take them *through* a large pipe and *over* some boards on sawhorses. The little child, of course, fails to go through and over on his first attempts, but his playmates help him to do it again, and he succeeds. The film ends with the children playing leap frog, running through each other's legs, and romping in a grassy plot.

The production of "Sesame Street" represents the first time that child watching research is being applied systematically to the design of televised instruction for young children. This research is proving to be of great value, not only in improving the quality of a specific set of programs, but in generating some general understanding of how young children learn, what moves them, and what catches their imagination.

Evaluation of Educational Programs as Research on the Educational Process

SAMUEL MESSICK

The author received his PhD in psychology from Princeton University in 1954. He is presently Vice-President for Research at Educational Testing Service, where his major interests are in education and human development, personality assessment, and the evaluation of educational programs and instruction.

During the past five years, a variety of pressing social problems have been attacked through the medium of innovative and compensatory education programs meant primarily to improve the lot of the culturally disadvantaged and the educationally alienated, with ultimate impact intended not only for students but for families, schools, and communities as well. These programs have been initiated, however, in a political climate marked by fierce competition for scarce economic resources. Given the seriousness of the problems and the scarceness of the resources, it is not surprising that demands should arise from several segments of society that these programs be both timely and effective. As a nation, we simply cannot afford to postpone action pending the results of preliminary research and development efforts that might increase the likelihood of positive effects. Nor can we afford the wasted time and resources of ineffectual programs. In H. G. Wells' (1956) aptly prophetic phrasing, "Human history becomes more and more a race between education and catastrophe." Time is of the essence, but rapid intervention is not enough—it must also be effective intervention.

Such pressures toward immediate program implementation have helped to create in some quarters an intellectual—or, more precisely, an antiintellectual—atmosphere in which research is seen as a frill. In this atmosphere, the watchwords are *action* and *accountability*: Primary concern is with the initiation and execution of programs and with demonstrating their overall effectiveness. The main question is whether or not the program works. With time running out, there is little inclination to pause to inquire why it works or even how it works, let alone to ask what aspects of the program work best and for what kinds of students under what kinds of circumstances. Under such conditions, program efforts can easily come to be animated more by a concern for vindication than by a concern for verification (Chapin, 1947), with more energy expended in justifying than in judging. But an unnecessarily high price is exacted for this emphasis on payoff to the exclusion of process: We do not obtain information about the dynamics of the program or the functioning of its components that could be used to improve the program or to modify it if conditions change (Cronbach, 1963).

Evaluative Research—Descriptive Phase

Fortunately, there is an alternative, and that is to undertake *evaluative research*. In other words, we should go ahead and do research on program functioning, to acquire information serving the ends of both accountability and program improvement, but within a time frame that will not delay program implementation. This may be accomplished by carrying out the research and the program simultaneously, by including within the administration of the program provision for collecting information relevant to its evaluation and improvement. In some educational programs it is even possible to embed the evaluative research directly into the program itself by capitalizing upon certain kinds of information, such as measures of pupil progress, for both evaluative and instructional purposes. Care must be taken, of course, to ensure that the evaluative research activities do not interfere with or contravene any program activities or intentions. For this reason, heavy reliance should be placed wherever possible on what Webb and his colleagues have called "unobtrusive measures" of program effects (Webb, Campbell, Schwartz, & Sechrest, 1966).

If evaluative research is to provide not only a basis for satisfying accountability concerns but also a base of knowledge and understanding that would permit program improvement, extrapolation to other settings and problem areas, and responsiveness to changing conditions, then the form it takes and the kinds of questions it asks must go far beyond the typical *engineering* model of evaluation studies. The engineering model focuses on input-output differences relative to cost. This provides information necessary for assessing overall program significance or impact but not sufficient for program revision or development. As Scriven (1966) has emphasized, the *medical* model is a more appropriate paradigm for educational research, and there are several important consequences of this view.

Medical Model Concept

To begin with, there is the recognition that a prescription for treatment and the evaluation of its effectiveness should take into account not only the reported symptoms but other aspects of the organism and its ecology as well. In the present context, this is essentially an affirmation of the need for a systems approach in educational evaluation that would attempt to deal empirically with the interrelatedness of psychological, social, environmental, and educational factors. In the area of human development, we are faced with a particularly complicated system composed of differentiated but overlapping subsystems that embrace family, peer, and community influences as well as school, teacher, and program influences. In such a situation it is possible that compensating trade-offs among variables will occur under different conditions to produce similar effects and that particular outcomes will frequently be multiply determined and sometimes overdetermined. One implication of all this is that evaluative research under such complex circumstances should routinely adopt a multivariate interactional strategy: It should employ multiple measures in each domain and methods of analysis sensitive to interacting influences. The evaluation question thus becomes elaborated within this framework from a straightforward comparison such as, "Is this new treatment more effective than the old one?" to something more complicated such as, "Do these treatments or treatment components interact with personality and cognitive characteristics of the students or with factors in their educational history or family backgrounds to produce differential effects upon achievement?" Note that such an elaboration is important, for if Personality × Treatment interactions occur or if background factors turn out to moderate treatment effects, then a simple comparison of average gains for different treatment groups will very likely be misleading (Messick, 1970, in press).

Another derivative of the medical model is a concern for monitoring possible side effects of the treatment. This also follows naturally from the system conception, for if the various elements and subsystems are interdependent, then a change in one part of the system may produce unanticipated and possibly adverse consequences in another part of the system. Because of this possibility, it is not enough to evaluate a program solely in terms of its stated goals, on the basis of how well it achieves its intended objectives. In addition to the *intended* outcomes, we should also assess a wide range of *possible* outcomes, for we might unearth in the process some alternatives that ought to be weighed in reaching a final appraisal of program impact (see Messick, 1970, in press). As Dyer (1967) has emphasized, "Evaluating the *side* effects of an educational program may be even more important than evaluating its intended effects."

Another implication of this medical analogy is that feelings and reactions should be assessed periodically throughout the course of the treatment and not just at the beginning and the end. This assessment should include, as is the custom in medical practice, a monitoring of attitudes toward the treatment itself.

Of course, underlying the entire metaphor is the notion that whenever possible in the evaluation of educational programs, as in the evaluation of drugs, we should go beyond a simple assessment of the size of effects to an investigation of the processes that produce the effects, because an understanding of these processes will provide a rational basis for changing programs if conditions change and for isolating possible danger zones where potential side effects should be monitored.

In this view, then, evaluative research should focus not only on the outcomes of education but also on the process and the context of education, thereby encompassing within its purview several broad areas of measurement concern—*input, context, process,* and *output* (Stufflebeam 1968; Worthen, 1968). In addition, it is probably wise to extend the range of the evaluation process even further in time. As in a medical case study, measures of *antecedent* conditions should be included, as well as follow-up measures of the *consequences* both of the treatment and of the termination of treatment. This approach thus emphasizes the importance of comparative longitudinal data in evaluating the effectiveness of educational treatments and stresses the need for analytical procedures that properly take into account those Student × Process × Environment interactions that produce differential results. For these purposes, the scope of measurement must be broad enough both to ensure adequate coverage of potentially interactive variables and to permit the monitoring of possible side effects of the educational programs, particularly in the affective and motivational domains. If possible, measures should be included to assess not only characteristics of the learners but also of their learning environments, including the home and community as well as the classroom and school, and of the educational processes at all levels, including characteristics of teachers, programs, and classroom dynamics (Anderson & Doppelt, 1969; Metfessel &

Michael, 1967). In this latter connection, it is particularly important to measure characteristics of the program as it is actually carried out, since the program as practiced is sometimes quite different from the program as planned (Stake, 1969).

Some persons might object at this point that this particular view of evaluative research is overly elaborate and complicated and that with all this emphasis on process and interacting influences, we are in danger of subverting the main aim of evaluation, which is an appraisal of outcome or product. This latter view has come to be called in some circles the "butter wrapping model" of evaluation (Wittrock & Wiley, 1970, in press). The main thing you want to know, if you have taught someone how to wrap butter, is how many pounds of butter he can wrap. For this purpose, it does not matter that different processes of butter wrapping are employed by different butter wrappers—one may use his right thumb, for example, and another his left forefinger. What matters is how many pounds of butter he can wrap after the training experience. But suppose one very effective butter wrapper has gained his speed and efficiency because of a particular stylistic quirk, namely, wetting his thumb with his tongue as he picks up the waxed paper. You may not be very happy with that particular style of butter wrapping even though it produces more wrapped butter than any other. It would seem that at least in some cases, then, it is necessary to take into account factors of style and process in order to evaluate the very desirability of the outcome.

It is thus being suggested here that, wherever possible, evaluative research should encompass both process and outcome in order to accrue information relevant for both program improvement and administrative decision making. At first glance, this may seem like a blurring of the conceptually useful distinction drawn by Scriven (1967) between "formative" evaluation, or evaluation for program improvement, and "summative" evaluation, or appraisal of the final product, but there really is no conflict involved. The terms "formative" and "summative" refer to different *roles* of evaluation not to different *forms* of evaluation, and data from a particular evaluation study can and usually should serve several roles. For example, the research design for the summative evaluation of the Children's Television Workshop series, discussed by Lesser, permits feedback from reactions to shows early in the broadcast year to serve as a guide to the development of shows not scheduled for production until later in the broadcast year (Educational Testing Service, 1969). The final product appraised in the summative evaluation is the series of shows actually telecast, but the shape of the latter part of that series may be drastically influenced by evaluations of the earlier part. Thus, it is possible for summative evaluations to serve formative purposes—whether immediately, as in the case of programs developed as a sequence of finished units like the Children's Television Workshop, or on a more delayed basis as in periodic program revision—as long as relevant data are collected a sufficient number of times during the course of the program, or under a sufficient number of varying conditions, to permit different program components to be evaluated separately.

Evaluative Research—Judgment Phase

Up to this point we have been discussing evaluative research in education primarily as the application of the methods of empirical social science to ascertain the nature and size of the effects of educational treatments. This covers the first or "descriptive" phase of evaluation, but we should not forget that the evaluation enterprise also includes a second or "judgment" phase, wherein decisions must be made as to whether or not the observed effects attain suitable standards of excellence or acceptability (Stake, 1969). The methods of social science research are clearly applicable to the descriptive phase, but it is not as generally recognized that they apply to the judgment phase as well. Thus, the concern of evaluative research properly extends to an examination of the criterion or goal scales, for example, and to an appraisal of the weightings and models used for combining performance information judgmentally in administrative decision making. Indeed, the purview of this research even extends to an evaluation of the goals themselves, and particularly to the investigation of the validity of assumptions underlying the goals (Suchman, 1967). Thus, an evaluation of the effectiveness of a program for educating mothers to place their infants on rigid feeding schedules might well involve an investigation of the validity of assumptions relating the expressed goals to underlying values.

As we exercise what Scriven (1968) has called "the scientific obligation to evaluation," we should recognize that social science faces not only obligation but opportunity and that evaluative research can serve to advance science as well as social welfare. As Suchman (1967) has summarized so well in his excellent treatise on the topic:

To some extent evaluative research may offer a bridge between "pure" and "applied" research. Evaluation may be viewed as a field test of the validity of cause-effect hypotheses in basic science. . . . Action programs in any professional field should be based upon the best available scientific knowledge and theory of that field. As such, evaluations of the success or failure of these programs are intimately tied into the proof or disproof of such knowledge. Since such a knowledge base is the foundation of any action program, the evaluative research worker who approaches his task in the spirit of testing some theoretical proposition rather than a set of administrative practices will in the long run make the most significant contribution to program development [p. 170].

References

Anderson, S. B., & Doppelt, J. (Chm.) *Untangling the tangled web of education. Research and measurement considerations related to assessing children's development in interaction with school, family, and community influences.* (Research Memorandum RM-69-6) Princeton, N. J.: Educational Testing Service, 1969.

Chapin, F. S. *Experimental designs in sociological research.* New York: Harper, 1947.

Cronbach, L. J. Course improvement through evaluation. *Teachers College Record,* 1963, **64,** 672–683.

Dyer, H. S. The discovery and development of educational goals. In, *Proceedings of the 1966 Invitational Conference on Testing Problems.* Princeton, N. J.: Educational Testing Service, 1967.

Educational Testing Service. *Evaluating "Sesame Street." A proposal for children's television workshop.* Princeton, N. J.: Author, 1969.

Messick, S. The criterion problem in the evaluation of instruction: Assessing possible, not just intended outcomes. In M. C. Wittrock & D. E. Wiley (Eds.), *The evaluation of instruction: Issues and problems.* New York: Holt, Rinehart & Winston, 1970, in press.

Metfessel, N. S., & Michael, W. B. A paradigm involving multiple criterion measures for the evaluation of the effectiveness of school programs. *Educational and Psychological Measurement,* 1967, **27,** 931–943.

Scriven, M. Student values as educational objectives. In, *Proceedings of the 1965 Invitational Conference on Testing Problems.* Princeton, N. J.: Educational Testing Service, 1966.

Scriven, M. The methodology of evaluation. In, *Perspectives of curriculum evaluation*. (American Educational Research Association monograph series on curriculum evaluation) Chicago: Rand McNally, 1967.

Scriven, M. The scientific obligation to evaluation. Paper presented at the annual meeting of the American Psychological Association, San Francisco, September 1968.

Stake, R. E. The countenance of educational evaluation. *Teachers College Record*, 1969, **68**, 523–540.

Stufflebeam, D. L. Toward a science of educational evaluation. *Educational Technology*, 1968, **8**, 5–12.

Suchman, E. A. *Evaluative research*. New York: Russell Sage Foundation, 1967.

Webb, E. J., Campbell, D. T., Schwartz, R. D., & Sechrest, L. *Unobtrusive measures: Nonreactive research in the social sciences*. Chicago: Rand McNally, 1966.

Wells, H. G. *The outline of history*. (Rev. ed.) New York: Doubleday, 1956.

Wittrock, M. C., & Wiley, D. E. (Eds.) *The evaluation of instruction: Issues and problems*. New York: Holt, Rinehart & Winston, 1970, in press.

Worthen, B. R. Toward a taxonomy of evaluation designs. *Educational Technology*, 1968, **8**, 3–9.

Technological Innovations: Computer-Assisted Instruction and Compensatory Education[1]

PATRICK SUPPES

The author received his PhD from Columbia University in 1950. He is presently a professor of philosophy, statistics, and education at Stanford University, where he also directs the Institute for Mathematical Studies in the Social Sciences.

MONA MORNINGSTAR

The author received her PhD in psychology from the University of Massachusetts in 1966. She is presently at Stanford University working as a research associate at the Institute for Mathematical Studies in the Social Sciences.

Computer-assisted instruction (CAI) has reached the operational stage in various parts of curricula in a number of places in the United States. Although the major purpose of CAI, that of instructing students, is constant for most CAI installations, the manner in which CAI fulfills this purpose varies from place to place. At a simple level, a curriculum can be written to serve as a supplementary drill for concepts learned in the classroom; the computer program presents each student in a given grade with the same set of materials, allows the student to respond, and then informs the student whether the response is correct. The complexities of CAI systems increase with the addition of tutorial curricula, the addition of specific error messages, and the addition of rules for individualizing the program as a function of the student's performance.

We are convinced that CAI offers a mode of instruction ideally suited for students from educationally deprived areas. Our convictions are based on our knowledge of learning theory, anecdotal evidence from teachers and administrators, intuitive feelings relative to the computer terminal and the student's response to it, and the results of evaluations of projects either completed or in progress at the Institute.

This paper is organized as follows. First, the history of CAI at Stanford is described. Next, the nature of student interaction with the computer terminal

---

[1] This paper is a somewhat expanded version of the presentation made by Suppes as part of the symposium "Early Learning and Compensatory Education." The research reported here has been supported by the National Science Foundation and the United States Office of Education.

is explained, as well as the ways in which CAI can provide the student who is performing below his ability level with a learning approach that can compensate for educational liabilities in his environment. Following this, examples are given of the evaluation of our arithmetic drill-and-practice program as implemented in educationally deprived areas in the United States. Finally, our latest arithmetic curriculum, which provides an unusual degree of individualization by explicit use of a global mathematical model, is described.

History of CAI at Stanford

The Institute for Mathematical Studies in the Social Sciences at Stanford University began a program of research and development in computer-assisted instruction in January 1963 that was supported by the Carnegie Corporation of New York and the National Science Foundation. In December 1963, construction of the Laboratory for Learning and Teaching on the Stanford campus was completed. The initial instructional system consisted of a medium-sized computer and 12 visual display devices, two in each of six student stations, placed within 100 feet of the computer. Microfilmed source material was presented on the 10 × 13 inch screen; the student responded by touching a light pen to the face of the screen.

The first operational program was in elementary mathematical logic and was demonstrated by fifth and sixth graders in December 1963. Between the spring of 1964 and the spring of 1965, students demonstrated logic lessons, two students completed a 20-lesson program in logic, and small groups of students worked on a first-grade arithmetic program. An important step was taken in April 1965 when student terminals were removed from the Stanford campus and placed in the classroom; the terminals were connected to the computer by telephone lines. At this time, 41 fourth-grade children did daily arithmetic drill-and-practice lessons on a teletype in their classroom.

During the 1965–66 school year, 60–75 students in each of Grades 3–6 participated in the arithmetic drill-and-practice program and an additional 60 students shared a teletype at a local high school. (For a description of this program, see Suppes, Jerman, & Brian, 1968.) Also, four teletypes with an audio line were used for a drill-and-practice program in spelling. The program in symbolic logic continued with 30 sixth-grade students and 7 fourth-grade students.

In addition to the laboratory at Stanford, the construction of the Brentwood Laboratory, a separate building at Brentwood Elementary School in East Palo Alto, California, was completed in the summer of 1966. Over 80% of the students at Brentwood are from some minority group, and many of them need compensatory education. This additional laboratory represented a portion of the funds provided to the Institute by the United States Office of Education to establish a computer-based instructional system at a public elementary school for the purpose of investigating CAI over an extended period of time. The Brentwood Laboratory was equipped with an IBM-1500 Instructional System operated by an IBM-1800 computer. For the two years the IBM system was in operation, we offered tutorial reading and tutorial mathematics curricula that presented material both aurally (tapes) and visually (film and cathode-ray tubes). The reading program for Grade 1 included 50 students in 1966–67 and 73 students in

1967–68; the mathematics program included 50 students in Grade 1 in 1966–67 and 76 students in Grade 2 in 1967–68. (A description of the laboratory, the curriculum, and the results of this program are described in Suppes & Morningstar, 1970; Atkinson, 1968; and Atkinson & Hansen, 1968.)

The activities of the Institute during the 1966–69 period included the expansion of the tutorial logic and algebra program (1966–69), the development of a tutorial program in first-year Russian (1967–68), and second-year Russian (1968–69) for university-level students, a drill-and-practice reading program for Grades 1–3 (1968–69), a tutorial program in computer programming for high school students (1968–69), and a dial-a-drill program in arithmetic for Grades 2–6 (1967–68). By the end of the 1968–69 school year the drill-and-practice program was available for Grades 1–9. Approximately 5,000 students from California, Illinois, Kentucky, Mississippi, Iowa, Ohio, Tennessee, and Washington, D.C., participated on a daily basis, with each student being processed via telephone line through the Institute's computer system on the Stanford campus.

The Institute's programs have involved various technological innovations: the development of computer-generated speech for the dial-a-drill program and the reading program, the use of both teletypes and audiotapes for the Russian program, the modification of teletype terminals for audio for the drill-and-practice reading program, and, possibly most important, the ability to present a program to students at a geographical location far removed from the central computer at Stanford. The computer facilities available for these programs were the PDP-1 with a 32,000-word core and an additional 4,000-word core interchangeable within the 32 bands of a magnetic drum on files stored on an IBM-1301 disc. The PDP-10 supported by 192,000 words of a 1-microsecond core and an IBM-2314 disc storage unit were installed in the fall of 1968. Additional support units attached to the PDP-10 include high-speed line units for interfacing with telephone lines, a digital audio system, and magnetic tape units.

Although we feel that the computer facilities and the diversity of programs available through the Institute are impressive, we realize that the student's performance is more affected by the curriculum than by the facilities necessary to present the material. That is, the most complex and sophisticated computer system cannot function as an effective educational tool unless the curriculum (*a*) is adequately developed in terms of content, (*b*) makes use of psychological variables known to have a positive effect on learning, and (*c*) is presented so that the student-machine interaction becomes a positive component in the student's learning environment.

Procedure at the Student Terminal

In most classes involved in the drill-and-practice mathematics program, the teletype (Model-33) is either in an enclosed area in the back of the classroom or in a separate room in the school. (See Figure 1.) Most students look forward to their turn at the teletype and leave the classroom at their scheduled time without disrupting the class. When the student initiates the program by pressing the "start key," the teletype prints the message PLEASE TYPE YOUR NUMBER AND NAME. The student types his assigned number, a space, his first name, and

Fig. 1. A student at the teletype. (Photograph supplied by RCA Instructional Systems, Palo Alto, California.)

another space. The teletype then prints his last name. Typing another space starts the presentation of problems.

If a student makes an error, the message NO, TRY AGAIN is typed, the problem is retyped to the point where the error occurred, and the student is given a second chance to make a correct response. After a second error the message NO, THE ANSWER IS____, TRY AGAIN is typed, and the problem is retyped to the point where the error occurred. After a third error, the error message giving the correct response is typed and, if the incorrect character was not the last character necessary to complete the problem, the problem is retyped with the correct answer. If a student does not respond within a given time, the error routine is followed with the message TIME IS UP, TRY AGAIN substituted for the error message. A new problem is presented when the student responds correctly to the preceding problem or when the teletype, after the third error, presents the correct answer.

When the problems for that day have been presented, the number of problems completed and the percentage correct on the first response are typed. The student is then signed off with the message GOOD-BYE, JOHN. PLEASE TEAR OFF ON THE DOTTED LINE.

Several characteristics of the procedure at the student terminal and of the drill-and-practice curriculum that enhance learning may be listed briefly since their effects have been documented empirically and do not require extensive justification. These characteristics are (*a*) an active response mode, (*b*) immediate knowledge of whether the response is correct, (*c*) an opportunity to correct an incorrect response, (*d*) an opportunity to respond correctly after the correct response has been supplied, (*e*) total time per problem controlled by the student, (*f*) provision of a permanent copy of the problems and a summary of the student's performance which he may take and use as he pleases, (*g*) difficulty of the problems related (within limits) to the capabilities of the student, and (*h*) review material based on the individual's performance history. (A more detailed description of the characteristics associated with the curriculum (*g* and *h*) may be found in Suppes & Morningstar, 1969, 1970).

Anecdotal evidence from teachers and students indicates several positive aspects of the CAI learning environment. For example, many educators have expressed fears that CAI is nonpersonal and mechanical and therefore cannot be "good" for children. Although no adult would deny that the teletype is mechanical (and therefore impersonal), the behavior of the children indicates that they perceive the system as a "person." Listening to students one hears: "Slow down, I'm not finished." "Stupid machine!" "Good, I thought you would say that [with an affectionate pat for the teletype]." "Don't use that one [teletype]; it's mad, gave me hard problems yesterday."

Verbal attacks directed at the teletype are quite frequent when the student gives an incorrect response—a behavior that would be unacceptable in the classroom. Few teachers are capable of continuing a lesson while ignoring the student's negative verbalization and would punish the student in some manner. Although the teacher must respond in a way that decreases such outbursts in order to maintain a manageable class, disciplinary responses to the student may have a negative effect on his learning. The teletype, however, responds with neither positive nor negative effect. The frequency of verbal attacks towards the teletype and the fact that they do not appear to interfere with the student's completion of the lesson indicate the possibility that such venting of emotion can be a positive aspect of the learning situation.

An example of the positive motivational aspects of CAI is provided by a teacher at Brentwood, a school in an underprivileged area in California. One student was absent from school, without parental permission, for a complete week yet arrived at the computer laboratory on the school grounds to take his turn to do arithmetic at the teletype. His truancy was not discovered until his teacher received the weekly teacher's report on mathematics performance from the computer laboratory.

Evaluation

As one example of the positive effects of the drill-and-practice program in mathematics, we present the evaluation of student performance in McComb,

Mississippi, during the 1967–68 school year. Although we found significant differences in performance when control groups were compared with experimental groups in both California (1966–67 and 1967–68) and Mississippi, the average performance level of students in some of the classrooms in Mississippi was as much as two years below their grade level. These students, therefore, provided an excellent example of the benefits of CAI in a situation in which the educational environment was not sufficient to produce "average" performance.

To evaluate the CAI program we administered the arithmetic portion of the Stanford Achievement Test (SAT) [2] in October for Grades 2–6 as a pretest, in February for Grade 1 as a pretest, and in May for Grades 1–6 as a posttest. Tests were given in 12 different schools in Mississippi; 8 of these schools included both experimental and control students, 3 included only experimental students, and 1 included only control students. Within the experimental group, 1–10 classes were tested at each grade level; within the control group, 2–6 classes were tested at each grade level. (For a description of the SAT and a listing of the levels administered as a function of grade, see Suppes & Morningstar, 1969.)

The response measure used to determine the change in performance level for the year was the difference between the posttest and pretest grade placement on the SAT computation section for each grade. The results of the t test applied to the difference between experimental and control groups on this measure and the average pretest and posttest grade placements for each grade are shown in Table 1.

TABLE 1

Grade-Placement Scores on the SAT: Mississippi 1967–68

Grade	Pretest Experimental	N	Pretest Control	N	Posttest Experimental	Posttest Control	Posttest-pretest Experimental	Posttest-pretest Control	t	df
1	1.41	52	1.19	62	2.55	1.46	1.14	.26	3.69*	112
2	1.99	25	1.96	54	3.37	2.80	1.42	.84	5.23*	77
3	2.82	22	2.76	56	4.85	4.04	2.03	1.26	4.64*	76
4	2.26	58	2.45	77	3.36	3.17	1.10	.69	2.63*	131
5	3.09	83	3.71	134	4.46	4.60	1.37	.90	3.43*	215
6	4.82	275	4.36	160	6.54	5.48	1.72	1.13	5.18*	433

* $p < .01$.

The performance of the experimental students improved significantly more than that of the control students in all six grades. The difference between the experimental group and the control group was the largest in Grade 1, where in only three months the average increase in grade placement for experimental students was 1.14 compared with .26 for control students.

In addition to the results from the computation section of the SAT, the performance of students in the experimental group was significantly better than that of the students in the control group on the concepts section of the SAT for Grade 3,

---

[2] The Stanford Achievement Test, revised in 1963, and the instructions for administration were written by T. Kelly, R. Madden, E. F. Gardener, and H. C. Rudman.

$t = 3.01$, $df = 76$, $p < .01$, and Grade 6, $t = 3.74$, $df = 433$, $p < .01$, and on the application section for Grade 6, $t = 4.09$, $df = 433$, $p < .01$. In Grade 4, the control group improved more than the experimental group on the concepts section, $t = -2.25$, $df = 131$, $p < .05$.

Although we have not presented the evaluation of our CAI program in California, a comparison of the results for California with those for Mississippi indicates, in a logical rather than statistical manner, that CAI is an advantageous tool for compensatory education. First, when significant effects were examined for all six grades, the CAI program appeared to be far more effective in Mississippi than it was in California. Second, the changes in performance level for the experimental groups were quite similar for California and Mississippi. However, the changes in performance for the control groups were very small in Mississippi compared with the changes for the control groups in California. Thus, although use of the CAI system resulted in equal changes in performance in two geographical areas, the program was more effective in terms of differences between experimental and control students when students were performing below grade level and were in need of extra education, as in the Mississippi area, than when students were receiving adequate education, as in the relatively affluent middle class neighborhoods in California.

Another example of the positive effects of CAI is provided by the evaluation during 1968–69 of a mathematics program in the New York City schools. More than 4,000 students in Grades 2–6 from 16 schools participated in the New York CAI program, a mathematics drill-and-practice curriculum modeled after the Stanford project. The New York system, with an RCA Spectra 70/45 computer and 192 student terminals, is currently the largest CAI project in any single school system in the country.

The Metropolitan Achievement Tests (MAT), Form C, were administered as a pretest in January 1969, and as a posttest in June 1969, to evaluate the program. The results of the testing[3] are shown in Table 2 for the 2,940 experimental students and 342 control students who took both the pretest and the posttest. The

TABLE 2

Average Raw Scores on the MAT: New York City 1968–69

Grade	Pretest Experimental Average	N	Pretest Control Average	N	Posttest-pretest Experimental Average	N	Posttest-pretest Control Average	N
2	17.20	340	18.44	79	6.78	340	3.50	79*
3	14.79	726	19.96	98	12.68	726	9.31	98*
4	26.26	790	31.36	93	8.34	790	6.10	93*
5	16.86	717	21.61	49	8.13	717	2.89	49*
6	22.79	367	35.34	23	5.54	367	2.69	23

*$p < .01$.

---

[3] This analysis was performed under the direction of M. Weiner of the City University of New York. For information about the project we are indebted to S. Umans, Director of Title III Projects in New York City.

average posttest minus pretest score on the computation section of the MAT was significantly greater for the experimental students than for the control students in Grades 2–5. The superiority of the experimental students appears to be greatest in Grade 5. We feel that the positive effects of CAI in New York City, especially when measured over a period of only five-and-a-half months, add further support for the use of CAI in compensatory education.

Strand Program in Mathematics

The most extensive curriculum development at the Institute has been in the drill-and-practice program in arithmetic. The final arithmetic curriculum appropriate for Grades 1–6 and, remedially, for Grades 7–9 was constantly revised during the years from 1964 to 1968. This curriculum, although utilizing the computer to present a program individualized in terms of difficulty of problems, immediate feedback, self-pacing, and review material, did not break away from the basic model of drill-and-practice provided in the traditional classroom.

During the summer of 1968, development began on a major revision of the drill-and-practice program. The revised program evolved when attention was diverted from a program which could duplicate and expedite classroom procedures for a given grade to a program which could provide the most efficient drill for a given individual from the start of Grade 1 through the end of Grade 6. The questions used to determine what types of problems a child should receive on a drill changed from "What grade is the child in?" and "What is usually taught at that grade level?" to "What concepts has this child mastered?" and "What should this child learn next?"

Attention to the child rather than to the classroom resulted in a reorganization of the drill-and-practice material in elementary-school mathematics into ungraded strands. The student, working on several strands simultaneously, begins at the bottom of a strand and moves upward on each strand as a function of his ability to perform correctly on that strand. Since movement along a strand depends on the student, the level of performance on one strand relative to the level of performance on other strands creates a problem set for one student different from the problem set for another student. Thus, unlike in the traditional classroom, each student is solving a different set of problems, and each set of problems contains problem types from each strand appropriate to the ability level of the student involved.

The strand system consists of three major elements:

1. A curriculum structure that classifies the problems appropriate for an elementary-school mathematics program;

2. A set of rules for determining the problems to be presented to each student;

3. A set of rules to define the progress of a student through the structure.

Curriculum Structure

The present curriculum structure contains 15 strands. Each strand includes all problem types of a given concept (e.g., fractions, equations) or of a major subtype of a concept (e.g., horizontal addition, vertical multiplication) presented in Grades 1–6. Table 3 shows the 15 strands and the portion of the six-year curriculum for which they are appropriate.

TABLE 3

Content and Duration of Each Strand

Strand	Content	Grade range
1	Counting and place value	1.0–7.0
2	Vertical addition	1.0–6.0
3	Horizontal addition	1.0–3.5
4	Vertical subtraction	1.5–6.0
5	Horizontal subtraction	1.0–3.5
6	Equations	1.5–7.0
7	Horizontal multiplication	2.5–5.5
8	Vertical multiplication	3.5–7.0
9	Fractions	3.5–7.0
10	Division	3.5–7.0
11	Large numbers and units of measure: time, money, linear measure, dozen, liquid measure, weight, Roman numerals, metric measure	1.5–7.0
12	Decimals	3.0–7.0
13	Commutative, associative, and distributive laws	3.0–7.0
14	Negative numbers	6.0–7.0
15	Problem solving	3.0–7.0

Within each strand, problems of a homogeneous type (e.g., all horizontal addition problems with a sum between zero and five) are grouped into equivalence classes. Each strand contains either 5 or 10 classes per half year with each class labeled in terms of a grade-placement equivalent. A problem count of problem types occurring in three major elementary-school mathematics texts (Clark, Beatty, Payne, & Spooner, 1966; Eicholz & O'Daffer, 1966; Suppes, 1966) and data collected during the past three years of the drill-and-practice program at Stanford were used to arrange the equivalence classes in an increasing order of difficulty and to insure that new skills (e.g., regrouping in addition) were introduced at the appropriate point in the curriculum. An example of the equivalence classes for the horizontal subtraction strand is shown in Table 4.

In addition to the ordering of the problems within a strand, we must know how much emphasis is needed on each strand at a given point in the year. To determine this, we divided the curriculum into 12 parts, each corresponding to half a year. A probability distribution function was developed for the proportion of problems on each strand for each half year. Both the problem count from the three textbooks and the average latency for problem types based on past data were used to develop the curriculum distribution. The final proportions in terms of time and problems for each half year for each strand are shown in Table 5, with the exception of Strand 15 (problem solving) which is handled separately.

Rules for Sampling Problems

Since the curriculum distribution is a function of the curriculum and in no way accounts for individual differences in performance, a sampling function was defined to determine which problems a given student would receive. The sampling function, calculated weekly for each student, is a weighted combination of the curriculum distribution and a subjective distribution.[4] A student's grade placement

TABLE 4

Revised Horizontal Subtraction Strand

Problem Limits	$a-b=x$ $0 \leq a \leq 4$	$a-b=x$ $5 \leq a \leq 9$ $b=0$ or 1 or a	$a-b=x$ $5 \leq a \leq 7$ $b \neq 0$ or 1 or a	$a-b=x$ $8 \leq a \leq 9$ $b \neq 0$ or 1 or a	$a-x=c$ $0 \leq a \leq 4$
Equivalence class	1.0	1.1	1.2	1.3	1.4
Problem Limits	$x-b=c$ $0 \leq x \leq 4$	$a-x=c$ $5 \leq a \leq 9$	$x-b=c$ $5 \leq a \leq 9$	$1a-b=xy$ $a>b$ a and b can $=0$	$1a-b=x$ $0 \leq a \leq 4$ $a<b$
Equivalence class	1.5	1.6	1.7	1.8	1.9
Problem Limits	$1a-b=x$ $1a-b=xy$ $5 \leq a \leq 8$	$1a-x=c$ $0 \leq a \leq 8$ $a<x$	$1x-b=c$ $0 \leq x \leq 8$ $x<b$	$a0-b0=x0$ $100-b0=x0$	$ab-c=xy$ $b \geq c$
Equivalence class	2.0	2.1	2.2	2.3	2.4
Problem Limits	$ab-cd=xy$ $b \geq d$	$1a0-b0=$ $1x0$	$1ab-cd=$ $1xy$ $b \geq d, a \geq c$	$2b-c=1x$ $b<c$	$ab-c=xy$ $b<c, a>2$
Equivalence class	2.5	2.6	2.7	2.8	2.9
Problem Limits	$ab-cd=x$ $b<d$ $a=c+1$	$ab-cd=xy$ $b<d$ $a>c+1$	$a-x=c+d$	$ab-xy=cd$ $b>y$	$xy-ab=cd$ $y>b$
Equivalence class	3.0	3.1	3.2	3.3	3.4

Note.—a,b,c,d = digits in problem as presented to student; x,y = digits in response; italicized characters do not appear in problem as presented to student.

on each strand is defined as the grade-placement equivalent associated with the equivalence class of problems he is being presented. For each student the curriculum distribution is selected to correspond to the half year that includes the student's average grade-placement performance on the strand curriculum. For instance, if the student's average grade placement is 3.3, then the curriculum distribution for the half year (3.0–3.5) will be used to calculate the sampling function, even if the student is enrolled in a fourth-grade class. The subjective function is a normalization of the distribution determined at a given point in time by subtracting the student's grade placement on each strand from his maximum grade placement at that time.

Thus, if sampling were from just the curriculum distribution, the proportion of problems from each strand for a given student would match the proportion of problems from each strand presented in an "average" textbook. If sampling were from just the subjective distribution, the proportion of problems for a given stu-

---

[4] The mathematical formulation of the distributions can be obtained by writing to the authors.

TABLE 5
Proportion of Time and Proportion of Problems for Each Strand in Each Half Year

Strand	1.0 PT	1.0 PP	1.5 PT	1.5 PP	2.0 PT	2.0 PP	2.5 PT	2.5 PP	3.0 PT	3.0 PP	3.5 PT	3.5 PP	4.0 PT	4.0 PP	4.5 PT	4.5 PP	5.0 PT	5.0 PP	5.5 PT	5.5 PP	6.0 PT	6.0 PP	6.5 PT	6.5 PP
1	50	36	24	18	24	16	17	12	10	10	5	4	7	8	7	8	8	10	11	14	14	20	10	10
2	10	14	10	12	9	12	19	22	19	20	7	6	8	10	2	2	3	4	1	2				
3	26	32	21	28	21	26	9	10	8	8														
4			9	12	8	12	15	18	22	20	10	8	13	10	3	2	3	4	1	2				
5	14	18	10	14	16	16	9	10	4	4														
6			17	10	12	10	16	12	17	16	14	12	17	20	7	8	5	8	7	12	7	12	8	10
7							7	10	3	6	8	14	5	10	3	6	2	8						
8											10	14	5	6	14	16	6	8	8	4	7	4	5	2
9											6	4	4	4	15	24	13	22	20	32	17	32	18	26
10					10	8	8	6	8	6	15	18	22	10	34	16	48	16	33	6	40	8	13	2
11			9	6					6	6	11	6	7	8	7	8	5	8	5	8	5	8	5	6
12									6	6	9	8	7	8	5	6	4	6	11	14	7	10	36	38
13									3	4	5	6	5	6	3	4	3	6	3	6	1	2	1	2
14																					2	4	4	4

Note.—PT = proportion of time; PP = proportion of problems.

dent would be largest from the strand for which his performance was lowest; the proportion from each strand would decrease as his performance on that strand came closer to the performance level of his best strand. To decide what proportion of the problems presented should be determined by the curriculum function and what proportion should be determined by the subjective function, we defined a weighting factor based on the amount of discrepancy between the student's maximum and minimum grade placement across strands. Applying the weighting factor to the curriculum distribution and the subjective distribution resulted in the final sampling function. Therefore, as the discrepancy between the maximum and minimum grade placement increases, the emphasis on the subjective distribution increases; if the student is performing at the same level on all strands, emphasis is on the curriculum function alone.

Progress through the Strand Structure

A student's progress through the strand structure is a function of his performance on each strand. As certain criteria of performance are satisfied for a given strand, the equivalence class from which the student is receiving problems changes, with a corresponding change in the student's grade placement on the strand. The criterion for a given equivalence class is a function of the strand and half year of which that class is a member.

For each equivalence class the criterion is stated in terms of three integers, W, Y, and Z. After every Y problems on a strand the student's performance is examined; if he did W or fewer problems correctly, he moves down one equivalence class; if he did more than W and fewer than Z problems correctly, he stays at the same equivalence class; if he did more than Z problems correctly, he moves up one equivalence class. An exception to the criterion for movement is made when a student is presented problems from a given equivalence class for the first time. In such a case, a check is made after the first three problems; if the student did all three incorrectly, he moves down one equivalence class.

The calculation of the values of W, Y, and Z for each equivalence class involved the combination of known facts, estimated facts, and several assumptions. First, knowing the amount of time a student would spend doing problems during a half year, estimating the average latency from presentation of a problem to a response from the student for each problem type (equivalence class), and assuming (for the purpose of calculations only) that the effect of the subjective distribution was negligible, we estimated the number of problems a student would receive from each strand during a half year. Then, assuming that a student has an average probability correct of .70, the values of W, Y, and Z were computed so that a student would increase his grade placement by .5 on all strands during a half year of time at the computer terminal.

Automaton Models

The components of the strand structure that provide an individualized curriculum for the student also provide a situation for data collection that allows great specificity in terms of the characteristics of individual students and the types of responses given as a function of problem type. The data available and the theory involved in developing the strand structure make it possible to conduct meaningful and sophisticated research on mathematical models of learning, and at the same time to demand that these models have direct relevance to the design and organization of individualized curriculum. Automaton models will be used extensively in our attempts to revise the curriculum and to learn which characteristics of arithmetic problems are important in the learning process.

An automaton is defined as a device with a finite number of internal states. When it is presented with one of a finite number of letters from an alphabet, as a function of this letter of the alphabet and its internal state, it moves to another of its internal states. (A precise mathematical formulation of both deterministic and probabilistic automata is given in Suppes, 1969.)

To apply the theory of automata to the performance of children solving arithmetic problems, we weld the two separate concepts of internal state and output into the single concept of internal state and identify them with the responses of the child. The letters of the alphabet correspond in a natural way to sets of stimulus elements presented on a given trial to the child.

For the analysis of student data it is necessary to move from deterministic to probabilistic automata. In terms of compensatory education, parameter estimates for the probabilistic automata can be compared to data sets obtained from students whose real grade level is equivalent to the grade placement of the problem type and from students whose real grade level was one, two, or three years above the grade placement identified with the problem. Any significant difference in parameter estimates, given a common error rate in the data sets, would indicate that below-average students encounter difficulties with that problem type that are different from those of the student who attempts the problem at the time specified by an "average" curriculum. Such differences might indicate changes in teaching emphasis necessary for the below-average student. Given probabilistic automata for many different problem types, the comparison of parameter estimates can possibly solve some of the problems involved in the teaching of the below-average child.

Once a number of automata are developed we will also be able to analyze a given student's approach to a group of problems of the same type. The individual approach leads in many directions. Consider the responses of four different students to the following set of problems:

	126	144	169
	− 52	− 71	− 93
Student A	74	73	76
Student B	178	215	262
Student C	134	133	136
Student D	1	3,859	41

A comparison of the responses of Student A with the responses of Student B indicates that Student A has chosen the correct automaton, whereas Student B has chosen the automaton which solves addition problems. Student C has chosen an automaton which, although wrong, has been used consistently; Student D has apparently behaved as an automaton which generates random numbers.

Of the three students responding incorrectly, it would be easier to get Students B and C to respond correctly than to elicit correct responses from Student D. To develop a system to aid Students B and C, we would have to perform an error analysis. From this analysis we could determine for a given problem type (*a*) which of the automata that should be in the student's repertoire are being applied incorrectly, and (*b*) which of the most common automata used should not be in the student's response repertoire. Given this information, the student could receive, after a number of responses to a given problem type, an error message more useful than a simple NO, TRY AGAIN.

A comparison of Student A with Student B also illustrates the necessity of developing a "control" automaton which selects from a set of automata the automaton needed for the problem presented. It is obvious that the input alphabet of the control automaton should include, among other stimuli yet to be determined, the operation symbol.

So far we do not know how many perceptual factors should be included in the automata to be developed. For example, if U is the automaton for a subtraction problem and U' is the automaton for an addition problem, does the probability of applying U' differ for the problems (with different location of the operation sign)

$$\begin{array}{r} 126 \\ -\ 52 \\ \hline \end{array} \qquad \begin{array}{r} 126 \\ -\ 52? \\ \hline \end{array}$$

If a difference in the probability of application of U' does occur, is it represented in a parallel way in differences in the parameter associated with the operation sign in the control automaton? If it does not occur, can a perceptual factor associated with either the subtraction automaton or the control automaton account for the the difference in performance for the two problems?

Perceptual factors also have to be examined within a given problem type. For example, can an automaton be developed with a parameter which accounts for the response 22 to the problem 71 + 5 = ____?[5] Again, an error analysis would lead to more information to help determine how many perceptual factors are operating when children are solving arithmetic problems.

Another application of the automaton models involves the examination of parameters to aid in determining the order of equivalence classes. The order of equivalence classes can be examined separately for the average students and the below-average students. The possibility exists that the structure of the curriculum can be further individualized to fit specific learning difficulties associated with the below-average student.

Strand Structure and Compensatory Education

It is perhaps evident how the strand structure is especially adapted to benefit those students who are in the bottom quartile or the top quartile of the distribution of performance in a class. However, for the purpose of the present symposium, it may be especially pertinent to spell out some of the ways in which we think

---

[5] In a sample of 270 students in the fourth grade, 71% responded correctly; the response 22 accounted for 55% of the error responses.

this structure is most directly relevant to compensatory education. Two aspects are to be stressed: One is the individualization of instruction, and the other is the individualization of diagnosis.

We have already commented at some length on the individualization of instruction provided by the strand structure. It cannot be stressed too strongly, however, that in dealing with students in rural areas or in the inner city, who for a variety of reasons have fallen badly behind in the basic skills of mathematics and reading, we must be realistic in providing them additional instruction. It is a common failing of most curriculum guides to assign grade placement of topics without detailed consideration of the actual achievement level of the students. If time and space permitted, we could give some good anecdotal evidence on the importance of being able to adjust the curriculum two or even three grade levels below normal grade level for a student who is having severe learning difficulties. We should provide him instruction in which he can make meaningful progress and which is not at a self-defeating level of difficulty. The strand structure is designed to do this on an individual basis without regard to the actual grade placement of the student. If a fourth grader, for example, operates at a first-grade level, then the strand structure is designed to place him there and to move him upward only as he is able to show a minimum mastery of basic skills. The problems of individualization are too easily ignored; it is simply not possible for a teacher operating with a group of 20–30 students to provide an adequate degree of individualization for the student needing compensatory work. The strand structure is designed to do this automatically within the conceptual framework of a dynamically organized curriculum.

The diagnostic aspect of the strand structure has not been stressed as yet, but plays an equally important role. In many cases in inner-city schools or in rural areas, teachers will be faced with classes that are depressed in terms of their level of achievement. The strand structure supplies to the teacher in the form of weekly reports a sharp diagnosis of those particular skills in which the class, as well as the individuals, is weakest. The teacher trained to use the teacher report and sensitive to the achievement level of his class will be able to emphasize for the class as a whole that skill which on the average is poorest, and also as time and effort permit to provide additional troubleshooting for individual children who are especially deficient in particular skills. The teacher receives as part of the teacher's report the grade placement of each student in each strand and the average grade placement of the class, as well as the *rate of change* of grade placement on the average for each student and for the class as a whole. This information can provide a continual basis for diagnosis of necessary changes in direction of teaching, especially in terms of casting the teaching at a more realistic level for students who are below grade level.

Finally, we wish to emphasize that we in no sense believe that the strand structure described represents a universal panacea for the problems of compensatory education. We want to stress as strongly as possible that we recognize the many difficulties of a cognitive and affective nature that must be solved before we can claim to have mastered in a serious way the problems of compensatory education. We do believe that the strand structure provides one step toward solving some of the problems, and is the kind of step that would be difficult to take without the on-line use of a computer.

The strand structure or, more generally, computer-assisted instruction certainly cannot solve in any simple fashion all the problems of compensatory education. We do believe that educational technology provides one rich resource that is just beginning to be used to attack these problems.

References

Atkinson, R. C. Computerized instruction and the learning process. *American Psychologist,* 1968, **23,** 225–239.

Atkinson, R. C., & Hansen, D. N. Computer-assisted instruction in initial reading: The Stanford Project. *Reading Research Quarterly,* 1966, **2,** 5–25.

Clark, C. H., Beatty, L. S., Payne, J. N., & Spooner, G. A. *Elementary mathematics, grades 1–6.* New York: Harcourt, Brace & World, 1966.

Eicholz, R. E., & O'Daffer, P. G. *Elementary school mathematics, grades 1–6.* Palo Alto, Calif.: Addison-Wesley, 1968.

Suppes, P. *Sets and numbers, grades 1–6.* New York: Singer, 1966.

Suppes, P. Stimulus-response theory of finite automata. *Journal of Mathematical Psychology,* 1969, **6,** 327–355.

Suppes, P., Jerman, M., & Brian, D. *Computer-assisted instruction: The 1965–66 Stanford Arithmetic Program.* New York: Academic Press, 1968.

Suppes, P., & Morningstar, M. Computer-assisted instruction. *Science,* 1969, **166,** 343–350.

Suppes, P., & Morningstar, M. Four programs in computer-assisted instruction. In W. H. Holtzman (Ed.), *Computer-assisted instruction, testing, and guidance.* New York: Harper & Row, 1970, in press.

Malnutrition, Learning, and Intellectual Development: Research and Remediation[1]

HENRY N. RICCIUTI

The author received his PhD in experimental-clinical psychology from Fordham University in 1949. He is currently a professor of human development and family studies at Cornell University, where he also serves as Director of the Cornell Research Program in Early Childhood Education. His major research interests center on the role of experience in emotional and cognitive development in infancy.

The devastating effects of severe malnutrition and disease in various regions of the world where conditions of extreme poverty prevail have been recognized for a long time. A variety of programs for alleviating these effects have been carried on particularly since the end of World War II, by public and private agencies in this country and others, as well as through the United Nations. It is only during the past several years, however, that the issue of malnutrition and its implications for human development and human welfare in the United States has become a matter of considerable and rather widespread public concern. The aroused public interest in the problem of malnutrition in this country may be viewed as a natural part of our society's increasing commitment, during the past 10 years or so, to wide-scale programs for improving the economic, educational, and health conditions of the poor, that is, our "war on poverty." At the same time, it seems to me, the increasing concern with malnutrition as a public health problem of particularly compelling priority is based in part on the growing conviction that malnutrition may adversely affect learning and intellectual development in children, perhaps to the degree of producing serious and irreversible mental retardation in some instances.

There has been ample research evidence for some time now that children's physical and biological development may be seriously and even permanently impaired by the combination of malnutrition, infection, and parasitic disease which is endemic in various poor populations (Graham & Morales, 1963; Pre-school

---

[1] Invited Address presented to the Division of School Psychologists at the Annual Meeting of the American Psychological Association, Washington, D. C., September 2, 1969.

Preparation of the paper was supported in part by the Cornell Research Program in Early Childhood Education, a component of the National Laboratory in Early Childhood Education, United States Office of Education Contract No. OEC–3–7–070706–3118. Points of view or opinions stated do not necessarily represent official Office of Education position or policy.

Child Malnutrition, 1966; Scrimshaw & Gordon, 1968). However, it is only during the past 12 years or so that concerted research efforts have been directed toward the question of the influence of malnutrition on mental development and learning in children (Latham, 1969; Scrimshaw, 1967). What I should like to do in this paper is to examine the status of our present knowledge on this rather complicated problem and to explore some aspects of recent research which might be of particular relevance to you in your work as school psychologists. At the same time, I want to consider some of the implications of our current knowledge about malnutrition and mental development with regard to public programs concerned with the alleviation of malnutrition and with the facilitation of intellectual development in children.

Malnutrition in America: A Current National Concern

Let me begin by briefly outlining some of the major features of our present national concern with the problem of malnutrition. You are familiar, I am sure, with two recent reports which effectively drew public attention to the existence of allegedly widespread and severe malnutrition in certain parts of the United States. One of these was the *Hunger U.S.A.* report, from the Citizens' Board of Inquiry into Hunger and Malnutrition in the United States (1968); the other was the CBS television program entitled "Hunger in America" which followed shortly thereafter in the late spring of 1968.[2] These reports were both applauded for drawing public attention to a seriously overlooked problem confronting our poor and criticized for presenting an inaccurate view of the problem.

At the present time, fortunately, with the support of Congress, the Department of Health, Education and Welfare, and professional organizations in nutrition and in pediatrics, major efforts are well under way to assess more precisely the nature and scope of malnutrition in this country, by means of systematic survey and examination techniques. One of these efforts is the Preschool Nutrition Survey, initiated under the sponsorship of the Children's Bureau beginning in late 1966[3] (Lowe, 1967). This study, which is still going on, is expected to provide detailed information concerning the growth and nutritional status of a large sample of children aged one to six, drawn from many regions of the United States. The other major effort is the National Nutrition Survey, also under HEW support, which will provide information on the nutritional status of a large sample of individuals of all ages, totaling 70,000–75,000 people or 18,000 families, approximately, with particular emphasis on people living in economically deprived areas[4] (see also Footnote 3). Thus, there will soon be forthcoming a great deal of hitherto unavailable factual information about the nature and scope of malnutrition at all age levels in various segments of the United States population.

In the meantime, a variety of programs to improve the nutritional status of children, pregnant women, and other adults who are particularly likely to be at

---

[2] C. Kuralt. "Hunger in America," CBS Television Network, May 21, 1968.

[3] W. J. Cohen. Statement on hunger and malnutrition in America before the Subcommittee on Employment, Manpower, and Poverty, Committee on Labor and Public Welfare, United States Senate, June 21, 1968.

[4] A. E. Schaefer. Statement on National Nutrition Survey before the Senate Select Committee on Nutrition and Related Human Needs, United States Senate, January 22, 1969.

risk are being continued and expanded (Egan, 1969). These include feeding programs for children in Head Start and other school settings, the Supplementary Food Program for needy infants, preschool children, pregnant and postpartum women, nutrition and health programs incorporated in the recently established parent-child centers and the maternity and infant care projects, and a variety of other nutrition-education programs. On the research front, for about the last six years private as well as public agencies, such as the National Institute of Child Health and Human Development, for example, have been exerting a good deal of leadership in stimulating and supporting a broad range of basic and applied research on malnutrition and development, with considerable emphasis on the particular problem of intellectual development and learning in children (National Institute of Child Health and Human Development Conference Reports, 1969a, 1969b). Thus, in the past few years, there has been a substantial increase in the number of investigators from different disciplines in this country who have begun to direct their research efforts toward this problem (Scrimshaw & Gordon, 1968).

It is obvious that regardless of the present status of our research evidence concerning the influence of malnutrition on learning and intellectual development in children, effective programs for combating malnutrition wherever it is found must continue to be developed and expanded. It has been pointed out and demonstrated over and over again that where malnutrition exists as a serious public health problem in disadvantaged populations, it is not an isolated phenomenon but part of a complex of interlocking social and biological conditions which take a heavy toll indeed in terms of human welfare (Collis & Janes, 1968; Scrimshaw, 1964). Severe educational and economic handicaps, infection, parasitic disease, malnutrition, complications of pregnancy and childbirth—all these conditions, which tend to be self-perpetuating, manifest their consequences in such problems as high rates of prematurity and infant mortality, impaired physical growth, and, as you are well aware, impaired intellectual development and school learning (Birch, 1968; Knobloch & Pasamanick, 1966; Pasamanick & Knobloch, 1966). Clearly, we need to remain committed to the development of programs which are aimed at eliminating this entire pattern of socially and physically debilitating conditions.

The Problem of Malnutrition and Mental Development

While necessary programs for combating malnutrition and the other conditions mentioned are continued and expanded, research efforts must continue to be directed toward these central questions: What is the influence of malnutrition on intellectual development, learning, and educational achievement in children? Can this influence be separated from the concomitant effects of the other social, environmental, and biological conditions typically associated with malnutrition? More specifically, how do the effects of malnutrition vary as a function of age of onset, severity, duration, and the particular type of malnutrition involved? How severe are the effects on intellectual development? Are they reversible with nutritional rehabilitation or must remediation occur at a particular point in development in order to be effective? Can the effects be assessed in terms of specific psychological functions and behavioral outcomes, not simply in terms of general intelligence measures? How are the effects on intellectual performance mediated—

through altered brain function, impaired learning capacity, reduced responsiveness to the environment, or through some other process?

These are important and difficult questions, of a sort familiar to most developmental and child psychologists. By their very nature, they are particularly difficult to answer in research with human subjects. Moreover, some investigators feel that definitive answers to many of these questions can be obtained only from the kinds of controlled experimentation that are possible in animal studies. As a matter of fact, an increasing amount of animal research related to these issues has been under way during the past few years, with the results being of considerable heuristic value insofar as malnutrition in children is concerned (Barnes, 1969; Harlow & Harlow, 1969; Scrimshaw & Gordon, 1968).

It should be clear that the research questions just posed concerning the influence of malnutrition on intellectual development are not only of theoretical importance to developmental psychologists and biologists, but they are also of very great practical significance, since answers to them should help us make wiser decisions and plans concerning specific programs aimed at facilitating the intellectual and educational development, as well as the physical development, of young children.

Malnutrition: Some Problems of Definition and Assessment

Before going on to a review of the research on malnutrition and mental development in children, let me spend some time on a few brief but necessary definitions and distinctions. First, what about the term "malnutrition" itself? A recent definition reflects current usage of the term as a rather broad concept referring to "an impairment of health and physiological function resulting from the failure of an individual to obtain all the essential nutrients in proper amount and balance [see Footnote 4]." According to this usage, as a generic term "malnutrition" would include: (*a*) *undernutrition,* representing a condition of impaired health due to the consumption of an insufficient quantity of food over an extended period of time; (*b*) *specific deficiencies,* due to the lack of particular essential nutrients, such as vitamins, iron, etc; and (*c*) *overnutrition,* impaired health due to the consumption of an excessive quantity of food, or of one or more nutrients, over an extended period of time (e.g., obesity).

My major concern in this paper will be with the first condition just mentioned, namely, malnutrition (or undernutrition) produced essentially by an insufficiency of protein and calories in the child's diet, commonly referred to as "protein-calorie malnutrition," which is regarded by many as the most serious nutritional problem on a worldwide basis (Jelliffe, 1959). I shall also examine briefly, however, some research on mental development and specific nutritional deficiencies.

Protein-calorie malnutrition includes the conditions of *nutritional marasmus,* involving a severe inadequacy of intake of all nutrients, usually from the earliest months of life, producing infants whose physical development is grossly impaired; and *kwashiorkor,* which is primarily an insufficiency of protein occurring in children typically toward the end of the first year or in the second year of life, usually after the birth of a younger sibling (Graham & Morales, 1963; Scrimshaw, 1963). Nutritional marasmus is usually a rather long-term condition beginning very early in life, while kwashiorkor often takes the form of a rather acute illness, occurring somewhat later on. Many combinations and mixtures of these conditions are found in practice, varying greatly in severity and duration. I should mention, incidentally, that when the nutritionist refers to marasmus in infants, he is not using the term as most psychologists have come to know it through the influence of Spitz (1945) particularly, implying a condition produced primarily by psychological deprivation.

One of the difficulties confronting researchers concerned both with nutritional surveys and with the relationships between malnutrition and intellectual development is the fact that it is not at all easy to secure reliable and valid assessments of nutritional status in children. This is particularly true if one is concerned with measurement throughout a broad range of nutritional variation, and not just with the identification of clinically obvious and severe malnutrition (Jelliffe & Jelliffe, 1968). In the current National Nutrition Surveys which were mentioned earlier, nutritional status is being assessed through three types of measures: (*a*) evaluation of food intake from detailed dietary reports; (*b*) physical or clinical evaluations, including various anthropometric and radiographic measures; and (*c*) biochemical evaluations of various specific nutrients from blood and urine samples.

The interpretation of such measurements as indicators of nutritional status is considered rather difficult, and many nutritionists feel that such measurements are most valid when used in combination with one another. Moreover, published standards for judging adequacy of nutritional status from a particular index vary considerably, resulting in variable estimates of the frequency of various specific nutritional deficiencies. It is for reasons such as these that the data collected in the National Nutrition Survey are to be reviewed and interpreted by panels of experts from several national scientific and medical groups.

I might mention parenthetically at this point that I do not believe I need dwell at length on the very similar and familiar problems which face us as psychologists when we try to obtain valid and reliable measurements of relevant perceptual-cognitive, learning, and motivational functions in young children from infancy through the elementary school years! We might take some slight comfort from the fact that our nutritionist and pediatric colleagues have just as many problems in the assessment of nutritional status in children!

A further definitional note concerns the necessity of distinguishing between "hunger" and "malnutrition," two terms which have tended to be blurred and used interchangeably in recent days. A child who frequently comes to school without breakfast, or who misses lunch often, may be hungry, but he may or may not be significantly malnourished. While it is conceivable that his school performance might be affected adversely by inattentiveness and distractability associated with hunger, we clearly need to differentiate these potential influences on school learning, about which we know very little, from those which might be the result of long-term protein-calorie malnutrition, perhaps in the form of altered central nervous system functions, reduced responsiveness to the learning environment, etc. Children sufficiently malnourished to undergo changes of this sort do not necessarily experience extended periods of "hunger," as commonly defined. In fact, many severely and acutely malnourished children tend to be characterized by apathy, withdrawal, and loss of appetite, rather than by the increased activity and restlessness associated with hunger (Cravioto, Delicardie, & Birch, 1966; Trowell, Davies, & Dean, 1954).

Now a final definitional comment. Because of space limitations, my discussion will deal primarily with protein-calorie malnutrition which occurs during postnatal and subsequent development in children. I must therefore omit consideration of the adverse influences on children's psychological development and educational achievement brought about by complications of pregnancy and childbirth, including prematurity, which are due in part, at least, to maternal malnutrition and ill health (Birch, 1968; Drillien, 1964). At the same time, I shall have to omit consideration of a number of problems which involve particularly complicated interactions of nutritional, psychological, and social difficulties in children, some of which you may deal with clinically as school psychologists. I refer here to such problems as the abused or neglected child who is also malnourished (Helfer & Kempe, 1968), the so-called "failure to thrive" babies sometimes found in socially advantaged and apparently benevolent homes (Leonard, Rhymes, & Solnit, 1966), "anorexia nervosa" or extreme loss of appetite (Kay & Leigh, 1954), and obesity or caloric overnutrition (Mayer, 1968), which some feel is one of our major nutritional problems in this country, rather than protein-calorie malnutrition.

Recent Research on Malnutrition and Mental Development

Preliminary Summary of General Conclusions

After these rather lengthy introductory comments, we are now ready to turn to the central question of the influence of protein-calorie malnutrition on learning and intellectual development in children. What conclusions can be drawn at this point from the research evidence based on humans? Let me start out immediately with the briefest kind of summary statement, with which I believe a good many of my nutritionist, pediatrician, and psychologist colleagues would concur.

First, there is reasonably good evidence that protein-calorie malnutrition occurring in the first year of life, which is severe enough to markedly impair physical growth and to require hospitalization and treatment, may have adverse effects on the child's mental development, perhaps even to the extent of producing in some instances borderline or more severe mental retardation which does not appear to be readily remediable under conditions of nutritional rehabilitation. Severe malnutrition beginning in the second year of life or later, often taking the form of kwashiorkor, appears to produce adverse effects on mental development which are not as severe and seem to be more amenable to treatment. In both instances, however, it is not entirely clear whether the condition of postnatal malnutrition is the sole or even principal determinant of impaired intellectual functioning, nor do we fully understand how its influences are mediated.

Second, when we consider the chronic, moderate-to-mild, protein-calorie malnutrition which appears to be endemic in many economically disadvantaged populations, then the evidence as to effects on intellectual and learning functions attributable to malnutrition as such, independent of the concomitant influences of social and environmental factors, is very weak and unclear indeed, and we need considerable further research on this question before it can be satisfactorily answered. I think it is reasonable to assume, however, in the light of our present knowledge of child development, that the effects of moderate or mild malnutrition on intellectual development and school learning are probably minimal, in comparison with the influences attributable to other major environmental, experimental, and genetic determinants of mental development.

Studies of Children Hospitalized for Malnutrition

Now let me briefly describe some of the major studies which have been done and summarize their findings in somewhat more detail. The great majority of investigations of protein-calorie malnutrition and intellectual development have been carried out in economically disadvantaged populations in Latin America, Africa, and Asia. Let us consider first some studies which have been concerned with the effect of malnutrition severe enough to require hospitalization and treatment in the first two to three years of life. Several of these studies have evaluated malnourished infants *during* their hospitalization and rehabilitation or shortly thereafter, while others have been concerned with effects observable *later* in the preschool or school-aged period.

One of the earliest and frequently quoted studies was done in Mexico City in the early 1960s by Cravioto, one of the foremost investigators in this field, and Robles (1965). Twenty infants hospitalized for severe protein-calorie malnutrition were examined with the Gesell infant scale every two weeks during treatment and rehabilitation, which lasted as long as 6 months for some infants. All infants were well below age norms on the Gesell when admitted, with developmental quotients (DQs) mainly below 60. During rehabilitation, 14 children who had been admitted for treatment between 15–42 months of age came progressively closer to age expectations on the Gesell. However, the 6 infants whose malnutrition led to hospitalization before the age of 6 months did not show any recovery of their developmental deficit during nutritional rehabilitation.

A study conducted in Venezuela at about the same time dealt with 60 children hospitalized at some time between 15–71 months of age for severe malnutrition, primarily of the kwashiorkor type (Barrera-Moncada, 1963). When examined after 7–12 weeks of treatment, these children had a mean DQ of 65 on the Gesell scale. Some of these children were reexamined two years later and achieved IQs approaching the normal range.

Several years ago Brockman and Ricciuti (1970) did a study with 20 children from 12–43 months of age who had been hospitalized for severe nutritional marasmus in Lima, Peru, sometime between 2½–42 months of age (see also Brockman, 1966). We attempted to assess cognitive functioning involved in primitive categorizing behavior in these infants by means of some simple sorting techniques which we had previously used with normal infants (Ricciuti, 1965). The test performance of the malnourished infants was substantially and significantly below that of a control group of children from the Lima slums, who had been selected on the basis of their being taller than the malnourished children, and hence presumably without a previous history of severe malnutrition.[5]

While there are many obvious technical difficulties in interpreting the results of studies like those I have just summarized, they indicate, as do a number of

---

[5] The use of stature as an index of nutritional background poses substantial interpretive problems (Pollitt & Ricciuti, 1969), as discussed later in this paper.

other studies in the literature (Geber & Dean, 1956; Pollitt & Granoff, 1967), that infants tested during and shortly after rehabilitation from severe protein-calorie malnutrition requiring hospitalization in the first several years of life show substantially reduced performance on developmental and cognitive tests. Moreover, some of the studies, at least, suggest that severe malnutrition which occurs in the second year of life or later may have relatively less severe and long-lasting effects on psychological development than seems to be the case for malnutrition occurring in the first year.

Now let us consider investigations in which the influence of severe malnutrition requiring hospitalization early in life is examined in regard to the intellectual status of the children somewhat later on in childhood. Two studies suggest that children hospitalized for malnutrition in the first year show appreciably reduced intellectual functioning when subsequently examined at about four years of age (Chase & Martin, 1969; Mönckeberg, 1968). As far as I know, the Chase and Martin study is the only investigation of protein-calorie malnutrition and intellectual development carried out on a sample of children in the United States. Working in Colorado, these investigators have recently found that 20 children who had been hospitalized for malnutrition before the age of one year had a mean DQ of 82 when examined approximately three and a half years later. This performance, based on the Yale Revised Developmental Examination, was significantly lower than the mean DQ of 99 achieved by a carefully matched control group of non-malnourished children.

When they contrasted the malnourished infants hospitalized before and after four months of age, those who had been admitted after the age of four months, and who presumably had been malnourished for a longer period of time without treatment, had a mean DQ of 70. On the other hand, children who were admitted and treated prior to four months of age had virtually normal DQs when examined three and a half years later, and were also less retarded in physical growth at that time than the later treated infants. (It should be mentioned that these infants were probably not as severely malnourished as those included in some of the previously mentioned studies from Latin America.) While the Chase and Martin study involved considerably more careful matching of the malnourished and control subjects on social and environmental factors than has ordinarily been the case, the authors themselves point out that from a research point of view "it appears impossible to completely separate undernutrition from associated environmental influences, as they are part of the same entity."

What about the intellectual functioning of *school-aged* children known to have been hospitalized for malnutrition during the first 2 or 3 years of life? A number of studies provide suggestive evidence, at least, that these children may perform less well than children without a history of early and severe malnutrition. One of the most recent of these investigations was carried out by Cravioto and his colleagues in Mexico City (Cravioto, Pinero, Arroyo, & Alcade, 1969). They tested 39 children 5–10 years of age, all of whom had been hospitalized at some time between 4–30 months of age for severe malnutrition, primarily of the kwashiorkor type. As control subjects they employed the nearest aged siblings of the experimental children. The previously malnourished children were found to have substantially lower WISC IQ scores, with nearly 50% of them scoring below 70, in contrast with nearly 30% of the control subjects. Furthermore, the malnourished children made more errors on a form recognition task and on a test of auditory-visual integration previously employed by Birch in his research in this country with retarded readers (Birch & Belmont, 1964).

In this report Cravioto and his collaborators caution against interpreting their results as evidence of a direct "causal relationship between malnutrition and mental competence" even with the use of siblings as controls. Nevertheless, they regard their results as suggesting that for children growing up in an environment generally capable of impeding intellectual growth, the added presence of an episode of severe malnutrition early in life increases the likelihood that there will be an impairment of the development of intellectual and learning functions important for the child to profit from the school experience.

A similar study was conducted very recently in India (Champakam, Srikantia, & Gopalan, 1968). Nineteen children hospitalized for kwashiorkor some time between 1½–3 years of age were examined when they were between 8–11 years of age on several tests of intersensory integration, and on a number of tests of memory, perceptual, abstract, and verbal ability. In comparison with the performance of control children matched for various social background factors, the previously malnourished children performed substantially less well, particularly in the 8–9 years group. Once again, with regard to problems of interpretation, these authors point out that the same environmental factors which might contribute to the development of kwashiorkor in some children and not in others in the same environment might well contribute directly to the reduced intellectual performance which was observed.

Studies of Nonhospitalized Children

Thus far we have been considering studies in which the malnutrition under investigation was clearly severe enough to warrant hospitalization during the first two to three years of life. A number of studies have dealt with children whose restricted physical growth, particularly in stature, is taken as suggesting a history of less severe but chronic malnutrition. In many respects, the results of these investigations are particularly difficult to interpret because of the problems involved in using extreme differences in physical stature, such as height, weight, or head circumference, as the principal indices of nutritional status. It is well known, for example, that while differences in height may reflect nutritional factors, they may also reflect a variety of other biological and social characteristics of the environment, or of the individual, which are capable of influencing intellectual development (Douglas & Blomfield, 1962; Pollitt & Ricciuti, 1969).

In a frequently quoted study by Stoch and Smythe in South Africa (1968), 20 children were selected for study when they were between 10 months and 3 years of age on the basis of markedly reduced height, weight, and head circumference. Their physical and intellectual development was checked periodically over approximately 11 years. During this follow-up period these children scored consistently and substantially lower than a control group, by 15 to 20 IQ points, on tests such as the Gesell, Merrill-Palmer, and, most recently, the New South Africa Individual Intelligence Scale. Educational placement of these children also was reported as lagging considerably behind average for age. While the consistency of these findings over an 11-year period is impressive, it is important to emphasize, as a number of people have already pointed out (e.g., Scrimshaw, 1967), that it is impossible to determine in this study to what extent malnutrition might account for the observed test score differences. The control children, although selected from the same socioeconomic class as the malnourished youngsters, came from more stable homes with markedly better living conditions, and they were attending an all-day nursery school when the study began.

Similar problems of interpretation arise in connection with two recent studies by Cravioto and his colleagues in which tall and short school-aged children were selected for study on the assumption that the likelihood of their having been previously exposed to nutritional risk was markedly different. Instead of relying on the usual measures of general intelligence, these investigators evaluated children's ability to integrate information from different sense modalities using procedures previously developed by Birch and Lefford (1964). In a Guatemalan village study of children from 6–11 years of age, the tall children tended to make fewer errors than the short children in identifying geometric forms on the basis of visual, haptic or tactual, and kinesthetic information, particularly in the younger age groups (Cravioto, Delicardie, & Birch, 1966). While the tall and short children did not differ significantly on a number of social-environmental background factors assessed as controls in the research, maternal education was markedly higher in the case of the tall children, illustrating again the difficulty of separating presumed nutritional differences in tall and short children from the influence of associated social factors such as parental education. A later study of auditory-visual integration in several hundred rural Mexican school children 7–12 years of age again revealed slight differences in favor of tall children, particularly at age 12 (Cravioto, Gaona, & Birch, 1967). No information is available in this latter report concerning possible social or environmental differences in the contrasting stature groups.

A number of recent investigations of malnutrition and intellectual development, such as the ones just mentioned, have begun to assess rather specific perceptual-cognitive functions in preschool or school-aged malnourished children. In some very interesting recent work in Guatemala, Klein (1969) gave several tests of short-term memory and simple incidental learning to 20 children five and a half years old, who had previously been sufficiently malnourished to be treated at a rehabilitation clinic (but not hospitalized). These children performed significantly poorer on the tasks mentioned than a taller control group with generally similar social background, including the presence of malnutrition in the home, in a sibling. In a rather rare replication study employing the same tests, these performance differences were not found by Klein, although significant differences were obtained in favor of control children on two new tasks involving memory and learning under conditions requiring rapid information processing. Klein has suggested that this failure to replicate the earlier findings might have been due to the presence of less severe malnutrition in his second study, or to the fact that the examiners in the second study were unaware of the differences in the nutritional histories of the experimental and control subjects.

At this point in my review, I hope I have given you some feeling both for the major suggestive findings coming from the research literature as well as the uncertainties and ambiguities we are confronted with when we try to evaluate the effect of protein-calorie malnutrition on intellectual development in children, as an influence separate from the other biological, social, and environmental conditions usually associated with it.

Studies Involving Nutritional Remediation and Biochemical Assessments

I would like to turn next to some brief examples of studies in which investigators have looked for changes in intellectual development as a possible consequence of rather extensive attempts to improve children's nutritional status by means of dietary interventions of various kinds. Interestingly enough, while there are some elaborate studies of this kind currently under way or in the planning stage in Latin America (Canosa, 1968; Latham, 1969; Velez, Vasco, Echeverri, & Vitale, 1969), this was a problem that nutritionists, home economists, and early childhood educators addressed themselves to in the United States as long ago as the early 1920s when, as part of the early child development movement, there was much emphasis placed on the school's role in improving the general health and nutritional status of children (Bliss, 1921; Smith & Field, 1926).

In more recent times, Kugelmass, Poull, and Samuel (1944) carried out a study in New York City in which 50 children two to nine years of age who were judged to be nutritionally deficient but in the normal IQ range were reported to have gained 18 IQ points, on the average, after two to three years of an unspecified nutritional improvement program. Since there is virtually no way of determining whether the IQ change was in fact due to the presumed nutritional changes or to other social and environmental variables, this study, while often quoted, has apparently not been taken too seriously for the most part.

Several years later, in a much more carefully controlled study, Harrel (1946) reported that orphanage children in Virginia who were given thiamine (vitamin B_1) daily over a one-year period scored significantly higher than a carefully matched placebo group of orphanage children on a number of tests of perceptual and intellectual functions important in school learning. It has recently been suggested that this improvement, which was not confirmed in a subsequent Canadian study (Robertson, Tatham, Walker, & Weaver, 1947), might have been achieved because the orphanage children were originally deficient in thiamine. Sandstead, Carter, and House (1969), who proposed the interpretation just mentioned, have recently completed a preliminary study of nutritional deficiencies in disadvantaged preschool children enrolled in a compensatory language program in Nashville, Tennessee. They found that children with biochemical evidence of a deficiency in thiamine (or vitamin B_1) tended to have lower initial Stanford-Binet IQs ($r = .45$). The IQ was unrelated, however, to other nutritional indices such as amount of iron, hemoglobin, or vitamin A.

Beller (1969) has also found no relationship between general intelligence and measures of iron deficiency anemia in disadvantaged preschool children in Philadelphia. However, he reports preliminary evidence suggesting that anemic children show more aimless manipulation, less purposeful activity, and a much lower attention span on several tasks than do nonanemic children.

The last few studies mentioned, which clearly are not conclusive as yet, are nevertheless illustrative of the currently increasing research interest in relating specific nutritional deficiencies, often biochemically determined, to specific perceptual, cognitive, and attentional processes, as well as to general intellectual functioning (see also Coursin, 1967).

Research Implications: Substantive and Practical

Having completed this brief overview and summary of some of the principal investigations of malnutrition and intellectual development in children, let us examine some of the main implications of these studies, first from the point of view of what we have learned in regard to some of the specific research questions I posed earlier, and then from the point of view of programs for facilitating physical, psychological, and educational development in young children, particularly in this country.

Does malnutrition adversely influence learning and intellectual development in children? If so, how severe are these effects, and are they enduring or remediable?

On the basis of the kinds of studies already summarized, and by inference from related research concerned with brain growth in severe malnutrition in both humans and animals (Dobbing, 1968; Winick, 1969), probably the most confident statement we can make in answer to these questions is that adverse effects on mental development in children are most likely to occur, to be rather severe and long lasting, to the extent that malnutrition begins early in the first year, is severe, and continues for a long period without treatment. When we speak of severe malnutrition at this point, we are talking about infants, for example, whose body weight when hospitalized for treatment at 5 or 6 months of age is no greater or even less than birthweight, and who have made little or no gain in height; or infants whose weight at 10 months is no greater than that of a normal month-old infant. When we speak of severe effects on intellectual development, we are referring to DQs or IQs well below 60, particularly in the Latin American studies.

Our direct evidence on such matters as the influence of age of onset and duration of malnutrition in children is very limited and unclear, even in the case of severe malnutrition, in part because in retrospective studies it is extremely difficult to get accurate information as to the time when malnutrition began, as well as its duration. Several longitudinal studies being carried on in Mexico (Cravioto, 1969) and Guatemala (Canosa, 1968) should eventually provide us with better data on these issues.

Whether or not the impaired intellectual functioning observed during or after exposure to severe or even moderate malnutrition is subject to remediation is still very much an open question, it seems to me. Our direct evidence on this matter is based almost exclusively on studies in which treatment was aimed primarily at the nutritional and medical needs of the child, as it had to be with severely ill children. In the case of long-term follow-up studies, our evidence is based on IQs which continue to be low in children who for the most part remain in the same social and physical environment which contributed to the development of malnutrition and impaired intellectual functioning in the first place. Would these children continue to function at a reduced intellectual level if it were possible to introduce appropriate environmental changes aimed at fostering learning and psychological development through day-care, preschool, elementary school, or home-based programs, combined with programs to insure good health and nutritional status? Until we can begin to answer this and other related questions, we certainly are in no position to conclude that malnutrition produces irreversible adverse effects on children's learning and intellectual development, as some people seem to believe.

Another major problem which still remains unresolved is one that has been referred to frequently in this paper, namely, the question of how malnutrition of varying degrees of severity might interact with other associated biological, social, and environmental conditions in influencing children's learning and intellectual development (Pollitt, 1969; Pollitt & Ricciuti, 1969; Richardson, 1968). Again, as implied earlier, it is probably reasonable to infer from our research that when postnatal malnutrition is severe, early, and long lasting, its relative influence, in comparison with the other conditions mentioned, is greater than it is when moderate or mild malnutrition is involved in children's development. In the latter case, as I have suggested previously, it is highly probable that moderate or mild malnutrition plays a relatively minor role in determining children's intellectual development and school learning, in comparison with the influences of other social, environmental, and genetic factors. Some time ago, a number of us suggested that we might begin to clarify some of these matters by means of experimental intervention studies in which we try to evaluate the influence of various nutritional and educational or experiential interventions, alone and in combination, in facilitating the intellectual development of children with moderate malnutrition (Ricciuti, 1968). Several promising investigations involving some of these approaches are now under way or are being planned by investigators in Guatemala (Canosa, 1968) and Colombia (Latham, 1969).

Meanwhile, I believe that both as scientists and as practitioners or program planners, we need to be very careful not to be drawn prematurely into inferring from our research the general conclusion that postnatal malnutrition, in and of itself, is a major determinant of severe and permanent impairment of intellectual functioning in children. While many research workers have been stressing the great difficulty of isolating the influence of malnutrition from that of other factors influencing mental development in children, the present climate of heightened concern with the alleviation of malnutrition has helped to produce viewpoints about the relationship between malnutrition, mental development, and mental retardation that are often oversimplified and sometimes misleading. A recent editorial (Editorial, 1969) in *Science,* for example, contains the statement: "Children reared in poverty tend to do poorly on tests of intelligence. In part this is due to psychological and cultural factors. To an important extent it is a result of malnutrition early in childhood [p. 17]." For reasons already indicated, the last part of this statement certainly requires a good bit of qualification. Another example is found in the Medical News section (1968) of a medical journal which contains the prominent headline: "Mental Retardation From Malnutrition: 'Irreversible' [p. 30]." The news article then briefly summarizes a report of a very interesting study in Latin America which requires just the kinds of careful interpretation we have been discussing before one can draw the kind of generalized conclusion so boldly suggested in the headline.

Let me hasten to emphasize here that the uncertainties in much of our research, which I have been pointing out in some detail, do not carry the slightest suggestion that we should be any less vigorous than we have been in developing programs to eliminate malnutrition and the other unfavorable educational, economic, and health conditions associated with it. To the extent that we are successful in alleviating these generally adverse conditions wherever they are found, we should not only bring about some improvement in children's nutritional status, but in their potential for learning and intellectual growth as well.

However, there are practical as well as scientific reasons for careful analysis and interpretation of our research findings and for avoiding premature and overgeneralized conclusions. I believe that in the long run we are more likely to be successful in developing and maintaining support for sound programs aimed at improving the physical and psychological development of disadvantaged children if we try to be very clear about the knowledge base and assumptions underlying our plans for such programs, as well as our expectations as to what these programs are likely to accomplish. For example, on the basis of our present knowledge I would say that it would be unwise to initiate large-scale food supplementation programs aimed at populations of mildly to moderately malnourished children on the *principal assumption* that improved nutritional status alone would produce a significant improvement in intellectual development and school learning. There are obviously many other important reasons for improving nutritional well-being, but it would be wrong to judge the success or failure of such a program primarily on the basis of inappropriate expectations concerning changes in intellectual functioning.

Similarly, if we consider various school or preschool settings in this country, there are obviously important reasons for schools to be concerned with helping to keep children in good health and nutrition. In many situations, well-planned school breakfast or lunch programs ought to make important contributions to the improvement of the general well-being of many children. But should these programs be undertaken *primarily* on the expectation that they will appreciably improve the general level of children's intellectual functioning and school learning through nutritional improvement? Again, I would say "No," although I suspect that premature and overgeneralized conclusions about the relationship between malnutrition and intellectual development might lead some people to regard this as a reasonable expectation for school lunch programs.[6]

It seems to me that our wisest strategy in dealing with issues of this sort is to begin with a careful analysis of the problem and a definition of our specific remediation goals, and then to plan our intervention programs and strategies accordingly. If our main goal in a particular situation, for example, is the facilitation of optimal psychological development and school learning in children, then

---

[6] The possible influence of school lunch or breakfast programs on school performance has apparently been investigated only rarely, with little or no evidence of effectiveness in this regard.

the proportion of our efforts which should go into nutritional remediation, relative to other program efforts, will depend mainly on the severity and scope of malnutrition in that particular situation and the influence which nutritional improvement is likely to have on children's learning in the context under consideration.

Our capacity to make wise judgments about such matters should be substantially increased, hopefully, as the Pre-School and National Nutrition Surveys begin to provide us with more factual information about the severity and scope of malnutrition in various parts of the United States, and as our continued research efforts begin to provide further clarification of the complicated relationships between malnutrition and mental development in children. Meanwhile, it seems to me, as psychologists concerned with the education of children of all ages and backgrounds, we must continue to develop the best possible educational programs to facilitate the psychological development of children in school, preschool, day-care, and home settings, while remaining sensitive to the important role which malnutrition and other biological factors may play in this process, particularly in the case of children in disadvantaged groups. At the same time, as psychologists and as members of the broader community, we must actively support the development of broad-gauged public programs which are aimed at ameliorating the adverse social, economic, and health conditions under which so many of our poor continue to live.

References

Barnes, R. H. Developmental consequences of malnutrition: Experimental studies in animals. Paper presented at the Conference on Nutrition, Growth and Development of North American Indian Children, Oklahoma City, May 1969.

Barrera-Moncada, G. *Estudios sobre alteraciones del crecimiento y del desarrollo psicologico del sindrome pluricarencial (kwashiorkor).* Caracas: Editora Grafos, 1963.

Beller, K. Effects of anemia on mental functioning in young children. Unpublished manuscript, Temple University, August 1969.

Birch, H. G. Health and the education of socially disadvantaged children. *Developmental Medicine and Child Neurology,* 1968, **10,** 580–599.

Birch, H. G., & Belmont, L. Auditory-visual integration in normal and retarded readers. *American Journal of Orthopsychiatry,* 1964, **34,** 852–861.

Birch, H. G., & Lefford, A. Two strategies for studying perception in "brain damaged" children. In H. G. Birch (Ed.), *Brain damage in children: Biological and social aspects.* Baltimore, Md.: Williams & Wilkins, 1964.

Bliss, D. C. Malnutrition, a school problem. *Elementary School Journal,* 1921, **21,** 515–521.

Brockman, L. M. The effects of severe malnutrition on cognitive development in infants. Unpublished doctoral dissertation, Cornell University, 1966.

Brockman, L. M., & Ricciuti, H. N. Severe protein-calorie malnutrition and cognitive development in infancy and early childhood. *Developmental Psychology,* 1970, **2,** in press.

Canosa, C. A. Ecological approach to the problems of malnutrition, learning, and behavior. In N. S. Scrimshaw & J. E. Gordon (Eds.), *Malnutrition, learning, and behavior.* Cambridge: MIT Press, 1968.

Champakam, S., Srikantia, S. G., & Gopalan, C. Kwashiorkor and mental development. *American Journal of Clinical Nutrition,* 1968, **21,** 844–852.

Chase, H. P., & Martin, H. P. Undernutrition and child development. Paper presented at the Conference on Neuropsychological Methods for the Assessment of Impaired Brain Functioning in the Malnourished Child, Palo Alto, June 1969.

Citizens' Board of Inquiry into Hunger and Malnutrition in the United States. *Hunger, U. S. A.* Washington, D. C.: New Community Press, 1968.

Collis, W. R., & Janes, M. Multifactorial causation of malnutrition and retarded growth and development. In N. S. Scrimshaw & J. E. Gordon (Eds.), *Malnutrition, learning, and behavior.* Cambridge: MIT Press, 1968.

Coursin, D. B. Relationship of nutrition to central nervous system development and function: Overview. *Federation Proceedings,* 1967, **26,** 134–138.

Cravioto, J. Malnutrition and inter-sensory development. Paper presented at the Conference on Neuropsychological Methods for the Assessment of Impaired Brain Funtioning in the Malnourished Child, Palo Alto, June 1969.

Cravioto, J., Delicardie, E. R., & Birch, H. G. Nutrition, growth and neurointegrative development: An experimental and ecologic study. *Pediatrics,* 1966, **38,** 319–372.

Cravioto, J., Gaona, C. E., & Birch, H. G. Early malnutrition and auditory-visual integration in school age children. *Journal of Special Education,* 1967, **2,** 75–82.

Cravioto, J., Pinero, C., Arroyo, M., & Alcade, E. Mental performance of school children who suffered malnutrition in early age. Unpublished manuscript, Hospital Infantil de Mexico, Mexico City, 1969.

Cravioto, J., & Robles, B. Evolution of adaptive and motor behavior during rehabilitation from kwashiorkor. *American Journal of Orthopsychiatry,* 1965, **35,** 449–464.

Dobbing, J. Effects of experimental undernutrition on development of the nervous system. In N. S. Scrimshaw & J. E. Gordon (Eds.), *Malnutrition, learning, and behavior.* Cambridge: MIT Press, 1968.

Douglas, J. W. B., & Blomfield, J. M. Environmental influences on physical growth. In Y. Brackbill & G. G. Thompson (Eds.), *Behavior in infancy and early childhood.* New York: Free Press, 1967.

Drillien, C. M. *Growth and development of the prematurely born infant.* Edinburgh & London: Livingstone, 1964.

Editorial: Malnutrition, learning, and behavior. *Science,* 1969, **164,** 17.

Egan, M. C. Combating malnutrition through maternal and child health programs. *Children,* 1969, **16,** 67–71.

Geber, M., & Dean, R. F. Psychological changes accompanying kwashiorkor. *Courrier,* 1956, **6,** 3–15.

Graham, G. G., & Morales, E. Studies in infantile malnutrition. I. Nature of the problem in Peru. *Journal of Nutrition,* 1963, **79,** 479–487.

Harlow, M., & Harlow, H. Malnutrition and learning in monkeys. Paper presented at the Conference on Neuropsychological Methods for the Assessment of Impaired Brain Functioning in the Malnourished Child, Palo Alto, June 1969.

Harrell, R. F. Mental response to added thiamine. *Journal of Nutrition,* 1946, **31,** 283.

Helfer, R. E., & Kempe, C. H. (Eds.) *The battered child.* Chicago: University of Chicago Press, 1968.

Jelliffe, D. B. Protein-calorie malnutrition in tropical preschool children. *Journal of Pediatrics,* 1959, **54,** 227.

Jelliffe, D. B., & Jelliffe, E. F. P. Field assessment of dietary intake and nutritional status. In N. S. Scrimshaw & J. E. Gordon (Eds.), *Malnutrition, learning, and behavior.* Cambridge: MIT Press, 1968.

Kay, D. W. K., & Leigh, D. The natural history, treatment, and prognosis of anexoria nervosa based on a study of 38 patients. *Journal of Mental Science,* 1954, **100,** 419.

Klein, R. Malnutrition and behavioral function. Paper presented at the Conference on Neuropsychological Methods for the Assessment of Impaired Brain Functioning in the Malnourished Child, Palo Alto, June 1969.

Knobloch, H., & Pasamanick, B. Prospective studies on the epidemiology of reproductive casualty: Methods, findings, and some implications. *Merrill-Palmer Quarterly,* 1966, **12,** 45–71.

Kugelmass, I. N., Poull, L. E., & Samuel E. C. Nutritional improvement of child mentality. *American Journal of Medical Science,* 1944, **208,** 631.

Latham, M. C. International nutrition and later learning. In, *Nutrition and intellectual growth in children.* Washington, D. C.: Association for Childhood Education International, 1969.

Leonard, M. F., Rhymes, J. P., & Solnit, A. J. Failure to thrive in infants. *American Journal of Diseases in Children,* 1966, **111,** 600–612.

Lowe, C. U. National nutritional survey of pre-school children. *Pediatrics*, 1967, **39**, 485–487.
Mayer, J. *Overweight: Causes, cost and control*. Englewood Cliffs, N. J.: Prentice-Hall, 1968.
Medical News Report. *Journal of the American Medical Association*, 1968, **206**(1), 30–31.
Mönckeberg, F. Effect of early marasmic malnutrition on subsequent physical and psychological development. In N. S. Scrimshaw & J. E. Gordon (Eds.), *Malnutrition, learning, and behavior*. Cambridge: MIT Press, 1968.
National Institute of Child Health and Human Development. *Nutrition, growth and development of North American Indian children*. (Conference report) Washington, D. C.: Author, 1970, in press. (a)
National Institute of Child Health and Human Development. *Neuropsychological methods for the assessment of impaired brain functioning in the malnourished child*. (Conference report) Washington, D. C.: Author, 1970, in press. (b)
Pasamanick, B., & Knobloch, H. Retrospective studies on the epidemiology of reproductive casualty: Old and new. *Merrill-Palmer Quarterly*, 1966, **12**, 7–26.
Pollitt, E. Ecology, malnutrition and mental development. *Psychosomatic Medicine*, 1969, **31**, 193–200.
Pollitt, E., & Granoff, D. Mental and motor development of Peruvian children treated for severe malnutrition. *Revista Interamericana de Psicologia*, 1967, **1**, 93–102.
Pollitt, E., & Ricciuti, H. Biological and social correlates of stature among children living in the slums of Lima, Peru. *American Journal of Orthopsychiatry*, 1969, **39**, 735–747.
Pre-school child malnutrition: Primary deterrent to human progress. Washington, D. C.: National Academy of Sciences, National Research Council, 1966.
Ricciuti, H. N. Object grouping and selective ordering behavior in infants 12 to 24 months old. *Merrill-Palmer Quarterly*, 1965, **11**, 129–148.
Ricciuti, H. N. Panel discussion: Social environment, learning, and behavior. In N. S. Scrimshaw & J. E. Gordon (Eds.), *Malnutrition, learning, and behavior*. Cambridge: MIT Press, 1968.
Richardson, S. A. The influence of social-environmental and nutritional factors on mental ability. In N. S. Scrimshaw & J. E. Gordon (Eds.), *Malnutrition, learning, and behavior*. Cambridge: MIT Press, 1968.
Robertson, E. C., Tatham, C. M., Walker, N. F., & Weaver, M. R. The effect of added thiamine on growth, vision, and learning using identical twins. *Journal of Nutrition*, 1947, **34**, 691–700.
Sandstead, H. H., Carter, J. P., & House, F. R. Nutritional deficiencies in disadvantaged pre-school children and their relationship to mental development. Unpublished manuscript, Vanderbilt University Medical School, August 1969.
Scrimshaw, N. S. Malnutrition and the health of children. *Journal of the American Dietetic Association*, 1963, **42**, 203–208.
Scrimshaw, N. S. Ecological factors in nutritional disease. *American Journal of Clinical Nutrition*, 1964, **14**, 112–122.
Scrimshaw, N. S. Malnutrition, learning and behavior. *American Journal of Clinical Nutrition*, 1967, **20**, 493–502.
Scrimshaw, N. S., & Gordon, J. E. (Eds.) *Malnutrition, learning, and behavior*. Cambridge: MIT Press, 1968.
Smith, A. J., & Field, A. M. A study of the effect of nutrition on mental growth. *Journal of Home Economics*, 1926, **18**, 686–690.
Spitz, R. A. Hospitalism. An inquiry into the genesis of psychiatric conditions of early childhood. *Psychoanalytic Study of the Child*, 1945, **1**, 53–74.
Stoch, M., & Smythe, P. M. Undernutrition during infancy, and subsequent brain growth and intellectual development. In N. S. Scrimshaw & J. E. Gordon (Eds.), *Malnutrition, learning, and behavior*. Cambridge: MIT Press, 1968.
Trowell, H. C., Davies, J. N. P., & Dean, R. F. A. *Kwashiorkor*. London: Arnold, 1954.
Velez, H., Vasco, J., Echeverri, L., & Vitale, J. J. Effects of a food supplement in addition to free medical care: A study in rural Heliconia, Colombia. In, *Proceedings of the eighth international congress on nutrition*. Amsterdam, The Netherlands: Elsevier, 1969, in press.
Winick, M. Malnutrition and brain development. *Journal of Pediatrics*, 1969, **74**, 667–669.

psychology and minority groups

Psychology and Minority Groups

The 1969 APA Convention saw considerable activity and concern for the problems of groups feeling the sting of discrimination. Numerous symposia, papers, and discussions not included in this volume focused on the needs particularly of black Americans but also of other groups. This section includes only those invited divisional addresses which the division chairmen felt to be especially relevant to the convention theme.

Thomas opens the section by taking psychology to task for its research to date on black Americans. He maintains that a racist bias has influenced this research and suggests that with a different value system, behavioral scientists would have gathered a very different set of data. In his other paper in this volume, "Black-White Campus Issues and the Function of Counseling Centers" (included in the section "Psychology and Campus Issues"), Thomas extends his attack to counseling. There he maintains that counselors with no understanding of black students' experience simply cannot serve them. One of the more obvious approaches to the problems which have concerned Thomas is to increase the number of black psychologists serving the black community.

Events resulting directly from activity at the 1969 convention may help to reach such a goal. At the convention the Black Students' Psychological Association (BSPA) petitioned the APA Council of Representatives for action to increase the numbers of black faculty and students in psychology and to increase the relevance of psychological education to the needs of the black community. This petition resulted in APA's establishing a Commission on Accelerating Black Participation in Psychology comprised of representatives of the APA, the BSPA, and the Association of Black Psychologists (ABP). This group is presently raising money to establish a Secretariat within the APA building in Washington to further the objectives of the ABP and the BSPA. They have met with officials from the National Institute of Mental Health and the Veterans Administration to explore ways in which they can further their goals. Through efforts such as these, perhaps in the future, Thomas will have a very different message for us.

Wilson in his paper "Toward a New Social Order" places the black struggle in a broader context. He suggests that the question "What can the social sciences do for the black community?" is a meaningless one. The forces leading to discrimination affect all groups and thus the significant question is rather "What can the social sciences do to build a more completely humane society?" He maintains that the struggles of the blacks for equality have uncovered the varieties of discrimination that permeate the society and have given members of other groups the courage to speak out for themselves.

Wilson's message is confirmed by the gathering momentum of women's groups, as exemplified at the convention. In particular, the women's petitions drafted at the convention for presentation to the APA appear to have roots in the black struggle. One petition, entitled "Sexism" (paralleling "racism"), under consideration by the 1970 Convention Committee, attacks practices of the convention itself which are discriminatory toward women. A second petition which resolved that abortion is a civil right of every woman was passed in the October 1969 meeting of the APA Council of Representatives, owing perhaps to the climate of opinion on civil rights established by the black civil rights movements. A third petition, requesting nonaccreditation for schools that discriminate against women, was not passed—just as the previous year a petition from the ABP which requested nonaccreditation for schools not reaching a particular quota of black psychologists had not been passed. Clearly as Wilson maintains, the struggles of groups suffering discrimination are intertwined.

While Thomas and Wilson speak broadly about the relation of minority groups to society, Havinghurst focuses his discussion on the needs of minority groups in the classroom. In his Thorndike Award lecture, he maintains that the students' experiences within their subculture determine what is rewarding to them. Thus, in making use of reward to strengthen particular behaviors, a teacher must be sufficiently aware of the cultural background of his students to be able to select appropriate rewards.

Hampton's paper deals with the problem of providing equal employment opportunity within the federal government. Speaking from his perspective as Chairman of the Civil Service Commission, Hampton contrasts the civil service of the nineteenth century with the present system, pointing out the improvements that advances in objective testing have made possible. However, he is by no means satisfied with our present testing ability. He challenges the psychological community to make tests more equitable for people of all backgrounds and to develop the ability to test a wider number of job-related factors.

Hallie closes this section with a discussion of the nature of cruelty, relating his discussion particularly to white institutional cruelty toward black Americans. He contrasts two types of cruelty which he labels institutional and Sadean (after the Marquis de Sade). Hallie suggests that although institutional cruelty is superficially the less horrifying of the two, it is ultimately the more cruel, and he explores the psychological effects of institutional racism upon black Americans.

Psychologists, Psychology, and the Black Community[1]

CHARLES W. THOMAS

The author received his PhD from Western Reserve University in 1961. He is presently Director of the Center for the Study of Racial and Social Issues in Los Angeles, where his major interests involve developing programs designed to reduce conflicts created by racism and poverty. He is also the National Honorary Chairman of the Association of Black Psychologists.

It is not entirely by accident that ghettoized people are saying, more and more, words to the effect, "Psychologists, take your psychology and go home." This growing development does not seem to disturb many men of science in psychology. If anything, research, educational, and service functions appear to be maintained by self-serving interests, as based on philosophical and scientific parameters nourished by a cover-up for a failure to see the human condition as it exists. It is around this basic flaw that psychology, in my opinion, has yet to achieve recognition as an extraordinary science that would in fact "promote human welfare in the broadest and most liberal manner." On the other hand, it would seem not only ethical but efficient to simply state that for some, the human condition will be promoted; for others, their human condition will be used to contain them. The problem is not really one whereby psychologists need to see the circumstances, for example, of ethnic minority people, but to simply see their whole society and their place in it as it is. Should that occurrence take place, they might see among other things how psychologists are sustained by and have contributed to those white racist values of society deemed too good to give up. Under the present conditions, changes will not come easily for a different fixation on scientific scrutiny, and certainly not before the traditional, cultural value system has had a more honest arrangement. The latter is difficult to achieve due, in part, to the proliferation of studies which seek to justify those social orders that reinforce the plight of those who do not fit into the dominant social group. So often the data accumulated give the curious aura of

---

[1] Invited Address presented to the Division of Psychological Aspects of Disability at the Annual Meeting of the American Psychological Association, Washington, D. C., September 2, 1969.

providing impressionistic confirmation which, according to Gutherie (1969) and K. B. Clark (1965), stems from the fantasy of aristocracy.

Another source of resistance to change can be seen in maintaining the meaning of too many conventional concepts. In conjunction with that reality, several implications have to be considered. As most of us know, theory is an important tool of science, which can be used in many ways. It is this mechanism, for example, that enables an analysis of structure or permits a description of a state of conditions as well as defining the major bearings of a discipline (Goode & Hatt, 1952). Of course, there is the circular condition also, in which theory predicts facts. The resulting circumstance is often more of the same in a more refined manner, and the best illustration of this can be seen in a review of the research findings about Afro-Americans, whereby the great majority of studies conclude that we are not only different but deviant or inferior.

The doctrine of white supremacy in social and behavioral sciences has been around for some time and has been useful in both explaining and justifying the dehumanized treatment of nonwhites (Garcia, Blackwell, Williams, & Simpkins, 1969). Conversely, it is also the use of a tradition of racism in scientific activities that maintains the testing business, publishing, government commissions, admission been the pacesetters of history. Rather, they fled from, or denied, the occurrence of white psychologists. These activities tend to promote racial tensions and by implication, at this point in time, to indicate that those social scientists want to assume responsibility for destroying society. As long as psychologists omit the resonance of experiences and desires of the oppressed as well as the oppressors, they cannot have experimental models that legitimately deal with the nature of scientific problems.

Withdrawing, or otherwise retreating from crucial social problems, will not contribute to the advancement of psychology as a science. Psychologists have not been the pacesetters of history. Rather, they fled from, or denied, the occurrence of most of the great social crises, only to merge at a later time, following the garden variety of people, but armed with some artificial distinctions made in the scientific enterprise. Professional activities have, in this connection, a significant way of repeating what society wants to hear. This situation appears to be a result of that peculiar cognitive world in which the professional has his existence; namely, "What a man sees depends both upon what he looks at and also upon what his previous visual-conceptual experience has taught him to see [Kuhn, 1962]." Along these lines, results of studies involving racial comparisons are illustrative.

Among Afro-Americans race itself is almost invariably cited as the factor that limits the human potential in some innate way. While conclusions based upon that assumption have come in for increasing criticism, as can be seen in the most recent case of the Jensen report (1969), the more subtle variations on the same theme can be observed in the work of those who have environmental orientations. With respect to the latter, one finds that attitudes, values, and patterns of social organization are learned, but little attention is devoted to the sociopolitical arrangements that determine the very special cultural behavior of those who are disengaged from the white, Anglo-Saxon, Protestant norm. Differences reported in sex roles, identity formation, child-rearing practices, social skills, and a variety of interpersonal functions have been extensively documented by a large variety of scholars. In one report, by way of illustration. David and Pearl Ausubel cited 130 different references by 114 professionals. Yet, the typical report seems to have two serious limitations. One is the orientation of psychology in the direction of pathology. The other involves an almost total lack of recognition of institutionalized racism as a basic factor influencing the life styles and particular motivational patterns of so-called disadvantaged, minority people. In a mutually reinforcing manner, these two assumptions have contributed to sustaining racial attitudes and the formation of laws and general social practices. At the least there are some notions about changing the individual to fit the existing social and legal structures (Ausubel & Ausubel, 1963).

Under these limitations those facts uncovered have not been particularly revealing of the nature of various personal-social arrangements found among ghetto people. If anything meaningful has been achieved, it seems to be in the direction of reducing the scope of problems around behavioral response sets, while increasing the accuracy of maintaining ghetto residents not only as different, but inferior and hopelessly deviant as well.

Racism: A Dilemma for Psychologists

For many social scientists, this is no easy dilemma to resolve. Racism, in its overt and latent manifestations, has been a part of their adjustment mechanisms throughout life. In addition, their education did not contain significant exposure to historical pararmeters as an important factor in referential processes and the latter's impact on behavioral response sets. Hence, one might state simply that social scientists are equipped neither by temperament nor by training to consider anything other than the universality of white cultural norms. In this connection, there has been no significant change in the community of psychologists that would alter the constellation of facts, theories, and methods. Scientific activities continue to be limited in both scope and precision with respect to extending knowledge of those facts inherent in the social system upon which experimental models are constructed.

A real discovery of the human condition of those who are socially disengaged by virtue of age, sex, race, or social class requires an awareness of how the demographic variable in and of itself does not account for more than a suggestion of a relationship between the variable and some personal-social circumstances. In actuality, however, it is not infrequent to find explanations of sociocultural patterns based on a personal trait. Normative differences in society, at the present time, would seem to require a revolution in conceptual schemes. Should that condition obtain it would encourage new questions about old data as well as the formulation of new conclusions from the existing evidence. Behavioral response sets would become the indices of social efficiency instead of the static, psychodiagnostic classifications that have little bearing on immediate social realities. No amount of humanistic disguise in the way of a social penalty for being too old, nonwhite, female, or having low test scores will lessen the trauma for receiving treatment at an infrahuman level. Nor will the continued use of the tools of science to sustain such circumstances serve the best interests of society. Kuhn (1962) stated it very well when he wrote, "Assimilating a new sort of fact demands a more than additive adjustment of theory, and until that adjustment is completed, until the scientist has learned to see nature in a different way, the new fact is not quite a scientific fact at all [p. 53]." Hence, the prevailing distinction of many behavioral activities has been not simply a focus on isolated events but isolated effects in a repeated social structure. Facts, theories, and methods assembled in the name of science are no better than the men of that science. Some will recoil from the indictment that in psychology as a whole, the actualization of institutionalized racism is quite apparent in the determination of significant facts, the matching of facts with theory, and the articulation of that theory.

A Challenge for Psychologists

The challenge to be confronted lies in working through that professional vanity which does not allow for radical social-scientific changes in treatment, organization of services, or expectations based on a single choice that is virtually impossible to pursue. Significant improvement in the applied, human-centered areas of psychology will come in direct proportion to the extent that findings from ethnological research are incorporated into the spectrums of psychological paradigms. Anthropological studies have underscored the importance of understanding the cultural context of relationships and have shown that behavior regarded as abnormal in one culture can be socially acceptable in another.

The same observations appear to hold with subcultural groups. Research involving Afro-Americans, for example, most often reflects interpretations that do not consider the cultural and social patterns within which behavioral events take place. Issues concerned with personality integration, role occupancy, communication processes, or motivation overlook normative prescriptions that are peculiar to the referential processes of Afro-Americans. Ignorance of the latter not only perpetuates normlessness as a myth but fails to appreciate developmental progressions that are critical to the total efficiency of distinctive behavior patterns in the matters of age-related expectancies or sex-related roles.

To the person outside a culture it is almost impossible to understand that the cues, feedback, and reinforcement of life styles within the culture are designed to assist the members of that culture in actively mastering their social environment. Within this context the established social order fosters differences in developmental experiences, differences in role responsibilities, and differences in standards of beliefs and behavior. Confusion surrounding these issues seems to come from those who lack training in dealing with psychocultural data (Leites, 1948). Then, there are the myths as expressed in the notion, "The Negro is only an American and nothing else. He has no values and culture to guard and protect [Glazer & Moynihan, 1963]." The latter denies, among other things, that the national character of our society has not changed significantly with respect to the treatment given Afro-Americans. Such value orientations also overlook the relation of personality to the functioning of major political and socioeconomic institutions (Inkeles, 1956). An understanding of these circumstances has not only some far-reaching implications but also helps to firm up some rather specific functions for the psychologist who would be engaged in those activities that pertain to Afro-Americans.

In an ideal sense, the psychologist who becomes involved in the humanity of Afro-Americans would have an education in the broad array of social sciences as well as specific experiences to equip him for dealing with the social realities of life in the ghetto. Under this arrangement, I believe one would see the clear interdependency of the diverse physical, social, political, cultural, and psychological features of the community. By contrast, there would be a rejection of the dependency syndrome in professional activities that has a way of furthering pathological accommodations. In this same vein, C. Clark (1969) has written, "White [largely liberal] thinking has brainwashed us all into believing . . . for example, if education is increased, better housing will ensue, etc. Such thinking is strongly dependency-oriented, and while it lends itself neatly to pre-packaged programs to 'help the disadvantaged'; it cannot deal with social reality. The fact of the matter is that the problems facing Black Americans are infinitely more complex and are related to *systemic* social forces and not due to a group of elements which operate independent of each other. To adequately deal with these forces necessitates a radical break with traditional modes of thinking [p. 5]." Accordingly, one might begin with a problem in education, but the solution becomes sterile unless education as a subsystem is related to the larger social system.

Meanwhile, it is virtually impossible for advocates of community psychology in the ghetto to be dissociated from the black movement which, in all of its parameters, involves primary prevention of identity confusion and the advancement of positive behavioral patterns. Furthermore, current mental health activities with common roots in the concepts and approaches to public health are congruent with significant aspects of the new black ethic. As a consequence, the organization and delivery of mental health services in the Afro-American community must be responsive to and accepting of the new black consciousness. Along these lines, the therapeutic community cannot be simply a treatment center with concerns around demographic characteristics at the expense of a sense of significance. This means that the primary goal must be directed toward the unfolding of creative powers to be used in such matters as a reduction of cognitive dissonance, the resolution of community disorganization, an elevation of self-esteem, and the promotion of changes in those social practices of life that have created and maintained pathological interdependency.

To do anything less would render such concerns as irrelevant to the most critical social issues. This approach is not only as it should be, but it is necessary if the humanity and sensitivity of social progress are to be achieved smoothly. Moreover, this is the only way that the transformation of conventional nonsense in the way of methods, techniques, and philosophy can be fused into an anthem that signifies significant reform.

This frame of reference makes the assumption that the treatment of Afro-Americans is directly tied in with the fate of society generally. It also recognizes that progress in various health, social welfare, educational, and political areas has its antecedents for change in the new black consciousness as a model for improving the quality of life.

In Afro-American communities, the psychologist is challenged to mobilize his vast body of knowledge, new and old, so that his consumers can be assisted in dealing with their environment more effectively. On the surface it would appear that this premise is not too different from what one might expect elsewhere. Yet, the reality is that neither psychology nor psychologists as a whole can be given that responsibility freely. This is especially critical since the context and definitions of the functional group have not been incorporated into the training of psychologists. Thus, the value of psychologists must be handled on an individual basis.

With aggressive assertion, seeking changes in social arrangements and content, the black man is no longer content with his lot as the end. Instead, he has cast his plight as the means for transforming society into one governed by truth and justice. Therefore, the basic goal centers around the unfolding of his creative powers and his becoming increasingly reactive to the choices available. A psychologist can make a significant contribution to changes in patterns of self-defeating behavior *if* he has a clear appreciation of the nature and properties of what is being changed. Likewise, it is no small matter to know how he arrived at the response to the challenge of working in the Afro-American community. In short, why is he paying his dues in this manner? Looking at the situation from the opposite point of view, if the psychologist has "paid his dues," so to speak, and is "doing his thing," he understands that the realities involve the following alternatives for Afro-Americans: (*a*) an acceptance of defeat by withdrawing; (*b*) an escape from the horrors of life through the use of alcohol, or drugs, or by suicide; (*c*) an acceptance of the expected, conforming mode of behavior; (*d*) a refusal to recognize defeat by adopting the values of the dominant group; or (*e*) a refusal to retreat from biosocial realities by searching for new meanings as expressed through blackness. The conceptual and behavioral contexts within which these choices arise are somewhat easy to recognize. Possible solutions and resources require another level of realization.

Social progress and conflict resolution, complex though they might be, if engaged in as they should be by the community psychologist, will take him to those necessary arenas beyond his parochial teachings. His life space will embrace participation, mobilization, communication, and confidence of the community people. These activities might include problems concerning (*a*) whether police departments are needed as they are presently organized to preserve law and order, (*b*) the social gains to be derived from decentralized schools, (*c*) the pathological dependency fostered by the welfare system, (*d*) the kind of social research needed, (*e*) whether developmental programs are responsive to community needs, or (*f*) coming to grips with some of the other by-products of racism. These conditions hold for psychologists of any ethnic group. However, as matters now stand, these activities appear to have more significance for the white psychologist because he is more readily identified as being from the Establishment.

This particular state of affairs cannot be managed successfully without a consideration of the facilitating, institutionalized social actions and circumstances. It is at this junction that the psychologist must be prepared to deal with his own values and social distinctions in terms of what Erikson (1968) has called the "wider identity" of the Afro-American. In much the same manner, the agent of change must firmly understand whether he is, in the words of Keniston (1968), "promoting another way of controlling deviant behavior under the disguise of community mental health." Conversely, one must know if he is influencing the course of events with new coping patterns that challenge existing structures. The achievement of that goal is dependent upon technically sound but socially productive programs that incorporate the interdependent effects of social class and ethnicity.

Implications of the Black Ethic for Social Science

As a social science model, the new black ethic holds promise, because it is based upon psychocultural factors involving racial awareness, identity, and pride that nurture biosocial acceptance in Afro-Americans. While somewhat limited in precision because it is still being articulated, there are several reasons that can substantiate the black ethic as a paradigm that offers more successful empirical propositions for productively stimulating human development than either the *bioasocial* or social deviance models.

The bioasocial or genotypic orientation, at best, seeks to maintain the brutality and inhumanity of society at the expense of actualizing the Afro-American's human potential. Studies involving cognition seem to use this type of model, and as Downs (1969) has pointed out, the results do not assess racial inheritance as much as they rank the social structure of the United States.

The social deviance model conceptualizes the Afro-American family as a pathological socializing agent transmitting cultural malignance. Studies involving our families have almost nothing to say about the resourcefulness and ingenuity that exist; and one also finds a conspicuous absence about the need for changes in the larger society that would foster a different type of family organization.

Perhaps the most compelling reason for the use of the black ethic as a social science model is its mental health implications. To this extent, it can be considered as a functional theory whereby Festinger's cognitive-dissonance in social psychology would be illustrative of what is being suggested. Both are based upon constructive explanations that allow for motivational determinism in a social definition of reality. Socially valued objectives and socially provided means to establish and pursue goal-directed activities are derived from the reliance on opinions of the group's functioning.

A healthy personality according to Jahoda (1958) actively masters his environment, shows a certain unity of personality, and is able to perceive the world and himself correctly. By comparison blackness is the manifestation of a specific form of behavior that enables the Afro-American to enhance his self-determined mastery over those political and socioeconomic institutions that would grossly impair his socially relevant behavior. For this reason Afro-Americans who have internalized their blackness tend to be seen not only as persons of high self-esteem but also as less susceptible to pernicious influences of the dominant group. The internalization of membership in their racial group may also be seen as a type of creative experience coming from adaptable deviance.

Social competence based upon biosocial acceptance would be more congruent with cognitive needs and seems to serve in the reduction of ambiguity between ideals and achievement. It strengthens the capacity to meet new challenges because confrontation with the self brings about or sustains a more authentic self-concept. The action patterns or motivational systems are characterized by the black man's aggressiveness, independence, and at times hostility, in dealing with groups and institutional failings that would maintain him as a passive, dependent, self-defeating person. "Life experiences inconsistent with self-awareness of the Black man have been the basis for inter-group tensions on the one hand; and, self defeating behavior on the other. This conflict could not change in any meaningful way until there was an acceptance of self. . . . As a result of his commitment to Blackness, the Afro-American thinks, feels, and sees himself as a member of a society in which he is no longer a passive onlooker [Thomas, 1969, p. 11]." The willingness among Afro-

Americans to commit themselves to a more competent sense of self and to seek the essence of collective manhood is related to centuries of symbolic childhood.

Two other circumstances around the use of the current black ethic as a theory are important. First, it can be viewed, to paraphrase Simon and Newell (1963), as a theory of man that takes into account his characteristics as an information-processing system. Next, "all theory," according to Marx (1963), "tends to be both a tool and a goal. This statement means that theory is seen to be useful as an aid, sometimes perhaps as essential aid, in directing empirical investigation (the tool function) and also to be something valued as an object in its own right (the goal function) [p. 5]." These conditions constitute the challenge that must be faced by those professionals who claim scientific interests and who require scientific status.

Conclusion

The strive for security or completion as an individual allows response sets that are no longer productive for personal-social constancy to drop out. In other words, if through psychological processes Afro-Americans internalize their blackness and cease to survive by clinging to a thread because they are confused about their worth as humans, benefits will also accrue to those who overtly or otherwise have been caught up in the historical assemblage of this same process. In short, it is not simply Afro-Americans who gain in mental health, because upon becoming black the black person also forces white people to respond in terms of some reaction formation that should promote a healthier meaning within whites. With respect to the latter, there is considerable doubt that any such essay on personality will gain widespread currency.

In different words but on the same theme, Murphy (1947) and K. B. Clark (1965) posed the question about who was to do what in making clear what the sense of fulfillment was in the individual himself, and, at the same time, understand implicit meanings in the social order.

Psychologists are in serious need of a reexamination of their philosophical commitment. The last few years have become increasingly characterized, not so much by a quest for truth, as by a search for power. Meanwhile, the social revolution has caught social scientists in the wilderness resting on a cot of science for science's sake, with their proverbial pants down.

References

Ausubel, D. P., & Ausubel, P. Ego development among segregated Negro children. In H. Passow (Ed.), *Education in depressed areas.* New York: Teachers College Press, 1963.
Clark, C. On racism and racist systems. *Negro Digest,* 1969, **XVIII**, 4–8.
Clark, K. B. *Dark ghetto dilemmas of social power.* New York: Harper & Row, 1965.
Downs, J. F., & Bleibtreu, K. K. *Human variation: An introduction to physical anthropology.* Beverly Hills, Calif.: Glencoe Press, 1969.
Erikson, E. *Identity, youth and crisis.* New York: Norton, 1968.
Goode, W. J., & Hatt, P. K. *Methods in social research.* New York: McGraw-Hill, 1952.
Glazer, N., & Moynihan, D. *Beyond the melting pot.* Cambridge: Harvard University Press, 1963.
Garcia, S. J., Blackwell, A., Williams, C. F., & Simpkins, G. Research in the black community: A need for self-determination. Paper presented at the meeting of the Western Psychological Association, Vancouver, B. C., June 1969.

Guthrie, R. V. The psychopathology of white folks. Paper presented at the meeting of the Western Psychological Association, Vancouver, B. C., June 1969.

Inkeles, A. Some sociological observation on culture and personality studies. In C. Kluckhorn & H. A. Murray (Eds.), *Personality in nature, society, and culture.* New York: Knopf, 1956.

Jahoda, M. Toward a social psychology of mental health. In M. J. E. Benn (Ed.), *Symposium on the health personality, Supplement II: Problems of infancy and childhood.* New York: Josiah Macy, Jr., Foundation, 1950.

Jensen, A. R. How much can we boost IQ and scholastic achievement? *Harvard Educational Review,* 1969, **39,** 1–123.

Keniston, K. How community mental health stamped out the riots. *Trans-action,* July/August 1968.

Kuhn, T. S. *The structure of scientific revolutions.* Chicago: University of Chicago Press, 1962.

Leites, N. Psycho-cultural hypotheses about political acts. *World Politics,* 1948, **1,** 102–119.

Marx, M. *Theories in contemporary psychology.* New York: Macmillan, 1963.

Murphy, G. *Personality: A biosocial approach to origins and structure.* New York: Harper, 1947.

Simon, H. A., & Newell, A. The uses and limitations of models. In M. Marx (Ed.), *Theories in contemporary psychology.* New York: Macmillan, 1963.

Thomas, C. W. On being a black man. Voice of America Presentation, February 1969. (Mimeo)

Toward a New Social Order[1]

CHARLES E. WILSON

The author received his Master of Science Degree in educational psychology from New York University in 1965. As Unit Administrator of the IS201 Complex Demonstration District, he has been interested in school reorganization, instructional reform, and active involvement of community members and parents. He is now an active staff member of the New Careers Training Laboratory.

The opportunity offered me to discuss with a nationwide assemblage of social scientists the relationship of psychology to the black community can be viewed as an honor, a challenge, and an awesome responsibility. It is an honor because so many of you have been in the very forefront of the struggle for human dignity, social progress, and the extension of citizenship privileges to men of every color and description. It is a challenge because for many of you the ideas that I hope to communicate may run counter to some of your most treasured assumptions. The challenge for me is how to reach you with words, so that you may begin to reexamine your own thoughts and assumptions about what role you will play in this current phase of man's seemingly never-ending struggle against tyranny. Finally, it is an awesome responsibility for I come before you as a representative of a point of view that has been frequently maligned, misinterpreted, and often deliberately denigrated. Whether I can rise to the occasion and put into words the thoughts, sentiments, and feelings of the various segments of the black community about what role that total community wishes from the discipline of psychology, with its numerous specialties, becomes an awesome responsibility to try to assume.

In such a circumstance I am not unmindful of the advice that arises from a Russian folktale attributed to former Premier Nikita Khrushchev. Khrushchev was a remarkably able, rather earthy and pithy man of action. He once told the story in the midst of the Cuban missile crisis of a tiny bird which was trapped by an early but heavy, wet snowfall while on a southward flight. During its flight, the bird became heavy with the wet snow and fell to earth damaging its wing. Through the afternoon's storm, the bird lay trapped in the snow. As the temperature dipped sharply, the bird was in real danger of freezing to death.

---

[1] Invited Address presented to the Division of School Psychology at the Annual Meeting of the American Psychological Association, Washington, D. C., August 31, 1969.

However, along came a peasant who picked up the bird, cleaned the snow from its feathers, and began to warm it, first with his own hands, then with his gloves. Finally, he placed the bird close to his bosom under his great coat. As the peasant trudged home with the bird, snug and warm, the signs of life slowly returned to the little winged creature.

When the peasant arrived at his farm shelter, he searched for a snug place for the bird. After some time the peasant found a fresh dung pile just outside the barn. Here he set the bird in a place much warmer than the peasant's hands, gloves, or great coat.

The next morning, spirits restored, and life slowly returning to it by a bright, warm, thawing sun, the bird was prompted to give vent to wonderous song. Its happy, beautiful song filled the air. A wolf lurking about heard the delightful song, darted out of the woods, and ate the bird. The tale has three morals for birds and men:

1. Not everyone who puts you in it is an *enemy*.
2. Not everyone who takes you out of it is a *friend*.
3. When you are in it up to your neck, do not sing out.

The question of what the black community wants from psychology seems strangely like two variations of the same question that has dogged minority groups through the past tumultuous decade. One variation is that of the pragmatic conservatives and reactionaries. The pragmatic conservatives, the active and passive reactionaries, have constantly asked, "What do you people want?" This question ignores the serious deficits in the existing social order while giving the appearance that those seeking change want some special privileges.

The question, as posed today, is not too unlike the question that has been posed repeatedly by the guilt-ridden segments who seem to lament, "What can we (those who are in) do for you (those who are still out)?"

It seems that both these variations on the same theme, similar to the question posed today and the historical antecedents of yesteryear, smack of a kind of convenient ignorance and patronization that are generally not the motivations for the kind of action that will be required to construct a more satisfying, more humane, less destructive social order in this country. In this, there is an awful lot that the black community has to do for itself. There are still other objectives that can be pursued in concert with other groups, and even more objectives that have to be pursued by other people to prepare the way for the change that is at hand. Thus, the social order could be characterized by four principles set down by Theobold (1968), namely: (*a*) a capacity for truth and accuracy in communication (honesty), (*b*) a capacity for change when change is needed (responsibility), (*c*) a restraint within the groups and individuals so that they no longer have an urge to dominate or take over the social order (humility), and (*d*) a capacity for flexibility to meet conditions of change (love).

The Real Question

Thus, the real question for psychology and for all the social sciences today as posed by blacks, by white students and black students, by poor black and white, and by women from all groups is not merely how the disciplines can help the separate groups. Rather the question is: Are the disciplines first ready and willing to use themselves and their resources to build a new kind of human social order with new institutional forms and more humane values? Second, how and when do the men of the disciplines plan to be about this work? Thus, the real question is one of what to do, the will to do it, the commitment, and a timetable for accomplishment.

A fundamental change is upon us—a process in which the emergence of the black community is just one part—a change that can transform human relationships and productive operations as well as, more importantly, basic human conceptions. *The presently powerless* are not going to be very patient about evolutionary rates of change and the *presently powerful* are not going to be very permissive about revolutionary disruptions. Somewhere between the "go slow" and the "right now," social scientists must take a stand, contribute their skills, and show their courage. It is all too clear that unless the expertise and commitment of the social sciences including that of psychology are not directed toward answering the real questions the entire community, black as well as white, is imperiled. It is an all too sad fact of American life today that "Those who have the knowledge, frequently don't have the power and those who have the power, frequently don't have the knowledge."

To date, the segments of the social sciences, those who have been long allied with those struggling for social justice, have not been recruited into this present struggle. The antics, gyrations, postures, oh yes, that rhetoric of the emerging communities often obscure the issues. Blinded by an all too appropriate sense of rage, the emerging communities often do not recognize friend or foe, for these communities have as often been victimized by their friends as by their foes.

It seems that only the intervention of men of action is required. But it soon becomes evident that motion cannot be substituted for thought, and that racism will not retreat from rhetoric no matter how brilliant the metaphors or how vile the cliches. Nor will new institutions needed to cope with the crisis appear by magic or without skill. It is all too conventional, but extremely naive, for those who are spectators to blame personalities for the present crisis. Social forces are at work with all kinds of potential for good as well as for evil.

The black community, students in general, other awakening nonwhite groups, and women's rights groups are each demanding in their own way *respect* for their human person, understanding for their legitimate aspirations, and an opportunity to realize themselves as individuals and as parts of new collectives. Blacks wish to see a change from an order rooted in racism and exploitation, though with an official dedication to "democratic ideals and processes," to a new social order committed to new humane values of honesty, responsibility, humility, and love. This is not to suggest that blacks see themselves or wish to use themselves as the only change agents for the society. Their current situation is more crucial, their needs more pressing.

Finally, each of the emerging communities seems to wish you to use your skills and commitment to make its often ill-defined dreams realities. This wish is indeed a compliment, and attaining the goal may be a feat worthy of a Houdini.

If You Don't Like It

The fuss and furor surrounding the painfully slow emergence of the demands for a "new order" have prompted too many of the social scientists to turn away and to dismiss these efforts—dismiss these efforts exactly at the very time when in fact the counsel of the social scientist might be listened to. If I were to give a few words of advice about this kind of behavior, it would be this: "If you don't like it and if you haven't tried it, don't knock it."

Psychologists, sociologists, and other social scientists today seem all too quick to evaluate, too quick to comment. Many rush to judgment about this movement or this segment without sufficient information. Others expect immediate miracles and rapid growth from people who for a long time have been effectively barred from interaction in this complex society. If this growth and change do not happen, the movement is written off. Together the rushers-to-judgment and the miracle watchers seem to spare no opportunity to point out the flaws in the new movements for the messengers of the mass media or any other audience willing to pay or willing to listen. The new groups, blacks, women, New Left, New Right, etc., of course, may lack finesse, sophistication, and may even be shortsighted.

The newly emerging black community is still subject to this kind of scrutiny. It may be facetious to point out that the shortsightedness of the new collectives including the blacks is inversely proportional to the long-windedness of their critics.

Yet many of these same critics and an entire cadre of the helping professions seem addicted to equate differences with deviance and pathology, to attempt to relate prejudice to the victim. It seems that by now McWilliam's observation (1962) of some 20 years ago should have struck home to some people. McWilliams observed that:

> The attempt to relate prejudice to the specific nature of its object is a cunning projection of the prejudice of the dominant group. Cunning because it passes as scientific curiosity. As long as the majority can pretend that the source of prejudice is inherent in the nature of their victim, social action can be postponed; there is always still another investigation which must be made [p. 250].

I am afraid that now as a nation including our social science fraternity we have exchanged the theory of genetic inferiority for the theory of social pathology. In doing so we have not changed the game, we have merely changed the name of the game. We will spend another 20 years or so examining the ghetto, researching the rural backwaters, rummaging through the enclaves of deprivation, studying the ghetto schools, exploring the pockets of discrimination, marveling at black anti-Semitism and white racism, examining signs and symbols, but not examining the very society that spawns such practices. These manifestations are not a fault of society or small flaws in an otherwise good life. These flaws are aspects of the way this society has been and is organized.

Therefore, as a basic precondition for dealing with the black community and all the other emerging new groups this paper urges psychologists and other social scientists to cease the dialogue that puts the downs down further while buttering up the already ups. The end to this kind of dialogue may in fact increase our capacity to secure more accurate, relevant data, as well as to make genuine contributions to the building of that new society.

Emerging Black Community—Many Ways to Help

I have mentioned repeatedly the "emergence of new collectives, new communities." When I speak of the black community, I am speaking of a community that is in the process of becoming. While we in America have referred to the people of African descent by various names, suggesting a solid grouping, it has been the deliberate deception of ourselves as well as the deception of the children of Africa, and a strategy of racial dominance to frustrate the formation of a genuine differentiated ethnic group among the children of Africa. Thus, today you may observe a black community struggling to come into being against a calculating system bent on maintaining the status quo. Comer (1967) once provided one cogent reason for the previous failures to achieve a sense of community among the descendants of Africa here in America. He wrote, "The power structure of the white society, industry, banks, the press, government can continue either inadvertently or deliberately to maintain divisions in the Negro community and keep it powerless [p. 23]." Yet today, a few short years after Comer's remarks, the struggle for a black community is on.

Unfortunately, for some scholars, the struggle has not followed classical lines, nor have black people, especially today's activists, turned to them for advice or counsel. The same scholars who have dismissed the movement or written off the participants now ask, "How could the young people bypass us?" Easily, very easily.

This same struggle for the emergence of a black community has highlighted more than just the inner divisions among blacks. The struggle in many areas within the limited states has uncovered the fact that in major cities the growth of the mass society has often produced a picture in which there are many more people compressed into a smaller area, but fewer viable communities—communities in which people are meaningfully related to one another and are involved in the key decisions that shape their lives and the lives of their children. Yet, few social scientists and few psychologists have described the deficits within local areas inhabited by poor whites and others. Perhaps, it may be important for social scientists to begin to identify related or similar phenomena so that no group that sees itself as different is wronged for no real reason. Disenfranchised white communities and black communities may learn to learn from one another's experiences. The deficits in the social order have been identified, deficits that the struggle of black people for a sense of community has helped them to perceive.

In the desire to help the newly emerging black community, it may be just as crucial for social scientists to help the still dormant white communities realize the dimensions of the societal crisis facing us all, as well as seeking to provide direct service to help black communities. For the black communities subject to deprivation and corrupted by powerlessness may be suspicious of you, hostile and fearful of your intended contribution. For the kind of humane society of which I have spoken is as unfamiliar to some blacks as it is to many whites, as unfamiliar to some women as it is to most men, as unfamiliar to some nonconforming students as it is to most of their professors. It will require an extra effort on all levels to win adherents to the cause of a new social order, a new way to approach problems and people.

The extent and direction of your contribution then depends *on you*. You can help black communities, and all human communities, by helping the various white enclaves to realize the necessity for a humane community, or you can help black communities more directly by your service. But here I must caution you that decision making will rest in the hands of the local groups. Some of you who do participate may still be disliked because of your contribution and disparaged because of your skin color. This conduct is in fact a legacy of our collective past history and nobody can pretend that the record of savagery and exploitation of the past was designed to enhance either the perpetrator or the victim.

I am trying to suggest that the helping professions have multiple and exceedingly challenging possibilities in terms of the emergence of a number of new collectives including the black community. Apertures exist for the inclusion of members of the new collectives in our efforts to provide services for these groups. If the rigidity of professional status and the intense subservience to credentialization can be dropped for the greater good of improved services to people, there may be still more opportunities to use our skills in a totally new way.

The emerging black community represents what Adler referred to as a final fictionalism. If blacks and whites act as if this fictionalism were true, it can provide the basis for far more constructive group life than is possible when unrelated individuals pursue what Franklin Frazier referred to as "self-seeking opportunism," at the expense of the total group. That professional participation may be more difficult than it was previously is not the issue. That often the leaders of the factions have not been able to see the relationship between their various separate demands and those of the other group is not earth shattering. That many of them have not been able to articulate these demands in a fashion designed to win adherents is not surprising. Yet, there is hope that as social scientists with skills, expertise, and commitment we can have as large or as small a role as we are prepared to play, either in direct relationship to the black community or in terms of helping to build the basis for a new society.

Man Is Beautiful

I suppose for some I have violated the rules of the game by daring to perceive the issue of change in a broader context than the needs of the emerging black community. For those who are offended I wish to assure them that I did so only in the hope that some of my audience might come to see the struggle for a humane community, yes, for a black community, in broader terms than heretofore realized. For this perception is fundamental to the struggle for a better life. There is a relationship between the demands of a host of submerged groups who no longer wish to be grouped at the bottom, victimized by all. It is unfortunate that for the most part the voices of the leaders of the blacks, of the white students, of the women's rights groups have been so unclear. These leaders often know more about what they are against than what they are specifically for. Yet, let no one believe these same leaders do not speak to and for a constituency. Many of their groups will struggle for their conception of cultural pluralism, that is, the right of minorities to have the right to choice, rather than the obligation of capitulation to oppressive popular standards.

If this pluralism is not possible, democracy as we have known it is doomed in the ghettos and the other societal backwaters, doomed despite this country's awesome military might and its frightening overkill capacity.

The hope is the people who are willing to struggle, people, black and white alike, who must struggle to transform the word "community" into a living reality. People cannot live unless they struggle to see that the transfer of power follows Goodwin's (1969) principle: "Power should be transferred to the smallest unit consistent with the scale of the problems." People must eventually learn that their individual and subgroup struggle can be merged into a broader, deeper channel, driving toward broad societal change.

The challenge, however, is ours as social scientists, as leaders of groups, to use our skills to build the new social order by relating the pieces to one another, by using our skills and expertise to help others to learn, to grow, and to develop.

"What can the field of psychology do for the black community?" then is a nonquestion hardly worthy of an answer. The bigger question, far worthier of you, is: When do you help to build the kind of social order that can produce human beings, a social order that binds the wounds of the past, sets about tackling the problems of the present, faces bravely toward the future?

In such a social order black is beautiful, white is beautiful, yellow is beautiful. In such a sound order, that black is beautiful does not mean that white is ugly—for all men and women are indeed beautiful.

References

Comer, J. P. The social power of the Negro. *Scientific American,* 1967, **210,** 16–23.
Goodwin, R. Reflections—sources of public unhappiness. *New Yorker Magazine,* January 4, 1969, 38–58.
McWilliams, C. *Brothers under the skin.* Boston: Little, Brown, 1962.
Theobold, R. The implications of American physical abundance. *Annals of the American Academy of Political and Social Science,* 1968, **378,** 11–21.

Minority Subcultures and the Law of Effect[1]

ROBERT J. HAVIGHURST

The author received his PhD in chemistry at Ohio State University. Later he changed his field of work to education, becoming a professor of education at the University of Chicago in 1941, a position which he still holds. He is interested in the field of human development, and presently is devoting much of his time to directing the National Study of American Indian Education.

Since the 1950s we in the United States have become more and more acutely aware of and concerned about the socially disadvantaged segment of our society. We have joined a "war on poverty." We have declared racial segregation in the public schools to be illegal. We have passed a Civil Rights Act. These things we have done out of our conviction that democracy is morally right and can be made to work better in our society than it has in the past.

We have also defined rather accurately the "socially disadvantaged" group as consisting roughly of the bottom 15% of our population in terms of income and educational achievement. Some people would argue that this is too small a proportion. They would add another 10% to make it a quarter of the population. Others would go as far as to define all manual workers and their families (about 60% of the population) as socially disadvantaged, but this kind of proposition could not be supported with data on inadequacy of income, educational achievement, stability of family, law observance, or any other major index of standard of living. While the stable working class (or upper working class), consisting of 40% of the population, is slightly below the white collar group in average income, educational level, and other socioeconomic indices, this group is not disadvantaged in an absolute sense, does not feel disadvantaged, and has an active interchange of membership with the white collar group between successive generations.

As for the truly disadvantaged group of 15–20% of the population, there is disturbing evidence that this group is in danger of becoming a permanent "underclass" characterized by absence of steady employment, low level of education and work skills, living on welfare payments, and social isolation from the remainder of society.

---

[1] The Annual Edward L. Thorndike Award Lecture presented to the Division of Educational Psychology at the Annual Meeting of the American Psychological Association, Washington, D. C., August 31, 1969.

The presence of this social and human problem cannot be passed off in any of the ways that might have been possible a century ago, or might be possible today in poor countries. It cannot be ascribed to inherited inferiority of the disadvantaged. It cannot be blamed on the country's poverty, since we are an affluent society. It cannot be passed off with the optimistic prediction that the current group of disadvantaged will soon become assimilated into the general society as most ethnic groups have done in the past—the Irish, Germans, Swedes, Poles, Italians, etc.

The problem is brought to a head by the clearly established fact that the children of this group are *not* doing as well in school or in the world of juvenile work as did the children of poor people 50 and 100 years ago.

Furthermore, most Americans believe that true democracy means equality of economic and educational opportunity. There is a growing conviction that the proof of the existence of equality of economic and educational *opportunity* is the achievement of economic and educational *equality* by the previously disadvantaged groups within a reasonable period of time, measured by decades and not by centuries or even by generations.

The War on Poverty?

For the past 10 years our principal attack on the problem of social disadvantage has been through the "war on poverty." We have spent much talent and energy and a good deal of money without raising the educational or occupational achievement level of this group appreciably, except in a few unusual situations. These unusual situations, in which disadvantaged children and youth have made normal or even superior progress, do not provide us with any broad program ideas that can be applied widely. They seem to tell us that:

1. No mere quantitative changes in the school program are likely to work. It does not bring a widespread improvement to extend the school day by an hour, or the school year by a month, or to reduce class size, or to revise school attendance boundaries.

2. Close and minute attention to the process of teaching a particular subject at a particular age may be useful.

3. We should look closely at children and their particular learning behavior for clues to action.

A Look at What We Know

Examination of known facts about school achievement of definable social groups in the United States shows that poor school achievement is not primarily a problem of ethnic subcultures, but rather is primarily a problem of the lowest socioeconomic group interacting to a limited degree with minority subcultures.

There are certain ethnic minorities that do very well—as well or better than the national average in school achievement. Outstanding among these are the Japanese, Chinese, and Jews. The adults of these groups have an average occupational status above the national average, and the children of these groups do better than the national average on tests of school achievement.

Other ethnic groups do poorly in these respects, but these groups also have substantial numbers who equal or exceed the national average. There is no single ethnic group of any size that can be said to be disadvantaged educationally and economically *as a group*. Negroes might be thought of as a disadvantaged group, and this would be true, historically. But at present there is a large and growing Negro middle class and a large and growing Negro upper working class, whose occupational status is average or above, and whose children do average or better work in school.

The same statement applies to Puerto Ricans, Mexican-Americans, and American Indians. It is the least educated and the least work-trained members of these groups who do least well in American society. These groups all have substantial and growing numbers of people who perform at average or higher levels of occupational status, and whose children do well in school.

Thus, when we speak of the group of socially disadvantaged people in America, we are speaking of some 15-20% of the population who are like each other in their poverty, their lack of education and work skills, but unlike each other in ethnic subculture. Crude estimates indicate that this group contains about 20 million English-speaking Caucasians, 8 million Negroes, 2 million Spanish-Americans, 700,000 Puerto Ricans, and 500,000 American Indians.

These people have poverty in common. Insofar as there is a definable "culture of poverty," they share that culture. Still, a small fraction of them, though poor, do not have the characteristics of the "culture of poverty."

It may be that their various ethnic subcultures have something to do with success or failure in school and in the labor market. If so, it must be the combination of poverty with the ethnic subculture that produces these effects. It may also be true that other ethnic subcultures, such as the Japanese and Chinese, serve to prevent poverty.

The Implicit Contract

It may be useful to examine the educational problem of the socially disadvantaged in terms of the *implicit contract* that a family and a school accept when a child is entrusted by his family to a school. The parents contract to prepare their child for school entrance, both cognitively and affectively. They further contract to keep him in school and to make home conditions appropriate for his success in school. The school contracts to receive the child, teach him as well as it can, taking account of his strengths and weaknesses and the ways in which he can learn most effectively.

Very little of this contract is put into legal codes, but the education of the child is successful only when both parties carry out their obligations fully. Sometimes one or both parties fail to understand the nature of these obligations.

In the case of the socially disadvantaged parents of this country, nearly all of them fail to meet the terms of the contract. But the schools generally fail also by failing to understand how the children of these families can learn most successfully.

The Human Reward-Punishment System

The principal proposition of this paper is that the job of educating socially disadvantaged children would be done much better if educators understood the nature of rewards and how they function in human learning, and applied this knowledge to their work with children and with parents of socially disadvantaged children.

Leads to this proposition exist in the literature of research on education, but do not force themselves on the educator. For example, Davis (1965) offered one of these clues in his paper "Cultural Factors in Remediation." He noted that his wife, then working as a substitute teacher in the Chicago public schools, made a discovery about the way disadvantaged children may learn arithmetic. In a second grade in a ghetto school she found several children, including one nine-year-old boy, who could not count beyond two or three. The following day was Valentine's Day, and she brought some candy hearts to school. She told the children they could have as many candy hearts as they could count. The *nine-year-old boy thereupon counted 14 candy hearts*. Davis goes on to say that teachers of "culturally low-status children" should learn how their children live, and then work out new materials and ways of teaching in order to *encourage* and *approve* those students who have experienced little except disapproval, stigma, and failure in the conventional school program.

In the years since 1960 a number of psychologists have studied the nature of rewards in human learning. Among others, the work of Zigler, Rotter, Katz, and Crandall has widened the field of research and has stimulated others to work in this field.

What these people have in common is the following proposition: Human learning is influenced by a variety of rewards, which are themselves arranged in a culturally based *reward-punishment system* which is learned.

This requires us to examine the nature of rewards. We cannot simply assume that "a reward is a reward and that is it," as we might be tempted to do if we were studying the learning behavior of cats, or pigeons, or rats. It was more or less obvious to researchers that reward systems might vary with social class, or with ethnic subculture. It seemed likely that a child learns his reward system mainly in the family, but also in the school, and the peer group, and the wider community.

Analysis of the Reward-Punishment Concept

The reward-punishment concept, and its related reinforcement theory, has been developed rather differently by each of three groups of psychologists.

Learning theorists, starting with E. L. Thorndike, have tended to use the concept to refer to something done *to* the learner by an experimenter or observer that influences the behavior of the learner. On the other hand, social psychologists and personality theorists have included the subjective experience of the learner as a source of reward-punishment. Thus a person may be rewarded or punished by his own feelings or by the attitudes of other people toward him.

Thorndike (1905) stated the law of effect as follows: "Any act which in a given situation produces satisfaction becomes associated with that situation, so that when the situation recurs the act is more likely to recur also [p. 203]."

Skinner's (1953) definition is, "We first define a positive reinforcer as any stimulus the presentation of which strengthens the behavior upon which it is made contingent [p. 84]."

These are broad enough to cover the other usages, though the social psychologists and personality theorists have stated them more fully. Thus, Hartley and Hartley (1952) say, "Reward . . . must be very broadly defined when we consider human learning. Because human beings are capable of retaining the effects of their experiences for long periods of time and because they are capable of generalization and transfer, functional rewards . . . may be far removed from physical rewards. When we speak of rewards we mean anything that operates as a source of satisfaction for the individual . . . the attitudes other people display and the individual's own feelings may come to serve as rewards [p. 275]."

Personality theorists make much of the distinction between external and internal sources of reward-punishment. Fenichel (1945) writes, "The superego is the heir of the parents not only as a source of threats and punishments but also as a source of protection and a provider of reassuring love. . . . Complying with the superego's demands brings not only relief but also definite feelings of pleasure and security of the same type that children experience from external supplies of love [p. 105]."

Theory of the Evolution of Reward-Punishment

It appears, then, that we can distinguish four major types of reward-punishments. The earliest, in terms of operation in human learning, is satisfaction or deprivation of physiological appetites—the physiological needs for food and pain avoidance. In this same category belong other material rewards that arise later in physiological development, either through the maturation of the organism or through experience—such rewards as release of sexual tensions, toys and play materials, money, and, perhaps, power over other people.

Next in order of appearance comes approval-disapproval from other persons, beginning with praise and reproof and expressions of affection and esteem from parents, and extending to approval-disapproval from others in the family and adults such as teachers, and from age-mates.

Next comes the self-rewarding and self-punishing action of the child's superego, or conscience. This is extremely important from the point of view of educational development, because it means that the child who has reached this level can become capable of pushing ahead with his own education without being stimulated and directed by his parents or his teachers or his peers.

Finally come the rewarding and punishing actions of the ego, the executive functions of the personality. This is more difficult to conceptualize as a source of reward or punishment, but it is essential for an adequate theory. It is essential as a means of *anticipation* of future reward or punishment, success or failure, which will result as a consequence of an action performed now, in the present.

Table 1 presents the theory of evolution of the human reward-punishment system, with additional considerations to be discussed in the following section of this paper.

There are six major propositions of educational significance that have received some research testing.

1. *Different subcultures carry their children along this evolutionary path at different rates and in different ways.*

Several researchers have tested this proposition using social class as the subcultural variable. Zigler and de Labry (1962) compared the performance of

TABLE 1
Evolution of the Human Reward-Punishment System

Age level in years	Nature of the reward-punishment	Giver of the reward-punishment	Action area
0–4	Satisfaction or deprivation of physical-physiological appetites (food, sex, pain, toys, money, power)	Parents	Basic motor skills Basic mental skills
5–10	Praise-disapproval from outside persons	Teachers and other adults in a teaching role	Social skills—social personality
		Self	Special motor skills (games)
	Approval-disapproval from superego	Peers and peer groups	Special mental skills reading, arithmetic, etc.
10–15	Approval-disapproval from ego	Wider community	Excitement Danger, uncertain outcome, sex Knowledge
15–25			Beauty Experience and expression
Adult years			Work roles Family roles

middle class and lower class six-year-old children on a task of classifying cards on the basis of color and shape, and using intangible reinforcement ("right" and "wrong") and tangible reinforcement (tokens to be cashed in for toys). They found middle class children to be superior with intangible reinforcement, but this superiority vanished when lower class children were given tangible rewards.

Lighthall and Cernius (1967) compared Caucasian middle class and working-class five- and six-year-old boys on a concept-switching task using intangible and tangible reinforcers. The tangible reinforcers were metal washers that could be traded in for a toy, a ball-point pen, a piece of candy, or a dime. They did *not* find a social class difference.

Zigler and Kanzer (1962) compared white middle class and working-class eight-year-old boys on a simple gamelike task, using two types of verbal reinforcers—praise and knowledge of how they were succeeding. They found that middle class boys did better when reinforced with "right" or "correct" than when reinforced with "good" or "fine," but lower class boys were more responsive to the praise reinforcement than to the level of performance reinforcement. The conclusion from this experiment is that middle class boys are more able to reward themselves by simple knowledge of how well they are doing than lower class boys, who are still at the stage where they depend mainly on external approval. However, a replication of this experiment by Rosenhan and Greenwald (1965) did not bear out these findings. McGrade (1966) made a similar study, using an administrator of the test game who was naive with respect to the purpose and hypotheses of the experiment. She failed to confirm the Zigler and Kanzer findings.

We know that this kind of experiment is complicated by side effects of the experimenter's sex in relation to the sex and age of the children, as was demonstrated by Stevenson (1961). It also seems likely that the social class variable was not sufficiently differentiated in some of these experiments. Probably there is very little difference between middle class and stable or upper-working-class families in the ways they teach their children to move up the evolutionary reward scale. Probably the big difference is between the stable upper working class and the "underclass" or lower working class. But it appears that most of the experiments reporting on social class differences used working-class samples of the upper-working-class level.

Two studies have clearly differentiated between these working-class levels. Hess and Shipman (1965) differentiated Negro lower class children into a group with stable upper-working-class characteristics and another group whose mothers were receiving Aid for Dependent Children. There was a substantial difference between the two groups in the mother-child relationship in a learning situation. Also, Davidson and Greenberg (1967) studied high achievers and underachievers among Harlem Negro lower class children, and found large differences in the orderliness of the home life between the two working-class groups.

2. *There are differences between ethnic subcultures among disadvantaged groups in the reward systems they teach their children.*

Although all of the severely disadvantaged families share some common characteristics of the "culture of poverty," they may also have different ethnic cultural traits which lead to different reward systems. There is evidence of such differences between Negro, Appalachian white, and some American Indian groups.

American Indians have a wide variety of tribal cultures, and therefore it is dangerous to generalize about "Indians." However, among contemporary Indian groups there appears to be a general virtue of cooperation and mutual support within an extended family and to a lesser degree within a tribal community. It might be inferred that praise-blame from family and from peer group is the most effective form of reward-punishment for Indian children living in Indian communities.

The hypothesis of peer-group rewarding power is supported by observations of school behavior in several different places. Wax (1969) reports that in both the Cherokee group in eastern Oklahoma and the Sioux of South Dakota the children tend to form a close-knit group with its own system of control that baffles the teacher. An observer in an Oklahoma Cherokee school writes, "Observing the upper-grade classroom, I concluded that the students regard it as their own place, the locus of their own society, in which the teacher is an unwelcome intruder, introducing irrelevant demands. It is rather as though a group of mutinous sailors had agreed to the efficient manning of 'their' ship while ignoring the captain and the captain's navigational goals [p. 101]."

Children do not tolerate an individual show of superior knowledge. Often a teacher cannot find any pupil who will volunteer an answer to a question that several of them know. In oral reading, the whole class tends to read together in audible whispers, so that the child who is supposed to be reciting can simply wait when he comes to a difficult word until he hears it said by his classmates. Generally, pupils like to work together, and to help each other. Consequently, the weak students are carried along by the stronger ones, and the stronger ones do not exert themselves to excel the weaker ones. This same kind of behavior was noted by Wolcott (1967) in his study of Kwakiutl children in British Columbia.

The peer group may be less effective as a source of reward-punishment for Appalachian disadvantaged children. They seem to get their rewards mainly within the family circle. Conceivably, the teacher may be a more potent source of reward for Appalachian than for Indian children, if the teacher develops a motherly or fatherly relation with them.

The Negro lower-lower class children may operate much more at the level of approval-disapproval from the teacher than the Indian or Appalachian children. They are less likely to have both parents in the home, and they probably get less parental approval-disapproval. They do not generally fall into the mutual help pattern of the Indian children. The peer group becomes a powerful influence on the Negro children probably after the age of 9 or 10, but its influence operates mainly in out-of-school contexts—on the playground or the street corner.

This proposition needs much more research before it can be pushed very far. But the contrasting school behavior and school success of the various minority groups argue for the existence of different systems of rewards and punishments, as well as different achievement goals to which these systems are directed.

3. *In general, external rewards (material or intangible) have positive values for disadvantaged or failing children.*

This proposition differs from the first in being valid for all social classes, leaving open the question of the relative effectiveness of these kinds of rewards in different social classes. There is a growing amount of solid, practical evidence for this proposition, growing out mainly from the *operant-conditioning* programs and experiments stimulated by Skinner. They all have in common the giving of a reward for every small step in the direction of the desired learning. Work with preschool children, such as that done by Bereiter and Engelmann (1966), is being studied widely and their practices repeated at primary grade levels.

It is not established whether material rewards, such as pieces of candy, are more effective than verbal praise. Intermediate between them is some kind of point system, whereby a child gets a point for every correct answer (sometimes a point is subtracted for errors), and the points may be "cashed in" later for material objects, or special favors such as a trip to the zoo.

Several school systems have established a "reinforcement technique" for working with children who have various kinds of school adjustment problems, academic and behavioral. This method seems to work equally well with middle class and lower-working-class children, as long as the child is having a school problem. The procedure is to diagnose the child's problem carefully, to work out a series of small steps from where he is to where he should be, and to reward him for each step. For example, an 11-year-old boy with a third-grade reading level but otherwise average intelligence may refuse to read with his sixth-grade class, and thus makes no progress. Rewarding him for reading with his class does no good, because he makes himself ridiculous in the eyes of his classmates. (The punishment is greater than the reward.) But if a counselor studies the boy, discovers his third-grade reading level, and then arranges for individual remedial work with rewards for each advance above the third-grade level, the boy may catch up with his age-mates within a few months.

Validity of a symbolic reinforcement program with underachieving children was indicated with a junior high school group in Chicago, in a situation in which one might expect social reinforcement to have relatively little value. Clark and Walberg (1968) experimented with a system of massive symbolic rewards in classes of sixth- and seventh-grade Negro children in a Chicago ghetto—all the children being in classes for after-school remedial reading, because they were from one to four years below grade level in their school work. The reward system consisted of tallies made by each child on a card containing numbered squares. Whenever a child made a correct response or showed some other sign of learning, the teacher praised him and asked him to circle the next number on his card with a special colored pencil that he was to use only for this purpose. The cards were collected at the end of the class period. No other rewards were given for the points gained.

Teachers of nine remedial classes were instructed to give praise rewards so that even the very slow ones would get several in a session. After six sessions of this sort, five of the nine teachers were selected at random, and confidentially asked to double or triple the number of rewards they gave, while the four control group teachers were told to "keep up the good work."

As a result, the experimental groups got many more tally numbers, while the control groups remained at the early levels. After five weeks a reading test was given, and the experimental groups exceeded the controls by a substantially and statistically significant amount.

4. *An effective reward system in a complex changing society must be based on a strong ego.*

This crucial step in the reward-punishment theory being developed here conceives the ego as a source of reward-punishment, as well as the executive and planning function of the personality. To develop this set of ideas we may turn to a recent article by Bettelheim (1969) entitled "Psychoanalysis and Education." Bettelheim starts with the conventional dynamic personality theory of learning by young children through rewards given first by the id (the physiological appetites) and then by the superego (the internalized praising and blaming voice of the parents). Therefore, learning based on the pleasure principle is supplemented by learning based on the superego, which carries a child from learning for fun to learning even if it is hard work because his superego rewards him for this kind of learning and punishes him for failing to learn. We all recognize that much necessary learning is hard work, and will not take place under the pressure of the id.

Perhaps this last sentence is not quite accurate. There are a number of creative teachers and writers about teaching who in effect take the position that the way to teach children successfully (whether they are socially disadvantaged or socially advantaged) is to get the id behind their learning experience, that is, to give their "natural drive to learn," their "native curiosity," free play, and to count on their learning "creatively" in this way throughout their school experience.

For example, Kohl (1967), in his book *36 Children,* describes how he worked for a year with a class of 36 Negro slum children who were below average in academic skills. He did get results. There is no reason to doubt this. His method of encouraging them to write about their fears, their hates, and their likes, about the bad and good things they experience in their homes and streets, loosened their pens and their tongues, added to their vocabulary, and got them interested in school. It seems that Kohl was helping them marshal the forces of the id on behalf of learning. But how far can this go? How far can a slum child (or a middle class child) go toward mastery of arithmetic, of English sentence style, of knowledge of science and history if he is motivated only by his drive to express his feelings, or possibly also by his desire to please his friendly and permissive teacher?

We do not know how far this kind of reward will carry a child's learning. We might guess that it would carry children up to about the seventh-grade level. Therefore, we should ask Kohl and others of this school of thought to prove that their methods will carry children to the eighth-grade level. No such claims appear to have been substantiated, except in the case of socially advantaged children, such as those attending A. S. Neill's school at Summerhill, England. And some observers of this school argue that it can only work with children who have a strong British middle class superego, and can profit from teaming their somewhat starved id with the superego in the pursuit of learning.

Bettelheim (1969) argues that the main function of education is to help the ego develop so that with the aid of the superego it controls the id, but at the same time it balances the superego by allowing reasonable satisfaction of the id. "The goal of education ought to be a well-blanced personality where both id and superego are subordinated to reality, to the ego [p. 83]." "Nothing automatically assures ego growth, neither punishment nor reward. The only thing that assures it is having the right experiences to stimulate and foster growth at the right time, in the right sequence, and in the right amount [p. 84]."

Thus, the ego becomes a source of reward and punishment through enabling the child to promise himself realistically a future reward for doing something unpleasant at the moment and through making the child take the blame for the future consequences of his mistakes of judgment or his mistakes of self-indulgence.

5. *A strongly developed ego gives a sense of personal control and personal responsibility for important events in one's life.*

The ego can only become an effective reward and punishment giver if the social environment is orderly enough to permit the ego to operate on the basis of a rational study of reality. This is substantially the case with the family and the community environment of the middle class and the stable working class in America. But the disadvantaged groups we have been considering do not experience this kind of orderliness in their environment, and do not transmit to their children a sense of confidence in an orderly environment.

Consider, for example, a child of a stable working-class home in which the family has supper at a regular time, the children have a time to play after supper, and a time to go to bed. A four-year-old child in this family has learned a routine for the evening. He finishes his supper and carries his dishes to the place where they will be washed. He then plays with toys for a while, and then goes to his bedroom, puts on his pajamas, and goes to his mother who has finished the supper dishes. He says, "I'm ready for bed. Now let's read." His mother gets out a picture book and they "read" together for a while, he nestled against his mother's body. Then she says, "Bedtime," and they go to his bed, where she kisses him goodnight. This is an orderly environment, in which the child's ego is developing so that it can promise him satisfaction if he does his share to bring it about.

Now consider a child of a mother with six children receiving welfare payments to care for them, because she has no husband at home. Rarely is there much order in this home. Hardly can this child count on starting a train of events by doing some household chore which eventually brings him into his mother's lap to read with her. She is just too busy, too preoccupied with a hundred worries and a few desires; she may not be able to read beyond the third-grade level, and she may dislike reading. She is not likely to have learned about the necessity of her children having regular rewards and punishments given consistently by her as a means of teaching them.

A good deal of research has been done on the acquisition by children of a sense of control of rewards. Rotter (Rotter, Seemann, & Liverant, 1962) has studied the "sense of personal control of the environment." Crandall (Crandall, Katkovsky, & Crandall, 1965) studied a child's feelings about whether his own efforts determine the rewards he gets from school and from important people or whether this is a matter of luck or the whims of important people. Battle and Rotter (1963) found that middle class and white skin color tended to be associated with a sense of self-responsibility and control of the outer world's rewards and punishments. Coleman (1966) in the National Survey of Educational Opportunity asked students to agree or disagree with three statements such as "Good luck is more important than hard work for success." Negro students had a greater belief in luck as the disposer. Coleman says, "It appears that children from advantaged groups assume the environment will respond if they are able to affect it; children from disadvantaged groups do not make this assumption, but in many cases assume that nothing they will do can affect the environment—it will give benefits or withhold them but not as a consequence of their own action [p. 321]." Negro children who answered "hard work" scored higher on a test of verbal performance than did white pupils who chose the "good luck" response.

Hall (1968) studied a group of young Caucasian and Negro men aged 18–20, all from working-class families in a big city. He divided these young men into three categories according to their work adjustment—one group who had a record of stable employment or went back to school and succeeded there; one group called "rolling stones" who had a recent history of frequent job changes or of going back to school and dropping out again; and a third group whom he called "lookers" who just loafed around, neither working nor going to school. He used with them a questionnaire aimed to measure their sense of control of the environment through their efforts. There was a clear difference in scores between the three groups, the "stable performers" having the most belief in their ability to control their environment.

From these studies it can be inferred that the ego is a less powerful source of reward, and the ego is itself weaker, in the socially disadvantaged groups. The child who can predict the consequences of his behavior can maximize his rewards.

6. *People learn to operate at all of the several levels of reward by the time they reach adolesence, and the level at which they operate varies with the action area.*

This proposition directs our attention to an important set of facts that are indicated on the right-hand column of Table 1. It is possible for a person at adolescence and later to operate in terms of physiological appetite rewards in one area of action, in terms of praise-blame from peers in another area, in terms of ego reward or punishment in yet another action area.

For example, a 17-year-old boy may seek id rewards or satisfaction of physiological appetite in his relations with the opposite sex. He also may seek the id rewards of excitement in doing perilous things such as driving a fast car, diving from a high diving board, rock climbing in the mountains, gang fighting, stealing cars. Some of these things he may do alone, thus cutting off rewards from others, and it is hard to see how one can get ego rewards from doing dangerous things for no purpose other than the thrill or from matching one's wits against nature.

This same boy may play a good game of tennis or basketball partly to get the reward of approval from his peers. He may work long hours at night on a high school course in calculus for advanced standing in college, primarily because his ego tells him he will be rewarded in the future by a successful occupational career.

Probably a social class and an ethnic subculture teaches a person to choose certain areas for certain kinds of rewards. For instance, some American Indian cultures may teach their children to rely on praise-blame from peers for much of their school behavior. A big city, Negro, lower-working-class culture may teach boys to learn to fight, to play basketball, to throw rocks at school windows, and to smoke "pot" through id rewards and peer-group rewards, while it teaches them to expect punishment from teachers for their behavior and lack of achievement in school.

But a particular Negro boy may become so accurate at "shooting baskets" on the park playground that he no longer gets much feeling of reward from being the best in his neighborhood. He may happen on an older high school athlete who rewards him by playing with him, or a man in the neighborhood who tells him that he might become a second Cazzie Russell, if he keeps on. At this point his ego may become effective as a promiser of future reward if he stays in school and makes his grades and then makes the school basketball team.

The study by Gross (1967) of "Learning Readiness in Two Jewish Groups" provides a striking illustration of action areas apparently selected by the minority group subculture for differential rewards. Ninety Brooklyn Jewish boys aged about six years and all middle class were given a set of tests of cognitive development. About half of the boys came from Sephardic families (immigrants from Arabic or Oriental countries) and half came from Ashkenazic families (immigrants from Europe). The mothers were all native born, and English was the household language. The boys with European family backgrounds were decidedly superior in the cognitive measures to the boys with Arabic-Oriental family backgrounds. There was a 17-point IQ difference on the Peabody Picture Vocabulary Test. Yet the parents were all middle class Jews living in the same big city. Intensive study of the family training and background experience of the two groups of boys revealed little difference except in the mothers' attitudes toward wealth. Twice as many Ashkenazic (European) mothers said that earnings were "unimportant" in their desires for their children, and three times as many Sephardic mothers said they wanted their sons to be "wealthy."

One may infer from this study that the reward systems in the two groups of families (which were very similar according to the sophisticated methods used to study them) were directed toward different areas of action.

Education of Disadvantaged Minority Groups

What can we say from this partially confirmed theory about the education of disadvantaged minority groups?

First, we can say that teachers would teach better if they had a systematic theory of the working of reward and punishment in the learning of children, and if they put this theory into practice. Their theory should include the concept of a hierarchy of reward levels, and they should understand what levels of reward are operating in their classes.

Second, we can assume that most socially disadvantaged children are lower on the evolutionary reward scale, at a given age, than are the advantaged children. Therefore, the teachers of these children should reward them with a great deal of praise, and perhaps with a point system that produces material rewards.

Third, a major goal of all teachers at all levels should be to help the child strengthen his ego as a controller and rewarder of his behavior. This means that the teacher cannot be content with using praise and other forms of external reward, although these should be used when they are needed. The teacher should help the child move up the reward scale.

Progress toward strengthening the ego can only be made in school by putting order and consistency into the school situation, so that the child can learn how to control his environment on the basis of the reality principle. This can be done for individual children partly by individualized instruction which enables them to learn and to predict their own learning in relation to their effort to learn. This can be done for a school class by an orderly program in which students know what their responsibilities are, participate in making decisions about their work, and get accurate information on their progress.

Since the family of the disadvantaged child so often fails to perform its part of the implicit contract, there is bound to be dissatisfaction by school teachers and administrators with the situation, and critics will sometimes blame the school and other times the family subculture. Probably the educator will have to spend much of his energy working with parents and leaders in the local subculture, helping them and receiving help from them to create an environment in the home and neighborhood that supports the learning experience of the child and directs it along socially desirable lines.

References

Battle, E., & Rotter, J. Children's feelings of personal control as related to social class and ethnic group. *Journal of Personality*, 1963, **31**, 482–490.

Bereiter, C., & Engelmann, A. *Teaching disadvantaged children.* Englewood Cliffs, N. J.: Prentice-Hall, 1966.

Bettelheim, B. Psychoanalysis and education. *School Review*, 1969, **77**, 73–86.

Clark, C. A., & Walberg, H. J. The influence of massive rewards on reading achievement in potential urban school dropouts. *American Educational Research Journal*, 1968, **5**, 305–310.

Coleman, J. S. *Equality of educational opportunity.* Washington, D. C.: United States Government Printing Office, 1966.

Crandall, V. C., Katkovsky, W., & Crandall, V. J. Children's beliefs in their own control of reinforcements in intellectual-academic achievement situations. *Child Development*, 1965, **36**, 91–109.

Davidson, H. H., & Greenberg, J. *Traits of school achievers from a deprived background.* (Cooperative Research Project No. 2805) Washington, D. C.: United States Office of Education, 1967.

Davis, A. Cultural factors in remediation. *Educational Horizons,* 1965, **43,** 231–251.

Fenichel, O. *The psychoanalytic theory of neurosis.* New York: Norton, 1945.

Gross, M. *Learning readiness in two Jewish groups.* New York: Center for Urban Education, 1967.

Hall, W. S. Levels of productive economic and educational involvement in the culture among lower class young men: A comparative study. Unpublished doctoral dissertation, Department of Education, University of Chicago, 1968.

Hartley, E. L., & Hartley, R. E. *Fundamentals of social psychology.* New York: Knopf, 1952.

Hess, R. D., & Shipman, V. Early experience and the socialization of cognitive modes in children. *Child Development,* 1965, **36,** 869–886.

Katz, I. Some motivational determinants of racial differences in intellectual achievement. *International Journal of Psychology,* 1967, **2,** 1–12.

Kohl, H. R. *36 Children.* New York: New American Library, 1967.

Lighthall, F. F., & Cernius, V. *Effects of certain rewards for task performance among lower-class boys.* (United States Office of Education & University of Chicago Cooperative Research Project No. S-283) Chicago: Department of Education, University of Chicago, 1967.

Marshall, H. H. Learning as a function of task interest, reinforcement, and social class variables. *Journal of Educational Psychology,* 1969, **60,** 133–137.

McGrade, B. J. Effectiveness of verbal reinforcers in relation to age and social class. *Journal of Personality and Social Psychology,* 1966, **4,** 555–560.

Rosenhan, D., & Greenwald, J. A. The effects of age, sex, and socioeconomic class on responsiveness to two classes of verbal reinforcement. *Journal of Personality* 1965, **33,** 108–121.

Rotter, J., Seeman, M., & Liverant, S. Internal versus external control of reinforcement. A major variable in behavior theory. In N. F. Washburne (Ed.), *Decisions, values, and groups.* Vol. 2. London: Pergamon Press, 1962.

Skinner, B. F. *Science and human behavior.* New York: Macmillan, 1953.

Stevenson, H. W. Social reinforcement with children as a function of chronological age, sex of experimenter, and sex of subject. *Journal of Abnormal and Social Psychology,* 1961, **63,** 147–154.

Thorndike, E. L. *The elements of psychology.* New York: Seiler, 1905.

Thorndike, E. L. *The fundamentals of learning.* New York: Bureau of Publications, Teachers College, Columbia University, 1932.

Wax, M. L. *Indian education in eastern Oklahoma.* (Research Contract Report No. O. E. 6-10-260 and BIA No. 5-0565-2-12-1) Washington, D. C.: United States Office of Education, 1969.

Wolcott, H. F. *A Kwakiutl village and school.* New York: Holt, Rinehart & Winston, 1967.

Zigler, E., & Kanzer, P. The effectiveness of two classes of verbal reinforcers on the performance of middle- and lower-class children. *Journal of Personality,* 1962, **30,** 157–163.

Zigler, E., & de Labry, J. Concept-switching in middle-class, lower-class, and retarded children. *Journal of Abnormal and Social Psychology,* 1962, **65,** 267–273.

Testing and Equality of Career Opportunity[1]

ROBERT E. HAMPTON

The author received a Bachelor of Business Administration Degree from the University of Chattanooga in 1949. Since 1950, he has held positions of increasing public service responsibility in the Department of State, the Department of the Air Force, and the United States Civil Service Commission. In 1958, he became a special assistant at the White House, a position he held until May 1961. In July 1961, he was appointed a United States Civil Service Commissioner, and in January 1969 was elevated to the position of Chairman.

I want to congratulate APA on its theme for the 1969 convention "Psychology and the Problems of Society." I recognize that many of you, as psychologists, in your individual efforts, are devoting substantially more and more time, thought, and resources to the complex issues of an ever increasingly complex technology. Life at a policy-making level in the area of public employment is, I think, equally complex, and you and I share many common concerns.

As complex as this life is now, it must have been even worse before public employment was covered by a merit system. In the days before 1883, the filling of federal jobs by patronage was an endless agony. President Lincoln managed to endure it by telling jokes about it. When Lincoln came down with a mild attack of smallpox and was confined to his bed, he said to his doctor: "Tell all the office-seekers to come in at once, for now I have something to give to all of them."

While I cannot pretend to have something for everyone, I am hopeful that coming nearer to one another will mean that we begin to work together in a more planned way toward the resolution of our common problems.

One of our common concerns is with the apparent erosion of confidence in the objective psychology in which you have been deeply involved professionally, and with the application of that psychology in public service employment, with which I have been concerned.

The measurement and evaluation of people, which has been of such importance to us, has now become society's concern and prerogative to criticize. Society's

---

[1] Invited Address presented to the Division of Evaluation and Measurement of the American Psychological Association, September 3, 1969. First published in *Civil Service News*, September 3, 1969, United States Civil Service Commission, Washington, D. C. 20415.

response cannot be dismissed. We have historic dependence on public confidence, and in particular in our ability to determine reliable and objective measures of job suitability and competence. The evolution of a federal merit system, which was born in 1883, was an outgrowth of failing public confidence in government employees and the widespread belief that favoritism toward special groups was inconsistent with a fair, efficient, and democratic society.

The creation of a merit system was a revolution in federal personnel administration. The concept that people should be evaluated according to how they met *job-relevant* criteria was a radical change. Radically new tools were needed—tools which met all the characteristics of objective tests. Every improvement in that merit system since its inception has been intended to maximize public confidence, to make the system a fair and equitable one for everyone.

While I am disturbed, as you are, by some of the similarities between the pre-1883 responses of society and the reactions of the 1960s, I believe the present system is sound. It is built on sound precepts devised through the contributions of sound measurement, and it has demonstrated willingness to respond to change. For example, the merit system was able to accommodate and absorb the tremendous personnel buildup of World War II. This rapid growth occurred while political balance was maintained at the higher levels of the career service. I do not see the need for another system, or, indeed, another revolution in personnel administration. I believe we can accommodate the complex needs of a growing society.

You, as psychologists, have traditionally been the first to challenge your own science, to work with other disciplines, to improve. Few professions are as willing as yours to examine and probe its own precepts and practices. While this may make problems for administrators such as myself who would like a more certain world in which to make decisions, it is healthy.

None of us is above criticism. However, to professionals accustomed to practicing this degree of self-criticism, it must be disturbing to be the subjects of uninformed criticism from other sources. Yet today, this is what is happening.

Current Criticisms of Testing

Let us take a look at the current wave of attacks on tests and testing. The attacks are general; they offer no remedies and no viable alternatives. Some of them come from extremists who seem to feel that anything not developed by and specifically for them is directed against them. The claim of these vocal few to being spokesmen for the minorities is a very dubious claim. The purpose of some has been to undermine public confidence and generate confusion.

As one who sees the value of your work, I want to answer this critical barrage. I recognize and appreciate your many contributions to the always difficult task of understanding man as he is. I want to emphasize, publicly, that without those contributions we would be back in an employment world of mobocracy. Without tests in a public personnel system, we would have chaos. (Incidentally, I define tests to include the entire spectrum of ways to measure human ability and performance.)

However imperfect they may be, objective tests have been basic instruments in working for equality in employment for everyone, including minorities. But the elimination of all testing leaves the door wide open to every kind of discrimination.

Those of us who must deal with today's problems need to understand their basis better, to modify practices and initiate changes where necessary, and to deal more effectively with the opposition. But we should not allow our critics to overrun us. We must uphold sound values and fair systems, where we know they exist. I am not prepared to abandon ship on tests—which would be, I believe, to move *away* from fairness and equality of opportunity.

The responsibility of the Civil Service Commission in law is for equality of career opportunity for *all*. But we must recognize, too, that not *all* people are qualified for the types of jobs or careers in the public sector. While we are concerned with equal career opportunity, and I believe the public service has demonstrated this, it must be carried out within the limits and context of the total personnel system. If it is not, I foresee the erosion of public confidence. Both equal opportunity and public confidence concern me, and they are inseparable in conception and in fulfillment.

Despite attacks, it would appear that confidence in and dependence on the public sector are on the *increase*. In the 1970s, governments at all levels, federal, state, and local, will be looked to for more and better solutions to social, economic, and other problems, and for more services to the public. At the same time, the pressure to keep government employment down is not likely to let up. The pressure on us to produce more with proportionately fewer people cannot be resolved through greater efficiency alone; it will require that the quality of workers be improved. It is likely that we will need people with greater skills.

The demand for people with graduate degrees over the baccalaureate is already on the increase. But it is not our intention to develop a work force selected more and more on the basis of credentials. Credentials make us uneasy, because demanding them often tends toward demanding greater skills than jobs need; as such, they are discriminatory. Also, the very validity of the credentials makes us nervous, for example, college grade point average. We need much more information on the *quality* of the educational experience, on motivation, and on other data beyond a transcript. The measurement of potential is critical in this improved quality search, for even small gains in quality are likely to generate large gains in productivity. I would offer this as an area in which psychologists could make large contributions.

I cannot compromise in the search for and insistence on improved quality of performance. We shall continue to explore ways to achieve fuller career participation in federal employment for minority groups. But the criterion must not be the popularity of a program, but its merit in the maintenance of a top-quality work force.

In applying this policy we are, I believe, reflecting the view of most of our citizens that reducing quality of performance is not the way to solve an unemployment problem. The federal government is not and should not be the first or last resort of persons seeking employment, but a partner in the response of the total economy to the need for employment. Despite its showcase role in American society, the federal government represents only 3% of the work force. We shall continue, however, to assume our proportionate share of national responsibility and our position of leadership in working toward full employment and full utilization of all our human resources.

In terms of numbers the federal government has increased its minority employment substantially. At the beginning of 1966, there were some 422,000 Negroes,

Spanish Americans, Orientals, and American Indians employed by the federal government. They represented a little over 18% of our total employment. Today these figures have increased to over half a million persons, representing almost 20% of our work force. While Negroes make up less than 11% of the *national work force,* they comprise about 16% of federal employees. I am sure that psychologists, more than any single professional group, know the pitfalls of quoting statistics. But the raw numbers do reflect something. They show the result of positive action programs, of more than indulgence in lip service to our beliefs in equal employment opportunity.

While the numbers reflect our concerns and successes in providing equal opportunity to be *selected* for a federal job, they perhaps do not reflect our equal concern with opportunity for personal fulfillment within a federal career. Many more personnel decisions are made *after* employment, and their impact is far more critical to assuring equal posture for minority groups. Our next tasks, then, are to stimulate the conditions that will allow all employees to use their capabilities to the fullest. This involves training, the redesign of work, and other innovative techniques. I believe that our responsibility is also to stimulate the private sector by providing examples of policy and workable programs that have been successful in providing equality of opportunity. To act as the pump primer, and also to get on with our next tasks, we must continue to depend on established sound measurement concepts, and at the same time to conceive new ones.

Areas of Progress in the Federal Personnel System

Without trying to make it appear that we have done everything that needs to be done, let me review some of the ways in which we have made progress. In the past, we, in the federal personnel system, have made major efforts in the following areas:

1. Jobs have been redesigned to provide more entry rungs. Here we have separated from professional, administrative, and technical jobs those tasks which might be performed by individuals with lesser skills. This is not *"make work."* It is providing an opportunity for many people to learn new skills, and to do useful work for which they have skills in support of others. At the same time, it is releasing the time of highly trained persons to cope with more challenges, and minimizing their underutilization. The college-trained professionals who are now entering the world of work are simply not going to allow us to saddle them with unchallenging work. They have told us so clearly. We cannot ignore their attitudes if we are to retain their commitment to public service.

2. We review continually and carefully the relevance of education and experience requirements for occupations. As I have said, it is our intention *not* to develop a credentialist work force. We intend to provide job opportunities for a wide range of individual skills.

3. Beyond our more traditional use of tests, we have some approaches which are designed to take the burden *off* written test scores. The job-element method is a systematic procedure for analyzing job demands and human abilities, and then matching people to jobs according to their *potential* for being successful. This general system now applies to the filling of over 600,000 jobs in trades. In this system, test scores become, properly, one of alternate methods by which an applicant can demonstrate possession of skills.

An extension of this concept—the worker-trainee program—emphasizes and attempts to measure the motivation to work rather than developed skills. For certain jobs, someone who has had no opportunity for skills development, but who wants to work, can find a job with us more easily than someone who has highly developed skills, but might be unwilling to do certain tasks.

This program is currently taking in over 1,200 people a month. It is frankly ahead of our knowledge of the measurement of motivation, but we do not find as accurately developed instrumentation in this area from your profession as we do in the cognitive area. We desperately need such dependable measures, based on sound precepts and fundamental research. I hope we can learn something about the objective measurement of motivation to work in less than the half-century it took us to get to where we are in written tests.

When tests are used in our own merit promotion programs, it is within the spirit of the APA guidelines on testing. It has been particularly distasteful for employees to be rated ineligible for promotion because of an arbitrary cut score. Therefore, tests are only alternate ways of getting promoted. No employee who takes a test as part of a promotion decision may be screened out on that basis alone. We have removed the bitter pill of "failing a test" for our employees—a concept which is clearly unacceptable for adults who are employed.

These are examples of significant steps that have been taken, but we still have much to do. For example, we need to develop better systematic methods for the identification of *all* employees who are being underutilized so that they can be trained and offered opportunity for advancement.

I think we need a federal aptitude and utilization scheme, especially at lower grades. We should measure not only aptitudes and abilities, but interests, motivation, self-perceptions, job concepts, etc. I am directing my staff to develop and test such a model so that all agencies may apply the principles. We may then have a more systematic approach to the identification of our training requirements, and our resources at these levels, and be able to do something about what we often refer to, too simply, as "good personnel utilization."

In addition, we need to continue fundamental research efforts so that we can more effectively guide *existing* practices. Along this line, as many of you know, the Educational Testing Service and the Civil Service Commission have been cooperating in a major research program to try to resolve the many questions concerned with the fairness of written tests for minority groups. The effort to date—a feasibility study—has been supported by the Ford Foundation, with a substantial contribution of ETS resources. The federal government is supplying subjects and technical partnership—and great interest. Minority groups, employee unions, personnel people, and others concerned with problems of testing also have a great interest in this program. It is with great pleasure that I am able to announce that the Ford Foundation has just made an additional grant of $358,000 to the Educational Testing Service for continuing support for the full study.

The results of this effort will have great action implications for employment in government and in industry. Certainly, they will have great impact on educational testing. This is an example of three large organizations expressing their willingness to cooperate in doing something about their common concerns for equal opportunity in our society.

While this is a fine example of cooperative effort on equal opportunity problems, I do not mean to imply that only major research programs can be effective. I believe that the smallest contribution to measurement knowledge can have great effects when applied. On the basis of measurements, we make very significant judgments. For example, the accuracy of the instruments we use—tests, or reflections of academic ability—has a direct relationship to the amount of money at which an individual is hired, hence how much he takes home. Our actions now which have a basis in measurement can determine who gets trained, placed, or promoted, and can have equality in our economy. An initial dollar differential as a reflection of measurement is compounded over the years in terms of ingrade increments, and is eventually reflected in the amount of retirement pay. These actions badly need sounder research support. I assure you that even small measurement improvements can have profound effects in a 20-billion-dollar federal payroll.

In reviewing the major actions we have taken and those which are in process or planned, I would conclude that they are *probably helpful* to meet some problems which have *erupted*. I concede that some of our solutions are probably of the band-aid variety. Others will be more permanent. Our policy is to search more intensively for the long-lasting variety. For example, in response to test-fairness issues, we would prefer to obtain valid answers through comprehensive research, rather than to tamper with tests without knowing whether the changes, though well intended, would actually help or hurt minorities.

In spite of the continuing need to cope with day-to-day problems as they erupt, we must now find the resources for longer range planning. I believe that social scientists should direct more of their thinking to long-range solutions and to anticipating issues, so that we may have help in properly planning for change.

Future Issues in Public-Service Employment

How far into the future can we plan? We can already foresee that issues in public-service employment in the 1980s will arise from: (*a*) the currently changing nature of work; (*b*) different occupational structures; (*c*) different educational systems; (*d*) changing relationships between workers, unions, and management; (*e*) new conceptions of occupational choice; (*f*) new attitudes toward career commitment; and (*g*) length of working life, etc.

These changes will undoubtedly place new pressures on the concept of equal opportunity, and we will need to know much more about how to handle them in a complex employment system. To be prepared to deal with the problems of the 1980s, we need new measures and methods to anticipate the effects of alternative policies, and to detect the outcome of policy changes made.

I am not sure any of us today knows what new measures must be taken. But I am convinced that no organization is better suited to try than yours. I believe that your profession and government should now actively join hands in developing models for an orderly future—a national goal, if you will, for the psychological measurement and public personnel professions.

We should establish a continuing group which would enable us to begin to identify the kinds of information we need to collect, the kinds of research that need to be done, and the kinds of support that will be needed in the next decade to provide public officials with the basic knowledge, precepts, and action plans for a broadened equal opportunity program. I am prepared to seek the resources, including asking other federal agencies to assign appropriate people to this effort.

Our goal should be the development of a federal civil service which by its one-hundredth anniversary shall have achieved true responsiveness to the needs for quality and equality in employment. By working now to develop the models and methods to deal with these problems, we can build for the establishment of these same standards throughout national employment. It is a goal consistent with American dreams—one not beyond our capabilities—if we but try.

Sadean and Institutional Cruelty[1]

PHILIP P. HALLIE

The author received his PhD in philosophy from Harvard University in 1952. He is currently the Griffin Professor of Philosophy and Humanities at Wesleyan University, Middletown, Connecticut. Presently, he is applying his analysis of cruelty (in his book *The Paradox of Cruelty,* 1969) to the broader concepts of evil and temptation, with special reference to both the image of the devil in literature and theology and to social degradation in poverty subcultures.

The *Oxford English Dictionary* (1961) defines "cruelty" as "a disposition to inflict suffering," and other dictionaries define it in terms of indifference to or delight in inflicting pain. They also agree that the antonyms of the word are words like "kindliness" and "charitableness."

This map of the logic of cruelty is profoundly misleading, especially for those of us interested in what the anticruelty societies call "substantial cruelty," fatal maiming. As a matter of fact, in this kind of cruelty, but especially in the kind we shall be confining ourselves to here, substantially cruelty towards human beings, pain is only an occasional symptom of a power relationship whereby stronger persons choose to smash the life styles of weaker persons. To confine our thinking about cruelty to pain is like confining our thinking about cancer to aches and aspirins.

Moreover, the opposite of cruelty is not the desire to give pleasure or avoid inflicting pain. The stronger party, whom we shall call the "victimizer," may be kind on occasion, or even at length, but his kindness, when his self-satisfied, condescending face appears before his victim, may be the hardest torture for that victim to bear. The opposite of cruelty is not kindness or charity; the opposite of cruelty is liberation from the cruel relationship between victimizer and victim. *From the victim's point of view* (most definitions are from the victimizer's point of view) the antonym of "cruelty" is "freedom." To understand all this is to understand better than most of us do not only the nature of cruelty in general but also the present black power movement in America, which is a response to 350 years of substantial cruelty, with white men as victimizers and black men as victims.

---

[1] Invited Address presented to the Division of Philosophical Psychology at the Annual Meeting of the American Psychological Association, Washington, D. C., September 3, 1969.

Personal and Institutional Cruelty

The destructive maiming of human beings by human beings can be done in various ways. The Marquis de Sade gave his name to victimization for the sake of erotic stimulation. His heroes and heroines wanted their "vital juices" to boil, and they needed bloody victims to achieve their orgasms. Like the locus of an orgasm the locus of the cruelties in Sade's writings is always an episodic, detached *now* when the flesh and will of what Sade called a "strong being" collide with the flesh and will of his victim.

Destructive erotic collision, however, is more than the relationship between two colliding bodies and two conflicting wills. Sadistic cruelty must collide with the customs, laws, and dominant morality of society before it can be stimulating, before it can make the "strong being" come to a boil. In a word, it must be *perverse,* that is, wrongdoing done for the sheer joy of causing and receiving irritation, for the sheer joy of conflict.

Still there is a curious fact about Sade's novels, plays, and essays: No victim ever really resists her victimizer; no strong arm of individuals or of society ever is turned against the Sadean hero or heroine. Sade's writings carefully imagine away all resistance, all substantial conflict between victim and victimizer. In fact, Sade is quite frank about this: Solid resistance from a victim would cool his victimizer's ardor, would destroy the delicious cruel relationship, and so he imagines it away in his writings, though in his life he could not do this, and spent about 30 years in jails and asylums because of the real resistance of his victims and their allies. The irritations of Sadean cruelty, as they occur in Sade's writings, are not conflicts as much as they are imaginative, masturbatory titillations. As Sade clearly saw, his kind of cruelty dissolves when the victim solidly resists. In fact, we shall find that the joys of all sorts of cruelty dissolve when the victim resists, and this follows logically from the fact that the cruel relationship requires a weak victim and an active, powerful victimizer. Without a difference of power between the two, cruelty modulates into *combat,* which is a different though related matter.

Now, living episodically and perversely in the Sadean *now* is quite different from living practically, as we usually use the word "practical." The man of practical wisdom, as Aristotle and so many others have pointed out, uses socially acceptable means to achieve long-range, socially acceptable goals; he has a clear insight into means and ends, and uses that insight to govern his impulses, his short-range goals. In every important respect, Sade's kind of short-term, perverse cruelty is the enemy of practicality; for example, Sade deliberately imagined away solid resistances, while the practical man sees them clearly and tries to remove them efficiently.

There is, however, a kind of fatal maiming that is practical. It is less perverse, less episodic, more long range, and more realistic than Sade's. I am referring not to Sade's person-to-person kind of cruelty, but to history's various forms of institutionalized maiming-unto-death. Capital punishment is one instance of public cruelty, and colonialism through the ages is another. Here, instead of perversity and orgasmic living in the moment, there are high, socially acceptable, eminently practical (for the Establishment) ideals that give unity and integrity not only to the various moments of individual lives, but also in some cases to the whole history of a nation. Such ideals as "law and order," "the white man's burden," and "freedom for the South Vietnamese" have justified fatal maiming very persuasively (at least to the victimizer and his friends) and have saved many men from lives of Sadean, perverse self-satisfaction.

Let us put aside violent, bloody, institutional cruelty and consider quiet maiming. Of course the two are not separate, but I shall treat them separately. Let us do this because this kind of human destruction of human beings is *the most elusive for its victims,* and we are studying cruelty with an emphasis on the victim's point of view (unlike the dictionaries). Sade's victims in the juicy world of his imagination always know what hits them, though they never do anything about it, except strike postures that make them even more delicious victims. Sade's victims are smashed candidly and perversely. But institutional cruelty does harm to large numbers of people efficiently, uneventfully, like the grinding of a large, well-oiled mechanism that still grinds exceedingly small. In fact, quiet public cruelty usually functions so smoothly that both the victimizers and the victims do not know that there is any other, better way for life to go! They all get used to it, and when doubts arise, or minor rebellions, the powerful ones can swiftly dig into the institutional archives (with the help of tame scholars) and come up with defenses that make a particular sort of maiming not only seem natural, but sometimes even a supernatural, divine necessity.

It is specifically in this kind of cruelty that our dictionary definitions offer us no map for the existing terrain of human destruction. The combination of immensely superior power on the part of the Establishment with high-flown justifications for maiming, and high, rigid abstractions for perceiving (or failing to perceive) individual victimizers and individual victims, this combination of physical power and mental persuasion masks or hides the cruelty that is happening from both the victimizers and the victims, at least for a while. The dangers, the high risks of revolt make it easier to be a live coward than a dead hero, and civilization has given victimizers elaborate vocabularies for describing the rotten act of calculated destruction. Nazis "exterminate" Jews, using the same word one uses for killing unindividualized rats; in America, bold, hardy pioneers make redskins "bite the dust"; and the history of institutional cruelty is the history of rigid stereotypes that make it seem that abstractions are destroying abstractions, not flesh and blood individuals destroying flesh and blood individuals.

Slavery: A Form of Institutional Cruelty

Let me clarify these generalizations by applying them to an instance of institutional cruelty as massive and profound as any in the history of the world, an instance we all can understand because it is still happening around and inside us, and its antonym, its opposite, is being explained to us every day by its victims. I am referring to the 350 years of slavery and its shadow, Jim Crow, which together compose one of the forms institutional cruelty takes in America. The black power movement happening to us all now is trying to explain the antonym, the opposite, of cruelty, as well as the very nature of cruelty itself.

The cruelty I speak of is not the castrations, the lynchings, the rapes, the whippings, etc.; these, remember, are the violent cruelties I spoke of at the outset, and if we confine ourselves to them, we become dazzled by the symptoms and fail to see the causes of these symptoms. No, slavery, and its shadow, Jim Crow employment, schooling, and housing, slavery as an institution helps us to see the cruel relationship stripped bare of distractions and of sentimental concerns for pleasures and pains. Slavery had benign masters, men who were never violent, or very seldom violent, with their slaves, who slashed off no ears and who even raped no black daughters or wives; but these benignities were another mask over the destructive relationship that is the center of cruelty of all sorts.

In 1740 the State of South Carolina passed legislation that provided that:

All negroes . . . mulattoes, or mestizos, who are or shall hereafter be in the province, and all their issue and offspring, born or to be born, shall be and they are hereby declared to be and remain forever hereafter absolute slaves . . . [Tannenbaum, 1947, pp. 66–67, quoted from Stroud's A Sketch of the Laws Relating to Slavery in America*].*

This is a legal formulation of the essence of cruelty: making a man the property of another without regard for the property's individual choices or powers. I could go on with a legal analysis of slavery and of the Jim Crow laws that perpetuated the idea that the blacks were property of the whites, property that could be packed in separate railway cars, schools, toilets, jobs, etc., without any regard for the individual choices or powers of the victim—absolute slaves, absolutely passive entities, as passive under the will of the white man as a biologically living being can be, almost as passive as a dead body.

I shall not examine the legal formulations of cruelty, however. Instead consider this advertisement in the *New Orleans Bee*:

Negroes for sale.—*A Negro woman, 24 years of age, and her two children, one eight and the other three years old. Said negroes will be sold* separately or together, *as desired. The woman is a good seamstress. She will be sold low for cash, or exchanged for* groceries.
For terms, apply to Matthew Bliss and Co., 1 Front Levee [Tannenbaum, 1947, p. 77, nonitalics added].

Contemplate this advertisement in all of its aspects and you begin to understand the cruel relationship. The whites have the power to buy and sell the members of this family separately or together, to use them, separately or together, as the whites wish, and to equate them with groceries. In fact, the whites have the power to use the blacks as groceries: to consume them as they wish so as to enhance their own pleasure and power, and then defecate them out of the body politic and out of life itself.

Cruelty is the rendering passive of a creature under the unlimited activity of another creature—and this goes for all the kinds of cruelty that there are, including quiet institutional cruelty. As Stowe (1965) put it in *Uncle Tom's Cabin*, in slavery "There is actually nothing to protect the slave's life, but the *character of the master* [p. 44, italics added]." That is, the slave's own initiative is nothing. The slave is groceries. "Sometimes I feel like I'm almost gone" is not only a line in a spiritual about motherless children; it is the victim's version of cruelty, and of the cruelty the whites in America have perpetrated on the blacks.

If this is still too abstract a discussion of cruelty to illuminate your ideas about the word, let me quote some passages from the autobiographies of runaway slaves. The first is from Northup's (1967) *Twelve Years a Slave*:

A slave never approaches the gin-house with his basket of cotton but with fear. If it falls short in weight—if he has not performed the full task appointed him, he knows that he must suffer. And if he has exceeded it by ten or twenty pounds, in all probability his master will measure the next day's task accordingly [pp. 39-40].

There is no sadistic torture here—just plain getting the most out of your property by keeping an eye on its productivity. It is all quiet fear, gentle dread, simple hopelessness. This dread is expressed in another passage from Northup's book:

It is an offence invariably followed by a flogging, to be found at the quarters after daybreak. Then the fears and labors of another day begin. . . . He fears he will be caught lagging through the day; he fears to approach the gin-house with his basket-load of cotton at night; he fears when he lies down, that he will oversleep himself in the morning. Such is a true, faithful, unexaggerated picture and description of the slave's daily life, during the time of cotton-picking, on the shores of Bayou Boeuf . . . [p. 40].

The Deep South was one thing, a hell presided over by good old, practical King Cotton. What of Maryland, with its genteel traditions for both field and house slaves? To get a hint of the undramatic cruelties involved in keeping a human being passive, consider this passage written by the hero of my book, *The Paradox of Cruelty* (Hallie, 1969), and in a sense the hero of my own life, Frederick Douglass, who, before he achieved international fame as an abolitionist orator and adviser to President Lincoln, had had a comparatively fortunate life as a slave in Maryland. A woman had been whipped:

The charge against her was very common and very indefinite, namely "impudence". This crime could be committed by a slave in a hundred different ways, and depended much upon the temper and caprice of the overseer as to whether it was committed at all. He could create the offense whenever it pleased him. A look, a word, a gesture, accidental or intentional, never failed to be taken as impudence when he was in the right mood for such an offense [p. 51].

Between the two charges of impudence and laziness the horror of slavery lived and moved and had its being, and both of these charges were completely in the power of the white master or his delegates. That power was slavery (and was to be its shadow), and that helplessness under arbitrary, alien power was the center of all those cruelties that are the history of the black man in our country.

This helplessness was supported as well as masked by those two forces mentioned a few moments ago: physical risk and imaginative stereotypes. The risks were obvious. Cash (1941) in his classic *The Mind of the South* summarized them briefly:

The lash lurked always in the background. Its open crackle could often be heard where field hands were quartered. Into the gentlest houses drifted now and then the sound of dragging chains and shackles, the bay of hounds, the report of pistols on the trail of the runaway. And, as the advertisements of the time incontestably prove, mutilation and the mark of the branding iron were pretty common [pp. 82–83].

Danger was everywhere, surrounding, infecting whatever gentility men affected towards slaves.

As to the stereotypes, our early history produced Sambo, the eternal child, dependent, happy, with unaccountable moods of depression, which he got over after some drink and some religion, lazy, watermelon eating—powerful only in his religious desires and in his love of music and the dance. Sambo, nigger, coon, these composed the stereotype that white men understood when they claimed to "understand their niggers."

They did everything they could to make the black people understand themselves this way, so that they would never think of emerging from their slavery, from their legal and spiritual passivity under the white man. The black people were, in the words of the great Frederick Douglass (1962), "trained from the cradle up to think and feel that their masters were superiors, and invested with a sort of sacredness . . . [p. 145]." This "slaveholding priestcraft," as Douglass labels it, led to many black people wanting to imitate whites by what Anna Freud called "passive adaptation," "survival through surrender," or "identification," or what Harry Stack Sullivan called "reflected appraisals" of the "significant others." But however one analyzes the conking of hair, the Brown Fellowship of Charleston with its aristocracy of Negroes who were lighter skinned, however one analyzes the self-concepts of black people, one sees the success of the white man's efforts to make them as passive as groceries under the white man's will.

These masks that kept the black man passive in his own mind, in the minds of his masters, and in his physical existence in the fortress that was his plantation, these masks hint at the deepest cruelty of all. Du Bois (1967) in *The Souls of Black Folks* describes that cruelty well:

The Negro is . . . born with a veil, and gifted with second-sight in this American world—a world which yields him no true self-consciousness, but only lets him see himself through the revelation of the other world. It is a peculiar sensation, this double-consciousness, this sense of always looking at oneself through the eyes of others, of measuring one's soul by the tape of a world that looks in amused contempt and pity. One ever feels his twoness,— an American, a Negro; two souls, two thoughts, two unreconciled strivings; two warring ideals in one dark body, whose dogged strength alone keeps it from being torn asunder [p. 16].

Lift a cup with that black hand, and you will find yourself asking: Is that the way it is supposed to be done? Is that the white way? After all, his is the highest way, the best, and his color is the best, and yet this hand is black, and you are trying to be white, hopelessly trying to be what you are not.

One aspect of this torture is what Myrdal (1944) called "an American dilemma" in his massive work of that name: the conflict between the American creed of a free society of equals and the firm belief that the black people must be neither free nor equal. The trouble with Myrdal's book is, as Charles Silberman has pointed out, that there is no American dilemma for white Americans. White Americans are not torn by two contradictory convictions—they are upset about trouble in the streets. Many whites can see no dilemma between Jeffersonian democracy and de facto Jim Crow in labor unions and in housing. Whites do not worry about reconciling contradictions as much as they worry about their businesses being interrupted or their peace being shattered.

There is no American dilemma except in the hearts of the victims of slavery and Jim Crow. The cruelty of two souls in one black body, a would-be white soul and an actual black soul, in Du Bois' words: "two souls, two thoughts, two unreconciled strivings; two warring ideals in one dark body . . . ." This is the tearing, the crushing, and the grinding that is the ultimate cruelty the white man has perpetrated upon the black: the wanting to be like whites, the inability to be white, and the deep conviction that the whites are not "superior" except in sheer brutal power. This witches' cauldron is the ultimate cruelty. When the victim renders himself weak by these tearings of his soul, the ultimate cruelty is happening, one's cruelty to oneself, one's hatred of the self one loves, of the only self one has. The white man made that cauldron because he wanted cheap labor and cheap self-esteem.

Unselfing: The Ultimate Cruelty

This then, in brief, is the cruel relationship: the "unselfing" of a weaker person by a stronger one by means of physical and mental intimidation. Pains are simply symptoms of this deep relationship, this deep disease. The dictionary that claims that cruelty has to do only with pain and that kindness, the refusal to countenance the infliction of pain, is the opposite of cruelty is plainly misleading. When a man is in the cruel relationship of being a living human being and yet being treated as passive groceries under another man's hand, the condescending kindness of his master is only another, more subtle means of torture for him. The smug face of the master when he presents a penny to one who has made that master rich, the face that sweetly and compassionately smiles upon a human being who is being "unselfed" because his initiative and his hope have been taken away from him, these kindnesses are tortures, because the victim sees that his victimizer is exonerating himself cheaply from responsibility and from guilt. For this reason and others Douglass (1962) wrote, "The kindness of the slave-master only gilded the chain. It detracted nothing from its weight or strength . . . [p. 155]." He could have gone further; he could have said that the kindness only added to the weight of the chain.

What then, despite our dictionaries, is the opposite of cruelty? From the victim's point of view, the opposite is freedom from being the passive member of a relationship between a man and his groceries.

Resistance: Mitigating Institutional Cruelty

However, I have promised not only an analysis of the disease and its masks; I have promised also a hint at its cure. Let me give you that hint by referring to an incident in the life of Frederick Douglass as he tells us about that life in his autobiography *Life and Times*.

Douglass was a young man, and had been beaten by the dreaded Covey, the so-called "Negro Breaker" with whom Douglass' master had left the young, spirited slave in order to break his will. After the beating he had run back to his master for help, and having not gotten it from his master, he had come back to the Negro Breaker. The incident I speak of occurred when Douglass, the day after his return, was in the barn getting ready to care for the horses. Covey had a way of moving like a snake, silently and close to the ground, in order to surprise and terrify the blacks he was breaking. Covey, while Douglass was beginning to work, "sneaked into the stable, in his peculiar way, and seizing me suddenly by the leg, he brought me to the stable floor, giving my body a terrible jar [p. 139]." At this moment came Douglass' birth into freedom from all those images and all those fears: He found himself fighting back, the way a person finds himself being born. At that moment, he says, "I was resolved to fight, and what was better still, I actually was hard at it." The young, strong black, his body still aching from the old beating and his long trip to his master and back, threw Covey to the manure-covered floor of the stable, threw him flat on his back in the muck. In the midst of the struggle, Covey, trembling in anger and unbelief, asked him "Are you going to resist, you scoundrel?" Still fighting, successfully, Douglass answered with a polite "Yes, sir." There follows in the autobiography an amazing statement, amazing to anyone who knows the immense danger, or rather the almost certain death, involved in striking a white man. Douglass writes, "During the whole six months that I lived with Covey after this transaction, he never again laid the weight of his finger on me in anger [p. 142]." For these two men, as individuals, the power relationship was changed, because the victim was no longer passive with fear and self-hatred. To use Douglass' words, "I was a changed being after that fight. I was nothing before—I was a man now . . . [p. 143]." He goes on to generalize the lesson he learned from fighting back: "A man without force is without the essential dignity of humanity. Human nature is so constituted that it cannot honor a helpless man, though it can pity him, and even this it cannot do long if signs of power do not arise [p. 143]."

In the mind of this young man, who was still a slave according to everybody else around him, and according to the law, the cruel relationship, the chain, was cracked. Covey *saw* Douglass as a resisting man, saw him as the Marquis de Sade's heroes and heroines never saw their gracefully unresisting victims. Douglass to himself and to Covey was, again in Douglass' words, "more than half free" because he was, again quoting him, "a power on earth." He could be killed, but he would no longer be a passive victim of that terrible crushing and grinding we have been calling "cruelty."

Of course, this event must be taken as only broadly symbolic, not as an accurate summary of the "cure" for institutional cruelty. Institutional cruelty is not broken by one act by one man—it may be cracked, weakened, but it is not broken. The years that followed brought Douglass into partnership with many blacks and whites (including John Brown and William Lloyd Garrison) as a leader in the abolitionist movement. And then there was the War Between the States—with the shadow of slavery, Jim Crow, even after all this, still lying on American minds and institutions at this moment. But the symbol of that cure is nonetheless there to be read: resistance, awakening from all those images and all those fears into self-respect and vigorous action; this awakening is at the living center of the cure, as even Sade knew when he frankly dreaded obstacles to his cruelty, resistance from his victims and their allies.

One point is clear: Douglass did not mitigate cruelty by waiting patiently for moments of kindness and generosity from the slave owners or their dependents. If the moments would have been more frequent than they were in his life, not only might they have continued to torture him, as we have noticed, but they might have softened his resistance and delayed his freedom. No, it is not only Winston Churchill who pledged never to preside over the dissolution of his people's empire—all those I know possessing absolute power have been very reluctant indeed to give it up to a supine victim. Kindness and generosity have little or nothing to do with the mitigation of substantial institutional cruelty. Only the breaking of the cruel relationship under the initiative of the victim and his allies outside of that relationship and within it can mitigate that kind of cruelty. The crucial beginning—if not the essence—of that mitigation is the full activity of the victim and his allies in all the dimensions of the human personality—physical, intellectual, and spiritual. This activity is freedom from the cruel relationship, and is what the black people have been trying to achieve, sporadically in previous centuries with the various revolts and concentratedly in recent years.

Of course, there are dangers they are discovering even now. When their resistance, and the resistance of their allies, escalates or intensifies in only one dimension of the human spirit, say physical violence, a dominant power structure may escalate its cruel treatment of them. Or when the pressures of despair and disagreement disorganize their resistance, the old relationship will quietly be strengthened, hardened. But there is reason for hope that the victims and their allies will help America to end its long history of cruelties by pressuring—in all the dimensions of human pressure—human beings in our country into facing each other with a little fear and with much respect.

There is a paradox of cruelty writ large across the history of mankind and written intimately into the minds of men: We find substantial maiming of other men totally unjustifiable, an object of disgust and horror, and yet we find it easy to justify in a hundred expediential and even religious ways. To mitigate this ambivalence that is shared, as I have shown, by both the victimizer and the victim is the task of the victim and his allies, and ultimately of their whole society. Smashing this paradox, this ambivalence in human relations, is the first step toward moral wisdom, which is a sad wisdom, and a dangerous wisdom, but one not without hope.

References

Cash, W. J. *The mind of the South*. New York: Knopf, 1941.
Douglass, F. *Life and times of Frederick Douglass: Written by himself*. New York: Collier, 1962.
Du Bois, W. E. B. *The souls of black folk: Essays and sketches*. Greenwich, Conn.: Fawcett, 1967.
Hallie, P. P. *The paradox of cruelty*. Middletown, Conn.: Wesleyan University Press, 1969.
Myrdal, G. *An American dilemma: The Negro problem and modern democracy*. New York: Harper, 1944.
Northup, S. *Twelve years a slave*. In M. Meltzer (Ed.), *In their own words: A history of the American Negro, 1619–1865*. Vol. 1. New York: Crowell, 1967.
Oxford English Dictionary. Vol. 2. London: Oxford University Press, 1961.
Stowe, H. B. *Uncle Tom's cabin, or, life among the lowly*. New York: Harper & Row, 1965.
Tannenbaum, F. *Slave and citizen: The Negro in America*. New York: Knopf, 1947.

psychology and the reduction of violence

Psychology and the Reduction of Violence

The issues uppermost in the minds of many—war, crime in the streets, urban riots, student unrest—reveal a common thread of concern over violence. If the proverbial "man in the street" were asked what contributions he thought psychology ought to make in solving the problems of society, he might well reply "Do something about all this violence." Can psychology contribute to the reduction of violence? The authors of this section feel that it can—through providing the understandings prerequisite to any real improvement in the situation. But understandings do nothing unless acted upon, and who is it that needs to act? Together these three authors indicate that action is needed from people at all levels. Wolfgang provides insights relevant to us all; Chein speaks particularly to those involved in coercive confrontations; and White directs his message to high-level diplomats and decision makers. Yet the understandings these authors offer must be absorbed throughout the society to create a climate in which violence can actually be reduced.

In the initial paper of this section, Wolfgang surveys violence in America. He presents a panorama of ways in which all elements of society unthinkingly encourage violence. Children are given toy weapons for play, adults are sold autos through appeals to aggression, and all are entertained with stories of violence. Urban decay nourishes norms of delinquency, masculine ideals encourage physical aggression, and the easy availability of guns extends the ability to kill. These are among the factors included in Wolfgang's review of sources of violence. While he does not prescribe solutions to the problem of violence, his analyses indicate clearly the kinds of changes we all need to make for its reduction.

Chein does offer advice, particularly to those involved in the coercive confrontations that so often result in violence. Out of his conceptual analysis of the nature of power, he highlights several assumptions that are often faulty and lead to the unnecessary use of coercion. One such assumption is that power per se is the basic issue at hand. Chein traces how this assumption often comes about and indicates how, in some cases, it can be avoided. Another assumption he examines is that power is a zero-sum quantity, and a third is that those holding power necessarily crave and value the degree and range of that power. Through a more analytical understanding of the nature of conflict, Chein suggests that alternatives to coercion and violence may be found.

Concluding the section, White focuses our attention on international violence. He places in an international context three psychological research findings which he feels are relevant to the quest for peace. The first is the finding that when an audience is both intelligent and initially in disagreement with a speaker, his persuasive message should demonstrate understanding of the opposing arguments. Extrapolating from this result, White suggests that in communicating with an adversary such as the Russians, we must search out common ground and indicate clearly our understanding of their views. His second point stems from research on self-images. He indicates that clarification and understanding of nations' territorial self-images could help avoid the wars which so often result when these images overlap. His final point involves the proposition that we tend to see others as being more supportive of ourselves than they actually are. Labeling this the "pro-us illusion," he suggests that its recognition might have helped us avoid the fiascos of both Cuba and Vietnam.

Violence and Human Behavior[1]

MARVIN E. WOLFGANG

The author received his PhD in sociology from the University of Pennsylvania in 1955. He is presently a professor of sociology and Chairman of the Department of Sociology at the University of Pennsylvania and Director of the Center for Studies in Criminology and Criminal Law.

I am honored to share some reflections on violence with my distinguished colleagues in psychology. As a sociologist-criminologist and Research Director of the National Commission on the Causes and Prevention of Violence during most of 1969, I have been writing, reading, and thinking about violence in a variety of forms, so that what I can say now is but a resume of many previous thoughts of my own and others.[2] I take no credit for original thinking, only the responsibility for the peculiar twists of the language to express some ideas.

I have been torn in preparation for this address between wanting to cover material on aggression from the laboratory, the psychological studies of reactions to films, electronic impulses imposed on critical centers of the brain, and the influence of the XYY gene syndrome, to interesting analyses of assassinations, firearms, crimes, and student violence. So extensive in scope and intensive in detail is our present national inquiry into violence that I can but hope that some of the dozen or so volumes that we expect to publish will have some interest to scholars and the public in general. My own remarks here are highly selective, more sociological than psychological, and generally devoid of the statistics needed to buttress argument. I shall concentrate on only a few general areas of concern.

When the dictatorial Duke of Athens was compelled by an angry mob to flee Florence in 1343, some of his political assistants were grabbed on the street, tortured, and murdered. The apex of the mob fury was reached in the scene described as follows by Machiavelli (1901):

---

[1] Invited Address presented to the Division of the History of Psychology at the Annual Meeting of the American Psychological Association, Washington, D. C., August 31, 1969. This address is essentially the same as a lecture given by the author at Churchill College, University of Cambridge, England, April 1969.

[2] I am drawing on materials from the National Commission on the Causes and Prevention of Violence, especially from the Task Forces on Individual Acts, co-directed by M. Tumin and D. Mulvihill, and Group Violence, directed by J. Skolnick.

I am also using some ideas that appeared in my previous writings, "Violence U.S.A." (1968) and "Youth and Violence" (1969), a report I recently submitted to the Office of Juvenile Delinquency and Youth Development, Department of Health, Education and Welfare.

Those who could not wound them while alive, wounded them after they were dead; and not satisfied with tearing them to pieces, they hewed their bodies with swords, tore them with their hands, and even with their teeth. And that every sense might be satiated with vengeance, having first heard their moans, seen their wounds, and touched their lacerated bodies, they wished even the stomach to be satisfied, that having glutted the external sense, the one within might also have its share [p. 100].

This mob action helped to sustain Machiavelli's insistence that "the rage of men is certainly always found greater, and their revenge more furious upon the recovery of liberty, than when it has only been defended [p. 100]."

My reason for referring to this scene is patent: to draw upon an example of riots and violence from a beautiful city at the most glorious time in its history, to show the brutal side of man's behavior in the midst of another period's affluence, political enlightenment, and highly humanistic culture.

Man is not innately criminal, violent, or aggressive. He responds to people, events, or other kinds of stimuli that precipitate violative, violent, or aggressive behavior. But he learns what is fearful or frustrating so that the things to which he reacts are interpreted by him as such, and the resolution of events which he defines as problems is also learned. Cats, dogs, and monkeys do not shoot their adversaries because they cannot or have not learned to use guns. Only man has the capacity to make and to use such artificial weapons designed to destroy himself and others.

This general introduction leads to my first major topic, the socialization into violence, with an emphasis on the fact that our culture provides a variety of learning processes that develop an acceptance of the use of violence, often labeled legitimate. Much of my concern is with America because I know it best and because I am involved in a national scrutiny of my own society. If I sound a bit critical of the United States at times, it is because we are critically analyzing our posture relative to violence.

I shall also discuss youth because youth is a time of movement and physical activity, and acts of physical aggression, whether performed by monkeys or homo sapiens, whether or not injurious to others, are most likely to be performed by the young.

Socialization into Violence

Legitimized Violence

Violence can be viewed as physical injury to persons and damage or destruction to property, and abstractly is neither legitimate nor illegitimate. Judgment of legitimacy is based on the agent, the target, the ends sought, and the context in which violence occurs. The decision of whether physical force is good or bad is always made within a cultural value setting. The positive or negatvie eufunctional or dysfunctional aspects of violence depend on the observer's perspective.

There is, however, no society that does not contain in its normative system elements of acceptable limits to violence. Thus, the use of physical force by parents to restrain and punish children is permitted, tolerated, encouraged, and is thereby part of the normative process by which every society regulates its child rearing. There are, of course, varying degrees of parental force expected and used in different cultures and times, and there are upper limits vaguely defined as excessive and brutal. The battered child syndrome is an increasingly recorded phenomenon in several Western societies.

The point is, however, that our norms approve or permit parents to apply force largely for their own ends against the child. The application of force is a form of violence and may be used consciously to discipline the child to the limits of permitted behavior, to reduce the domestic noise level, to express parental disapproval, and even unconsciously as a displacement for aggression actually meant for other targets. This model of parent-child interaction is a universal feature of all human societies. The model is one that the child himself comes to ingest; that is, that superior force is power permitting manipulation of others and can be a functional tool for securing a superordinate position over others, for obtaining desires and ends.

The violence in which the child himself engages is but an expressed extension of this basic model. The use of physical restraint and force is not a feature only in lower class families, although studies have shown that its persistent use, and its use in greater frequency over a longer span of childhood, is more common in that social class. The substitutions, by middle class parents, of withdrawal of rights and affection, of deprivation of liberty, and of other techniques are designed to replace the need for force. They are also ways of masking the supreme means of control, namely, physical force.

Violence and the threat of violence form the ultimate weapons of any society for maintaining itself against external and internal attacks. All societies finally resort to violence to solve problems that arise from such attacks. War is aggressive force between nations and is legitimized within reach. Relativity of moral judgments about violence is quite clear in the case of war. When the American colonies collected themselves together in the eighteenth century to sever metropolitan ties, we called the action revolution and good despite the violence it engendered. When some states in the nineteenth century sought to bifurcate the nation, we called the action civil war and bad, and lamented the bloodshed. The Nazis gave justice to our bombs and enlisted the world's generation of youth to react violently to violence. Violence becomes viewed as a rapid collective problem solver, from the "three and twenty stabs in Caesar," according to Suetonius, to riots in city streets or on college grounds.

There are international conflicts in which the United States has been involved and for which the label of legitimacy has been seriously questioned by substantial numbers within our own territory. Vietnam is such an episode. When this happens, a society becomes more conscious of the process of socializing its own youth to accept violence as a mode of response. When war is glorified in a nation's history and included as part of the child's educational materials, a moral judgment about the legitimacy of violence is surely and firmly made.

Socialization means changing the individual into a personality; it is the process of cultural transmission, of relaying through the social funnel of family and friends a set of beliefs, attitudes, values, speech, and habits. When the frontline instruments of war become part of the physical features of a child's life space, when cannons, rifles, grenades, and soldiers are moved from real battlefields to the mind of the child and the plastic world of his playroom and are among the objects touched and manipulated by the child in the process of becoming, then some set of values associated with the legitimacy and recognition of the superiority of violent activity is also transmitted.

It is our youth who man the weapons of war. But they must be trained to have reduced fear and increased anger, to rationalize their being mobilized into a phalanx of force. Youth must be socialized into acceptance of the collective will that drives and flies them into battle against their individual desires. From Roman troops who marched through Britain to United States soldiers who struggle in Vietnam, the still-forming limbs of youth have been used to push political philosophies through history.

It is always an older generation that thrusts its younger ones into battle. Decisions made with maps and oval tables in the conference halls of power are made by men whose own youth has passed. Not privy to the policies that formed their own fate, the young are used to play the games of violence imposed on them by their elders. I am not here questioning, but only describing, the process which creates its own cultural justification. But I am implying that the process and justifications that envelop it are part of the socialization of generations into violence. We might question whether it is the generation that designs or the generation that fights the war that is the truly violent one.

There are many other areas of social life that witness the protection of order by representatives of control. In their roles and persons, they corporealize the actual or potential use of legitimized violence. The police and national guard are the most obvious of these agents, but there are also the less visible and more silent cadres of guards in prisons, mental institutions, banks, parks, and museums. Even less seen but subjectively self-legitimized are unofficial groups like the lynching mobs of yesteryear, the minutemen and vigilantes of the rural South and urban North, and certain black militants who have armed their members for assault. The presence of all these groups, ranging from the culturally prescribed to the barely tolerated, has diffusive effects that are part of the socializing experience of youth into the acceptance of violence as a means of control. The more these agents of real or potential aggression are used, the more impact such use has in socializing others to the functional utility of violence. If the official legitimacy of violence is stressed, many of the young generation exposed to such values will have heightened acceptance of its use. On the other hand, many who are identified with the targets of officially legitimized violence will respond in like manner, thereby confirming their need to use violence to combat violence. And this message is passed on to yet another group of the younger generation that learns to attack the guardian executors of the larger society with its own contrived version of legitimate violence.

Masculinity

Social scientists, psychologists, and psychiatrists have often stressed the importance of the theme of masculinity in American culture and the effect this image of the strong masculine role has had on child rearing and the general socialization process. Today the middle class child has some difficulty if he seeks to match himself to the old masculine model, and he may sometimes become neurotic and insecure. Among the lower classes, says Walter Miller, the continuity of the physically assertive male is still one of the "focal concerns." The desire to prove one's masculinity, added to the desire to become a successful male adult member of the lower class culture, requires adolescent "rehearsal" of the toughness, heavy drinking, and quick aggressive response to certain stimuli that are characteristic of the lower class adult male. Such rehearsal involves activities not necessarily delinquent, but often involves participation in conduct that is defined as delinquent by the middle class. *Machismo* is still a viable term in various cultures, and especially among the young in the lower class, which equates maleness with overt physical aggression. The genesis reaches far into the biological evolution of the species, into the history of civilization; it was found on the peripheries of expanding colonial powers, on the frontiers of America, and it has been at the core of the less verbally articulate classes. Efforts to explain its persistence include rejection by the male child of female dominance at home and school and rejection of the association of morality with femininity; the result is the antithesis, that of being physically aggressive, which in turn often leads to delinquency and crime.

Males commonly carry the role of committing the required deeds of assault, of investigating homicides and suicides, of being mortician assistants, of handling the injuries on highways; in short, men are required to assume responsibility for the physical public injuries and tragedies of humanity. Women are protected, their faces are turned, from such displays. It is also the male who is expected to use violence in prescribed ways and at prescribed times, during which he must be sufficiently desensitized to the pain he inflicts, whether in the street or playground, on a battlefield or in a bomber. It should not be unexpected, therefore, that most delinquent acts of physical injury are also committed by males.

Mass Media

Other features of our culture in general, such as the mass media, may promote acceptability of male violence or make violence so banal that large segments of the population are no longer sensitive to expressions of violence. At least these features fail to encourage nonviolence. Whether television viewing or otherwise vicariously experiencing violence functions as a catharsis is not a scientifically resolved issue. The weight of most research seems counterindicated. The sheer frequency of screened violence, its intensity as well as context, and the myriad forms it takes cannot be claimed to instill firm notions of nonviolence in the children who are witnesses. Unless the logic of the assertion that violence in mass media encourages violent behavior is destroyed by scientifically acceptable evidence, we play dangerous games with the socialization process and its adult products.

Automobile Advertising

Even automobile advertising in America evokes many of the attributes of aggression, particularly male aggression, and seeks to affect purchasing habits by drawing on the existing pool of socializing forces. Despite pamphlets distributed to young drivers by car manufacturers to encourage courteous driving habits, these same manufacturers advertise aggression behind the wheel by linking their cars and the drivers to masculine might. In a short time I can only give the tenor of their appeal.[3]

Glamour and thrill in the cars are meant to be associated with speed and power through such verbs as "roars," "growls"; adjectives like "dynamic," "powerful," "exciting," "wild," "ferocious," "swinging"; nouns like "missile," "rocket," "tiger," "stinger." Phrases of advertising include: "just pull the trigger"; "start billing yourself as the human cannon ball"; "want action?"; "fire the second stage"; and "aim it at the road." Longer excerpts make clear the intended associations: (a) "For stab-and-steer men, there is a new 3-speed automatic you can lock in any gear.... Make small noises in your throat. Atta boy tiger"; (b) "Bring on the Mustangs, Wildcats, Impalas.... We'll even squash a few Spyders while we're at it. Dodge has made it a little harder to survive in the asphalt jungle. They just uncaged the Coronet"; (c) "This year let yourself go for power"; (d) "All new! All muscle! ... with Advanced Thrust engineering ... and an almost neurotic urge to get going. Drive it like you hate it—it's cheaper than psychiatry"; (e) "Nobody said a nice car can't play mean now and then."

There are appeals to virility and masculinity: "Get with man-sized Dart." "Sleek, lean, muscled new style ... improved cat-quick handling"; "Burly and businesslike"; "Go ahead, be rebellious. Demand more 'big.' More 'hot' "; "Come rid yourself of prematurely gray driving"; "The 300 has muscle"; "Bold Plymouth Fury"; "A man's kind of action! Bold! ... It's the man's car for men who like their action big ... gives a man that 'in charge' feeling."

It is difficult to factor out the contribution this kind of advertising makes to the traffic accidents of the young, both as victims and agents. That the association is present is clear. Traffic accidents are the leading cause of death among children and youth. Of all youth 13–25 years of age who died in a recent 10-year span, 42% died as the result of traffic accidents. The young are our worst drivers, as reflected in part by insurance rates. Persons under 25 are 19% of all licensed drivers but cause over 30% of the accidents. Two-fifths of all teenage drivers are involved in traffic accidents each year (O'Connell, 1967).

Such advertising through car magazines read by thousands of youths reaches into the later adolescent socializing process and can be faulted for adding to the violence in our culture if not on the road.

Guns

Much the same can be said about guns in American society, but I shall not burden you long with this problem. The Firearms Task Force Report of the National Commission on Violence (1969) has now been published and calls for more control over handguns. The appeal to masculinity is again present, and the general awareness of young males about guns forms yet another part of the socialization into violence. The best current estimate is that there are at least 100 million guns in the United States. If evenly distributed, there would be one

---

[3] From a report entitled "Automobile Safety; Speed and Racing Advertising," submitted to the United States Federal Trade Commission November 15, 1966, by C. B. Yarley and C. A. Sweeney. A careful comparison between the automobile industry's safe-driving publications and magazine advertisements has been made by O'Connell (1967).

for every male in the country. But they are not evenly distributed. The southeastern and south central regions have the highest gun possession, as do males under 25. These are also the regions and the age group of highest rates of homicide.

Nearly 3,000 persons in the United States are fatal victims of firearms accidents each year, and at least another 20,000 are injured by firearms accidents. About 65% of our criminal homicides involve firearms.

The ease with which guns can be purchased is well documented. During the past decade about 30 million new guns have been added by domestic production and importation. Weak or unenforced control statutes on possession or use make guns available to almost anyone who wants one. To this availability is added the stimulus of advertising not unlike that which I have mentioned about automobiles.

Mail-order advertisement in America, the highest gun-to-population ratio in the world, the virtual glorification of guns in our history, and the daily displays on television of guns in the hands of heroes can surely play no role in minimizing violence in the socialization process.

I have spoken of guns, automobile advertising, and legitimized violence because they are features given scanty attention among the socializing forces that mold the personalities, shape the values, and form the mentality of many youths in our society. As we unpack the mixed bag of cultural inputs presented to youth, we become increasingly aware that a high proportion are violence laden, and that they are often offered for absorption with the palliative of legitimacy and social acceptability. They can now be seen more clearly as further extensions of the basic model of physical force found in parent-child interaction. Violence, thus viewed, is a continuous variable, measured in degrees of severity and intensity, legitimacy and illegitimacy.

Illegitimate violence is not qualitatively different from, but is continuous with, and dynamically similar to legitimate violence. It is to the clearly illegitimate forms of violence—the delinquencies and crimes—and the more blatant criminogenic forces of our society that I should now like to turn briefly in order to understand another dimension of the relation between culture and violence.

Urban Violence

Subculture of Violence

The forces that generate conditions conducive to crime and riots are strongest in our urban communities. Urban areas with mass populations, greater wealth, more commercial establishments, and more products of our technology also provide more frequent opportunities for theft and greater chance of violence. Victims are impersonalized, property is insured, consumer goods in more abundance are vividly displayed and are more portable.

Urban life is commonly characterized by population density, spatial mobility, ethnic and class heterogeneity, reduced family functions, and greater anonymity. When, on a scale, these traits are found in high degree, and when they are combined with poverty, physical deterioration, low education, residence in industrial and commercial centers, unemployment or unskilled labor, economic dependency, marital instability or breaks, poor or absent male models for young boys, overcrowding, lack of legitimate opportunities to make a better life, the absence of positive anticriminal behavior patterns, higher frequency of organic diseases, and a cultural minority status of inferiority, it is generally assumed that social-psychological mechanisms leading to deviance, crime, and violence are more likely to emerge.

It is abundantly clear even to the most casual observer that Negroes in American society are the current carriers of a ghetto tradition in our cities. More than any other socially defined group, they are the recipients of urban deterioration and the social-psychological forces leading to legal deviance. For this reason, concern with crime in the American city is commonly a concern with Negro crime.

Although there are good reasons for raising serious questions about criminal statistics that report race of the offender and the fact that official crime rates for Negroes are in general three or four times higher than white rates, and although Negroes probably suffer more injustices than whites in the law enforcement process from arrest to imprisonment, it is no surprise that the most valid efforts to measure crime still find Negro crime rates high. When the untoward aspects of urban life are found among Italians, Germans, Poles, or almost any other group, their crime rates are similarly high. Relative deprivation and social disqualification are thus dramatically chained to despair and delinquency.

All of this is not meant to obscure the fact that poverty also exists in small towns and rural areas. But when multiplied by congested thousands and transmitted over generations, poverty, as Oscar Lewis has claimed, becomes a culture. The expectations of social intercourse change, and irritable, frustrated parents often become neglectful and aggressive. The children inherit *a subculture of violence* (see Wolfgang & Ferracuti, 1967) in which physically aggressive responses are either expected or required by all members sharing not only the tenement's plumbing but also its system of values. Ready access and resort to weapons in this milieu may be essential to protection against others who respond in similarly violent ways. Carrying a knife or some other protective device becomes a common symbol of willingness to participate in violence, to expect violence, and to be ready for its retaliation.

A subculture of violence is not the product of cities alone. The Thugs of India, the *vendetta barbaricina* in Sardinia, the *mafioso* in Sicily have existed for a long time. But the contemporary American city has the major accoutrements not only for the genesis but also for the highly accelerated development of this subculture, and it is from this subculture that most violent crimes come.

The use of violence in such a subculture is not viewed as illicit conduct, and the users do not have to deal with feelings of guilt about their aggression. Violence can become a part of the life style, the theme for solving difficult problems, and is used primarily between persons and groups who themselves rely upon the same supportive values and norms. A carrier and user of violence will not be burdened by conscious guilt, then, mainly because the recipient of his violence shares in the same subculture and has similar class, occupation, residence, age, and other attributes that characterize the subuniverse of persons sharing in the subculture of violence.

Delinquency in a Birth Cohort

Now there is a relatively small cadre of young citizens who are born into and grow up in a subculture pocket of residential propinquity, poverty, and psychological depression, ungoverned households and unwed mothers, where the subculture of violence is nurtured and transmitted across generations as well as city streets. Yet, this relatively small group, fostered by inadequate urban renewal, occupational, educational, and housing programs, and unchecked by community service agencies or correctional strategies, can and does inflict most of the serious, violent social harm on a community.

Relative to this assertion are some new kinds of evidence about juvenile crime and particularly about violence that are being analyzed by the Center for Studies in Criminology and Criminal Law at the University of Pennsylvania under support from the National Institute of Mental Health. The data constitute a unique collection of information in the United States about a birth cohort of boys born in 1945. Approximately 10,000 males born in that year and who resided in Philadelphia at least from ages 10–18 have been analyzed in a variety of ways. Using school records, offense reports from the police, and some military information, the Center has, among other things, followed the delinquency careers of those boys in the cohort who *ever* had any contact with the police. The cohort is probably typical of other urban cohorts in the United States.

Some of the findings from this Philadelphia study are particularly pertinent for a better understanding of youth and crimes of violence. Of the total birth cohort of 9,946 boys born in 1945, about 85% were born in Philadelphia and about 95% went through the Philadelphia school system from first grade on. From the entire cohort, 3,475 (35%) were delinquent, meaning that they had at least one contact with the police before reaching age 18. Of the 7,043 white subjects, 2,017 (29.64%) were delinquent. Of the 2,902 nonwhites, 1,458 (50.24%) were delinquent. It is a dramatic and disturbing fact that slightly more than half of all Negro boys born in the same year were delinquent—more than were nondelinquent.

Of special significance is the fact that only 627 boys were classified as chronic offenders, or heavy repeaters, meaning that they committed five or more offenses during their juvenile court ages. These chronic offenders represent only 6.3% of the entire birth cohort. Yet, these 627 boys were responsible for 5,305 delinquencies, which is 52% of all the delinquencies committed by the entire birth cohort.

Chronic offenders are heavily represented among those who commit violent offenses. Of the 815 personal attacks (homicide, rape, aggravated and simple assaults), 450 (53%) were committed by chronic offenders; of the 2,257 property offenses, 1,397 (62%) were from chronic offenders; and of 193 robberies, 135 (71%) were from chronic offenders. Of all violent offenses committed by nonwhites, 70% were committed by chronic boys; of all violent acts committed by whites, 45% were performed by chronic boys.

Clearly, these chronic offenders represent what is often referred to as the "hard-core" delinquents. That such a high proportion of offenses—particularly serious acts of violence—is funneled through a relatively small number of offenders is a fact that loudly claims attention for a social action policy of intervention. Under the assumption that these offenses are the most serious ones and the ones to reduce in any deterrence or prevention program, and that most of the other forms of delinquency are relatively trivial, the pivotal point of social cost reduction appears to be when juveniles have committed their first offenses. To produce delinquency desisting at this stage in the biography of the child might thus be considered the most efficient procedure. More nonwhites go on after the first offense, and perhaps the major concern should be with this racial group. Nearly 30% of the nonwhite boys, as compared to only 10% of the white boys, fall into the chronic offender category of having committed five or more offenses.

Urban Riots

There is a still more serious form of violence today—that of group violence. The United States has recently experienced race riots that offer fundamental threats to the entire social system. To deny the political utility of such violence would be neither easy nor valid. Not until violence erupted did the United States Congress move to enact the first major civil rights legislation since the Civil War.

Nearly every major city in the land has experienced riots and civil disorder during the past few years. There were 239 violent outbursts by Negroes that involved at least 200,000 people and resulted in more than 8,000 casualties, including 191 deaths, most of them Negroes. More than 30,000 white Americans have taken part in violent clashes with civil rights demonstrators, causing more than 150 injuries. Some 200 major acts of white terrorism against blacks and civil rights workers have resulted in approximately 20 deaths and more than 100 serious casualties.[4]

When men perceive oppression as their lot and know of others not oppressed, when ordered avenues of change are blocked by kings or legislators or some vague variety of any social system, the oppressed will either resign themselves to fate or rise up to taste the fruit of freedom, and having tasted will want the feast.

Like whites, Negroes are men who have learned of their oppression. By forced migration they became slaves. The politics of war redefined their citizenry but did little to redefine their status. Slaves became servants in the economics of change. The quiet process of elevation has been too slow for all but a trickle of black humanity to enjoy white privilege, and today color is a description not of the skin but of one's status. That status is a depressed, deprived, and now frustrating one.

Group violence, however, is not a new phenomenon in American society. Our history suggests violence as severe as or worse than now. We might discount the Revolution and the War Between the States, the latter of which took approximately half a million lives. But we cannot neglect the Shay and Whiskey Rebellions over debts and taxes; the slaughter and subjugation of American Indians; the Know-Nothings who fought rising Irish political power, who had a 48-hour orgy of mob violence in St. Louis in 1854 in which a dozen persons were killed and 50 homes

---

[4] These compilations have been made by the staff of the National Commission on the Causes and Prevention of Violence and appear in the progress report (1969).

of Irish Catholics wrecked and looted, who killed 20 persons in a two-day riot in Louisville the next year and burned two churches and two parochial schools in Philadelphia; and the Irish antidraft riot in New York in 1863 that killed nearly 2,000 and injured 8,000 in four days.

There were the bloody railroad strikes in 1877 that killed 150; the Rocky Mountain mining wars that took the lives of 198, including a governor, at the turn of the century; the brutal Molly Maguires, a secret band of Irish miners in Pennsylvania; the Wobblies, or Industrial Workers of the World; the industrial and railroad police who brutally beat laborers from Pennsylvania to California; the garment workers' strike in Chicago in 1910 that resulted in 7 deaths, an unknown number of seriously injured, and 874 arrests; the 20 lives lost in the Illinois Central Railroad strikes in 1911; the 1919 steel strike in which 20 persons perished; the national cotton textile labor dispute of 1934 that spread from Georgia and South Carolina to Alabama, even to Rhode Island and Connecticut, with 21 deaths and 10,000 soldiers on strike duty (Taft, 1966).

By 1871 the invisible empire of the Ku Klux Klan "had a membership of over half a million, and a Congressional investigation that year uncovered hangings, shootings, whippings, and mutilations in the thousands. In Louisiana alone, two thousand persons had been killed, wounded, or injured in a short few weeks before the election of 1868. The commanding general of federal forces in Texas reported: 'Murders of Negroes are so common as to render it impossible to keep accurate accounts of them' [Forster, 1966, p. 143]."

That violence is not unique to the United States is an assertion that needs no more than a few illustrations. The aftermath of the French Revolution had a kind of terror and bloodshed never witnessed in this country; the 1843 student riots in France spread throughout Europe; assassinations occurred from Austrian Archduke Francis Ferdinand in 1914 to Prime Minister Vervoerd in South Africa. The Nazis need not even be mentioned. There is still fresh in history the tortures in French Algeria; the Stalinist terrors of a generation; the mob violence and riots off and on for another generation involving Pakistanis and Indians; the recent Nigerian civil war; the student and union violence in France; the *violencia* of Colombia for nearly 20 years that resulted in the assassination of Dr. Jorge Gaitan in 1948 and an estimated 200,000 deaths up to 1967; the confused "cultural revolution" in mainland China; and the horrendous, little-publicized massacre of 400,000 persons in recent years in Indonesia.

Violence in America's past and in the past and present of other nations does not diminish it in our current scene. But its present dimensions and our instant explanations should be viewed within these perspectives.

While not having a firm political ideology any more than students who riot on campus, the "young militant" Negroes responsible for the fire bombing and the sniping—the bitter and alienated activists—surely perceive the bureaucrats and the broader social order as distant, impersonal targets for distaste and disruption. Having seen that it is possible to get attention and dethrone the complacency of the white establishment, and having gained hope that their lot can be improved, they regard their present deprivation as unendurable. In referring to the French Revolution, De Tocqueville (1949) said: "A people which has supported without complaint, as if they were not felt, the most oppressive laws, violently throws them off as soon as their weight is lightened. The social order destroyed by a revolution is always better than that which immediately preceded it. . . . The end which was suffered patiently as inevitable seems unendurable as soon as the idea of escaping from it is conceived [p. 186]."

To riot is a crime in any state penal code definition. To incite to riot, to loot, burglarize, set on fire, destroy property, rob, assault, shoot, carry deadly weapons —each of these is a crime. Surely the unrecorded number of crimes and of unapprehended offenders in riots is enormous.

However, in another sense, not compatible with a legalistic proximate cause notion, the white society, as the Kerner Commission noted, is responsible for inciting to riot. While displaying before the Negro poor the democratic idealism of opportunity, it has inflicted on them the prejudice, the economic blockage of opportunities, the subjugation, and the alienation from power and participation in democracy that have produced among Negroes the power to respond, exploding now in attacks to express their feelings. The urban riots thus far are a mixed bag of some confusing revolutionary ideology among a few, anomic acts expressive of social malaise among many, and almost adventuresome play among still others. Should there be another round of rioting, it will be either moderate skirmishes in more muted tones, reflecting a skewness toward dissipation of the ghetto thrust, or more violent guerilla warfare that can result only in more stringent repressive force by the state. If riots this summer are few or more moderate, we might conclude that the massively diffused efforts for better police-community relations, coalitions of white businessmen with the Negro community, and all our other strategies of solution that reject tokenism and gradualism are beginning to pay off.

I am inclined to link the causes of urban riots and those of urban crime. Where riots have begun, crime rates have been highest, especially for crimes of violence. The social forces that have generated crime overlay the forces that erupt into riots. The players in both dramas are the same or similar. The parallelism is too strong to ignore or deny. Correct the conditions causing the one phenomenon and we change the other concomitantly.

Student Violence

Student violence is yet another and slightly different form of group violence experienced in most societies today. I can only touch lightly on this topic, but I would like to underscore the element of cultural contagion and the fact that many protests are peaceful demonstrations. But some escalate into violence, often as a result of excessive reaction by the police.

During 1967–68 in the United States, about 700,000 antiwar and antidraft protestors staged more than 170 demonstrations in cities and universities across the country. Of these, only 36 involved violence, including 15 in which counterdemonstrators initiated violence. Only 8 resulted in reported injuries, a total of 800. During last year, student demonstrations on war and campus issues involving more than 100,000 participants occurred on more than 100 campuses. About 220 demonstrations took place. A few resulted in seizure of university facilities, police intervention, riots, property damage, injury, and even death; and several institutions were brought to a halt (see Footnote 4).

Here are a few descriptions commonly reported in news accounts:

(a) *Over 4,500 police with shields rushed into [the] University early this morning and, using tear gas, tried to force out 300 students barricaded in . . . the main building.*

(b) *Hundreds of students today ransacked the office of [the] University Rector and tried to throw him out a window. . . . After a wild meeting of 2,000 students in the central university building, about 500 rushed toward the rector's office, painting slogans on the walls as they went.*

(c) *A month's old student strike was complicated by a partial walkout by teachers. Mounted police charged groups of students along off-campus streets; rocks flew and the toll of arrests and injuries climbed steadily.*

(d) *The Dean . . . was imprisoned for eight days in an occupied university building and subjected to "mass collective bargaining" until he was finally allowed to leave, exhausted, on a stretcher.*

(e) *A hard core of about 150 radical students caused havoc at the . . . University . . . today. They smashed doors and windows, broke into cupboards, flung files around, piled up furniture as barricades, and manned hoses ready to fight the police.*

These are a few typical reports of student violence during the early part of 1969. There is at least a score of specific criminal offenses lodged in these activities. The locale in each report has been deleted in order to demonstrate clearly how widespread and similar the violence is. The difficulty one has in distinguishing the universities attests to the extent and similarity of the conditions. The following list identifies the sources of information and the universities where the student violence occurred: (*a*) *The Times* (London), January 18, 1969—Tokyo University; (*b*) *International Herald Tribune,* January 18, 1969—Barcelona University; (*c*) *Time,* January 17, 1969—San Francisco State College; (*d*) *The Times* (London), January 8, 1969—Tokyo University; (*e*) *The Times* (London), January 24, 1969 —Free University of Berlin. In some cases it is instrumental violence to obtain clarified parochial goals; in other cases it is a generalized effort at sheer confrontation for the sake of disruption. Often, in either case, "The commitment to violence is clear-cut. Said an anarchist leader of the . . . students who first began the dispute . . .: 'Simply, the situation is a battle against the entrenched and direct power of the State. This power equals violence. To fight back we must employ direct violence. There is no other choice' [Quoted from *The Times* (London), January 19, 1969]." This is a quotation from a student at Tokyo University, but the comment is heard in similar tones from San Francisco State to the Sorbonne.

It is important to keep in mind that most student protest has not been violent, that it has captured the sentiments of many who are no longer young, and that the social effects of youthful protest are systemic. Most students are not radically, wholly, or injuriously involved in the activism on campuses. Reports rather consistently indicate that only about 1–2% of all students in America are actively involved in protests. This figure may be most misleading, however, for some students weave in and out of periods of activity, but the ardor and forcefulness that the active members bring to their tasks have indeed created political, economic, and international attention. Events seem to move more swiftly than the pen. The analysis made last month, however sophisticated at the time, may seem outmoded this month. The liberal who gained his stance 10 years ago for integration of the races is today fighting a new style of segregation suggested by the militant blacks who want not only separate Afro-American departments, faculty, and budget for black students at San Francisco State College, but who want separate black dormitories there, at Yale, and elsewhere. Black power is a term that takes on more meanings as time goes on, adding money and guns to the former meaning of dignity and identity. The desire to participate in decision-making episodes affecting one's own life shifts partly to a wish for confrontation. Dialogue changes into "duologue," a term Abraham Kaplan uses to refer to two parties who talk *at,* rather than *to,* one another without listening. Responses to student demands range from repression to reasoned arguments that student leaders often do not heed.

Whether or not student protest becomes violent depends on the intensity of the protestors' feelings, the response of the forces who try to control the protest, the leaders' rhetoric, and many other things. But escalation into violence is not the usual pattern of demonstrative protest.

Nor should student activists necessarily be viewed as rebelling against the values of their parents. On the contrary, our current studies in the United States (and apparently in England as well) indicate that students appear to be trying to implement those very values through their actions. Student activists are recruited from the better students; they were raised in families that have valued esthetic and intellectual interests over money and material success, and have transmitted to the children notions of humanitarianism and free expression that sometimes question authority, convention, and tradition. It is not "permissiveness" so much as parental interests in political and socially conscious activity that are commonly related to this group of active youth.

The growth and complexity of the university structure have combined with increasing involvement in issues of national policy and inadequate channels for expression of disagreement and participation of student and faculty in the decisions that affect their lives on campus. At the same time, radical student activists concerned with these issues have been attracted to such movements as the Students for a Democratic Society (SDS), which claims 7,000 dues-paying national members and about 35,000 members in its several hundred local chapters.

Scores of other single-issue groups on campuses across the United States and in England range from civil rights support groups to leagues for sexual freedom. They are generally not involved in violence concerning these issues, but their numbers reflect increased student participation in public affairs and the volatile potential of campus politics. They are showing, instead, their desire for more personal autonomy, greater latitude for self-expression.

Until recently, Negro university students were smaller in number, politically impotent if not indifferent, and considerably individualistic. Black power groups on campus have offered direction and organizational vehicles for young educated Negro students to find collective expression of grievances and identification with the black community as well as with fellow black students. Black student unions and Afro-American associations have recently emerged on many campuses with increasing numbers of black students. The black student leaders are as militant and violent or more so than the white radicals, especially in terms of tactics used. The principal difference appears to be that black student groups wish to negotiate specific reforms and concessions while the white student radicals often seek only confronting authority with their protests and serve no guiding ideology or specific target. The militancy and violent tactics of black students seem to augment the militant stance of white students. Moreover, internecine battles for power are beginning to occur among the black organizations and may occur eventually between white and black radicals. The white radical commitment to justice and equality is often answered with derision and skepticism by blacks.

Much of the white student movement and whatever violence it engenders is without many ideological supports. There are, nonetheless, values expressed but not always followed: compassion instead of coercion, people above property, total involvement (to the point of holding administrators hostage or running risks of urban guerrilla fighting), distrust of constituted authority (white or black), sexual freedom, privacy of one's own organism (to ingest what one wants, including drugs), rejection of bureaucratic hierachicalism and hypocrisy. From an earlier external interest in poor blacks in Mississippi, students from relatively affluent middle class families shifted to more militancy as they became interested in the Vietnamese. Then, almost suddenly, they were fighting less for others and more for themselves. Abstract principles of justice and equality through student power, and the problems of the war in Vietnam, were concretized by specific objections to university-military contracts and were personalized by threat of the draft. In the process of these shifts increasing use of violence was the accompaniment. Ironically, a kind of romantic element has mixed with the personal as attention is also focused on the sterility of the power structure and an emphasis on human values. Dissent finds targets in mass production, creature comforts, and industrial technocracy. But these features of the New Left have little thrust toward politicization that could resemble an earlier era's underpinning of labor unrest with Marxism.

Some observers have noted that violence most often erupts, or occurs in most intense fashion, when the university authorities and police overract. Perhaps this is a lesson learned from the Columbia and Harvard riots. Daniel Bell, of the sociology department at Columbia, views the behavior of the police as the major cause that "radicalized" the Columbia student body.

Confrontation is a militant and violent means of arousing moderates to join in the movement and the action. It is used to alert the public to the issues. It may dislodge the qualities of patience and quietude from young middle class radicals whose traditional ethics of nonviolence have been politically inhibiting. Confrontation can cause many of the otherwise docile students who have been living only the quiet revolution of thought to commit themselves seriously to the revolution of action, however violent it may become. These are a few of the tenets of the tactics used by the SDS and other radical students. They are the kinds of tactics that elicit, if not encourage, violence.

Because many students are still committed to pacifist or liberal democratic ideals and are as much concerned with university courses as with causes, they are becoming disturbed by the new waves of violence, uncomfortable with the rude, uncouth attacks and the increasingly antiintellectual stance of the radical student movement. As this movement becomes more militant with its strategy of confrontation, it may grow more isolated and loose and fail to attract the large cadre of moderate students whose sense of social justice is being offended by a violence more "nasty and brutal" in its Hegelian prepoliticality than the power structure they at first rejected.

The response to student protest places the major burden on the universities themselves. University administrators are the front-line forces who must cope with the challenges of most of the protest of middle class youth when it becomes violent.

The university today appears to have accepted the assertion that it is a microcosm of society. The university is also a step beyond this minimirror of its context. It is a community of young citizens and of scholars who not only harbor and enrich the knowledge so tediously acquired in the past, but who should engage constantly in questioning and reassessing that knowledge, which includes ideas about the functions and values of the present society. The capacity to inquire and to analyze the results of inquiry is the most fundamental feature of a university, to which I might add Sir Eric Ashby's cogent comment that the university should provide an "environment for the continuous polishing of one mind by another." To maintain and strengthen this capacity is the purpose of every university administration.

The concept of stern authority by the university over the *civil* life of its students is now nearly anachronistic. The traditional intradisciplinary measures used by the university to regulate, in assumed parental role, the personal lives of its younger citizens cannot much longer be of adequate utility for most universities in the United States. Few, if any, universities enjoy the collegiate loyalty of Cambridge and Oxford. The judicial structure of the contemporary university does not reproduce the rules of evidence, qualified judges, accredited legal counsel, and the other features of legal authority to handle major civil and criminal violations. Many of the violent violations on campus today are far beyond the internal differences of a family affair.

The distinction between academic and civil roles must therefore somehow be made both for the university administration and the students. If students are violent and disruptive, they must be judged by the proper role they are taking and by the proper agency of response. If they question what is *academic* in character, the university cannot resort to a claim for allegiance to campus spirit and loyalty to an old-fashioned authority. Their questioning should be honored with respect and they should be engaged by the administration in full debate if courses, curriculum, and other academic affairs are at issue. Where the right of the university to assert authority over certain matters is questioned, it must be earned by argument, if necessary.

Conclusion

When violence occurs in crime or protest, youth is often its vehicle. But most crimes and most protests are not violent, even when young people are involved.

There are many different kinds of violence; some of it is legitimized by the norms of the society and ranges from the force used in parent-child interaction to the conduct of national war. The older generations of most societies are not entirely free from the use of violence, either in the earlier version of their own youth or in the context of their later years. The conduct of a war is but one of the more obvious examples. Moreover, an older generation may be but slightly removed from the posture of most proximate cause for various kinds of violence that a society comes to tolerate. Not yet having arrived at positions of power where responsibilities are shared, youth cannot be blamed for a society that yields violence because it fails to make automobiles and highways safer, fails to reduce high rates of infant mortality, fails to move more vigorously to reform cities of bright and organized crime, and fails to control the manufacture and sale of guns.

Violence is largely a learned response. If in everyday life man witnesses the display of violence in an abundance of styles, it takes on a banality and he may come to accept its use in encounters with his own environment.

It might be said that for all their protest against their established elders, young people in a sense rely on the patience, understanding, tolerance, and responsibility of the older generation to check their escalating demands at the crunch point of the utterly impossible. One of the privileges of youth is having the ability to afford to complain and question (Lorber & Fladell, 1968). The older generation becomes immersed in running the system and must rely on the younger one to provide the pressure needed to question and reform it. Even when it shows displeasure at the tactics of student protest and rioting, the older generation may have sneaking suspicions that youth could be right about many things. Like the ordinary German who a generation ago slowly became aware that something terrible was going on at the edge of town, so those in middle age are having their conscience aroused by youth and feel that more than a few things around them may not be well. There is merit in some of the disturbance from the student youth who are often idealistic, if not well clothed with an ideology. "You'd never believe," said one professor in the midst of student protests at the London School of Economics, "that a group could be so dedicated and saintly and such a terrible nuisance."

If the response to youthful violence is exclusive repression, the response may well assume the violence it seeks to halt. Perhaps, instead, a growing flexibility to change and an understanding of youth's requests will be the older generation's final weapon. The thrust of youth's protests may be dissipated in the soft belly of the Establishment; and violence will be dethroned. Whatever the outcome of current crises, the annual layer of each newly arriving cohort folds into the fabric of society and continues to enrich the cloth.

Violence is a means of seeking power and may be defined as an act of despair committed when the door is closed to alternative resolutions. It comes from the failure to have a more abundant repertoire of means to gain a goal.

The lessons to be learned from current collective violence seem clear: As Columbia University officials remarked recently, acts wherein muscles usurp the role of minds are alien to a university. I suggest the same dictum for the larger society. Where reason is ruined and collective violence is viable, the social system has failed to provide the kind of participatory democracy we basically extol.

In the abstract there can be no side of violence with virtue. The course of the dominant society built on law and intrinsically the inheritor of the value of nonviolence must be to maintain itself. The black militant who would burn cities or the student who would destroy an administration building harbors no better way of life than the Ku Klux Klaner who would burn crosses or bomb Sunday schools. But the responsibility of that dominant society is to offer alternatives for expression, provide reasonable access to the thrones of power, permit grievances to be known, and execute the provisions of our Constitution with dispatch.

Change occurs in all societies, albeit the change in some may be slow or unplanned. It is when persons opposed to change become intransigent and those who wish to promote change are willing to resort to violence that order becomes disorder. When protest moves to riot and riot to rebellion, dissent is transformed into disruption. The right to exercise dissent peaceably is our basic political guarantee. But when physical harm occurs, another guarantee is called into focus and is used to force assaulters to retreat. This kind of balance is a fundamental that the police and the courts were designed to protect and maintain.

Perhaps Abraham Lincoln asked the basic question about violence most succinctly: "Must a government of necessity be too strong for the liberties of its own people, or too weak to maintain its own existence?" I trust that our country is sufficiently sensitive to the liberties of all to listen to its people and strong enough to maintain these liberties with justice under the rule of law.

References

de Tocqueville, A. *L'Ancien regime.* (Trans. by M. W. Patterson) Oxford, England: Blackwell, 1949.
Forster, A. Violence in the fanatical left and right. *Annals of the American Academy of Political and Social Sciences,* 1966, **364,** 141–148
Lorber, R., & Fladell, E. The generation gap. *Life,* January 26, 1969.
Machiavelli, N. *History of Florence and of the affairs of Italy.* London: Dunne, 1901.
National Commission on the Causes and Prevention of Violence. *Firearms and violence in American life.* Vol. 7. Washington, D. C.: United States Government Printing Office, 1969.
O'Connell, J. Lambs to slaughter. *Columbia Journalism Review,* Fall 1967, 21–28.
Taft, P. Violence in America labor disputes. *Annals of the American Academy of Political and Social Sciences,* 1966, **364,** 127–140.
Wolfgang, M. Violence, U.S.A. *Crime and Delinquency,* October 1968, 289–305.
Wolfgang, M. *Youth and violence.* Washington, D. C.: Office of Juvenile Delinquency and Youth Development, Department of Health, Education and Welfare, 1969.
Wolfgang, M., & Ferracuti, F. *The subculture of violence.* London: Tavistock, 1967.

The Concept of Power[1]

ISIDOR CHEIN

The author received his PhD in psychology from Columbia University in 1939. He is presently a professor of psychology at New York University, where his major research interest involves the advancement of knowledge relevant to the solution of social problems.

Conflict and turmoil over the distribution of social power are by no means novel events in human history. If only because of our greater proximity to them, however, they seem to have been getting a lot noisier and far more disturbing of our peace and quiet than were the conflicts of the relatively distant past. The noise and turmoil—and perhaps even the issues—demand some attention.

What is all of the shouting, picketing, mass demonstrating, rioting, kidnapping of deans, seizure of buildings, head cracking, police violence, etc., about? Generically, that is, so that we do not have to deal with each and every instance in its own idiosyncratic particularity. Almost anyone can tell you. Many of those who have less power than they think they should have are demanding more, and are meeting with resistance. Anger mounts, and torrents of words about the substance, form, and style of both demands and resistance escalate into contests of brawn and outbursts of destructiveness.

Alas, the answer is scarcely informative. What, for instance, is being demanded or denied when relative power is at stake? Do the demander and denier have the same thing in mind when they, respectively, demand or deny? Does either comprehend what is in the mind of the other? And, for that matter, is either clear in his own mind as to what it is he is demanding or denying?

If the turmoil is about the distribution of power, we need to go to the nature of "power" to comprehend what it is all about. We turn to the relevant scientific literature only to discover that—given the sophistication of the scientists, their highly cultivated ability to discriminate conceptual and factual issues, and their diverse specialized interests even within the framework of a particular behavioral science—the term "power" can be read in a bewildering welter of meanings, not all of which go to the heart of our particular inquiry.

---

[1] An abridged version of this paper was presented as the Presidential Address to the Division of Philosophical Psychology at the Annual Meeting of the American Psychological Association, Washington, D. C., September 3, 1969.

Irrelevance of Some Familiar Conceptualizations

In one class of definitions, "power" is understood as the ability of a person, P, to induce one or more other persons, O, to behave in a particular way or to carry out a certain action. There are many difficulties with such definitions that, in effect and often explicitly, equate social influence with social power. Social influence may be a tool of power but there are instances of social influence no one would think of as involving power in any sense that occasions interpersonal or intergroup conflict. Take, for instance, the case of P serving as a model for O, often without P's knowledge or intent. We might speak of P's power over O, but this power is vested in O, not in P. With whom—rationally, that is—shall O struggle to change the distribution of power? Or take the continued influence of persons long since dead, say, Aristotle or Darwin. Are they still powerful? Or the most general case of P influencing O who in turn influences Q who is never in a common unit with P. The *influence* is transitive but is the *power* necessarily so? Or the case of O echoing the behavior of P because the behavior is governed by a symmetrical, normative relationship. Thus, P waves his arm and says, "Hi," whereupon O likewise waves his arm and says, "Hi." Thus, P's behavior has undoubtedly influenced O's in that he, in a sense, seized the occasion for the relevance of the norm, but it is not within his provenance or control whether O will abide by it. Moreover, if O had spotted P sooner or if his "reflexes" had been quicker, it would have been P echoing O rather than vice versa. Is this the kind of power that occasions demands for its redistribution?

More fundamentally, however, a glance at some recent power conflicts indicates that while it may be possible to stretch such a definition to cover the cases, it would still distort the focus. In the noisy incidents at least, it seems that P is not concerned with inducing some action by O, but with changing a situation in a way that would increase P's degrees of freedom. Thus, the recent conflict between the local school board in the Ocean Hill-Brownsville section of New York City and the United Federation of Teachers was unquestionably a power conflict between the two, but each was only derivatively and incidentally concerned with the activities of the other. At stake were *rights* rather than activities.

Happily, then, we find a class of definitions of power that emphasizes rights established by rule, as, for example, the powers of branches and agencies of government or those defined in contractual agreements. Not all rights, of course, are powers. One would not, for instance, think of rights that do not involve the taking of action as powers (e.g., the right to *be,* the right to life); nor would one, under these definitions, think of as a power the right to do whatever is not expressly forbidden unless such a right were explicitly established by rule.

Rights as powers can, I think, be subsumed under a broader conceptualization of power. My immediate concern, however, is that this class of definitions distorts the focus with respect to what happens in many struggles over power as much as do the definitions that emphasize P's control of the behavior of O. If the *rights* definitions were relevant in the Ocean Hill-Brownsville situation, for example, one would have expected the conflict to center on changing the rules, but it seems to me that each of the parties was convinced that it was operating properly under the relevant and applicable rules. The crux of the conflict was not over the rules but over the state of affairs that rules, at best, signal and formalize. Negotiated settlements were repeatedly arrived at and agreed-upon operating rules were announced each time. But, since the underlying sources of the conflict were not disposed of, the struggle was renewed each time almost as quickly as the announcements could be issued.

My basic point has been that much of the conceptualization of power found in the literature of the behavioral sciences seems to be largely irrelevant to the power struggles we have been witnessing. And, if the conceptualizations are irrelevant, so in the main and except by accident must be the findings of studies guided by these conceptualizations. To be sure, I have not demonstrated the point. I have illustrated it with one instance of a power conflict, but I believe that almost any headline-making instance involving struggles over black power or student power or labor power or from the arenas of international relations would have served as an equally good illustration.

A Relevant Conceptualization

Many definitions of power are so broad in scope as to be quite manifestly not very helpful, failing to distinguish any particular class of referents. Clark (1965), within a few paragraphs of criticizing another writer on this score, commits essentially the same sin by joining some writers who have virtually identified the concept of power with the concept of causality. "Social power," he tells us, means "the force or energy required to bring about, to sustain or to prevent social, political or economic change." On the face of it, a riot compels a redeployment of the police and, if extensive enough, of the military reserves; and it often induces political backlash. The riot is demonstrably a release of force and energy that brings about change, but this is *not* what the riot was about.

I am criticizing the definition and not its author. Clark quickly shows himself to be as immersed in human affairs of moment as we have long known him to be. Immediately with the definition, for instance, he adds the caveat that we must think of demonstrability as part of the definition. I have already shown that this caveat does not save his definition. Clark's caveat, however, expresses a concern, the concern of one who knows what is going on in the world and not the concern that most behavioral scientists would be expressing by it. It is not about semantically empty statements. Clark is warning us that, "Pseudo-power, verbal power or substitute claims of power or denials of power" must be distinguished from actual power. Note that word "denials." It assures us that Clark is saying something more than what is implied in the not uncommon distinction between *attributed* and *actual* power. He is rather saying, in effect, "No thank you. I'll have none of that baloney about power in a democracy being vested equally in all of the people; and please don't give me any of those disclaimers of power as rationalizations of failure to correct inequities. If we want to be responsible scientists, we have to be realists."

Let me give but one among many possible examples of how Clark is entrapped by his faulty definition. It involves his discussion of the "exercise of excessive power." To my knowledge, the issue has never come up in laboratory studies. To someone who has seen people crushed by the abuse of power, however, such a notion is only a natural. Still, an "exercise of excessive power" is, as Clark himself indicates, clearly a violation of his suggested law of the economy of power. He writes that, "Evidence of the violation of this principle in a social, or governmental, or international system would be found in any signs of the exercise of excessive power, that is, a power markedly disproportionate to the nature of the challenge or under conditions where there is no observable challenge or under conditions where the excessive exercise of power itself generates the opposition. By its very violation it betrays the inherent instability, the tenuous integration, or the incipient disintegration of the system." That is, the law holds except when it does not, and the failure is per se pathognomic of (NB since it is per se pathognomic of, it defines) systematic instability, tenuous integration, or incipient disintegration. But calling the violation pathological—or even amending the statement to indicate that any exercise of excessive power should alert one to the likelihood of other signs of the instability, etc., of the system—does not change the fact that the law actually follows inexorably from Clark's basic definition of power. Increasing force beyond the minimum needed to effect change merely results in an increased rate of change and, when Clark talks of excessive power, he is not referring to rate of change.

What Clark misses is *intention*. We may reasonably speak of an expression of power as excessive when at least one of the following conditions obtains: (*a*) The amount of power brought to bear is more than is needed to accomplish the *manifest* intentions of the wielder, (*b*) the amount of power brought to bear is more than is needed to accomplish *any* intention that would be considered normatively appropriate to the situation, or (*c*) the intention of the wielder or the means adopted to achieve it violate the rights of others. But then the conceptualization of "power" needs to acknowledge its intentionality.

Clark is, of course, quite right when he suggests that excesses in the deployment of power may breed increased resistance and opposition, but he offers no explanation of the phenomenon. Yet it is not hard to understand. Such excess is, at the very least, manifestly unreasonable and capricious, and hence is likely to infringe on the rights of others; and, in the more extreme cases, it is damaging and hurtful to them.

However, he is only partly right when he suggests that such excess is necessarily pathognomic of instability, etc.; that is, the apparent excess may sometimes be rooted in insecurity, but this is not necessarily so. To begin with, there is a diagnostic or assessment operation involved, and the error in judgment may be in the diagnosis or assessment of excess. Moreover, the diagnosis may depend on which side of the conflict you are on. In the second place, given the intentional aspects of power and assuming the nonindependence of intentional and cognitive processes, Clark overlooks the possible misconstruction of the amount of power needed. Such misconstructions may be chronic as a consequence of fixed and unchallenged assumptions, poor communication, and other kinds of lack of access to relevant information, etc. It is understandable, of course, that Clark, involved as he is, should overlook these matters. Such an oversight is not trivial, however, and may indeed be direly consequential. Assuredly, the faulty conceptualization, if not directly responsible for the oversight, nevertheless does not help guard against it.

We find ourselves in a situation, then, in which much of what behavioral scientists have to say about power seems to be irrelevant, largely as a consequence of their deliberate self-detachment from what goes on in the world, and in which others among us are blinded to significantly relevant aspects by our very involvement.

A Modified Weberian-Heiderian Conceptualization

I have touched upon the basic components needed for a relevant definition of power in much of the preceding discussion. People, either individually or through some collective entity, want certain things or states of affairs, and various factors stand in the way of their getting what they want. In this connection, let me define the following terms: a "social element" is an individual person or collective entity; a "social unit" is a set of social elements among whom there is some interdependence with respect to their respective powers; "will" is the weighted summation of what is desired by a social element; "resistance" refers to the factors that stand in the way of a social element's effecting its will. Then, I may define "social power" (or when the context is clear, simply "power"), as *the ease with which an element in a social unit can carry out its will against resistance.* By extension, when reference is made to the expenditure or activation of power, the reference is to the mobilization and activation of "possessed" means of overcoming resistance. Among such "possessed" means are *rights* which are normatively sanctioned. The assertion of a right and resort to the supports for enforcing it is an expression of power.

Several observations concerning this definition are in order. First, there are several close, explicit precedents to my definition. Weber defined "power" as "the probability that one actor within a social relationship will be in a position to carry out his own will despite resistance, regardless of the basis on which this probability rests [1947, p. 152]," and as, "the possibility of imposing one's will upon the behavior of other persons [1954, p. 323]." He was, of course, not using the term "will" as I have just defined it and he was also referring only to resistance emanating from other persons. Heider (1958) offers a broader but related definition of "power" as a function of the ratio of the difficulty of a task to the amount of exertion needed to accomplish it: The more difficult the task (i.e., the greater the resistance to carrying it out) and the more easily a person performs it, the greater is that person's power.

Second, it is obviously possible, following Weber and Heider, to define "will" more narrowly than I have, so that "power" would be defined for specific arenas of activity and even for a particular action at a given time. Such definitions of "power" properly imply that the powers of a social element are generally not homogeneous through all of the arenas of its activities and are not necessarily stable over time. I have, however (and this rests on my definition of "will"), defined "power" for our present purpose as a net and comprehensive attribute of a social element. The major conflicts and turmoil of our time over power are, it seems to me, over the generalized attribute, a general property of a social element, even when they seem to explode in specific arenas. Thus, the contemporary struggles over student power involve, among other things, many matters that are remote from the campus—the war in Vietnam, for instance. Similarly, black separatism emphasizes a concern with the enhancement of the power of Negroes in all matters that affect their lives.

I have, therefore, not specified and do not intend that the weighted summation of things wanted should involve a common list of wants or identical weights for related wants or even the same number of wants for each of the elements in the unit. The degree of dissatisfaction with one's ration of power cannot be unrelated to one's unfulfilled wants, and the priorities assigned to relatively hard-to-fulfill wants are not likely to be the same as they would be were they much easier to satisfy. Both the list of wants and their weights, and the need for power itself, must depend then, at least in part, on the general level of power that one has. It follows that the phrase "weighted sum" in my definition is not there to satisfy a passion for quantification, but is there to express the notion of total wants and to acknowledge that not all wants are of equal moment to a given element and that a given want is not of equal moment to diverse elements.

Third, there can be no power where there is no will, and there can be no power where there is no resistance. There is no place for power in either nirvana or paradise.[2] It is a paradox of unconditional omnipotence that it must be powerless for it can have neither occasion to want anything nor any resistance to overcome. An unconditionally omnipotent being would have to create its own sources of frustration to experience or enjoy power. Maybe that is why God created willful Man.

Fourth, there is no implication that resistance can emanate only from another social element. It is an entirely impersonal force, gravity, that has to be counteracted to satisfy man's desire to fly. Other sources of resistance may be social in origin, but are essentially impersonal in character if not in consequence—poverty, for instance. Where funds are needed to satisfy a want, an insufficiency of funds is, within the meaning of the terms adopted here, a source of resistance. So is lack of access to relevant information. Knowledge, to paraphrase an old aphorism slightly, may be a source of power. There are also intrapersonal sources of resistance. Incompetence, indecisiveness, and rigidity, as a rule, diminish power.

Fifth and finally for present purposes, since my basic definition of power deals with the latter as a potential, it is necessary to say something about the distinction between potential and activated power. The distinction, however, is not as simple as it sounds. When potential energy is translated into kinetic, it is diminished as potential to the extent that it is kineticized. This, however, is not true of the nonphysical power we are discussing. When Clark, for instance, talks of the expression of power, he does not mean to imply (as we would expect from his physical analogue) that the store of power is in any way expended or diminished. Indeed, potential power may be increased through the very process of its expression. Also, the potential energy of physics does not do anything except when and to the extent that it is kineticized. Similarly, when you buy a light bulb rated at 100 watts, a measure of physical power, the rating means that the bulb will deliver 100 joules of work per second when and if it is incorporated into a suitable closed circuit, but it does not do any work unless and until it is so incorporated. Social power, how-

---

[2] See my contrast of nirvana and paradise in Chein, Gerard, Lee, and Rosenfeld, 1964.

ever, can be effective without ever being activated (Nagel, 1968). That a social element, E, need not actually do anything for its power to be felt by other elements, O, is a consquence, in part, of attributed power (which is itself a source of real power, see Lippitt, Polansky, & Redl, 1958) and in part, of norms related to status position.[3] Element O's overt resistance to E may not only be diminished as a consequence, but O may actively, albeit reluctantly, take the initiative to comply with E's will.

Another aspect of the distinction between potential and activated power bears examination. Activated power is, as such, always specific and concrete. Element E, so to say, twists O's arm, or threatens to do so, or withholds some desired goal object, or offers some reward, or mobilizes his troops to induce O to act in a certain way. But the potential of social power is, in its nature, abstract—and particularly so in the broad way in which I have defined it—so that its implicative reach is never completely explicit. Every concrete instance of activated power must, as a consequence, be not only an event per se but must also be a test of the abstract potential. Every specific conflict must to the degree of its specificity be limited to its manifest concerns; that is, to the extent that it is specific it may *involve* but it is not *concerned* with power. Whether the white church groups should pay reparations for past and present sufferings of blacks may or may not become a power struggle over reparations depending on whether it retains and is limited to this specificity, and granting the reparations solely as a matter of social justice is not a concession of power. It becomes a struggle for power or part of such a struggle only to the extent that the outcome symbolizes something beyond reparations, something that can never be completely specified with assurance. One may argue that the abstraction is coextensive with some common property of all its possible concrete manifestations, but the hitch is in the word "possible" since it covers *actual* possibilities that may exclude some *thought of* possibilities and include some that are *unthought of*.

This is one reason why so much of what behavioral scientists have to say about power seems so irrelevant. With their positivistic biases and passion for operational definitions, they are preoccupied with specifics—specific conditions of influence, specific settings, etc.—a preoccupation that shuts out what the major struggles over power are about.

"Come Now and Let Us Reason Together [Isaiah, 1:18]"

If behavioral scientists have left something wanting in their discussions of power, it does not follow that persons involved in power conflicts as participants or as bystanders have any better comprehension of what they are caught up in. They are, to start with, likely to be suspicious of and impatient with conceptualizations and fine distinctions. Words, after all, not only help to guide but they also

---

[3] Nagel attributes the effect to the anticipation by O of the reactions of E to noncompliance. Such a dynamic is, of course, sometimes operative, but it is not necessary. Not only may any calculated awareness of such reactions be bypassed, but the reactions of others (support, condemnation, etc.) may also be relevant, as may be the simple expectation of the futility of resistance. Most commonly, I suspect, the relevant norms and proprieties simply function as a *set*.

delay, inhibit, and often substitute for more vigorous action; and more vigorous action does often offer greater promise of effectiveness. Moreover, when *change* is at issue, reason and reasonableness are not, as most might suppose, fully impartial. For, even though all elements involved be dedicated to dealing justly under the rules of reason, the status quo sets out with two counts in its favor: First, the burden of proving the necessity for change rests on its advocates; and, second, no matter how much one agrees on the evils of the status quo, its properties are at least known and it is of demonstrated viability or it could never have settled into a status quo, whereas one cannot be certain that the proposed change does not hide within itself greater evils. This bias of reason may be reasonable, but it scarcely eases the discomfort of those whose shoes are pinching and who are therefore crying for a change. In any case, we cannot assume a universal dedication to justice; and the tones of reason are all too readily diverted into the service of sophistry, rationalization, Machiavellian manipulation, the masking of uncertainties that becloud its premises, and the ignoring of relevant terms that are felt but for which we have not yet found words.

Let us also not forget that, when it is the distribution of power that is at issue, the more powerful elements are far more likely than the less powerful to be skilled in the use of words and the abuse of reason and they are far more likely to have access to means of exploiting these skills. Finally, we dare not overlook the fact that if only some of the contenders are willing to be governed by the disciplines of reason, the reasonable ones are generally at a great disadvantage. In such a conflict, coercion normalizes countercoercion as a means of mediating claim versus counterclaim, and brute force normalizes brute force.

So! Words, fine distinctions, logic, reason, and reasonableness are all suspect, and properly so when there is a conflict of interest, but only when they are appealed to by the opposition or when, in one's own thinking, their use shows signs of inhibiting the free examination of alternatives. It may be that we should not let ourselves become slaves to reason, but it is surely wise to hear it out. Suspicion itself may blind one to opportunity and bar the way to fulfillment. It is, after all, a feature of the human condition that we are constantly beset with the challenges of finding our way between excesses of one kind or another, and always in the absence of *total* intelligence. The heat of combat only aggravates this aspect of our existence. Still there are periods of lull in even the fiercest of combat. During these periods, it behooves us, assuming that we are not utterly exhausted, to examine ourselves, and our situation, including the wants and premises of our opponents. The results of such cogitation may reinforce or lead us to modify our course of action, or may be set aside for continued examination when opportunity arises, or even discarded as worthless. If we must be unreasonable or if we find cause to mistrust the results of finite reason, let us, if we can, at least make sure that we have considered what reason has to offer.

What troubles me most about the current disturbances, domestic and international—apart from the bloodshed and human wreckage, that is—is that very little advantage is taken of lulls for the reexamination of basics. Much attention is given by both participants and bystanders to thoughtful consideration of the conflicts, but the thought tends to get lost in specifics or in ethical decisions. Separate schools of Afro-American studies should or should not be established and they should or should not be run by blacks. Students have or have not been exploited and cheated, and they should or should not be given representation with or without a vote on university senates. It is or is not understandable that black students should appear on campus carrying rifles. Discriminating conscientious objection to particular wars should or should not exempt one from military service. The poor, the underprivileged, one or another or all minority groups, workers, students, or you name them, should or should not be granted what they are asking for. The goals are good but the means are not. When no alternatives are available, ends do or do not justify the means. There can or cannot be sufficient provocation to justify violation of law. But somehow the underlying and generic issues of power are overlooked or ignored with the consequence that available options and possible directions of peace-making action are overlooked.

When power per se is at issue, it is, for instance, a well-nigh universal assumption that the conflict is zero sum; that is, what one element gains must be counterbalanced by the losses of other elements. With this assumption comes its almost inevitable corollary: Conflicts focused on power can only be resolved by coercion or by shifting the focus.

Resolution by coercion may involve extension of the conflict to include social elements not originally involved, either through the formation of alliances and coalitions with other elements or through the imposition of a resolution on the original contenders by noncombatant elements. But, however accomplished, such resolution is, as a rule, only temporary, because the original tensions generally remain and because the very success of coercion—even though on the side of goodness, law, or God—validates the use of coercion as a means of resolving conflict.

Resolution by shifting the focus of conflict, often conjoined with coercion, involves provision for the satisfaction of wants by inducing a change in manifest wants or by reducing resistance through some form of "bribery." Thus, the United States may promise the Viet Cong and North Vietnam, "Be good fellows and lay down your arms. We will then pour great wealth into Vietnam. Everyone will be secure and prosperous." The effort is to shift the focus from power to prosperity and security. Such a maneuver may sometimes work, but not when power per se rather than the particular applications of power has become the burning issue. The desire for power may be generated by the indignities of powerlessness and past inabilities to help oneself; but, once generated and crystallized as the answer to unspecified *possibilities* of insult and helplessness, it becomes exceedingly tenacious and resistant to diversion or bribery.

The premise that the resolution of conflict over the distribution of power must be coercive and sum to zero is, however, false. There are at least three ways in which the net power in a social unit can increase with a gain, or at least no loss, for every element. First, as I have already noted, resistance does not necessarily stem from the counterposition of motives of different social elements. To the extent that more effective devices are developed for coping with the impersonal sources of resistance, therefore, there is a net increment in power for the entire social unit. Second, to the extent that the structure of the social unit is altered so that its various elements can communicate and otherwise deal with one another more effectively, each element becomes to some degree a power resource of the others and, again, there is a resulting net gain in power.[4] Third, chronic coercive confrontations not only intensify the resistances of some elements to the will of others but also demand the diversion of resources (time, effort, etc.) and sometimes result in the destruction of resources (e.g., school buildings, books, etc.). The elimination of instigations to such confrontations, therefore, results in net saving of power, a saving that is effectively an increment in power.

The three ways of increasing power offer the possibility of redistributing power without loss to any element—providing, of course, that no element desires to control other elements as one of its major and fundamental wants.

Foci of Conflict in Power Struggles

It would be naive to ignore the fact that much of the contemporary turmoil over the distribution of power centers on the demand by some elements for greater control over their own fate and that this demand offers a direct challenge to other elements that want to continue their control of the challengers. In such cases, there may be no alternatives to coercive confrontations, although presumably the preferred form of coercion would resort to bargaining as its instrument, introducing other wants into the negotiations. There is, of course, no sharp line of demarcation between the bargaining table and brute force; the latter, too, enlarges the range and variety of stakes involved in the interchange, gambling on the aversiveness of pain, disruption, destructiveness, and exhaustion, and brute force may be a necessary step to bring the contenders to the bargaining table. On the other hand, it is an increasing practice in bargaining to rely on physical exhaustion to induce a readiness to compromise and possibly to overwhelm the opposition. Let me repeat, however, what I have already said in other words: When power is, by whatever name, explicitly one of the stakes, the character of the bargaining situation is unique in that the values of all other gratifications and need-satisfactions are markedly diminished because power holds the key to the possibilities of unspecified need-satisfaction in the indefinite future. At best, a coerced settlement creates an interlude opportune to building up the mutual trust, dependability, and support that make coercive power irrelevant to the interactions of elements within the unit, thus reducing the valence of differentials of power; but, even at best, such an interlude comes under the worst of circumstances.

At any rate, I am not claiming that there are never any circumstances that offer no realistic alternatives to coercive confrontation. But often—more often, I think, than not—there indeed are alternatives that are missed because of blindness induced by fixed assumptions.

It often happens, given our hierarchically structured social order, that an element, E, does, in fact, control significant aspects of the life and fate of O and thereby possesses great power over the activities of O. In the light of the history of both successful and unsuccessful bloody revolutions and of ideologies stemming

---

[4] What a complicated way of saying that "in unity, there is strength"! But the complexity seems appropriate to the context. I hope that it will be forgiven.

from such diverse sources as Karl Marx, Max Weber, and Alfred Adler, we generally take it for granted that E craves its power over O. Now, I submit, the assumption is not necessarily valid and the sheer possibility that it is not should alert us to inspect more carefully the conflicts that arise. An error can be catastrophic, contributing to a vicious circle and self-fulfilling prophecy that can only lead to a coercive showdown.

Envision, for instance, some sequence of events such as the following: Element O wants something access to which is controlled by E and comes to E with some appropriate request. The request does not quite fit the way E construes the world. Therefore, E does not comprehend or rejects it. Then O's request, reasonable from its viewpoint, becomes a demand, and, in style and intensity, violates one or more norms that regulate the interactions of elements differing in social position. Element E is caught off balance in a structure that trembles under the impact of the violation. The substance of O's request or demand becomes of even less concern to E than it was. Thinking its world is at stake, E mobilizes its resources to restore its balance and the stability of the structure. Element O is overwhelmed; its request is lost. It develops new needs to which it expects E to be more responsive, but E's perceptual field is not that of O. Next, O's expectations become requests, the requests become demands, and the process repeats. Sooner or later, O begins to apprehend that its troubles are rooted in its lack of power and—especially if it is influenced by the ideologies of power—in the imbalance of power, and its demands become more and more focused on the distribution of power. However, E has by now become convinced that O is unreasonable and undisciplined and, therefore, unfit to wield power. Element E is impelled to resist O's bid for power, not because it craves power nor even the privileges that go with power, but because it must preserve an orderly world. Order is a necessary condition of human security and E may well see itself as acting for O's benefit as much as for its own.

What difference does it make if E is primarily concerned with preserving its power or if it is primarily concerned with preserving order if the consequences for O are the same? The difference is that when and if order and stability are E's primary concern, there are, at least hypothetically, describable conditions for winning a redistribution of power that do not require escalation into a coercive struggle.

It will be recalled that the escalating process I have just described began with O's request, E's failure to accede, and the construction that E placed on O's response to this failure. Hidden in this account and the subsequent abstract narrative are two critically important normative factors that hold the key to the outcome. Each is a necessary but not sufficient condition of power when there are social elements with counterposed desires. Even together, the two factors may not be sufficient for any real increase in power, but often the real issue concerns one or the other factor, or both, rather than power per se. I shall refer to the first as "dominion" and to the second, adapting an important concept of Horwitz (1958), as "weight." Let me start with a brief consideration of "dominion" and its bearing on our problem. Then I will go on to a similar treatment of "weight."

Dominion and Weight versus Power

By "dominion" (NB not "domination") I mean the arena within which, and the range of events with respect to which, a social element may properly and legitimately express a desire that demands acknowledgement and consideration by other social elements. It does not follow that the other elements must necessarily accede or that dominion is exclusive.

Many a quarrel over power is, at least in its onset, a quarrel over the bounds of an element's dominion. In the preceding example, E did not attend to O's request. Why not? If we know nothing more about it, the simplest hypothesis is that such a request, whatever it may have been, was not expected to emanate legitimately from O; hence, a considerable likelihood that it would not be heard or, if heard, not comprehended or, if comprehended, not taken seriously or, if taken seriously, apprehended as offensive. When students first proposed that they be given a voice and vote in the hiring and firing of faculty, many a professor did not believe his ears or the seriousness of the proposal—or, believing, took the proposal as a bit of unmitigated gall. Why such reactions? Because the proposal intruded into affairs that these professors took to be totally outside of the dominion of students.

The extent and range of dominion is normatively sanctioned and, with the force of the normative system behind it, it is a major aspect of power. Still, it is not quite the same thing to establish that some unexpected matter is within one's legitimate sphere of interest so that one's desires must be given serious consideration, that is, that the matter is within one's dominion, as it is to declare that one demands a greater share of power, and, often, the extension of dominion is all that is being sought.

Dominion is as a rule established by precedent, particularly precedent associated with status and possession (e.g., a woman's dominion extends over her kitchen), but also the negative precedent of failure to register objection or resistance to repeated extensions of an element's domain of concern. There are also other kinds of precedent that sound odd when put into words, but that are nevertheless well grounded in some moretic systems; for example, doing favors for another extends the dominion of the latter over some seemingly unrelated affairs of the doer. One may have a right to expect and to demand, for instance, that someone who has been serving you voluntarily should meet certain canons of respectability.

Generally, even though there may be no established precedent, the dominion of an element extends to all matters that affect its welfare, provided that it is conceivable that ways can be found to fulfill the related desires without intolerable violations of the normative system of the social unit. The term "intolerable" in the proviso does not designate a rigid limit, and the amount of "give" that can be tolerated is a function of how incommutably vital these matters are to the legitimate welfare of the element. In other words, in a noncoercive relationship, any social element may properly and legitimately express desires and expect them to be taken seriously to the extent that it is clear that its welfare is at stake and that the net damage to others and to the common welfare will not exceed socially tolerable limits—and this even though these desires may not conform closely to established ways of doing things.[5] This principle, I think, is normative, although not necessarily explicitly so, in any social unit not founded on coercion, and it may even be operative in some ways in coercive units. It is the noncoercive basis for change in the distribution of power.

The way the principle operates is as follows: An element, E, makes some request. If there is no response, E proceeds on the assumption that O does not regard the matters involved as falling within E's dominion. Instead, therefore, of escalating the request into a demand, mobilizing its coercive resources, and taking other aggressive action, E accepts the nonresponse as a challenge to demonstrate that the matters involved do indeed affect its welfare and that ways can be found to implement its desire without disproportionate cost to the welfare of others, the common weal, and accustomed ways of doing things. Indeed, even before making the request, E would be well advised to anticipate, not O's probable response, but O's probable view of E's dominion. Element E cannot afford to assume, no matter how self-evident this assumption may seem, that O will readily comprehend and grant E's dominion. The initial negotiations will focus, therefore, not on the substance of the request, but on the dominion with respect to the matters involved. Only when and to the degree that the issue of dominion is settled, can the negotiations constructively turn to the substance of the request.

What if E does not operate in this way? Then it is up to O to raise the issues of dominion if this is what its reluctance to accede to the request is based on. I am not saying that every request that meets with resistance must be dealt with in this way, but that every request that entails a significant redistribution of power should be handled in this way if one wishes to minimize the likelihood of a coercive showdown.

There is a special kind of request, not necessarily articulated as such, that is particularly crucial in transactions involving power. Such a request entails what Horwitz has called "weight."

By established custom, some elements of a social unit carry more weight than others. (Cp. the fifth commandment which, in the original Hebrew, reads literally: [Give] weight [to] your father and your mother.) In any conflict of desire between two elements, given that the desires are equally legitimate and of about equal intensity, the element with less weight is expected to give way; and even a marked difference in the strengths of legitimate desire may be more than compensated for by a difference in weight, so that the element with the greater desire may still be

---

[5] A common condition for granting powers to an element, E, that is, giving E social support in getting its way against resistance, is that E can be trusted on both grounds of competence and concern to use these powers responsibly, that is, to give due weight to its own welfare, the welfare of others who might be affected, and the common weal. It follows from what was said in the text that E's dominion can be established by establishing the involvement of its welfare and its responsibility. I have preferred the more general statement, however, because it is my point that in many instances in which it is assumed that E is bidding for power, E is actually bidding for dominion. Element E itself may assume that what it wants is an extension of its *power* where it would actually be fully satisfied with an extension of its *dominion*. In such instances, it makes no sense to say that a condition of the extension is that E can be trusted to act responsibly. What is at issue is not E's possible actions, but whether E's wishes are to be listened to and given due consideration.

expected to give way to the one with greater weight. This is the sense in which Horwitz used the term "weight." In everyday usage, the term applies to matters of opinion and belief rather than to desire; that is, when there is a difference of opinion, certain social elements are expected to, and generally do, defer to others. We may also note that there is a similar weight differential with respect to the setting, definition, and determination of relevance of social norms, for example, style setters, chairmen, parliamentarians, and arbiters of etiquette being among those receiving greater weight. The three kinds of weight (as applied to desire, opinion, and norms) are interrelated and interdependent in many ways and all three play roles in determining the outcomes of interactions of social elements. Individual social elements, thus, differ in the weights that they carry in identifying and specifying what *is* and/or what *should be* (both desires and norms, of course, involve *what-should-bes*). It is in this broad sense that I am using the term "weight."

Weight may be associated with status (hereditary, conferred, or achieved), with roles, with expertise, with earned credits, etc. But any failure to abide by expectations based on the comparison of weighted desires carries a challenge to the established order and an insult (the insult of unilateral weight reduction) to the element of greater weight.

An extension of E's dominion is of little moment from the viewpoint of power if it is not accompanied by a significant increase in weight in the new areas that have come into its dominion. Weight is, however, with a qualification I shall shortly note, a zero-sum quantity; that is, what E gains must be lost by O. Moreover, I suspect, weight is a far more precious commodity than is power per se. The experience of the weight accorded to one's self is a major ingredient of the self-image and of self-respect. Transactions with regard to weight are therefore inherently delicate affairs. All quarrels with respect to power are basically quarrels over dominion or over weight or simultaneously over both. When dominion is conceded, the actual quarrel is always over weight.

Despite the fact that weight is a zero-sum quantity, there are three mitigating factors that affect contentions over it. The first is that it is a commonplace of human experience that increased weight is freely granted to social elements as they earn it and the corresponding reduction of one's own weight is freely accepted with no, or barely any, notice of the loss. The compensatory feature that makes this possible is that, in the long run, the lot of all is improved with the optimal distribution of earned weights.

The second mitigating factor is that the zero-sum property of weight is situation specific; that is, when we refer to this property, we mean that the gains and losses involved in the redistribution of weights counterbalance one another *in specific situations*. When different social elements add up weights across situations, however, they will commonly attach different weights to the situations; that is, the between-element weights are themselves situationally weighted, and they are not weighted in the same way by different social elements. In the long run, it is these net weights (the weighted sums of between-elements weights) that matter most to the various social elements, and these net weights are not interrelated by the zero-sum principle. The gains and losses in net weight over time are not necessarily mutually counterbalanced. If everyone can gain in self-esteem, everyone can gain in net weight as just defined.

The third mitigating factor is that it often happens that there is an accrual of credit in one's earning of weight as a consequence of not being overly fussy and picayune about one's weight. There is often a long-range premium in weight as a result of conceding weight. The meek may be a long way from inheriting the earth, but some of the most influential persons in history have been individuals who never made an issue of their weight; apart from certain great religious leaders, one may think of such persons as Socrates. On the other hand, it is widely believed that persons who repeatedly "pull rank" lose in authority thereby.

Disagreements over weight will, however, become coercive engagements, with all the hostilities that such engagements entail, if E simply tries to assume more weight for itself. Horwitz has, for instance, shown that even in laboratory situations with arbitrarily assigned weights and essentially trivial desires, the violation of the weighted-desire balance will generate hostility. Disagreements over weight can, however, be dealt with in exactly the same way as disagreements over dominion, that is, through negotiations in which the first real item on the agenda is E's establishment of the propriety of its request for change. In other words, to avoid coercive conflict, E's first task is to establish that its status or condition has changed so as to merit greater weight and/or that its welfare is at stake, that the welfare of the entire social unit will not be damaged by the change, and that the elements that have to give up some weight will not suffer insult or other undue injury. Still another way of putting the point is that E has first to establish that its desire for greater weight comes within its dominion and then to argue its full case. If a good case can be made for E, it will stand in its good stead that the distribution of zero-sum commodities comes under normative rules of fair play.

Recapitulation

It is one of the functions of a psychologist to advance the understanding of human behavior. It is the special function of a psychologist concerned with the social significance of psychology to develop psychological understanding in ways that are relevant to the diagnosis and solution of social problems. It is the function of a philosopher to clarify and guide thought with respect to whatever matters come into his purview. It is, therefore, presumably the function of a philosophical psychologist to clarify and guide thought bearing on the understanding of human behavior. What I have attempted to do here is to conjoin these functions specifically with respect to the problem of conflict over power. Whether I have discharged my self-imposed task well will have to be judged by others. There are obviously many matters upon which I have not even touched. I have not said anything, for instance, about the role of such psychological processes as pride and personal identity in the genesis of power conflicts. Nor have I attempted to deal with the philosophical value issues entailed in such conflicts. And, from the point of view of a social engineer, I have said little more than that the proper definition of a problem is a step toward its solution. In my presentation, I did particularly want to emphasize the following points:

1. Power is best defined as the ease with which an element in a social unit can carry out its will against resistance.

2. When power is itself the focus of contest, it is as a generic potential with reference to unspecified needs and desires in the unspecified future.

3. Coercive confrontations in conflicts over the distribution of power rarely, if ever, offer the possibility of stable, satisfactory outcomes.

4. There may be instances of such conflicts in which an element in a social unit can realistically find no alternatives to coercive confrontations but, perhaps more often than not, there are alternatives that are not perceived because of blindness induced by fixed assumptions. It may also be that at least short-term success in coercive confrontations may be, in some situations, necessary to establish conditions that permit more rational coping with problems; but the very success of coercion tends to validate the use of coerciveness in interpersonal and intergroup affairs and, thereby, to undermine the availability and potential effectiveness of other means. On a rational basis, therefore, resort to coercive confrontation must be a heavily assured matter of last resort.

5. It is a mistake to assume that power is a zero-sum quantity, some elements necessarily suffering losses to balance the gains of others.

6. It is a mistake to assume, even in instances in which some elements fight against any concession of power, that these elements necessarily crave and value their degree and range of power; they may really be fighting for the preservation of a familiar universe.

7. When and to the degree that resistance to change in the distribution of power is rooted in the desire to preserve a familiar universe, there is a basis for noncoercive negotiation.

8. In noncoercive negotiation for change in the distribution of power, it is a mistake to assume that power as such must necessarily be an item on the explicit agenda, but it is equally a mistake to assume that the key and primary issues that need to be negotiated are those the winning of which would symbolize and betoken a change in the distribution of power.

9. Issues that are taken as symbolizing and betokening power may be important objects of negotiation in their own right, but such issues should either be dealt with as specifics sharply shorn of their power-betokening aspects or postponed until the key issues of power have been negotiated successfully.

10. The key, and often sufficient, issues for noncoercive negotiation over power are issues of dominion and/or of weight, that is, the right of the element seeking change to extend the arena within which and the range of events with respect to which it has a right to express desires that demand acknowledgment from and consideration by other elements in the unit, and the right to have its desires, either with respect to certain kinds of matters or in general, given greater weight in the process of arriving at consensus than they have been receiving. Often it may turn out that, if these issues are properly identified, power per se is not even in contest. I have described briefly the terms that are relevant to the negotiation of these issues.

11. It should perhaps be added as a final point of emphasis that the goal of rational noncoercive negotiation is never compromise but rather the changing of

minds. Compromise itself entails a compromising of that goal. Compromise inherently involves coercion although each of the engaged parties bears some of the brunt of it—as coercer and as coerced. Compromise is, therefore, ideally, a matter of next-to-last resort—next, that is, to unyielding, uncompromising, coercive confrontation.

References

Chein, I., Gerald, D. L., Lee, R. S., & Rosenfeld, E. *The road to H: Narcotics, delinquency, and social policy.* New York: Basic Books, 1964.

Clark, K. B. Problems of power and social change: Towards a relevant social psychology. *Journal of Social Issues,* 1965, **21,** 4–20.

Heider, F. *The psychology of interpersonal relations.* New York: Wiley, 1958.

Horwitz, M. The veridicality of liking and disliking. In R. Taguiri & L. Petrullo (Eds.), *Person perception and interpersonal behavior.* Stanford: Stanford University Press, 1958.

Lippitt, R., Polansky, N., & Redl, F. The dynamics of power: A field study of social influence in groups of children. In E. E. Maccoby, T. M. Newcomb, & E. L. Hartley (Eds.), *Readings in social psychology.* New York: Holt, 1958.

Nagel, J. H. Some questions about the concept of power. *Behavioral Science,* 1968, **13,** 129–137.

Weber, M. *The theory of social and economic organization.* (Trans. by A. M. Henderson & T. Parsons) New York: Oxford University Press, 1947.

Weber, M. *Max Weber on law in economy and society.* (Trans. by M. Weinstein & E. Shils, Ed. by M. Rheinstein) Cambridge: Harvard University Press, 1954.

Three Not-So-Obvious Contributions of Psychology to Peace[1]

RALPH K. WHITE

The author received his PhD in psychology from Stanford University in 1937. He is presently a professor of social psychology and a member of the Institute for Sino-Soviet Studies at George Washington University. He is primarily interested in the psychological background of war, especially the Vietnam war and the East-West conflict in general.

There are two things in this world that do not quite fit together. One is that mushroom cloud. We try not to think about it—but it is *there,* rising, enormously, behind everything else we do. Then there is the other thing: the whole complicated spectacle of all the old causes of war going on as usual. There is the arms race and ABM, and—much worse than ABM— that hydraheaded monster, MIRV. Most of all, there is the war in Vietnam. It stands there as a continual, glaring reminder that the United States—our own peace-loving United States—is capable of the kind of bungling that got us into that war. And then comes the thought: *If* even the peace-loving United States could bungle itself into a little war like Vietnam, what guarantee is there that we will not bungle ourselves into a big war—a nuclear war? It might be possible to exorcize the specter of that mushroom cloud if the Vietnam war did not exist. But it does exist.

The sense of bafflement is especially great perhaps among psychologists, because a good many psychologists feel that the bungling that got us into the Vietnam war, and could get us into a nuclear war, consists largely of ignoring certain fundamental *psychological* truths. Most of our American policy makers (both Johnson and Nixon, for instance) behave as if they do not recognize certain things that we psychologists take for granted, things such as the necessity for empathy (including empathy with our own worst enemies), the dangers of black-and-white thinking, and the role of the self-fulfilling prophecy in the vicious spiral of the arms race.

All of this strengthens the case for better communication—better communication directly between us and the policy makers in Washington, and also better

---

[1] Kurt Lewin Memorial Address presented to the Society for the Psychological Study of Social Issues at the Annual Meeting of the American Psychological Association, Washington, D. C., August 31, 1969.
Reprinted from the *Journal of Social Issues,* 1969, **25**, No. 4. Copyrighted by the Society for the Psychological Study of Social Issues, 1969.

communication between us and other scholars, such as historians, political scientists, and area specialists, who in turn influence the policy makers a good deal more than we do.

One difficulty in communicating with these people is that from their standpoints we often sound like a little boy trying to teach grandma to suck eggs. Many of them are experts in their own fields, people from whom we really could learn a great deal. And then we come up with these ideas that they think they have heard many times already—ideas that they often think we have dressed up in pretentious new terminology but that they regard as essentially old, familiar, and, in a sense, obvious.

The paradox is that it is precisely these so-called obvious ideas that we often see the top policy makers ignoring when it comes to concrete action decisions. We see that mushroom cloud coming closer because policy makers *act* as if they could not see what to *us* seems obvious. Thus, in order to define the problem accurately, it looks as if we need three categories. First, there are the things that really are obvious on the verbal level *and* on the action level. Second there are the things that seem obvious on the verbal level but that are often ignored on the action level. Third, there are the things that are not obvious on either the verbal level or the action level.

Obvious Concepts Ignored in Action

It is the second category, although it is not my main focus in this discussion, that is the most important, namely, the things that seem obvious on the general, abstract, verbal level but that are often ignored on the specific, concrete, action level. As examples, let us take the three ideas I have already mentioned: the necessity for empathy, the dangers of black-and-white thinking, and the role played by the self-fulfilling prophecy in the vicious spiral of the arms race.

When empathy is defined in common-sense phrases like "understanding the other fellow's point of view," any policy maker is likely to say, "Sure, I believe in that, and I try to do it all the time." He is likely to pride himself on understanding the other fellow's point of view even when he does not. Or take the black-and-white picture. Anyone who has ever seen a western movie and knows about the good guys and the bad guys is likely to have some notion on the verbal level of the dangers of black-and-white thinking even if in practice he engages in black-and-white thinking most of the time. Or take the role of the self-fulfilling prophecy in the vicious spiral of the arms race. To some, the self-fulfilling prophecy may be a new and interesting idea—Senator Fulbright found it new and interesting when he heard it from Jerry Frank—but the vicious spiral of the arms race is an old idea that has been heard many times and probably would be accepted in theory even by people like Melvin Laird who in practice ignore it. What can we do then? The things we feel are being most dangerously ignored are the things most likely to make our listeners yawn.

The answer certainly is not to ignore the things we are most anxious to say. My own feeling is that our most important task is to keep our focus on these fundamental things and to communicate them in such a way that they become really familiar and really used, on the action level as well as the verbal level. That means, among other things, giving concrete examples.

For instance, take the notion of empathy. It seems to me that a flagrant concrete example of a violation of the principle of empathy was our bombing of North Vietnam. That bombing was urged and continually supported by our most flagrant nonempathizers—the military. But its effect included a continual solidifying of opposition to us among the people in North Vietnam. It was as if we were doing our best to persuade every man, woman, and child in North Vietnam that America really is the devil, the wanton, cruel aggressor, that Communist propaganda has always said it was. Most of our military men in active service not only failed to empathize with the North Vietnamese, but it looks as if they actively, though unconsciously, resisted the temptation to empathize. They shut their eyes to the best evidence available: the firsthand testimony of people like Harrison Salisbury, Cameron, Schoenbrun, Gerassi, and the Quakers of the Phoenix who went to North Vietnam and came back saying that our bombing was solidifying opposition to us. They shut their eyes also to the evidence that the bombing was tending to alienate from us most of the other people in the world. And, most surprisingly, they shut their eyes to the evidence of history, represented by our own Strategic Bombing Survey after World War II which described how our bombing of Germany and Japan had the same solidifying effect.

This kind of concrete example may jolt and antagonize some people, but it will not make them yawn. Focusing on such examples should help to make abstract concepts like empathy become more and more a part of the reality world of the listener, on the concrete action level. It matters very little whether a policy maker talks about empathy. It matters a great deal whether the impulse to empathize keeps coming up in his mind at those particular moments when wisdom in action requires that he should at least try to understand the other fellow's point of view.

Nonobvious Psychological Principles

Then there is that third category of psychological ideas and psychological facts that are relatively unfamiliar to the decision makers on both levels. They do not call for the kind of special tactful treatment that the familiar ideas call for. I am going to talk about three of them, "three not-so-obvious contributions of psychology to peace." (Of course, when I say "contributions" I mean potential contributions. What we have done is to learn certain things about the psychological causes of war. Whether these insights and the facts that support them will ever actually contribute to peace depends on our own effort and our own skill as communicators.) Also, it should be clear that these are not necessarily the most important of the not-so-obvious contributions. There are others that seem to me just as important or more so: Osgood's GRIT proposal, for instance, and the experimental work Morton Deutsch has been doing, and the monumental job Kelman (1965) did editing that big volume *International Behavior*. But those are pretty well known. I am going to focus on three that are not very well known.

The Hovland Principle in Communicating with Communists

First, there is a corollary of the Hovland principle that a two-sided presentation of an argument is more persuasive than a one-sided presentation when you are talking with people who initially disagree with you. This corollary is that *we Americans should publicly accept as much as we can honestly accept of the Communist point of view.*

To some psychologists this may seem obvious, but most of our politicians and foreign-policy makers are likely to regard it as very far from obvious. To many of them it must sound like subversive doctrine—like being "soft on communism." That is precisely why we psychologists, if we think the evidence supports it, ought to be saying so, clearly, and often, and with all the research evidence that we can bring to bear.

Let us look at the evidence. You are probably familiar with the impressive body of experimental data accumulated by Hovland and his colleagues Janis, Lumsdaine, Kelley, and others on the general advantages of a "two-sided" form of persuasion, which includes stating fairly the stronger arguments of the other side before trying to refute them, and also acknowledging any elements in them that the speaker himself regards as valid. Their findings show that this two-sided approach is likely to be more effective when the audience is intelligent, or initially in disagreement with the viewpoint of the speaker, or both intelligent and initially in disagreement. Now comes the corollary, which is especially interesting from the standpoint of our relations with the Communist world. The Communist leaders fit exactly the Hovland prescription for the kind of people with whom one should use the two-sided approach. They are intelligent. They could hardly have maintained stability in a vast nation like the USSR if they were not at least fairly intelligent. And to put it mildly, they are initially in disagreement with us. So it would follow that in communicating with them we should use the two-sided approach.

What would it mean, concretely? It would not mean soft-pedaling any of the things we believe to be wrong and dangerous on the Communist side: the invasion of Czechoslovakia, for instance, or the recent regression toward Stalinism in the Soviet Union, or the anarchy and cruelty of the "great cultural revolution" in Communist China, or the assassination of village leaders in Vietnam. But it would mean coupling candor about what we think is wrong with candor about what we think is right. That raises the question: What *is* right in communism? Is anything right? Each of us would probably have a different answer, but just to make the main point concrete I am going to go out on a limb and mention some of the things that I personally think are right.

Most important, probably, is the depth and intensity of the Russians' desire for peace. They hate and fear war at least as much as we do. How could they not hate war after the searing experience they went through in World War II? We can also give them credit for bearing the brunt of World War II—and winning on that crucial Eastern front. I know from my own experience in Moscow that nothing touches the heart of a Russian more than real appreciation by an American of what they suffered and what they accomplished in our common struggle against Hitler. There is real common ground here, both when we look back on World War II and when we look ahead to the future. We and the Communists, looking ahead, find ourselves on the same side in the rather desperate struggle that both they and we are waging against the danger of nuclear war.

Some other things that I personally would acknowledge include Soviet space achievements, which really are extraordinary, considering how backward Russia was in 1917; the case for Communist Chinese intervention in Korea after Mac-Arthur crossed the 38th Parallel; the case for Communist China in the matter of Quemoy and Matsu; the Vietnamese Communist case against Diem and his American supporters; a very large part of their case against what we have been doing in Vietnam since the death of Diem; and, more basically, the proposition that the Communist countries are ahead of us in social justice. In spite of striking inequalities, my reading of the evidence is that they are definitely ahead of us in eliminating unearned income ("surplus value") and somewhat ahead of us in diminishing the gap between the rich and poor.[2]

If all this has a subversive sound, please recall again the Hovland experiments, and also the rather large number of other experiments that bring out, in one way or another, the desirability of discovering common ground if conflict is to be resolved. For instance, there are the experiments of Blake and Mouton on how each side in a controversy ordinarily underestimates the amount of common ground that actually exists between its own position and that of its adversary. There is all the research on the non-zero-sum game, and the need to keep the players on both sides from treating a *non*-zero-sum game, in which the adversaries actually share some common interests, as if it were a zero-sum game in which loss for one side always means gain for the other. There is the so-called Rapoport Debate (actually originated by Carl Rogers, apparently), in which neither side is permitted to argue for its position until it has stated, to the other side's satisfaction, what the other side is trying to establish. There is Hammond's recent work on the importance of implicit assumptions that differ on the two sides of an argument. There is Sherif's Robbers' Cave experiment in which conflict was replaced by cooperation where a superordinate goal—an overriding common goal—demanded cooperation. There is Rokeach's work on the importance of common beliefs as a basis for good will. All of these have as a common element the idea of common goals or common ground, and the desirability of common ground for conflict resolution.

There is also my own content analysis (White, 1949) of the values in various ideologies (American, Nazi, and Communist) using the value-analysis technique (White, 1951), a project carried a good deal further recently by William Eckhardt. The main upshot of that analysis was that there has apparently been a convergence of the value systems of the Communist East and the non-Communist West. From a study of opinion and attitude surveys in a number of non-Communist countries, and of behavioral data and political speeches and writings on both sides of the East-West conflict, a picture emerged of a good deal more common ground, shared by us and the Communists, than the embattled partisans on either side have ever recognized. Neither they nor we depart very far from the most commonly held political philosophy—I call it the "modal philosophy"—which with minor variations seems to characterize most of the politically conscious people in the world (White, 1957). (It is the great piling

---

[2] For a fuller statement of this and related problems, see White, 1967–68.

up of people in the middle zone, a very large "mode" in the statistical sense of the word "mode," that justifies the term "modal philosophy.")

It includes three main elements: first, a preference for private ownership and free enterprise in at least the smaller economic units, the grocery store, the laundry, the repair shop, the small farm. In that respect the global majority seems to lean more toward our American way of life than toward that of the thorough-going Socialists or Communists. A second element, though, is a strong emphasis on social welfare—helping the poor. In that respect the modal philosophy is more like communism. And, third, there is a belief in political democracy, including free speech. Most of the people in the global majority reject dictatorship, and most of them reject the word "communism" because to them it implies dictatorship, while they more or less accept the term "socialism," which to them implies democracy. In fact, the term "democratic socialism" probably comes closer than any other single term to representing what this modal philosophy is. This pattern of values and beliefs, or some not-very-wide variation from it, constitutes the great common ground that liberal Americans share not only with millions of people who call themselves Communists but also with an actual majority of the politically conscious members of the human race.

Mirror-Image Wars and Territorial Self-Images

A second not-so-obvious proposition is that *the mirror-image type of war is most likely to break out where there is overlapping and conflict of territorial self-images.*

There are two kinds of wars. There is the mirror-image war in which each side really believes that the other side is the aggressor. And there is the non-mirror-image war in which one side really believes that the other side is the aggressor, while the other side, though feeling justified, does not really literally believe that it is the victim of aggression.

An example of a mirror-image war would be World War I. A great many Americans do not realize how well Bronfenbrenner's term, the "mirror-image," applies to what happened in 1914. A great many still picture that war as a case of outright German aggression, comparable to Hitler's aggression in 1939. The historical facts, as we know them now, do not support that belief. The Germans believed, with some factual justification, that they were the victims of aggression. They pictured Russia, France, and England as ganging up on them and felt that unless they struck first they would be overwhelmed by enemies on two fronts. North and Holsti, with their content analysis of the documents of 1914, have confirmed what historians such as Fay and Gooch had already shown, that when the war actually broke out the Germans were motivated mainly by fear.

Another mirror-image war is the Vietnam war. The militants on each side clearly believe that the other side is the aggressor. The North Vietnamese see the United States as aggressing against the soil of their homeland, and, in mirror-image fashion, militant Americans see the North Vietnamese as aggressing against South Vietnam, both by a campaign of assassination in the villages and, now, by actual troops invading the South.

There is a supreme irony in this mirror-image type of war. It seems utterly ridiculous that *both* sides should be fighting because of real fear, imagining the enemy to be a brutal, arrogant aggressor when actually the enemy is nerving himself to fight a war that he too thinks is in self-defense. Each side is fighting, with desperate earnestness, an imagined enemy, a bogey man, a windmill. But you cannot laugh at this kind of joke. It is too bloody, too tragic. You can only stand aghast and ask: How is it possible, psychologically, for one country, or perhaps both, to be *that* much deluded?

Then there is the other kind of war, a non-mirror-image war. Any conflict regarded by neutral onlookers as outright aggression is a case in point, Hitler's attack on Poland, for instance. He must have known, and other Germans must have known, that Poland was not attacking or threatening to attack Germany. Whatever their other justifications may have been, in this respect the German perception of the war was not a mirror image of the perception in the minds of Germany's victims.

Since most people probably assume that the Hitler type of outright aggression is the typical way for wars to start, I did a rough check to see whether that is actually true by looking at 37 wars that have occurred since 1913 and putting each of them, to the best of my ability, in one category or the other. The result was surprisingly even; 21 of the 37 wars (a little more than half) were in my judgment the mirror-image type, and 16 (a little less than half) were the non-mirror-image type. The method was rough, but it does seem clear that mirror-image wars, such as World War I and the Vietnam war, are not unusual exceptions. Their frequency is at least comparable with the frequency of non-mirror-image wars.

Now, what can psychology contribute to an understanding of mirror-image wars, aside from applying to them Bronfenbrenner's apt and vivid term "mirror-image"?

Actually it can contribute a number of things, several of which I have discussed in a book called *Nobody Wanted War* (White, 1968). In this paper, I want to focus on just one of them, the notion of the overlapping and conflict of territorial self-images.

It was a striking fact that most of the mirror-image wars in my list, 16 out of 21, grew out of territorial conflicts in which there was reason to think that each side *really* believed that the disputed territory was part of itself. The surface of the world is dotted with ulcerous spots that have been the source of an enormous amount of bad blood and, often, of war: Bosnia, Alsace-Lorraine, the Sudentenland, the Polish Corridor, Northern Ireland, Algeria, Israel, Kashmir, the Sino-Indian border, South Korea, Taiwan, Quemoy, South Vietnam. Every one of these ulcerous spots is a zone of overlap, where one country's territorial image of itself overlaps with another country's territorial image of *it*self.

The historians and political scientists are in general quite aware of this as a cause of war, and, under labels such as "irredentism," or simply "territorial disputes," they have given it a fair amount of emphasis. But I do not think they have given it nearly enough emphasis, and, as far as I know, they have never suggested an adequate psychological explanation of it. Their favorite formula, the international struggle for power, does not adequately cover it, because what needs to be explained is the special emotional intensity of the desire for power over a certain piece of territory when that territory is perceived as part of the national *self*, even though it may make little contribution to the overall power of the nation. Taiwan is a good case in point. The Chinese Communists seem fanatically intent on driving the invaders out of Taiwan (the "invaders" being us and Chiang Kai-shek) even though Taiwan would add only a little to their national power.

Psychologists can offer some useful clues to an understanding of this phenomenon. One is the notion of the self-image itself, and of how, by a process of identification, the self-image comes to include many things that were not originally part of it. We use a variety of names in referring to the self-image; many would call it simply "the self," Kurt Lewin called it the "person." (His use of the term was broader, but I will not go into those complexities here.) But whatever we call it, I think most of us would agree that the concept of self-image plays a central role in psychology, and that the process of identification, by which other things come to be incorporated in the self-image, is also very important. Lewin, for instance, spoke of how a person's clothes come to be psychologically a part of the "person." If clothes are identified with to such an extent that they seem to be part of the person, or part of the "self," then surely the territory that represents one's own nation on the map can also be part of it.

Another clue is the analogy with the territorial fighting of animals. Lorenz, Ardrey, Carpenter, and others have described how an animal will spring to the defense of territory that it has identified with and that it seems to regard as its own. Now, of course, we need to be on our guard against overly hasty parallels between animal behavior and complex human behavior such as war making, but at this point the parallel seems valid since the mechanism of identification is involved in both. In both cases, too, there is emotional disturbance when strangers —alien, unpredictable, presumably hostile strangers—are seen as impinging on land that is regarded as one's own and therefore as part of the self.

Still another clue lies in the notion of intolerance of ambiguity. What calls for explanation, you remember, is the rigidity of overlapping territorial claims, usually on both sides, and the special emotional intensity of those claims. Usually each side refuses to grant for one moment that there could be a particle of validity in the other side's claim. There is a cleancutness, a simplicity, an all-or-none quality in these territorial perceptions that is clearly a gross oversimplification of the complexity of reality. In each side's world that land just *is* its own; that is all there is to it.

As an example let us take Dean Rusk and his perception of what land belongs to whom in Vietnam. Of course Rusk did not see South Vietnam as belonging to America, but he did apparently see it as self-evidently part of something called the "free world," and he did assume an American responsibility to resist any Communist encroachment on the free world. If he had not seen the problem in these simplistic terms, he would hardly have kept coming back, as he did, to the simple proposition that the Communists have to be taught to "let their neighbors alone." To him it apparently seemed self-evident that South Vietnam was a "neighbor" of North Vietnam rather than, as the Communists apparently perceive it, a part of the very body of an independent nation called "Vietnam," into which

American invaders have been arrogantly intruding. To Rusk the notion that American troops might honestly be regarded by anyone as invaders was apparently an intensely dissonant thought and therefore unthinkable.

South Vietnam, I think, is almost a classical case of an area in which territorial self-images overlap and in which, therefore, each side honestly feels that it *must* expel the alien intruders. On both sides ideology is to a large extent rationalization; the underlying psychological factor is pride—the virile self-image—defined as having the courage to defend one's "own" land when foreigners are perceived as attacking it. In a sense you could also say that fear is a fundamental emotion in wars of this type, but it is important to recognize that this fear is mobilized by cognitive distortion, by the mistaken assumption that the land in dispute is self-evidently one's own, and that therefore anyone else who has the effrontery to exist on that land, with a gun in his hand, must be a diabolical alien "aggressor." Neither fear nor pride would be intensely mobilized—as both of them are—if it were not for this cognitive distortion. Each side feels that its manhood is at stake in whether it has the courage and toughness to see to it that every last one of those intruders is thrown out of *its* territory. To Ho Chi Minh this proposition was apparently as self-evident and elemental as the mirror image of it was to Dean Rusk. Neither one of them, apparently, could tolerate overlapping, and, therefore, ambiguous, territorial images. Frenkel-Brunwik would probably say that neither could tolerate ambiguity. We have, then, in the concept of intolerance of ambiguity another clue to an understanding of why it is that territorial claims have such rigidity and emotional intensity. And we have the implication that pulling apart these overlapping images—clarifying boundaries and getting agreement on them—is one of the things that most needs to be done if we want peace.

The "Pro-Us Illusion"

A third not-so-obvious proposition is that *there is a tendency to see the people in another country as more friendly to one's own side than they actually are*. Let us call this the pro-us illusion. It is a form of wishful thinking, obviously, but like various other forms of wishful thinking, it is seldom recognized as such by those who indulge in it.

One major example of it would be the long-lasting, hard-dying delusion of many Americans that most of the people in the Soviet Union are against their present rulers and on the American side in the East-West conflict. From 1917, when the Communists first came to power, until perhaps the middle 1950s, this was a very widespread belief in the United States, and it contributed much to the rigidity of the anti-Communist policy of American policy makers such as John Foster Dulles. The Harvard research by Bauer, Inkeles, Kluckhohn, Hanfmann, and others did a lot to put an end to this delusion, but it lingers on in some quarters. Not so very long ago a prominent United States senator declared that the Soviet Union is "seething with discontent and hostility to its present rulers."

Another example was the belief of many Americans, at the time of our Bay of Pigs adventure, that most of the Cuban people were intensely hostile to Castro in the same way we were, and perhaps ready to rise up against him. It is hard to tell just what was in the minds of our policy makers at that time, but it looks as if they thought there would be some kind of uprising if we could just provide the spark to ignite it. The sad thing is that they could have known better. They had easy access to the research of Lloyd Free, a good, solid piece of public-opinion survey work indicating that most of the Cuban people, less than a year earlier, were quite favorable to Castro (Cantril, 1968). But Free's evidence was ignored. According to Roger Hilsman (1968), the policy makers just did not try to find out what real evidence existed on the attitudes of the Cuban people. They made no genuine effort to get evidence that was free from obvious bias. (The testimony of refugees in Miami, which they apparently did get, was obviously biased.) That much seems clear; their curiosity was inhibited. As to the reasons for their inhibition of curiosity, one can speculate along various lines. Perhaps it was a defense against dissonance; Festinger might say that they were embarked on an enterprise, and any doubts about the wisdom of that enterprise would have been cognitively dissonant. Or perhaps it was a defense of their black-and-white picture; they may have sensed that the information they did not inquire into would have impaired their all-black image of Castro's diabolical tyranny over the Cuban people and their all-white image of themselves as liberating the Cuban people from a diabolical tyrant. In any case, it looks as if they shut their eyes because they were unconsciously or half-consciously afraid of what they might see. They cherished too fondly the pro-us illusion—and we know the fiasco that resulted.

Now, more disastrously, there is the case of Vietnam. There, too, we more or less kidded ourselves into believing that the people were on our side. In some ways it is very much like the case of Cuba. In both cases there has been a great overestimation of the extent to which the people were pro-us, and consequently a gross overestimate of the possibility of achieving a quick military victory. In both cases, too, there has been a striking lack of interest, on the part of top policy-making officials, in the best evidence that social and political science could provide.

The irony is increased by our solemn official dedication to the great objective of enabling the people of South Vietnam to determine their own destiny. President Johnson, McNamara, Rusk, and others continually talked about helping "the Vietnamese" to defend themselves against the Vietcong and invaders from the North—as if the Vietcong were not Vietnamese, and as if it were self-evident that most of "the Vietnamese" were gallantly resisting these attacks from within and without, and eager for our help in doing so.

Actually that was always far from self-evident. Some of you may have read my long article, "Misperception and the Vietnam War," nearly three years ago in the *Journal of Social Issues* (White, 1966). If so, you may remember the 25 pages of the article that were devoted to a rather intensive effort to cover the evidence on both sides of that question and to find out how the people of South Vietnam really felt about the war. The upshot of that analysis was pessimistic; I estimated that probably there were at that time more South Vietnamese leaning in the Vietcong direction than leaning in our direction.

Since then I have revised and updated the analysis on the basis of three more years of accumulating evidence. The new information includes all that I was able to glean during two months on the spot in Vietnam, where I had an unusual opportunity to interview well-informed Vietnamese. It includes the CBS-ORC opinion survey, in which more than 1,500 South Vietnamese respondents were interviewed, the writings of Douglas Pike, the outstanding authority on the Vietcong, and a good deal of other miscellaneous evidence. None of this information is conclusive. For instance, the CBS survey obviously never solved the problem of getting peasants to speak frankly with middle class, city-bred interviewers. But by putting together all of the various sorts of information, which is what I did in my book *Nobody Wanted War* (pp. 29–84), we can, I think, make some fairly educated guesses.

The general upshot of the revised analysis differed from the earlier one chiefly in giving a good deal more emphasis to sheer indifference on the part of a great many of the South Vietnamese. It looks as if a large majority are now so disillusioned with both sides that their main preoccupations are simply with their efforts to survive and with a fervent hope that peace will come soon, regardless of which side wins. It is a "plague on both your houses" attitude. But the results of the earlier analysis did seem to be confirmed in that it still looks as if, among those who do care intensely about which side wins, the Vietcong have the edge. My own very rough and tentative estimates, representing the situation in 1967, were these: Something like 20% were really dedicated on the side of the Vietcong, about 10% were equally dedicated on the anti-Vietcong side, and the remainder, approximately 70%, were relatively indifferent. Since in any political conflict the people who count are the people who care, what matters here is the estimate that, among those who *are* dedicated to one side or the other, more are against the position of the United States than for it. The upshot still seems to be that the psychological balance tips *against* the Saigon government and the intervening Americans. That is probably true even now, in 1969, and in previous years it was apparently much more true. For instance, my estimate is that in early 1965, when we first became very heavily involved, it was more like 40 to 10, not 20 to 10, in favor of the Vietcong.

Suppose our policy makers had known that, and had known it clearly, at the time they were making those fateful commitments and staking American prestige on the outcome. Suppose that in 1962 when John Kennedy made his major commitment, or in 1965 when Johnson made his, they had said to themselves: "Of course we know that if we fight in Vietnam we will be supporting a small minority against a much larger minority." Would they have done it? Would we now have all the tragedy of the Vietnam war? All the blood, all the guilt, all the moral ignominy in the eyes of most of the rest of the world, all the sensitive, intelligent young people here at home estranged from their own country? I doubt it. The American superego, *if* well informed, is too genuinely on the side of national self-determination, too genuinely against any clear, naked form of American domination over little countries on the other side of the world, even in the name of anti-communism. If Kennedy and Johnson had clearly realized that the attitudes of the South Vietnamese people at that time were much more anti-us than pro-us, would this whole Vietnam mess have been avoided? I think so. Vietnam was avoidable, just as the Bay of Pigs was avoidable. The one essential factor in avoiding both of these tragedies would have been to look hard, and honestly, at the best available evidence. Our policy makers in 1962 and 1965 did not look hard and honestly at the best available evidence; and the chief reason they did not, it seems to me, was that they were clinging to an image of America as helping a beleaguered and grateful South Vietnam—not intervening in a nasty civil war in which most of those who were emotionally involved would be against us. Like the adventurers who planned the Bay of Pigs they were not really curious, because they half knew what the answer would be if they did look honestly at the facts. They, too, shut their eyes and put their hands over their ears because they were cherishing too fondly the pro-us illusion. And we know now the disaster that resulted.

In summary, the three not-so-obvious contributions, or potential contributions, of psychology to peace are:

1. A corollary of the Hovland two-sided approach, namely, that we Americans should strenuously seek common ground with the Communists and publicly accept all we can honestly accept of the Communist point of view;

2. The proposition that the mirror-image type of war is most likely to break out when there is overlapping and conflict of territorial self-images;

3. The pro-us illusion, with the further proposition that neither the Bay of Pigs nor the Vietnam war would have occurred if we Americans had not been indulging in it.

References

Cantril, H. *The human dimension: Experiences in policy research.* New Brunswick, N. J.: Rutgers University Press, 1968.

Hilsman, R. *To move a nation.* New York: Delta, 1968.

Kelman, H. C. (Ed.) *Internationl behavior: A social-psychological analysis.* New York: Holt, Rinehart & Winston, 1965.

White, R. K. Hitler, Roosevelt and the nature of war propaganda. *Journal of Abnormal and Social Psychology,* 1949, **44,** 157–174.

White, R. K. *Value analysis: The nature and use of the method.* Glen Gardner, N. J.: Society for the Psychological Study of Social Issues, 1951.

White, R. K. The cold war and the modal philosophy. *Journal of Conflict Resolution,* 1957, **2,** 43–50.

White, R. K. Misperception and the Vietnam war, *Journal of Social Issues,* 1966, **22,** 167.

White, R. K. Communicating with Soviet Communists. *Antioch Review,* 1967–68, **27,** 467–476.

White, R. K. *Nobody wanted war: Misperception in Vietnam and other wars.* New York: Doubleday, 1968.

psychology and campus issues

Psychology and Campus Issues

The turbulence of today's campuses spills into this section about students which includes discussions of the explosive topics of violent and nonviolent disruptions, drug use, and black-white relations. In the symposium "Factors Underlying Student Unrest," we see that even convention participants did not escape the arena of protest, as the meeting itself was taken over by a group of young psychologists. Providing two different perspectives on the events leading up to the symposium takeover are the prefatory remarks by Clark, the symposium chairman, and Sawyer, a spokesman for the protestors.

The protestors' speeches follow these remarks in a transcript which, having received only minor editing, presents nearly exactly what the audience heard. It is included to convey to the reader the full context of the symposium and to present the message that these young psychologists felt was so important to communicate. As the protesting speakers indicate, they represent no particular group; but it is clear that they share the sense of impatience, discontent, and desire for change evident in so many campus disruptions. They are angry about research on student unrest which focuses on characteristics of the protestors and on superficial aspects of their institutions rather than on the issues they are protesting. It is the inequities in society which they discuss as the real sources of student unrest.

At the point where the transcript ends, about two-thirds of the audience left the charged atmosphere of the protestors' session for the relatively calm presentations by the formal symposium participants which had been rescheduled in an adjoining room. In the papers which follow the transcript, each symposium member examines the relationship of certain aspects of educational institutions to incidents of student protest. Astin reports on his survey of disruptions at United States institutions of higher education, statistically relating the type and issue of the disruption to characteristics of the institution at which each occurred. Although his data are subject to various interpretations, one that Astin offers is that schools having less concern for the individual student are more protest-prone. Peterson's data support this interpretation in the finding that colleges most concerned with undergraduate learning seldom experience protests. Peterson's data further indicate that it is the factors characteristic of the large multiversity which are most strongly related to incidence of protest. Heist then specifically examines the faculty's role in contributing to student discontent through such factors as impersonalized relationships with students, heavy commitments outside of teaching, and narrowness of research interests.

In closing the symposium, Smith puts into perspective both the protestors' viewpoints and the research offered by the symposium members. He takes a firm stand for recognizing the value of all kinds of evidence and the value of free inquiry. He admonishes the protestors for their objections to research of the type presented, suggesting at the same time that factors in the society at large be included in a total research effort aimed at discovering the roots of student unrest.

Nowlis, in her invited address to the Division of Developmental Psychology, focuses on another topic charged with emotion—that of student drug use. She begins by examining the terms "drug," "drug use," and "drug effects," noting how carelessly these terms tend to be used and with what misleading effects. For example, she notes that when a term such as "regular use" is clearly defined, the evidence indicates that contrary to many headlines only a very small percentage of students can be considered to be regular users of a drug such as marihuana. She goes on to look at student drug use first in the context of drug use throughout our society and then in the developmental context of the emerging adult. She calls our attention to the large number of legal drugs promoted through the mass media and widely used by adults for many of the same reasons that the young use their illegal ones, pointing out the inconsistency in society's attitudes. She closes by commenting on the extension of the period of "nonadulthood" created by our educational process, and suggests that rather than lashing out at symptoms such as drug use, we would do better to integrate these young people more fully into the society at large.

In the final paper of this section, Thomas touches a third emotion-laden topic—that of black-white relations. He discusses in particular the need for black Americans to fully accept and appreciate their blackness, pointing out how essential this is to their psychological health. He then suggests that to build such appreciation is an essential part of counseling for black students, thus highlighting the need for black counselors.

Factors Underlying Student Unrest

Editors' note: This symposium was partially disrupted by a group of young psychologists. The prefatory comments by Clark and Sawyer provide background information concerning the events of this symposium. To provide the reader with the fullest context of the events of the symposium, an edited transcript of the protestors' program is presented. Following the transcript are the originally scheduled papers of Astin, Peterson, Heist, and Smith which were delivered 45 minutes later than originally planned.

A resolution from the Council of Representatives and the Board of Directors at the 1968 APA Convention specified that there should be a theme for the 1969 meeting, the theme to be Psychology and the Problems of Society. A special committee of three persons, with Stuart Cook as chairman, was appointed as a subcommittee of the APA Convention Committee to deal with this part of the overall program. Members of the Association were invited to write to the chairman with any suggestions they might have about the program.

I was assigned the responsibility for assembling a panel to deal with the problems of student unrest on the campus. After consultation with a variety of persons in the area, plans for a program were completed in March and April of 1969. These arrangements met the usual deadlines for submission of contributions to the APA program, and led to the publication of the program in the *Convention Program*. In the middle of August, while on vacation, I received a letter suggesting that a student be added to the panel which was planned and listing the names of about 10 persons who might be considered as candidates for inclusion in that panel program. On arriving at the APA meeting, August 30, I consulted with the writer of that letter to see whether we might identify a person who could arrange to read the papers ahead of time, to meet with the members of the panel, and to provide some comments. However, this did not seem to be a critical aspect of the program, since the intent from the beginning had been to provide at least one hour in which a large number of persons might comment, critically or otherwise, on the content of the papers. It seemed clear to all of the participants in the panel that the work being reported was only a small beginning of the work that ought to be done in this area and that this particular program was intended to stimulate members of the American Psychological Association to bend more efforts toward the study of matters relating to student unrest on our college campuses.

The planned program did not develop as scheduled because at the time of the beginning of the meeting the platform was occupied by a number of young psychologists wearing red armbands who announced that they planned to take over the meeting. As chairman of the session, I discussed the intentions of the disrupters with their chairman and proposed a number of alternatives. These alternatives would have involved the participation of some members of that group in the program as scheduled. As is evident from the remarks made by members of that group in later parts of this report, they felt that the planning of the schedule was improper, and they were not willing to use the usual procedures of APA for scheduling a meeting of their own, preferring to take over the very large audience that would be attracted to this particular session. They also were unwilling to play any role in the session unless they themselves were in charge of the session and determined precisely how matters would proceed. Their chairman indicated that they had a planned program and that they intended to occupy the platform and use the auditorium during the period for which the regular symposium was scheduled.

I then announced to the audience that the persons on the platform were unwilling to vacate the platform and suggested to the audience that they might profit by staying for 45 minutes to hear at least the first part of the program planned by the group. I also announced that at the end of 45 minutes the regularly scheduled symposium would take place in an adjoining ballroom. At the end of the 45 minutes the announcement was repeated and a substantial portion of the audience moved to the next room to hear the regularly scheduled program.

KENNETH E. CLARK
Symposium Chairman

The chairman is Dean of the College of Arts and Sciences and a professor of psychology at the University of Rochester. He received his BS and PhD from Ohio State University. He is currently the editor of the *Journal of Applied Psychology*.

Establishing the Right to Be Heard: The Development of a Program Takeover[1]

JACK SAWYER

The author received his PhD in 1955 from Purdue University and was a postdoctoral fellow in mathematical statistics at the University of Chicago. He is presently an associate professor of psychology and sociology at Northwestern University, where his major interests involve social conflict and social change.

At a "radical caucus" held Sunday evening, August 31, 1969, and attended by some 200 persons, many suggestions were made for both long-range programs and more immediate activities that would highlight and enhance the possibility for psychology to work actively toward the solution of human problems. Strong dissatisfaction was expressed with the generally unrecognized tendency for the implicit values of psychology to greatly favor the status quo. This was felt to be glaringly so in the orientation of the convention theme sessions on "Psychology and the Problems of Society." The Monday morning theme session particularly epitomized the bias by looking for "Factors Underlying Student Unrest" in the personalities of the protestors rather than in the conditions of society. It was considered important not to let the myth that such research is value free go completely unquestioned. At least once in the official APA program, this prevailing doctrine should be openly challenged.

The session on student unrest was convention-wide, preempting on the presumed behalf of all psychologists, any other programs at that time. It seemed particularly audacious to study a group of which many young psychologists were a part, yet to exclude their viewpoint from the panel. The earlier suggestions of another group—Psychologists for Social Action—for speakers with less status-quo orientation had already been ignored. A separate session by the radical caucus at some time and place APA might possibly be willing to provide could hardly counteract the misimpression of value-free solidarity the plenary session would give. Many of the psychologists who attended this session would continue to be unaware of how deeply immoral significant numbers of their colleagues felt such research to be and of their reasons for feeling this way. The presentation of a replacement program was intended to inject a corrective into at least this one session—to make

---

[1] At the request of the editors of this volume, I have obtained the approval of the speakers to have their material appear in a transcript of their session and have written this introduction to attempt to convey how the replacement program came into being.

patent the implicit bias of such research, and to put forth the real "factors underlying student unrest." At the same time, it would generally assert the right to be heard of other voices other than those in accord with the established values.

At the Monday morning session, a number of representatives presented themselves on the platform and indicated their intention to present a replacement program. Other persons distributed to the audience an explanation of their position ("Research . . . or Cool Out?"). At this point, the chairman of the originally scheduled session promptly took up the previously ignored suggestion and offered to permit some of the protestors to speak within the framework of the scheduled session. He also threatened to turn off the microphone if the protestors did not accept this and went ahead with their plans to present a program. The moderator of the replacement session made this threat public to the audience and indicated the intention of the protestors to proceed. The microphone was then left on, but the original chairman intervened to propose that the audience express its preference to stay to hear the protestors or leave to hear the original papers elsewhere. Strong audience reaction followed, and the chairman dropped the proposal for an immediate move and suggested instead that the protestors be heard for at least half an hour. Applause followed, and he set the presentation of the planned papers for 45 minutes later.

Thus the broadening of the program was steadfastly resisted at every step, starting with the written suggestion in advance of the convention. It was eventually achieved only through the presence of persistence of persons willing to brave censure by confronting established and biased procedure. Yet in the end, the program so recently eschewed was embraced by the original chairman, and he told the audience, "I would like to encourage you to remain for at least half an hour, because I believe that you do need to hear from representatives of the oppressed student groups." Thus after the replacement program appeared inevitable, it was suddenly proclaimed desirable and given the chairman's sanction, thereby reestablishing official control over the platform. Nonetheless, it is clear that this program modification would not have occurred in the absence of the protest. APA, like other institutions, modified its behavior only with the continued application of pressure.[2]

After it had been generally established that the replacement program was going ahead, the new moderator, Larry Rabinowitz, called me from the audience and I gave a history and rationale supporting the right of these dissenting views to be heard. Remarks by Geri Steiner, Bert Garskof, and Howard Gadlin then presented the main message of the replacement program. These presentations were essentially spontaneous, since only the evening before—the first day of the convention—had people been able to meet to express the widespread dissatisfaction

---

[2] How to minimize the effect of dissent on the normal operation of conventions has been of general concern to professional associations, as illustrated by a lead article of *Association Management* (Charles Louis Schafer, "What to Do about Convention Protesters?" October 1969, 21(10), 30–37, 65). The article is concerned mainly with smooth-running conventions, and does not comment upon the legitimacy of the grievances (being similar in this lack to the study of student unrest). A more thorough analysis of recent convention protests (including an accurate description of action at the APA) appears in *The Chronicle of Higher Education,* 1969, 3(22).

and to discuss courses of action. Following the main presentations, reactions were volunteered by Howard Gruber and Barbara Pliskow.

Then the original chairman intervened to announce the presentation of the scheduled papers, and about half the audience left. After a few more brief remarks, persons divided into small groups. Lively discussion extended far past the scheduled ending time on such topics as the psychology of social change, student rights, psychology and the military, rights of patients and subjects, and the content of a radical psychology.

In preparing this section, transcripts of the speeches were submitted to the speakers, but to aid in preserving the flavor of the moment, the speeches are printed here with only minor stylistic editing.[3] Of course, these brief remarks do not pretend to present the serious analysis of the relations of psychology and politics that is warranted and would have been more nearly possible in scheduled presentations. The speakers have agreed to the inclusion of these incompletely formulated remarks because they feel that it is desirable to begin to establish a forum where persons whose psychology includes political views contrary to the official ones can be heard.

---

[3] Thanks are due to two members of the audience who happened to be tape-recording this session and kindly made their tapes available for transcription: Kurt Konietzko, Institute of Rational Living, Philadelphia, and Victor Jackson, West Side Veterans Administration Hospital, Chicago.

Transcript of the Protestors' Session[1]

[*Editors' note*: Prior to their formal speeches the protestors handed out a sheet entitled "Research . . . or Cool-out" which follows.]

Research . . . or Cool-out?

1. What's happening right now at this meeting and how did it come about?
2. What are the implications of the ACE study of student protest?
3. How long will you tolerate the duplicity of research which serves to maintain intolerable social conditions?

The American Psychological Association nods its head at social problem-solving by presenting these token two-hour didactic sessions, conducted by persons whose commitment to social change is not clear. This meeting which you are attending its particularly offensive to us; it will present for your evaluation research destined to detect, control, and neutralize the growth of radical beliefs among American youth—a nascent Early Warning System for administrators.

This activity must not continue under the guise of effective attention to social problems. We as members of APA and as participants in this convention feel compelled to clarify the disastrous potential of the dynamics behind this kind of symposium and the research it represents.

The very composition of this panel indicates that something has gone wrong: to discuss STUDENT unrest, students are notably underrepresented. The one student on the panel was notified of his participation only a day ago. Psychologists for Social Action submitted a list of names of persons who could sensitively discuss the issues of student unrest. None of those suggested are present on this panel. We regret that you are being denied an essential perspective, and we are deeply disturbed by the illusion of full information created.

One of the panelists will be describing research studies conducted in the last four years by the ACE, using assessment devices to identify those students most likely to become radically involved. While we are concerned about oppressive governmental agencies utilizing this research to screen out prospective radical students from universities, we are more deeply worried about the possibility that these same agencies may use this data to blunt the thrust of the entire radical movement via allegedly "neutral" selection procedures. Although, in correspondence with the National Student Association, Dr. Astin defends this study on the grounds that 1) objective scientific inquiry is not dangerous, 2) that his subjects' anonymity is protected, and 3) that the study is "relevant" to a social problem, all three defenses are of questionable validity. Furthermore, any outcry regarding this by psychologists is discouraged by Dr. Astin's statement that making public the controversial nature of the study would contaminate his sample, in causing college students to think twice before filling out his questionnaires.

How truly objective can this study be if a board supervising this ACE study has publicly stated:

"There has developed among some of the young a cult of irrationality and incivility

---

[1] *Editors' note*: To most fully convey the flavor of the protestors' session, audience reactions are indicated. However, the proportion of the audience reacting in the manner indicated is not mentioned and may vary from a small minority to a sizable majority.

which severely strains attempts to maintain sensible and decent human communication . . . Disruption and violence have no part on any campus."
(*Science,* 11 July 1969, p. 161.)

Dr. Astin stresses that the research division and its studies are independent of control by policy statements of their boards of directors . . . BUT WE WONDER. Ken Kenniston wonders too, suggesting that these "guidelines" will not prevent misuse of the data—they will merely absolve committee members of guilt. The objectivity of the study is even further threatened by the fact that, through Dr. Rubenstein, a member of this panel, the study has funding from NIMH ($114,000) and from the Office of Education ($35,000).

Dr. Astin's own understanding of the movement seems dubious, in addition, in the light of his statements in earlier research on aggression, in which he equated food fights and panty raids with Vietnam protests.
—distributed by vigilant and concerned members of APA

Larry Rabinowitz:

It is a pleasure to welcome you to today's program entitled "Factors Underlying Student Unrest." I would only like to announce that the participants of the program have been changed to be more in line with the title.

We have been informed that if we go ahead with our plans the microphone will be turned off. It is our position that the program as scheduled, under the listed title, is an illegitimate program. (Booing.) I think if you want to find out about why people who experience social injustice, or who claim to experience social injustice, are unhappy and what causes them to protest, then you had better talk to the victims of social injustice rather than to the oppressors of these people. (Applause.) We see the program or at least I see the program—because we are not a group of any organized sort—as analogous to a program that might have been scheduled in 1944 Germany where German psychologists, working for the Establishment, were invited to speak on factors underlying prisoner unrest in concentration camps. That is a very immoral thing to do. (Applause, booing.) Having been advised that if we continue the mikes will be turned off, I can only say that we *plan* to continue and I would like to introduce Jack Sawyer. (Applause.)

Kenneth E. Clark:

May I inquire of the audience whether you would prefer to remain and listen to this, or whether you would rather move to the next auditorium where you can hear the prepared speakers. You have your option. (Shouting.)

I would like to encourage you to remain for at least half an hour, because I believe that you do need to hear from representatives of the oppressed student groups. (Applause.) I would like, however, to inform you that the planned papers that are prepared to be presented will be presented about 45 minutes hence in the ballroom immediately behind me. Thank you. (Applause.)

Jack Sawyer:

My name is Jack Sawyer. I'm at Northwestern University, and I am national co-chairman of Psychologists for Social Action, though I speak here purely as an individual. I am pleased to be offered the opportunity to speak because I would like to say that the persons who have made themselves a part of this program, without being asked, have both the right to be heard and a contribution that will bring the program more in line with its purported purpose.

Let me say why. The theme of the convention—"Psychology and the Problems of Society"—was adopted a year ago by suggestion of Psychologists for Social Action and through the goodwill of persons like John Lacey, the convention manager. APA has responded significantly. It has devoted two hours of each day solely to these morning symposia. But the result has been disappointing—in the elitist way in which the program was formulated, in the restricted, establishment-oriented content of the program, and in its nonparticipatory format.

After making the time commitment—which I believe indicated a sincere effort to deal seriously with the theme—APA's effort went awry. It went awry because it was carried out as a top down, imposed solution by a leadership that does not represent its constituency and does not know their needs. The way to facilitate persons being socially responsible is not to tell them what to do. It is to involve individuals themselves, directly. (Applause.)

It was only after the repeated suggestion of Psychologists for Social Action that any provision for member participation was made. It then involved one hour of discussion after two hours of lecture—two hours for four or five persons to tell you how it is and one hour for 5,000 persons to explore their own concerns. The committee thought there might be as many as 5,000 attending these symposia, with 40 discussion groups. Yesterday there were 500, and only enough stayed for one discussion group.

Why did the committee anticipate members' interests so poorly? Because, as psychologists should know, no one can know perfectly what others are thinking and feeling—but even if they could, people must do things themselves. The APA structure cannot rightly act for psychology as a whole because it is illegitimate. It does not represent psychologists. The APA Council has 130 persons, only 11 women, 8 persons under 40, and no black persons. The new Council will have one black. Whom does such a Council represent? It surely does not represent students, and increasingly many APA members who are black, young, or female are seeing that the APA does not represent their concerns either.

With the best of will, a top down solution cannot satisfy; witness the present program. It is on student unrest, yet until a day ago it included no student. It does include, however, the director of one study that has been widely criticized for obtaining politically and legally incriminating information from students without adequate safeguards against disclosure. Such a symposium is part of the problem, not part of the solution.

Recognizing how limited the programs were, how establishment oriented, how ironically irrelevant—or repressively relevant—the programs were, PSA wrote APA. We suggested such psychologists as Bert Garskof, fired from Michigan State, where he had developed participatory programs that were popular with students but unpopular with administrators; Richard Flacks, a founder of SDS and a leading researcher on youth and social change; William Domhoff of Santa Cruz, author of *Who Rules America?* Our letter was not even answered.

Since coming to the APA Convention, however, PSA has been sought out by the committee to provide "relevant" participants, and we have helped bail it out; the one student added to this panel yesterday was contacted through PSA. Perhaps the committee doesn't know any students it could ask. (Laughter.)

Well, students and other disenfranchised psychologists are here now, on this platform. I believe they will make a contribution to this session that it would otherwise lack, that they have acted with genuineness, and that they have a legitimate right to be heard. Let us hear them. (Applause.)

Larry Rabinowitz:

I don't know what's going to happen next. We had hoped last night when we planned our program today to have someone speak on the politics of such studies as the ACE study on student unrest. Is someone prepared to speak to us? If not, I apologize. It's difficult to organize a program in about three hours.

Geri Steiner:

I am not a student any longer myself, but I've been one on and off for a fairly long time. I started out in the silent generation and I think moved along with many of the students and other groups in this country since the early fifties. I believe that this generation of students is the best educated generation of students in the United States during its entire history. I do not believe that that is a function of the public education system in this country, except insofar as they learned to read and read well, that the communications media are so widespread, and that they travel. They have learned to see the world in perspective; to see their country in a perspective of the whole world rather than the narrow context which is generally taught.

After the McCarthy era, the first big lesson which these students learned was through the civil rights movement, in which they made a very serious attempt to change attitudes toward racism. They found that there was a real contradiction: The racist mood was not eliminated by the civil rights movement. After this huge campaign to make the public aware of racism, it somehow just went on—and they looked further into the facts. They discovered a 22 billion dollars a year wage differential between black and whites in this country adding to profits. If there is an objective material factor like that inherent in the system, then it is very difficult to start by changing attitudes.

When the war in Vietnam came about, the students again discussed, read, discovered, and tried to put the war in the context of the entire international situation. They discovered again that there were contradictions between attitudes and objective interests. They found that over half the population of their country really wanted to end this war, thought it was unjust, immoral, and so forth. But the arguments about the immorality, injustices, and so forth didn't seem to hold water, because the behavior of the government didn't change.

Each of these contradictions led them to further research. What a scientist generally does, when he finds contradictory facts, is to look for alternative theoretical models. Not all of the students became social-political analysts, but some of them began to study alternative models. They found that the Marxist model explained the contradictions as no other model could. It is hardly surprising that many of them adopted it, and that when they spoke to their fellow students about it, they found a receptive audience. That is what a scientist does; he looks first for a model that fits the data. The data on poverty, racism, Vietnam, etc., were very confusing until cast into the framework of a class society.

The danger to the class on top in this society comes from the fact that many groups have found they have a common interest. It is not just the students showing unrest, and I don't think their movement should be treated in isolation. Once the Marxist class analysis was made, they understood why black people rebel, why poor people rebel, why women rebel, why workers rebel, and why all these groups were coming together and talking to each other and understanding the fact that they have common interests.

In discovering the nature of this society historically, the students found that, through the Constitution, the behavior of this country was geared to the vested interests of a small group which had the power to control the lives of the larger group. As long as a "democratic" procedure can be used to vote people into power peacefully, this is obviously in the interest of that small group. When the procedure no longer serves the interest of that small group, they will use force to maintain their position. The students studied history not taught in school; they studied our violent traditions, which include shooting down workers on strike in this country. They know that democracy is a facade of common interest over a system set up in the interest of a small class. They saw that very contradictory values are instilled in a society where one obscenity carved into a piece of furniture belonging to a dean promotes more outrage than all the bloody fire of bombing children in Vietnam. (Applause.)

Now, if a serious scientific investigation were to be conducted about the causes of student unrest, surely you would be looking at factors in the economic, political, and social structure of the country and not conducting a demographic and statistical survey of what kinds of actions in occupying buildings or taking deans captive are correlated with what kind of school and family background, etc. (Applause.) This kind of study can only be used to gather information for behavioral control and containment or redirection of the student movement. (Applause.) If understanding student unrest is the goal, the students are acting in a far more scientific way about how they conduct their research than the people who are trying to contain them. (Applause.)

Bertram Garskof:

Let me try to relate student unrest to our own feelings as we attempt to be teachers and scientists. This is the kind of society that no one escapes from. I suppose even the Rockefellers are oppressed in some ways and that even they would be happier if this present system were changed. But I'm not speaking to the Rockefellers, I'm concerned with you, a group of people, many of whom see yourselves as teachers, living under this system and working at universities. We work at universities that, because of their fundamental nature, prevent us from doing much real teaching and keep us from relating to students as people —because of the caste system and because of the university's involvement in the draft, war research, racial tracking, and other symptoms of the relations between the university and other established institutions. I think that the best way in which you can relate, any of you who are teachers, to the student-youth movement is to let some of those feelings of frustration come out a little bit, come out past your carefully rationalized cynicism. Look at the feelings you have trying to be a teacher, trying to be an honest person working for the kind of institution that most of us work for, feeling that you could do more, feeling that you could reach students but never quite doing it and never quite understanding why the best of them protest their lot.

We, too, as teachers, are oppressed by this system. We too would be freer, freer to teach, to be whole people, more fulfilled if we could gain the demands and make the changes being raised by the students. We are, in truth, among the victims of this society. If you have some of these students in your class, listen to them as they explain the functional relationship between the structure and content of your classes and the production of the kinds of citizens needed for this kind of society—the kinds of personalities that are molded through the educational system from preschool right up, through child psychology, molded to fit the manpower needs of industrial capitalism. If you begin to see your classroom in this light, then you will come to realize that you need the victory of the protestors to fulfill your own lives. (From the audience: Garbage!) I will be glad to talk to anyone who thinks that's garbage afterwards. We'll break up soon into small groups.

Now, let us talk about our other role, that of researcher. Are we free or are we victims? We are free to get grants like the ones being sold here. In case people aren't hip to what I just implied, what is being peddled here at this meeting is a pipeline to big research money to do the kind of research that was going to be presented here. (Applause.) We are free to do studies psychologicalizing the activists' backgrounds, trying to say that they became activists because they hate their father, because of something that happened when they were kids, or because of their ethnic background. We are free to do more studies like Astin's.

Astin challenged me; he said that I didn't know what was in his study. Well I haven't read his report but I am willing to bet that the study does not include analysis of the corporate holdings of the trustees of Columbia University. (Applause.) In fact Astin's questionnaire asked only a few superficial questions about the nature of the institutions at which protests occurred: like whether they were publicly or privately funded and whether they were denominational or not—nowhere near as detailed a set of questions as that asked about the protestors themselves and their associates. There was little interest in the nature of the institutions; the reason for the protests was to be found within the psyches of the demonstrators. The political bias of such work is clear. People in the audience who like might get together afterwards to develop a parallel grant proposal to study the nature of the institutions, including corporate interconnections, war research, the tracking system, etc. It might be fun to work up such a proposal and submit it to NIMH. (Applause.)

In the meantime, as researchers in a society in crisis, in a society which increasingly coerces its people to continue to support the privileges of the few, we, as psychologists, supposedly interested in people and their betterment, have no pipelines to funds and no training or perceptions to facilitate research which really serves the needs of the peoples of the world as they strive to throw off the oppressions of the American system. In that very real sense, as researchers, we are oppressed, unfree in this same system. This is a subtle point and all too often we are misled in this matter by our perceptions of our seeming freedom to do any research we wish. What we wish is in itself unfree.

All I'm trying to say here is that your lives are involved, too. You are not neutral observers. No one is neutral at this moment or really any time. You are not neutral scientists. You are scientists with a built-in bias. For example, Division 3 [the Division of Experimental Psychology] voted against anything of a political nature occurring at APA. But they do not think of Astin's work or military psychology as political. So there is a bias in the perception of what is neutral and what is inappropriately political. There is politics in APA and we want to bring it out to the surface. (Applause.) This symposium as it was scheduled was goddamn political on a particular issue, student protest. The panel's politics is where psychology presumably stands. Now, people in the world are saying it is time to stand up and say where you are at. There was a guy up on stage before who said, "I am in sympathy with what you protestors are doing but I am going to get off the stage." [*Editors' note*: This remark occurred in discussions among protestors on the platform before opening addresses and hence is not included in this transcript. The speaker elaborates on his remark below.] OK. Well, I've heard that a long time from a lot of people on the campuses, from a lot of professors about the war, etc., and there is no more time. We entitled our initial leaflet yesterday, "No Hiding Place Down Here." I think that this is the message I'll leave you with: There is no hiding place anymore for the kind of politics Astin and these other folks were going to run through. No hiding place anymore. We will find them anyplace they are.

Now I think that rather than going on in a large group—and your acquiescence is amazing, by the way (laughter)—it would be good if in some way we break down—those interested—into smaller groups to continue this discussion, if that's what the audience wants. . . . Someone has suggested questions from the floor first, then breaking down into small groups. . . . Is that OK? (Applause.) Could we have the side mikes turned on, please?

From the audience: I have a question from the floor: What do you mean that teachers are oppressed?

From the audience: What do you have to do with the CIA, buddy?

Garskof: Is there another question? (Laughter.)

From the audience: Answer that one.

Garskof: I tried to already. I'm sorry that you did not catch on.

Howard Gruber:

If you turn the side mikes on, I would like the floor. If not I'll manage without them. I am the person who was referred to who was in sympathy with what the students were doing but did not want to be on the platform.

My name is Howard Gruber. I am professor of psychology at Rutgers University and I, too, am co-chairman of Psychologists for Social Action. PSA is a group of academic psychologists, clinical psychologists, all sorts of psychologists, including a large number of students, and we are a group that entertains disagreement within its ranks. There *is* disagreement within our ranks. Jack Sawyer and I, the co-chairmen of the organization, both agree, and we have agreed for some time, with the criticisms that you have heard of the official APA plan for today's session and other symposia on social problems: that they were planned from the top down, that they do not reflect a genuine concern for social activism, that they are unrepresentative, and that a panel yesterday concerned essentially with the problems of black people had no black people on the program. Today's panel, concerned with student activism, originally had no students on the program. (Applause.) I am asked to get up to the front mike. Am I permitted? (Applause. Gruber goes to the platform.)

Garskof: I think it would be in the spirit of what we are trying to do if . . .
From the audience: Let him speak. (Shouting.)

Gruber: There are many forms of student and faculty and adult activism. I believe that the best response that the—I don't know if we should call ourselves adults—the somewhat older members of the dissenting community can make to the younger members is to develop forms of responsible protest. As I have said, I have very great sympathy for what the students have done today. On the other hand, I am mulling over whether I think that the form they adopted—disrupting someone else's meeting rather than planning their own—is the right form. (Applause.) I do want to point to another form that is possible. It's one that requires the intimate collaboration of young and old, of student and faculty. (Applause.)

On October 15 there will be a nationwide anti-Vietnam war Moratorium calling for the immediate cessation of this detestable war. (Applause.) That Moratorium—in other words an academic strike, one day in October—will probably increase in magnitude as time goes on, if necessary. That Moratorium is a continuation of the type of activity begun last March 4th by a group of radical student activists who were graduate students at MIT.

If psychologists want to participate in helping to plan their roles in this Moratorium, Psychologists for Social Action has planned a mechanism by which you may do so. Today at 5:15 p.m. in the Washington Hilton, Room 7157, or the Sheraton Park Hotel, Room C640, I will be chairing one Peace Action Workshop and Fred Wright of Atlanta will be chairing the other one. At that time, we will be planning work for the Wednesday Walk-for-Peace in which psychologists from this convention are invited to walk with us to the White House to protest against the war in Vietnam and demand the reordering of American priorities for health, education, and welfare. You can participate in planning for that walk and for its success, and you can help to plan participation in the October 15th Moratorium. Thank you. (Applause.)

Geri Steiner:

I would like to say a few words on responsible protest. If I may be permitted a quotation from Chairman Mao, "The tree would prefer calm, but the wind will not subside." (Booing.)

It is a fact that revolution is not historically a polite situation. It is also a fact that in this country we do not have a nonviolent and polite situation. (Applause.) Ten million people (according to *The New York Times*) are living under conditions where children suffer malnutrition; 85% of the kids in some countries have worms in their bellies. (Booing.) This is not polite; this is violent. We know of even worse conditions around the world: In Brazil, half the babies don't reach one year of age; India spends a quarter of its GNP on children who don't reach productive adulthood. We know that there is a great deal of violence, that maintaining the status quo in the world each year kills more people than have all the revolutions of this century. (Applause.)

I think that all of us wish very heartily that it were possible to change this society with polite and responsible protests. We've seen over a decade of them now, and they've occurred before in our history, but they don't seem to get the result of true social change. We are going to have to expect a great deal of conflict, and many of us will have to find a great deal of courage. I don't find it easy to be up here speaking to a large audience of my colleagues, having to say things like this to them when I know that I incur their censure for it. But the situation in this country is an increasingly contradictory situation, and we are going to see increasing violence directed at student, worker, black, and women's movements, which will not be contained via sociological analyses! That is what we are going to be facing. (Applause.)

Howard Gadlin:

Again, in answer to Howard Gruber's comments: There are a couple of very fundamental misperceptions of what we are doing here—misperceptions of the movement and of what the idea behind the takeover of this meeting was, and I think they ought to be clarified. I think a part of the problem we have is that we've been too polite—we're trying not to offend. We are trying to change attitudes.

First of all, this is not a protest and it is not a part of a protest movement. Let's make that very clear. The protest movement beginning with the civil rights movement took place from the end of the fifties to the beginning of the sixties. There was an attempt to demonstrate the existence of injustice. The idea behind a protest movement is that you assume that the people to whom you are protesting are rational beings operating freely on the basis of some objective response to reality and that all you have to do is to present facts to these people, they will understand the true nature of the situation, and change their position.

That did not happen with the civil rights movement because it wasn't a matter of changing attitudes. It was a matter of changing a racist society. It did not happen with the case of the Vietnamese war. Very clearly and factually, the protest movement demonstrated what was wrong with the Vietnamese war from a variety of perspectives, most of them not radical. But there was no rational authority. We were appealing to an authority, a rational authority that did not exist. And so what has happened, as a function of these experiences, is that people have come to understand that they are dealing not with a rational authority but with a basically oppressive system. And the basis of that system is primarily its social and economic structure.

Now, with respect to attitude change, for the most part, our attempts at converting people by our political activity initially centered around the attempt to change people's attitudes. That represented the bias that could exist only in a group of middle class academicians who think that holding an idea is taking an action. Bullshit. We have learned, time and time again, that to change people's attitudes is not the way to produce social change. We have learned that actions are necessary, and that attitude change follows and rationalizes the actions that you are involved in. It is not the thing that leads people to change. (Applause.)

We don't particularly care about the attitudes—and I say this very seriously—of the people involved here. What we would hope to do, for some of you at least—the younger people, the graduate students who object to their own oppression, whose oppression is more clearly defined and who are, daily, more in touch with the sources of their oppression—is to help you identify a position and to change your behavior as a function of this.

As for the rest of you, since you function very often in the position of oppressors, and since you are in many ways privileged, you are afraid of what you have to give up. It is not a very optimistic venture to attempt to change the behavior of people who are oppressors until we can help you to come to realize in some of your own ways the areas of your oppression. An interesting kind of thing happens among psychologists and it reflects their privileged position. They come to realize, for example, many of the ways in which their oppression manifests itself in their everyday lives in terms of their interpersonal relationships, in terms of the way in which people get messed over when they try to relate to each other as human beings.

And what psychologists do, then, is to develop techniques for the people who objectively are relatively privileged to deal with the symptoms of their oppression. And so you have the development of sensitivity training which now functions so that people can go off in a corner of some room or some hotel, take off their clothes, and play touch-me-feel-me games while there are still millions of people running around the country hungry, while there are still millions of people being killed and deprived of a basic standard of living throughout the world because of the United States capitalist system. It is to this system that our movement is addressed. We are not a protest movement, we are not attempting to change attitudes. We are attempting to overthrow this system.

Barbara Pliskow:

I would like to speak. I am also a member of PSA. My name is Barbara Pliskow. What I want to talk about is why some people in the PSA find it very necessary to support this action. Some of us feel that this convention has really been a kind of model of polite oppression or what some people like to call cooptation. It seems to me that we fought so hard in San Francisco [the 1968 APA Convention was held in San Francisco] to say to our colleagues, "Look, we live in a society, let's look at it and talk about it." We've all talked about the kind of traditional research papers that have been presented in the 10 to 12 o'clock sessions [*Editors' note*: During each of the five days of the convention, a symposium was held from 10–12 a.m. on a topic related to the convention's theme "Psychology and the Problems of Society." These five symposia are included in this volume.] and also our traditional disinterest in them. I think we have to get to the point where we stop researching at people and about them and talk and listen to them at least occasionally. And the only way it seems this can be done is through this kind of disruption. I think that it is terribly important that we do not allow our protest to be coopted. (Applause.)

Kenneth E. Clark:

May I announce that the meeting of the scheduled papers will begin in about five minutes in the ballroom immediately behind. Those of you who wish to hear those papers are invited to move there. The rest of you have the option of remaining.

HOWARD GADLIN
The speaker received his PhD in experimental psychology from the University of Michigan in 1966. He is currently an assistant professor of psychology at the University of Massachusetts, and is interested in teaching and in the political and ideological functions of the social sciences.

BERTRAM E. GARSKOF
The speaker received his PhD in experimental psychology from the University of Michigan in 1963. He is an associate professor at Federal City College, Washington, D.C., where he is involved in the study of the psychology of social movements.

HOWARD E. GRUBER
The speaker received his PhD in experimental psychology in 1950 from Cornell University. He is presently a professor of psychology and Co-Director of the Institute of Cognitive Studies at Rutgers University, Newark, where his research interests include perception, thinking, and the history of science.

BARBARA PLISKOW
The speaker is a doctoral candidate in social psychology at Wayne State University, where her research interests include social movements and primate social behavior.

LARRY RABINOWITZ
The speaker completed two years of graduate work in psychology at the University of California, Los Angeles. He is presently a student at Rutgers University Law School and is interested in law in the service of revolution.

GERI STEINER
The speaker received her PhD in experimental psychology in 1969 from Dalhousie University, Halifax, Nova Scotia. She is a National Institute of Mental Health postdoctoral fellow at the American Museum of Natural History, where she is conducting research on brain function in fish.

Campus Disruption, 1968-69: An Analysis of Causal Factors

ALEXANDER W. ASTIN

The author received his PhD in psychology from the University of Maryland in 1957. He is presently Director of Research at the American Council on Education, where his major research interest involves the comparative effects of different types of college environments on a student's development.

The increasing intensity and frequency of campus unrest during the past academic year has generated great national disquietude, reflected in public statements by academicians, students, and others, as well as in several bills proposed recently in the state legislatures and the national Congress. The high level of tension and emotionality expressed by all parties concerned with campus unrest suggests that an objective appraisal of the facts of the situation is needed. The study that I shall discuss involves disruptions on the campus during the past academic year 1968–69. Its major objectives were to determine the frequency and extent of student unrest and related events during that period and to identify possible causal factors in the student body, the administrative structure of the institution, the issues of the protest, and the protest tactics.[1]

The data were collected by means of a questionnaire [2] mailed to a stratified national sample of 427 colleges and universities that have been participating in the Council's Cooperative Institutional Research Program, which is designed primarily to assess the impact of different college environments on the student's development.[3] After several follow-ups, we were able to obtain usable responses from 382 institutions, or nearly 90% of the sample originally polled. Designed to gather factual rather than subjective data, the questionnaire was concerned mainly with the incidence of protests, their mode, the issues involved, the immediate consequences, and any institutional changes which occurred during the same academic year.

The 382 responding colleges and universities were matched against the Council's master institutional file, which contains published information about

---

[1] This research was carried out in connection with a larger three-year national study of campus unrest being conducted by the American Council on Education and supported in part by a grant from the National Institute of Mental Health.

[2] Detailed tabulations of the data from this survey have been presented in an earlier report (Bayer & Astin, 1969).

[3] For a fuller description of the program, see Astin, Panos, and Creager, 1969.

the institution's administrative characteristics as well as data on its environmental attributes. In this way, it was possible to obtain complete data from a subsample of 200 institutions.

Mode of Protest

The questionnaire inquired as to whether the institution had experienced any of 14 categories of protest tactics. For purposes of analysis, we identified 6 of these tactics as both disruptive and violent and an additional 5 as nonviolent but disruptive. Although we are conducting analyses of nondisruptive and nonviolent forms of protest, this discussion focuses on protests that are either violent or disruptive. (These are listed in Table 1.) The table also gives the estimated frequency of occurrence for each type of incident in the institutional population during 1968–69. These weighted percentages are based on the Council stratification scheme for populations, which is designed to control error with respect to the type of institution, its quality, and its size.[4]

TABLE 1

Estimated Number of United States Institutions Experiencing Incidents of Violent or Disruptive Protests for the 1968-69 Academic Year

Protest incident	Institution at which incident occurred	
	N	% of population
Violent		
Burning of building by protestors	43	1.8
Breaking or wrecking of building or furnishings	80	3.4
Destruction of records, files, papers	21	0.9
Campus march, picketing, or rally with physical violence	62	2.6
One or more persons killed	8	0.3
Some persons injured	45	1.9
Total of institutions experiencing violent protests	145	6.2
Disruptive (nonviolent)		
Building or section of building occupied	275	11.7
Entrance to building barred by protestors	83	3.5
Officials held "captive" by protestors	4	1.0
Interruption of school function (e.g., class, speech, or meeting)	260	11.1
General campus strike or boycott of school function	141	6.0
Total of institutions experiencing disruptive or violent protests	524	22.4

Note.—Data have been adapted from Bayer and Astin (1969).

Note from Table 1 that a total of 22% of the institutions in the country experienced some kind of disruptive protest during the past academic year, but less than one-third of this total had violent protests. The most frequent modes of protest were the occupation of buildings and the interruption of school functions such as classes, speeches, or meetings. Of the violent modes, damage to buildings or

---

[4] For a description of the sampling design, see Creager, 1968.

furnishings and campus marches or rallies involving physical violence occurred most frequently.

By scanning the last column of percentages from Table 2, you can see that the likelihood of disruptive protests varied markedly as a function of type of institution. None of the 25 two-year private colleges, for example, experienced disruptive protest, whereas 70% of the private universities experienced such protest. Incidents involving violence were also most likely to occur at the private universities. (It should be remembered, however, that disruptive protests also include all those classified as violent.) By comparing the pairs of percentages for any one type of institution, you can get a notion of its "proneness to violence." Nearly half of the disruptive protests in the private universities, for example, involved violence, whereas this was true for less than one-fourth of the disruptive protests occurring at private, nonsectarian colleges.

TABLE 2
Incidence of Major Campus Protest Activity: 1968-69

Type of institution	Sample N	Population N	Estimated % of total population with Violent protests	Estimated % of total population with Disruptive protests
Public universities	54	244	13.1	43.0
Private universities	28	61	34.4	70.5
Four-year public colleges	44	336	8.0	21.7
Four-year private nonsectarian colleges	85	411	7.3	42.6
Four-year Protestant colleges	49	292	1.7	17.8
Four-year Roman Catholic colleges	43	234	2.6	8.5
Two-year private colleges	25	226	0.0	0.0
Two-year public colleges	54	538	4.5	10.4
Total	382	2342	6.2	22.4

Note.—Data have been adapted from Bayer and Astin (1969).

In order to get a better picture of the causal factors involved in these various protest events, we conducted an extensive series of regression analyses, using the subsample of 200 institutions for which complete data on environment, administrative characteristics, and student characteristics were available from earlier American Council on Education research.

The first set, the results of which are shown in Table 3, involved possible relationships between issues and tactics. War-related protests included protests against the Vietnam war, United States military policy elsewhere, selective service policy, ROTC, military research, and recruiting by government or industry. Student power protests included demands for changes in parietal rules, disciplinary practices, and censorship policies, and demands for greater student participation in decision making and faculty evaluation, hiring, etc. Services to students included quality of instruction, food, and physical facilities. Racial policies included protests for special educational programs for minority groups, for special admissions policies, and for the hiring of more minority group faculty members. While much finer distinctions are possible (some analyses involving more categories are currently in progress), we decided first to generate these broader groupings in order to increase the base rates of occurrence of various issues and tactics.

TABLE 3
Correlations (phi coefficients) between Protest Issues and Protest Tactics

Tactic	Protest issue			
	War related	Student power	Services to students	Racial policies
Disruption[a]	.51	.51	.31	.49
Violence	.29	.25	.13	.33
Sit-in	.44	.39	.22	.46

Note.—$N = 200$ institutions.
[a] Includes violence and sit-ins.

It should be pointed out that the phi coefficients in Table 3 are highly affected by the base rates of occurrence of each tactic and each issue. Thus, the correlations involving the use of violence are small primarily because violent protest did not happen as often as either sit-ins or general disruption. The same is true for services to students, which were the least frequent issues of protest. The patterns of correlations do, however, manifest some relationships between issues and tactics not solely attributable to base rates. Violent incidents, for example, appear to have occurred most frequently in protests involving racial policy and were least likely in the case of protests involving services to students. In the regression analyses to be discussed some of these relationships appear even more clearly.

Our next set of analyses concerned causative institutional factors. Since earlier research (Astin, 1968b) has shown that the occurrence of protest is highly dependent upon the characteristics of the students at an institution, we performed a series of stepwise regression analyses in which we first permitted all the measures of student characteristics to enter the regression analysis and then examined the partial correlations between protests and institutional characteristics.[5] The partial

TABLE 4
Partial Correlations between Protest Tactics and Institutional Characteristics, after Control for Student Input Characteristics

Institutional characteristics	Partial correlation with occurrence of:	
	Disruptive protest	Violent protest
University	.22**	.28**
Four-year college	−.19**	−.30**
Coeducational college	.25**	.16*
Technical school	−.20**	−.10
Liberal arts college	−.07	−.21**
Private, nonsectarian college	−.05	−.17*
Public college	.10	.22*
Concern for the individual student (ICA factor)	−.13	−.19

* $p < .05$.
** $p < .01$.

---

[5] The student characteristics that predicted the occurrence of disruptive or violent protests were similar to those identified in previous research: a high proportion of nonreligious and Jewish students, a low rate of conventional religious behavior, and a high degree of interest in musical and artistic activities.

correlations are shown in Table 4. Apparently, institutions that experienced more disruptive and violent protests than would be anticipated from the characteristics of their entering students tended to be universities, coeducational colleges, and public colleges. Institutions that had fewer protests than one would expect from their student inputs tended to be four-year colleges, technical schools, liberal arts colleges, and private, nonsectarian colleges and to have environments characterized by a high degree of concern for the individual student. These findings suggest that campus unrest, at least that of a disruptive or violent nature, is in part a response to a feeling that the welfare of the individual student is slighted. Another possibility is that students feel freer to engage in violent or disruptive protest if their institution manifests little interest in their individual development.

Protest Issues

Table 5 shows the partial correlations between each of the four categories of issues and various institutional characteristics after control for differential student inputs to the 200 institutions. We have included in the table all institutional characteristics that were significantly correlated with at least one of the four. The patterns of coefficients from issue to issue are almost identical, at least with respect to sign. This finding would indicate the existence of a general tendency toward "protest-proneness" at certain institutions, independent of the issue. War-related issues appear to be the best single indication of this tendency, since they are more highly correlated with institutional characteristics than are any of the other three types of issues. Paradoxically, issues concerning institutional services to students seem to be least dependent upon institutional characteristics.

The data in Table 5 indicate that protests against the Vietnam war or against other matters related to United States military policy were most likely to occur in universities, coeducational institutions, and public institutions. These same institutions tended to have environments that were incohesive. Moreover, students and faculty had little involvement in the class, students were not on warm, friendly terms with the instructor, and they were not verbally aggressive in the class. Finally, these institutions had relatively permissive policies concerning student drinking. Students in the protest-prone institutions tended to feel that there was little concern for their individual welfare but a high degree of school spirit and an emphasis on social activities. Once again, these data indicate that the emergence of protest—particularly against the Vietnam war and against racial policies—is in part a response to an environment that lacks cohesiveness (measured primarily by number of close friendships among the students) and that shows little regard for the student's welfare.

Community and Institutional Response to Protest Issues and Tactics

A topic of great interest, but one that has received very little systematic study so far, is the nature of institutional and community response to student protest. By "response," I mean both immediate response, which is often disciplinary or even legalistic in nature, and more general institutional change that may result from protest. We conducted several regression analyses to examine these relationships.

TABLE 5
Partial Correlations between Protest Issues and Institutional Characteristics, after Control for Student Input Characteristics

Institutional characteristics	Protest issue			
	War related	Student power	Racial policies	Services to students
Type of institution				
University	.32**	.24**	.20**	.18**
Four-year college	−.19**	−.16*	−.16*	−.13
Two-year college	−.14*	−.10	−.04	−.05
Men's college	−.19**	−.13	−.11	−.06
Coeducational college	.20**	.17*	.15*	.10
Liberal arts college	−.10	−.08	−.14*	−.05
Public	.19**	.05	.13	.02
ICA Factors[a]				
Cohesiveness	−.19**	−.09	−.17*	−.06
Use of the library	−.19**	−.11	−.07	.02
Involvement in the class	−.30**	−.10	−.09	−.08
Verbal aggressiveness	−.22**	−.01	.02	−.02
Extraversion of the instructor	−.18**	.00	.03	.05
Familiarity with the instructor	−.16*	−.05	−.05	−.04
Severity of policies against drinking	−.23**	−.09	−.13	−.05
Concern for the individual student	−.28**	−.12	−.09	−.12
School spirit	.23**	.09	.24**	−.01
Emphasis on social life	.18**	.04	.15*	.03
Permissiveness	.14	.11	.17*	.06

Note.—$N = 200$ institutions.
[a] Environmental factor scores from Astin (1968a).
* $p < .05$.
** $p < .01$.

In the first series, we were interested in two types of immediate response to protest behavior: "legal response" such as arrests and indictments of students by civil authorities, and "significant institutional response," which included dismissal or expulsion, suspension, probationary action, and withdrawal of financial aid from protestors. We did *not* include in this second category such relatively minor responses as reprimands.

Two somewhat different questions concerned us: First, (*a*) "what effects do tactics and issues have on legal and institutional discipline?" and (*b*) "What institutional factors are related to legal or institutional discipline, independent of tactics or issues?" Table 6 shows the independent effects of tactics and issues. What we did here was to regress the legal consequences and institutional discipline variables on student input characteristics, tactics, and issues. The values shown in the table are therefore the F ratios associated with each of these variables in the final regression equation. These F ratios are proportional to the *unique* contribution of each variable, in the sense that the residual sum of squares would be increased in proportion to a particular F ratio if that variable were removed from the final equation.

Clearly, legal consequences, that is, arrests or indictments by civil authorities, were almost entirely a response to violent tactics. The use of disruptive but nonviolent tactics, including sit-ins, had no direct relationship to arrest or indictment.

Violence was also the only one of the various tactics related to institutional discipline, although the relationship was much weaker than in the case of legal consequences.

It is somewhat curious that, whatever the tactics used, legal action was more likely to result when the protest concerned the Vietnam war or some related issue regarding United States military policy. Perhaps this finding reflects a bias on the part of civil authorities; it could also indicate that war-related protests are more apt to arouse public interest. The only other significant connection between issue and disciplinary response was that protests concerning the racial policy of the college were most likely to result in some sort of institutional discipline. Again, this finding is somewhat odd, considering that protest tactics have been statistically controlled. Several explanations can be offered. Perhaps racial protests involve levels of disruption or violence not reflected accurately in our measures. (The same argument could be made in the case of the effects of war-related issues on legal responses.) Another possibility is that institutions overreact, in terms of disciplinary procedures, when the protest involves demands for changes in racial policies. These alternative explanations provide challenging hypotheses for our future research.

TABLE 6

Effects of Protest Tactics and Protest Issues on Legal Consequences and Institutional Discipline, after Control for Student Input

Independent effect	Legal consequences (arrests/indictments)	Institutional discipline
Tactics[a]		
Disruption	− .03	1.5
Violence	44.9 **	4.2*
Sit-ins	0.0	− 1.3
Issues[a]		
War related	3.9 *	1.6
Student power	0.7	0.6
Services to students	− 2.5	− 0.2
Racial policies	1.8	12.8**
Nonresponse to previous protests	2.1	1.0

Note.—$N = 200$ institutions.

[a] F ratios are those associated with unique or independent contribution of each variable to the reduction of residual sums of squares in the final regression equation.

* $p < .05$.
** $p < .01$.

The effects of institutional characteristics on legal and institutional discipline are shown in Table 7. Again, it is important to note that, in arriving at these partial correlations, we have controlled for student inputs, tactics, and issues. Legal action was more likely to result in public institutions and in institutions located outside the western states. Officials at public institutions may be more inclined to call in the police, perhaps because of the closer connection between public institutions and civil authorities necessitated by the nature of institutional control. Whatever the explanation, the law seems to be unevenly applied in the case of protest in public versus private institutions.

Our next series of analyses dealt with substantive changes in institutional policy during the year surveyed. We developed two major categories of institutional changes, those concerning racial policies and those concerning increases in student power. The first category comprised the establishment of black studies programs or departments, the institution of special admissions programs for minority group members, and efforts to hire more black faculty. Increases in student power were defined as liberalization of parietal rules, increased student representation on existing committees or other policy bodies in the institutions, and miscellaneous other changes in institutional rules and regulations governing students. *Not* included were minor changes in institutional policy such as the formation of special study groups or ad hoc committees involving students.

Table 8 shows the independent effects of protest tactics and issues on these two types of institutional change. It is interesting to note that disruptive and violent tactics, as opposed to sit-ins, were related to changes in racial policies. The same was not true of increases in student power, which occurred independently of protest tactics. Institutions seem more willing to make concessions to black students if their tactics are extreme. Or possibly, as was suggested before, protests over racial policies involve degrees of disruption or violence not measured well enough in our crude dichotomies.

TABLE 7

Partial Correlations of Institutional Characteristics with Legal Consequences and Institutional Discipline, Independent of Student Inputs, Protest Tactics, and Protest Issues

Institutional characteristics	Partial correlation with:	
	Legal consequence (arrests/indictments)	Institutional discipline
Western region	−.16*	−.06
Public control	.27**	.05
Private, nonsectarian	−.17*	.06
ICA factors[a]		
Verbal aggressiveness	−.16*	−.11
Familiarity with the instructor	−.14*	−.09
Concern for the individual student	−.17*	.03
School spirit	.16*	.04
Cooperativeness	.07	.16*
Emphasis on athletics	.11	.17*

Note.—$N = 200$ institutions.
[a] Environmental factor scores from Astin (1968a).
* $p < .05$.
** $p < .01$.

As would be expected, changes in racial policies were directly related to protests over that issue. Of special interest here, protests in response to previous institutional handling of protest (the last item in Table 8) were also related to changes in institutional racial policies. In addition, it is important to note that protests over racial policies seem to be in competition with protests over other institutional policies. Thus, when protest is concerned with student power or institutional services to students, the institution is less likely to change its racial policies than when there are no such policies. In this case, our data indicate that protests about institutional policies other than those concerning race are a kind of diversion.

TABLE 8
Effects of Tactics and Issues on Changes in Institutional Policy

Independent effect	Type of change	
	Racial policies	Increased student power
Tactics[a]		
Disruption	3.9*	0.6
Violence	2.8	− 2.2
Sit-ins	− 3.9*	− 0.8
Issues[a]		
War related	− 2.3	2.1
Student power	− 4.8*	14.5**
Services to students	− 5.3*	5.6*
Racial policies	33.1**	0.0
Nonresponse to previous protests	8.0**	.1

[a] F ratios are those associated with unique or independent contribution of each variable to the reduction of residual sums of squares in the final regression equation.
* $p < .05$.
** $p < .01$.

Table 9 shows the partial correlations between institutional characteristics and the two types of institutional changes after control of student inputs, protest tactics, and protest issues. It appears that universities are changing their racial policies at a much slower rate than four-year colleges, considering the type and frequency of protest that they encounter. No institutional characteristic, however, was related to changes in student power, which suggests that different types of institutions are making such changes at about the same rate and in proportion to the amount of protest activity they experience. It should be clear from Table 8, however, that increases in student power were directly related to the occurrence of protest and were more likely to occur in institutions where there were such protests than in institutions where there were not.

TABLE 9
Partial Correlations of Institutional Characteristics with Changes in Institutional Policy, Independent of Student Inputs, Protest Tactics, and Protest Issues

Institutional characteristics	Type of change	
	Racial policies	Increased student power
Type of institution		
University	−.34**	.00
Four-year college	.20**	.01
Size	−.20**	−.02
Art school	.17*	.06
ICA factors[a]		
Verbal aggressiveness	.19**	−.01
Concern for the individual student	.15*	−.01
Involvement in the class	.20	−.01

[a] Environmental factor scores from Astin (1968a).
* $p < .05$.
** $p < .01$.

Although our findings show clearly that universities were more likely to experience protest than were other types of institutions and that they apparently were less responsive to such protest, some interesting alternative hypotheses were suggested by some additional analyses.

One of these analyses was based on the fact that the percentage of blacks in the student body was not related to the occurrence of protest concerning racial policies. To explore this question further, we eliminated the predominantly black colleges from our sample (no such protests had occurred at these institutions) and computed the correlation between the percentage of black students and the occurence of black protest at the predominantly white colleges. We obtained a very low correlation, indicating at best a trivial relationship.

Our findings with the universities, however, suggested a different possibility, namely, that it is not the percentage of black students that matters so much as their *absolute numbers*. Thus, given a sufficient number of black students, an institution is more likely to experience black protest than not, regardless of its size and other attributes. To explore this hypothesis, we plotted the likelihood that protests involving racial policies would occur as a function of the absolute number of blacks enrolling in the college. The results of this analysis are shown in Table 10. Note that as the absolute number of blacks enrolling in the college increases so does the likelihood of black protest. Assuming that we could develop an appropriate method for scaling the number of blacks, it should be possible to obtain a substantial correlation between these two variables. We are currently attempting to develop such metrics, which we shall then apply to cross-validation samples in order to avoid the old problem of the "foldback" design.

TABLE 10

Racial Protests in 1968-69 as a Function of Freshman Black Student Enrollment in Fall 1968

Number of blacks in Fall 1968 entering freshman class	Number of institutions [a]	Percentage of institutions experiencing protests involving racial policies during 1968–69
0–1	33	6.1
2–4	34	17.6
5–9	39	25.6
10–29	60	36.7
30 or more	19	52.6
Total	185	27.0

Note.—$N = 185$ institutions.

[a] Six predominantly black colleges have been removed from the sample.

In brief, the data in Table 10 suggests that the apparent effects of universities on the occurrence of protest may result in part from their sheer size: The larger the institution, the more likely it will have a "critical mass" of students who can organize a protest. This suggestion is, of course, rival to the hypothesis stated earlier about the university's impersonal atmosphere and lack of concern for the individual student. Within the next year, we hope to gain more insight into the relative validity of these opposing hypotheses by analysis of data on independent samples.

References

Astin, A. W. *The college environment.* Washington, D.C.: American Council on Education, 1968. (a)

Astin, A. W. Personal and environmental determinants of student activism. *Measurement and Evaluation in Guidance,* 1968, **1,** 149–162. (b)

Astin, A. W., Panos, R. J., & Creager, J. A. A program of longitudinal research on the higher educational system. *ACE Research Reports,* 1966, **1**(1).

Bayer, A. E., & Astin, A. W. Violence and disruption on the U.S. campus, 1968–1969. *Educational Record,* Fall 1969, 337–350.

Creager, J. A. General purpose sampling in the domain of higher education. *ACE Research Reports,* 1968, **3**(2).

The Student Protest Movement: Some Facts, Interpretations, and a Plea

RICHARD E. PETERSON

The author received his PhD in education from the University of California at Berkeley in 1962. At the time of the APA Convention, he was Staff Director for the Special Committee on Campus Tensions, established by the American Council on Education He is currently a research psychologist at Educational Testing Service, Berkeley, where his research interests center on human and institutional factors in higher education.

I would like to divide this paper into two unequal and quite distinct parts. In the first, I will try to summarize the research I have done on the student protest movement and some of its correlates. In the second, I would like to discuss some things that are on my mind by virtue of my work as Staff Director for the recently established Special Committee on Campus Tensions (of which Brewster Smith, our discussant, is a member).

Research on Student Protest

First the research. Let me begin by describing two roughly comparable national surveys of organized student protest that I carried out, the first in 1965, the second in 1968. The academic year 1964-65 probably marked the beginning of serious, organized student protest directed against the university. As we all know, the free speech movement erupted at the University of California at Berkeley in the fall of 1964, a year that has turned out to be truly a watershed in the recent history of American higher education. Other scattered student uprisings that year, combined with extensive coverage in the mass media, led to the beginnings of public unease about the situation on the campus. At any rate, in the spring of 1965 I was struck by the need for some reasonably accurate information on a national scale about what looked like a social phenomenon of more than passing significance. I sent questionnaires to the deans of students at all 1,000 accredited four-year colleges in the country, asking them to indicate for each of 27 issues whether there had been organized protest during the past academic year and, if so, what percentage of the student body was involved (Peterson, 1966).

The second survey, carried out in the late spring of 1968, was identical to the earlier study, with the exception that several new issues were substituted for matters that were judged not to have been important causes of protest during the academic year 1967-68 (Peterson, 1968). Dow Chemical recruiters on campus would be an example of a "new" issue. Response rates on both surveys were close to 85%.

One purpose of these surveys, as I said, was to document a social fact. Another purpose was to provide interested people, especially college and university leaders, with something of a perspective on what was taking place. Thus, I had hoped that people on a given campus might look back on the past year and consider what had happened or had not happened on their campus in relation to the national data, and then perhaps begin to do some serious thinking about what the student protest movement would and should mean for their campus. The data from the two surveys made a number of things about the student movement quite clear, for example:

1. Relatively small minorities of students, 2–10% depending on the issue, were generally actively involved in protests, and issues bearing on college controls on the personal lives of students, for example, dormitory or student dress regulations, stirred up larger numbers of students than educational issues or even off-campus issues such as the Vietnam war or civil rights.

2. There are very large differences in the extent of student protest according to type of institution. For most issues, protest was most frequent at the independent and public universities and least frequent, quite infrequent in fact, at the Catholic- and Protestant-affiliated colleges and at the vocationally oriented institutions such as teachers colleges and technical institutions.

3. Campus protest over off-campus issues such as the war, the draft, civil rights, etc., is less frequent in the South than elsewhere in the country.

4. Organized protest occurred much more frequently on the large rather than the small campus.

5. Student Left groups such as the Students for a Democratic Society were functioning on one-fourth of the campuses in 1965 and on one-half of the campuses in 1968.

6. The surveys also provided people with an idea about the relative national significance of various issues. In 1965, civil rights, dormitory regulations, and food service led the list. In 1968, the Vietnam war, dormitory regulations, and student participation in campus governance, in that order, were the major issues. Black student activism was reported on roughly one in five colleges during the year.

One problem with surveys like these is that the descriptions they provide rapidly become obsolete. The radical movement will not stand still. The kind of study that probably has somewhat more permanence is one that looks at relationships, say, between the fact of protest and other relevant variables. (Some relationships, of course, were illuminated by the surveys, those between protest and size and type of institution, for example.)

In the interim between the two surveys, Sasajima, Davis, and I did a correlational study involving, for 109 colleges, the protest data from the 1965 survey and the scales in the College and University Environment Scales (CUES), an instrument developed by C. Robert Pace at UCLA (Sasajima, Davis, & Peterson, 1968). With CUES, students report their perceptions of the climate of the college in terms of dimensions labeled Practicality, Community, Awareness, Propriety, and

Scholarship.[1] Summarizing quickly, the combination of the Awareness and Propriety scales, Propriety weighted negatively, gave a multiple correlation of .63 with civil rights protest as the criterion; and Awareness and Community (the latter weighted negatively) yielded a multiple of .71 with Vietnam war protest. We also found, however, that CUES was not predictive of protest over internal campus problems and issues—like the quality of instruction, paternalistic regulations, student participation in decision making, etc.

Again in the interest of continuities in social research, a fourth study I want to mention is in a number of ways comparable to the third one just described. Using the same analytic strategy (zero order and multiple correlation) and a sample of 50 colleges, Centra and I are studying relationships between protest data from the 1968 survey and a new set of predictors—the scales in a new instrument known as the Institutional Functioning Inventory (IFI) (Peterson & Centra, 1969; Peterson, Centra, Hartnett, & Linn, 1970).

Under development for several years by Hartnett, Centra, and myself, the IFI relies primarily on faculty perceptions to obtain measures of a number of institutional functions and orientations. The inventory consists of 11 12-item scales; their reliabilities—coefficient alphas for college means—range between .84 and .96. Brief definitions of these measures are as follows:

IAE: *Intellectual-Aesthetic Extracurriculum* refers to the availability of activities and opportunities for intellectual and aesthetic stimulation outside the classroom.

F: *Freedom* has to do with academic freedom for faculty and students as well as freedom in their personal lives for all individuals in the campus community.

HD: *Human Diversity* deals with the degree to which the faculty and student body are heterogeneous in their backgrounds and present attitudes.

IS: *Concern for Improvement of Society* refers to a desire among people at the institution to apply their knowledge and skills in solving social problems and prompting social change in America.

UL: *Concern for Undergraduate Learning* has to do with the degree to which the college, in its structure, function, and professional commitment of faculty, emphasizes undergraduate teaching and learning.

DG: *Democratic Governance* deals with the extent to which individuals in the campus community who are directly affected by a decision have the opportunity to participate in making the decision.

MLN: *Meeting Local Needs* refers to an institutional emphasis on providing educational and cultural opportunities for all adults in the surrounding area, as well as meeting needs for trained manpower on the part of local businesses and government agencies.

---

[1] *Practicality*: the degree to which the environment is structured and orderly, where rules and procedures are important, and where interest in ideas for their own sake tends to be deemphasized.

Community: the degree to which a warm, cohesive atmosphere is emphasized and where there are close relationships between students and faculty and among students.

Awareness: the degree to which interest in philosophy, the arts, and national and international affairs gives evidence of personal awareness in relation to society.

Propriety: the degree to which proper forms and conventions are emphasized, where good manners are evident, and where there tends to be an absence of unconventional behavior.

Scholarship: the degree to which the pursuit of knowledge and ideas and the attainment of scholarly achievement is highly valued.

SP: *Self-Study and Planning* has to do with the importance college leaders attach to continuous long-range planning for the total institution, and to institutional research needed in formulating and revising plans.

AK: *Concern for Advancing Knowledge* has to do with the degree to which the institution, in its structure, function, and professional commitment of faculty, emphasizes research and scholarship aimed at extending the scope of human knowledge.

CI: *Concern for Innovation* refers, in its highest form, to an institutionalized commitment to experimentation with new ideas for educational practice.

IE: *Institutional Esprit* refers to a sense of shared purposes and high morale among faculty and administrators.

Table 1 contains a matrix of product-moment correlations between the 11 IFI scales and reported incidence of organized student protest over each of 27 issues. Only correlations of .20 or higher are given. The protest data were gath-

TABLE 1
Correlations between IFI Scales and Incidence of Student Protest over Various Issues in 1967–68

Issue	IAE	F	HD	IS	UL	DG	MLN	SP	AK	CI	IE
1. Class size	30	20	34	41	−37				51		
2. Senior faculty absent		25	31	32	−43				60		
3. Quality of instruction				22	−40	−24			33		
4. Testing and grading					−37	−25	22		29		
5. Curriculum inflexibility						−23				−21	
6. Academic freedom											
7. Tenure policies		−26				−32				−24	
8. Controversial instructor		24	41	28			23		−22		−32
9. Alleged censorship						−33	21			−29	−20
10. Rules: controversial visitors		−40									
11. Visits by leftists	23										
12. Visits by rightists	22			28	−23				33		
13. Living group regulations						−25					
14. Food service	−28				−25	−22					
15. Dress regulations		−38	−21			−39			−26	−26	
16. Drinking regulations									−20		
17. Drug regulations		21				20					
18. Disciplinary actions				25		−25					−32
19. Alleged racial discrimination	29	22	32	35	−36				32		
20. Student-administration communication					−26	−22			−25	−25	
21. Student participation in governance			26	27	−36				21		−21
22. Civil rights		34	43	50	−20				34	20	
23. The draft	42	36	44	54		40			42	29	
24. Armed services recruiters	20	31	45	29		24					
25. Other recruiters (Dow, etc.)		43	61	51	−31	26			40		
26. Vietnam	42	31	50	65		35			41	34	
27. Classified research	33		37	40	−40				55		

Note.—*N* = 50 institutions.

ered in the summer of 1968; the IFI information, in February and March of the same year. There are a number of interesting, if not altogether surprising, patterns in the Table 1 data. For example, all the correlations involving the Undergraduate Learning (UL) scale are negative, meaning that colleges that stress or do a good job of teaching undergraduates seldom experience organized protest. Democratic Governance (the DG scale) tends to be associated with satisfaction with, or lack of protest against, the college, but with protest over off-campus issues (the war, civil rights, etc.)—a situation liberal administrators might consider to be ideal. Scales that tend to define the large multiversity—Human Diversity (HD), Improvement of Society (IS), Advancement of Knowledge (AK), and Intellectual-Aesthetic Extracurriculum (IAE)—all tend to be positively related to campus activism, especially protest arising from off-campus issues.

As had been done in the earlier study with CUES, the 27 protest issues were grouped, on the basis of a prior factor analysis, into a smaller number of protest criterion measures. In this present study the 27 issues were reduced to seven scales that were labeled Unconcern with Teaching, Instruction and Curriculum, Faculty Affairs, Politically Extremist Visitors, Administrative Paternalism, Student Power, and New Left Issues.

Multiple correlations were statistically significant for three of the seven protest criteria: New Left (mainly war-related) Issues, Unconcern with Teaching (which contained the classified-research-on-campus item), and the Faculty Affairs measure (student protest stemming from, say, a negative rehire decision or the behavior of a "controversial" professor). Only in the last instance, Faculty Affairs, however, did the use of multiple predictors materially improve the prediction. The highest zero-order correlation with the Faculty Affairs criterion, as one might expect, involved the Institutional Esprit (IE) scale—a rather modest $-.34$. However, adding the Improvement of Society, (IS), Advancement of Knowledge (AK), and Undergraduate Learning (UL) scales, with all but IS weighted negatively, yielded a multiple correlation of .74. This particular pattern of institutional characteristics suggests a seriously demoralized campus, where the faculty believe that the college may not be doing anything particularly well. Perhaps the institution is in transition or for some other reason is unclear about its purposes. Such a climate could easily give rise to open faculty conflicts, in which students could be expected to take sides. Are there such institutions, or are we speaking only of a statistical figment?

In view of the ability of the IFI to predict the two categories of protest arising totally or in part from off-campus issues, and only one of the five clearly campus-issue protest criteria, I came to the same general conclusion that was drawn from the earlier study: Protest over off-campus issues is more readily predictable than protest over campus conditions. As a general explanatory hypothesis, I would suggest that New Left militance, which has tended to focus on conditions external to the campus, is almost entirely a function of the values of the students involved. Indeed, Astin (1968) has shown Vietnam and civil rights protest behavior to be quite predictable on the basis of personal characteristics of the protesting students. By contrast, campus-issue protest is determined not only by students' values, but also by a host of college policies, practices, personalities, and the like. Because of its relative causal complexity, the incidence of protest over campus conditions is less amenable to statistical prediction than Student Left protest directed at broad social issues.

Special Committee on Campus Tensions

So much for the research. Let me begin this last part with a few words about the recently established Special Committee on Campus Tensions. The Committee was created in response to an awareness, rather belated perhaps, of both the escalation of hostilities on the campus and the mounting political backlash off the campus. In its report, it will urge the nation's colleges to accelerate reforms directed at the on-campus causes of unrest, and to improve mechanisms for self-regulation and for timely yet just response in the event of serious disruption. We hope our efforts will be understood by people in public life as an earnest effort by the academic community to manage its own affairs. We intend, however, to impress upon people in public life, once again, the clear fact that campus unrest springs in very large part from a consciousness on the part of hundreds of thousands of students that there is great injustice in American society and that our national priorities are grossly wrong.

I am appealing to the social science community for help. The Special Committee plans to center its deliberations and recommendations on a fairly wide range of topics, many of which fall within the general purview of psychology—especially social psychology—and the other social sciences. Listed below are some of the areas in which we intend to concentrate, and we would welcome receiving relevant materials from social scientists. These areas of concentration include: (*a*) modern interpretations of the history and philosophy of dissent, civil disobedience, and revolt; (*b*) the breakdown of authority in American life, to include analyses of emerging bases of legitimacy; (*c*) the dynamics of institutional change, to focus especially on factors affecting an institution's ability to respond to the need for change; (*d*) institutional governance, especially models based on a commonality of interests rather than factionalism; and (*e*) effective communication in complex organizations.

The second plea I would like to make to the social science community, and many will not be sympathetic, is that those who are on campuses become involved in efforts to head off violence at their institution. More so than most other academics, people in the social sciences, especially psychologists, ought to possess the skills and sensitivities necessary to spot sources of potential conflict and to help conflicting groups reach satisfactory accommodations. I urge these people to work with student and faculty groups toward making their actions essentially *non*violent. I am *not* speaking about a deescalation of goals, only a deescalation in tactics. I am absolutely convinced that this will be a critical year for the American university. If very many colleges erupt with the violence of Berkeley, Columbia, or Harvard, no number of blue-ribbon committees will be able to prevent a public backlash that potentially could crush the university as a functioning intellectual enterprise.

References

Astin, A. W. Personal and environmental determinants of student activism. *Measurement and Evaluation in Guidance,* 1968, **1,** 149–161.

Peterson, R. E. *The scope of organized student protest in 1964–1965.* Princeton, N. J.: Educational Testing Service, 1966.

Peterson, R. E. *The scope of organized student protest in 1967–1968.* Princeton, N. J.: Educational Testing Service, 1968.

Peterson, R. E., & Centra, J. A. *Organized student protest and institutional functioning.* (Research Bulletin 69–77) Princeton, N. J.: Educational Testing Service, 1969.

Peterson, R. E., Centra, J. A., Hartnett, R. T., & Linn, R. L. *Institutional functioning inventory: Preliminary technical manual.* Princeton, N. J.: Educational Testing Service, 1970.

Sasajima, M., Davis, J. A., & Peterson, R. E. Organized student protest and institutional climate. *American Educational Research Journal,* 1968, **5,** 291–304.

Activist Students Challenge the Social Scientists

PAUL HEIST

The author received his PhD from the University of Minnesota in 1956. He is presently a research psychologist at the Center for Research and Development in Higher Education and a professor of higher education at the University of California at Berkeley. His major research interests center on personality theory and studies of change and development.

The historians in 1984, at the beginning of the next century, and in 2069, 100 years from today, will probably find this period of higher education one of tremendous interest and provocation. From their vantage points of extended hindsight, increasing with the years, we would expect to find them a somewhat less perplexed group than many contemporary administrators, faculty, and social scientists. One reason for a future historian's interest in the current period of turmoil and confrontation between students and the more established segments of our society may well be a direct evolution of continuing and related events from this past decade to dates 2 to 10 decades removed. However, in spite of the years intervening, a lesser degree of perplexity on the part of historians may not be matched by a lesser degree of disturbance.

If we can take our cues from the very slow pace of institutional change and the acknowledged inertia of social lag, notwithstanding the rapidity of scientific progress and change since the beginning of World War II, as well as the more recent mild revolutions in ethical and social mores, future students are likely to protest the "System" in 1984 even more diligently than students today. By then, with only minimal elimination of social ills, they will have numerous additional precedents and successes to serve as their models. As long as a minority of college youth persist in effectively showing us the error of our ways, with smaller numbers suggesting various means to a more just and democratic society, the occurrences of arrests, convictions, and even police aggression are not likely to deter them from a long sequence of involvement, if not confrontation.

The following comments imply a certain bias on the part of the author. The status of our examination and reexamination of present social and educational problems cannot be discounted or go unrecognized, limited as that accomplishment may be after only one decade of student discontent and challenge. Whatever the attitudes and sentiments of teachers and professors, they can hardly fail to recognize that the so-called student movement(s) has(have) brought us closer to the portals, if only the portals, of a new tomorrow. In the field of higher education and in the areas of some persistent social problems, the power of enlightened but troubled youth is not likely to permit a return to the quiescence and the suppressed evils of a previous day. The increased horizons, now possible for all discerning people, and the enhanced opportunities for comprehending and dealing with issues and problems, in ways never before attempted, are not to be negated.

With the trauma and the violence, the latter having been introduced from both sides, by the oppressor as well as the discontented and oppressed, have come respectable gains and new directions. Many activist college youths have been skeptical about the latter, and the journalists have been remiss in not revealing or "giving equal time" to this side of the story. This may be a responsibility and a task that social scientists should not be loath to undertake. In reality, although as yet no revolution in education has taken place, neither the public nor the students are informed of the variety of mild and major changes in progress on numerous university and college campuses. For example, since the gradual introduction since 1962 of a new breed of student on the University of California campus at Davis, which blossomed into serious efforts on the part of students in promoting other changes by 1965, and since the dramatic events during the fall of 1964 on the Berkeley campus, many persons would be amazed by the breadth and complexity of what both students and faculty have set into motion on these two campuses.

However, the effects and accomplishments which may be traced in large part to the "press" of student efforts, often very negatively perceived and received in their inception, are not the topic of the moment. After I only briefly acknowledge the successful and increasing role of a minority of students, the focus here will be on the situation in the general academic world which provides a controversial setting, leading to growing student concern on more and more campuses.

A Decade of Activism and Challenge

At least a resume of some of the available information about modern, protesting college youth seems in order. By now, near the end of this decade, all interested educators and political leaders have had ample opportunity to discover the facts about the backgrounds, attitudes, and orientations of the majority of activists and the leaders of both general movements and specific campus encounters.

This matter of characterizing the discontented and protesting student minorities has become more complicated as greater divergency in thought and behavior has become pervasive in the ranks of these social deviates. The results of studies of the political activists in the days of the free speech movement led to a number of fairly common attributes (Heist, 1965; Somers, 1965). These students came from upper-middle-class homes, were brighter as a group when compared to other students, had maintained good academic records, and were nonauthoritarian and intellectual in their general orientation. Among the activists high on these last two categories, we find a smaller group that accepts or lays claim to the label "radical." Those involved in the more recent forms of campus confrontation, where the activities have had direct or indirect political overtones, are similarly described as an exceptional, nonrandom sample of students. Such capable and committed students are not found in abundant numbers across campuses, but significant minorities seem to be concentrated on relatively few campuses.

Unfortunately, neither the positive characterizations of activist leaders and participants nor their underlying reasons for becoming involved in the causes of social, political, or educational issues have impressed the authorities and legislators. For them, actions, whether violent or nonviolent, have spoken louder than words, and the repeated disruptions of law and order on major campuses across the land have led to a submersion of the most frequently professed student concerns and the distortion of the sincere and defensible rationale of many youths.

It seems that the elders most deeply ingrained in the educational administrative hierarchies and academic disciplines, as well as those in the political-industrial superstructures, are unable to get beyond the overt acts of students. For those who have patiently listened to and understood some of the concerns and anguish expressed by hundreds of capable and committed youths, white and black, they seem to be unable to comprehend the students' recourse to bitter antipathies and aggressive tactics. But why should they comprehend the problems, concerns, and behavior of these latecomers, that is, the dissenting students, when they and we have seldom heard or responded to the endless frustrations and aggravations of our black and brown citizens, even after many have highlighted their anxieties and resorted to the destruction of their own communities?

In the latter analogy there lies some essence of the truth; like the ethnic minorities of darker hues who were never understood or accepted, eventually granted legal but never human citizenry, and usually dealt a separate form of justice, so the mass of students, with few exceptions, have been treated as lesser creatures, with few of the rights and privileges of educational citizenship, only infrequently accepted and seldom understood. The latter has become increasingly true, for as in our relationships with certain ethnic peoples, we have dealt with students chiefly as a mass and rarely as individuals. And, as many of them have become discontented and overtly obstreperous, whether tackling intra- or extramural issues, we fell naturally into categorizing all activist youths as those immature, disrespectful, rebellious, violent, and immoral others.

The once almost definable movement and behavior of the *political* student activists, to use the most frequent classification of an earlier period, have proliferated to a variety of movements and trends, with little integration or formal coordination among the different activist organizations on widely scattered campuses. There are, nevertheless, some common, persistent concerns and themes among some of the current subgroups or separate movements, but these have seldom won the attention or respect of the concerned public or the legislators. Admittedly, a minority of administrators and faculty on numerous occasions have learned to respect some of the complaints and pleas. However, faculty and students have as yet to join forces to effectively and consistently protest the Vietnam war, to tackle persistent problems of urban society and interracial living, or to protect themselves from their own trustees or state and federal politicians. Such collaboration, interestingly enough, has been initiated or, in part, effected on intramural concerns in a surprising number of institutions.

Students on many fronts have asked for involvement and a voting voice, and rights of participation, in various forms, have been granted in a surprising number of instances. Such participation runs the gamut from having voting representation on 95% of the administrative and faculty committees on one campus to serving on curriculum reorganization committees and a presidential selection committee on another. For example, where ethnic studies have been instituted and developed, much of such development has to be credited to the efforts of minority group students.

As already implied, the institutional changes and improvements resulting as a direct outgrowth of student concern and agitation, however insignificant they may seem to students, are breakthrough steps, pointing toward new directions and changed campus climates. Such developments are too seldom given the publicity of the press. It is doubtful that existing improvements of this nature will be seen as the essential or necessary changes by the students, but the fact that they may not will get more attention from communication media than growing cooperative efforts and gradual steps to effect additional changes.

Whatever the specific changes and renovations to date, on the campuses seeing the most of such changes student activism is more likely to be continued, probably in stepped-up fashion, than on other campuses where nothing has happened. Thus, to iterate, student activism, whether in the form of collaboration, confrontation, or violence, should be seen and understood as a continuing phenomenon. But the extremes of aggression and violence are least likely to be seen where institutional flexibility and mechanics for change are recognized as part of a functional policy and where ready communication channels are well established. From this perspective, students will have to be given the credit for at least opening the vista of the new tomorrow, as well as initiating very necessary reconsiderations in administration and curriculum. The faculty cannot do less than be encouraging and participative in the very developments that it may have viewed initially as unwelcome or unimportant.

Situational Context for Discontent and Protest

The preceding remarks introduce, at least by implication, an important but frequently neglected consideration. For the most part, the modern, protesting students are viewed and criticized as entities in a vacuum. What they do and say may or may not be seen as self-generated, and at most it is viewed as behavior in mutual response to each other or to student organizers. Strange as it may seem, their behavior is only seldomly interpreted as a reaction to or interaction with events, people, and problems in their perceived environments. The students very frequently, and quite eloquently in their speech, songs, and posters, inform us of their general and specific aggravations, their frustrations, and the sources or causes of their agitation and unhappiness. However, the mass of responding adults appear not to hear or catch the message. They criticize, berate, judge, and condemn as if the only errors to behold were in the spoken words or immediate acts of the students. Not viewing or not wanting to understand modern youths as *people in a situation,* or in the larger social-political context, restricts most elders to looking for the key problem only in the aggressor rather than in the environmental conditions, and seldom in the unending relationship between man and environment.

This same inadequacy of perception has led others, the researchers of students, to commit similar errors. Their search for explanations is often conducted in a way that can at best lead to half "truths" or no "truths." To attempt to establish causality, or even meaningful relationships, between events and a situation, by seeking significance in single dimensions, whether describing the actor or the situation, completely misses the total unity, the social-cultural raison d'etre, and the essence of committed, unalienated behavior. When the social scientists, who by definition and design cannot utilize or establish appropriate controls for their kind of field research, attempt to adhere to the law of parsimony in seeking answers in an area of fluctuating complexity, the "truth is not in them," and neither the subject nor the situation is being assessed fairly.

In the approaches and analyses of some researchers directed to activists per se or events on individual campuses, especially in their attempts to reach for understanding or predictability in a small web of several related facts, they are being misled about the importance of a challenging and revealing phenomenon. In the name of feasible science and scientific methods, researchers have been lured into studying symptoms rather than causes. To the sincere, activist youth, major concentration on his personality traits or his overt acts must seem like the ultimate "put-down," when rather it is the history, logic, or defense of his personal involvement that should be considered or his thinking and feelings about the never-resolved social problems. If both understanding and control of protest and violence are the objectives of recent research, it must appear to intelligent youth that too many efforts are being invested in solving the wrong problem(s). If it is not too late, there may be little to lose in asking a sample of activists and radicals what they think might be profitably studied and how, and what more is to be gained by studying them.

With those few remarks, concerns about the extramural world may be shelved, except as social and political problems come under consideration for the social scientist who teaches and does research in the position of a faculty member. The comments that follow have their locus in the positions of present-day psychologists and sociologists, particularly the work of those directed to the life and welfare of man as a social-psychological creature. The basis of some of the comments is found in research evidence from several projects in the last 10 years which included information from faculty samples in a diversity of institutions.[1]

An underlying question or theme running through these considerations about faculty members is centered on their general orientation toward the education and welfare of students, especially as they, the faculty, may behave as candidates to support or help clarify the numerous concerns of the committed and activist college student. In other words, one possibly important aspect of the students' academic situations is here subjected to cursory review and scrutiny.

Perhaps one should start with a positive perspective on faculty members, from the standpoint of their work with students and their potential relationships with activist movements. A primary concern in most if not all research on faculty members has been their commitment to teaching and student learning, and here the variation among institutions and disciplinary subgroups within schools is less great than on other topics. A large majority of those faculty members surveyed in several investigations strongly professed a primary interest in the teaching-learning process, and presumably they do not intentionally shortchange the students in this respect.

---

[1] From studies conducted at the Center for the Study of Higher Education, University of California, Berkeley.

In a most recent study conducted at six institutions, Wilson and Gaff (1969) found that approximately 90% of a sample of over 1,000 faculty members acknowledged that teaching was a major source of satisfaction; approximately the same percentages subscribed to the primary importance of teaching, to the importance of responsible teaching practices, and to the importance of giving time to advising students.

If we accept this expressed intensity of interest in teaching and students as valid, we might have a first clue to some of the antipathy to overt discontent and disturbance. As indicated in other studies, protests and strikes would be seen as disruptive of the teaching-learning environment and the teachers' objectives and schedules. Such activity would also tend to bring more students to a critical orientation and the possible questioning of purposes and methods in an area where most teachers are reluctant to relinquish their assumed prerogatives (Wilson & Gaff, 1969).

This strong faculty commitment to teaching, whatever it may mean for each professing pedagogue, is not paralleled by excellence or quality of instruction, if one is to accept the reports and opinions of students. Through various means and in different studies students have been asked to appraise the quality of the instruction experienced during one or more college years; the form of appraisal has usually been on a comparative basis, with estimates made about the instructors who qualify as excellent, average, or poor.[2]

The most common finding regarding instruction is that students are much more dissatisfied than satisfied with the faculty they have encountered. Whether the institutions are large or small, whether a liberal arts college or a technical institute, approximately 20–25% of the teachers are rated as good to excellent, 30–40% as mediocre or average, and the rest as poor. Allowing for some truth in these findings, on the basis of reliability established in the opinions of numerous judges, the implications are that any student will receive excellent teaching only a minimal amount of his classroom time. Those students who have become increasingly concerned about the curriculum and their academic experiences will have little difficulty finding support for their cause among at least a proportion of the students. The majority, though recognizing mediocrity, have always been willing to settle for whatever instruction they received, outside of complaining about boredom and too much work. In this heyday of protest, they may eventually join forces to make many instructors face up to the mediocrity of courses and programs.

From the reports by Wilson and Gaff (1969), there is essentially only one other area where a majority opinion, in the students' favor, is obtained across their faculty sample. Two-thirds were supportive of giving the students the major responsibility for regulating or determining their own social life and ways of living. As these authors intimate, however, this positive attitude toward students is not based on a conviction of their goodness, maturity, or potential for responsibility. More likely, it is the result of a need or desire not to become too involved and not to be taken too far from academic concerns. Also, American faculty members have

---

[2] Unpublished results to date from projects conducted at the Center for Research and Development in Higher Education, University of California, Berkeley.

become accustomed to the fact that the extracurricular aspects of student life have been the responsibility of nonacademic personnel. In most cases, they seem to prefer that or a complete abnegation to the modern student.

After we get beyond the self-acknowledged faculty members' concern about teaching, whether genuine or pseudo, what else do we find to typify their commitments—their interests in the students and their concerns? What are other facets to the academic story for the social scientists? Or are they still the ivory-towered scholars and pedants of another day, if such were ever the case? Some of this story is not hard to come by and is probably known to all within the ranks. The following sampling of generalizations, taken from interviews and observations in longitudinal studies conducted inside and outside the Center for Research and Development in Higher Education, must be seen in the light of the exceptions and reservations brought to all gross explanations. But in such generalizations we find the composite of several stories which represent the faculty man and the tenuous commitment he presents to our modern college-going youth.

1. In many large universities and in a smaller sample of colleges the well-known but increasing nonteaching roles of many faculty members necessarily negate the concern and time for teaching. Admittedly, this grievous problem exists chiefly in the institutions with either major and/or numerous research contracts, and it is literally absent in a great many other campuses. Although this campus problem of being a man-in-demand has been well exposed, the actual curtailment in responsibilities and negative effects on the teaching in particular departments and classrooms remain to be established. Suffice it to say, the obvious diversifying of interests, commitments, and use of time, for whatever reasons, cannot be overlooked when the instruction and welfare of students are primary concerns.

2. Although it is still only a minority of faculty members, across the many institutions of higher education, that are involved in the nonteaching roles of externally financed research and consulting, the latter takes on a special significance for more and more persons in some of the social sciences (e.g., political science, economics, and sociology). Increasingly, assignments as consultants or resource staff to state and federal governments, as well as large industries, take men beyond the pale of their disciplines and primary tasks and responsibilities, especially when asked to confer on governmental policy or the ethics of scientific advancements. The available, albeit inadequate, evidence regarding the questionable aftereffects of these involvements warrants serious attention from both colleagues and students if teaching continues to be the chief or only reason for salaried positions.

3. As with many disciplines, especially those outside the natural sciences, the social sciences are caught up with both an overstabilizing traditionalism and a rampant professionalism, which tend to perpetuate the "tried and the true," even in this era of rapid scientific transformations. These status quo "forces" have discouraged and chased out many a talented and creative student, while binding the majority of old and young faculty to the extent of preventing or crippling innovation, change, and stimulating experimentation, both in the classroom and in research activities. The disciplines in the social sciences, when the blocks or protests to present innovation and new developments are occasionally overcome, tend to break up into splinter groups or subdepartments which must go through a struggle for acceptance, status, and existence. The development of dichotomies and divi-

sions within disciplines has caused much tribulation for both graduate and undergraduate students within respective departments. (The counteracting but struggling movements of free universities and innovative programs are likely to experience resurgent swings as the slow fight with traditionalism continues inside the established educational systems.)

4. The traditional and established curricula pervading much of the academic world, notwithstanding continuing efforts at innovation, are premised on the same old unquestioned assumptions and routine methods of teaching, with poor or second-rate lecturing being maintained as the chief form of carrying out the teaching-learning process. The education of college teachers, first, to a concern about diverse and effective *learning* processes and, second, to the possibilities of varied instructional methods and more effective means of introducing subject matter, remains on the horizon as a development of the future. The disciplines in the social sciences which deal most closely with the human variable must be given more than a fair share of credit for encouraging and maintaining this anchorage in the traditional. Only a very minimal number of professional personnel have dared the controversial stance of manifesting a concern and interest in either sound, defensible, pedagogical practices or the student as an individual learner.

5. Mentioning the other participant in academic life, namely, the student, brings us to the *cause celebre* of academia. Underlying much that both the exceptional and ordinary student find to criticize in the social sciences, as well as other disciplines, is the failure to grant them the respect of individuality. Along with the hue and cry about the lack of relevancy of much in the modern curriculum, students repeatedly address themselves to the amazing absence of personalization in what should be some of the most significant relationships of their lives. It would be difficult to deny that here college youth have caught us in one of our most grievous sins—failing to recognize that knowing and understanding the individual is basic to teaching him most effectively. Granted this is difficult in mass education, but even an address to this concern is hardly part of the orientation and motivation of our associates and colleagues.

6. Respect for students as individuals takes on a second dimension when we add the fact of sex. Among the problems faced by women in this Western culture, at least the problems more frequently encountered by them than by men, is that of becoming professionals and established members of the social science disciplines. At least from the female perspective, this is seen as a problem with numerous facets, only one of which may be considered here all too briefly. Among the several problematic facets that the social sciences cannot overlook or suppress is the simple matter of encouraging the complete education and acceptance of capable women, as well as working with them as equals at all echelons in these academic spheres which also tend to remain predominantly male. Besides the obvious advantages of more thoroughly utilizing and profiting from the diversity introduced by those of another sex, there is the very important matter of "keeping the faith" with our adolescents and postadolescents.

Scientists and educators cannot be unconcerned, as the youth would have us understand, about what it means to be a member of any socially assigned minority, be it black, brown, female, or under 21, 25, or 30. There is much more to be understood than has been the case to date about the different ways we can or do introduce acceptance, respect, and status for all "outsiders" currently tagged as minorities. There is much for those in the social sciences to comprehend and appreciate, especially in the contemporary period, about what it means to be a woman, whatever the age, whether enrolled in these disciplines or not.

Where the half dozen above points either directly or indirectly relate to both faculty and students in their academic roles, the remaining points, more unique to the social sciences than to all disciplines, deal with the scientist chiefly in non-teaching roles.

7. Much of the activity in the social sciences which comes under the classifications of research and scholarship is not contributing, at least directly, to a functional body of applicable knowledge about human behavior or interaction, nor is it adding to the bases for policy making or direction giving in the contemporary society. Although the presumably more basic research and scholarship of this nature has always been seen as legitimate in the academic world, activist students will probably raise more and more questions about the amount of time and effort concentrated on basic, pure, or overly specific research. It is not a large step between picketing a university or an industry for war-related activities and demonstrating against a departmental faculty for the amount of funds allocated to studying what appear to be inconsequential specifics.

On the contrary side, there is an obvious trend, in part traceable to pressure from students, for some programs in the social sciences to give increasing time to both field and action research and also to instruction regarding social issues and problems. However, much of such work is handicapped by very inadequate funding and will continue for some time to receive only secondary consideration. Obviously, there are at least two sides to this question when viewed in the light of the purposes and functions of the university. Nevertheless, in the modern period there seems little question that numerous disciplines will need to reconsider the earlier imbalance of their concerns and efforts.

8. With a few exceptions, individuals or groups of social scientists have failed to set up comprehensive or long-range research projects, with adequate funding, where the staff has both the freedom and time to address itself to the totality of persistent social or educational problems. This failure is especially glaring in the light of funds that the physical sciences have enjoyed in pursuing a host of "no-payoff" projects. It is difficult to predict a specific direction here for the immediate future, with those in charge of the sources of large funds, whether federal or private, presently considering the granting of money for other problems than extensive and intensive studies on human behavior in academic settings.

The point to be made is that the search for valid facts regarding the effective education of varied youth has a long way to go. Although valuable information and insights have been products of earlier investigation, such results have only scratched the surface of what could or should be known about learning, change, and development in formal education settings. There have not been enough capable disciplinarians addressing themselves to the important issues and problems either within or outside the institutions.

In the past 15 years a variety of investigations of college students—directed to their education and development—can be characterized as much for their failures as their successes. The social scientists involved have, for the most part, only touched upon the countless failures of educational institutions and upon what actually happens developmentally to students who succeed or fail, and then have come up with a multiplicity of conflicting findings on different aspects of the student protests. Such failure is not unrelated to the question of funding (mentioned previously) and the inadequacy of methods in the fields of psychology and sociology, but it is also not unrelated to shallow theoretical frameworks, the limited conceptualizations of some projects, and the still lacking interests and concern of many in these disciplines.

9. The right or privilege of being apolitical, especially under the defense of neutral scholarship, seems due for reexamination in the present period. Many social scientists, as well as physical scientists, attempt a lifelong nonpolitical stance and avoid addressing themselves to issues of continued warfare, racial problems, interracial living, the drug culture, and the modern distress of concerned college youth. This right of not being politically or socially concerned or active is presumably respected in a democratic governmental system, but it may also be a privilege that we can no longer afford to extend to educated men and women.

The previous point is obviously conjectural, but the continuing "trend" of increased political activism in the student world is likely to put many more scientists through the task of rethinking their basic political beliefs and precepts. However, the latter is secondary to student concern about the number of scientists who maintain a position of neutrality and diligently avoid exhibiting any overt stance on persistent domestic and international issues. The students have looked for and sought leadership, direction, and support from the social scientists in recent years, with only a modicum of visible activity along these lines being realized. Not having obtained aid and support in the struggle to change both education and society, the persistent student has already shown that the desired help will be sought from other fronts.

From Today to Tomorrow

The implications for the years ahead which may derive first from the new emphasis on old and new problems posed by activist and radical minorities, and second from the strong anchorage in the past and the status quo exhibited by members of professional disciplines, are a little difficult to read, but some of the handwriting is on the wall.

Along with numerous analysts of the disturbing events and developments of the last decade, it is safe to predict that the ranks of discontented youth, discontented to the extent of taking action, will continue to increase. With the continuation of the Vietnam war, the slow and begrudging admission of ethnic minorities to social and political citizenship, and the oppression and ostracization of many young people, students will believe that they have only one recourse. Their voice and participation will remain on the academic agenda, whether collaborative and constructive or directed to an impatient destruction of the ineffective traditionalism of the past. An uneasy "peace" at best will be the continuing campus climate in a large number of institutions, while undulating conflict and partisanship will be the continuing theme in a minority of the high-ranking universities.

Neither the policies of state and federal governments nor the rigamarole of educational practices, as both have developed out of an imbalance of hindsight rather than foresight, can be changed rapidly enough to appease the committed, capable clientele that seek out an education in the big-image institutions. A new tomorrow devoted to the peace and welfare of mankind is not on the immediate horizon. If the radicalism of the members of the Students for a Democratic Society or single ethnic groups can no longer draw upon their dissatisfactions and talents, other activist groups, some with a somewhat greater willingness to build on the present, are already asking for their chance to tackle the issues as they see them.

The social scientists could and may have a distinctive part to play in the challenging, changing plot on the stage of higher education. However, this enactment will demand the earlier leadership of younger and more recent entrants to the disciplines, many of whom found their commitments through their own student activism, and some representing reconversions, having won their spurs in a previous era. Also, and as already under way, though out of coercion, the contributions of educational leaders of minority groups must be more thoroughly incorporated into the totality of systems which will respect and accommodate the needs of all youth and which will be directed to an education for the learner, for community living, and, perhaps, to the resolution of problems rather than their piecemeal study.

Needless to say, the order poses an impossible challenge, but the mass of educators have never really addressed themselves to the impossible. Both in the earlier period of academic cloisterism of most college faculty members and in the last two decades when many have been drawn off campus part time to consult with government and industry, diligent and effective involvement in the issues and problems of a democratic republic and a united world have not been seriously addressed by the majority of the seemingly relevant disciplines. In reality, the mass of educators have never come forth from their "hidden arenas," and they have yet to learn to teach the essentials of their disciplines to the advantage of both the student at hand and the society in which they live a privileged existence. For the older younger generation it may be too late to relearn or to understand the challenge, but the succeeding generations of committed youth are not likely to misread or reject their cues nor to give up their efforts to reeducate the educational establishment.

References

Heist, P. Intellect and commitment: The faces of discontent. In O. W. Knorr & W. J. Minter (Eds.), *Order and freedom on the campus*. Boulder, Colo.: Western Interstate Commission for Higher Education and the Center for the Study of Higher Education, Berkeley, Calif., 1965.

Somers, R. N. Mainsprings of the rebellion: A survey of Berkeley students in November 1964. In S. Lipset & S. Wolin (Eds.), *Berkeley student revolt*. New York: Anchor, 1965.

Wilson, R., & Gaff, J. Student voice—faculty response. In, *The research reporter*. Berkeley, Calif.: Center for Research and Development in Higher Education, 1969.

Comments on the Symposium "Factors Underlying Student Unrest"

M. BREWSTER SMITH

The author received his PhD in social psychology from Harvard University in 1947. He is presently a professor of psychology and Chairman of the Psychology Department at the University of Chicago, where he is currently interested in the social psychology of self-determination and other aspects of psychological effectiveness.

The previous papers in this symposium have been tough going. Particularly, the empirical reports by Astin and Peterson are intrinsically hard to listen to or to read. The trees dwarf the forest. The authors are still too close to their data to give us much help in seeing the broader patterns of significance.

So it may be easy for you to identify with the protesting young radicals and to write off such gritty research as "irrelevant" or (there seems to be an inconsistency in the charges) self-serving and possibly vicious.

This, it seems to me, would be too easy—and mistaken. The facts in regard to campus unrest *are* complicated. If there are any facts that are important for members of the academic world to understand, they are surely these. They are important to a wider audience, too. If you believe, as I do, that our society is heading toward multifaceted disaster if we continue to slip along our current trends in the spirit of "business as usual," you will want to understand as clearly and as critically as you can the dissidents who purport to represent the winds of change —as catalysts, as sources of ferment, and as prophets true and false. Only if we are committed, as some of the protesting young people obviously are, to simplistic, prejudged interpretations and solutions can we forego the attempt to search out and understand the facts in their complexity.

Indeed, as scientists and as members of college faculties, we had better give up entirely if we cannot stand by the value of evidence and by the right to seek it and to discuss and evaluate it freely. This is our special obligation. If the young protestors are specialists in the advocacy of values of equality, peace, and justice, academics are specialists, too, in the realm of values—guardians of free inquiry as a precious aspect of the democratic heritage. We must not abdicate this guardianship in response to protest, even when we respect the protestors.

The papers before us provide a wealth of provocative data. Rather than comment on each in detail, I will attempt to see them in the perspective of the larger task of understanding the recent wave of student protest. Schematically, there are at least four facets to the phenomena that need to be investigated: (*a*) the distinctive characteristics of student dissidents—both leaders and followers; (*b*) institutional characteristics as determinants of student unrest and its outcomes; (*c*) characteristics of the extrainstitutional situation as they bear on student protest; (*d*) social-historical trends and factors that underlie student protest.

The early wave of research that began soon after the Berkeley free speech movement of 1964 emphasized the first of these topics. From many mutually confirming studies we learned that the protesting students tended to be good students from liberal middle class backgrounds—facts that were initially news but are no longer. We learned something of their personalities, values, moral style, and socializing experiences. There are still unanswered questions in this realm, including the question of whether the succession of increasingly disruptive styles of protest has led to the progressive recruitment of different sorts of leaders and followers. But the student radicals who were very critical of such research focused on student characteristics were surely right in their contention that, as an approach to understanding protest, its partial truths tended to deflect our attention from considerations that call for realistic correction. Thus, it is healthy that recent research exemplified in the Astin and Peterson papers now focuses on characteristics of academic institutions as these relate to campus protest. It is also healthy to be reminded, as we are by Heist's paper, that college faculties and how they carry out their tasks of teaching are a salient and relevant part of the institutional environment. But we have only begun to explore the factors that fall into this broad second category. As we are able to examine in more detail the effects of educational and administrative policies and of how they are implemented, knowledge may become more useful in helping faculties and administrators to turn conflict in the direction of constructive, not destructive, outcomes.

The third facet—the part played by the extrainstitutional situation—remains more in the sphere of journalistic speculation (even if it is social scientists who speculate) than in that of hard data. What is the impact of the Vietnam war, the draft (which holds unwilling students to the campus and adds a grim multiplier to academic penalties of suspension and expulsion), the minor commitment of government resources to the solution of urban problems, the contrasting investment in the moon venture? We get hints from the data on *issues* in campus conflicts, as in the Astin and Peterson papers. Studies planned to provide adequate time series, as in the Astin program, may begin to disentangle the part played by these situational factors as the historical situation shifts over the years.

If the third category has been dealt with more in the spirit of journalism than of social science, the fourth, social-historical trends and predisposing factors, has been the province of social criticism and essay writing almost unchallenged by data. Yet it is here that questions and answers about student protest may have the broadest significance. Are the protesting students—and the hippie quietists—symptomatic of our sociocultural impasse? Are they pointing to new answers to the unsolved problems of how to preserve and advance humane values in a technological society? It is easy—and fascinating—to speculate about these matters, but very hard to develop types of data that begin to become relevant to them. Whatever headway research on student protest can make in this direction should contribute to our appraisal of present quandaries and our sense of direction for the future.

Student Drug Use[1]

HELEN H. NOWLIS

The author received her PhD in psychology from Yale in 1939. She is currently a professor of psychology and a research consultant on student affairs in the Office of the Provost, University of Rochester. Her primary interests are in developmental psychology, especially the college student, but she has strayed into such areas as parent-child relationships, the effects of drugs on social, emotional, and motivational behavior, and university administration.

Student drug use is a highly emotional topic for virtually everyone. For an increasing number of people "student" arouses bewilderment, frustration, even anger, and "drug" adds a measure of panic, fear, revulsion, and indignation. Together they provide a climate that is not conducive to clear thinking and constructive action.

I would like to share with you some of the experiences I have had during the past three years as a psychologist, an educator, and an erstwhile psychopharmacologist who has been concerned with all aspects of this complex problem. I have managed to become involved with students who use a wide variety of drugs in a variety of ways and for a variety of reasons, with students who do not use drugs, with scientists from biochemists to sociologists, with professionals from medicine and education and the mass media, with judges, with lawyers, with legislators, and with enforcement personnel, as well as with diverse segments of the general public.

I hope that many of you will not be disappointed that I will be discussing only incidentally the prevalence of student drug use, the kinds of drugs they use, and the outcomes of drug use. There are others who can do this better than I. In this connection I would strongly recommend that anyone who is concerned with any aspect of student drug use become familiar with both the methodology and the conclusions of Blum and his associates (1969a, 1969b) in their two important recently published volumes *Society and Drugs* and *Students and Drugs*. My own role has been that of a psychologist analyzing the problem, interpreting the research of others, assessing the current state of our knowledge, and relating it to what is considered by many to be one of society's major prob-

---

[1] Invited Address presented to the Division of Developmental Psychology at the Annual Meeting of the American Psychological Association, Washington, D. C., September 2, 1969.

lems. At least a dozen bills related to drug use and abuse have been introduced in the current session of Congress.

Although I shall be discussing one particular problem, I would like to suggest that it is a prototype for many other problems that involve individuals and groups of individuals, society's response to some of the things they do, and psychology's role in contributing to the understanding of these problems and, hopefully, to their solution. I would also suggest that, without being aware of it or without intending to do so, many of us actually contribute to these problems simply by the way we report our research. Once was the time when we could talk only to each other and we developed a special elliptical discourse that, in most instances, communicated effectively and efficiently. We no longer talk only to each other and our discourse (jargon for others) with all of its implicit assumptions is getting us into trouble. Our so-called conclusions are spread abroad by and to people who do not understand sampling and correlation, experimental controls, significance of difference, and the prevalence of error, who do not read or understand our operational definitions, our null hypotheses, or the limited validity and reliability of our measures. They surround every word we use with their own apperceptive mass.

The current "drug problem" is an excellent example of what can happen. One scientist reports chromosome breakage in a "significant" number of white blood cells as a result of adding LSD to blood samples in a test tube and the word spreads across the nation and reverberates in the halls of Congress that LSD is threatening future generations. I am not at all sure how we can cope with this problem, but it might be helpful if each of us reread his "Summary and Conclusions" as if he were John Doe and perhaps added a "may" or an "in some cases," hopefully specified. We may even have to include a new final paragraph, "Cautions." It may not enhance one's ego or one's pleasure over significance at the $p=.01$ level of confidence, but it certainly would help in educating nonscientists in the proper use of scientific information. The real challenge is to do this for individuals who are seeking simple yes-or-no answers to complex questions, and to do it without stretching their tolerance for complexity and uncertainty to the point where they ignore us completely.

"Student drug use" has been widely interpreted as the "spread of narcotic addiction from the ghetto to our middle class and suburban youth," a "threat to the future of our society." In the wake of this increasingly widely held feeling it is almost impossible to discuss student drug use objectively. In the face of society's decision to consider much of this drug use criminal it is difficult even to study it. In estimating incidence of use, of adverse effects, of any drug-related phenomenon we have many numerators but virtually no reliable denominators. The challenges involved in persuading students that their admission to having committed a felony will be confidential and, indeed, in being able to guarantee that confidentiality are sometimes great.

Definition of Terms

Within the limits of the space available I would like to discuss the nature and extent of student drug use, its meaning and significance, society's response to it, and some of the problems resulting from efforts to control it. But before we do this we must define some terms lest we add to, rather than reduce, the confusion and controversy that exist.

The first term we must define is "drug." In our society there are two widely accepted definitions of "drug" and both of these contain many implicit assumptions. One defines "drug" as a chemical useful in the art and practice of medicine; the other defines "drug" as a "narcotic," with "narcotic" defined not pharmacologically or medically, but as a socially disapproved substance or an otherwise approved substance used for socially disapproved reasons. Many problems result from definitions based on the purpose for which a drug is used. For example, there is the fact that one and the same substance may be a medicine under one circumstance and a "narcotic" under another or not even a drug under still another. Second, there is a great temptation to study one type of drug or drug use out of the context of all drugs. Third, there is a tendency to assume that the use of all drugs that fall under one definition has the same significance and the same effects. The use of heroin as a model for all drugs labeled "narcotic" is a case in point. This has led to complete confusion in the design and interpretation of surveys of student drug use. One investigator will define "drug use" as use of any drug without the advice or supervision of a physician; another will define it as use of specific socially disapproved drugs, with the list varying from survey to survey; and at least one has defined it as use of a wide span of drugs, including social drugs such as alcohol and tobacco, home remedies, painkillers, prescription drugs, over-the-counter drugs, as well as exotic and illicit drugs. Only the latter is in any real sense a survey of student drug use. You will note that I have carefully avoided the word "abuse." We will come to that later.

What is needed is a definition of "drug" that is objective and descriptive and does not have within it a variety of implicit value judgments, which are the source of much of the confusion and controversy that abounds in discussions of drugs and drug use. The basic pharmacological definition of "drug" as any substance that by its chemical nature affects the structure or function of the living organism is about as descriptive and objective as one can be. This definition includes a wide range of substances. It includes both medicines and socially disapproved substances. It also includes a wide range of substances that we do not ordinarily call drugs, such as beverage alcohol and caffeine, nicotine, agricultural, industrial, and household chemicals, pollutants, even food. For many purposes this is too broad a definition, but it forms a base from which we can select groups of drugs and it forces us to make explicit the basis on which we make a given classification. Hopefully, it reminds us that a drug is a drug and the principles by which it interacts with the living organism are the same whether we call it a medicine, a "narcotic," or by some other name.

The other term that we must define is "use." Again, there are certain advantages in starting from a descriptive and objective base. "Use" is often defined in terms of frequency—as ever having tried, occasional, regular, or excessive. But even these terms leave plenty of room for value judgments. It is necessary to specify each in terms of actual frequency of use over a specified time. Whatever one's definition of excessive, it is then at least explicit.

This is perhaps the point at which we should consider "abuse" and to recognize that, as currently used, both socially and legally, it has little correspondence to "use" as I have defined it. In other contexts and even for our national drug, alcohol, "abuse" is defined as a pattern of use that interferes with the psychological, social, academic, or vocational functioning of a given individual. As far as many other drugs are involved, if we call them drugs, "abuse" is legally defined as *any* use of a non-medically approved drug or of a medically approved drug for a non-medically approved purpose. Our effort to justify and support this as abuse in terms of "effects" of drugs so used is one of the main factors in the current controversy over drugs. When research indicating that monosodium glutamate injected peritoneally into pregnant mice produces offspring with neural damage, ataxia, obesity, and sterility (Olney, 1960) is presented as evidence that it is dangerous and should not be added to baby food, eminent experts testify that this is irrelevant because it "has no relationship to the amount of MSG consumed conventionally nor does it have any relationship to the usual rate of entry into the body."[2] When the same type of evidence is presented for LSD, it is used as at least partial grounds for labeling LSD society's most dangerous drug, placing it in a category with heroin and singling it out for the severest criminal penalties. I am not making a case for LSD. I am merely pointing out that we are changing the rules to suit our purposes and are inviting controversy and charges of hypocrisy.

Surveys of Student Drug Use

With all of these qualifications and with the recognition that we have no research from which we can confidently generalize to all students, what can we say about student drug use? Most students use drugs. In Blum's 1967 survey (Blum et al., 1969a, 1969b) of a random sample of approximately 200 students from each of five different west coast colleges and universities, 68–81% had used tobacco one or more times, 89–97% had used alcohol, 11–32% had used amphetamines, 18–31% had used sedatives, 11–28% had used tranquilizers, 10–33% had used marihuana, 2–9% had used any of a variety of hallucinogens, and 1–2% had used a variety of narcotics and painkillers. Lest you forget, let me remind you that these percentages represent reports of having used once or more. They include both legal and illegal use for most drugs. A follow-up survey in 1968 on marihuana use in the school that had shown 21% marihuana use in the initial survey showed 57% marihuana use. Reports of regular use had increased from 4 to 14%. The rate of hallucinogen experience had increased from 6% to perhaps as high as 17%. Opium use (not heroin) was estimated to have increased from 1 to 10%. Again, a word of caution: We know on the basis of a variety of surveys of institutions around the country that use of illicit drugs varies from institution to institution and from area to area. We also know that the west coast tends to be a relatively high-use area. Even there, it is a small minority of students who are involved in regular use of marihuana or hallucinogens, with regular use defined as more than once a week but less than daily.

---

[2] P. L. White. Testimony before the Select Committee on Nutrition and Human Needs, United States Senate, 1969. (Quoted in Associated Press Washington dispatch, July 18, 1969.)

There are two surveys in the planning stage that should provide us with more adequate data on which to base generalizations. One will involve a sample of 200 colleges of varying sizes and locations, hopefully with a follow-up after two years. The other will involve a sample of high schools together with their feeder junior high schools in a four-year longitudinal study.

Estimates currently made by Stanley Yolles, Director of the National Institute of Mental Health,[3] on the basis of results of a majority of studies that have been done throughout the country, are that 20–40% of high school and college students have tried marihuana at least once. Of these about 65% are experimenting (from 1 to 10 times and then discontinuing use), 25% are social users, smoking on occasion when it is available, and 10% of those who have tried it at least once use it regularly, with regular defined as devoting a significant portion of their time to obtaining and using the drug. This would mean that somewhere between 2–4% of the students are regular users. This would seem to bear little relationship to statements by prominent people headlined in the news media that 1 out of 10 students is "hooked" on marihuana.

The National Institute of Mental Health (see Footnote 3) also estimates that the use of LSD, even in relatively high-use areas, is low, with probably not more than 5% ever having tried, and an even smaller percentage country-wide.

There can be little doubt that use of illicit drugs is increasing and that use is spreading both up and down the age scale. In recent years it has begun to appear at the junior high and elementary school levels. A large number of middle class adults are believed to be using marihuana. We do not have and probably will not have good data on this group (or any group) as long as possession of marihuana is a felony. In all cases it is the spread of marihuana use that is predominant. The fact that there is increasing use of a mood-changing drug should not surprise us. Mood-changing drugs are the largest single type of drug used, even in prescriptions. The thing that is significant is that marihuana is a drug that carries the heaviest criminal penalties and a degree of social disapproval equivalent to that of heroin to most people.

The reasons for nonmedical drug use are predominantly the same reasons for which man has used drugs throughout the ages: to relieve pain, to allay anxiety, to produce euphoria, and to modify experience, perception, and thought. It is tempting to speculate that modern man's increased use of mood- and mind-altering substances is at least in part an indication that modern man has more pain, more anxiety, less euphoria, and less satisfying experiences, but this is the kind of speculation that has gotten us into trouble. Many of the reasons that young people use drugs are in large measure the reasons that adults use drugs: for fun, to facilitate social interaction, to feel better, to relieve boredom, to escape from problems, even to protest a little. The main difference is that most adults get their stimulants, sedatives, and tranquilizers legally from physicians and their social drug, alcohol, is legal. Their tension, anxiety, fatigue, and depression are judged to be legitimate consequences of their full participation in pursuit of socially approved social and economic goals or values. That the outcomes of their drug use are not always good is attested to by the fact that increasing

---

[3] S. F. Yolles. Statement before the Subcommittee on Alcoholism and Narcotics, Committee on Labor and Public Welfare, United States Senate, August 6, 1969.

numbers of hospital admissions are directly attributable to drug-related illness and that we have 6–9 million alcoholics, depending on how one defines "alcoholic."

Concept of "Drug Effect"

Please note the use of "outcomes of drug use" rather than "drug effects." The concept of drug effect is an example of a term which may be used to communicate effectively among scientists who understand how drugs act that the "effect" of any drug is a function of dose level, route of administration, and many nondrug factors, and that drugs do not have within them the power to produce a specifiable and reliable effect. The average layman with his "magic-potion-notion" of drugs does not understand that we are really involved in a numbers game. For example, the effective dose (ED50) of any drug is that dosage level or amount of the drug *by* which, not at which, 50% of a given population show whatever effect is desired, among many others. The official toxic dose (TD50) depends on how one defines toxic. Even the lethal dose (LD50) is that dosage level *by* which 50% of a group of animals die under specified conditions. The lethal dose may vary with the temperature under which the animals are kept and with whether they are housed singly or in large groups. The reason for this numbers game is that the "effect" of many drugs is largely a function of many nondrug factors.

"The effect" of any drug is a myth. All drugs have multiple effects. No effects are completely reliable or predictable. All drugs are chemicals that are absorbed into the bloodstream and interact with the complex, delicately balanced biochemical system that is the living organism. It is a system that varies from individual to individual and from time to time in the same individual. It varies with age. It varies with sex. It varies in sickness and in health. One needs only to read the counterindications and the list of idiosyncratic reactions and side effects, the "diseases of medical progress," in the advertisement of drugs in medical and scientific journals to be aware of the complexity of factors influencing the effects of a drug. Effects also vary with psychological characteristics of the individual, with his expectations, and with the setting in which the drug is taken or administered. "Outcomes of" or "reactions to" *use* of a drug at least put the organism, physiologically and psychologically defined, into the picture and leave room for discrimination among patterns and circumstances of use.

Whether outcomes or reactions are good or bad is a value judgment. In some cases there is general agreement, in others, violent disagreement. The widely hailed outcome of treating mentally disturbed patients with the major tranquilizers, that is, "emptying our mental hospitals," is considered by at least one prominent psychiatrist to be the equivalent of putting the patient in a chemical straightjacket and depriving him of his right to attempt to solve his problems. The methadone treatment for heroin addiction is regarded by many, including some addicts, as a bright hope and by others as no treatment at all and as outright immoral, because it substitutes dependency on one drug for dependency on another. It is just a matter of values, to be dependent or to be free of supporting one's habit on the black market. There is bitter disagreement within the medical profession as to the propriety and effectiveness of the use of LSD in therapy.

Somewhat guardedly, Blum (Blum et al., 1969b) concludes from his data, "It is clear . . . that a variety of unpleasant outcomes can occur but one gets the impression that very few suffer anything damaging over the long run. Thus, one can conclude, as we do, that anything but acute toxic ill effects are unlikely and that illicit-exotic drugs when used as students are now doing, for the most part, do not seem to pose serious hazards to school performance or to health [p. 378]." He hastens to point out, and properly, that his sample did not include any information on students who had dropped out of school and that those who remained and were studied were a select group. He also points out that his data give no indication of the possible outcomes of long-term low-dosage use.

Yolles (see Footnote 3) reports from NIHM that the incidence of serious adverse reactions to marihuana use appears to be low, but also points out that as the total number of users increases the number experiencing adverse reactions will increase, that the effects of the drug on judgment and perception *might* very well be a factor in automobile accidents, and that users with significant psychiatric problems *might* avoid seeking psychiatric treatment as a result of this form of "self-medication." There are no adequate research data to support the latter statements.

Both of these statements function as projective tests. Those who, because of their personal beliefs, attitudes, and values, believe that illicit drugs are by definition "bad" and that illicit drug use can bring nothing but harm to the individual and to society will dismiss the data and seize on the questions raised by limitations of research design or the absence of research results. Those who hold the other view will seize on the data and dismiss the questions. Those who attempt to be objective will advise caution until we have more data based on research. The irony is that more research will probably leave us with essentially the same dilemma. Such is the nature of drug, of drug action, and of complex human behavior.

I cannot conceive of a research design that could provide the definitive answers the public wants. The number of and interactions among the independent variables involved in, for instance, the driving performance of individuals who have used marihuana are staggering. Administering marihuana of known composition in known amounts in a double-blind situation in the laboratory to naive subjects of equivalent driving skill as measured on a simulator will tell us very little about the driving performance of individuals who, for a variety of reasons, have chosen to use an unknown amount of an illegal drug of unknown strength and purity obtainable only on the black market, who have expectations and varying amounts of experience as to the "effects" of that drug, who choose to drive cars of varying type and condition under various road conditions at some time after having used some amount of the drug, and who have had varying degrees of experience in coping with whatever reactions they as individuals experience when they "use marihuana."

We do need laboratory research on all drugs. We need to know the ways in which they modify the biochemical and neurochemical organism. But beyond this we need to know how these changes are related to changes in behavior. This is the greater challenge. In the meantime, differences "significantly greater than chance" in situations in which so many important independent variables have been controlled will not provide us with the answers to social problems, especially when they are used inappropriately by people grasping at anything that seems to support what they believe about drugs that have historically been labeled "bad," "dangerous," or "evil."

The use of virtually all drugs involves adverse reactions or bad outcomes, including death or, in some cases, life imprisonment, *at some dosage level in some people under some circumstances.* This includes aspirin, smallpox vaccine, penicillin, alcohol, nicotine, barbiturates, amphetamines, as well as heroin, LSD, and marihuana. In this regard, it is of interest that, to my knowledge, there are no verified deaths directly attributable to either LSD or marihuana *as pharmacological agents* except for one elephant. Official records show approximately 185 deaths per year from aspirin.

Societal Reactions to Student Drug Use

As we turn to the meaning and significance of student drug use, society's response to it, and efforts to control it, I want to make it very clear that I am speaking as one psychologist who is acutely aware of the fact that background, training and experience, beliefs, attitudes, and values, even basic beliefs about the nature of man, are important factors in any analysis and assessment of these phenomena. One always hopes that awareness inspires caution. My only special qualifications to comment on this social problem are that, because of commitments entered into almost adventitiously, I have been forced to look at student drug use from almost every possible point of view and have had the privilege of interacting with many representatives of disciplines and professions who espouse these many points of view, including students of all shades of opinion and involvement.

If one wants to understand drug effect and drug use, one must look not solely at the pharmacological agent, but at the person who chooses to use drugs, how much he uses, when and where and how, and what he expects, wants, or believes will result from that use. We are learning to our dismay that to try to control drug use by limiting the supply of the particular drug used does not decrease drug use in general. Many users merely turn to another substance that may involve even more risk, and in our society drugs are everywhere, legal drugs, illegal drugs, and substances which we do not call drugs.

In addition, we have mounted a gigantic campaign to persuade the public that there is a drug for every ill or misery—anxiety, depression, tension, and the physical symptoms associated with these, irritability, fatigue, lack of success in business, in social life, in the family. If there is not a chemical cure, there soon will be. This has rocketed the pharmaceutical industry to the number-one profit-making industry in the country, passing the automobile industry in 1967. All of this, of course, has to do with the promotion of legal drugs, both prescription and over-the-counter drugs, obtained through legal means. But I seem to remember learning in introductory psychology about a principle known as generalization. It should not surprise us that young people do not understand why we are so excited about their use of drugs for their miseries and ills. It is also relevant to note that there has been an almost equally vigorous campaign on behalf of their drugs via the news reporting of the drug scene. It has been suggested that the chemical most responsible for the current drug scene is printer's ink. Just because most of us who are over 30 do not ordinarily seek adventure, new experience, insight into one's self, independence, and have either found or given up looking for new insights, meaningful social relationships, creative expression, even a dash of rebellion against the restrictions that we accept as inevitable in a modern technological society, and a pinch of fun, we should not underestimate the appeal to the young of anything that promises any or all of these, regardless of whether those promises can be fulfilled. This particular characteristic of many drugs does not seem to deter many of us from seeking what is promised. In addition, we have learned that many drugs are much more effective if we believe that they will be, and that "sugar pills" have cured great ills and produced profound negative effects. One physician has been reported to have said somewhat facetiously, "Whenever a new drug comes on the market, rush to your physician while both he and you still believe in its powers."

It is almost trite to point out to an audience of psychologists that drug use serves different functions for different individuals. Despite this, "escape to nowhere" has become the banner for numerous efforts to dissuade everyone from any use of certain drugs. It is astounding to note how often mere use of illicit drugs is taken as an indication that the user needs psychiatric treatment. This would seem to be, in part, the result of our concept of drug abuse as a disease and our definition of any use of illegal drugs as abuse. We seem to assume both that drugs are to cure illness and that if one takes drugs, he is, almost by definition, ill. There is no doubt that some young people use drugs to escape from pressure, from anxiety, from impulses which threaten them, from the stresses and strains of growing up. There is also no doubt that some people who are ill use drugs. But unless one defines doing anything that is not socially approved as illness, the great majority of young people who use drugs illegally are not ill and are not in need of psychiatric treatment. Many use them because they think it is fun. Many try them out of curiosity. Many use marihuana much as we use alcohol to facilitate social interaction. Some use them as occasional respite from the pressures of increasing academic demands.

Fun, curiosity, social interaction, and change of pace are all rather normal motivations. There are many ways to satisfy them. The important question is why increasing numbers of students are choosing to risk severe legal penalties by choosing to use illegal drugs. It could have something to do with society's response to their use of drugs or, perhaps more important, society's response to young people.

The very small minority of students who use illegal drugs regularly and who devote a considerable portion of their time to obtaining drugs, to using them, and to talking about their drug experiences are also a varied group. Many of them are bright enough and well enough put together to manage their drug use and still fulfill their academic obligations. Others are not. Some are convinced that drugs will solve any of a variety of problems, some developmental and some pathological. Some are sick. Again we should ask the question, "Why illegal drugs?"

Society's undiscriminating response to all student drug use has been emotional and extremely punitive. It is outraged at many of the things some young people are doing and saying these days. There are those who would pass laws against them and even some who would shoot a few students in the belief that that would serve as a deterrent. If one watches the faces of those who suggest the latter, one gets the impression that shooting students might also serve to reduce their anger and frustration. But there are calmer voices to be heard and as yet the more violent reactions have been held in check in most cases. But the drug issue is different. For a great variety of historical and cultural reasons we have carefully nurtured attitudes, beliefs, and stereotypes about all drugs which are outside of medicine or used for nonmedical reasons. Beginning with the Harrison Narcotic Act we have forged a system of criminal penalties, including mandatory jail sentences, denial of probation and parole, for possession and "sale" ("to sell" is legally defined as to sell, to give, or otherwise to dispose) of "narcotics" that would suggest that these were greater than any crimes other than treason or first-degree murder. I would suggest the hypothesis that the drug issue may represent a rallying point for frustration, resentment, and anger generated by many things that young people are saying and doing and that the existing drug laws and the attitudes that support them are rough-and-ready weapons for retaliation. Many are quick to blame drugs for everything from dropping out, criticizing, and protesting to violence and crime on the streets. If drugs are to blame, we can concentrate on controlling them and look no further. Historically, nonmedical drug use has been associated primarily with minority groups and, with the persistent "magic-potion-notion" of drugs, drug use has been a convenient scapegoat and a ready target for aggression against these groups. Students are our fastest growing and increasingly vocal minority.

Estimates of the number of persons in the United States who have used marihuana vary from 8 to 20 million. The NIMH (see Footnote 3) considers that 8 million is a conservative estimate and that there may be 12 million. All of these people are criminals because they have committed a felony: They possessed marihuana. Psychology has something to say about the effects of labeling. Psychology and common sense certainly have something to say about punishment as a deterrent when the chances of being punished are somewhere between 1 in 500 and 1 in 1,000. But it either is not being said or is not being heard.

Because of these laws, because of the nature of the law enforcement approach to the control of drug use, and because of the persistent attitudes and beliefs which support that approach, the drug issue has also become a target and a rallying point for many young people's frustration, resentment, and charges of hypocrisy against a society that promotes the use of alcohol, is unwilling even to require the registration of guns, and seems unwilling to regulate much behavior that results in thousands of deaths and injuries.

Educational Approach to Drug Control

The other major approach to control of illegal drug use is that of education. I use the word reluctantly because most so-called drug education has until very recently consisted of preaching and of attempts to scare with statements that are inaccurate and often patently false. Much of it still does. It seems to be designed to preserve and justify our attitudes and beliefs and our laws. It obviously has not reduced illegal drug use. Some of it may even have instigated use.

Drug education is desperately needed: Students need it; parents need it; legislators need it; physicians need it; the general public needs it. We are living in an increasingly chemically dominated environment. Drugs are an important part of that chemical environment. One of our most urgent social problems is to learn to live wisely in that environment, but we cannot learn as long as we do not understand what drugs are and how they act, what risks are involved in all drug use, and how these risks can be minimized. We also need to expand our concept of drug to include the many substances that by their chemical nature affect the structure and function of the living organism.

To do honest, sound, and effective drug education we will need all of our skills in communication and persuasion. We will have to change long-held beliefs and attitudes about drugs. We will have to separate the problem of drugs as pharmacological agents from the problem of people who make value judgments about drugs, about "drug effects," about the reasons for using drugs, and about people who use drugs. The *people* problem will be the more difficult to solve, but a solution to the *drug* problem should make it easier.

Conclusion

I would like to close by addressing myself particularly to Division 7, the division of APA primarily concerned with growth and development from infancy to adulthood. The problem of student drug use is extremely complex. It has very little to do with drugs as pharmacological agents. At the core of it is a phenomenon that has relatively recently been created by our society primarily in the interest of technological and economic development. It has recently been intensified by the arrival of the baby boom at college age. This phenomenon is that of increasingly prolonged adolescence. Having created it we generally choose to pretend that it does not exist.

"Nonadulthood" has been stretched 5–10 years beyond physiological maturity. It has been stretched farthest for the brightest and most talented. Our young people between the ages of 16 and 25 are our fastest growing minority, a minority that has very little power and influence even on their own destinies. In other times they would have been married and dutifully, even happily, contributing to the gross national product or being "liberally educated" while waiting to assume the positions which had been prepared for them.

Our failure to integrate today's young people into society, to give them any significant role except to fight our wars, to provide them with a realistic arena in which to accomplish the tasks of adolescence, however you wish to define them, to examine these tasks in the light of the world in which we now live has left them largely to their own devices. We tend to react violently against many of these.

All is not well with many of our young people. We are not facing the very difficult problems involved in understanding and dealing with the process of becoming an adult in a rapidly changing and highly technological society. No society will flourish whose institutions—family, religion, education, business, government—do not effectively challenge substantial numbers of its most gifted young people to grow, to use their talents in constructive and satisfying ways, to develop a sense of worth and accomplishment, to develop meaningful and humane social relationships, to feel that they have an increasing role in the control of their destinies and some influence on the society in which they must live, work, play, establish a home and raise a family, and eventually to assume responsibility for that society and its problems.

Instead of facing basic problems we are lashing out at symptoms, at drug use, at protest, at dropping out, at manner and dress and language, and are feeling satisfaction and relief at doing "something." Much of what we are doing is at best keeping us from dealing with the basic problems and at worst intensifying those problems. As pointed out by Barber (1967) and many others, social policy is itself one of the major determinants of the nature and severity of a social problem, particularly the "drug problem."

Perhaps we should be among the first to accept George Miller's (1969) advice in his Presidential Address and spread the word that young people are not basically bad and need not be coerced into work and responsibility. Given half a chance they will grow and develop and make wise decisions, but only if we expect that they will and provide the freedom and opportunity for them to learn to do so.

References

Barber, B. *Drugs and society*. New York: Russell Sage Foundation, 1967.

Blum, R. H., & Associates (Eds.) *Society and drugs*. Vol. 1. *Drugs*. San Francisco: Jossey-Bass, 1969. (a)

Blum, R. H., & Associates (Eds.) *Students and drugs*. Vol. 2. *Drugs*. San Francisco: Jossey-Bass, 1969. (b)

Miller, G. A. Psychology as a means of promoting human welfare. *American Psychologist,* 1969, **24,** 1063–1075.

Nowlis, H. H. *Drugs on the college campus*. New York: Doubleday, 1969.

Olney, J. W. Brain lesions, obesity, and other disturbances in mice treated with monosodium glutamate. *Science,* 1969, **163,** 719–721.

Black–White Campus Issues and the Function of Counseling Centers[1]

CHARLES W. THOMAS

The author received his PhD from Western Reserve University in 1961. He is presently Director of the Center for the Study of Racial and Social Issues in Los Angeles, where his major interests involve developing programs designed to reduce conflicts created by racism and poverty. He is also the National Honorary Chairman of the Association of Black Psychologists.

Among the basic challenges confronting social science professionals in contemporary society is an understanding of what racist values have done to whites, on the one hand, and how to facilitate in Afro-Americans an appreciation for what it means to be black, on the other. To be black, by way of definition for this presentation, is a biosocial acceptance of membership in the racial group. This membership becomes manifested through a specific form of behavior that enables the Afro-American to enhance his self-determined mastery over those political and socioeconomic institutions that would grossly impair his socially relevant behavior. In Afro-Americans, blackness is productive of the most healthy personality due to the emphasis on self-regarding attitudes that serve to increase self-esteem. Furthermore, upon internalization, changes in the cognitive world nurture not only self-determination, but give rise to an effective stage for a closer interaction between feelings and activities.

Upon becoming black, there is a more extensive repertory of choices which accompany the personal-social freedom. The therapeutic gains are remarkably similar to the nature of counseling. For example, Tyler (1958) has defined counseling as "one kind of psychological helping activity, the kind that concentrates on the growth of a clear sense of ego identity and *the willingness to make choices* and commitments in accordance with it [p. 8, italics added]." With a substitution of blackness for counseling, the definition would also be appropriate for the former, that is, blackness.

In much the same manner, the criteria for mental health provide useful insights as to what blackness is. Jahoda (1958) cites the following criteria: (*a*) attitudes of an individual toward his own self; (*b*) growth, development, or self-actualizatism; (*c*) integration; (*d*) autonomy; (*e*) perception of reality; and (*f*) environmental mastery. Any combination of these principles would also reflect social-psychological underpinnings of blackness. Admittedly, this was not the intent

---

[1] Invited Address presented to the Division of Counseling Psychology at the Annual Meeting of the American Psychological Association, Washington, D. C., September 2, 1969.

of current concepts in mental health, but they are useful in clarifying the pedestrian reactions to significant aspects of blackness.

More appropriate recognition of what is taking place will not occur until the fantasies and myths society promotes and rewards have been dispelled. For members of the group in control to sustain their sense of personal adequacy and security at the expense of those who are lacking in such resources negatively reflects upon those professionals who by training should know better. There is, for example, something terribly inadequate about the science of psychology, if, as black students have found, James Baldwin is able to present a more cogent discussion of referential processes than the standard fare in social psychology.

The furor about black studies is another case in point. Few black instructors will fail to deny that white students, in general, are naive to the point of impeding the progress of the class. This observation has nothing to do with the popular question, "Should they or should they not be admitted to black studies?" It does, however, concern the quality and level of instruction.

By way of illustration, this issue was recently discussed by a variety of black scholars from across the country. The consensus was best summarized by a law professor who said:

If anything, white students are more in need than Blacks of a Black teacher in a course seeking to deal in a rewarding way with the significance of racism as a dehumanizing factor in this society. While a white teacher of competence and sensitvity, working with adquate materials may convey a sense of the problem, there is perhaps, uniquely in this area of education, a more serious problem of unlearning than teaching students. . . . A Black instructor brings not only intellectual competence to his subject but also the weight of professional involvement and personal experiences. A Black, capable of combining all these qualities has at least the chance of breaking through the "I understand your problem" barrier that is particularly difficult to penetrate in the liberal white. The white teacher with all of the best intentions in the world, just can't do it.[2]

Issues concerning the meanings of behavior and the confusion in attempting to understand commitments with respect to roles and responsibilities will become more critical on college campuses.

Irrelevancy of Present Counseling Services

Problems in this area will be accentuated by the increasing number of students whom colleges are ill-equipped to educate On the other hand, the present generation of students is less inclined to remain silent about the quality of what is taught, or to submit to the many mystical rites that went unchallenged by the preceding generations of students. The demand that every part of the college operation be examined in terms of contemporary social problems will not end soon. Mix these issues with problems in human development and it becomes clear as to what the magnitude of the challenge is to an efficiently but relevantly operated counseling center.

In an ideal way, student personnel services would be the vanguard when it comes to removing social barriers that interfere with the inherent growth force of

---

[2] Derrick Bell, personal communication, 1969.

clients. The traditional activities in counseling, however, have had a social control rather than a social change context for people of Afro-American ancestry. It is this paradox that has caused counseling programs to reflect an ambiguity about eradicating racism as a mental health problem.

The manifestations of injustice because of race are impossible to ignore. Students have been advised, for example, not to enter a particular field on the basis of a counselor's void in personal knowledge of any Afro-Americans engaged in the occupation under consideration; or a high school freshman might be programmed into taking non-college preparatory courses even when the student has both the potential and interest. Then, of course, there are the "How does it feel to be a Negro?" and "What does one call you people these days?" type questions. That such experiences are not isolated events but integral parts of too much counseling is understood quite well by black students.

The apparent emphasis in counseling seems to be on a continual molding of black students to fit into the existing social system rather than on strategies for changing social institutions to accommodate the needs of students. Perhaps that factor explains the unimpressive record of success in counseling services for Afro-Americans and others who do not fit into the normative requirements of the larger society. In the absence of reasons that would hold due to theoretical considerations, the discrepancy has to be found in who is conducting the counseling. Tyler (1961) comes close to this situation when she states that there is "some uncertainty and ambiguity in the minds of counseling psychologists . . . that deal with conflicts between one's responsibility to his client and his responsibility to society [p. 258]."

When it comes to difficulties in counseling with black students, it seems to me that counselors so often fall into those diagnostic categories reserved for their clients. In counselors one finds "lack of assurance, lack of information, lack of skill, cultural self-conflict, interpersonal-self conflicts or choice conflict [Tyler, 1961, pp. 78–79]. For black students there appears to be a lack of confidence about the rewards of counseling in handling the agonies of life experiences. Less than positive feelings are also expressed about the perception of counselors who do not understand the social realities of what is taking place. As a black student remarked recently, "They want to put a white tag on the solution of my set of problems which does not apply as I see things. I can't accept that kind of a trick bag."

The goodness of fit between social ideals and social practices will require different criteria for defining, implementing, and evaluating effective behavior changes. However, significant progress in the resolution of conflict around human problems in living will come in direct proportion to the extent that restructuring in the control of the larger social units is possible.

With the gap closing between mental health and vocational adjustment, which in turn shifts the emphasis in counseling, different types of specialists and changes in some activities will be necessary. Such changes in direction, however, will not automatically bring about more humanistic orientations in a larger sense. As Amos and Grambs (1968) have noted:

This total person was the verbally oriented middle class youth or adult who, in most cases had the ability, values and experiences to talk through his particular problem and decide on a course of action. In recent years we have found that with many of our disadvantaged youth such an approach is not effective. Increasingly, one hears that the most successful counselor with the disadvantaged youth is the nonprofessional from the youth's own social or cultural group who can communicate on the youth's own terms and understand his problem because he has experienced them. Even though such a position has some merit, the long term danger to the counseling profession is obvious. Unless counselors and counselor educators recognize this threat and are willing to modify curriculum, roles, techniques and procedures, additional criticism will be forthcoming [p. 2].

Similar ideas have been expressed by a variety of clinical and counseling psychologists. Many of the advocates for such changes recognize that if changes do not come from within the profession, they will come from external forces.

The Drive for a More Humanistic Society

Vast humanitarian movements, committed to solving current living problems, are already under way that will have an impact on the counseling profession. Avoidance behavior in any form will not lessen the drive for a more humanistic society. Black people in a variety of human service areas have become organized, to paraphrase Philips and Wiener (1966), in the tradition of the Promethean reach for creative control, the human reach for mastery of self and environment, and the breaking of chains forged by concepts of chance, mythology, and overwhelming complexity. As such, one cannot dismiss lightly the efforts of policemen, social welfare workers, public elected officials, psychiatrists, educators, public health workers, nuns, engineers, nurses, students, and psychologists who are organizing in order to address themselves to the significant social problems affecting Afro-Americans particularly but also other segments of society whose needs have not been fulfilled.

Time is not on the side of those of any ethnic hue or social class who would conduct business as usual. Every segment of society can take its choice of working to facilitate the realization of goals that Afro-Americans perceive as important or resigning itself to increasing oppressive measures that will constrain the freedom of all men. As of now the social order has not changed in any meaningful manner, so much of what appears to be new is nothing more than another crop of duplicates that maintain not only tribal wisdom but the rites of passage as well. The failures and false steps in improving the quality of life for minority people are abundant. Furthermore, ethnic minority people seem to have reached a critical social-psychological point where a growing number feel that the majority group has neither the will nor the ability to deal with legitimate social problems stemming from race and social class.

These circumstances have contributed to the growing pessimism of Afro-American students and an increasingly expanding number of their middle-aged, middle-income elders about the hope for real social progress. But, as Pierce (1969) has stated, "Black people are not emotionally prepared to continue the present state of affairs. We have, indeed, a sense of urgency as we proceed to eradicate the old social order that has as its most visible symbol . . . moral failure [p. 2]." Much of the mounting mistrust and open dislike for whites can be explained by the fact that a very large number of white people neither understand nor accept equal dignity of all human beings. It is these harsh social realities that black students, more than any other group, are highly sensitive to, in their struggle for an education that would be related to their needs.

Issues and Innovations in Counseling

With the existing social climate, the challenge in operating a counseling center is far from easy. The primary question is not a center for *what* but a center for *whom*. It is entirely possible that an expansion in the scope and variety of services to be performed should be provided by experts trained in other areas or by those who have experience in other areas. Let me hasten to add that I do not look forward to that development any time soon, and certainly not as a voluntary effort by any substantial number of counseling center personnel. On the other hand, the issue of manpower has to be confronted and resolved.

More than ample evidence is available indicating that professionals are desensitized and unable to communicate with clients who have a different sociocultural life style. Furthermore, with the advent of the "war on poverty" and the new careers movement, it became quite clear that graduate training was not necessary in order to perform many of the activities that professionals were doing. In a very similar manner, studies have rather consistently shown that theoretical orientation is not a significant factor in treatment outcome. A different type of expert counselor does not mean that he will pollute the profession. It is far from a convincing argument that those presently identified as professionals are equipped to cope with the problems of black students. Also, given the less than calm atmosphere between blacks and whites generally, it is illogical to assume that black students in large numbers would seek help from white professionals.

Related to the manpower consideration is the location of the counseling center. Too many are situated in places that contribute to inaccessibility and fragmentation of services. With the growing emphasis on mental health, it would be efficient to have counseling centers in student health buildings and to have satellite programs in dormitories, student unions, and other places where students meet. Such an arrangement would allow for mental health teams to operate and to provide broader support for students in their efforts to cope with the circumstances of their lives. These changes in the established operations would also enable counseling centers to engage in outreach activities by taking services to the students.

Changes in operational conditions alone, however, are not sufficient. The quality of the personnel who conduct the services is a key to the success of the program, particularly if there is concern about Afro-American students and their problems. In this regard, 80 black upper division and first-year graduate students were polled recently about their impressions of counseling services at a state college in Los Angeles. (A formal study of larger scope is under way.) The following is presented acknowledging the limitations found in clinical compilations that have not been subjected to empirical analysis. However, these shortcomings not withstanding, the responses can be used to gain additional appreciation for the perceptions provided.

Most of the students seen stated that they would go to a counseling center if compelled to do so for reasons concerning academic difficulties, financial need, or employment opportunities. Even in these areas, they believe that it would be difficult to confer with a white counselor. Conversely, with problems of a more personal nature, they would prefer to take these to a counselor who was considered to be a black "militant." However, most indicated that since there was no such counselor available, they had attempted to solve their problems with assistance from friends or their parents.

The counseling center was assessed as providing the best services for native white, moderate-to-conservative students from middle-income homes. It was not seen as providing very effective services, however, for students of any color with serious problems. Impressionistic differences existed between males and females with respect to preferences for a male or female counselor. For these young black men, their choice was for a male counselor. Women, by contrast, considered the sex of the counselor to be inconsequential.

Both male and female blacks did agree that it would be quite important to the counseling relationship for the counselor to be: (*a*) of the same race, (*b*) as black in thinking and feeling as they, (*c*) no younger in age than they, (*d*) able to understand and use street language, (*e*) able to listen and to help find the best solution to the problem, and (*f*) able to understand social-psychological issues through training or experience. Although these are anecdotal references, and are to be respected as such, they do tend to be supported by the results of empirical studies.

As more Afro-American students are recruited into predominately white colleges and universities, the sheer number, in and of itself, will not constitute a problem. Difficulties will come about because the programs and institutions will not be adapted to the needs of the students. Educational experiences also have to be more than another form of social containment in order that a few people may live in the fantasy of respectability. Thinly veiled games passed off as innovations may contribute momentarily to the special arrogance displayed so well by academicians with their recently acquired expertise, but it must be recognized that such behavior encourages a culture of distrust.

Conclusion

The morally destructive forces of racism are embedded in every segment of life in our society. It is these forces that have become the agents of social control that subvert man as a thinking, feeling, becoming being. There is an abundance of ideas about what the nature of these problems are and how they should be solved. If, as the existentialist (Sartre, 1947) teaches, "Man is nothing other than what he makes himself," I believe those of us in the mental health sector at this historical period need to ask of ourselves, "What is the purpose of man?" Is it to take a giant step on another planet in the name of humanity while on earth there are all of the ills ever known to man? The same society that places a man on the moon closes its eyes to hunger and pain in its own children, spends more money on a war in another land (that really does not serve the cause of justice) than it spends on developing the human potential of its own citizens, and fosters the myth that some of its citizens are the goal rather than a bridge to a more humanistic community. The black movement, if for no other reason, in all of its diverse forms serves as a needed transfusion for a wider and more cogent view of courage and of freedom in the perception of social reality.

Difficulties in human relations are similar to a problem in Zen (Reps, 1962). "It is too clear and so it is hard to see. A dunce once searched for a fire with a lighted lantern. Had he known what fire was, he could have cooked his rice much sooner (Mu-Mon) [p. 19]."

References

Amos, W. E., & Grambs, J. D. *Counseling the disadvantaged youth.* Englewood Cliffs, N. J.: Prentice-Hall, 1968.

Jahoda, M. *Current concepts of positive mental health.* New York: Basic Books, 1958.

Phillips, E. L., & Wiener, D. N. *Short-term psychotherapy and structured behavior change.* New York: McGraw-Hill, 1966.

Pierce, W. The black psychologist and current revolution—the case for the indigenous professional. Paper presented at the meeting of the Western Psychological Association, Vancouver, B. C., June 18, 1969. (Mimeo)

Reps, P. *Zen flesh, Zen bones.* Garden City, N. J.: Anchor Books, 1962.

Sartre, J. P. *Existentialism.* New York: Philosophical Library, 1947.

Tyler, L. E. *The work of the counselor.* New York: Appleton-Century-Crofts, 1961.

Tyler, L. E. Theoretical principles underlying the counseling process. *Journal of Counseling Psychology,* 1958, **22,** 3–10.

psychology and society's future

Psychology and Society's Future

The two papers in the closing section of this volume contain broad perspectives on the problems of society along with glimpses of alternative futures. A note of gloom touches both papers, tempering Bennis' basic optimism and pervading Etzioni's outlook. Both see a need for basic reform which will allow the individual to experience a greater sense of identity and authenticity.

Bennis provides us with his second thoughts as he reviews the predictions he made in 1964. At that time, being primarily oriented toward large, science-based, expanding organizations, he had an optimistic view of the future. He predicted that organizations would become increasingly democratic as they became more flexible and allowed their members greater opportunities for meaningful participation.

Five years later, with the intervening national agonies of Vietnam, riots, assassinations, and confrontations, plus his own personal administrative experience at a large public university, Bennis' outlook is less optimistic. While many of his earlier predictions are already being realized, they have turned out to be more problematical than he had previously envisioned. As he now observes, increasing participation does not necessarily lead to greater commitment to organizational goals, but rather often leads to conflict and confrontation. He cites a number of factors that interfere with the increasing democratization of organizations including: (*a*) the frequent impossibility of consensus, particularly when a group's members represent subsystems with conflicting goals; (*b*) the impatience and rigidity which result from the frustrations caused by the ambiguities of modern life; and (*c*) the diminished psychological attractiveness of bland democratic processes compared to the heady excitement of disruption. Thus, while again Bennis predicts a continuing trend toward greater participation, this time he adds a trend toward increasing confrontation, negotiation, and bargaining.

Etzioni also sees increasing participation as the trend of the future, a trend which he suggests will provide the individual with a greater sense of authenticity. Noting that some societies are better designed to meet human needs than others, Etzioni suggests that modern, pluralistic, democratic societies do not adequately meet certain psychological needs, particularly the need for authentic participation. He points to numerous areas where such participation is blocked. He notes that the political process is responsive not to votes, but to organized groups, and hence those who are not organized have little opportunity for real political participation. In the educational process, he suggests that individual authenticity is submerged in the quest for the rounded personality. In suburban living, he finds among neighbors little in the way of authentic relationships. And in industry he points to human relations programs aimed at teaching managers to give their subordinates a feeling of participation without really sharing the power.

However, regarding the future, he observes that increasingly the alienated are stirring against these blocks to their authentic participation in society. Whether these stirrings will result in greater societal responsiveness to individual needs or in a showdown between those holding power and those seeking more, Etzioni leaves us to ponder.

A Funny Thing Happened on the Way to the Future[1]

WARREN G. BENNIS

The author received his PhD in social sciences and economics from the Massachusetts Institute of Technology in 1955. He is presently Vice-President for Academic Development at the State University of New York at Buffalo, where his major interest involves the building of a great new campus at SUNY/Buffalo.

Analysis of the "future," or, more precisely, inventing relevant futures, has become in recent years as respectable for the scientist as for the shaman. Inspired by Bertrand de Jouvenal, Daniel Bell, Olaf Helmer, and others, there seems to be growing evidence and recognition for the need of a legitimate base of operations for the "futurologist." Writing in a recent issue of the *Antioch Review,* groping for a definition of the future I wrote:

For me, the "future" is a portmanteau word. It embraces several notions. It is an exercise of the imagination which allows us to compete with and try to outwit future events. Controlling the anticipated future is, in addition, a social invention that legitimizes the process of forward planning. There is no other way I know of to resist the "tyranny of blind forces" than by looking facts in the face (as we experience them in the present) and extrapolating to the future—nor is there any other sure way to detect compromise. Most importantly, the future is a conscious dream, a set of imaginative hypotheses groping toward whatever vivid utopias lie at the heart of our consciousness. "In dreams begin responsibilities," said Yeats, and it is to our future responsibilities as educators, researchers, and practitioners that these dreams are dedicated [Bennis, 1968, p. 227].

Most students of the future would argue with that definition, claiming that it is "poetic" or possibly even "prescientific." The argument has validity, I believe, though it is difficult to define "futurology," let alone distinguish between and among terms such as "inventing relevant futures," scenarios, forecasts, self-fulfilling prophecies, predictions, goals, normative theories, evolutionary hypotheses, prescriptions, and so on. Philosophers and sociologists, for example, are still arguing over whether Weber's theory of bureaucracy was, in fact, a theory, a poignant and scholarly admonition, an evolutionary hypothesis, or a descriptive statement.

---

[1] This paper is a combination and revision of two papers given at professional meetings in early September 1969: an invited address to the Division of Personality and Social Psychology, American Psychological Association, September 2, Washington, D.C., and a speech for a panel on "political science and the study of the future," given before the American Political Science Association, September 4, New York.

However difficult it may be to identify a truly scientific study of the future, most scholars would agree that it should include a number of objectives:

1. It should provide a survey of possible futures in terms of a spectrum of major potential alternatives.

2. It should ascribe to the occurrence of these alternatives some estimates of relative a priori probabilities.

3. It should, for given basic policies, identify preferred alternatives.

4. It should identify those decisions which are subject to control, as well as those developments which are not, whose occurrence would be likely to have a major effect on the probabilities of these alternatives [Helmer, 1969].

With these objectives only dimly in mind, I wrote a paper on the future of organizations (five years ago to the day that this paper was delivered to the American Political Science Association) which was called "Organizational Developments and the Fate of Bureaucracy [Bennis, 1964]." Essentially, it was based on an evolutionary hypothesis which asserted that every age develops a form of organization most appropriate to its genius. I then went on to forecast certain changes in a "postbureaucratic world" and how these changes would affect the structure and environment of human organizations, their leadership and motivational patterns, and their cultural and ecological values. A number of things have occurred since that first excursion into the future in September 1964 which are worth mentioning at this point for they have served to reorient and revise substantially some of the earlier forecasts.

Perhaps only a Homer or Herodotus, or a first-rate folkrock composer, could capture the tumult and tragedy of the five years since that paper was written and measure their impact on our lives. The bitter agony of Vietnam, the convulsive stirrings of black America, the assassinations, the bloody streets of Chicago have all left their marks. What appears is a panorama that goes in and out of focus as it is transmitted through the mass media and as it is expressed through the new, less familiar media, the strikes, injunctions, disruptions, bombings, occupations, the heart attacks of the old and the heartaches of the young. Strolling in late August 1969 through my own campus, lush, quiet, and sensual, I am almost lulled into thinking that nothing fundamental has happened to America in the past five years. Only the residual grafitti from last spring's demonstrations ("Keep the Pigs Out!" "Be Realistic—Demand the Impossible!"), hanging all but unnoticed in the student union, remind us that something has— though what it is, as the song says, "ain't exactly clear." One continually wonders if what has happened is unique and new ("Are we in France, 1788?" as one student asked), whether what is happening at the universities will spread to other, possibly less fragile institutions, and, finally, whether the university is simply the anvil upon which the awesome problems of our entire society are being hammered out. No one really knows. Despite the proliferation of analyses attributing campus unrest to everything from Oedipal conflicts (the most comforting explanation) to the failure of the Protestant Ethic, the crises continue relentlessly.

In his *Report to Greco,* Nikos Kazantzakis tells us of an ancient Chinese imprecation: "I curse you; may you live in an important age." Thus, we are all damned, encumbered, and burdened as well as charmed, exhilerated, and fascinated by this curse.

In the rueful words of Bob Dylan:

> *Come, writers and critics*
> *Who prophesize with your pen*
> *And keep your eyes wide*
> *The chance won't come again*
> *And don't speak too soon*
> *For the wheel's still in spin*
> *And there's no tellin' who*
> *That it's namin'*
> *For the loser now*
> *Will be later to win*
> *For the times are a-changin'.*

Reactions to our spastic times vary. There are at least seven definable types:

1. First and most serious of all are the *militants,* composed for the most part of impotent and dependent populations who have been victimized and infantalized, and who see no way out but to mutilate and destroy the system which has decimated their group identity and pride. Excluded populations rarely define their price for belated inclusion in intellectual terms, which confuses and terrifies the incumbents who take participation for granted.

2. The *apocalyptics,* who with verbal ferocity burn everything in sight. So, in *The Age of Overkill,* Benjamin DeMott assumes the persona of a future historian and casts a saddened eye on everyone from the Beatles to James Baldwin, from the *Berkeley Barb* to Alfred Kazin, while contemplating the age of megaweapons. He writes: "By the end of the sixties the entire articulate Anglo-American community . . . was transformed into a monster-chorus of damnation dealers, its single voice pitched ever at hysterical level, its prime aim to transform every form of discourse into a blast." These voices are as hot as flamethrowers, searing all that get in their way and usually fired from a vantage point several terrain features away.

3. The *regressors,* who see their world disintegrating and engage in fruitless exercises in nostalgia, keening the present and weeping for a past: orderly, humane, free, civilized, and nonexistent. Someone recently recommended that the university insulate itself from outside pollutants—I suppose he meant students and the community—and set up, Medieval Oxford style, a chantry for scholars which he warmly referred to as a "speculatorium."

4. There are the *retreaters,* apathetic, withdrawn, inwardly emigrating and outwardly drugged, avoiding all environments except, at most, a communal "roll your own" or a weekend bash at Esalen, longing for a "peak experience," instant nirvana, hoping to beat out reality and consequence.

5. The *historians,* who are always capable of lulling us to sleep by returning to a virtuous past, demonstrating that the "good old days" were either far better or worse. "The good old days, the good old days," said a Negro comedienne of the '30s, "I was there; where were they?" I learnt recently, for example, that the university as a quiet place devoted to the pursuit of learning and unaffected by the turbulence of the outside world is of comparatively recent date, that the experience of the medieval university made the turbulence of recent years seem like a spring zepyhr. It was pointed out that a student at the University of Prague

cut the throat of a Friar Bishop and was merely expelled, an expedient that may have had something to do with the fact that in dealing with student morals university officials were constrained to write in Latin.

6. The *technocrats,* who plow heroically ahead, embracing the future and in the process usually forgetting to turn around to see if anybody is following or listening, cutting through waves of ideology like agile surfers.

7. And, finally, the rest of us, "we happy few," the *liberal-democratic reformers,* optimists believing in the perfectibility of man and his institutions, waiting for a solid scientific victory over ideology and irrationality, accepting the inevitability of technology and humanism without thoroughly examining *that* relationship as we do of all others, and reckoning that the only way to preserve a democratic and scientific humanism is through inspiriting our institutions with continuous incremental reform.

The 1964 paper I mentioned earlier was written within the liberal-democratic framework, and it contained many of the inherent problems and advantages of that perspective. The main strategy of this paper and its focus of convenience will be to review briefly the main points of that paper, to indicate its shortcomings and lacunae in light of five years experience (not the least of which has been serving as an administrator in a large, complex public bureaucracy), and then to proceed to develop some new perspectives relevant to the future of public bureaucracies. I might add, parenthetically, that I feel far less certainty and closure at this time than I did five years ago. The importance of inventing relevant futures and directions is never more crucial than in a revolutionary period exactly and paradoxically at the point in time when the radical transition blurs the shape and direction of the present. This is the dilemma of our time and most certainly the dilemma of this paper.

The Future: 1964 Version

Bureaucracy, I argued, was an elegant social invention, ingeniously capable of organizing and coordinating the productive processes of the Industrial Revolution, but hopelessly out of joint with contemporary realities. There would be new shapes, patterns, and models emerging which promised drastic changes in the conduct of the organization and of managerial practices in general. In the next 25 to 50 years, I argued, we should witness, and participate in, the end of bureaucracy as we know it and the rise of the new social systems better suited to twentieth-century demands of industrialization.

This argument was based on a number of factors:

1. The exponential growth of science, the growth of intellectual technology, and the growth of research and development activities.

2. The growing confluence between men of knowledge and men of power or, as I put it then, "a growing affinity between those who make history and those who write it."

3. A fundamental change in the basic philosophy which underlies managerial behavior, reflected most of all in the following three areas: (*a*) a new concept of **man**, based on increased knowledge of his complex and shifting needs, which **replaces** the oversimplified, innocent push-button concept of man; (*b*) a new

concept of power based on collaboration and reason, which replaces a model of power based on coercion and fear; and (c) a new concept of organizational values based on humanistic-democratic ideals, which replaces the depersonalized mechanistic value system of bureaucracy.

4. A turbulent environment which would hold relative uncertainty due to the increase of research and development activities. The environment would become increasingly differentiated, interdependent, and more salient to the organization. There would be greater interpenetration of the legal policy and economic features of an oligopolistic and government–business controlled economy. Three main features of the environment would be: interdependence rather than competition, turbulence rather than a steady, predictable state, and large rather than small enterprises.

5. A population characterized by a younger, more mobile, and better educated work force.

These conditions, I believed, would lead to some significant changes:

• The increased level of education and rate of mobility would bring about certain changes in values held toward work. People would tend to: (a) be more rational, be intellectually committed, and rely more heavily on forms of social influence which correspond to their value system; (b) be more "other-directed" and rely on their temporary neighbors and workmates for companionships, in other words, have relationships, not relatives; and (c) require more involvement, participation, and autonomy in their work.

• As far as organizational structure goes, given the population characteristics and features of environmental turbulence, the social structure in organizations of the future would take on some unique characteristics. I will quote from the original paper:

First of all, the key word will be temporary: Organizations will become adaptive, rapidly changing temporary systems. Second, they will be organized around problems-to-be-solved. Third, these problems will be solved by relative groups of strangers who represent a diverse set of professional skills. Fourth, given the requirements of coordinating the various projects, articulating points or "linking pin" personnel will be necessary who can speak the diverse languages of research and who can relay and mediate between various project groups. Fifth, the groups will be conducted on organic rather than on mechanical lines; they will emerge and adapt to the problems, and leadership and influence will fall to those who seem most able to solve the problems rather than to programmed role expectations. People will be differentiated, not according to rank or roles, but according to skills and training.

Adaptive, temporary systems of diverse specialists solving problems, coordinated organically via articulating points, will gradually replace the theory and practice of bureaucracy. Though no catchy phrase comes to mind, it might be called an organic-adaptive structure.

(As an aside: what will happen to the rest of society, to the manual laborers, to the poorly educated, to those who desire to work in conditions of dependency, and so forth? Many such jobs will disappear; automatic jobs will be automated. However, there will be a corresponding growth in the service-type of occupation, in organizations such as the Peace Corps and AID. There will also be jobs, now being seeded, to aid in the enormous challenge of coordinating activities between groups and organizations. For certainly, consortia of various kinds are growing in number and scope and they will require careful attention. In times of change, where there is a wide discrepancy between cultures and generations, an increase in industrialization, and especially urbanization, society becomes the client for skills in human resources. Let us hypothesize that approximately 40% of the

population would be involved in jobs of this nature, 40% in technological jobs, making an organic-adaptive majority with, say, a 20% bureaucratic minority) [Bennis, 1966a, pp. 41–45].

Toward the end of the paper, I wrote that "The need for instinctual renunciation decreases as man achieves rational mastery over nature. In short, organizations of the future will require fewer restrictions and repressive techniques because of the legitimization of play and fantasy, accelerated through the rise of science and intellectual achievements [Bennis, 1966]."

To summarize the changes in emphasis of social patterns in the "postbureaucratic world" I was then describing (using Trist's framework, 1968), the following paradigm may be useful:

From	Towards
Cultural Values	
ACHIEVEMENT	SELF-ACTUALIZATION
SELF-CONTROL	SELF-EXPRESSION
INDEPENDENCE	INTERDEPENDENCE
ENDURANCE OF STRESS	CAPACITY FOR JOY
FULL EMPLOYMENT	FULL LIVES
Organizational Values	
MECHANISTIC FORMS	ORGANIC FORMS
COMPETITIVE RELATIONS	COLLABORATIVE RELATIONS
SEPARATE OBJECTIVES	LINKED OBJECTIVES
OWN RESOURCES REGARDED AS OWNED ABSOLUTELY	OWN RESOURCES REGARDED ALSO AS SOCIETY'S RESOURCES

I hope I have summarized the paper without boring you in the process. One thing is clear, in looking backwards, reexamining one's own work five years later is a useful exercise. Aside from the protracted decathexis from the original ideas, new experiences and other emergent factors all help to provide a new perspective which casts some doubt on a number of assumptions, only half implied in the earlier statement. For example:

1. The organizations I had in mind then were of a single class: instrumental, large-scale, science-based, international bureaucracies, operating under rapid growth conditions. Service industries and public bureaucracies, as well as nonsalaried employees, were excluded from analysis.

2. Practically no attention was paid to the boundary transactions of the firm or to interinstitutional linkages.

3. The management of conflict was emphasized while the strategy of conflict was ignored.

4. Power of all types was underplayed while the role of the leader as facilitator—"linking pin"—using an "agricultural model" of nurturance and climate building was stressed. Put in Gamson's (1968) terms, I utilized a domesticated version of power, emphasizing the process by which the authorities attempt to achieve collective goals and to maintain legitimacy and compliance with their

decisions rather than the perspective of "potential partisans" which involves diversity of interest groups attempting to influence the choices of authorities.

5. A theory of change was implied based on gentle nudges from the environment coupled with a truth–love strategy; that is, with sufficient trust and collaboration along with valid data, organizations would progress monotonically along a democratic continuum.

In short, the organizations of the future I envisaged would most certainly be, along with a Bach Chorale and Chartres Cathedral, the epiphany to Western Civilization.

The striking thing about truth and love is that, whereas I once held them up as the answer to our institution's predicaments, they have now become the problem. And, to make matters worse, the world I envisaged as emergent in 1964 becomes, not necessarily inaccurate, but overwhelmingly problematical. It might be useful to review some of the main organizational dilemmas before going any further, both as a check on the previous forecast as well as a preface to some new and tentative ideas about contemporary human organizations.

Some New Dilemmas

The problem of legitimacy. The key difference between the Berkeley riots of 1964 and the Columbia crisis of last May is that in the pre-Columbian case the major impetus for unrest stemmed from the perceived abuse or misuse of authority ("Do not bend, fold, or mutilate"), whereas the later protest denied the legitimacy of authority. The breakdown of legitimacy in our country has many reasons and explanations not the least of which is the increasing difficulty of converting political questions into technical–managerial ones. Or, put differently, questions of legitimacy arise whenever "expert power" becomes ineffective. Thus, black militants, drug users, draft resisters, student protestors, and liberated women all deny the legitimacy of those authorities who are not black, drug experienced, pacifists, students, or women.

The university is in an excruciating predicament with respect to the breakdown of legitimacy. Questions about admissions, grades, curriculum, and police involvement—even questions concerning rejection of journal articles—stand the chance of being converted into political–legal issues. This jeopardizes the use of universalistic-achievement criteria, upon which the very moral imperatives of our institutions are based. The problem is related, of course, to the inclusion of those minority groups in our society which have been excluded from participation in American life and tend to define their goals in particularistic and political terms.

Kelman (1969) cites three major reasons for the crisis in legitimacy: (*a*) serious failings of the system in living up to its basic values and in maintaining a proper relationship between means and ends, (*b*) decreasing trust in leadership, and (*c*) dispositions of our current youth. On this last point, Flacks (1969) "suggests the existence of an increasingly distinct 'humanist' subculture in the middle class, consisting primarily of highly educated and urbanized families, based in professional occupations, who encourage humanist orientations in their offspring as well as questioning attitudes to traditional middle class values and to arbitrary authority and conventional politics . . . . Although this humanist subculture represents a small minority of the population, many of its attributes are more widely distributed, and the great increase in the number of college graduates suggests that the ranks of this subculture will rapidly grow."

In short, as the gap between shared and new moralities and authoritative norms (i.e., the law) widens, questions of legitimacy inevitably arise.

Populist versus elite functions. Can American institutions continue to fulfill the possibly incompatible goals of their elitist and populist functions? Again, the American university is an example of this dilemma, for the same institution tries to balance both its autonomous-elite function of disinterested inquiry and criticism and an increasingly service-populist-oriented function. This has been accomplished by insulating the elite (autonomous) functions of liberal education, basic research, and scholarship from the direct impact of the larger society, whose demands for vocational training, certification, service, and the like are reflected and met in the popular functions of the university. As Trow puts it:

> These insulations take various forms of a division of labor within the university. There is a division of labor between departments, as for example, between a department of English or Classics, and a department of Education. There is a division of labor in the relatively unselective universities between the undergraduate and graduate schools, the former given over largely to mass higher education in the service of social mobility and occupational placement, entertainment, and custodial care, while the graduate departments in the same institutions are often able to maintain a climate in which scholarship and scientific research can be done to the highest standards. There is a familiar division of labor, though far from clear-cut, between graduate departments and professional schools. Among the faculty there is a division of labor, within many departments, between scientists and consultants, scholars and journalists, teachers and entertainers. More dangerously, there is a division of labor between regular faculty and a variety of fringe or marginal teachers—teaching assistants, visitors and lecturers—who in some schools carry a disproportionate load of the mass teaching. Within the administration there is a division of labor between the Dean of Faculty and Graduate Dean, and the Dean of Students. And among students there is a marked separation between the "collegiate" and "vocational" subcultures, on the one hand, and academically or intellectually oriented subcultures on the other [Trow, 1969, p. 2].

To a certain extent, the genius of American higher education is that it *has* fulfilled both of these functions, to the wonder of all, and especially to observers from European universities. But with the enormous expansion of American universities, proportional strains are being placed on their insulating mechanisms.

Interdependence or complicity in the environment. The environment I talked about in 1964, its interdependence and turbulence, is flourishing today. But my optimism must now be tempered, for what appeared then to be a "correlation of fates" turns out to have blocked the view of some serious problems. The university is a good example of this tension.

The relationship between the university and its environment has never been defined in more than an overly abstract way. For some, the university is a citadel, aloof, occasionally lobbing in on society the shells of social criticism. Both the radical left and the conservative right seem to agree on this model, maintaining that to yield to the claims of society will fragment and ultimately destroy the university. Others, for different reasons, prefer a somewhat similar model, that of the "speculatorium" where scholars, protected by garden walls, meditate away from society's pollutants. Still others envisage the university as an "agent of change," a catalytic institution capable of revolutionizing the nation's organizations and professions. In fact, a recent sociological study listed almost 50 viable goals for the university (Gross, 1968) (a reflection of our ambivalence and confusions as much as anything), and university catalogues usually list them all.

The role of the university in society might be easier to define if it were not for one unpalatable fact. Though it is not usually recognized, the truth is that the university is not self-supporting. The amount available for our educational expenditures (including funds necessary to support autonomous functions) relates directly to the valuation of the university by the general community. The extent to which the university's men, ideas, and research are valued is commensurate with the amount of economic support it receives (Parsons, 1968). This has always been true. During the Great Awakening, universities educated ministers; during the agricultural and industrial revolutions, the land-grant colleges and engineering schools flourished; during the rise of the service professions, the universities set up schools of social welfare, nursing, public health, and so on. And, during the past 30 years or so, the universities have been increasingly geared to educate individuals to man the Galbraithean "techno-structure."

Thus, the charge of "complicity" of the universities with the power structure is both valid and absurd; without this alleged complicity there would be no university, or only terribly poor ones. In the early '50s, the allegations came in intensified form from McCarthyism. In the late '60s, the same attack comes from the New Left. The paradox can be blinding, and often leads to one of two pseudosolutions, total involvement or total withdrawal—pseudosolutions familiar enough on other fronts, for example, in foreign policy.

If I am right that the university must be valued by society in order to be supported, the question is not should the university be involved with society, but what should be the *quality* of this involvement and *with whom?* For years, there has been tacit acceptance of the idea that the university must supply industry, the professions, defense, and the technostructure with the brains necessary to carry on their work. Now there are emerging constituencies, new dependent populations, new problems, many without technical solutions, that are demanding the attention of the university. We are being called upon to direct our limited and already scattered resources to newly defined areas of concern— the quality of life, the shape and nature of our human institutions, the staggering problems of the city, legislative processes, and the management of human resources. Will it be possible for the modern university to involve itself with these problems and at the same time to avoid the politicization that will threaten its autonomous functions? One thing is clear, we will never find answers to these problems if we allow rational thought to be replaced by a search for villains. To blame the establishment or Wall Street, or the New Left, for our problems is lazy, thoughtless, and frivolous. It would be comforting if we *could* isolate and personalize the problems facing the university, but we cannot.

The last two dilemmas that I have just mentioned, elitist versus populist strains vying within a single institution and the shifting, uncertain symbiosis between university and society, contain many of the unclear problems we face today, and I suspect that they account for much of the existential groaning we hear in practically all of our institutions, not just the university.

The search for the correct metaphor. Metaphors have tremendous power to establish new social realities, to give life and meaning to what was formerly perceived only dimly and imprecisely. What *did* students experience before Erikson's "identity crisis"? Greer (1969, p. 46) wrote recently:

[But] much of our individual experience is symbolized in vague and unstandardized ways. There is, as we say, no word for it. One of the great contributions of creative scientists and artists is to make communicable what was previously moot, to sense new meanings possible in the emerging nature of human experience, giving them a form which makes communication possible. The phrase-maker is not to be despised, he may be creating the grounds for new social reality. (On the other hand, he may merely be repackaging an old product.)

Most of us have internalized a metaphor about organization life, however crude that model or vivid that utopia is—or how conscious or unconscious—which governs our perceptions of our social systems. How these metaphors evolve is not clear although I do not think Freud was far off the mark with his focus on the family, the military, and the church as the germinating institutions.

Reviewing organizational metaphors somewhat biographically, I find that my first collegiate experience, at Antioch College, emphasized a "community democracy" metaphor, obviously valid for a small, town-meeting type of political life. In strong contrast to this was MIT, which employed the metaphor (not consciously, of course) of "The Club," controlled tacitly and quite democratically, but without the formal governing apparatus of political democracies, by an "old boy network," composed of the senior tenured faculty and administration. The State University of New York at Buffalo comes close, in my view, to a "labor-relations" metaphor, where conflicts and decisions are negotiated through a series of interest groups bargaining as partisans. There are many other usable metaphors: Clark Kerr's "City," Mark Hopkins' "student and teacher on opposite ends of a log," "General Systems Analysis," "Therapeutic Community," "Scientific Management," and my own "temporary systems," and so on, that compete with the pure form of bureaucracy, but few of them seem singularly equipped to cope with the current problems facing large-scale institutions.

Macro- versus microsystems. One of the crude discoveries painfully learned during the course of recent administrative experience in a large public bureaucracy turns on the discontinuities between micro- and macrosystems. For quite a while, I have had more than passing *theoretical* interest in this problem, which undoubtedly many of you share, but my interest now, due to a sometimes eroding despair, has gone well beyond the purely theoretical problems involved.

My own intellectual "upbringing," to use an old-fashioned term, was steeped in the Lewinian tradition of small-group behavior, processes of social influence, and "action research." This is not terribly exceptional, I suppose, for a social psychologist. In fact, I suppose that the major methodological and theoretical influences in the social sciences for the last two decades have concentrated on more microscopic, "manageable" topics. Also, it is not easy to define precisely where a micro social science begins or where a macro social science ends. Formally, I suppose, microsystems consist of roles and actors, while macrosystems have as their constituent parts other subsystems, subcultures, and parts of society. In any case, my intellectual heritage has resulted in an erratic batting average in transferring concepts from microsystems into the macrosystem of a university.

An example of this dilemma can be seen in a letter Leonard Duhl wrote in response to an article by Carl Rogers which stressed an increased concern with human relationships as a necessary prerequisite for managing society's institutions. Duhl (1969, pp. 279–280) wrote:

Though I agree with [Rogers] heartily, I have some very strong questions about whether, indeed, this kind of future is in the cards for us. I raise this primarily because out of my experiences working in the U.S. Department of Housing and Urban Development and out of experiences working in and with cities, it is clear that in the basic decision making that takes place, the values Dr. Rogers and I hold so dear have an extremely low priority. Indeed, the old-fashioned concerns with power, prestige, money and profit so far outdistance the concerns for human warmth and love and concern that many people consider the latter extremely irrelevant in the basic decision making. Sadly, it is my feeling that they will continue to do so.

The following examples from my own recent experience tend to confirm Duhl's gloomy outlook:

• The theory of consensus falters under those conditions where competing groups bring to the conference table vested interests based on group membership, what Mannhein referred to as "perspectivistic orientation." Where goals are competitive and group (or subsystems) oriented, despite the fact that a consensus might rationally create a new situation where all parties may benefit—that is, move closer to the Paretian optimal frontier—a negotiated position may be the only practical solution. There was a time when I believed that consensus was a valid operating procedure. I no longer think this is realistic given the scale and diversity of organizations. In fact, I have come to think that the quest for consensus, except for some microsystems where it may be feasible, is a misplaced nostalgia for a folk society as chimerical, incidentally, as the American search for "identity."

• The collaborative relationship between superiors and subordinates falters as well under those conditions where "subordinates"—if the word is appropriate —are *delegates* of certain subsystems. Under this condition, collaboration may be perceived by constituents as a threat because of perceived co-option or encroachment on their formal, legal rights.

• Or, to take another example, in the area of leadership, my colleagues at SUNY/Buffalo, Hollander and Julian (1969), have written for *Psychological Bulletin* one of the most thoughtful and penetrating articles on the leadership process. In one of their own studies (1966), reported in this article, they found that aside from the significance of task competence, the "leader's interest in group members and interest in group activity" were significantly related to the group acceptance of the leader. Yet, in macro-power situations, the leader is almost always involved in boundary exchanges with salient interorganizational activities which inescapably reduce, not necessarily interest in group members or activities, but the amount of interaction he can maintain with group members. This may have more the overtones of a rationalization than an explanation, but I know of few organizations where the top leadership's commitment to internal programs and needs fully meets constituent expectations.

In short, the interorganizational role set of the leader, the scale, diversity, and formal relations that ensue in a pluralistic system place heavy burdens on those managers and leaders who expect an easy transferability between the cozy *gemütlichkeit* of a Theory Y orientation and the realities of manpower.

Current sources for the adoption or rejection of democratic ideals. I wrote (Bennis, 1966b), not long ago, that "While more research will help us understand the conditions under which democratic and other forms of governance will be adopted, the issue will never be fully resolved . . . I. A. Richards once said that 'language has succeeded until recently in hiding from us almost all things we talk about.' This is singularly true when men start to talk of complex and wondrous things like democracy and the like.[2] For these are issues anchored in an existential core of personality." Today I am even more confused about the presence or absence of conditions which could lead to more democratic functioning. Somedays I wake up feeling "nasty, brutish, and short," and, other times, feeling benign, generous, and short. This may be true of the general population, for the national mood is erratic, labile, depending on repression or anarchy for the "short" solution to long problems.

Let us consider Lane's (1962) "democraticness scale," consisting of five items: (*a*) willingness or reluctance to deny the franchise to the "ignorant or careless"; (*b*) patience or impatience with the delays and confusions of democratic processes; (*c*) willingness or reluctance to give absolute authority to a single leader in times of threat; (*d*) where democratic forms are followed, degree of emphasis (and often disguised approval) of underlying oligarchical methods; (*e*) belief that the future of democracy in the United States is reasonably secure.

Unfortunately, there has been relatively little research on the "democratic personality," which makes it risky to forecast whether conditions today will facilitate or detract from its effective functioning. On the one hand, there is interesting evidence that would lead one to forecast an increased commitment to democratic ideals. Earlier I mentioned Flacks' work on the "transformation of the American middle-class family," which would involve increased equality between husband and wife, declining distinctiveness of sex roles in the family, increased opportunity for self-expression on the part of the children, fewer parental demands for self-discipline, and more parental support for autonomous behavior on the part of the children. In addition, the increase in educated persons, whose status is less dependent on property, will likely increase the investment of individuals in having autonomy and a voice in decision making.

On the other hand, it is not difficult to detect some formidable threats to the democratic process which make me extremely apprehensive about an optimistic prediction. Two are basically psychological, one derived from some previous assumptions about the environment, the other derived from some recent personal experience. The third is a venerable structural weakness which at this time takes on a new urgency.

1. Given the turbulent and dynamic texture of the environment, we can observe a growing uncertainty about the deepest human concerns: jobs, neigh-

---

[2] See Sartori (1957, p. 112), "Democracy." "No wonder, therefore, that the more 'democracy' has become to be a universally accepted honorific term, the more it has undergone verbal stretching and has become the loosest label of its kind."

borhoods, regulation of social norms, life styles, child rearing, law and order; in short, the only basic questions, according to Tolstoi, that interest human beings: how to live? what to live for? The ambiguities and changes in American life that occupy discussion in university seminars and annual meetings and policy debates in Washington, and that form the backbone of contemporary popular psychology and sociology, become increasingly the conditions of trauma and frustration in the lower middle class. Suddenly the rules are changing—all the rules.

A clashy dissensus of values is already clearly foreshadowed that will tax to the utmost two of the previously mentioned democraticness scales: "impatience or patience with the delays and confusions of democratic process" and the "belief that the future of democracy in the United States is reasonably secure."

The inability to tolerate ambiguity and the consequent frustration plus the mood of dissensus may lead to the emergence of a proliferation of "minisocieties" and relatively impermeable subcultures, from George Wallace's blue-collar strongholds to rigidly circumscribed communal ventures. Because of their rejection of incremental reform and the establishment, and their impatience with bureaucratic-pragmatic leadership, their movements and leadership will likely resemble a "revolutionary-charismatic" style (Kissinger, 1966).

2. The personal observation has to do with experience over the past two years as an academic administrator, experience obtained during a particularly spastic period for all of us in the academy.[3] I can report that we, at Buffalo, have been trying to express our governance through a thorough and complete democratic process, with as much participation as anyone can bear. There are many difficulties in building this process, as all of you are undoubtedly aware: the tensions between collegiality and the bureaucratic-pragmatic style of administrators, the difficulty in arousing faculty and students to participate, etc. I might add, parenthetically, that Buffalo, as is true of many state universities, had long cherished a tradition of strong faculty autonomy and academic control. Our intention was to facilitate this direction as well as encourage more student participation.

When trouble erupted last spring, I was disturbed to discover—to the surprise of many of my colleagues, particularly historians and political scientists—that the democratic process we were building seemed so fragile and certainly weakened in comparison to the aphrodisia of direct-action, mass meetings, and frankly autocratic maneuverings. The quiet workings of the bureaucratic-democratic style seemed bland, too complex and prismatic for easy comprehension, and even banal contrasted to the headiness of the disruptions. Even those of us who were attempting to infuse and reinforce democratic functioning found ourselves caught up in the excitement and chilling risks involved.

Erich Fromm said it all, I reflected later on, in his *Escape from Freedom,* but what was missing for me in his formulation was the psychic equivalent for democratic participants.

---

[3] I am reminded here of Edward Holyoke's remark, written over 200 years ago on the basis of his personal experience: "If any man wishes to be humbled or mortified, let him become President of Harvard College."

During this same period I came across a paper by Argyris (1969) which reinforced my doubts about the psychological attractiveness of democracy. Using a 36-category group observational system on nearly 30 groups, in 400 separate meetings, amounting to almost 46,000 behavioral units, he found that only 6 of the 36 categories were used over 75% of the time and these 6 were "task" items such as "gives information, asks for information," etc. Almost 60% of the groups showed no affect or interpersonal feelings at all and 24% expressed only 1% affect or feelings. These groups represented a wide cross section of bureaucratic organizations, research and development labs, universities, service and business industries.

Argyris' data, along with my own personal experience, have made me wonder if democratic functioning can ever develop the deep emotional commitments and satisfactions that other forms of governance evoke, as for example, revolutionary-charismatic or ideological movements? The question which I will leave with you at this time is not the one from the original paper ("Is Democracy Inevitable?") but "Is democracy sexy?"

3. The structural weakness in present-day democracy, using that term in the broadest possible political sense, is the 200-year-old idea first popularized by Adam Smith in *The Wealth of the Nations*. This was "the idea that an individual who intends only his own gain is led by an invisible hand to promote the public interest." The American Revolution brought about a deep concern for the constitutional guarantees of personal rights and a passionate interest in individuals' emotions and growth, but without a concomitant concern for the community.

In a recent issue of *Science,* Hardin (1968), the biologist, discusses this in an important article, "The Tragedy of the Commons": Herdsmen who keep their cattle on the commons ask themselves, "What is the utility to me of adding one more animal to my herd?" Being rational, each herdsman seeks to maximize his gain. It becomes clear that by adding even one animal, as he receives all the proceeds from the sale of the additional increment, the positive utility is nearly $+1$, whereas the negative utility is only a fraction of -1 because the effects of overgrazing are shared by all herdsmen. Thus, the rational herdsman concludes that the only sensible course for him to pursue is to add another animal to his herd. And another . . . and another, until each man is locked into a system that compels him to increase his herd without limit. Ruin is the destination toward which all men rush. Freedom in a commons brings ruin to all.

A recent, less elegant example along these lines occurred at my own campus where there is a rather strong commitment against institutional racism. A recent form this commitment has taken is the admission of at least double the number of black students ever before admitted. However, more disadvantaged students could have been accepted if the students had chosen to vote for "tripling" in the dormitories. It was voted down overwhelmingly, and it was interesting to observe the editor of the student newspaper supporting increased admission for black students and at the same time opposing tripling.

The democratic process as we know it, expressed through majority vote, contains many built-in guarantees for individual freedom without equivalent mechanisms for the "public interest," as Gans' (1969) recent article in the Sunday Magazine section of *The New York Times* argues.

A character in Balchin's (1949) *A Sort of Traitors* expresses this structural problem with some force:

> You think that people want democracy and justice and peace. You're right. They do. But what you forget is that they want them on their own terms. And their own terms don't add up. They want decency and justice without interference with their liberty to do as they like.

These are the dilemmas as I see them now: the threat to legitimacy of authority, the tensions between populist and elitist functions and interdependence and complicity in the environment, the need for fresh metaphors, the discontinuities between micro- and macrosystems, and the baffling competition between forces which support and those that suppress the adoption of democratic ideology. All together, they curb my optimism and blur the vision, but most certainly force a new perspective upon us.

A New Perspective

These profound changes lead me to suggest that any forecast one makes about trends in human institutions must take into account the following:

• The need for fundamental reform in the purpose and organization of our institutions to enable them to adapt responsively in an exponentially changing social, cultural, political, and economic environment.

• The need to develop such institutions on a human scale which permit the individual to retain his identity and integrity in a society increasingly characterized by massive, urban, highly centralized governmental, business, educational, mass media, and other institutions.

• The significant movement of young persons who are posing basic challenges to existing values and institutions and who are attempting to create radical new life styles in an attempt to preserve individual identity or to opt out of society.

• The increasing demands placed upon all American institutions to participate more actively in social, cultural, and political programs designed to improve the quality of American life.

• The accelerating technical changes which require the development of a scientific humanism: a world view of the social and humanistic implications of such changes.

• The necessity of a world movement to bring man in better harmony with his physical environment.

• The need for change towards a sensitive and flexible planning capability on the part of the management of major institutions.

• The rising demand for social and political justice and freedom, particularly from the American black community and other deprived sectors of society.

• The compelling need for world order which gives greater attention to the maintenance of peace without violence between nations, groups, or individuals.

A New Forecast for Public Bureaucracy

The imponderables are youth and tradition and change. Where these predicaments, dilemmas, and second thoughts take us, I am not exactly sure. However, by way of a summary and conclusion—and at the risk of another five-year backlash, there are a number of trends and emphases worth considering.

The organization's response to the environment will continue to be the crucial determinant for its effectiveness. Economists and political scientists have been telling us this for years, but only recently have sociologists and social psychologists, like Terreberry (1968), Emery and Trist (1965), Levine and White (1961), Litwak and Hylton (1962), and Evan (1966), done so. To quote Benson Synder,[4] concerning a recent trip to Californian universities:

> There is another consequence of this limited response to rapid change. The climate of society becomes suffused and distrait, positions ossified, and one hears expressions of helplessness increase, like dinosaurs on the plains of mud. Each in his own way frantically puts on more weight and thinks this form of strength will serve him. He doesn't know he has lost touch until the mud reaches the level of his eyes....

Three derivatives of this protean environment can be anticipated: First, we will witness new ecological strategies that are capable of anticipating crisis instead of responding to crisis, that require participation instead of consent, that confront conflict instead of dampening conflict, that include comprehensive measures instead of specific measures, and that include a long planning horizon instead of a short planning horizon.

Second, we will identify new roles for linking and correlating interorganizational transactions—"interstitial men."

Third, and most problematical, I anticipate an erratic environment where various organizations coexist at different stages of evolution. Rather than neat, linear, and uniform evolutionary developments, I expect that we will see both more centralization (in large-scale instrumental bureaucracies) and more decentralization (in delivery of health, education, and welfare services); both the increase of bureaucratic-pragmatic and of revolutionary-charismatic leadership; both the increase in size and centralization of many municipal and governmental units and the proliferation of self-contained minisocieties,[5] from the "status-spheres" that Tom Wolfe writes about like Ken Kesey's "electric, kool-aid, acid-heads," and the pump-house gang of La Jolla surfers to various citizen groups. Ethnic groups organize to "get theirs," and so do the police, firemen, small property owners, and "mothers fighting sex education and bussing," and so on.

Large-scale public and private bureaucracies will become more vulnerable than ever before to the infusion of legislative and juridical organs. These probably will become formalized, much like the Inspector General's office in the army. In one day's issue of a recent *New York Times,* three front-page stories featured: (*a*) the "young Turks" within the State Department who are planning to ask the Department to recognize the Foreign Service Association as the exclusive agent with which the Department would bargain on a wide scale of personnel matters, (*b*) antipoverty lawyers within the Office of Equal Opportunity who have organized for a greater voice in setting policy, and (*c*) the informal caucus of civil

---

[4] B. Snyder, personal communication, 1969.

[5] Sometimes it is difficult to distinguish the reform groups from the reaction groups, except that the affluent, particularly the young, uncommitted affluent, have already begun to invent and manage environments, cutting across class and ethnic lines, that reflect unique life styles. And these begin and end as rapidly as boutiques on Madison Avenue, which in many ways they resemble, rather than the massive, more familiar conglomerates of yesteryear.

rights lawyers in the Justice Department to draft a protest against what they consider a recent softening of enforcement of the civil rights laws.

I have always been fascinated by Harold Lasswell's famous analogy between the Freudian trinity of personality and the tripartite division of the federal government. Most bureaucracies today contain only one formal mechanism, that is, the executive or ego functions. The legislative (id) and the judicial (super ego) have long been underrepresented; this will likely change.[6]

There will be more legitimization for "leave-taking" and shorter tenure at the highest levels of leadership. One aspect of "temporary systems" that was underplayed in the 1964 paper was the human cost of task efficiency. Recently, James Reston observed that the reason it is difficult to find good men for the most responsible jobs in government is that the good men have burnt out, or as my old infantry company commander once said, "In this company, the good guys get killed." Perhaps this creates the appearance of the Peter Principle; that is, that people advance to the level of their greatest incompetence. What is more likely is that people get burnt out, psychologically killed. Many industries are now experimenting with variations on sabbaticals for their executives, and I think it is about time that universities woke up to the fact that a seven-year period, for a legalized moratorium, is simply out of joint with the recurring need for self and professional renewal.[7]

It may also be that leaders with shorter time horizons will be more effective in the same way that interregnum Popes have proven to be the most competent.

New organizational roles will develop emphasizing different loci and commitments of colleague-iality. Aside from consultants and external advisory groups, organizations tend to arrogate the full working time and commitments of their memership. One works for Ford, or HEW or Macy's or Yale. Moonlighting is permitted, sometimes reluctanly, but there is usually no doubt about the primary organization, or where there might be a possible "conflict of interest." This idea of the monoorganizational commitment will likely erode in the future where more and more people will create pluralistic commitments to a number of organizations.

---

[6] The labor unions have been relatively unsuccessful in organizing either top levels of management or professionals. They have failed to do so, in my view, because they have operated at the lowest level of the Maslow Hierarchy of Needs, economic, physiological, safety, failing to understand the inducements of most professionals: achievement, recognition, intrinsic quality of work, and professional development. Ironically, this has provided more "due process" and, in some cases, more legitimate participation to nonsalaried employees than to higher level personnel. It is no coincidence that the cutting edge of last year's French revolution, in addition to the students, were middle-class professional employees and technicians.

According to William Evan, the lack of "due process" for the high-ranking managerial and professional personnel has led to or reinforced the "organization man."

[7] At Buffalo, we have tried to develop a policy whereby all administrators would hold an academic appointment as well as an administrative post. They would be expected to return to their academic calling after no longer than five, possibly ten years. The response to this formulation was less than positive and I suspect that the basic reason for its unpopularity was the psychological blow to the self-concept which equates role leaving (without manifest promotion) to failure.

To use my own university as an example once again, we have set up one new experimental department which includes three different kinds of professors, different in terms of their relatedness and loci to the department. There is a core group of faculty with full-time membership in the department. There is an associated faculty with part-time commitment to the department, but whose appointment is in another department. And finally, there is a "network faculty," who spend varying periods of time in the department but whose principal affiliation is with another university or organization. Similar plans are now being drawn up for students.

Similarly, a number of people have talked about "invisible colleges" of true colleagues, located throughout the world, who convene on special occasions but who communicate mainly by telephone, the mail, and during hasty meetings at airports. I would wager that these "floating crap-games" will increase and that we will see at least three distinct sets of roles emerge within organizations: those that are *pivotal* and more or less permanent, those that are *relevant* but not necessarily permanent, and those that are *peripheral*. A person who is pivotal and permanent to one organization may have a variety of relevant and peripheral roles in others.

There are many reasons for this development. First and most obvious is the fact that we live in a jet age where air travel is cheap and very accessible. (A good friend of mine living in Boston commutes daily to New York City for his analytic hour and manages to get back to his office by about 10:30 a.m.) Second, the scarcity of talent and the number of institutions "on the make" will very likely lead more of the top talent to start dividing their time among a number of institutions. Third, the genuine motivational satisfactions gained from working within a variety of comparable institutions seems to be important not for all, but among an increasingly growing fraction of the general population.

We must educate our leaders in at least two competencies: (*a*) to cope efficiently, imaginatively, and perceptively with information overload. Marxist power was property. Today power is based on control of relevant information. (*b*) As Michael (1968) says in his *The Unprepared Society,* "we must educate for empathy, compassion, trust, nonexploitiveness, nonmanipulativeness, for self-growth and self-esteem, for tolerance of ambiguity, for acknowledgement of error, for patience, for suffering."

Without affective competence, and the strength that comes with it, it is difficult to see how the leader can confront the important ethical and political decisions without succumbing to compromise or to "petite Eichmannism."

We will observe in America a society which has experienced the consequences of unpreparedness and which has become more sanguine about the effects of planning—more planning not to restrict choice or prohibit serendipity, but to structure possibilities and practical visions.

Whether or not these forecasts are desirable, assuming their validity for the moment, really depends on one's status, values, and normative biases. One man's agony is another's ecstasy. It does appear as if we will have to reckon with a number of contradictory and confusing tendencies, however, which can quickly be summarized:

1. More self- and social consciousness with respect to the governance of public bureaucracies.

2. More participation in this governance by the clients who are served as well as those doing the service, including lower levels of the hierarchy.

3. More formal, quasi-legal processes of conflict resolution.

4. More direct confrontations when negotiation and bargaining process fail.

5. More attention to moral–ethical issues relative to technical efficiency imperatives.

6. More rapid turnover and varying relationships within institutions.

I think it would be appropriate if I concluded this paper with a quote from the earlier 1964 paper which still seems valid and especially pertinent in light of the new perspectives gained over the past five years. I was writing about the educational requirements necessary for coping with a turbulent environment:

Our educational system should (1) help us to identify with the adaptive process without fear of losing our identity, (2) increase tolerance of ambiguity without fear of losing intellectual mastery, (3) increase our ability to collaborate without fear of losing our individuality, and (4) develop a willingness to participate in social evolution while recognizing implacable forces. In short, we need an educational system that can help make a virtue out of contingency rather than one which induces hesitancy or its reckless companion, expedience [Bennis, 1966].

References

Argyris, C. The incompleteness of social-psychological theory: Examples from small group, cognitive consistency, and attribution research. *American Psychologist,* 1969, **24,** 893–908.

Balchin, N. *A sort of traitors.* New York: Collins, 1949.

Bennis, W. G. Organizational developments and the fate of bureaucracy. Paper presented at the annual meeting of the American Psychological Association, Los Angeles, California, September 1964.

Bennis, W. G. Organizational developments and the fate of bureaucracy. *Industrial Management Review,* 1966, **7,** 41–55. (a)

Bennis, W. G. When democracy works. *Trans-action,* 1966, **3,** 35. (b)

Bennis, W. G. Future of the social sciences. *Antioch Review,* 1968, **28,** 227.

Duhl, L. Letter to the editor. *Journal of Applied Behavioral Science,* 1969, **5,** 279–280.

Evan, W. M. The organization-set: Toward a theory of interorganizational relationships. In J. D. Thompson (Ed.), *Approaches to organizational design.* Pittsburgh: University of Pittsburgh Press, 1966.

Emery, F. E., & Trist, E. L. The causal texture of organizational environments. *Human Relations,* 1965, **18,** 21-32.

Flacks, R. Protest or conform: Some social psychological perspectives on legitimacy. *Journal of Applied Behavioral Science,* 1969, **5,** 127–150.

Gamson, W. A. *Power and discontent.* Homewood, Ill.: Dorsey Press, 1968.

Gans, H. J. We won't end the urban crisis until we end majority rule. *New York Times Magazine,* 1969, **119** (Aug. 3), Section 6.

Greer, S. *The logic of social inquiry.* Chicago: Aldine, 1969.

Gross, E. Universities as organizations: A research approach. *American Sociological Review,* 1968, **33,** 518–544.

Hardin, G. The tragedy of the commons. *Science,* 1968, **162,** 1243–1248.

Helmer, O. Political analysis of the future. Paper presented at the annual meeting of the American Political Science Association, New York, September 1969.

Hollander, E. P., & Julian, J. W. Contemporary trends in the analysis of leadership processes. *Psychological Bulletin,* 1969, **71,** 387–397.

Julian, J. W., & Hollander, E. P. A study of some role dimensions of leader-follower relations. Technical Report No. 3, April 1966, State University of New York at Buffalo, Department of Psychology, Contract 4679, Office of Naval Research.

Kelman, H. C. In search of new bases for legitimacy: Some social psychological dimensions of the black power and student power movements. Paper presented for the Richard M. Elliott Lecture, University of Michigan, April 1969.

Kissinger, H. A. Domestic structures and foreign policy. *Daedalus,* 1966, **96,** 503–529.

Lane, R. E. *Political ideology.* New York: Free Press, 1962.

Levine, S., & White, P. E. Exchange as a conceptual framework for the study of interorganizational relationships. *Administrative Science Quarterly,* 1962, **6,** 583–601.

Litwak, E., & Hylton, L. Interorganizational analysis: A hypothesis on coordinating agencies. *Administrative Science Quarterly,* 1962, **6,** 395–420.

Michael, D. *The unprepared society.* New York: Basic Books, 1968.

Parsons, T. The academic system: A sociologist's view. *Public Interest,* 1968, No. 13, 179–197.

Sartori, G. Democracy. In E. R. A. Seligman (Ed.), *Encyclopedia of social sciences.* New York: Macmillan, 1957.

Terreberry, S. The evolution of organizational environments. *Administrative Science Quarterly,* 1968, **12,** 590–613.

Trist, E. *The relation of welfare and development in the transition to post-industrialism.* Los Angeles: Western Management Science Institute, University of California, 1968.

Trow, M. Urban problems and university problems. Paper presented at the twenty-fourth All-University Conference, University of California at Riverside, March 1969.

Man and Society: The Inauthentic Condition[1]

AMITAI ETZIONI

The author received his PhD in sociology from the University of California at Berkeley in 1958. He is presently a professor of sociology at Columbia University and Director of the Center for Policy Research. His major interest is macro-sociology.

Among sociologists and social psychologists the concept of "basic human needs" is held in low regard. Inkeles (1964), in reviewing the field, said:

Man's "original nature" is seen largely in neutral terms, as neither good nor bad. It is, rather, a potential for development, and the extent to which the potential is realized depends on the time and society into which a man is born and on his distinctive place in it. If it does not quite treat him as a "tabula rasa," modern sociology nevertheless, regards man as a flexible form which can be given all manner of content.

Socialization, the process of learning one's culture while growing out of infant and childhood dependency, leads to internalization of society's values and goals. People come to want to do what from the point of society they must do. Man is, therefore, seen, in his inner being, as mainly moral, by and large accepting and fulfilling the demands society makes on him [p. 50, nonitalics added].

Cohen (1966) stated recently:

Nobody has ever been able to formulate an inventory of original or unsocialized tendencies that has commanded more than scattered and temporary agreement. In the second place, the very meaning of "original human nature," in any other sense than a range of possibilities, each of them dependent upon specific experiences for its development or maturation, has always proved exceedingly elusive and obscure [p. 60].

Basic Human Needs Debate

This is not to suggest that these disciplines do not recognize the existence of tensions between social roles (modes of conduct which are socially prescribed and reinforced) and personal needs or preferences. But the discrepancies between a person's inclination and that which is socially expected are accounted for by imperfect socialization, inadequate social control, or conflicting social demands, all *social* factors. True, these sociologists and social psychologists will concede, we do

---

[1] Revised version of an Invited Address presented to the Division of Personality and Social Psychology at the Annual Meeting of the American Psychological Association, Washington, D. C., September 1, 1969.

Reprinted from Human Relations (London). Copyrighted 1970 by Tavistock Publications.

encounter what seems like a conflict between a person's private self and his public self (or between a person and his fellow men), but since the private self is shaped by previous socializations, this conflict really amounts to a clash between the *social* past and the present. One cannot even retreat, grant that private selves are "socialized" and that all that is "socialized" is by definition a social product, and suggest that unsocialized elements in the infant's conduct are indicative of basic human needs. This is because sociologists and social psychologists will be quick to point out that unsocialized conduct is animal-like (illustrated by studies of children adopted by a wolf or left in attics) or like a free-floating libido, which has no shape of its own. The *human* element, they stress, is socially provided, and the "animal" needs—the physiological requirements for nourishment, liquids, and slumber—can be provided for in such a wide variety of socially approved ways that they set only very lax limits on that which is socially feasible. This is where the collective wisdom of mainstreams of modern sociology and much of social psychology stand; the concept of basic human needs cannot be used to account for tensions between specific attributes of private and public selves.

The counterarguments—and we are dealing with debates among schools rather than with findings of "critical" experiments—advance the proposition that human nature is significantly less malleable than these disciplines tend to assume, that unsocialized beings have *specific* needs. When social arrangements run counter to these needs, human beings can be made to "adapt" to them, but the fact that adaptations had to be made can be learned from the level of personal "costs" inflicted, such as mental disorganization and psychosomatic illness. Modern industrial society is often depicted as such a frustrating structure, one which causes various kinds of neurosis, interpersonal violence, and craving for charismatic leadership. Excessively "instrumental" (or "cold"), it is said to provide only inadequate opportunities for "expressive" (or "warm") relations.

A second set of costs is social rather than personal. It manifests itself, we suggest, in that efforts which must be spent to socialize men into roles or cultures which are unresponsive to basic human needs are much greater than those needed to socialize men into more responsive ones. The same holds, as we see it, with regard to the costs of social control; that is, those expenditures required to keep men in frustrating roles and to prevent them from being altered are higher than those which would be required to keep men in less frustrating roles. It seems more costly, for instance, to educate a man to be a good bureaucrat (e.g., one who disregards family, friendship, and political bonds and allows his decisions and acts to be governed by abstract and "universalistic" criteria) than to be a public servant who follows the opposite rules; that is, we suggest that it is more natural to be "particularistic." [2] The same difference is expected to be found between roles which require substantial deferment of gratification versus those which allow more frequent gratification, even if there is no difference in the sum total of rewards received.

Evidence that some social roles and cultural patterns are less "natural" as compared to some others may be gleaned from cross-cultural comparative studies,

---

[2] We draw here on the well-known opposition between universalistic and particularistic orientations presented by Parsons (1951).

which show that certain modes of required conduct generate frustration in a large variety of societies, which suggests that such conduct violates a universal set of human needs. The frustration found could not be caused by a specific socialization, cultural pattern, or institutional structure of any one society, for these vary greatly among the societies compared. Austerity, for instance, is found objectionable (and generates pressure to overcome it) in as different situations as the Soviet Union a decade after the revolution, contemporary Israeli kibbutzim, and Catholic orders a generation after their foundation.

The implications for critical view and social research of these two divergent views of the malleability of human nature are extensive. By the first view, persons who do not accept the social prescriptions are "deviants." Even when no moral connotations are attached to the term, attention focuses on the factors which generated the deviancy and the ways these factors can be altered to engender conformity to social prescriptions. In contrast, the second view implies that a society is the "deviant" if it sets prescriptions which are contrary to human nature. According to this view, it is society that ought to be altered, to make it more responsive to man.

While this debate, as briefly outlined, is often viewed as one between the "integration" school (of which G. H. Mead and Talcott Parsons are main proponents) and the "conflict" or alientation school (whose representatives are numerous), scholars of the Marxist branch of the conflict school tend to reject human nature conceptions even more resolutely than those of the "integration" school. This is because they see the concept of a universal set of basic human needs as ahistorical. Conflicts, the Marxist writers stress, are determined by technological and economic relations which have grown apart from other social relations in the process of history. They are not due to personality variables. Actually, the notion of basic human needs and of historical processes can be quite readily reconciled. Human needs, such as a need for regular and frequent affection and recognition, may be universal, while the social conditions, which determine the degree to which they are satisfied, may be historically shaped.

From Alienation to Inauthenticity

If we ask the extent of responsiveness of society in the present historical stage, and limit our answer to Western societies, a rather central transformation from past stages suggests itself. This is the transformation from scarcity and the alienation generated by instrumentality toward rising inauthenticity of affluence and pseudo-expressive relations. Before this trend can be explored, a note on the place of participation in our conceptual scheme is necessary. Of the many definitions of alienation, the following seems the most essential: A social condition is alienating if it is unresponsive to the basic needs of men in that condition; if it is beyond their understanding and control. The question arises as to how a responsive social structure may be generated. How are the members' needs and preferences to be related to societal forms? The answer seems to us to lie in the members' participation in shaping and reshaping these forms. Maximal societal responsiveness will be attained under the utopian condition in which all the members participate in the shaping of all aspects of their societal life. Even this condition would be expected to encounter some alienation (which Marcuse, 1955, refers to as irreducible), the result of the fact that not all members' needs are mutually complementary, and hence the compromises inevitably worked out leave each less than fully satisfied. Participation, though, provides the most effective way to reach such compromise; any other procedure, for example, a wise and open-minded monarch taking his country's needs into account, would be expected to leave a greater residue of alienation than broadly based participation. This is because under such a system upward communication of members' needs would be both more accurate and more powerful as compared to any other system. While maximal participation is utopian, we may compare social systems in terms of the extent to which they are participatory, and expect that those which are relatively more participatory will also be relatively less alienating.

This brings us to the historical stage and situation in which we find ourselves. In contrast to previous ages of scarcity, the contemporary period, for industrialized societies, has been characterized as one of abundance (at least for the private sector and the "upper" two-thirds of the members). The lower the level of scarcity, the lower the extent of irreducible alienation. This is because the more basic needs of members can be satisfied without necessarily depriving anyone.

When a society lives close to the subsistence level, existing allocative patterns often entail the deprivation of the most basic human needs to some categories or groups of members—baby girls or minorities, for instance. Here, reallocation aimed at improving the lot of these members may entail inflicting such deprivation on some other segment of the membership. In the age of affluence, reallocation is aimed at creating a society which satisfies the basic needs of all members and which does not inflict deprivation of basic needs on any member; it can draw on "slack"; that is, rather than redistribute the burden of societal alienation, the total level can be reduced. Moreover, it is not only that material needs can be more widely satisfied, but also that more time and energy can be freed for expressive pursuits. For example, all other things being equal, the mother who need not labor to add to the family's income will find it easier to provide affection for both her husband *and* her children, reducing the rivalry between them over this overscarce "commodity." In *this* period of affluence the role of participation becomes more crucial; if alienation is not reduced here, this can be attributed more to exclusion and unresponsiveness than to objective inability to respond, as compared to *much* less affluent earlier periods or other societies.

The difference between our own and earlier societies, it may be argued, is much smaller than we suggest, because scarcity is a state of mind as well as of the economy. For a suburban matron, inability to acquire a new fur, when all her friends acquire them, may be as frustrating as a Burmese village matron's inability to fill her rice bowl with rice or any other food. But, even if there are no "real" (physiological) differences, and if the status race has no level of satiation, it still must be noted that the basic reason the suburban matron is caught in a status race is lack of authentic expressive relations, while the sources of hunger in the Burmese village are at least in part economic and technological. The suburban "scarcity" can be treated to a large extent by providing for authentic participation; the hunger in Burma can be so treated only to a very limited degree.

Sources of Societal Unresponsiveness

The resistance to making affluent societies more responsive, to reallocating, and to opening the society to extensive participation has both "real" and symbolic sources. In part, this resistance draws on existing privileged power and economic positions, which would be undermined in such a societal change. While there is, on the one hand, a rise in and a spread of societal consciousness and of the capacity to act politically among the deprived collectivities due to the mass education and means of communication, there is also in contemporary industrialized society an increasing capacity of those in power to manipulate. This is because of the communication revolution and the growing utility of social science, especially market and voting research. Aside from sustaining the existing pattern of privileges and restricted participation, mass manipulation is said to provide for the unloading of the ever-increasing produce the affluent economy manufactures. The ultimate manipulation, some empirical evidence for which is cited below, is found in sustaining the legitimacy of a system that is unresponsive to the basic needs of its members, in that it offers a sense of participation—and, more broadly, of responsiveness—where there is only a pittance.

In pursuing the idea of alienation with the eyes of a sociologist, our attention focuses first on the array of societal institutions. In earlier writings on unresponsiveness attention would typically focus on work and economic institutions as the source of alientation. But in seeking to understand the affluent age, attention ought to focus on the main source of inauthentic participation, the politics of pluralistic, democratic societies. On the face of it all, authentic democracy is assured by the structure of the government interests and by the values of all members. It is asserted that these can find their way into the political give-and-take, out of which consensual policies and acceptable structures emerge. These claims tend to minimize or view as temporary the unresponsiveness of this political system to those significant segments of the population which have no effective vote, the role played by the mass media and the elites in producing endorsement of unresponsive policies (policies which are against the interests of the members and which they would reject if they were better informed and less tranquilized), and the fact that the political alternatives among which choice is offered constitute a narrow range, one which excludes many options—especially for fundamental changes leading to increased responsiveness on the society-wide level. The 1964 choice between the Vietnam policy Senator Goldwater advocated and the rather similar one President Johnson followed up to the election (let alone after it) is a case in point.

Pluralism by itself, without substantial equality in power among the political contenders, does not provide for a responsive political system. Groups of citizens (such as classes or ethnic groups) have a say in accordance with their assets, power, and, above all, extent of organization for political action, such as lobbying and campaigning. As these resources are unevenly distributed among groups of citizens, the consensus produced is about as responsive to the needs of the weaker members as an agreement between an international oil company and a street-corner gasoline-pump owner. Pluralism "works" not mainly via elections, but via private and public interest groups (McConnell, 1966). New administrative policies and major pieces of legislation are "cleared" with the "relevant" groups, that is, labor and management, churches, and civic associations. In the process those interests which are not organized (and part of their deprivation is their relative lack of the educational background and experience which organization necessitates) are neglected. Farm hands, excluded from the minimum-wage legislation in the United States, are a typical case in point.

Inauthenticity in other institutional areas is frequently reported. Studies of education show the stress which is placed on a uniform personality format, the "rounded personality" capable of smooth handling of others. This is a format which, first, does not provide for expression of the variety of personality needs young men exhibit, and which, second, promotes relations among men which are devoid of deep affection and adequate releases (Freidenberg, 1965). Studies of suburbia have shown the pseudoquality of the *Gemeinschaft* generated. Here, it is reported, the instrumental orientation penetrates even the relation between mother and child, the former using the latter to score points in a status race, disregarding the child's deeper needs (e.g., to get dirty sometimes), and failing to provide authentic, unconditional affection (Seeley, 1956). Studies of "human relations" training programs for management show programs whose aim is to teach supervisory personnel how to provide their underlings with a sense of participation in industrial decision making without real sharing of power or interest in responsiveness (Bendix & Fisher, 1961), and of labor unions which are so committed to industrial peace and cooperation that they serve much more as a mechanism of downward control ("part of the labor relations department of the plant"), than of upward representation of workers' needs (Whyte, 1955).

Inauthenticity in one area sustains that in others. "Rounded" education prepares for pseudoparticipation in the realm of work (with "don't rock the boat" as the prime tenet). Consumer races provide an outlet for an avalanche of products which answer no authentic need, but produce the demand to work, even at alienating conditions, in order to obtain them. Inauthentic politics close the circle by not providing an opportunity to mobilize for fundamentally different systems, and the mass culture provides "escapes" which drain protest and which, in turn, serve to conceal the "flatness" (Marcuse, 1964) of the mass-society, consumption-and-work world.

The total effect is one of a society which is not committing, to which members are not "cathected," one which provides no effective channels for expression of frustrations, grievances, and needs. Hence, the rise of demonstration democracy, as men take to the streets to express, release, or communicate feelings upward; the rise in wildcat strikes, as labor unions become part of the managerial structure;[3] the rise in *middle class* dropouts among students; and the rise in the number of demonstrators and the increasingly "respectable" kinds of social groups which take to the streets (teachers, social workers, and, at least in one case, doctors).[4] More deeply, the high rate of alcoholism, neuroses, divorce, addiction, and other such symptoms seem traceable in part to the noncommitting social world. The best evidence that lack of involvement is a major factor in causing these personal "costs" and societal problems is that when social life becomes more committing—as for the members of

---

[3] On the nature of wildcat strikes, see Raskin (1967); for engineers on the picket line, see *American Engineer News* (January 1968, p. 13).

[4] Doctors demonstrated in front of the automobile displays at Columbus Circle in New York City to call attention to unsafe cars.

a social movement—there is a sharp decline in these symptoms.[5] It seems that not only are members of such movements less likely to be alcoholics, have fewer "breakdowns," etc., when compared to other less-involved citizens of similar class, ethnic, and educational background, but also that the same persons—for instance, Malcolm X—experience a sharp decline in particular symptoms and/or asocial behavior when they are authentically activated.[6] In the final analysis, even the members of a social movement are, of course, not free of their society, and only a society which would become more active and less inauthentic could expect to overcome these problems on a broader base.

Psychological Focus on Alienation and Inauthenticity

Shifting from a sociological focus to a psychological one, the difference between alienation and inauthentic involvement seems to lie first in the difference between having a clear and external target for aggression and keeping aggression at least in part "bottled up" inside. The "purely" alienated person—barred from voting, joining a labor union, or attending a university—may feel "shut out," as if facing a heavy locked door in a passage he seeks to travel. He can, with relative ease, identify an "enemy" and release part of his frustration by anger and even physical violence against the "bosses," the Establishment, etc. The inauthentically involved person is allowed to vote, to organize, to join; but all of this does not make the system more responsive to his needs. It is like being caught in an invisible nylon net. He is often unable to identify the sources of his frustrations. He frequently has a sense of guilt because had he not played along it would have been impossible to sustain the system and he would not have ended up being manipulated. His resentment against being caught is in part a resentment against himself for allowing himself to be taken.

Rejection, which lies at the root of both conditions, is much more impersonal and hence less psychologically damaging in the pure alienating situation as compared to the inauthentic one. Jews, usually excluded during the Middle Ages from the political and economic power centers of society, could make a comparatively healthy psychological adjustment by focusing their identity on the ingroup and limiting their expressive ties to other Jews. But with emancipation, as Jews were

---

[5] A study of narcotics addiction among Negroes in the United States for a decade by the Federal Bureau of Narcotics (quoted in *The New York Times*, March 6, 1967) showed a 15% decline (27,321 as compared to 29,482) from 1955 to 1965; the first factor listed among four was "growing racial pride among Negroes has accompanied the fight for civil rights." See also Clark, 1965, pp. 101, 216. On similar evidence for Los Angeles, see Druz, 1967, p. 131. It is said that rates of neurosis were much lower during the London Blitz, and that those mobilized by a social movement had a low criminal record. See also Rude, 1964, especially chap. 15, pp. 195–268. See also Reid, 1961. It is necessary, though, to use as indicators antisocial behavior as defined by a social science model and not by the middle class or the alienating society. Thus, it is not clear at all that the smoking of marihuana (as distinct from heroin or opium) is more antisocial than moderate drinking. Its prevalence in a mobilized group is not a sign that activation does not reduce deviancy. But interpersonal violence, for instance, seems more antisocial, and we would expect a lower rate in active groups, unless this happens to be a pattern the group picks up as its rebelling symbol. The question of an absolute base for the study of deviant behavior will be explored further in a later publication.

[6] For a story of a deviant who becomes a political innovator through mobilization, see *The Autobiography of Malcolm X* (1965).

allowed, for instance, to study at German universities, they lowered their defenses and moved emotionally closer to non-Jews. When rejection came here, it was often more damaging to self-identity and emotional security (Wirth, 1957). Similar experiences are now the fate of educated Negroes in the United States. More technically it may be said that pure alienation exists when the social distance scale is great and encompasses all the major expressive relations; authentic relations reduce the scale to a minimum; inauthentic ones stand midway on the scale and are "uneven," allowing for closer relations in some expressive areas, and less in others, a particularly strained imbalance. Much more needs to be found out about the differences in the psychological problems and dynamics of persons who live in these two kinds of social conditions. Are there differences in psychosomatic illness, for instance? Do alienated persons have more speech defects while inauthentic ones have more asthma and ulcers? etc.

Conclusion

I conclude with a brief note on the conditions under which alienation and inauthenticity may be reduced. In part these are "structural" conditions, as, for instance, those under which a more equal distribution of political power among the members of society can be brought about. These, in turn, are a prerequisite of more widely distributed opportunity for participation and thus for a more broadly based responsiveness. Here the central question is does not the very structure of inequality which generated excluded and underprivileged groups also prevent their effective mobilization for societal change, which such a redistribution of power would constitute. The answer, which cannot be spelled out here, seems to be that while the existing structure does make it more difficult, if only because of differential access to education, for some groups to mobilize themselves, other factors prevent control from being watertight. The spread of education (which the economy's needs foster) and the unbalanced upward mobility of those groups which did gain admittance (e.g., the Jews in the United States) are among these factors (see Etzioni, 1968).

In addition, there are psychological factors. The fear to challenge the existing social structure or its rhetoric, for example, has some roots in the reality of experiences in earlier periods or even present ones (e.g., where political activeness on the side of change, as in parts of the South, causes loss of one's job, land, or life); but it may also be grossly magnified because of internal weakness or lack of a tradition of collective action (Wilson, 1960).

Attempts by those who share similar fears, underprivileged statuses, *and* the social sources of alienation to confront their difficulties serve, first, to reduce the inauthenticity by more clearly marking the true opportunities for participation and by pointing out the false ones. They then serve to make the system less alienating by promoting some reallocation of resources and power, which, in turn, makes society somewhat more participatory and responsive. Whether this leads to a continual reformation of society, until it gradually becomes a highly responsive one, or leads to full-fledged confrontation between the rising collectivities and those who see their interest in preserving the satus quo it is too early to tell. In either case, should mobilization of the uninvolved lead to a gradual transformation or a showdown, inauthenticity—the mark of the affluent society—will be much reduced.

References

Bendix, R., & Fisher, L. The perspectives of Elton Mayo. In A. Etzioni (Ed.), *Complex organizations.* New York: Holt, Rinehart & Winston, 1961.

Clark, K. B. *Dark ghetto dilemmas of social power.* New York: Harper & Row, 1965.

Cohen, A. K. *Deviance and control.* Englewood Cliffs, N.J.: Prentice-Hall, 1966.

Druz, E. *The big blue line.* New York: Coward, McCann, 1967.

Etzioni, A. *The active society: A theory of societal and political processes.* New York: Free Press, 1968.

Friedenberg, E. Z. *Coming of age in America.* New York: Random House, 1965.

Inkeles, A. *What is sociology?* Englewood Cliffs, N.J.: Prentice-Hall, 1964.

Malcolm X. *The autobiography of Malcolm X.* New York: Grove Press, 1965.

Marcuse, H. *Eros and civilization.* Boston: Beacon Press, 1955.

Marcuse, H. *One-dimensional man.* Boston: Beacon Press, 1964.

McConnell, G. *Private power and American democracy.* New York: Knopf, 1966.

Parsons, T. *The social system.* New York: Free Press, 1951.

Raskin, A. H. Why labor doesn't follow its leaders. *The New York Times,* January 8, 1967.

Reid, D. D. Precipitating proximal factors in the occurence of mental disorders: Epidemiological evidence. In, *Causes of mental disorders: A review of epidemiological knowledge, 1959.* New York: Milbank Memorial Fund, 1961.

Rude, G. *The crowd in history.* New York: Wiley, 1964.

Seeley, J. R. *Crestwood Heights.* New York: Basic Books, 1956.

Whyte, W. F. *Money and motivation.* New York: Harper, 1955.

Wilson, J. Q. *Negro politics.* New York: Free Press, 1960.

Wirth, L. *The ghetto.* Chicago: University of Chicago Press, 1957.